Antarctica

Jeff Rubin

LONELY PLANET PUBLICATIONS
Melbourne • Oakland • London • Paris

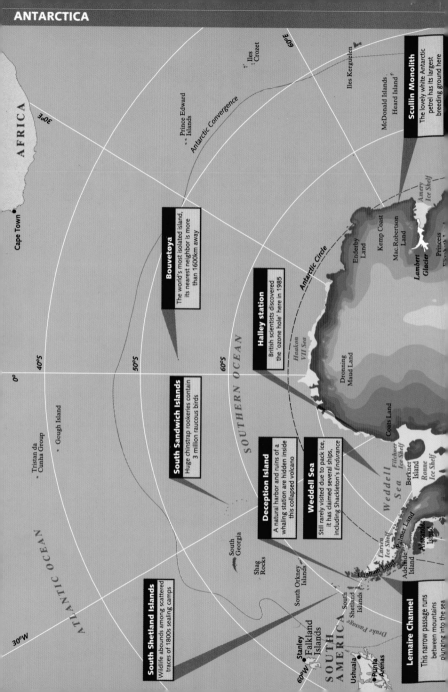

AFRICA

Cape Town

30°E

60°E

Iles Crozet

Prince Edward Islands

Antarctic Convergence

Iles Kerguelen

McDonald Islands
Heard Island

Scullin Monolith
The lovely white Antarctic petrel has its largest breeding ground here

Amery Ice Shelf

Kemp Coast

Enderby Land

Mac.Robertson Land

Princess Elizabeth Land

Lambert Glacier

Bouvetøya
The world's most isolated island, its nearest neighbor is more than 1600km away

Antarctic Circle

Halley station
British scientists discovered the 'ozone hole' here in 1985

Haakon VII Sea

Dronning Maud Land

40°S

0°

50°S

60°S

SOUTHERN OCEAN

South Sandwich Islands
Huge chinstrap rookeries contain 3 million raucous birds

Coats Land

Deception Island
A natural harbor and ruins of a whaling station are hidden inside this collapsed volcano

Weddell Sea
Still rarely visited due to pack ice, it has claimed several ships, including Shackleton's *Endurance*

Filchner Ice Shelf

Berkner Island

Ronne Ice Shelf

Weddell Sea

South Georgia

Shag Rocks

30°W

Tristan da Cunha Group

Gough Island

ATLANTIC OCEAN

South Shetland Islands
Wildlife abounds among scattered traces of 1800s sealing camps

South Orkney Islands

South Shetland Islands

Larsen Ice Shelf

Graham Land

Adelaide Island

Palmer Land

Alexander Island

Drake Passage

Lemaire Channel
This narrow passage runs between mountains plunging into the sea

60°W

Stanley
Falkland Islands

Ushuaia
Punta Arenas

SOUTH AMERICA

ANTARCTICA

East Antarctica
Antarctica's 'Far Side' spawns spectacular tabular bergs

Commonwealth Bay
Mawson's 'Home of the Blizzard' is one of the windiest places on Earth

Macquarie Island
This is the only place where rocks from the Earth's mantle are actively being exposed above sea level

Vinson Massif
This oft-climbed 4897m peak is Antarctica's highest

Ross Ice Shelf
The 'Barrier' glistens in the summer sun like bright white Carrara marble

Ross Island
Explorers' huts are eerie, ghost-filled time capsules

Dry Valleys
Otherworldly beauty marks an area that has had no rain for several million years

AUSTRALIA

Tasmania

Hobart

NEW ZEALAND

Stewart Island
Auckland Islands
The Snares
Campbell Island
Antipodes Islands
Bounty Islands
Christchurch

INDIAN OCEAN

West Ice Shelf
Davis Sea
Shackleton Ice Shelf
Wilhelm II Coast
Queen Mary Coast
Bunger Hills
Hills

SOUTHERN OCEAN

Wilkes Land

East Antarctica

Terre Adélie

South Magnetic Pole (June 1995)
64°42'S · 138°36'E

George V Coast

Dumont d'Urville Sea

Balleny Islands

Oates Land

Victoria Land

Dry Valleys

Cape Adare

Scott Island

Transantarctic Mountains

Geographic South Pole

Queen Maud Mountains

Ross Ice Shelf

Ross Island

Roosevelt Island

Bay of Whales

Ross Sea

Rockefeller Plateau

Edward VII Land

Marie Byrd Land

West Antarctica

Hollick-Kenyon Plateau

Patriot Hills
Vinson Massif 4897m

Ellsworth Land

Peter I Øy

Amundsen Sea

PACIFIC OCEAN

Antarctic Convergence

90°E
120°E
150°E
180°
150°W
120°W
90°W

70°S
60°S

Elevation

4500m
4000m
3500m
3000m
2500m
2000m
1500m
1000m
500m
Sea Level

1000 km
600 miles
0   500
0   300

Antarctica
2nd edition – September 2000
First published – November 1996

Published by
Lonely Planet Publications Pty Ltd ABN 36 005 607 983
90 Maribyrnong St, Footscray, Victoria 3011, Australia

Lonely Planet Offices
Australia Locked Bag 1, Footscray, Victoria 3011
USA 150 Linden St, Oakland, CA 94607
UK 10a Spring Place, London NW5 3BH
France 1 rue du Dahomey, 75011 Paris

Photographs
Many of the images in this guide are available for licensing from
Lonely Planet Images.
email: lpi@lonelyplanet.com.au
Web site: www.lonelyplanetimages.com

Front cover photograph
Near Deception Island (Donna Carrol/International Stock)

Title page photograph
Wildlife Guide (David Tipling)

ISBN 0 86442 772 7

Printed through Colorcraft Ltd, Hong Kong
Printed in China

**Although the authors
and Lonely Planet try
to make the informa-
tion as accurate as
possible, we accept
no responsibility for
any loss, injury or
inconvenience sus-
tained by anyone
using this book.**

Contents

INTRODUCTION 11

FACTS ABOUT ANTARCTICA 12

Formation of the
Continent 12
History & Exploration . . . 13
Geography 53
Geology 54
Climate 54
Ecology & Environment . . 55
Flora & Fauna 56
Government & Politics . . . 59
Population & People 62
Society & Conduct 62

FACTS FOR THE VISITOR 64

Highlights 64
Planning 64
Tourist Offices 71
Visas & Documents 71
Customs 72
Money 73
Post & Communications . . 74
Books 76
Film & Video 88
CD-ROMS 90
Magazines & Journals . . . 91
Photography & Video . . . 92
Time 94
Electricity 94
Laundry 94
Health 94
Disabled Travelers 98
Senior Travelers 98
Travel with Children 98
Useful Organizations 99
Dangers & Annoyances . 101
Legal Matters 102
Special Events 102
Activities 102
Work 102
Accommodations 103
Food 103
Drinks 103
Shopping 105

GETTING THERE & AWAY 108

Sea 108
Air 124

WILDLIFE GUIDE 129

ENVIRONMENTAL ISSUES 161

Exploitation of Marine Life . 161
Exploitation of Minerals . . 164
Global Changes
Affecting Antarctica 165
Environmental Impact
of Science 166
Environmental Impact
of Tourism 170
Your Own Presence 173

ANTARCTIC SCIENCE 174

Living on a Scientific
Station 175
The Southern Ocean 176
Antarctic Marine Life 177
Antarctica Terrestrial Life . 183
Geology, Geomorphology
& Paleontology 185
Ice on Land & Sea 188
Atmospheric Science 190
Geomagnetism 192
Astronomy 192
Medical Research 193

PRIVATE EXPEDITIONS 196

Evolution of Private
Expeditions 196
British Joint-Services
Expeditions 200
Major Private Traverses . 200
Adventure Network
International 202
Mountaineering 206
Airborne Adventures . . . 208
Seaborne Adventures . . 208
Skydiving over
the South Pole 210
The Future 211

ANTARCTIC GATEWAYS   212

Cape Town 212   Hobart 221   Stanley 228
Christchurch 216   Punta Arenas 225   Ushuaia 230

SOUTHERN OCEAN & SUB-ANTARCTIC ISLANDS   235

Southern Ocean 235   Îles Kerguelen 244   Scott Islands 259
Cape Horn 235   Heard & McDonald   South Shetland Islands. . . . 260
Islas Diego Ramirez 237   Islands. 246   South Orkney Islands 271
Sub-Antarctic Islands 237   Macquarie Island. 251   South Georgia. 273
Prince Edward Islands 240   New Zealand's   Tristan da Cunha Group . . 281
Îles Crozet. 241   Sub-Antarctic Islands. 255   Falkland Islands 284

ANTARCTIC PENINSULA & WEDDELL SEA   292

Antarctic Peninsula 292   Wiencke Island. 297   Weddell Sea 302
Cuverville Island. 296   Paradise Bay. 299   Ronne Ice Shelf 307

ROSS SEA   308

Cape Adare 308   Terra Nova Bay 312   Dry Valleys 312
Possession Islands 311   Drygalski Ice Tongue . . . 312   Ross Island 314
Cape Hallett 311   Franklin Island 312   Ross Ice Shelf 328
Mount Melbourne 312   Nordenskjöld Ice Tongue 312

EAST ANTARCTICA   330

Neumayer Station 330   Mawson Station 333   Bunger Hills 336
SANAE IV 332   Scullin Monolith 334   Casey Station 336
Novolazarevskaya   Amery Ice Shelf 334   Dumont d'Urville
Station 332   Larsemann Hills 334   Station 338
Maitri Station 332   Davis Station 334   Commonwealth Bay . . . 340
Syowa Station 332   Vestfold Hills 335   Vostok Station 341
Molodezhnaya Station . 333   Mirnyy Station 335

SOUTH POLE   342

History 342   Climate 347   Amundsen-Scott
Geography 347   Visiting the South Pole . 347   South Pole Station 349

APPENDIX: THE ANTARCTIC TREATY   357

GLOSSARY   362

ACKNOWLEDGMENTS   367

INDEX   369

MAP INDEX

OTHER MAPS
Antarctica at Front of Book
Ice Sheet Thickness page 15
Continents page 20
Snow Accumulation & Extents of Sea Ice page 21
Territorial Claims & Stations page 50-51
Southern Ocean Whale Sanctuary page 163
Sub-Antarctic Islands page 239
Nonexistent Islands page 243
Explorers' Routes to the South Pole 343

Capetown
page 213

0   700   1400 km
0   400   800 miles

Grytviken
Whaling Station
page 279
South Georgia
page 274

South Sandwich
Islands page 280

Falkland Islands
(Islas Malvinas)
page 286-287

South Orkney Islands
page 272

East Antarctica
page 331

Stanley
page 229

Ushuaia
page 231

*see South Shetland
Island inset*

Antarctic
Peninsula
page 293

Weddell Sea Region
page 303

Punta Arenas
page 225

Cape Horn
& Vicinity
page 236

Heard Island
page 246

Amundsen-Scott
South Pole Station
page 350

Ross Sea
page 309

Ross Island
page 315
McMurdo Station
page 317

0   60 km
0   40 miles

South Shetland Islands
page 261

Macquarie Island
page 251

New Zealand's
Sub-Antarctic Islands
page 255

Hobart
page 222

King George Island
page 263

Christchurch
page 217

Deception Island
page 267

The Author

Jeff Rubin

Jeff loves cold places, but after graduating from Kalamazoo College in Michigan, he moved to Western Australia. There he worked as a newspaper reporter, general laborer, jackaroo on a cattle station in the Kimberleys and, eventually, as a Sydney correspondent for *Time* magazine's Australian edition. He first visited Antarctica in 1987 while writing a story about Australia's Antarctic science program – a trip that stretched to nearly three months when the ship that was to take him home became trapped in pack ice and could not reach Davis station, where Jeff was staying. Since then, he has returned to Antarctica many times. Jeff lives in Connecticut with his wife, Stephanie Wiles, and daughter, Emily.

STEPHANIE WILES

FROM THE AUTHOR

This book is dedicated to my grandfather Norbert C Rubin, who by his example inspired me to go see the world, and to my parents, Carolyn and Howard Rubin, who helped me do it.

I would especially like to thank Bob Headland, Ron Naveen and John Splettstoeser for their valuable comments, and I'm grateful to John Cooper, Maj De Poorter, Colin Monteath and David Walton for the excellent chapters they contributed on their specialties.

I appreciate the wonderful articles written by these experts in their fields: Graham Bell, Martin Betts, Joe Bugayer, Gary Burns, Robert Burton, Fauno Cordes, Annie Dillard, Bill Hammer, Ralph Harvey, Bob Headland, Jo Jacka, Andrew Jackson, Valmar Kurol, Phil Kyle, Phil Law, Des Lugg MD, Don & Margie McIntyre, Steven McLachlan, Jim Mastro, Mike Masterman, Rita Mathews, Ray Morris, Ron Naveen, Baden Norris, Andy Parsons, Sally Poncet, Ricardo Ramos, Collin Roesler, Robert Stephenson, Diana Wall, David Walton, Tony Wheeler and Bill Zinsmeister.

Thanks also to shipmates who have provided friendship and wisdom: Graham 'The Birdman' Bell, Lilliana Carosso, Laurie Dexter, Adam Gilbert, Jon Green, Tomas Hollick, Graham Lewis, Herbert McCoy MD, Lani McCoy, Colin McNulty, Nick Mooney, the Neely Family, Nikolai, Tom O'Connor, John Pickard, Ian Pritchard, Rob & Jen Reader, Katarina Salen, Sasha, Patrick Shaw, Vitaly Smirnov, Adam Sperling and David & Elizabeth Tomlinson.

In Australia, I received great assistance from Martin Betts, Peter Boyer, Stewart Campbell, Phil Crosby, Andrew Darby, Damien Gildea, Bernadette Hince, Mark Hindell, Sally Jacka, Andrew Jackson, Silvija Karklins, Tony & Sue Maiden, Nick Mooney and Michael Whitehead.

In New Zealand, Paul Chaplin, John Charles, Phil Doole and David Harrowfield were very helpful.

Ian and María Strange gave me useful information about the Falklands.

In the UK, I'm thankful for advice from Mike Richardson at the FCO's Polar Regions Section, and John Killingbeck and Anita Robinson.

In the US, Lynn Simarski at the National Science Foundation and Scott Borg, David Friscic, Guy Guthridge, Nadene Kennedy, Julie Palais and Polly Penhale in NSF's Office of Polar Programs are always great sources of information. Others in the US whose help and advice I'm grateful for include: Martha Añez and Adriana Gómez for their translations; Jeff Blumenfeld; Beth Marks Clark at the Antarctica Project; Paul Dalrymple; Tom Danziger; Stephen Dibbern; David Fischer for his South Pole expertise; Mary Laura Gibbs; Vina M Hoover; IAATO; Elsa Jiminez; Svetlana Kuzmina and Mary Hostetler for their much-appreciated help with Emily; Denise Landau; Florette Lyew; Margot Morrell; ; Keith Piercey; Lisa Reiss; Helen A Rubin; Darrel Schoeling; R Tucker Scully and Harlan K Cohen at the Department of State; Brian Shoemaker; Ruth Siple; the Olin Library and the Science Library at Wesleyan University; and Gretchen Wesselhoeft.

Others who were very helpful are Bjorn Basberg and Gustav Rossnes in Norway; Dave Burkitt at Port Lockroy; Mike Douglas in North Vancouver, BC; Dr Ing Pietro Giuliani in Rome; and Eric Leyes in France. Sara Vial in Viña del Mar, Chile gave permission to reprint her haunting poem about Cape Horn.

At Lonely Planet, I'd like to thank Elaine Merrill for her thoughtful editing and cheerful disposition; Brigitte Barta and Eric Kettunen for their assistance; John Spelman for the terrific maps in this book; and John Spriggs for his technical assistance. For their help on this and the previous edition, I thank Tom Downs, Caroline Liou, Carolyn Hubbard, Michelle Gagné, Sandra Lopen Barker, Chris Salcedo, Alex Guilbert, Hugh D'Andrade, Hayden Foell, Rini Keagy and Scott Summers.

Thanks also to the authors of the Lonely Planet guides whose material makes up the bulk of the Antarctic Gateways chapter and the Falkland Islands section: *Cape Town* (Jon Murray), *New Zealand* (Peter Turner, Jeff Williams, Nancy Keller and Tony Wheeler), *Tasmania* (Lyn McGaurr, John Chapman and Monica Chapman), *Argentina, Uruguay & Paraguay* (Wayne Bernhardson) and *Chile & Easter Island* (Wayne Bernhardson).

Most of all I would like to thank Stephanie for making everything better, easier and a lot more fun.

SPECIAL SECTION AUTHORS

Dr John Cooper, Wildlife Guide author, has undertaken ecological, physiological and taxonomic research on African, sub-Antarctic and Antarctic seabirds over more than 25 years at the University of Cape Town. His major interests include the conservation of seabirds and their breeding islands. He is Chair of the Scientific Committee on Antarctic Research Bird Biology Subcommittee, Vice-Chair of the World Conservation Union's Antarctic Advisory Committee and Editor of the international journal *Marine Ornithology*, which he founded in 1976. He is currently the global coordinator of BirdLife International's Seabird Conservation Programme.

Dr Maj De Poorter, who contributed the Environmental Issues section, worked with Greenpeace as an Antarctic campaigner from 1984 to 1996. She participated in five of their expeditions (three as leader), and has personally carried out inspections on more than 35 bases throughout Antarctica to check their environmental performance. She has attended official meetings of the Antarctic Treaty System as an NGO observer since 1986. Dr De Poorter is a member of the World Conservation Union's Antarctic Advisory Committee and serves as a senior advisor to the Antarctic and Southern Ocean Coalition (ASOC).

Dr David Walton, Science section author, first became interested in the Antarctic while a teenager. After a first degree in botany from Edinburgh University, he began work in 1967 with the British Antarctic Survey, studying sub-Antarctic plants. He still works for BAS and is now responsible for all of its information and public relations as well as the conservation and environmental management done by the UK in the Antarctic. Dr Walton also chairs the international Antarctic scientific committee on environmental affairs and conservation and represents the interests of Antarctic science at Antarctic Treaty Meetings. He is the author of more than 80 scientific papers, the editor of several books and the editor in chief of the international journal *Antarctic Science*.

Colin Monteath, who wrote the Private Expeditions section, has had 23 seasons in Antarctica since 1973, including 10 years with the New Zealand Antarctic Programme. Since 1983, he has been a freelance photographer and writer specializing in polar and mountain regions. With his wife Betty he runs the Hedgehog House New Zealand photo library. Colin has climbed many new routes on Antarctic peaks and has been involved in seaborne tourism since 1983.

This Book

The first edition of Antarctica was researched and written by Jeff Rubin and edited by Tom Downs. This second edition was updated and amended by Jeff Rubin. Special sections were contributed by Dr John Cooper, Dr Maj De Poorter, Colin Monteath and Dr David Walton, all recognized experts in their particular Antarctic fields. Both the first and the second editions were produced in Lonely Planet's US office in Oakland, CA.

From the Publisher

This second edition of Antarctica was edited by Elaine Merrill, working under the excellent guidance of Brigitte Barta and Michele Posner. Kevin Anglin meticulously proofread the text and the maps, while Maria Donohoe and Ben Greensfelder helped get the project off the ground during its early stages. Ken DellaPenta created the index.

Alex Guilbert, Kimra McAfee and Tracey Croom oversaw the making of the icy-cool maps, which were drawn by John 'S-P-E' Spelman with the assistance of Patrick Phelan.

Shelley Firth masterfully designed the book, with guidance from Susan Rimerman. Henia Miedzinski made the climate charts. Beca Lafore was invaluable in coordinating the illustrations. Rini Keagy designed the cover and contributed drawings. Jennifer Steffey and Hayden Foell also did illustrations, along with superartist Justin Marler, who drew the intrepid penguins that grace the chapter ends. Credit goes to Andy Redline for the illustration accompanying the boxed text 'They Come from Outta Space,' and to Hugh D'Andrade for the watercolor whale portraits in the Wildlife Guide.

Special thanks to Tony Wheeler for sharing all of his Antarctica notes and ideas, and for contributing his tale about the tiny boat.

Thanks also to all those authors and in-house staff who worked on the LP titles from which the bulk of the Falklands Islands section and the Gateways chapter was taken.

THANKS
Many thanks to the travelers who used the last edition and wrote to us with helpful hints, advice and interesting anecdotes. Your names appear in the back of this book.

Foreword

ABOUT LONELY PLANET GUIDEBOOKS

The story begins with a classic travel adventure: Tony and Maureen Wheeler's 1972 journey across Europe and Asia to Australia. Useful information about the overland trail did not exist at that time, so Tony and Maureen published the first Lonely Planet guidebook to meet a growing need.

From a kitchen table, then from a tiny office in Melbourne (Australia), Lonely Planet has become the largest independent travel publisher in the world, an international company with offices in Melbourne, Oakland (USA), London (UK) and Paris (France).

Today Lonely Planet guidebooks cover the globe. There is an ever-growing list of books, and there's information in a variety of forms and media. Some things haven't changed. The main aim is still to help make it possible for adventurous travelers to get out there – to explore and better understand the world.

At Lonely Planet we believe travelers can make a positive contribution to the countries they visit – if they respect their host communities and spend their money wisely. Since 1986 a percentage of the income from each book has been donated to aid projects and human-rights campaigns.

Updates Lonely Planet thoroughly updates each guidebook as often as possible. This usually means there are around two years between editions, although for more unusual or more stable destinations the gap can be longer. Check the imprint page (following the color map at the beginning of the book) for publication dates.

Between editions, up-to-date information is available in two free newsletters – the paper *Planet Talk* and email *Comet* (to subscribe, contact any Lonely Planet office) – and on our website at www.lonelyplanet.com. The *Upgrades* section of the website covers a number of important and volatile destinations and is regularly updated by Lonely Planet authors. *Scoop* covers news and current affairs relevant to travelers. And, lastly, the *Thorn Tree* bulletin board and *Postcards* section of the site carry unverified, but fascinating, reports from travelers.

Correspondence The process of creating new editions begins with the letters, postcards and emails received from travelers. This correspondence often includes suggestions, criticisms and comments about the current editions. Interesting excerpts are immediately passed on via newsletters and the website, and everything goes to our authors to be verified when they're researching on the road. We're keen to get more feedback from organizations or individuals who represent communities visited by travelers.

> Lonely Planet gathers information for everyone who's curious about the planet – and especially for those who explore it firsthand. Through guidebooks, phrasebooks, activity guides, maps, literature, newsletters, image library, TV series and website, we act as an information exchange for a worldwide community of travelers.

Research Authors aim to gather sufficient practical information to enable travelers to make informed choices and to make the mechanics of a journey run smoothly. They also research historical and cultural background to help enrich the travel experience and allow travelers to understand and respond appropriately to cultural and environmental issues.

Authors don't stay in every hotel because that would mean spending a couple of months in each medium-size city and, no, they don't eat at every restaurant because that would mean stretching belts beyond capacity. They do visit hotels and restaurants to check standards and prices, but feedback based on readers' direct experiences can be very helpful.

Many of our authors work undercover; others aren't so secretive. None of them accept freebies in exchange for positive write-ups. And none of our guidebooks contain any advertising.

Production Authors submit their raw manuscripts and maps to offices in Australia, the USA, the UK or France. Editors and cartographers – all experienced travelers themselves – then begin the process of assembling the pieces. When the book finally hits the shops, some things are already out of date, we start getting feedback from readers and the process begins again....

WARNING & REQUEST

Things change – prices go up, schedules change, good places go bad and bad places go bankrupt – nothing stays the same. So, if you find things better or worse, recently opened or long since closed, please tell us and help make the next edition even more accurate and useful. We genuinely value all the feedback we receive. A well-traveled team reads and acknowledges every letter, postcard and email and ensures that every morsel of information finds its way to the appropriate authors, editors and cartographers for verification.

Everyone who writes to us will find their name listed in the next edition of the appropriate guidebook. They will also receive the latest issue of *Planet Talk*, our quarterly printed newsletter, or *Comet*, our monthly email newsletter. Subscriptions to both newsletters are free. The very best contributions will be rewarded with a free guidebook.

We may edit, reproduce and incorporate your comments in all Lonely Planet products, such as guidebooks, Web sites and digital products, so let us know if you don't want your comments reproduced or your name acknowledged.

Send all correspondence to the Lonely Planet office closest to you:

Australia: Locked Bag 1, Footscray, Victoria 3011
USA: 150 Linden St, Oakland, CA 94607
UK: 10a Spring Place, London NW5 3BH
France: 1 rue du Dahomey, 75011 Paris

Or email us at: talk2us@lonelyplanet.com.au

For news, views and updates, see our Web site: www.lonelyplanet.com

HOW TO USE A LONELY PLANET GUIDEBOOK

The best way to use a Lonely Planet guidebook is any way you choose. At Lonely Planet, we believe the most memorable travel experiences are often those that are unexpected, and the finest discoveries are those you make yourself. Guidebooks are not intended to be used as if they provided a detailed set of infallible instructions!

Contents All Lonely Planet guidebooks follow the same format. The Facts about the Country chapters or sections give background information ranging from history to weather. Facts for the Visitor gives practical information on issues like visas and health. Getting There & Away gives a brief starting point for researching travel to and from the destination. Getting Around gives an overview of the transport options available when you arrive.

The peculiar demands of each destination determine how subsequent chapters are broken up, but some things remain constant. We always start with background, then proceed to sights, places to stay, places to eat, entertainment, getting there and away, and getting around information – in that order.

Heading Hierarchy Lonely Planet headings are used in a strict hierarchical structure that can be visualized as a set of Russian dolls. Each heading (and its following text) is encompassed by any preceding heading that is higher on the hierarchical ladder.

Entry Points We do not assume guidebooks will be read from beginning to end, but that people will dip into them. The traditional entry points are the list of contents and the index. In addition, however, some books have a complete list of maps and an index map illustrating map coverage.

There may also be a color map that shows highlights. These highlights are dealt with in greater detail later in the book, along with planning questions and suggested itineraries. Each chapter covering a geographical region usually begins with a locator map and another list of highlights. Once you find something of interest in a list of highlights, turn to the index.

Maps Maps play a crucial role in Lonely Planet guidebooks and include a huge amount of information. A legend is printed on the back page. We seek to have complete consistency between maps and text, and to have every important place in the text captured on a map. Map key numbers usually start in the top left corner.

Although inclusion in a guidebook usually implies a recommendation, we cannot list every good place. Exclusion does not necessarily imply criticism. In fact, there are a number of reasons why we might exclude a place – sometimes it is simply inappropriate to encourage an influx of travelers.

Introduction

Antarctica is one of the most beautiful places on Earth. Its gigantic icebergs and ice shelves are found nowhere else on the globe. Its vast mountain ranges and the enormous emptiness of the polar plateau boggle the mind.

Antarctica is still very difficult to reach. As the most isolated continent, it must be earned, either through a long, often uncomfortable voyage or an expensive flight. Weather and ice – not clocks or calendars – set the schedule, and Antarctic tour companies always emphasize that their itineraries are completely at the mercy of the continent's changing moods.

Little wonder. Antarctica's wind speeds top 320 km/h, its temperatures plunge as low as -89°C, and its average precipitation is comparable to that of the driest deserts. These extremes merely confirm that Antarctica is a spectacular wilderness, a wilderness of landscapes reduced to a pure haiku of ice, rock, water and sky, filled with wildlife still unafraid of humans.

But saying that Antarctica is a wilderness means more than merely that it has no indigenous people and that even today it is essentially unpopulated. Antarctica is also a wilderness of the mind. Traveling there is like visiting no other country. At times in Antarctica, the activities of the rest of humanity seem utterly insignificant; your ship or camp or research station becomes a world unto itself. Indeed, the personnel handbook issued by one national government funding research in Antarctica talks about 'when you return to the world.'

No one owns Antarctica, and no one ever should. It is too big and too important to belong to any single nation. The international treaty that governs Antarctica works unprecedentedly well not just because it has been carefully crafted by consensus, but also because Antarctica's real value lies in no animal, mineral or vegetable riches that can be extracted from it. The continent's true wealth, the nations of the world appear to agree, lies in the continuation of its unique status as a peaceful, free, open, unmilitarized land of international cooperation, scientific research and unsullied beauty.

The first tourists to reach the Antarctic continent didn't arrive until 1957, when a Pan American flight from Christchurch landed briefly at McMurdo Sound. Its lucky passengers bought the chance to see a tiny portion of the frozen 14.25-million-sq-km continent, which until then had been the sole domain of sealers, whalers, explorers, scientists and soldiers – nearly all of them men. Antarctic tourism only really got under way in 1966 when Lars-Eric Lindblad began offering annual trips, which gave well-heeled visitors a chance to see The Ice.

There are some people who come to Antarctica simply to 'bag' their seventh continent, or to check off one more destination on their roster of obscure places. But it's also true that many Antarctic cruises include a high percentage of repeat visitors. As one tour leader has put it, Antarctica is 'highly addictive.'

Tourism to Antarctica has increased tremendously during the past decade. The collapse of the Soviet Union forced cash-strapped Russian research institutes to lease their ships in order to earn hard currency. As word of mouth has spread news of the continent's beauty, demand has risen steeply. Today, the variety of Antarctic travel itineraries, activities and prices is wider than ever before, making now the perfect time to head south…to the Far South.

Tourism has turned out to be Antarctica's growth industry, not mining or oil drilling, as many people once feared. Tourists come to Antarctica to experience a clean white continent unlike any other. Provided their visits are properly managed, these tourists just might turn out, paradoxically, to be one of the best assurances that this vast wilderness can remain (nearly) as pure as the driven snow. Let us hope!

Facts about Antarctica

FORMATION OF THE CONTINENT

Around 200 million years ago, Antarctica was joined with Australia, Africa, South America, India and New Zealand in the supercontinent Gondwana. Ten million years later, Gondwana began the enormously slow process of breaking into the pieces we recognize today, and the continents, subcontinent and islands began moving into their present positions. By about 70 million years ago, the continents were becoming widely separated and the Drake Passage opened. After making its final detachment from another continent, Australia, about 40 million years ago, Antarctica settled into its present polar position and began to cool dramatically.

German naturalist Alexander von Humboldt, noticing the shapes of the continents bordering the Atlantic, was the first to suggest (c1800) that they might once have been joined. In 1851, British botanist Joseph Hooker wrote to Charles Darwin about similarities he noticed among plants in New Zealand, Tasmania, Iles Kerguelen and the Falkland Islands. At about the same time, French geologist Antonio Snider-Pellegrini, noticing identical fossil remains in both Europe and North America, theorized that the continents must have been joined. He too fit two pieces of the supercontinent puzzle together, proposing the childishly simple idea that Africa's west coast once abutted South America's east coast.

Austrian Eduard Suess, in 1885, was the first to propose that there had been a southern supercontinent. Suess gave it the name Gondwana, derived from the historic region in central India occupied by the Gond people where fossil strata similar to that of other widely removed continents was found – thus supporting the supercontinent theory. In 1908, American Frank Taylor suggested that mountain ranges had been formed in ancient times by the collision of drifting continents.

German Alfred Wegener came up with the first fully articulated theory of continental drift in 1912, which envisioned a supercontinent he called Pangaea ('all lands'). For his hypothesis, Wegener quickly received much scorn from the world scientific community, mostly because no one could conceive of continents being able to move.

Later scientists – mainly working in the Southern Hemisphere – followed Wegener's work, and in 1937 South African geologist Alexander Du Toit refined the idea of Pangaea to include two continents, Gondwana to the south, and another called Laurasia to the north. Australian geologist S Warren Carey found evidence that the fit between the continents was even better along the offshore continental shelves, but he believed that was explained by an expanding-Earth model, in which the planet's diameter was slowly increasing.

Exploration of the sea floor in the 1950s and '60s provided new data and new ideas, leading to the theory of plate tectonics. Geologist HH Hess postulated that the sea floors are spreading away from the mid-ocean ridges, thus providing the mechanism to drift the continental land masses as Wegener's theory and geologic data had suggested.

Among the fossil evidence found in Antarctica that clearly supports the supercontinent theory is a deciduous conifer (*Glossopteris*), a fern (*Dicroidium*) and a terrestrial reptile (*Lystrosaurus*). All of these species lived on Gondwana and their fossil remains have been found in rocks of the same age in such widely separated locales as India, South America, Australia, Africa and Antarctica. Because *Glossopteris*' seeds and *Dicroidium*'s spores could not have been blown, and *Lystrosaurus* could not have swum across the oceans that separate these continents, their fossilized remains offer certain proof that the continents were all once united.

HISTORY & EXPLORATION
Ancient History

Antarctica, unlike any other continent, was postulated to exist long before it was actually discovered. The ancient Greeks, beginning with Pythagoras in about 530 BC, believed the Earth to be round, an idea Aristotle supported and refined further, suggesting that the symmetry of a sphere demanded that the Earth's inhabited northern region should be balanced by an equally inhabited – or, at the very least, inhabitable – southern region. Indeed, without it, the top-heavy globe might tumble over. This idea of earthly balance gave rise to the name we give the southern continent today: Antarktos, or 'opposite Arktos,' the constellation in the northern sky. The Egyptian Ptolemy agreed that geographical equilibrium required an unknown southern continent, but he believed that the unknown land would be populated and fertile. A map he drew c150 AD showed a large continent linking Africa and Asia.

Two factors conspired, however, against anyone actually going out to look for this mysterious undiscovered continent. First, ancient thinkers as far back as Parmenides (460 BC) believed that between the two temperate regions of the Earth would be found a zone of fire and perhaps even monsters. This may have been wisdom somehow gleaned from an early traveler who had experienced a tropical summer. In any case, this torrid zone was thought impassable and deadly. If mortal fear was not enough to dissuade would-be discoverers, perhaps eternal damnation did the trick, for the Church found the idea of a southern continent – with its own population, and thus its own separate relationship with God – unacceptable. The idea that the Creator could possibly have made two sets of humanity was deemed heretical, and the flat-Earth theory was given full backing.

That is not to say that intrepid voyagers did not push back the boundaries of their known worlds. As early as 700 BC, the Greek historian Herodotus records, a Phoenician fleet sailed from the Red Sea south along the African coast and around Cape Agulhas to the Straits of Gibraltar. This incredible voyage was not to be repeated for nearly 2000 years. In 650 AD, according to Rarotongan legend, a Polynesian navigator named Ui-te-Rangiora sailed so far south that he reached a place where the sea was frozen. These voyages were neither repeated nor widely known, however, and it was not until late in the 15th century that further progress was made on answering the question of Antarctica.

The Explorers

The Portuguese made the first important penetrations south, beginning with a naval voyage in 1487-88 led by Bartholomeu Días de Novaes and João Infante, who sailed around the southern tip of Africa, Cape Agulhas, as far as present-day Mozambique. Their voyage opened the way for another naval expedition, led by Vasco da Gama in 1497, to discover the way around Africa to India. These expeditions proved that if there was a great southern continent, it was not attached to Africa.

Likewise, the Portuguese Fernão de Magalhães (Ferdinand Magellan), leading the first circumnavigation of the globe from 1519-22, discovered and named Tierra del Fuego ('Land of Fire,' named not for the ancients' torrid regions, but for the campfires, built by the native Yahgan people, that had been spotted on shore). By sailing through the straits that now bear his name, Magellan proved that the southern land was not connected to South America either, though it remained possible that it was attached to Tierra del Fuego.

What is remarkable about these discoveries is that their makers were *disproving* rather than proving the existence of a great southern land. Antarctica was a mysterious place whose extent was originally imagined to be enormous: it was thought to cover the whole Southern Ocean and connect to the southern extremes of the known continents. Although each subsequent voyage of discovery pared off great sections of open ocean where Antarctica obviously was *not* located, few people seemed able to conceive that the continent might not exist at all; instead the belief persisted strongly that Antarctica – a greatly diminished Antarctica, to be sure – must lie just a little farther south. But the Southern Ocean's terrifying storms and impenetrable pack ice conspired to keep the continent's white face shrouded from inquiring eyes for centuries more.

Glaciology

The Antarctic Ice Sheet The Antarctic ice sheet has an area of about 13.3 million sq km (1.7 times the size of Australia, 1.4 times the size of the US or 1.3 times the size of Europe). It is thicker than 4km in some locations and on average is about 2.7km thick – giving a total ice volume of about 32.4 million cubic km.

This enormous amount of ice has formed through the accumulation of snow over millions of years. The amount of snow deposited in any one year is relatively very low – Antarctica is a desert, and it is the driest continent on Earth. Because the snow has been deposited over so many years without melting, the ice sheet provides a natural archive that glaciologists and climatologists study for evidence of past environments and of climatic changes.

As snow is deposited year after year in the interior of the ice sheet, it consolidates to form ice. Due to pressure created by its own weight, the ice flows from the high interior toward the Antarctic coast, where large slabs break off to form icebergs.

Glaciologists from several countries measure the amount of snow falling on the ice sheet and compare this with the amount of ice flowing toward the coast, and ultimately with the amount of ice breaking off as icebergs or melting in the warmer coastal margins of the continent. These quantities would be the same if there had been no change in the climate during the thousands of years since the ice in the icebergs was falling as snow.

The mass of the ice sheet is balanced only when the amount of ice coming in is equal to the amount flowing out, a condition called steady state. A positive mass budget – meaning more snow is falling than is flowing out to the coast – suggests that there has been a climate change in which more snow is falling now than did some time (maybe thousands of years) in the past. A negative mass budget suggests that less snow is falling now than in the past.

To calculate the mass budget of a particular section of the Antarctic ice sheet, glaciologists make measurements of ice surface height and thickness, then determine the rate of snow accumulation and the speed of the ice as it moves toward the coast. By flying over the ice sheet, or by traversing it with over-snow tractor trains, glaciologists are able to use satellite surveying techniques to measure ice surface height. Ice thickness is measured using downward-looking radars. Global positioning satellites accurately measure the positions of markers in the ice sheet, which over time reveal the speed of the ice flow.

Although such measurements have been made over much of the Antarctic ice sheet, it is not feasible to measure the whole ice sheet directly. But remote sensing from satellites is used to provide observations of large areas and long time intervals, and computer modeling studies are carried out to estimate the mass budget of different areas of the ice sheet and of the whole Antarctic ice sheet.

Drilling into the Past As snow is deposited on the surface of the Antarctic ice sheet, different chemicals and gases that have dissolved and mixed in the snow and in the atmosphere become trapped in the ice. By drilling through the ice sheet and analyzing the ice and air trapped in the bubbles, glaciologists access an archive of past climate change.

The oxygen isotope ratio (or 'delta value') of melted ice samples is related to the temperature when the ice was deposited as snow. Thus, a climate history can be built up by measuring delta value from the surface of the ice sheet down. At Russia's Vostok station in central Antarctica, an ice core has been

Terra Australis – the term was first used by Flemish mapmaker Oronce Finé in 1531 – continued to exert its southerly attraction, however. Englishman Francis Drake, sailing in *Pelican* (later named *Golden Hind)*, made the second circumnavigation of the globe from 1577-80. Drake discovered the passage that now is named for him, definitively

Glaciology

drilled to a depth of 3348m. The ice at the bottom of this core is about 426,000 years old, and the delta values show several glacial cycles; that is, several ice ages and warmer interglacial periods.

Air pockets between snow grains on the surface of the ice sheet become bubbles under high pressure deep down in the ice. These bubbles contain tiny samples of the atmosphere from earlier times. Analysis of the air trapped in the bubbles allows glaciologists to examine how the concentrations of different gases in the atmosphere have changed over time.

While some ice cores (such as the one drilled at Vostok) can give us a climate history extending back hundreds of thousands of years, they cannot be dated accurately. Others, however, drilled at locations where the snow accumulation is relatively high, can provide very precise dating. This is because if the annual snow layer is thick enough, several samples can be analyzed for each year of snow. However, these ice cores do not extend back in time as far as the deeper, low accumulation cores, so the shallower, high snow accumulation ice cores provide very accurately dated climate and environmental data, but only for the past few thousand years.

Because the delta value is related to temperature when the snow was deposited, it has an annual cycle: it is colder in winter, warmer in summer. The chemical compound hydrogen peroxide, which is dissolved in the ice, also shows an annual cycle. Hydrogen peroxide is formed in the atmosphere naturally by a chemical reaction that requires ultraviolet light. In Antarctica, where the sun is above the horizon for 24 hours per day at midsummer, yet below the horizon at midwinter, there is a large variation in ultraviolet light throughout the year and thus a marked annual cycle of hydrogen peroxide in the ice cores. Once the annual cycles in the ice core have been detected, the core is dated very easily by counting the number of cycles.

There is a third technique (completely independent of the above-described annual cycles) for dating an ice core. Sulfate is a chemical which is blasted into the atmosphere from time to time by erupting volcanoes. It is then distributed around the globe in the atmosphere, and dissolved in rain and snow. By measuring sulfate concentration in the ice cores, glaciologists can 'see' past volcanic eruptions. By collaborating with volcanologists, they can then determine which sulfate signals in the ice correspond with which volcanic eruption and, more importantly, when that eruption occurred.

— **Dr Jo Jacka,** glaciologist at the Antarctic Cooperative Research Centre and the Australian Antarctic Division

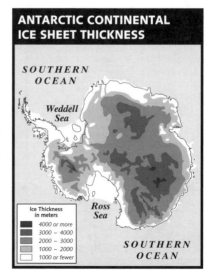

ANTARCTIC CONTINENTAL ICE SHEET THICKNESS

SOUTHERN OCEAN

Weddell Sea

Ross Sea

SOUTHERN OCEAN

Ice Thickness in meters
- 4000 or more
- 3000 – 4000
- 2000 – 3000
- 1000 – 2000
- 1000 or fewer

proving that no great southern continent was connected to either South America or Tierra del Fuego. As the sub-Antarctic and Southern Ocean archipelagoes were found in succession – the Falklands, the South Sandwich Islands, South Georgia, Bouvetøya, Iles Kerguelen – some were initially thought to be northerly projections of *Terra Australis*, but each eventually proved merely insular. Dutchman Abel Janszoon Tasman's voyages charting parts of Tasmania and New Zealand in 1623-25 and again in 1644 also sparked hope, at first, that they might be part of the great missing continent, but these hopes, too, soon died.

Cook Yorkshireman James Cook (1728-1779), once apprenticed to a shopkeeper, was the widest-ranging explorer who ever lived. He circumnavigated the globe three times and discovered more territory than anyone else in history. At the age of 40, he undertook the first of his three great voyages of discovery, and between 1768 and 1771, he found New Zealand and the whole east coast of Australia, claiming them for Britain. On his third voyage, from 1776 to 1779, he explored the Arctic coasts of North America and

Captain James Cook

Siberia before being killed by natives in Hawaii in 1779. Not the least of Cook's accomplishments was his virtual defeat of scurvy among his crews, thanks to such provisions as sauerkraut, salted cabbage and 'Mermalade of Carrots.'

Cook's Antarctic discoveries came on his second voyage, beginning in 1772 aboard HMS *Resolution* and HMS *Adventure*. Like HMS *Endeavour*, Cook's previous ship, these vessels were colliers from the north country of England. Part of Cook's genius lay in persuading the Royal Navy of the value of these ships that he had come to know in his earliest seagoing days as a deckhand on the coal run from Yorkshire to London: he knew that these shallow-drafted barques could explore close inshore without risk of running aground. With them on his second voyage, he sailed 109,500km and penetrated farther south than anyone else before. He crossed the Antarctic Circle on January 17, 1773, becoming the first person to do so, and crossed it twice again without ever sighting land, despite pushing to a record 71°10'S. On his third pass through the pack ice, Cook landed on South Georgia, which he called the Isle of Georgia, and discovered the South Sandwich Islands.

Despite his remarkable first circumnavigation of Antarctica – which he did without losing a single person – Cook failed to find the southern continent itself. It's almost more remarkable that he *didn't* find Antarctica, given that he managed to get so much farther south than anyone before him. Cook simply had poor luck: in the longitudes where he managed to penetrate farthest south, the coast of Antarctica itself also swerved southward. Upon leaving the frozen southern seas for the last time, Cook wrote:

Thick fogs, Snow storms, Intense Cold and every other thing that can render Navigation dangerous, one has to encounter and these difficulties are greatly heightned by the enexpressable horrid aspect of the Country, a Country doomed by Nature never once to feel the warmth of the Suns rays, but to lie for ever buried under everlasting snow and ice.

If there were any remaining doubt how he felt about the prospects of a still-undiscovered Antarctica, Cook later underscored this opinion:

…whoever has resolution and perseverance to clear up this point by proceeding farther than I have done, I shall not envy him the honour of discovery, but I will be bold to say that the world will not be benefited by it.

So convincing were the pessimistic sentiments recorded in his journal that Cook discouraged other explorers from seeking the great southern continent for decades afterward. But he also recorded his observations of large numbers of seals and whales in the southern waters – and others, more commercially minded than the Royal Navy, took notice.

Sealing Voyages The sealers, motivated not by discovery but by profit, came from Britain, the Cape Colony (now part of South Africa), France, New South Wales (in present-day Australia), New Zealand, Tasmania and the United States.

Sealing was an extremely hard life. Gangs were typically dropped off on a promising beach and left to live and work for months at a time while the ship continued in search of other sealing grounds. The sealers lived in tents, rude huts, or occasionally in small 'caves' among the rocks. None offered more than a little shelter from the wind and weather.

Greed was the watchword as the sealing gangs slaughtered without thought for the future of their industry. Captain James W Budington, a Connecticut sealer who worked in the Antarctic for more than 20 years, testified to the US Congress in 1892:

We killed everything, old and young, that we could get in gunshot of, excepting the black pups, whose skins were unmarketable, and most all of these died of starvation, having no means of sustenance, or else were killed by a sort of buzzard, when the mother seals, having been destroyed, were unable to protect them longer . . . The seals in all these localities have been destroyed entirely by this indiscriminate killing of old and young, male and female. If the seals in these regions had been protected and only a certain number of 'dogs' (young male seals unable to hold their positions on the

beaches) allowed to be killed, these islands and coasts would be again populous with seal life. The seals would certainly not have decreased and would have produced an annual supply of skins for all times. As it is, however, seals in the Antarctic regions are practically extinct, and I have given up the business as unprofitable.

Another Connecticut sealer, George Comer of East Haddam, testified to the Congress in the same year about the enormous waste of life involved in the sealing business:

In the first part of a season we never disturbed the rookeries we visited, always letting the seals come on shore; then we would kill them on land with clubs or rifles. During the latter part of a season the seals became very wild, and we used to shoot them in the water from boats. When we shoot them in the water, we lose certainly three out of five we kill by sinking, and we also wounded a great many more. Shooting seals in the water is the most destructive method of taking them as compared with the number of skins we have to show for our work.

A different kind of waste that resulted from the 'gold rush' mentality of the seal hunters was described by another professional sealer: 'To so great an extent was this indiscriminate killing carried that in two years (1814-15) no less than 400,000 skins were obtained from Antipodes Islands alone, and necessarily collected in so hasty a manner that many of them were imperfectly cured. The ship *Pegassus* took home 100,000 of these in bulk, and on her arrival in London, the skins, having heated during the voyage, had to be dug out of the hold, and were sold as manure, a sad and reckless waste of life.'

Elephant seals also were hunted, though not as frequently, for the oil that can be rendered from their blubber rather than for fur, which they lack. Elephant seals grow to massive sizes, particularly the males, but the sealers found 'sea elephants,' as they called them, easy prey. 'To the skilful hunter their overthrow is but the work of a moment,' wrote one sealer on Kerguelen. 'He fearlessly approaches the animal in front, and, as it raises the left forepaw to advance upon him, with great address plunges his lance, 10 or 12 feet [3m-3.5m] long, into its heart.'

Earliest Antarctic Landings

Antarctica's definite – rather than speculative – history is very short, and there is confusion in some accounts regarding the details of the continent's first sighting, earliest landing and first wintering.

The earliest crossing of the Antarctic Circle was made during the circumnavigation of the continent by Captain James Cook on January 17, 1773, but Cook saw no land. There are uncorroborated reports of early sightings, but these are very doubtful. It's far more likely that a dirty iceberg was observed during poor weather and reported as land. The first corroborated sighting was made by a Russian expedition led by Fabian von Bellingshausen aboard *Vostok* (East) accompanied by Mikhail Lazarev aboard *Mirnyy* (Peaceful). This expedition circumnavigated Antarctica in high southern latitudes and extended some of Cook's work. On January 27, 1820, two coastal areas in Kronprinsesse Martha Kyst and Prinsesse Ragnhild Kyst were mapped at about 69°35′S, 02°23′W. These were parts of the ice shelf and, although not reported then as such, they were the first part of the mainland to be seen, as well as the first land south of the Antarctic Circle confirmed. Three days later, Edward Bransfield discovered Trinity Peninsula, and many US and British sealers working from the newly discovered South Shetland Islands saw, and some mapped, this part of the continent.

The South Shetlands were discovered in February 1819, and a large number of sealers exploited them starting the following austral summer. This began what was in effect a three-year 'gold rush,' which ended with the seals' near extinction. There is evidence that during the 1820-21 austral summer two sealing masters working from the islands independently landed on the Antarctic Peninsula – thus becoming the first humans on the continent. They were John Davis aboard *Cecilia* from Nantucket, on February 7, 1821, and John McFarlane aboard *Dragon* from London, at an unknown date. Few details are known of these landings because no fur seals were found, thus the trips were of little interest to those involved. These are the only recorded landings (their order is equivocal) from more than 60 sealing vessels from Britain and the United States that worked at the South Shetlands and searched the region for seals during that season. Just two more continental landings by sealers during the rest of the century are known, one on the Antarctic Peninsula and the other in the vicinity of Cape Adare. It is likely that several other landings were made, but because of the absence of seals they were regarded with little interest and weren't recorded. During the sealing period, about 1780 to 1892, more than 1100 sealing ships visited Antarctic regions, compared to barely 25 exploratory vessels – thus discoveries, especially of the islands, were inevitable.

An oft-cited, but spurious, claim to a first Antarctic landing dates from 1895. A Norwegian sealing and whaling exploration, led by Henrik Bull aboard *Antarctic*, and commanded by Leonard Kristensen, reached Cape Adare and landed on January 24. The assistant biologist, Carsten Borchgrevink, claimed to have been the first ashore and thus to be the 'first on the Antarctic continent.' The captain also claimed to have been first and thus to be 'the first man who ever put foot on South Victoria Land.' Alexander Tunzleman (a boy recruited in Stewart Island) may, however, have preceded both: he claimed to have got off first to steady the boat for the captain to disembark. The expedition leader, Henrik Bull, indicated no precedence, stating only 'The sensation of being the first men who had set foot on the real Antarctic mainland was both strange and pleasurable… .' They dispute an empty claim – for there had been at least five earlier landings by sealers. In defense of *Antarctic*'s crew, however, earlier landings may not have been known to them.

Borchgrevink does have, however, a firm claim to fame as the leader in 1899 of the first expedition to winter on Antarctica. Traveling aboard *Southern Cross*, this expedition landed on Ridley Beach near Cape Adare and built two huts which still stand today.

– **Robert Headland,**
archivist and curator at the Scott Polar
Research Institute, Cambridge, England

Sealing voyages far outnumbered expeditions that could be called strictly scientific – there were about 44 times as many sealing voyages made – and nearly a third of the sub-Antarctic and Southern Ocean islands were discovered by sealers. But they considered their discoveries proprietary information and kept them to themselves as much as possible (though drunken sailors in port taverns were not always able to restrain themselves from boasting about newfound sealing grounds). So it remained for kings and czars and governments to send out expeditions to explore and chart new territory, in hopes of extending their sovereignty over ever-greater empires.

Bellingshausen Fabian von Bellingshausen (1778-1852), an Estonian who was a captain in the Russian Imperial Navy, led the first Russian circumnavigation in 1803-06. In 1819, Czar Alexander I called Bellingshausen to St Petersburg and dispatched him on a voyage of discovery into the Southern Ocean, a dream assignment for Bellingshausen, who had long admired Cook's voyages. With his flagship *Vostok* ('East'), a newly launched corvette with a copper-sheathed hull, and the older, sluggish *Mirnyy* ('Peaceful'), which constantly slowed the expedition, Bellingshausen sailed from Kronstadt, an island off St Petersburg, in July 1819. Unique to his expedition was the shipboard sauna he constructed as a hygienic measure for his crew and their clothing; heated cannonballs inside a tent on deck supplied the healthful steam for bathing and washing.

They crossed the Antarctic Circle on January 26, 1820, and the next day Bellingshausen became the first person to sight the Antarctic continent. Through a heavy curtain of falling snow, at 69°21'S, 2°14'W, he saw 'an icefield covered with small hillocks.' The trouble was, he didn't realize the importance of his discovery; he merely noted the weather conditions and his position in the ship's log before continuing. The two ships sailed eastward, pushing farther south than anyone else had previously done. Eventually they tacked north to escape the oncoming

winter, spending four months in the South Pacific. Turning south again, they crossed the Circle six more times, eventually probing as far as 69°53'S, where they discovered Peter I Øy, the southernmost land known at that time. They also found a second piece of ice-free land below the Circle, which Bellingshausen called Alexander Coast after the czar. It is now known to be an island joined to the Antarctic Peninsula by an ice shelf.

Returning north through the South Shetlands, Bellingshausen met American sealer Captain Nathaniel Brown Palmer, in the sloop *Hero*, who claimed to know well the coast that he had just explored. A legend created by Palmer's biographer, sealer Captain Edmund Fanning, claims that Bellingshausen was so impressed by Palmer's claims of knowledge that he named the new territory after Palmer, but the meticulous Bellingshausen never noted this alleged act in his diaries or charts, and the story appears to be fantasy.

Despite Bellingshausen's discoveries – and his duplication of his hero Cook's circumnavigation of Antarctica – he returned to Russia to find that his countrymen had little interest in his voyage. It took nearly 120 years and the start of the Cold War before his accomplishments were fully appreciated – by a Soviet Union newly anxious to assert its right to authority in the Antarctic.

Weddell Scotsman James Weddell (1787-1834), an upholsterer's son who became a Master in the Royal Navy, rejoined the merchant service in 1819 and took command of the brig *Jane* on a sealing expedition to the recently discovered South Shetlands. Although the voyage was a financial failure, he independently discovered the South Orkney Islands, which had just been sighted by American sealer Nathaniel Brown Palmer and British sealer George Powell, who were working together. In 1822, Weddell persuaded *Jane*'s owners to send him on another voyage. This time accompanied by the cutter *Beaufoy*, he sailed again from England in September. It was a hard passage for both ships, small and fragile in the huge rollers of the Southern Ocean. The sailors' unenviable

THE RELATIVE SIZE OF ANTARCTICA

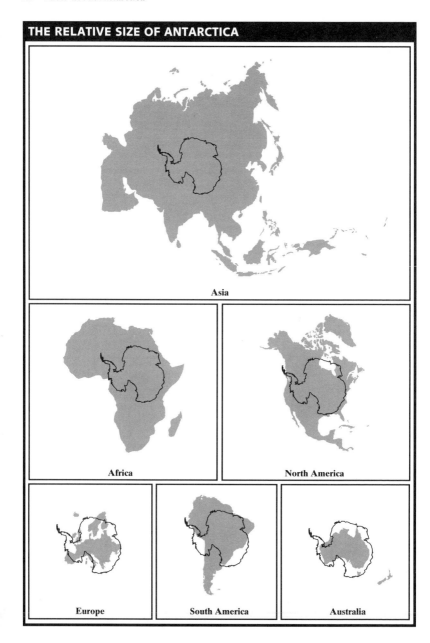

Asia

Africa

North America

Europe

South America

Australia

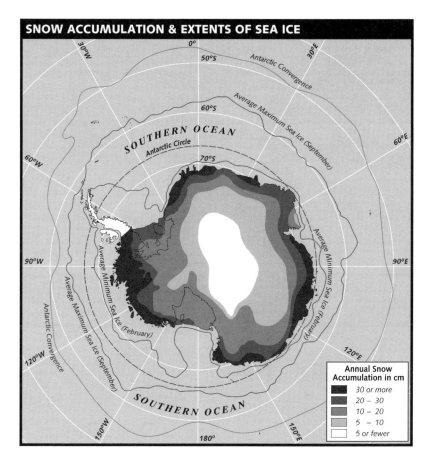

SNOW ACCUMULATION & EXTENTS OF SEA ICE

Annual Snow Accumulation in cm

- 30 or more
- 20 – 30
- 10 – 20
- 5 – 10
- 5 or fewer

jobs were made somewhat more tolerable by their daily ration of rum: three full wine-glasses per man.

By the end of January 1823, the two vessels had reached the eastern end of the South Orkney chain, and a landing was made at Saddle Island. Weddell himself went ashore, and six skins of a new species of seal were collected; today this animal is known as the Weddell seal. But by early February, Weddell had given up on finding a harvestable population of fur seals, so he changed course southward into a sea normally covered in impenetrable ice as far north as 60°S.

Constant gales soaked the crew, but on February 16, when the 70th parallel was crossed, the weather took a turn for the better. The breeze backed to the northeast and *Jane* and *Beaufoy* began a fine run south. Well aware of the remarkable conditions he was encountering, Weddell made the following notation in his log on February 18: 'NOT A PARTICLE OF ICE OF ANY DESCRIPTION WAS TO BE SEEN.'

By February 20, they had reached an amazing 74°15'S – a new southing record, 344km farther south than Cook. But Weddell was worried. The season was getting on, and despite the open water that lay ahead to the south, he ordered a retreat. But first a gun was fired in celebration and the sea named to honor the sovereign, King George IV (the name was changed in the next century to honor Weddell's discovery). The ships' crews, disconsolate at not pursuing further progress, were no doubt cheered by the extra ration of rum allotted to them that day.

Dumont d'Urville Long before Frenchman Jules-Sébastien-César Dumont d'Urville (1790-1842) sailed for Antarctica, he had earned for himself a footnote in history. In 1820, while surveying the eastern Mediterranean, Dumont d'Urville heard about a remarkable statue that had recently been excavated on the island of Milos. Struck by its rare beauty, he urged the French government to buy it, something the government agreed to do 'whatever it might cost.' Today, that purchase – the Venus de Milo – graces the Louvre in Paris.

Already a veteran of two circumnavigations (and fluent in English, German, Greek, Hebrew, Italian and Spanish), Dumont d'Urville sailed from Toulon in 1838 with *Astrolabe* and *Zélée*, which, like Bellingshausen's ships, were clad in copper for protection from the ice. Though Dumont d'Urville hoped to reach the South Magnetic Pole – magnetism was then one of science's hottest questions – his orders from King Louis Philippe were simply to proceed as far south as possible in the Weddell Sea. Indeed, the explorers were promised a bonus of 100 gold francs if they reached 75°S and another 20 francs for each additional degree gained toward the Pole. But the ice in the Weddell Sea that season extended much farther north – indeed, this is its normal configuration – and much to his frustration Dumont d'Urville was unable to penetrate anywhere near as far as Weddell did. At the end of February he discovered (or rediscovered, since sealers had probably already landed there) Louis Philippe Land and Joinville Island at the northern tip of the Antarctic Peninsula. By this time, scurvy plagued his ships, and on the return to Tierra del Fuego a sailor died of the dread disease.

After a year spent making ethnological voyages in the Pacific, during which 23 men died during an outbreak of dysentery and fever, Dumont d'Urville headed south again in January 1840. On the 19th, they spotted what they felt certain was land, confirmed the next day by a clearer sighting. Unable to go ashore because of the massive ice cliffs, they sailed west before coming upon a group of islets just a few hundred meters offshore. A group was landed, a few chips of granite hacked off as proof that they had found *terra firma*, and the discovery claimed for France. An officer who had anticipated success brought out a bottle of Bordeaux and a toast was raised to the King.

Alone among the early explorers, Dumont d'Urville honored his wife by naming the newfound territory for her. Terre Adélie was dedicated to 'the devoted companion who has three times consented to a painful separation in order to allow me to accomplish my plans for distant exploration.' Heading east in search of the Magnetic Pole, Dumont d'Urville's lookouts were astonished one afternoon to see an American man-of-war emerge from the fog, running before the wind straight toward them. The ship was *Porpoise*, part of Charles Wilkes' US Exploring Expedition, but thanks to a misunderstanding, the two ships did not stop to exchange communication. Each side later blamed the other for raising sail and blowing past. Returning to France to great acclaim after a 38-month voyage, Dumont d'Urville and his men were rewarded by the French government with 15,000 francs to be divided by the expedition's 130 surviving members.

Smith & Bransfield Though he was once credited with being first to sight Antarctica, it is now agreed that Edward Bransfield (c1795-1852) was beaten to that honor by Bellingshausen by three days.

After English merchant Captain William Smith announced his discovery of the South Shetlands in 1819, the Royal Navy chartered Smith's ship *Williams* to survey the islands. Bransfield was put in command with Smith as pilot, and they sailed south from Valparaiso, Chile. Two months were spent charting the coastlines of what they called New South Britain; a landing was made at George Bay on King George Island to claim the group for – surprise – George IV, the British sovereign.

Continuing south, Bransfield sighted the Antarctic Peninsula on January 30, 1820, calling it Trinity Land. One of his midshipman, quoted in the *Literary Gazette and Journal of Belle Lettres*, called it 'a prospect the most gloomy that can be imagined…the only cheer the sight afforded was in the idea that this might be the long-sought Southern Continent.' They charted the islands along it for another 20 days before being stopped by pack ice and turning north.

Palmer American sealer Nathaniel Brown Palmer (1799-1877), the son of a shipyard owner, left his home of Stonington, Connecticut at the age of 14 to go to sea. On his second sealing voyage to the South Shetlands in 1820, commanding the sloop *Hero* (which carried a complement of five, including Peter Harvey, born in Philadelphia in 1789, the first black to reach such a high latitude), Palmer sailed south with a small fleet of other sealers. Upon arrival in the South Shetlands, the need for a more secure anchorage for the five ships drove Palmer to push south ahead of the others. He dropped anchor inside the caldera of Deception Island, almost certainly the first person ever to do so. On November 16, from a high lookout at Deception, he caught sight of Trinity Island to the southeast and probably the Antarctic Peninsula beyond. The next day Palmer sailed to investigate, but due to heavy ice thought it imprudent to try to land. In later years, Palmer claimed that he had found the Antarctic continent, calling his discovery Palmer Land. But even if he did spot Antarctica on that occasion, his sighting came ten months after Bellingshausen's (January 27) and Bransfield's (January 30) in that same year.

Nevertheless, Palmer has another clear Antarctic discovery to his credit: a year later, while commanding the sloop *James Monroe*, Palmer was searching for seals in the South Shetlands with British Captain George Powell of *Dove*. Finding no seals,

they steered east, and on December 6, 1821, discovered a large island of a new group, the South Orkneys. Finding no seals, Palmer had no further interest in the island, but Powell went ashore and claimed it for the British crown, calling it Coronation Island.

Biscoe Another Briton, John Biscoe (1794-1843), joined the Royal Navy at 18 and fought in the 1812 war against the US. Dispatched by the London firm of Enderby Brothers in July 1830, he made the third circumnavigation of Antarctica, sailing in the brig *Tula*, accompanied by George Avery in the cutter *Lively*. The ships sighted what they called Enderby Land on February 24, 1831, and confirmed the discovery three days later, the first sighting of the Antarctic continent in the Indian Ocean sector. Biscoe also was struck by the ethereal beauty of the aurora australis, which, he recorded in the ship's log, 'at times (appeared) not many yards above us.' Oncoming winter forced the ships to head north to Hobart, but scurvy so ravaged *Tula*'s crew that only Biscoe, three other men and a boy were able to work. Aboard *Lively*, which had become separated from *Tula*, all but three of the crew died of scurvy or other diseases.

Sailing again with both ships in October 1831, on what after all was supposed to be a commercial voyage, Biscoe spent three months searching for whales or seals off New Zealand. Finding none, he headed south once more, and discovered Adelaide Island (which he named for the consort of King William IV) on February 16, 1832. Biscoe discovered land again (now thought to be present-day Anvers Island) on February 21, and claimed the territory for King William IV. Still seeking seals or some other valuable cargo to bring home, he was forced to sail for England after *Tula* damaged her rudder. (En route home, *Lively* was wrecked in the Falklands.) Although he returned to London in January 1833 with empty holds and one ship missing, Biscoe was fortunate to have extremely open-minded bosses. Instead of being reprimanded or fired, he received the highest award of the newly established Royal Geographical Society.

After Biscoe's return, the stretch of coast he discovered was named Graham Land, for James RG Graham, First Lord of the Admiralty. Although this was in fact a southern portion of the Antarctic Peninsula, which had already been sighted by Bransfield, Smith and Palmer, the name eventually came to be applied to the entire Antarctic Peninsula on British maps, while the name Palmer Land was used by American chart-

A Low-Latitude Antarctic Gazetteer

There could be a bit of Antarctica just down the street from you. If you can't visit The Ice itself, the next best thing may be to go to a 'low-latitude' site with an Antarctic connection.

Many museums, of course, have interesting collections of Antarcticana (see also the boxed text 'Antarctic Museums' in the Facts for the Visitor chapter). The **Oates Museum**, Selborne, Hampshire, UK is filled with artifacts associated with Captain Lawrence Oates, who died with Captain Robert Scott. The **Cheltenham Art Gallery & Museum**, Cheltenham, Gloucestershire, UK features an excellent exhibit on native son Edward Wilson, physician, zoologist and artist and Scott's closest friend. The **Navy Museum**, Washington, DC has probably the US's largest collection of Antarctic material. Scott's sledge journal is on display at the **British Library**, London.

Antarctic sites also abound in churches, in the form of memorial plaques, stained- glass windows and, of course, graves. **St Peter's Church** at Binton, Warwickshire, UK has a marvelous set of four windows memorializing Scott and his men. Two plaques commemorate Henry 'Birdie' Bowers, who died with Scott – one in **St Ninian's Church**, Rothesay, Scotland and a duplicate in **St Thomas' Cathedral** in Bombay, India. One of the larger church memorials is in the south transept of **St Paul's Cathedral**, London, commemorating Scott's polar party. James Clark Ross is buried in the churchyard of **St James the Great**, Aston Abbots, Buckinghamshire, UK and there is a memorial window in the church. Nearby is his house and in the garden is a pond with two islands that he named Erebus and Terror after his ships.

Other interesting graves include two in Paris for France's most famous Antarctic explorers: a large reddish obelisk in the **Cimetiére du Montparnasse** marks the final resting place of Jules-Sébastien-César Dumont d'Urville, while across the Seine at the **Cimetiére de Montmartre** is Jean-Baptiste Charcot's mausoleum. Edward Bransfield is buried in the **Brighton Extra-Mural Cemetery**, Brighton, East Sussex, UK, his grave recently restored after years of neglect. Nathaniel Brown Palmer is buried in the idyllic **Evergreen Cemetery**, Stonington, CT, US. Nearby is his house, which features some Antarctic items in its displays. My favorite grave is at the **Pine Ridge Cemetery for Small Animals**, Dedham, MA, US. Here a pink rock reminiscent of a large iceberg marks the grave of Igloo, the loyal terrier that accompanied Admiral Byrd more than once to the Antarctic. The inscription reads: 'Igloo. He was more than a friend.'

Antarctic statues, memorials and monuments are more common than you might guess. Among the most familiar is the Scott statue in London's **Waterloo Place**, sculpted by his wife, Kathleen. A duplicate version in Christchurch, NZ (see the Gateways chapter) was done in marble because of wartime bronze shortages. Edward Wilson is well portrayed by a statue on **The Promenade**, Cheltenham, also sculpted by Kathleen Scott. Wilson's birthplace is not far away at 91 Montpellier Terrace (now a bed and breakfast). A fine bronze statue of Roald Amundsen can be found in **Tromsø**, Norway, and there's a bust in **Spitsbergen**. By far the most forceful of all Antarctic statuary is the one of Ernest Shackleton, dressed in polar clothing, on the facade of the **Royal Geographical Society**, London. For size and monumentality, the most impressive memorial is one to Scott and his men at **Mt Wise**, Devonport, Plymouth, UK, combining bronze statuary, bas-relief portraits and carved stone.

makers. (This difference continued until 1964, when the US and the UK agreed to use the name Antarctic Peninsula for the entire northward-reaching extension of the Antarctic continent, with the northern part to be called Graham Land and the southern, Palmer Land.)

The British discoveries in the Antarctic Peninsula region had not escaped the attention of the US government, however, and

A Low-Latitude Antarctic Gazetteer

Houses with Antarctic associations are numerous. Shackleton had many, two of which bear the blue plaques that indicate residences of the famous in Britain: **12 Westwood Hill**, London SE26, where he spent most of his boyhood, and **14 Milnthorpe Rd**, Eastbourne, Sussex, UK. One Shackleton address worth remembering is 11 Vicarage Gate in London's Kensington, now the **Abbey House Hotel**. Scott had several London addresses, though the one given a blue plaque is at **56 Oakley St**, close to the Thames. Byrd's house is at **9 Brimmer St** at the foot of Beacon Hill in Boston. The home of Bellingshausen, Antarctica's discoverer, is now a mental hospital in Estonia. Amundsen's house, **Uranienborg**, south of Oslo, Norway is open to the public.

Artifacts are widely scattered. Scott's skis are in the **City Museum & Art Gallery**, Plymouth, UK, while Otto Nordenskjöld's reside at New York City's **American Museum of Natural History** and Amundsen's are at the **Ski Museum**, Oslo. There's a Scott sledge at the **Naval Academy Museum**, Annapolis, MD, US, along with one of Byrd's. Other sledges with Scott connections are at the **Marine Biological Association**, Plymouth, UK, at the **Cheltenham Art Gallery & Museum**, at the **Scott Polar Research Institute**, Cambridge, UK and at the **Otago Museum**, Dunedin, NZ. This last was briefly removed from the museum in 1939 to haul food to a stranded radio station during the worst snowstorm in the city's history.

Ships and bits and pieces of ships are likewise well distributed. The bell from Scott's *Terra Nova* is used to announce morning coffee and afternoon tea at the Scott Polar Research Institute, and the lovely figurehead is at the **Welsh Industrial & Maritime Museum** in Cardiff, Wales. The crow's nest from Shackleton's *Quest* rests in the crypt of **All Hallows Barking**, a church close to the Tower of London. That most famous of boats, *James Caird*, is nicely displayed at **Dulwich College** in London's southern suburbs.

Planes have not been overlooked. Byrd's *Stars and Stripes* is at the **Virginia Aviation Museum**, Richmond, VA, US, and his Ford Trimotor *Floyd Bennett* is at the **Henry Ford Museum**, Dearborn, MI, US. Lincoln Ellsworth's *Polar Star* is at the **National Air and Space Museum** in Washington, DC.

One of the more offbeat Antarctic sites I've encountered is **Little America** near Rock Springs, WY, US, now a truck stop and resort hotel, its name inspired by Byrd's base in Antarctica. There's a stuffed Emperor penguin on display.

I have saved the best for last: pubs and hotels with an Antarctic connection. In Cardiff, there's the **Royal Hotel** (sadly threatened and boarded up), where Scott and his men enjoyed their last dinner in Britain on June 13, 1910. Best of all is **The South Pole Inn**, Anascaul, County Kerry, Ireland, originally kept by Tom Crean, associated with both Scott and Shackleton. Tom Kennedy, the present publican, displays some artifacts, including a sledge made for the film *Scott of the Antarctic.*

– Robert Stephenson,
website coordinator at www.antarctic-circle.org, where all of these sites and
several hundred more can be found under Low-Latitude Antarctic Gazetteer

after nearly a decade of being urged to do so, the US Congress voted to send crews and ships south to explore the region.

Wilkes By the time American Lieutenant Charles Wilkes (1798-1877) was offered command of the US Exploring Expedition in 1838, the position had already been declined by several senior officers. Perhaps they knew something Wilkes didn't, for this inauspicious beginning foretold great hardship for the expedition. In the words of polar historian Laurence P Kirwan, it was 'the most ill-prepared, the most controversial, and probably the unhappiest expedition which ever sailed the Antarctic seas.'

For a start, the six ships selected were poor choices: three of them, *Vincennes*, *Peacock* and *Porpoise*, were naval warships with gun ports that let heavy seas pour into the ships; *Sea Gull* and *Flying Fish*, former New York pilot boats, were odd choices for Antarctic exploration; and the sluggish storeship *Relief* rounded out the sorry fleet. As might be expected of an expedition planned by committee, the US Ex Ex, as it became known, had a distinct lack of focus. Antarctica was to be only one area of its endeavor, and a minor one at that: Wilkes was also directed to explore the whole of the Pacific, from Chile to Australia to the northwest coast of North America. Meanwhile, a jealous Navy Department did all it could to exclude civilian scientists from the expedition, though Wilkes did manage to take with him artist Titian Ramsey Peale. One unsuccessful applicant for the position of expedition historian was American writer Nathaniel Hawthorne.

By the time the expedition sailed on August 18, 1838, a depressed Wilkes confided to his private diary that he felt 'doomed to destruction.' After sailing down the east coast of South America to Orange Harbour, near the tip of Tierra del Fuego, Wilkes divided the fleet into three parts. He directed *Peacock* and *Flying Fish* to sail southwest to try to better Cook's southing record; *Vincennes* and *Relief* were to survey the coast of Tierra del Fuego. Placing himself aboard

Porpoise, he set off south with *Sea Gull* to see how far he could penetrate the pack ice. The ships soon lost contact with one another, each undergoing its own trials. Gales blew out sails and tangled rigging, boats were crushed by ice, men were injured and frozen. Wilkes himself, in the flagship, narrowly missed running aground on Elephant Island in fog. *Sea Gull* was lost with all hands off Chile. But *Peacock* and *Flying Fish* managed to cross the 70th parallel, little more than a degree away from beating Cook's record.

Diminished by two, *Relief* having been sent home as unsuitable for ice work, the expedition reconvened in Sydney in November 1839 after surveying in the South Pacific. After a month's recuperation, the four ships sailed south again on December 26, with Wilkes commanding *Vincennes*. On board was one of the first recorded canine visitors to the Antarctic, a dog acquired in Sydney and named after that port. Again the ships were quickly separated, and in late February *Flying Fish* gave up its search for the others and returned to New Zealand alone. The other three vessels managed to rendezvous, however, and on January 16, 1840 – three days before Dumont d'Urville made his discovery – they sighted land in the region of 154°30'E, putting a boat ashore three days later to confirm it. Separating again, *Vincennes* continued west, sighting and charting discoveries until reaching the present-day Shackleton Ice Shelf, which Wilkes named Termination Land. The massive ice shelf, which today extends nearly 290km out to sea, convinced him that it was time to head home, which he did on February 21.

Having followed the Antarctic coast for nearly 2000km, Wilkes announced the discovery of an Antarctic continent upon his return to Sydney. Although he was the first to do so, his only reward upon his homecoming in New York was a court-martial. Petty jealousy from some of his officers, coupled with his harsh shipboard discipline, entangled Wilkes in a messy trial in a Naval Court of Inquiry held at the Brooklyn Navy Yard. Two long months later, all of the charges against him – save one – were dismissed. Found guilty of ordering a too-severe punishment for some thieving seamen, Wilkes was officially reprimanded by the Secretary of the Navy. The US Congress, however, handed Wilkes his bitterest defeat, authorizing publication of just 100 copies of the expedition's official report. Today, the full set of the *Narrative* is one of the rarest – and most valuable – polar books.

Ross Scotsman James Clark Ross (1800-1862), considered one of the most dashing figures of his time, had all of the advantages for Antarctic exploration that Wilkes lacked. After joining the Royal Navy at the tender age of 11 or 12, Ross went on to a career filled with Arctic discovery. Between 1818 and 1836, he spent eight winters and 15 summers in the Arctic, and in 1831, as second-in-command of a voyage led by his uncle, John Ross, he located the North Magnetic Pole. In 1839, he was asked to lead a national expedition to explore the south, and if possible, to locate the South Magnetic Pole. The contrast between his commission and Wilkes' could not have been greater. With his government firmly behind the effort, both philosophically and financially, Ross was given excellent ships, officers and provisions; the sailors on the expedition were volunteers on double pay.

Setting sail in September 1839 in *Erebus* and *Terror*, shallow-drafted three-masted barques specially strengthened for ice navigation, the expedition stopped in Hobart on its way south. There, the Governor of Van Diemen's Land (Tasmania) was John Franklin, himself a veteran Arctic explorer who would later and tragically sail Arctic waters again – in the very same *Erebus* and *Terror* – before disappearing and triggering the greatest polar search in history.

In Hobart Ross heard troubling news: Both Wilkes and Dumont d'Urville were exploring the area in which he intended to search for the magnetic pole. In the same whining tone that Robert Scott would later use upon hearing that Roald Amundsen (or Ernest Shackleton, for that matter) was heading to 'his' territory, Ross expressed his unhappiness that the Americans and the French would even consider sailing into 'his' area. The petulant Ross also refused to acknowledge a generous gesture made by Wilkes, who had left for him a chart tracing his track and discoveries, but took the useful data with him – and later used it to denounce Wilkes. Meanwhile, Ross reacted quickly, changing his plans to a more easterly longitude for the push south.

Good fortune was to be on his side, though the elements made Ross earn it. Sailing south along the 170°E meridian, he pushed through pack ice for four days, trusting that his reinforced ships would be able to go where none had gone before. On January 9, 1841, he broke through to open water, becoming the first to reach what we know today as the Ross Ice Shelf. The next day, Ross sighted land, a completely unexpected development. A boat was landed two days later on an islet named Possession Island and the new territory claimed for Queen Victoria.

Exciting though the discovery was, Ross' goal was the South Magnetic Pole, which had been calculated to lie both north and west of his current position. To follow the coast south and eastward would appear to be the 'wrong' way to get there, but to sail west would mean following in the tracks of Wilkes and Dumont d'Urville, something equally unappealing. Ross may have been thinking of the islands and channels of the Arctic he knew so well; perhaps sailing south and eastward would reveal a passage back toward the expected pole. So he stayed his course, discovering High (now called Ross) Island, and naming its two mountains – Erebus, the steaming volcano, and Terror, its easterly sister – for his ships.

Lying in Ross' path, however, was a formidable obstacle, one which so overwhelmed him that he called it simply 'the Victoria Barrier,' an enormous wall of shimmering ice towering 60m above the sea. It was, Ross wrote, 'a mighty and wonderful object far beyond anything we could have thought or conceived. What was beyond it we could not imagine.' But this mass, today known as the Ross Ice Shelf, also frustrated

Icebergs

The Antarctic ice sheet is the iceberg 'factory' of the Southern Ocean. The total volume of ice calved from the ice sheet each year is about 2300 cubic km, and it has been estimated that there are about 300,000 icebergs in the Southern Ocean at any one time. Individual icebergs range in dimensions from a few meters (these are often called 'growlers') to tens of meters ('bergy bits') to kilometers.

From time to time, particularly large icebergs break off the ice sheet. These can be tens of kilometers to even 100km long. At any one time there might be four or five gigantic icebergs in excess of 50km in length in the Southern Ocean, usually close to the Antarctic coast. It has been estimated that as much as 70% of the total volume of ice discharged from the Antarctic ice sheet is accounted for by icebergs of greater than a kilometer in length.

These larger icebergs are tabular in shape and form by calving from the large Antarctic ice shelves (the Ross, Filchner or Amery ice shelves, for example). Typically, these icebergs are about 30 to 40m high (above sea level) and as much as 300m deep. After erosion from wind and waves, and melting from the warmer sea temperatures away from the Antarctic coast, the tabular icebergs become unstable and roll over to form jagged irregular icebergs, sometimes with spikes towering up to 60m into the air and with even greater protrusions deep under the ocean surface. Ultimately, icebergs melt completely as they drift to more northerly, warmer water.

– Dr Jo Jacka

Ross: 'We might with equal chance of success try to sail through the cliffs of Dover.' The two ships, tiny by comparison, cruised along the Barrier for 450km, the sailors in awe of its unchanging face, which was oblivious to even the most gigantic wave crashing against it. After reaching a new southing record of 78°9'30'S on January 22, 1841, Ross ordered the yards braced 'round and headed for Hobart.

Sailing south again in November 1841, Ross this time aimed for the eastern extremity of the Barrier. New Year's Day found *Erebus* and *Terror* moored beside a large ice floe, on which the crews held 'a grand fancy ball,' complete with carved-ice thrones for the captains and a refreshment bar cut into the ice. Then, after surviving a horrifying storm amongst ice fragments 'hard as floating rocks of granite' which nearly destroyed both ships' rudders, they again reached the Barrier. It appeared to join a range of mountains, but winter's onset forced a retreat. Ross' third season was equally disappointing: trying to best Weddell's southing record in Weddell's namesake sea, Ross found conditions similar to those previously encountered by everyone but Weddell. He was forced to head home after reaching 71°30'S. The expedition reached England on September 2, 1843, after nearly 4½ years away. When Ross married later that year, his bride's father set one condition: he must promise to end his exploring days, a pledge Ross made and faithfully kept.

After Ross' important discoveries, Antarctica was once again ignored by the rest of the world. Ironically, this was due in part to Ross' old ships, *Erebus* and *Terror*, which John Franklin took to the Arctic in 1845 to try to navigate the Northwest Passage. When Franklin failed to return, Britain's naval resources were diverted for more than a decade in the search for some sign of his fate.

Larsen Norwegian Carl Anton Larsen (1860-1924) went to sea at 14, and at 25 became master of his first whaling ship. His first brush with polar fame came when he sailed in *Jason* on the same voyage that carried Fridtjof Nansen to Greenland for his famous east-to-west crossing in 1888. Whaling entrepreneur Christen Christiansen dispatched Larsen in *Jason* in 1892 to search for whales in the Antarctic. In 1893, having found fur and elephant seals but no whales of species he could catch, Larsen returned home. He went south again independently later that year, this time with three ships: *Jason*, *Hertha* and *Castor*.

The expedition explored both coasts of the northern Antarctic Peninsula, and made the first use of skis in Antarctica. Larsen also discovered petrified wood on Seymour Island. He went on to captain Otto Nordenskjöld's ship *Antarctic* in 1901 (see the section on Nordenskjöld later in this chapter), and to set up the whaling station at Grytviken on South Georgia in 1904.

Bull Norwegian-born Henrik Johan Bull (1844-1930) traveled to Australia in 1885 and set himself up in business. Convinced that a fortune could be made by reviving the Antarctic whaling trade, but unable to convince any Australians to join him, Bull returned to Norway in 1893. There he persuaded Svend Foyn, the wealthy inventor of the exploding harpoon gun, to back an expedition to assess the Ross Sea's potential as a whaling ground. Whales in the Northern Hemisphere had been hunted to commercial extinction, and though petroleum products had to some degree replaced whale oil, baleen (whale bone) was as prized as ever for women's fashions.

Sailing from Norway in 1893 in a refitted whaling steamer, *Antarctic*, Bull's expedition encountered many misfortunes in their hunt for whales, of which it saw few. A £3,000 profit made from sealing in Iles Kerguelen evaporated when the ship ran aground at Campbell Island. Putting in for repairs at Melbourne, the ship picked up a young Norwegian naturalist, Carsten E Borchgrevink (see the section on Borchgrevink later in this chapter), who signed on as assistant biologist. On January 18, 1895, *Antarctic* landed on the Possession Islands, where Borchgrevink discovered lichens, the first time vegetation had been found south of the Antarctic Circle.

Six days later, a party from *Antarctic* went ashore at Cape Adare in what was claimed to be the first landing ever made on the continent outside the Peninsula. Although Borchgrevink himself asserted that he had leapt out of the landing boat as it neared the shore in order to ensure himself a place in history – and made a widely reproduced drawing showing himself in the act – two others in the landing party disagreed upon just who first

placed his foot on the frozen shore, and their differences were eventually aired in the correspondence columns of the *Times* of London. In any case, the landing was only one of several disputed 'first landings' on the continent (see the boxed text 'Earliest Antarctic Landings' in this chapter). Penguins, rock specimens, seaweed and more lichens were collected, and though the voyage was not commercially successful, it helped to revive interest in Antarctica. Bull himself continued sealing and whaling, and at the age of 62 was shipwrecked and marooned on Iles Crozet for two months.

De Gerlache Belgian Adrien Victor Joseph de Gerlache de Gomery (1866-1934), a lieutenant in the Royal Belgian Navy, persuaded the Brussels Geographical Society to finance a scientific expedition to Antarctica. Sailing in a refitted three-masted sealing ship (with an auxiliary engine) that he purchased in Norway and rechristened *Belgica*, de Gerlache left Antwerp in 1897 with a decidedly international crew. The Belgian Antarctic Expedition included a Romanian zoologist, a Russian meteorologist, a Polish geologist (Henryk Arctowski, for whom the Polish research base on King George Island is named) and a Norwegian who offered to join the expedition as first mate, without pay: Roald Amundsen. As the ship's surgeon, de Gerlache signed an American, Frederick A Cook, who joined *Belgica* in Rio de Janiero.

The expedition got a late start sailing south, leaving Punta Arenas on December 14. Some now speculate that this tardy departure was a deliberate attempt by de Gerlache to ensure that *Belgica* would be beset in the ice and thus be forced to remain in the Antarctic for the winter. Others have correctly pointed out that Antarctic pack ice was known to be at its most navigable late in the summer. By early February, the expedition had discovered and mapped the strait which now bears de Gerlache's name on the west side of the Antarctic Peninsula, as well as the islands on the west side of that strait: Brabant, Liège, Anvers and Wiencke (the last named for a sailor who fell overboard and drowned). They also charted the Danco

They Come from Outta Space

One special night in 1969, the world watched with amazement as humanity planted its first steps on the moon, changing forever the point from which we view our planet. I was one of those viewers, and as an eight-year-old, was filled with visions of a future exploring the planets, piloting spacecraft and fighting ferocious aliens.

On a cold summer's day six months later, something nearly as momentous occurred, this time witnessed by only a few Japanese glaciologists. They discovered the first concentration of Antarctic meteorites, nine specimens in all, near the Queen Fabiola Mountains in East Antarctica. They had no idea their discovery would prove as important as the Apollo program in opening doors to the exploration of our solar system. Their serendipitous discovery evolved into a collection of more than 20,000 specimens, our only current and continuous source of macroscopic extraterrestrial materials. While the Apollo program ended just three years later, the Antarctic search for meteorites continued to grow and thrive. In the end, I did end up exploring other planets – by going to one of the most otherworldly places on Earth, searching for rocks from outer space.

There are two principal reasons Antarctica is the world's best place to look for meteorites. First, if you want to find objects that fall from the sky, simply spread out a giant white sheet and see what lands on it. Indeed, almost any rock you find on the East Antarctic ice sheet had to fall there. Second, there's a more subtle and dynamic mechanism concentrating meteorites in Antarctica. Meteorites falling randomly across the ice sheet get buried and travel with it as it flows out toward the Antarctic coast. The vast majority of these imbedded meteorites are lost to the Southern Ocean as the ice sheet calves icebergs. But in a few places, particularly where the ice sheet tries to squeeze through the Transantarctic Mountains, the flow of the ice can be dramatically slowed or stopped. If that happens where the ice is also exposed to the fierce winds of the plateau, massive amounts of ice sublimate, or change directly from solid to vapor. Where sublimation is strong, the loss of ice can be as much as several centimeters per day, producing beautiful deep-blue expanses of old glacial ice. Littered across this ice are meteorites, left behind because they can't evaporate. If we're really lucky, we find a place where this process has gone on for hundreds of thousands of years or more, allowing the meteorites to pile up until there are hundreds in an area the size of a football field.

Who cares? Why recover meteorites from anywhere, let alone Antarctica? Meteorites are rare scientific specimens – and outside of Antarctica, only a few are recovered each year. With the exception of a few lunar specimens, meteorites are the only samples we have of the extraterrestrial materials making up our solar system. Some represent the primitive building blocks from which our solar system formed, and are essentially unchanged since its birth 4.56 billion years ago. Others represent fragments of small planetary bodies broken up by impacts, providing samples from their deep interior. Still others are samples of intermediate planetoids with active and alien geological processes. A very small set of meteorites are pieces of the Moon and Mars, knocked loose by giant impacts and sent on a collision course with Earth. Among these is the now-famous ALH84001, a Martian sample within which some NASA researchers have suggested may be traces of ancient biological activity on Mars.

The most consistent Antarctic meteorite recovery program has been ANSMET (the Antarctic Search for Meteorites), whose annual expeditions, with support from the US National Science Foundation, have recovered nearly 10,000 specimens since 1976. The only other nation currently supporting active recovery of Antarctic meteorites is Japan, whose expeditions in Queen Maud Land have recovered even more specimens. Meteorites, like all Antarcticspecimens, are

They Come from Outta Space

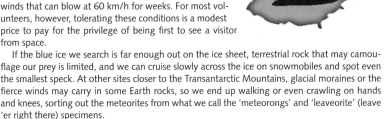

collected only for scientific purposes and are protected by the Antarctic Treaty.

The life of a meteorite hunter is scenic, cold and a little lonely. We camp near blue ice areas on the margins of the high-altitude polar plateau, sometimes with little to see but ice and snow in all directions. Many of these areas are literally off the map, and we give them colorful, unofficial names such as Footrot Flats and Mare Meteoriticus. We make our homes in double-walled Scott tents and depend on the 24 hours a day of sunshine to keep warm in temperatures as low as -40°C and winds that can blow at 60 km/h for weeks. For most volunteers, however, tolerating these conditions is a modest price to pay for the privilege of being first to see a visitor from space.

If the blue ice we search is far enough out on the ice sheet, terrestrial rock that may camouflage our prey is limited, and we can cruise slowly across the ice on snowmobiles and spot even the smallest speck. At other sites closer to the Transantarctic Mountains, glacial moraines or the fierce winds may carry in some Earth rocks, so we end up walking or even crawling on hands and knees, sorting out the meteorites from what we call the 'meteorongs' and 'leaveorite' (leave 'er right there) specimens.

The quarries we hunt are rarely as glamorous or beautiful as the meteorites you see in museums. The average find is about 10g in mass and smaller than a golfball. They range from unweathered specimens still dressed in the formal, glossy-black fusion crust they acquired during their fiery plunge through the Earth's atmosphere, to crumbling, rusty-grey fragments nearly indistinguishable from road gravel. To the meteorite hunter, of course, all meteorites are beautiful. But it's too hard to stay warm, and there are too many specimens for sentimentality – they get mundane names like EET96538. In a typical season we recover between a few hundred and a thousand specimens, each one bagged quickly, cleanly and efficiently to avoid human contamination (and frozen fingers).

At the end of a six-week season, we've recovered a suite of meteorites representing the rocky fragments our planet has swept up from space. The specimens are shipped, still frozen, to the Johnson Space Center in Houston, TX, for initial characterization and curation. Scientists knock off a few chips, looking for minerals or textures that help define the kind of meteorite it is, and write up an initial description of the sample. Twice a year, the JSC lab issues the Antarctic Meteorite newsletter, detailing recently recovered specimens and offering samples to interested researchers around the globe. Spreading the 'treasure' out this way has made ANSMET expeditions a unique example of cooperation in science, worthy of the international spirit shown by so many Antarctic endeavors.

– Dr Ralph P Harvey,
who has spent 10 summers in Antarctica as the principal investigator of the
Antarctic Search for Meteorites program (www.cwru.edu/affil/ansmet/)

Coast of the Peninsula, along the east side of the strait, named for the ship's magnetician, who also died during the expedition.

Photography was first used in Antarctica on this expedition, and Cook recorded that 'as the ship steamed rapidly along, spreading out one panorama after another of a new world, the noise of the camera was as regular and successive as the tap of a stock ticker.' (Seem familiar?)

On February 15, 1898, *Belgica* crossed the Antarctic Circle, and by March 1, already deep into the heavy pack, she reached 71°31'S. The next day began a long imprisonment in the ice. In fact, the ship would not be freed for 377 days – and then only by enormous effort and a great deal of luck. During this, the first time anyone had wintered south of the Antarctic Circle, the expedition underwent great hardships: midwinter darkness toyed with the men's sanity, and the lack of vitamin C made them ripe for scurvy.

Frederick Cook, who had been on the North Greenland Expedition with Robert E Peary in 1891 and then returned to Greenland twice more in the next three years, likely saved the ship. To prevent scurvy, he urged de Gerlache to set an example by eating fresh seal and penguin meat, which the men detested. He organized elaborate betting games to take the crew's minds off their desperate circumstances and encouraged them to think of their own amusements. One popular event, held on Belgian King Leopold's birthday, was a 'Grand Concourse of Beautiful Women,' in which 464 illustrations of beauties 'representing all kinds of poses and dress and undress' were selected from a Paris journal and judged according to 21 characteristics, including 'rosy complexion,' 'underclothes,' 'most beautiful face' and 'sloping, alabaster shoulders.' It was the men's hope that once the expedition returned to civilization the winners would agree to appear before the committee to receive their prizes.

That they *would* return to civilization was by no means certain, however. By January 1899, Cook suggested that they attempt to liberate themselves by hand-sawing a canal 600m long from a *polynya*, or stretch of open water, back to the ship, pushing the ice pieces that they cut from the canal out into the open water. They worked like dogs for a month. When they were within 30m of the ship, a wind shift tightened the pack ice and their hard-won canal closed up within an hour. Two weeks later, the ice opened and they steamed into the polynya, only to be forced to wait another month until they could gain the open sea. *Belgica* finally reached Punta Arenas on March 28, 1899.

The primary achievement of the Belgian Antarctic Expedition – surviving the first Antarctic night – proved that bases could be set up on the continent itself, enabling a full-time program of exploration. That knowledge was crucial for the next phase of Antarctic discovery.

Adrien de Gerlache remained involved in Antarctic affairs. In 1903, he joined Charcot's *Français* expedition (see the section on Charcot later in this chapter), but resigned in Buenos Aires. He later launched a business venture he called 'polar safaris,' taking tourists to East Greenland and Spitsbergen, but the enterprise collapsed in its initial phase, and de Gerlache sold his ship, *Polaris*, a 300-ton barquentine, to Ernest Shackleton, who renamed it *Endurance*. De Gerlache's son, Gaston de Gerlache, joined the Belgian Antarctic Expedition of 1957-59.

Borchgrevink Carsten Egeberg Borchgrevink (1864-1934), the son of a Norwegian father and an English mother, got his start in Antarctic exploration shipping out with Bull in *Antarctic* in 1894. His landing at Cape Adare convinced Borchgrevink that it would be possible to survive an Antarctic winter ashore, so he decided to organize his own expedition with the goal of being the first to accomplish it.

After failing to raise any money for his expedition in Australia, Borchgrevink visited Britain, where he met with rejection after rejection – until 1897, when he convinced a wealthy magazine publisher, Sir George Newnes, to sponsor the expedition, to the tune of £40,000. Borchgrevink's stunning fundraising success infuriated the British exploration establishment, headed by the

The *Akademik Shokalski* navigating the Ross Sea

Relaxing on deck

Climber on Brunhilde Peak, Asgard Range

Swimmers enjoying volcanically heated water, Deception Island

Royal Geographical Society, because it was preparing to mount its own voyage of Antarctic discovery. Even more galling was the fact that Borchgrevink's 'British' Antarctic Expedition of 1898-90 was British in name only; just three (two Englishmen and one Australian) of the 31 men were not Norwegians. The expedition ship *Southern Cross*, a converted Norwegian sealer equipped with powerful engines, sailed under the Union Jack only at the insistence of its magnanimous sponsor.

Southern Cross departed London on August 22, 1898, and arrived at Cape Adare on February 17, 1899. Two weeks later, after a pair of simple wooden huts were erected on Ridley Beach, which Borchgrevink named for his mother, *Southern Cross* departed to winter in New Zealand. The 10 men left behind were some of the most solitary in history, having the entire Antarctic continent to themselves.

They had plenty of canine companionship, however, for Borchgrevink had brought 90 sledge dogs with him, the first dogs ever used in Antarctic work. The expedition also pioneered the use of kayaks for sea travel, and was the first to bring to Antarctica the Primus stove, a lightweight, portable pressure stove invented in Sweden six years before. Although the kayak never became an important mode of Antarctic transport, the Primus stove was carried by nearly every expedition that followed Borchgrevink, and is still in use today.

Unfortunately, the expedition marked another first – the first human death on the continent – when Norwegian zoologist Nicolai Hansen died on October 14, 1899, and was buried on the ridge above Cape Adare. Aside from Hansen's death, there were other accidents – including a nearly disastrous fire and a narrow escape from asphyxiation by coal fumes – but the expedition escaped the dietary and psychological dangers experienced by *Belgica*'s crew during their long Antarctic night. By the time the ship returned on January 28, 1900, to pick up the expedition, it had proven a critical fact: humans could survive Antarctica's fiercely cold, dark winter ashore, using a wooden hut as a base for travels along the coasts and inland towards the Pole.

Borchgrevink's expedition produced many positive results, including excellent maps of the Ross Sea area produced by the expedition's English surveyor and magnetician, William Colbeck of the Royal Navy, which would prove invaluable to later explorers. Nevertheless, Borchgrevink's return to England was all but unheralded. The exploration establishment was still embittered by his fundraising success – and absorbed by Robert F Scott's impending expedition. Not until 1930 did the Royal Geographical Society see fit to award Borchgrevink its Patron's Medal. He died in Norway four years later.

Drygalski University of Berlin geography Professor Erich Dagobert von Drygalski (1865-1949), leader of a four-year expedition to Greenland, was given command of the German South Polar Expedition in 1898. Three years later, Drygalski and 31 other men sailed from Kiel on August 11, 1901, in *Gauss*, a three-masted schooner fitted with auxiliary engines. Drygalski named the ship after German mathematician Johann Karl Friedrich Gauss, who had calculated the position of the South Magnetic Pole, the accuracy of which James Clark Ross had set out to test.

Stopping en route at Cape Town and Iles Kerguelen (where it picked up 40 dogs), the expedition sighted land on February 21, 1902, in the region of 90°E, a territory which Drygalski named Kaiser Wilhelm II Land (now called Wilhelm II Land). On the same day, the ship got caught in the ice, soon becoming, in Drygalski's words, 'a toy of the elements.'

With *Gauss* trapped in the west-drifting pack, the men settled into a routine of scientific work by day and card games, lectures, beer and music by night. With snow drifted up over the ship, its warm, humid interior was infused with a very German *gemütlichkeit*, or coziness. A sledging party journeyed 80km to the Antarctic coast, discovering along the way a low hill they named Gaussberg after their ship. On March 29, 1902,

Drygalski ascended to 480m in a large, tethered hydrogen balloon and used a telephone to report his observations to the ship. This was the second use of aviation in Antarctic history, after Scott's tethered flight during the *Discovery* expedition (see below). The men also recorded penguin sounds with an early phonograph, and undertook two more sledging trips to Gaussberg, on the last of which Drygalski and his companions nearly became lost in the trackless white wasteland of snow-covered sea ice.

Being beset during the winter was one thing, but when spring and then summer arrived, the men began to feel desperate, especially after sawing, drilling and even dynamiting the 5m- to 6m-thick ice did nothing to free the ship. *Gauss*' captain suggested that they toss message-filled bottles into the sea – and launch others by balloon – in hopes that a rescue party might find them. In the end, they were liberated thanks to a basic principle of physics luckily observed by Drygalski himself during a walk on the ice. He remarked that cinders from the ship's smokestack caused the ice on which they landed to melt, since the dark ashes absorbed the sun's heat. Devising an ingenious method of escape, he ordered his men to lay a trail of coal ash, supplemented by rotting food and other garbage, across the 600m of ice that separated *Gauss* from open water.

As hoped, the trick worked, and soon there was a 2m-deep channel filled with water. Two months passed, however, before the bottom of the canal cracked open, on February 8, 1903, and the ship was freed. The expedition then spent seven weeks trying to chart the Kaiser Wilhelm II coast, but constantly shifting sea ice threatened to trap *Gauss* once more, and Drygalski reluctantly ordered the ship north on March 31. After reaching Cape Town, he wired Berlin for permission to return to the Antarctic the following season. But the Kaiser, apparently disappointed that more new territory was not discovered and claimed for the Fatherland, refused the request. Despite his disappointment, Drygalski spent the next three decades writing up the expedition's reports, which occupy 20 full volumes.

Nordenskjöld Swedish geologist Nils Otto Gustav Nordenskjöld (1869-1928) had previously led expeditions to both the Yukon and Tierra del Fuego, and his uncle, the North Polar explorer Nils AE Nordenskjöld, made the first transit of the Northeast Passage around Siberia. So he was well suited for the task that was assigned to him in 1900: leadership of the Swedish South Polar Expedition, which would be the first to winter in the Antarctic Peninsula region.

Sailing in *Antarctic*, the stout former whaler used by Henrik Bull in 1893-95, the expedition left Gothenburg on October 16, 1901. At *Antarctic*'s helm was Captain Carl Anton Larsen, the Norwegian who had already discovered Oscar II Land during a previous expedition in 1892-94 (see above), and who would later set up Antarctica's first whaling station at Grytviken, South Georgia. By late January 1902 *Antarctic* was exploring the western side of the Peninsula, making several important geographical discoveries in the area (among them, the fact that the Orleans Strait connected with the Gerlache Strait, and not with the Weddell Sea, as had been believed) before sailing back to the tip of the Peninsula. There, they crossed between the Peninsula and off-lying Joinville Island, naming the strait for their ship, *Antarctic*.

Next, the expedition attempted to penetrate south into the Weddell Sea, but its infamous ice stopped them, and instead Nordenskjöld and five men set up a winter base on Snow Hill Island, off the east coast of the Peninsula, in February 1902. *Antarctic*, meanwhile, sailed for the Falklands to winter there. Poor weather confined the shore party to its small hut for most of the winter, but in December Nordenskjöld was able to sledge to Seymour Island, directly north of Snow Hill, where he found some striking fossils, including the bones of a giant penguin, bolstering earlier fossil finds made by Captain Larsen on the island in 1893.

But December is midsummer in Antarctica, and the men were getting distinctly anxious about their ship, which should have arrived by then. Their fears were justified, though they were not to learn why for many months. After wintering in Patagonia and South Georgia, *Antarctic* had returned south, again surveying the western side of the Peninsula. Trying unsuccessfully to cross through her namesake strait to reach the Peninsula's east coast – and the men at Snow Hill Island – *Antarctic* stopped at Hope Bay on the Peninsula's tip to drop off three men, who would try to hike the 320km to Snow Hill. The ship then sailed around Joinville Island and headed south, soon becoming caught in the pack ice, whose relentless grip inexorably crushed it. The end, on February 12, 1903, was recorded by one of the men, Carl Skottsberg:

Now the name disappears from sight. Now the water is up to the rail, and, with a rattle, the seas and bits of ice rush in over her deck. That sound I can never forget, however long I may live...the streamer, with the name *Antarctic*, disappears in the waves. The bowsprit – the last mast-top – She is gone!

The ship sank 40km east of tiny Paulet Island, and the men sledged for 14 days to reach it.

The three men left at Hope Bay, meanwhile, found their way to Snow Hill Island blocked by open water, so they settled down to wait for *Antarctic*'s return, according to a prearranged plan. The Swedish Antarctic Expedition was now split into three groups, two living in very rough conditions, with no group aware of the others' fates. How they all managed to survive is one of the greatest examples of good fortune in Antarctic history.

The Hope Bay trio, after eking out the winter in a primitive hut and living primarily on seal meat, set out again for Snow Hill Island on September 29. By a lucky coincidence, Nordenskjöld and another man were dog-sledging north at the same time on a research journey, and on October 12, the two groups met. Nordenskjöld was so struck by the Hope Bay men's remarkable appearance – they were completely soot-blackened, and wearing odd masks they had fashioned to prevent snow blindness – that he wondered if they were from a previously unknown race of men. Nordenskjöld's companion, Ole Jonassen, considered that an

unholstered revolver might be a necessary precaution in facing these disconcerting apparitions. But they quickly established the identities of their fellow expeditioners, renaming the point of their rendezvous 'Cape Well Met.'

Antarctic's crew, meanwhile, wintered on Paulet Island. They built a stone hut and killed 1100 Adélies for food before the birds left for the winter. On June 7, just before midwinter, one of the party who had been sick for weeks, Ole Wennersgaard, died. On October 31, Larsen led a group of five others in an open boat to search for the trio at Hope Bay. Finding a note the three had left at their hut, Larsen decided he would have to follow by sea the route that the Hope Bay men were taking to Snow Hill Island.

Even as Larsen's group rowed their boat south, outside help was on its way to Snow Hill Island. Since nothing had been heard of the Swedish expedition, three search parties had been dispatched. Argentina sent a naval ship, *Uruguay*, to search for it in 1903. On November 8, *Uruguay*'s crew found two of the men from Snow Hill Island camped at Seymour Island, and after waking them, joined them in the short trek to Snow Hill – arriving, by incredible coincidence, only a few hours ahead of Larsen and his group. After a joyful reunion, all that was left to do (on November 11) was to pick up the remaining *Antarctic* crew members back on Paulet Island, who, ironically, had just finished collecting 6000 penguin eggs, their first surplus food supply.

Although Nordenskjöld's expedition is remembered primarily for its survival against nearly overwhelming odds, it also performed the most important research in Antarctica undertaken up to its time.

Scott's *Discovery* Expedition Even as Nordenskjöld's men were struggling for survival, British explorer Captain Robert Falcon Scott (1868-1912) was working from a base established on Ross Island. The son of an upper-middle-class brewer, Scott had joined the Royal Navy's training ship *Britannia* as a cadet at the age of 13, and advanced through the ranks, being promoted to commander in June 1900. A month later he was named leader of the British National Antarctic Expedition, which the country's exploration establishment had been planning since the mid-1880s. It was this expedition on which Borchgrevink stole a march by securing his large grant from Sir George Newnes in 1897.

When Scott's well-financed expedition sailed from England on August 6, 1901 in *Discovery*, a specially built wooden steam barque, it was the best equipped scientific expedition to Antarctica to that date. After stopping in New Zealand for refitting and reprovisioning, the expedition got off to an inauspicious start when a seaman fell to his death from the top of the mainmast. By January 3, 1902, *Discovery* crossed the Antarctic Circle, and six days later stopped briefly at Cape Adare. Penetrating the Ross Sea, Scott cruised along the Ross Ice Shelf, discovering King Edward VII Land on the shelf's eastern margin. He also made the first flight in Antarctica, on February 4, 1902, in a tethered balloon called *Eva*. From a height of 240m, Scott saw the undulating surface of the Ross Ice Shelf rising toward the polar plateau. Camera-toting expedition member Ernest Shackleton went up next, making himself Antarctica's first aerial photographer.

By mid-February 1902, Scott's men had established winter quarters at Hut Point on Ross Island. Although a hut was built ashore, *Discovery*, frozen into the sea ice, served as the expedition's accommodations, with officers and crew separated into wardroom and messdeck, befitting the quasi-naval expedition that it was. The shore building was reserved for scientific work and recreation, including theatrical performances, when it was called 'The Royal Terror Theatre.' But life in McMurdo Sound was not all research-and-games: In a violent snowstorm during a sledge trip, a young sailor named George Vince slipped over a precipice to his death. The winter passed fairly quietly otherwise, the group's accommodations made cheerier by another Antarctic first – electric lights (powered by a windmill). With Shackleton as editor, the expedition published Antarctica's

first magazine, the monthly *South Polar Times*, as well as one issue of a more ribald alternative, the *Blizzard*, whose title page featured a figure holding a bottle, captioned 'Never mind the blizzard, I'm all right.'

With spring, the expedition's real work began. To the cheers of *Discovery*'s men, Scott set out for the South Pole on November 2, 1902, with Shackleton, scientific officer Dr Edward A Wilson, 19 dogs and five supply sledges hitched up in train formation. Despite initial optimism and a large depot of food laid by an advance party, the trio soon struck harsh reality, Antarctica-style. They had never tried skiing or sled dog driving, and their inexperience produced predictably poor results.

Through sheer willpower, they reached 82°16.5'S on December 30 before turning back. Actually, Scott and Wilson reached that point, Shackleton having been ordered to remain at camp that morning to look after the dogs. This may or may not have been an intentional slight on the part of Scott (though certainly it was petty), but Shackleton smarted at the gesture.

For all of them, the trip home was miserable. The remaining dogs by now were nearly worthless, and soon were hitched *behind* the sledge, which the men pulled themselves. On at least one occasion, a dog was carried on the sledge. As dogs weakened, they were shot and fed to the others. The men, meanwhile, were also breaking down. Shackleton especially was suffering from scurvy, and suffering badly – but those accounts of the trip that say he had to be carried on the sledge are false.

Two weeks before the southern party's return home on February 3, the relief ship *Morning* had arrived in McMurdo Sound. *Morning*'s captain, William Colbeck, had been the surveyor on Borchgrevink's *Southern Cross* expedition. Colbeck and Scott, upon his return, decided that with *Discovery* still frozen into the ice, *Morning* should not wait to depart. With the prospect strong that he would have to remain another winter, Scott sent home eight men, including Shackleton, who went only upon being ordered to do so. The following summer, after Scott led a sledging party in southern Victoria Land, *Morning* returned, in company with *Terra Nova*, sent by the British government. The two vessels bore a distressing order: if *Discovery* could not be freed within six weeks, it would have to be abandoned. After weeks of cutting and blasting with explosives, Scott was nearly ready to give up, but nature relented, and the ice gave way. One final blast, on February 16, 1904, released *Discovery* for the long journey home.

Bruce Scotsman William Spiers Bruce (1867-1921), the physician son of a surgeon, joined a whaling voyage to the Antarctic from Dundee in *Balaena* in 1892 as surgeon and naturalist. He would have joined Bull's *Antarctic* expedition in 1894-95, but was unable to reach Melbourne in time to meet the ship. Bruce also later made many trips to the Arctic. In 1901, he declined the offer of a position on Scott's expedition because he was in the midst of planning his own, the Scottish National Antarctic Expedition.

Sailing from Troon on November 2, 1902 in *Scotia*, a renamed Norwegian steam sealer with extremely elegant lines, the expedition pushed south into the Weddell Sea. By 70°S, *Scotia* was beset, and after freeing herself, headed north to winter at Laurie Island in the South Orkneys. There the expedition set up a meteorological station, hand-built of stone and called Omond House, on April 1, 1903. Midwinter's Day (June 22) 1903 was celebrated with a barrel of Guinness porter, a brew made more potent by the freezing of its water, unintentionally yielding concentrated alcohol. At the end of the first season, *Scotia* sailed to Port Stanley and Buenos Aires. Bruce asked the British government to continue staffing Omond House, but his request was refused. Instead, at the invitation of the British Ambassador, the Oficina Meteorológica Argentina agreed to assume responsibility for the station. This duty the Argentine government maintains to the present day, making the station (now called Orcadas) the oldest continuously operated scientific base in the Antarctic.

Pushing south again in January 1904, Bruce was able to penetrate the Weddell Sea

to 74°S. There he discovered Coats Land, named for the expedition's patrons, Andrew and James Coats of Paisley, Scotland. *Scotia* followed the coast for 240km, but always the fast ice kept the ship two or three frustrating kilometers offshore, and no landing could be made. The Scottish expedition, however, could claim an important milestone: moving pictures were made in the Antarctic for the first time. There was another pioneering achievement: a remarkable series of photographs, documenting the first known use of bagpipes in the Far South, shows an emperor penguin, head thrown back and beak agape, being serenaded by a kilted piper. Although an observer noted 'only sleepy indifference,' some of the photos show that the bird was tethered by a line to prevent escape.

Though Bruce later became a world authority on Spitsbergen in the Arctic, he must have retained a special love for the Antarctic; upon his death in 1921, his ashes were carried south and poured into the Southern Ocean.

Charcot French physician Jean-Baptiste Etienne August Charcot (1867-1936) inherited 400,000 gold francs and a Fragonard painting, *Le Pacha*, from his father, a famous neurologist whose work influenced Freud. Charcot used this entire fortune to finance construction of a three-masted schooner, *Français*, and to outfit it with laboratory equipment. His original intention had been to sail north to the Arctic, but when word arrived that Nordenskjöld's expedition was missing in Antarctica, Charcot decided to go south. Meanwhile, French citizens rallied to the French Antarctic Expedition, contributing 450,000 francs.

Français sailed from Le Havre on August 15, 1903 – into immediate tragedy. Just minutes off the quay a hawser parted, striking and killing a sailor; the expedition was delayed 12 days before departing without further incident. Belgian explorer de Gerlache accompanied the expedition as far as Buenos Aires, where he told Charcot that he missed his new fiancée too much to continue. Also in Buenos Aires, the expedition learned that the Argentine ship *Uruguay* had already rescued Nordenskjöld and his men, so Charcot decided instead to investigate the west coast of the Peninsula. He deliberately chose to avoid the Ross Sea, with its potential for international rivalry, an act for which the territorial Robert Scott later called him 'the gentleman of the Pole.'

By February 19, 1904, Charcot had discovered Port Lockroy on Wiencke Island. Sailing on, he decided to winter at a sheltered bay on the north coast of Booth Island, a place he named Port Charcot. The bay was so small that the explorers were able to stretch a hawser across its mouth to keep out ice that might otherwise crush their ship. Winter passed with various amusements (including reading and discussing old newspapers) and sledging expeditions to nearby islands. The peace was marred only by the death of the ship's pet pig, Toby, who ate a bucketful of fish – along with the hooks that caught them.

After the spring breakup, the expedition sailed north, running into trouble on January 15, 1903, when *Français* struck a rock. Despite attempts at plugging the hole and round-the-clock pumping, the ship continued to flood. Temporary repairs effected at Port Lockroy enabled the expedition to continue to Tierra del Fuego and Buenos Aires, where Charcot sold *Français* to the Argentine government. Then he headed home to a hero's welcome from all of France – except his wife (a granddaughter of Victor Hugo) who divorced him for desertion.

Four years later, Charcot returned to Antarctica, this time as head of an expedition sponsored by the French government, which granted him 600,000 francs. On August 15, 1908, he again sailed from Le Havre, this time in the newly built and amusingly named *Pourquoi Pas?* ('Why Not?'), which he had once christened his toy boats as a child. Among those aboard was Charcot's second wife, Meg, who sailed as far as Punta Arenas. (Wary of repeating his failed first marriage, Charcot had secured a prenuptial agreement from her that she would not oppose his explorations.)

After a stop at Deception Island's whaling station, where Charcot saved a man from a

hideous death by amputating his gangrenous hand, *Pourquoi Pas?* sailed on Christmas Day 1908, and continued the survey work on the west side of the Peninsula that Charcot had begun with *Français*. As on his previous voyage, unfortunately, Charcot struck a rock, damaging *Pourquoi Pas?*, which had pumps that were able to manage the water pouring in through the seam. The expedition pushed on, discovering and naming the Fallières Coast, circling Adelaide Island and proving its insularity, and discovering Marguerite Bay and naming it for Meg. Most useful for this survey work was a small, iron-prowed motorboat carried in *Pourquoi Pas?*. The ship also boasted electric lighting and a 1500-volume library.

Those amenities proved valuable during the winter of 1909, when the expedition wintered at Petermann Island, with *Pourquoi Pas?* frozen into the ice at a bay they called Port Circumcision. The group set up a shore station, with huts for meteorological, seismic, magnetic and tidal research, and passed the winter with reading, lectures, meetings of the 'Antarctic Sporting Club' and recitations from a novel being written by one of the officers.

At winter's end, they returned north to resupply with coal at Deception – where a whaling-company diver inspected the ship's damaged hull and warned against further exploration. This advice Charcot ignored, heading south a final time. On January 11, 1910, he made his most personally treasured discovery, sighting an uncharted headland at 70°S, 76°W. This he called Charcot Land (since proven to be an island) – not after himself, but after his esteemed father. Twenty-six years later, Charcot and *Pourquoi Pas?* were again sailing in treacherous waters, this time off Iceland, when a gale arose and claimed captain, ship and all but one of 43 crew.

Shackleton's *Nimrod* Expedition Irishman Ernest Henry Shackleton (1874-1922), second of 10 children born to a doctor and his Quaker wife, had been badly stung by his breakdown on the return from Scott's furthest south in 1902. Indeed, Shackleton lived by his family motto: *Fortitudine Vincimus* (By Fortitude We Conquer). Even as he was being sent home as an invalid by Scott, Shackleton resolved that he would one day return to Antarctica – which he did in 1908. An indefatigable worker with a charming and forceful personality, Shackleton inspired fierce loyalty and admiration from his men, who called him 'The Boss.'

Following his return from *Discovery* expedition, Shackleton had married and fathered the first of his three children, at the same time holding a succession of jobs: magazine journalist, secretary of the Scottish Royal Geographical Society, (unsuccessful) candidate for Parliament, and finally, PR man for a big Glasgow steelworks. The works' owner, William Beardmore, took a liking to Shackleton and agreed to sponsor an Antarctic expedition.

The British Antarctic Expedition sailed from Lyttelton, New Zealand, on New Year's Day 1908, in *Nimrod*, a three-masted sealing ship with 40 years' experience in the Arctic. To conserve coal, the ship was towed part of the 2700km to the ice edge by the steel-hulled *Koonya*. Although Shackleton had originally intended to use *Discovery*'s old base at Ross Island, Scott wrote to him describing his own plans for another Antarctic expedition and asking him to establish his shore base elsewhere, a show of territoriality that seems presumptuous today. Shackleton agreed to seek his own headquarters, but when he arrived at the Ross Ice Shelf in January 1908, he was dismayed to find that the inlet where *Discovery* had launched its balloon just six years before, the Bay of Whales, had disappeared. Evidently the great ice shelf had calved, and if so, it would be very risky to try to set up a base on top of it. But *Nimrod* was unable to push farther east, due to pack ice, so Shackleton reluctantly decided to use Ross Island as his base – breaking his promise to Scott.

Unforgiving ice blocked his path to Hut Point, however, and Shackleton was compelled to build his hut at Cape Royds on Ross Island, 30km farther from the polar goal. While he didn't bring sledge dogs, neither did Shackleton agree with Scott's ro-mantic but misguided notion that manhauling was 'more noble and splendid' than dog-driving. Instead, Shackleton brought with him ponies from Siberia, which unfortunately were unsuited to the task. Although they managed to pull loads a considerable distance across the Ross Ice Shelf, they did not have the stamina or versatility of dogs.

With three companions – Jameson Adams, Eric Marshall and Frank Wild – Shackleton pioneered the route up to the polar plateau (which he claimed, and named, for King Edward VII) via the Beardmore Glacier, which he named for the expedition's patron. By January 9, 1909, the foursome had trudged on foot to within 156km (later sources figure it was more like 180km – but who's counting?) of the Pole before being forced by dangerously dwindling supplies of food to turn and run for home. It was the hardest decision of Shackleton's life. He told his wife Emily later: 'I thought you'd rather have a live donkey than a dead lion.' Still, they had achieved a remarkable run, beating Scott's furthest south by 589km, discovering almost 800km of new mountain range, and showing the way to anyone who would attempt the Pole after them. They also found coal and fossils at Mt Buckley at the top of the Beardmore Glacier.

The expedition achieved other firsts as well. Six men, led by Professor TW Edgeworth David, ascended Mt Erebus for the first time, reaching the rim of the volcano's crater on March 10, 1908 after a five-day climb. While the polar party was out, three of the expedition's members – Douglas Mawson and Alistair Mackay with Professor David again leading – hiked nearly 1600km to the South Magnetic Pole, reaching it on January 16, 1909, the first time it had ever been visited. (Today the pole is offshore in the Dumont d'Urville Sea, and Antarctic tour ships routinely sail over it.) The expedition also saw the Antarctic's first motor car, an Arrol Johnston, tested at Cape Royds (it was no good in snow, but proved useful for transporting loads across the sea ice), and produced about 80 copies of *Aurora Australis*, the first – and only – book published in Antarctica.

Amundsen Norwegian Roald Engebreth Gravning Amundsen (1872-1928) was already a veteran explorer by the time he sailed in 1910 from Christiana (modern-day Oslo) on his way to what only he and a few others knew was the Antarctic. Amundsen had been with the first group to winter south of the Antarctic Circle, the *Belgica* expedition, and in 1903-06 had accomplished the first navigation of the Northwest Passage, a goal sought by mariners for centuries. He spent three winters in the Arctic, learning much from the native Eskimos about polar clothing, travel and dog-handling that would later prove invaluable.

The Arctic had always been Amundsen's first interest, and he had long dreamed of reaching the North Pole. Indeed, he was well into the planning for an expedition to freeze his ship into the ice and drift with the current across the Pole when news reached him that American Robert E Peary claimed to have reached 90°N on April 6, 1909. Amundsen quickly – and secretly – turned his ambitions 180°.

Fram, Amundsen's aptly named ship (it means 'Forward'), which had been used by Norwegian explorer Fridtjof Nansen on his unsuccessful attempt to reach the North Pole, sailed from Norway on June 6, 1911. *Fram* had a diesel engine, allowing quick start-up (as opposed to a coal-fired steam engine), as well as a rounded hull so that it would rise up out of pressing ice floes rather than being nipped as a standard hull would. In order not to let his rival Robert Scott know of his plans, Amundsen kept quiet about his intentions – revealing them to just three members of the expedition – until he reached Madeira. There he told his stunned men, and soon after, sent his infamous telegram to Scott in Melbourne: 'Beg leave to inform you *Fram* proceeding Antarctic Amundsen.'

Amundsen did not share Shackleton's fear of a dangerously calving Ross Ice Shelf. Instead, he established his base, Framheim ('home of *Fram*'), right on the shelf at the Bay of Whales, where Scott had previously made Antarctica's first balloon flight. There, in a small prefab wooden hut, nine men spent the winter. Outside, some of the 15 identical tents served as store sheds – and some as doghouses for the expedition's 97 North Greenland dogs. From Framheim, Amundsen had the advantage of starting 100km closer to the Pole, but he also had to pioneer a route up to the polar plateau from the Ross Ice Shelf. Scott, following Shackleton's lead, could take the charted course up the Beardmore Glacier.

Setting out from Framheim on October 19, 1911, after making one false start too early in season, Amundsen and his four companions had four sledges, each pulled by 13 Greenland dogs. Dogs and skis made the difference for them. As Norwegians, they were well trained in the use of skis, and during his years in the Arctic, Amundsen had developed excellent dog-driving skills. He also planned meticulously, took three or four backups of every critical item, and laid 10 extremely well-marked depots as far as 82°S, which together contained 3400kg of stores and food.

The five men – Amundsen, Olav Bjaaland, Helmer Hanssen, Sverre Hassel and Oscar Wisting – reached the South Pole on December 14, 1911, camping for three days at what they called *Polheim*. Amundsen claimed the polar plateau for Norway, calling it King Haakon VII Land, and wrote a note to Scott in the dark green tent he left behind. Then, they turned for home.

'On January 25, at 4 am,' Amundsen laconically recorded in his diary, 'we reached our good little house again, with two sledges and 11 dogs; men and animals all hale and hearty.' Despite his near-flawless success, there were those who felt Amundsen's achievement was tainted by several factors. In some ways, he had made the polar journey look *too* easy. There was also the view taken by some that Amundsen's surprise assault on the Pole had forestallen Scott, as though the British explorer had the 'right' to reach the Pole first (though Amundsen, in fact, preceded him to the Antarctic). Finally, the tragic drama of Scott's expedition was much more the stuff of legend than was Amundsen's cool triumph of technical skill.

Scott's *Terra Nova* Expedition When Amundsen's startling cable reached him, Scott became deeply distressed, though he worked hard not to show it. He had first watched Shackleton come close to snatching what he regarded as his prize, and now a dangerous new threat had arisen.

Sailing from New Zealand on November 29, 1910, in *Terra Nova*, the old Scottish whaler that had been one of the two relief ships sent at the end of the *Discovery* expedition, Scott's British Antarctic Expedition got off to a rough start. Just three days after weighing anchor, *Terra Nova* was hit by a screaming gale that lasted 36 hours and nearly sank the ship. Arriving at Ross Island in January 1911, Scott found ice blocking the way to his old *Discovery* hut on Hut Point, so he established winter quarters at Cape Evans, named after his second-in-command, ERGR 'Teddy' Evans. As soon as the hut was built, Scott commenced an ambitious program of depot-laying. He also introduced a useful innovation to Antarctica: A telephone line was established between Cape Evans and Hut Point. Mules, ponies, motor-sledges and dogs were employed to set up supply caches, but once again, when these methods failed, the expedition resorted to the old British standby, manhauling.

The next spring, on October 24, Scott dispatched a party with two motor-sledges, and eight days later followed with a larger group of men and 10 ponies. Various teams relayed the supplies and laid depots until, on January 4, 1912, the last support party turned back. For the final push to the Pole, Scott had chosen his companion on his previous furthest south, Edward Wilson, along with Lawrence Oates, Edgar Evans and Henry Bowers, who was added only the night before. (Another tactical error, since the food, tent and skis had been planned for four-man teams.)

What happened next is the most famous Antarctic story of all: the five arrived at the South Pole on January 17, 1912, to find that Amundsen had beaten them by 35 days. Nothing tells the tale better than Scott's diary itself, unless it is one of the many biographies that deconstruct what has grown to be a hoary legend. Their return home was a haunting, desperate run of barely sighted depots, slow starvation and incredible cold. A delirious Evans died on February 17. A month later, Oates was in such bad shape that he prayed not to wake upon retiring. The next morning, deeply disappointed to find himself still among the living, Oates walked out of the tent during a raging blizzard, telling his companions simply, 'I am just going outside and may be some time.' Another blizzard kept the three remaining men in their tent from March 21 onwards. Scott's last entry was dated March 29.

(In a depressing fin-de-siécle postscript to the story, Captain Scott's descendants decided to sell several artifacts from his last expedition at an auction in London in late 1999. They had been kept in a bank vault for half a century by Sir Peter Scott, Captain Scott's son. Parts of the Primus stove on which the three last members of the polar party may have cooked their final hot meal brought £27,600. A Union Jack found with the bodies, possibly flown by the party at the Pole, sold for £25,300.)

Despite being beaten to the Pole, Scott's last expedition accomplished a great deal of important science. (In fact, the push for research had itself contributed to the polar party's destruction, since the men dragged a sledge which carried, among other items, 16kg of geological samples.) The infamous three-man midwinter trek to Cape Crozier, which Apsley Cherry-Garrard chronicled so eloquently in *The Worst Journey in the World*, braved 24-hour darkness and temperatures as low as -59°C – so cold that the men's teeth cracked in their mouths and they were 'beginning to think of death as a friend,' as Cherry-Garrard wrote – all so that they could be the first to collect emperor penguin embryos. A separate Northern Party, led by Victor Campbell, discovered Oates Land (named for Lawrence Oates) and spent a winter of terrible privation in a snow cave at Terra Nova Bay on the western shore of the Ross Sea. And a six-man group led by geologist Griffith Taylor explored the mysterious, otherworldly Dry Valleys, which Scott had found on the *Discovery* expedition.

Shirase Coming from a country with no tradition of exploration, Nobu Shirase (1861-1946), a lieutenant in the Japanese Navy and the eldest son of a Buddhist priest, was a surprise. Despite the Japanese public's outright scorn of his fundraising efforts, Shirase organized an Antarctic expedition in 1910. Sailing from Tokyo on December 1 in *Kainan Maru* ('Southern Pioneer'), the expedition reached Victoria Land in March 1911. Unable to land, however, it returned to winter in Sydney, where Shirase and his countrymen set up camp in the garden of a well-to-do resident of suburban Vaucluse.

By mid-January 1912, *Kainan Maru* was back in the Ross Sea, where it met Amundsen's expedition at the Bay of Whales on the Ross Ice Shelf. Amundsen – and Scott, too – had by this time already reached the Pole,

though Shirase, of course, could not know it. Despite being far behind, Shirase and six of his men formed a 'dash patrol' and in a symbolic gesture, headed south with dogs and sledges. First, however, they had to claw their way to the top of the Ross Ice Shelf, which towered nearly 90m over the sea where *Kainan Maru* stood offshore. The patrol pushed 260km to a furthest south of 80°5'S, reached on January 28, 1912. There, Shirase claimed all the area of the Ross Ice Shelf within sight as the 'Yamato Yukihara,' or 'Yamato Snow Plain.' This claim has never been taken seriously (even by Japan), given that Amundsen had already traveled through the area on his way south to the Pole. Nevertheless, the expedition's members were welcomed as heroes when they returned to Yokohama on June 20, 1912.

The Origins of ANARE

The Australian National Antarctic Research Expedition (ANARE) was established in 1947, partly because Douglas Mawson was urging that Australia send another expedition to Antarctica. The word 'Expedition' was later changed to the plural, 'Expeditions,' to reflect the ongoing nature of ANARE's work.

During its first season, ANARE sent naval vessel *HMALST 3501* to establish bases on Heard Island (in December 1947) and on Macquarie Island (in March 1948). Meanwhile another ship, HMAS *Wyatt Earp*, which had sailed to Antarctica four times with American aviator Lincoln Ellsworth, was dispatched to find a site suitable for a permanent Australian Antarctic base. Bad ice conditions and the lateness of the season, however, prevented *Wyatt Earp* from reaching the Antarctic coast.

Wyatt Earp had proved quite unsuitable for our purposes, and in the absence of any other vessel, further efforts in Antarctic waters were not possible, so I concentrated on building up the scientific programs at our island stations. In 1952, I learned that the Lauritzen shipping line in Denmark had built a polar ship, *Kista Dan*, for work in Greenland, and I was able to interest them in chartering it to us during the Northern Hemisphere winter. I explained this to the Australian government and obtained approval to mount an expedition in 1954 to establish an Antarctic station. My book *Antarctic Odyssey* describes this in greater detail.

Aerial photographs of the Antarctic coast taken by the US Operation Highjump helped me to select a suitable site for the station. The area appeared as a horseshoe-shaped expanse of rock attached to the fringe of the continental ice. Mawson station, established in February 1954, was built in the head of the horseshoe. The two arms of the horseshoe circled around to the entrance, where the water was deep enough to allow a ship to enter and stand with hawsers running to the shore.

It was an exciting moment for me as we raised the Australian flag over the site. I had been brought up on the stories of Scott and Shackleton and other explorers – and here I found myself

Mawson Australian geologist Douglas Mawson (1882-1958) had been asked by Robert Scott to accompany *Terra Nova*, but he declined the invitation in favor of leading his own expedition. Already a veteran of Shackleton's *Nimrod* expedition, Mawson wanted to explore new territory west of Cape Adare. With the Australian government granting him more than half the expedition's cost, Mawson escaped some of the financing worries that plagued other explorers.

The Australasian Antarctic Expedition (AAE) sailed from Hobart on December 2, 1911, in *Aurora*, an old sealer with years of experience in the Arctic and the relief of Shackleton's Ross Sea party to its credit. Its master was Captain John King Davis, and on board was the first airplane taken to the Antarctic, a Vickers REP monoplane that had crashed during a test flight before the expedition even left Australia. Mawson brought the wingless aircraft with him anyway, hoping to use it as an 'air tractor,' but it failed at this task too when its engine seized while towing a heavy load.

Aurora arrived at the ice edge in January 1912, then headed west and followed the coast to new territories, which Mawson called King George V Land and claimed for the British crown. At Cape Denison on Commonwealth Bay, he set up his base, unaware that the roaring katabatics – gravity-driven winds – made the spot one of the windiest places on Earth. He later gave it the memorable name 'the home of the blizzard.' A party of eight men, led by Frank Wild, also a veteran of Shackleton's *Nimrod*

The Origins of ANARE

in a similar position, on virgin territory, raising a flag and claiming the land in the name of the English sovereign.

Today, Mawson is the oldest permanently occupied station south of the Antarctic Circle. It is fascinating for me to look back and remember Mawson as it was when I first walked to the rocky area, with our airplane waiting on the frozen sea offshore. Over the years, from a fixed point in the rock area, I photographed the gradual development of the station, chronicling the steady growth of the number of buildings and the total space occupied by the station.

When the International Geophysical Year (1957-58) was mooted, I approached my government again, suggesting a second station on a rocky expanse of land known as the Vestfold Hills, where Lincoln Ellsworth had once landed. We established Davis station (550km east of Mawson) in January 1957.

At the end of the IGY, the US Antarctic Program, in order to cut back its extensive activity, decided to close its Wilkes station (1300km east of Davis). Several US scientists approached me, suggesting that because of its value as a scientific observatory, it would be fine if Australia could agree to take it over and continue its programs. I was able to persuade my government to accept this offer. For several years, Wilkes was run as a joint US-Australian station, before coming under total Australian control. About 10 years later, the station, which had deteriorated badly, was evacuated, and a new station that we built nearby – Casey – was opened.

'Hit and run' landings from ships were also made at numerous points along unknown coasts, while men from ANARE stations made long inland traverses. Memorable exploits include a 700km dogsled journey from Enderby Land to Mawson in 1958, a 2900km tractor train journey from Wilkes to Vostok and back in 1962-63, and a four-man winter occupation of a camp on the Amery Ice Shelf for glaciological research in 1967.

– **Dr Phillip G Law,** leader of ANARE from 1949 to 1966
In 1987, Australia established Law Base, named in his honor, in the Larsemann Hills

expedition, was landed at the Shackleton Ice Shelf, 2400km west of Cape Denison. Battling wind speeds that occasionally reached more than 320 km/h at Commonwealth Bay, the expedition systematically explored King George V Land as well as neighboring Terre Adélie during the summer of 1912-13. On one of these sledging trips, the first Antarctic meteorite was found. The expedition also made the first radio contact between Antarctica and another continent, on September 25, 1912, using a wireless relay at the five-man station the expedition established on Macquarie Island.

Despite those accomplishments and the comprehensive research done by the expedition, it is remembered primarily for the ordeal that its leader endured on a deadly dog-sledging journey. With Belgrave Ninnis, a British soldier, and Xavier Mertz, a Swiss mountaineer and ski champion, Mawson left Cape Denison on November 10, 1912, to explore east of the expedition's base. By December 14, after crossing two heavily crevassed glaciers (later named for Mertz and Ninnis), they had reached a point 500km from their base. That afternoon, Ninnis disappeared down an apparently bottomless

Ninnis is gone!

crevasse with his team of dogs – and most of the party's food, all of its dog food and its tent. Wrote Mawson later: 'It seemed so incredible that we half expected, on turning round, to find him standing there.'

Thus began a harrowing trek home. Battling hunger, cold, fatigue and, possibly, vitamin A poisoning from the dog livers they were forced to eat, Mawson and Mertz struggled on. After Mertz died on January 7, when they were still more than 160km out, Mawson sawed the remaining sledge in half with a pocket knife to lighten his load. By now his body was literally falling apart: hair coming out, toenails loosened and even the thick soles of his feet sloughing off. Somehow he got back to Cape Denison – only a few hours after *Aurora* had sailed away.

Six men had remained behind at the hut, hoping against hope that the missing party might return. Though they radioed the ship, heavy seas prevented *Aurora* from reaching Cape Denison, and they were forced to spend another winter, arriving back in Australia in late February, 1914.

In 1929-31, Mawson returned to Antarctica, leading the two summer voyages of the British, Australian and New Zealand Antarctic Research Expedition (BANZARE) to the west of Commonwealth Bay, where they discovered Mac.Robertson Land.

Filchner With the Pole won, Bavarian army Lieutenant Wilhelm Filchner (1877-1957) decided to tackle another problem of Antarctic discovery: the question of whether the Weddell and Ross seas were joined by a channel, as some geographers posited. Educated at the Prussian Military Academy and a veteran of a pioneering horseback journey through the Pamirs and another expedition to Tibet, Filchner hoped to cross the continent, starting from the Weddell Sea, to solve this puzzle. When he was unable to raise the large amount of money such a two-ship expedition would require, he decided merely to push as far south as he could into the Weddell Sea.

Sailing from Bremerhaven on May 4, 1911 in a Norwegian ship renamed *Deutschland*, the Second German South Polar Expedition called in at Buenos Aires on the way south. There, Filchner met aboard *Fram* with Amundsen, who was on his triumphant return from the Pole. By mid-December, *Deutschland* reached the Weddell Sea pack ice. After 10 days of pushing through narrow leads, the ship penetrated to the sea's southern coast, William Bruce's Coats Land. Sailing west, Filchner reached new territory, which he called 'Prinz Regent Luitpold Land' (now Luitpold Coast). He also discovered a vast ice shelf, naming it 'Kaiser Wilhelm Barrier' for his emperor (who later insisted that it be renamed after Filchner). Filchner then tried to establish a winter base ('Stationseisberg') on the ice shelf, but these plans had to be hastily abandoned when a huge section of the shelf – carrying the expedition's nearly completed hut – calved into the sea.

The Antarctic winter closed in before *Deutschland* could escape to lower latitudes and the ship was beset and drifted for nine months. In contrast to the wintertime hardships experienced by the *Belgica* expedition, the Germans had a fairly uneventful winter, both ship and crew managing well. Filchner even led a three-man party on a dangerous midwinter dog-sledging trip over some 65km of sea ice to the charted location of 'New South Greenland,' which American sealer Benjamin Morrell claimed to have sighted in 1823. Finding nothing but frozen ocean, Filchner proved the nonexistence of Morrell's 'discovery.' Successfully navigating back to the ship was a great feat, since the instruments were nearly destroyed by the -34°C cold – and *Deutschland* had drifted almost 65km with the current-driven pack ice.

On November 26, 1912, the decaying ice released the ship, which sailed to South Georgia and home. Back in Germany, armed with his newly won knowledge of the Weddell Sea coast, Filchner again tried to raise interest in a crossing of Antarctica, from the Weddell to the Ross Sea. But Germany's attention, on the eve of WWI, was elsewhere.

Shackleton's *Endurance* Expedition

After losing his most sought-after prize – but saving himself and his companions –

on the *Nimrod* expedition, Ernest Shackleton had also set his sights on an Antarctic crossing. The threat of a German expedition attempting the same journey helped Shackleton to raise funds, as nationalistic Britons sent in contributions to the 'first crossing of the last continent.' His plan was simple but ambitious: Shackleton would sail in *Endurance* to the Weddell Sea coast, establish a base, then trek across the continent via the South Pole. At the top of the Beardmore Glacier, the crossing party would be met by another group, which would have been landed at Ross Island by *Aurora*, sailing from Hobart.

Even as *Endurance* prepared to sail, the firestorm ignited by the assassination of Archduke Franz Ferdinand and his wife on June 28, 1914 was engulfing Europe. Britain declared war on Germany on August 4, and Shackleton immediately offered *Endurance* and her crew for service. Winston Churchill, then First Lord of the Admiralty, wired his thanks, but the expedition was told to proceed. *Endurance* sailed from Plymouth on August 8 'to carry on our white warfare,' as Shackleton put it. After calling at Madeira, Buenos Aires and South Georgia, the expedition pushed into the Weddell Sea pack and soon found itself squeezing through ever-narrower leads.

By January 19, 1915, *Endurance* was caught. The events that followed have grown to legend, becoming nearly as famous as the story of Scott's last expedition. The ship, inexorably crushed by the grinding ice floes, finally sank on November 21. Shackleton and his men lived on the pack ice for five months before they sailed three small boats to Elephant Island in the South Shetlands. Since the island was uninhabited, Shackleton and five others were forced to sail another 1300km across the open sea in one of the boats, the 6m *James Caird* (which the ship's carpenter had decked over with spare timbers) to seek help from the whalers at South Georgia. After 16 exhausting days at sea, they landed at South Georgia, completing one of history's greatest feats of navigation.

But their landfall was at King Haakon Bay, on South Georgia's bleak, uninhabited southwest coast, and the whaling stations were on the island's northeast side. Although no one had previously penetrated farther than a kilometer or so from the coast, Shackleton had no choice but to try to cross the island. He and two of the six men who had sailed *James Caird* with him, Tom Crean and Frank Worsley, hiked for 36 straight hours over the 1800m mountains and crevassed glaciers to reach the whaling station at Stromness Harbour. As they neared the station, impassable ice cliffs forced them to lower themselves down an icy, 9m waterfall. Upon their arrival at the station, on May 20, 1916, their long beards, matted hair, ragged clothes – and fierce body odor, no doubt – caused the first three people they met to flee in disgust.

At the home of the station manager, where they bathed and were fed and clothed, Shackleton asked, 'When was the war over?' 'The war is not over,' the manager answered. 'Millions are being killed. Europe is mad. The world is mad.' That night a whaler was dispatched to pick up the three men left behind at King Haakon Bay. After three failed rescue attempts over the next four months, Shackleton enlisted the help of *Yelcho*, a steamer lent by the Chilean government, and was finally able to pick up all 22 men stranded at Elephant Island on August 30.

Still, Shackleton's troubles were not over, for the Ross Sea party had encountered its own difficulties. *Aurora* had intended to winter at Ross Island, but a blizzard blew the ship from its moorings, stranding at Cape Evans 10 men who spent a miserable winter with minimal supplies. *Aurora*, meanwhile, was beset for 10 months, finally getting free on March 14, 1916. Shackleton met the ship in New Zealand and after an extensive refitting *Aurora* was able to relieve the marooned Cape Evans party on January 10, 1917. The war, meanwhile, raged for another 22 bloody months, long enough for two of Shackleton's men to die in the fighting.

Shackleton himself lived to mount one final assault on the Antarctic, the ill-defined *Quest* expedition. Upon reaching South Georgia, he suffered a massive heart attack

and died January 5, 1922 aboard his ship, moored alongside at Grytviken.

Wilkins Australian George Hubert Wilkins (1888-1958), a Balkan War combat photographer and veteran of two Antarctic expeditions including Shackleton's final voyage in *Quest*, decided in 1928 that the time was right to attempt a flight in Antarctica. He had already flown 4000km across the Arctic Ocean earlier in the year, becoming the first to cross the region by air, and now Wilkins took the same pilot (Carl Ben Eielson) and the same plane (now called *Los Angeles*) south to tackle The Ice.

With his Arctic success guaranteeing him a well-funded expedition – including a lucrative US$25,000 news rights contract with American press baron William Randolph Hearst – Wilkins was transported on a whaling ship, *Hektoria*, which called at Deception Island. He also brought with him a backup pilot, Joe Crosson, and a second wood-framed Lockheed Vega monoplane, christened *San Francisco*. These planes were revolutionary for their time, having no wires or exposed controls to offer extra wind resistance.

Wilkins had equipped the Vegas with pontoons to enable them to take off from the protected waters of Deception's Port Foster, but on test runs he encountered a uniquely Antarctic obstacle: hundreds of albatrosses, attracted to the open water created when the ship broke the harbor ice. So Wilkins and his men – aided by crews from the nearby whaling station – cleared a rough runway on shore. Rough it was: running 800m up a hill, down across ditches, up another hill, and down to the harbor. If a plane hadn't gotten up enough speed to take off by then, it would plunge into the water. On November 16, 1928, Wilkins and Eielson took off in the *Los Angeles*, flying for just 20 minutes before the weather closed in. Still, it was a useful shakedown – and it made history as the first powered flight in Antarctica.

Little more than a month later, Wilkins and Eielson were ready to tackle a longer flight. Although they hoped to fly from the Peninsula to the Ross Sea, bad weather made that impractical. But on December 20, taking off again from Deception, they flew for 11 hours across the Peninsula and along its eastern side, covering 2100km and reaching as far south as 71°20'S. Eight years before, as a member of the British Imperial Expedition to Graham Land, Wilkins had been frustrated by 'the slow, blind struggles' to make progress over the difficult terrain. 'This time,' he exulted, 'I had a tremendous sensation of power and freedom – I felt liberated...for the first time in history, new land was being discovered from the air.' Important though the flight was, Wilkins was deceived by the appearance of the Peninsula from above and wrongly concluded that it must be an archipelago.

Wilkins returned to the Antarctic the next summer, making more flights and discoveries. All told, he mapped 200,000 sq km of new territory, proving beyond any doubt the efficacy of the airplane in Antarctic work. He later supported Lincoln Ellsworth (see the Ellsworth section later in this chapter) with his flights over Antarctica.

Byrd Wilkins scared American flier Richard Evelyn Byrd (1888-1957). A graduate of the US Naval Academy at Annapolis, Byrd had in 1926 claimed to be first to fly over the North Pole (the claim remains controversial to this day). In 1927, he was narrowly beaten by Charles Lindbergh in the era's greatest race: solo across the Atlantic. Soon after, he made it his goal to become the first to fly over the South Pole.

Crowned with his Arctic 'success' (almost no one then knew that it was, in fact, a failure), Byrd raised nearly a million dollars from such eminent sponsors as Charles Lindbergh (US$1000), the National Geographic Society and the *New York Times*, which paid US$60,000 for exclusive rights and the privilege of sending its own reporter, Russell Owen, on the expedition. Byrd's United States Antarctic Expedition was the best-funded private expedition to Antarctica in history. It sailed from Hoboken, New Jersey, in August 1928, in the square-rigged *City of New York* with not one, but three separate aircraft. 'Accompa-

nied by business managers, physicians, cameramen, dog trainers, scientists, aviators, newspapermen,' *Time* magazine wrote of the departing expedition, 'the size and diversity of its personnel suggests a circus.'

The expedition's base, 'Little America,' was established at the Bay of Whales on the Ross Ice Shelf in January 1929. Byrd quickly set up a flying program with his three planes – the big aluminum Ford trimotor *Floyd Bennett*, named for his North Pole pilot who had died of pneumonia earlier in 1928; the smaller, single-engined Fairchild, *Stars and Stripes*; and a single-engined Fokker Universal named *The Virginian* for his home state.

In March the expedition suffered Antarctica's first plane crash, but luckily no one was in *The Virginian*. A five-man party had been flown south to survey the Rockefeller Mountains (named for an expedition sponsor), when a blizzard blasted them for 12 days. Although the Fokker was tied down, so furious was the wind that when the pilot made a radio call back to Little America from inside the plane, he noticed that the airspeed indicator read 140 km/h. A few mornings later, the men awoke at their nearby camp to find that the plane had flown itself 800m to an inevitable crash. Byrd and the others eventually rescued the stranded party.

With winter's onset, the two remaining planes were cached in snow shelters. The men settled down to an under-snow routine of research, repair work, radio training, and recreation, which included watching some of the expedition's 75 movies, specially selected for their nonprovocative story lines. On August 24 the sun rose again, and preparations for the big flight began. By November, a fuel depot was set up at the foot of the Axel Heiberg glacier (the same glacier Amundsen had used) leading up to the polar plateau, since *Floyd Bennett*'s fuel tanks couldn't carry enough to reach 90°S and back.

On November 28, an expedition field party working in the Queen Maud Mountains far to the south radioed to Little America that the weather was clear. Four men – Byrd as navigator; Bernt Balchen, chief pilot; Harold

June, second pilot and radio operator; and Ashley McKinley, photo surveyor – climbed into the big Ford trimotor. Flying up the Liv Glacier, an icy on-ramp to the polar plateau, the plane was unable to climb due to the cold, thin air, forcing the men to ditch 110kg of their emergency rations. Balchen, an experienced Arctic pilot, gained a little more altitude by throwing the aircraft into a hard turn toward the towering rock face on his right and catching an updraft amidst the rush of air flowing down the glacier.

From there, it was simply a four-hour drone to the Pole, praying that *Floyd Bennett*'s engines would keep beating out their powerful rhythm. They did, and at 1:14 am, on November 29, 1929, the plane reached the Earth's southern axis. 'For a few seconds we stood over the spot where Amundsen had stood December 14, 1911, and where Scott had also stood,' Byrd wrote. 'There was nothing now to mark that scene; only a white desolation and solitude disturbed by the sound of our engines.'

Byrd returned to the US as a national hero, fêted with ticker-tape parades, a promotion to rear admiral, and a special gold medal struck in his honor. He went on to lead four more Antarctic expeditions including the second USAE of 1933-35 (during which he nearly died of carbon monoxide poisoning while living alone at a tiny weather station called 'Advance Base') and the massive US Government exercise known as Operation Highjump (see the Operation Highjump section later in this chapter). But this was his finest hour.

Ellsworth American Lincoln Ellsworth (1880-1951), scion of a wealthy Pennsylvania coal-mining family, had whetted his appetite for polar exploration in 1925, when he made the first flight toward the North Pole with Roald Amundsen. The flight failed, but he did reach the Pole in 1926, three days after Byrd claimed he did.

In 1931, Ellsworth began what would become a long and productive association with Hubert Wilkins – with the goal of crossing Antarctica by air. For the first of their four expeditions together, Ellsworth bought a Northrop Gamma monoplane, which he named *Polar Star*, and a stout Norwegian fishing vessel, named *Wyatt Earp* after his hero, the gun-slinging marshal of the Old West, whose wedding ring Ellsworth wore and whose gun and holster he carried with him everywhere. For his pilot, Ellsworth chose Bernt Balchen, chief pilot on Byrd's expedition.

The first Ellsworth Antarctic Expedition in 1933-34 ended after just one short flight from skis in the frozen-over Bay of Whales. The plane was parked overnight on an ice floe, and a massive breakup early the next morning left the aircraft dangling by its wingtips from two separate pieces of the floe. The expedition was forced to retreat north, where Ellsworth's money soon funded the plane's repair.

In late 1934, he was back in the Antarctic, with a new flight plan: the expedition would fly from Wilkins' old base at Deception Island to the Ross Sea via the Weddell Sea. But the season's first try was another disaster – an engine seized up after its heavy preserving lubricant was not drained before starting. The expedition again retreated north, to pick up a spare part that Ellsworth had flown in from the factory to a South American port. The next flight was equally frustrating: Balchen turned the plane around after little more than an hour, citing heavy weather to the south, though Ellsworth saw only a small squall. While he retained respect for Balchen, Ellsworth never hired him again.

The third try, in 1935, was lucky for Ellsworth, but only on the season's third attempt. Ellsworth's new pilot, English-born Canadian Herbert Hollick-Kenyon, made two false starts – the first aborted by a leaky fuel gauge and the second by a threatening storm. *Polar Star* finally took off from Dundee Island at the tip of the Peninsula on November 22, 1935, headed for the Bay of Whales on the Ross Ice Shelf. As the pair flew south, sighting and naming the Eternity and Sentinel ranges, Ellsworth was overcome with realization that his years of effort were finally paying off: 'Suddenly I felt supremely happy for my share in the opportunity to unveil the last continent in human history.'

The 3700km flight was intended to last just 14 hours, even with landings to refuel. But poor weather stretched the actual trip to two weeks, during which time the pair established four separate camps. Unfortunately, their radio went dead during that period, prompting fear that they had perished. Even on the last leg of the flight, problems plagued them: *Polar Star* ran out of fuel 25km from the Bay of Whales on the Ross Ice Shelf, and they trekked eight days to reach it. Australia, meanwhile, urged on by Douglas Mawson and John King Davis, dispatched a 'rescue' attempt, although Wilkins and *Wyatt Earp* had already made detailed plans to pick up Ellsworth and Hollick-Kenyon at the Bay of Whales after their flight. The Australians met the explorers at Byrd's former base, Little America II, where the explorers had been living comfortably for nearly a month. Heavy ice, meanwhile, slowed *Wyatt Earp*, which arrived four days later. After returning to a heroes' welcome in the US, Ellsworth made a final expedition to Antarctica with his faithful friend Hubert Wilkins in 1938, and then retired from exploration for good.

The Contemporary Era

Wilkins' flight was one of the last large private expeditions made to Antarctica. WWII severely interrupted the plans of many explorers, and after the war the cost of mounting a major expedition pushed nearly everyone but national governments out of the game. In 1943, Britain began the permanent occupation of Antarctica, establishing Base A at Port Lockroy on Wiencke Island.

Operations 'Highjump' & 'Windmill' In 1946 the US launched 'Operation Highjump,' the largest-ever Antarctic expedition. Officially called the US Navy Antarctic Developments Project, it was primarily a training exercise that gave US forces experience in polar operations, which would have been valuable had the Cold War, then developing with the Soviet Union, flared into an all-out Arctic fight. Highjump sent 4700 men, 33 aircraft, 13 ships and 10 Caterpillar tractors to the continent, and used helicopters and ice-breakers for the first time in the Antarctic.

Tens of thousands of aerial photographs were taken along nearly three-quarters of the continent's coast (though their usefulness for mapmaking was limited by a lack of ground surveys). A smaller, follow-up expedition the next year (later nicknamed 'Operation Windmill' for its extensive use of helicopters) surveyed major features sighted by Highjump.

ANARE In February 1954, Phillip Garth Law and the Australian National Antarctic Research Expeditions (ANARE) set up Mawson station in East Antarctica. (See the boxed text 'The Origins of ANARE' in this chapter.) Named for Douglas Mawson, this was the first permanent scientific station set up on the continent, and the only one outside the Peninsula. Today, Mawson is one of Australia's three continental stations.

International Geophysical Year (IGY) A growing interest in Earth and atmospheric sciences during the late 1940s prompted the declaration of the International Geophysical Year. The IGY, which ran from July 1, 1957, to December 31, 1958, was timed to coincide with a peak level of sunspot activity. Its objective was to study outer space and the whole Earth, with 66 countries participating from locations all around the planet. But the IGY left its greatest legacy in Antarctica.

Twelve countries – Argentina, Australia, Belgium, Chile, France, Japan, New Zealand, Norway, South Africa, the UK, the US and the USSR – established more than 40 stations on the Antarctic continent and another 20 on the sub-Antarctic islands. Among these were the US base at the South Pole, created through a massive 84-flight airdrop of 725 tonnes of building materials, and the Soviet Vostok station at the Geomagnetic South Pole. Many countries also operated tractor traverses across great sections of the continental interior. The British Commonwealth Trans-Antarctic Expedition, led by Vivian Fuchs, was the first to cross the continent overland (see also the Private Expeditions chapter). The international cooperation promoted by the IGY led to the creation of the Antarctic Treaty (see Government & Politics, later in this chapter).

TERRITORIAL CLAIMS & YEAR-ROUND STATIONS

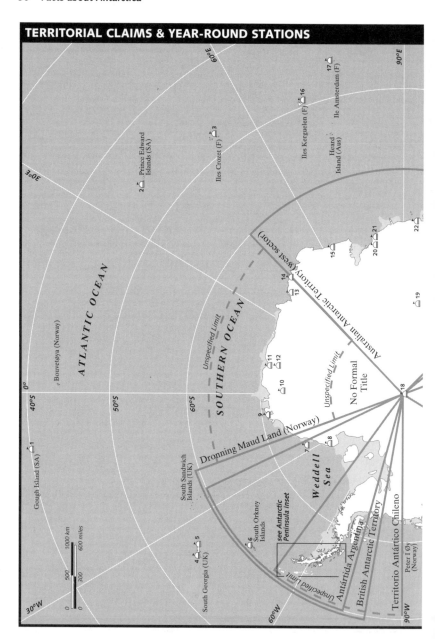

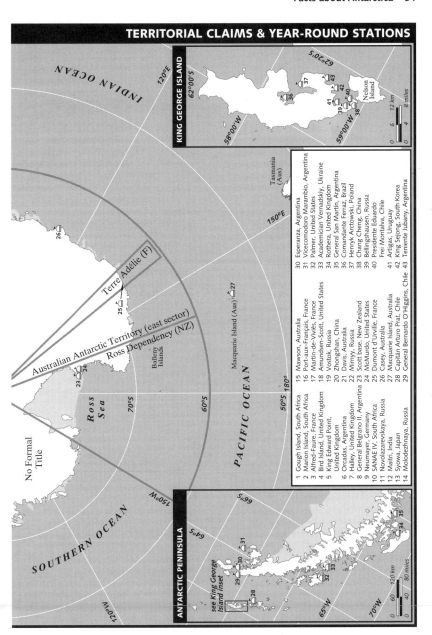

TERRITORIAL CLAIMS & YEAR-ROUND STATIONS

KING GEORGE ISLAND

Nelson Island

INDIAN OCEAN

Terre Adélie (F)

Australian Antarctic Territory (east sector)

Ross Dependency (NZ)

Balleny Islands

Macquarie Island (Aus)

Tasmania (Aus)

Ross Sea

No Formal Title

PACIFIC OCEAN

SOUTHERN OCEAN

ANTARCTIC PENINSULA

see King George Island inset

1 Gough Island, South Africa	15 Mawson, Australia
2 Marion Island, South Africa	16 Port-aux-Français, France
3 Alfred-Faure, France	17 Martin-de-Viviès, France
4 Bird Island, United Kingdom	18 Amundsen-Scott, United States
5 King Edward Point, United Kingdom	19 Vostok, Russia
	20 Zhongshan, China
6 Orcadas, Argentina	21 Davis, Australia
7 Halley, United Kingdom	22 Mirny, Russia
8 General Belgrano II, Argentina	23 Scott base, New Zealand
9 Neumayer, Germany	24 McMurdo, United States
10 SANAE IV, South Africa	25 Dumont d'Urville, France
11 Novolazarevskaya, Russia	26 Casey, Australia
12 Maitri, India	27 Macquarie Island, Australia
13 Syowa, Japan	28 Capitán Arturo Prat, Chile
14 Molodezhnaya, Russia	29 General Bernardo O'Higgins, Chile

30 Esperanza, Argentina	
31 Vicecomodoro Marambio, Argentina	
32 Palmer, United States	
33 Academician Vernadskiy, Ukraine	
34 Rothera, United Kingdom	
35 General San Martín, Argentina	
36 Comandante Ferraz, Brazil	
37 Henryk Arctowski, Poland	
38 Chang Cheng, China	
39 Bellingshausen, Russia	
40 Presidente Eduardo Frei Montalva, Chile	
41 Artigas, Uruguay	
42 King Sejong, South Korea	
43 Teniente Jubany, Argentina	

Women in Antarctica Women were largely excluded from the work done in Antarctica until recently. Norwegian Caroline Mikkelsen, the first woman to set foot on the continent, landed at the Vestfold Hills with her husband Klarius, captain of a whaling ship, on February 20, 1935. It was to be another 40 years before women had any kind of significant presence on The Ice.

'Oh My God, It's Female!'

That was all I heard as I climbed a rope to the ceiling of the aircraft hangar at McMurdo. 'How the hell does he know from that angle?' was my first thought. 'I'm wearing the same trousers as everyone else.' I'd been at McMurdo for almost three weeks and thought I had run the gauntlet of male mumblings, fumblings and assaults. After all, here I was with my peers – scientists from all over the world – learning to prusik (the mountaineering word for climbing a rope) in a survival skills course.

I was also learning, however, that as a woman in Antarctica I needed to master another, entirely different set of survival skills. The Antarctic had always been a men's club. When I first arrived, I got the distinct feeling that the men thought we women were there just to have a look, much as you used to be allowed to peek in on the exclusive men's clubs in the big cities. I arrived in 1978, just four years after the first woman had wintered at McMurdo. We were still treated as strange animals – but the opinions about exactly how we should be handled differed as much as the individual men on the station. There were 650 men on base, and their treatment of the 42 women ranged from abject deference to out-and-out solicitation, from respect to contempt.

Being a biologist, I was interested to find that the men fell into three natural categories. The Predators were the big nuisance. They would lie in wait at every turn. I could go nowhere – except the women's toilet – without encountering a Predator waiting to pounce. The best thing to do was hook up with someone, which I discovered stopped most of the Predators, the way it does among wolf packs. (The strongest male wolf gets to the female first and all the others wait around in a circle without interfering until he's finished. How far above the animals or below the angels are we?)

That brings me to the Scavengers. They served a most useful purpose in scavenging the pieces left after the gauntlet of the Predators. The Scavengers were considerate enough to stay away and wait for a signal from a woman – so, after several dinners in the mess hall sitting next to what I thought were the most attractive of the men, I hooked up with one. He accompanied me most places, and this kept the Predators at bay.

The Herbivores were a different matter. They apparently would have nothing to do with the flesh. In fact, they usually gathered in groups at any function, including meals. They would not even look at a woman. Conversation with a female was evidently a no-no, and even a curt nod of the head or a sly glance was too much. They did not want to be bothered with females, and since we were in such short supply, maybe they didn't have such a bad idea. Out of sight, out of mind – with no subsequent longings or problems. Don't stir or heat, and it won't boil!

Within this framework, we all had a great time. We shared the work, the troubles and the fun as good companions. And there was lots of work: from 6 am to 10:30 pm every day except Sunday, when we had brunch instead of breakfast and went to chapel afterward. Then, of course, back to work.

– Dr Rita Mathews,
retired biologist, who frequently lectures on polar cruise ships

In fact, the Antarctic programs operated by various national governments had an official ban on women for decades. This sexism was justified by rationalizations about physical strength and the difficulty of providing separate toilet facilities. The real difficulty, in all likelihood, would have been experienced by the women left at home by male Antarctic expeditioners, who doubtless felt pressure from those women to prevent other females from going south. Indeed, many people say that the sexual tensions that build in Antarctica's isolation *are* exacerbated by mixed company.

The first women wintered on Antarctica in 1947, when Edith ('Jackie') Ronne and Jennie Darlington spent a year with their husbands on Stonington Island in the Antarctic Peninsula region during the Ronne Antarctic Research Expedition. They had planned to accompany the expedition just as far as Valparaiso, Chile. Only at the last minute did leader Finn Ronne convince his wife to stay with the expedition to help write its newspaper dispatches. Jennie Darlington, asked to remain as well, became pregnant during the expedition and nearly gave birth to the first native Antarctican. She later wrote *My Antarctic Honeymoon* (see Books in the Facts for the Visitor chapter) about the expedition's trying personal relationships.

The first women to see the South Pole were two flight attendants, Patricia Hepinstall and Ruth Kelly, aboard the first commercial flight to Antarctica, a Pan Am stratocruiser that departed Christchurch and landed at McMurdo on October 15, 1957.

In 1956, Russian marine geologist Marie V Klenova worked for part of the austral summer at Russia's Mirnyy station, and in 1968-69, four Argentine women did hydrographic research in the Antarctic Peninsula region.

In 1969 the US finally allowed women to participate in its national Antarctic program. A four-woman group of geologists and a husband-and-wife team worked on The Ice that year, and New Zealand also sent a woman biologist to Antarctica. On November 11, 1969, the first women to reach the Pole arrived by US Navy aircraft and spent a few hours there before flying back to McMurdo; they included a reporter from a Detroit newspaper.

In 1974, American biologist Mary Alice McWhinnie, who had spent nearly a decade doing research in Antarctic seas aboard the research vessel *Eltanin*, became chief scientist at McMurdo. McWhinnie and her colleague Sister Mary Odile Cahoon, a teaching nun from Minnesota, wintered at McMurdo that year, the first women to do so. Sister Mary later said, in Barbara Land's excellent book *The New Explorers: Women in Antarctica*, that the US Navy and the National Science Foundation 'felt more comfortable having a couple of maiden aunts test the situation.' The first woman to winter at the South Pole, physician Michele Eileen Raney, was the station's lone female during the winter of 1979.

Artist Nel Law was the first Australian woman to set foot in Antarctica, accompanying her husband Phillip Law there in 1960-61. It was another 15 years before the first Australian women were allowed to work in Antarctica, and the first Australian woman (Louise Holliday) wintered only in 1981, at Davis station. The first woman head of an Antarctic station was Australia's Diana Patterson, who was station leader at Mawson in 1989.

Other nations took longer to allow women to participate in their Antarctic programs. Japan, for instance, sent its first two women to winter in Antarctica only in 1997.

In December 1990, Germany's Georg von Neumayer station was staffed by the first all-female group to winter in Antarctica. Eight women spent 14 months at the station, nine of them in complete isolation. The group's physician, Monica Puskeppeleit, was the station leader.

GEOGRAPHY

Viewed on a map, Antarctica resembles a giant stingray with its tail snaking up toward South America's Tierra del Fuego and its head swimming into the Indian Ocean. Without the 'tail,' the continent is roughly circular, with a diameter of about 4500km and an area of about 14.2 million sq km.

Antarctica's coastline measures 30,500km. It is the fifth-largest continent, ahead of Australia and Europe. If Antarctica were a country, it would be the world's second largest after Russia. It is also the most arid and – with an average elevation of 2250m – the highest continent. Surrounded by the Southern Ocean, it's the most isolated continent as well.

Antarctica is divided by the 2900km-long Transantarctic Mountains into East Antarctica (sometimes referred to as 'Greater Antarctica') and West Antarctica (or 'Lesser Antarctica'), with the directions deriving from 0° Longitude. The continent's highest point is 4897m Vinson Massif.

The Antarctic Peninsula separates the two great embayments into the continent, the Weddell and Ross seas. Each of these seas has its own ice shelf – the Ronne Ice Shelf and the Ross Ice Shelf, respectively – which are extensions of the great Antarctic ice sheet. The Ross Ice Shelf, which is roughly the size of France, is the world's largest ice shelf. The largest glacier in the world is the Lambert Glacier, which flows onto the Amery Ice Shelf in East Antarctica.

Although Antarctica is routinely described as being 98% ice-covered, analysis of satellite images of the continent shows that, in fact, ice covers 99.6% of Antarctica. Antarctica's ice sheets contain 90% of the world's ice – 30 million cubic km – which contains nearly 70% of the world's fresh water. This ice is up to 4775m thick, and in some places its enormous weight has depressed the underlying landmass by nearly 1600m. Antarctica's continental shelf is about three times deeper than that of any other continent. In the unlikely event of the Antarctic ice sheet melting, the world's oceans would rise by up to 70m. West Antarctica would become an archipelago of small, mountainous islands (much like Indonesia), while East Antarctica would be a continental landmass about the size of Australia.

In September, Antarctica's late winter, the size of the continent effectively doubles with the freezing of the sea ice, which can extend more than 1000km from the coast.

The Antarctic Convergence is a temperature and salinity boundary of the Southern Ocean. North of this seasonally and longitudinally varying line, the summer surface seawater temperature is about 7.8°C, while south of it the temperature drops to 3.9°C. In winter, the temperature drops to around 2.8°C north of the Convergence and to 1.1°C south of it. The Convergence is an area of great biological importance, for the meeting of the cooler southern seas with the warmer northern waters acts as a great mixing agent, bringing an upwelling of nutrients to the surface.

GEOLOGY

The rocks of East Antarctica are at least 3 billion years old, among the oldest on Earth. In fact, some of the oldest terrestrial rock yet discovered was found in Enderby Land (roughly between 40° and 60°E) by Australian geologist Lance Black in 1986 – it's estimated at 3.84 billion years old. West Antarctica is relatively new: only 700 million years old.

CLIMATE

Antarctica is synonymous with cold, thanks to its polar location, its high elevation, its lack of a protective, water-vapor-filled atmosphere and its permanent ice cover, which reflects about 80% of the sun's radiation back into space. Interestingly, the South Pole is not the coldest part of the continent. The lowest temperature ever recorded on Earth's surface was -89.6°C at Russia's Vostok station on July 21, 1983. The warmest temperature ever recorded for Antarctica was +15°C on January 5, 1974 at New Zealand's Vanda station. Mean temperatures in the Antarctic interior range from -40°C to -70°C during the coldest month, and from -15°C to -35°C during the warmest month. On the coast, temperatures are considerably warmer: -15°C to -32°C in the winter, and from +5°C to -5°C in the summer. The Antarctic Peninsula experiences the highest temperatures year round.

The interior of Antarctica, despite its ice cap, is the world's driest desert, since the extreme cold freezes water vapor out of the air. Annual snowfall on the polar plateau is equivalent to less than 5cm of rain.

Antarctica experiences the strongest winds on the planet: the katabatics caused by denser, colder air rushing down off the polar plateau to the coast. These can achieve velocities of up to 320 km/h. The winds on the polar plateau, by contrast, are usually very light.

Antarctic blizzards are quite common. During a typical one very little, if any, snow actually falls. Instead, the snow is picked up and blown along the surface by the wind, resulting in blinding conditions in which objects less than a meter away may be invisible. Obviously such conditions are extremely dangerous, and several people have perished just meters from safety when they couldn't find their way to shelter.

Whiteouts are another peculiar Antarctic condition, during which there are no shadows or contrasts between objects. A uniformly grey or white sky over a snow-covered surface can yield these whiteouts, which cause a loss of depth perception – for both humans and birds.

ECOLOGY & ENVIRONMENT

With its extremely harsh climatic conditions, Antarctica has a sensitive ecology. Visitors must respect that sensitivity to ensure that no damage is done – and also to avoid penalties, including fines of up to US$10,000 (for US citizens) or even imprisonment (for British citizens)! The Antarctic Treaty system's Protocol on Environmental Protection is legally binding on all visitors to Antarctica who are nationals of its signatory countries, whether they are on governmental or private visits. (See the Environmental Issues chapter.)

Although tourism to Antarctica is sometimes criticized as being harmful to the Antarctic environment, in truth the impact made by tourists is absolutely minimal when compared to scientific activities on the continent. Using the unit of a 'person-day' (that is, one person spending 24 hours on the Antarctic continent or a sub-Antarctic island), tourists accounted for about 0.5% of all person-days logged in Antarctica during the 1995-96 season. Ship-based tourists leave

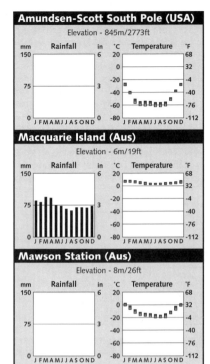

behind almost no trace of their stay (hopefully!), and those few who spend the night on the continent are not supposed to leave behind any evidence of having done so.

Some scientists like to raise the point that cumulative visits to the same place (by tourists, for example) may have long-term effects not yet understood. In fact, there are several places on Antarctica that do get remarkably high tourist traffic (see the chart of Most Visited Sites, in the Antarctic Peninsula chapter). Many of these locations, however, are being studied (see the boxed text 'Antarctic Site Inventory' in this chapter). Scientific stations – permanent facilities – represent the largest possible number of cumulative visits to a single site. As any visitor to one can attest, it's clear that by far the most serious environmental impacts in Antarctica occur at scientific

Antarctic Site Inventory

The 1991 Protocol on Environmental Protection to the Antarctic Treaty (the 'Protocol') is an exciting development (see the boxed text 'The Antarctic Treaty' in this chapter and 'Guidance for Visitors' in the Facts for the Visitor chapter). The Treaty parties have long grappled with Antarctic environmental issues, and this new regime of assessments and monitoring is aimed at protecting Antarctica's environmental riches over time. But assessments and monitoring will have little use unless they are supported by data that allows a fair analysis of whether environmental changes are occurring at visitor sites. Unfortunately, sufficient information is presently unavailable. Such analysis is complicated, as visitors' impact depends on many variables, including the physical and biological features of the sites visited, the frequency and timing of visits, the number of visitors and what visitors do while on site.

The Antarctic Site Inventory project, which began field work in 1994, is intended to fill this void. The Inventory has begun assembling a database to assist the Treaty parties in determining how best to minimize any potential adverse impacts from tourism or other activities. At key times during the course of the Antarctic spring and summer field season, the project places two-person field teams aboard ships to collect three kinds of information.

The first, Basic Site Information, includes descriptions of key physical and topographical characteristics; latitude and longitude; locations of floral assemblages (lichens, mosses and grasses); haul-out sites and wallow areas of Antarctic seals; discrete groups of breeding penguins and flying birds; penguin molting areas and guano-melt streams; glacial-melt streams; and how the site is accessed and exited.

The second category, Variable Site Information, includes specific data on weather and other environmental conditions (sea ice extent, cloud cover, snow cover, temperature, wind direction and speed); biological variables relating to penguins and flying birds (numbers of adults or individual animals, active nests, numbers and ages of chicks); and the nature and extent of any

stations, where personnel eat, sleep, work, drive, fly and eliminate on shore every day for years on end.

By the time their ship reaches the continent, many tourists are better-versed in environmental concerns in Antarctica than some members of national Antarctic programs. Despite all this care, however, Antarctica is unable to remain completely unsullied by the industrial world. Studies by Italian researchers at Terra Nova Bay station have found that minute particles of lead from gasoline combustion are blown to Antarctica as soon as one month after they have left exhaust pipes in South America, Australia and New Zealand.

FLORA & FAUNA

Plant species are actually more numerous than first impressions of Antarctica would lead one to believe, but they are far smaller and less conspicuous than plants in other latitudes. Some 350 species of lichens, 100 species of mosses and hundreds of species of algae, including 20 species of snow algae – which form colorful patches of pink, red, yellow or green on areas of permanent snow – live in Antarctica. Some remarkable lichens and algae can even live *inside* rocks, inhabiting the spaces between individual grains of the rock. There are no trees or shrubs in Antarctica and just two species of indigenous vascular plants: Antarctic hair grass *(Deschampsia antarctica)* and Antarctic pearlwort *(Colobanthus quitensis)*. The sub-Antarctic islands, of course, have much more diverse floras, with South Georgia alone boasting at least 50 species of vascular plants.

Antarctica's native land animals are all invertebrates, with nearly all terrestrial macrofauna belonging to the phylum *Arthropoda*, including mites, lice, springtails, midges and

Antarctic Site Inventory

visitor impacts observed (footprints or paths through moss beds, cigarette butts, film canisters and other litter). It is important for the field teams to visit sites during the peak of penguin egg laying, when the best nest counts are obtained, and then five to six weeks later, when chick numbers are at their peak, because the numbers of chicks produced per active nest indicates a colony's productivity.

At each site, investigators attempt to select and establish control colonies (those that are seldom visited) and experimental colonies (frequently visited) to count. The intent is to repeat censuses regularly, both near and far from landing beaches, to allow for comparisons over time between frequently and infrequently visited areas.

The third information category is Maps and Photodocumentation. The project has produced accurate, up-to-date maps of each site, showing the major physical features of the site, locations of the principal colonies and assemblages of fauna and flora, and points that offer clear vantage for photographing penguin colonies, seal haul-out sites, floral associations and other features.

The most frequently visited (by tourists) locations on the Antarctic Peninsula are the ones likely to generate the most attention – and possibly concern about potential adverse environmental effects – under the Protocol on Environmental Protection. At 47 different Peninsula sites, 299 locations have been established for conducting counts of penguins, flying birds and seals. Sixty of these 299 locations have been selected as potential 'control sites' to allow comparisons between visited and nonvisited colonies.

The Antarctic Site Inventory's database should assist the Treaty parties in fulfilling the environmental assessment and monitoring requirements of the Protocol. It should also lead to a better understanding of the environmental impacts of tourists – and all visitors to Antarctica.

– **Ron Naveen,**
principal investigator of the Antarctic Site Inventory project

fleas, many of which are parasites of seals and birds. The largest animal that permanently dwells on land in Antarctica is a wingless midge *(Belgica antarctica)* that grows to just over 1cm long.

Approximately 45 species of birds breed south of the Antarctic Convergence, including seven of the 17 living species of penguins. Just a few bird species breed in Antarctica, among them emperor, Adélie and gentoo penguins, snow petrels, Antarctic petrels and South Polar skuas.

The Southern Ocean, by contrast to Antarctica's relative barrenness, teems with life. With the 5cm-long, shrimplike krill *Euphausia* as the basis of its food chain, the Southern Ocean supports a wealth of fish, seal, whale and seabird species.

For more information regarding Antarctic fauna, refer to the color Wildlife Guide later in this book.

When viewing Antarctic wildlife, it is important to keep your distance. For one thing, the Guidelines for Visitors to the Antarctic require it – as does your safety. There's another reason to keep back: your photos won't turn out as well if you press in close: the animals are more likely to move, blurring your picture. Your presence changes the animals' behavior, so the farther back you keep, the more natural the animal will act. While wildlife may not seem to be concerned about your presence, it may in fact be under considerable stress. A single thoughtless gesture can cause the loss of a bird egg or chick, or the crushing of a seal pup by a frightened adult.

Species Conservation

International measures adopted in 1964 provide overall protection for *all* animal and plant species in Antarctica. No animal or plant in Antarctica may be collected or killed without a license, except in an emergency as food. For details about international measures to further protect Antarctic wildlife, see the Environmental Issues chapter, and for information regarding the status of individual species, refer to the color Wildlife Guide.

Protected Areas

Since no nation indisputably owns any part of Antarctica, there are no national parks. But the Antarctic Treaty System does offer protection to different kinds of areas.

Specially Protected Areas (SPAs) are designed to preserve unique ecological systems. Sites of Special Scientific Interest (SSSIs) protect areas where research is either underway or planned.

Tourists – and all other unauthorized people – must stay out of both SPAs and SSSIs. While many of these areas are not marked by any signs or markers, tour leaders should know where they are. It is their responsibility to ensure that their passengers do not stray into them. Pay attention to your cruise staff so that you are aware of any SPAs or SSSIs on your visits ashore.

Exploitation

Antarctica's exploration was tied directly to the exploitation of its marine mammals, specifically seals and whales. Throughout the 19th century, the discovery of new sealing grounds on sub-Antarctic islands was in each case immediately followed by the near-extinction of the local population (see the Southern Ocean & Sub-Antarctic Islands chapter).

Until 1870, when Norwegian Svend Foyn patented the exploding harpoon, whaling had been practiced from small boats, as Herman Melville famously depicted in *Moby Dick*. With Foyn's invention, the harpoon, once embedded in the whale's flesh, exploded and killed it. No more being pulled along in a tiny whaleboat by an angry leviathan on a 'Nantucket sleigh ride.'

The Antarctic whaling boom soon followed. South Georgia was one catching ground, important in the beginning years. The South Shetlands were the other early whaling area, with the first modern floating factory ship, *Admiralen*, operating in Admiralty Bay on King George Island in 1906. By the 1920s, advancing technology – particularly the stern slipway, which allowed the entire whale to be winched aboard a floating factory ship for processing – shifted predominance to pelagic, or open-ocean, whaling. Whalehunting also shifted from being a mainly Norwegian and British business to one dominated by the Japanese and Soviets in later years.

To give some idea of the numbers of whales that were caught, it is useful to look at the records from South Georgia, the main site of land-based operations. From 1904 to 1965, when whaling at South Georgia ceased, a total of 41,515 blue whales were caught, along with 87,555 fins, 26,754 humpbacks, 15,128 seis and 3716 sperm whales. The total slaughter: an astounding 175,250 animals. Little wonder that so few whales exist today. Some species, such as the mighty blue whale, are so diminished in number that individuals may have a hard time even finding another of their species to mate with.

About 400 minke whales (out of some 760,000 minkes that the International Whaling Commission estimates live in Antarctic waters) are now killed each year by Japan. To help fund its research, which includes data collected on age, calves and gestation, Japan's Institute of Cetacean Research sells the approximately 2000 tonnes of meat taken from the minkes, mainly to canned-food processors. These sales earn more than US$30 million each year, more than half the cost of running the research program. The retail price of prime-quality red whale meat was set by the government at just under $US100 per kg for the 1997 season. The meat is also used in school-lunch programs and served in *kujira-ya*, or 'whale restaurants,' 22 of which throughout Japan have joined together to form the National Association to Continue the Tradition of Whale Cuisine.

Krill have been fished commercially since 1972; the catch reached a peak in 1985-86, when 425,870 tonnes were caught. Japan is now the primary harvester. In the 1998-99 season, Japan took about 69% of the 103,000-tonne catch of the pink, 5cm-long crustaceans, followed by Poland (18% of the catch), Argentina (6%), Ukraine (5.5%) and Korea (1%). Nearly half of the annual catch is canned or frozen and sold as 'Antarctic shrimp.' Brochures marketing krill suggest masking its strong taste by using a pungent flavoring such as soy sauce or garlic. Even in the former Soviet Union – a major krill harvester – where food's palatability was not always the prime consideration for cost-conscious consumers, the 'ocean paste' made from krill tended to remain on store shelves, unsold. Krill is also used as cattle and fish feed.

Fish and squid are caught in large numbers, and around South Georgia, crabs are taken. An unfortunate – and completely unnecessary – 'bycatch' of the long-line fishermen looking for tuna in the Southern Ocean are some 40,000 albatrosses (including 8000 female wandering albatrosses, which feed at a more northerly latitude than do males), which are drowned when they are hooked while stealing bait, which gets dragged down to enormous depths. More recently, one fishery has focused on taking *Dissostichus eleginoides*, known as Patagonian toothfish or Chilean sea bass. Because most toothfish is caught illegally, the slow-growing species is in immediate danger of being fished to commercial extinction. Environmentally-conscious consumers should avoid buying it at the market or ordering it in restaurants.

Iron ore, coal and other minerals have been found in the Antarctic, but their quantities – and qualities – are unknown. At present, exploiting any of these deposits would be highly uneconomical, the equivalent, in one scientist's words, of 'mining on the moon.' Although it is theorized that oil and natural gas exist beneath Antarctica's continental shelf, no commercial-size deposits have ever been found. As Stephen J Pyne writes in his masterful portrait of Antarctica, *The Ice* (University of Iowa Press, 1986), '...overall The Ice is not a source or a cornucopia of biotic and mineral resources but a sink that will absorb vast quantities of money, labor and information before it will yield returns.'

In 1988, the Antarctic Treaty parties agreed to a Convention on the Regulation of Antarctic Mineral Resources Activities (often known by the awkward acronym CRAMRA). But Australia and then France repudiated their signatures of CRAMRA, favoring instead another international agreement, the Protocol on Environmental Protection. Signed in Madrid in 1991 by all 26 consultative parties to the Antarctic Treaty (see the Government & Politics section in this chapter), the Protocol on Environmental Protection – also known as the Madrid Protocol – prohibits all mining in Antarctica for 50 years. (See the Environmental Issues chapter.)

Although many believe that the Madrid Protocol is the best possible protection for the Antarctic environment, others think it would have been better to have CRAMRA in place instead, ready for a time when its regulations might become necessary. In the future, they worry, resource-hungry nations might decide to reverse any ban on Antarctic mining. If no regulations controlling Antarctic mining exist at that time, it will be very difficult to enact laws as strict as those agreed to in CRAMRA.

GOVERNMENT & POLITICS

No country holds indisputable title over any part of Antarctica, and since there are no indigenous people, it has no native government. During the years of its discovery, parts of Antarctica were being 'claimed' in the name of various queens, kings, emperors, potentates, dictators and presidents. Argentina, Australia, Chile, France, New Zealand, Norway and the United Kingdom all claim territory in Antarctica. As long as very little was going on in Antarctica, no one cared too much about these sovereignty claims. It is also important to note that many world powers – the US and Russia, for example – have made no formal territorial claims on Antarctica. But they have carefully preserved their right to do so in the future. (See the Territorial Claims and Stations map earlier in this chapter.)

The Antarctic Treaty: A Unique Pact for a Unique Place

Imagine a world where there has (almost) never been war, where the environment is fully protected, where research has priority. This is the land the Antarctic Treaty parties call a natural reserve, devoted to peace and science.

The Antarctic Treaty is a landmark agreement through which countries active in Antarctica consult on the uses of the whole continent. The Treaty, which applies to the area south of 60°S, is surprisingly short but remarkably effective. (For the full text of the Treaty, see Appendix.) In its 12 articles, the Treaty

- stipulates that Antarctica should forever be used exclusively for peaceful purposes and not become the scene or object of international discord
- prohibits nuclear explosions, the disposal of nuclear waste and any measures of a military nature
- guarantees freedom of science and promotes the exchange of scientists and research results
- allows on-site inspection by foreign observers to ensure the observance of the Treaty
- removes the potential for sovereignty disputes between Treaty parties.

The Treaty was negotiated by the 12 nations present in Antarctica during the International Geophysical Year (IGY) (1957-58). They wanted to maintain the cooperation that characterized the IGY, when science proceeded unhindered. Such cooperation was particularly important in the context of the Cold War, which was at that time causing international tensions elsewhere. Since entering into force on June 23, 1961, the Treaty has been recognized as one of the most successful international agreements ever negotiated. Problematic differences over territorial claims have been effectively set aside, and as a disarmament regime the Treaty has been outstandingly successful. Treaty parties remain firmly committed to a system still effective in protecting their essential Antarctic interests.

Membership continues to grow. There are (as of October 1999) 44 parties to the Treaty. Twenty-six are Consultative Parties on the basis of either being original signatories or by conducting substantial research in Antarctica. The parties meet annually to discuss issues as diverse as scientific cooperation, measures to protect the environment, management of tourism and preservation of historic sites – and they are committed to taking decisions by consensus.

In the wake of the IGY, scientists and diplomats decided to codify the spirit of international cooperation developed during that 18-month period. They wrote an incredible and unprecedented document, the Antarctic Treaty, which has governed the continent since 1961. Although countries such as Malaysia have complained that the Antarctic Treaty member nations constitute an elite 'club' and should be replaced by a United Nations-ruled Antarctica, in fact Treaty members represent about 80% of the world's population. Also, the Treaty is open to any UN member state that wishes to accede to it. Any such state performing

significant scientific research in Antarctica can become a 'consultative party,' or full voting member.

Despite the Treaty's 'freezing' of territorial claims, various methods have been employed by different countries to try to reinforce their 'sovereignty' over large sections of Antarctic real estate. Chief among these have been flagpoles, plaques and even large representations of national flags painted on the sides of buildings. Conflicting claimants used to remove offending physical representations of sovereignty placed there by rivals, and pointedly, though politely, return them via diplomatic channels. Antarc-

The Antarctic Treaty: A Unique Pact for a Unique Place

Protection of the Environment Protecting Antarctica's unique ecosystem is a priority of the Treaty system. Specific environmental measures include:

The **Agreed Measures for the Conservation of Antarctic Fauna and Flora** (1964) protect native animals and birds. In addition, areas of outstanding ecological interest may be set aside as Specially Protected Areas. The category Sites of Special Scientific Interest was later added to protect significant scientific values.

The **Convention for the Conservation of Antarctic Seals** (1978) provides a means to regulate commercial sealing activities, in the unlikely event that they should ever be resumed. Three species of seal are totally protected and catch limits are set for others.

The **Convention on the Conservation of Antarctic Marine Living Resources** (1980) was adopted in response to fears that unregulated fishing for krill, at the center of the Antarctic food chain, might threaten the marine ecosystem. It ensures that the Southern Ocean's living resources are treated as a single ecosystem. Measures under CCAMLR identify protected species, set catch limits, identify fishing regions, define closed seasons, regulate fishing methods and establish fisheries inspection.

The **Protocol on Environmental Protection to the Antarctic Treaty** (1991) was negotiated following the failure of the Antarctic minerals convention in 1989. Also known as the Madrid Protocol, it arose out of proposals for a comprehensive regime that would guarantee protection of the environment. The Protocol integrates a number of existing measures in a single legally binding form. Among its provisions, the Protocol

- designates Antarctica as a 'natural reserve, devoted to peace and science'
- establishes environmental principles for the conduct of all activities
- prohibits mining for 50 years
- subjects all activities to prior assessment of their environmental impacts.

Annexes to the Protocol detail measures relating to environmental impact assessment, conservation of Antarctic fauna and flora, waste disposal, marine pollution and management of protected areas.

– Andrew Jackson,
Manager of Antarctic Policy at the Australian Antarctic Division

tic historian Robert Headland imagines that a typical scene might have involved an ambassador being called in by a rival head of state, who would have said something like 'We found this in *our* territory recently and wondered if you might like it back....'

Only a few times in Antarctic history has this careful diplomacy nearly disintegrated into 'political relations...by other means,' as Clausewitz famously euphemized war. One such incident occurred in 1952 at Hope Bay, when British expeditioners arriving to reestablish a base that had burned down earlier were greeted with a decidedly unfriendly welcome from their Argentine neighbors, who fired a machine gun over their heads. The governor of the Falkland Islands responded by dispatching two gunboats to reassert British 'sovereignty,' and the commander of the Argentine station was recalled. In 1953, Argentina and Chile got together and each built a hut on an airstrip used by Britain at Deception Island. Royal Marines arrived to oust the Argentines and Chileans from 'British territory,' and several Argentines were brought to Grytviken in South Georgia and deported to Argentina. In 1975, Britain's HMS *Shackleton* was fired on by an Argentine navy ship, which demanded that it proceed to

Ushuaia, a demand *Shackleton* ignored, sailing to Stanley instead.

Acts of war – or even of physical destruction – are extremely rare in Antarctica. More common are subtle, even somewhat pathetic, attempts made by countries to bolster their territorial claims – usually completely ignored by their rivals. As part of its effort to 'colonize' Antarctica, for example, Argentina has frequently sent women and children to its Esperanza station at Hope Bay on the Antarctic Peninsula. One such woman, Silvia Morello de Palma, was married to Army Captain Jorge de Palma, Esperanza's station leader, and was flown to Antarctica when seven months pregnant. On January 7, 1978, she gave birth to Emilio Marcos de Palma, the first 'native-born' Antarctican.

Other methods used by governments to assert territorial 'sovereignty' include the issuing of Antarctic stamps, which, being prized by philatelists, offer the added benefit of generating a profit at the same time. The leaders of national bases in Antarctica are often given titles reflecting a governmental or administrative role over their slice of The Ice: justice of the peace, for example, or local administrator. Some countries go so far as to 'naturalize' foreign citizens at their Antarctic stations. Britain levies a special tax on its citizens who work in the 'British Antarctic Territory,' which goes to the colonial government of the territory and is used for activities such as producing publications or restoring old research stations as historic sites. The territory is governed by a British Government-appointed commissioner, so its residents must endure 'taxation without representation,' something that got Britain in trouble with another of its colonies long ago! Interestingly, the commissioner makes no effort to collect taxes from other residents of the British Antarctic Territory, including the nationals of at least eight other countries that maintain stations there.

The US has found a practical way to put other countries at a distinct disadvantage in the Antarctic 'competition.' It bans the licensing to anyone but the American military of LC-130s, the ski-equipped Hercules cargo planes that are so useful in resupplying its continental stations at McMurdo and the South Pole. The powerful aircraft would be just as useful in the Arctic as well, so the US Government considers their use a security issue, but the restriction also neatly hampers other nations' Antarctic efforts and ambitions.

POPULATION & PEOPLE

Antarctica has never had a native population. Even today, its harsh environment assures that all residents are temporary. The continent's winter population is around 1200; one-third are scientists, and the rest are support personnel. During the 1999 austral winter, 43 stations – operated by 18 countries – were open in Antarctic regions recording meteorological data and doing other scientific research. In summer, the population increases sevenfold.

SOCIETY & CONDUCT

Antarctica's social rules are fairly straightforward: anytime you're inside a building, even one as simple as a hut or tent, you're a guest in someone else's home, and you should treat it accordingly. Antarctic bases, especially small ones, can be somewhat fragile societies, each with its own national character. Discretion is always advised.

When tourists visit Antarctic stations, residents must adjust their schedules in order to balance their desire to be hospitable and at the same time complete their work before the season ends. While this may not seem difficult to do, remember that yours is not the only visit the station will receive. Many get visitors practically every week during the austral summer.

Never enter any building unless specifically invited to do so. You might interfere with scientific work, or you might simply invade someone else's privacy, an all-too-rare commodity in Antarctica. Take off your shoes or boots whenever you enter a station building, especially accommodations, living quarters or dining areas. Cleaning up mud or guano dragged in by 110 pairs of tourist boots can be a real drag, and might make a station reluctant to allow visitors in the future. Be a courteous guest.

Another rule to remember: *Never* ask to use the station toilet. First, you're coming from a well-equipped ship – it's environmentally inexcusable to leave your waste on Antarctica when other alternatives exist. Second, although it appears to be a small favor to ask, imagine multiplying the task of emptying or cleaning the toilet by several dozen, and you can understand what a hassle tourists can be for station staff. Just make sure to go before you leave the ship!

Facts for the Visitor

HIGHLIGHTS

Although the whole of the Antarctic with its stark beauty and abundant wildlife is the highlight of a voyage to the continent, there are some extra special places within its realm. It's impossible to see them all in one trip, so you'll have to come back. The narrow passage of the **Lemaire Channel**, with its reflected mountains plunging straight into the sea, is particularly spectacular. The **Dry Valleys** with their otherworldly beauty and sculpted ventifacts are unlike anywhere else on Earth. The **historic huts of the Ross Sea region** are eerie, ghost-filled time capsules. The **aurora australis'** ethereal shimmering curtains of pale color are mysterious and awe-inspiring. A huge chinstrap penguin rookery at **Zavodovski Island** in the South Sandwich Islands, home to about 1 million birds, is one of the largest penguin colonies in the world. **Paradise Harbor** is one of the Antarctic's most heavily visited areas; Zodiac cruising among its icebergs and glacier-and-mountain reflections is wondrous. The **Ross Ice Shelf** glistens in the summer sun like bright white Carrara marble. **Deception Island**'s natural harbor is entered through the sea-breached wall of a volcanic crater, and the thermally heated waters at Pendulum Cove are warm enough for bathing.

PLANNING

When to Go

No tourists visit Antarctica during the winter, when the pack ice extends its frozen mantle for 1000km around most of the continent, barricading it against all ship traffic. In any case, few people would pay thousands of dollars to experience the Antarctic winter's near round-the-clock darkness and extreme cold – the thermometer can plummet to -50°C. At that temperature, boiling water thrown into the air freezes instantly – and noisily – into a cloud of snow.

So the Antarctic tour season is short – about four months, with each offering its own highlights. November is early summer: spring pack ice is breaking up, and birds – especially penguins – are courting and mating. December and January, when penguins are hatching eggs and feeding chicks, are the height of the austral summer, bringing warmer temperatures and up to 20 hours of sunlight every day. In the late summer month of February, whale sighting is best, penguin chicks are beginning to fledge and adult penguins are ashore molting.

There are other factors to consider: cruises later in the season may be less crowded, so there may not be as much waiting around for Zodiacs and station tours. However, the later you wait to go, the greater the risk that much of the wildlife will already be gone to sea. For those wishing to see Ross Island's historic huts, the best bet is to go as late in the season as possible. Even with an icebreaker, it may be impossible to penetrate the pack ice that far south earlier in the season.

Because of the heavy ship traffic sailing from Ushuaia for Antarctica, it may be possible for independent travelers to find bargain prices there. Since the ships are ready to sail, if they have open berths they may be willing to negotiate the fare, on the theory that making some money is better than none at all. Be warned, however, that most Antarctic ships are fully booked, though you'll probably find that late in the season – particularly during the month of February – there are open cabins.

What Kind of Trip

The vast majority of tourists visit Antarctica by ship. This is both practical – hotel, restaurant and sightseeing vehicle are all combined in one unit – and environmentally sound, since there is no tourism infrastructure ashore to compete for the already scarce areas of ice-free rock. This bare rock is needed by birds and seals for breeding grounds and used by national Antarctic programs for their stations.

Pack ice

Tabular iceberg with striations

Fractured iceberg

Ice crystals hanging from an iceberg

Old ice

Ice edge, East Antarctica

COLIN MONTEATH (HEDGEHOG HOUSE)

Storm cloud and iceberg, Paradise Bay, Antarctic Peninsula

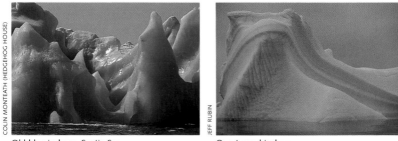

COLIN MONTEATH (HEDGEHOG HOUSE)

Old blue iceberg, Scotia Sea

JEFF RUBIN

Overturned iceberg

JEFF RUBIN

Heavily crevassed ice

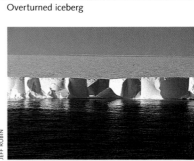

JEFF RUBIN

Ross Ice Shelf

Not everyone is content to restrict themselves to the coast, however, and tourists can visit the continent's vast interior, parts of which are still largely unexplored. At present there is only one company offering visits to the interior mountains, ice sheets and even the South Pole itself (see the Getting There & Away chapter). Predictably, the complicated logistics of these visits make them very expensive.

Questions to Ask Your Tour Operator
What kind of ship is it? Is it designed for safe polar travel and ice-strengthened? Or is it an unstrengthened cruise liner that just happens to be routed south to The Ice for a cruise or two? An icebreaker is able to push its way through far thicker ice than a vessel that has merely been ice-strengthened. If you're hoping to visit the Ross Sea region, choose *only* an icebreaker voyage, as non-icebreaking ships almost never penetrate deep enough to permit landings in the area, even with helicopters – and there are no refunds for missed landings. However, an icebreaker's shallower draft means it will roll more in heavy seas, causing discomfort for those prone to motion sickness.

What – *exactly* – is included in the quoted price of the trip? Find out whether port taxes and other non-tour fees are included; some companies leave these charges out in order to make their advertised prices appear more competitive, but they can add US$600 or more to your cost. What about airfare? Some tour operators include this in their prices, but most do not. Price, however, should be just one factor in your decision.

How many days will you actually spend in Antarctica? Some tour operators include as many as three nights in South America as part of a 14-day 'Antarctica' program. How long is the voyage? Cruises to the Peninsula from South America are generally more popular because they require the least amount of time at sea (about

two days each way, as opposed to three or more, each way, for non-Peninsula destinations), an activity that many people find uncomfortable or boring. But there are many attractions in the other parts of Antarctica that make the longer voyages worthwhile.

How many other passengers will be on board? Some ships are much more crowded than others. The smallest ships accommodate just 38 passengers, while the largest carry more than 1000. In general, the smaller the passenger complement, the better. Fewer than 100 passengers per cruise is best, and any ship carrying more than 150 passengers to Antarctica is simply ridiculous. This is not simply a matter of having two or more seatings in the dining room. Lectures become standing-room-only affairs, and shore landings become assembly lines – creating unnecessary stress on fragile Antarctic landing sites. The rules governing visits to the historic hut sites in the Ross Sea area, meanwhile, allow no more than 40 people ashore at one time, and at one of them, no more than three passengers are allowed inside at once. Many scientific stations are reluctant to welcome more than 80 passengers in a single visit.

Another factor to consider: in the unlikely event of an accident, rescuing more than 200 people would be very difficult, if not impossible. Larger vessels visiting Antarctica have become a major cause of concern for the countries operating national programs there, since personnel in such programs would be the ones called upon to render assistance in any disaster.

The International Association of Antarctica Tour Operators (IAATO) is so concerned about the negative effect of larger ships visiting Antarctica that it recently reaffirmed its commitment to limiting member companies to those whose ships carry fewer than 400 passengers, though this number is still more than double what it should be.

Although all members of IAATO pledge themselves to put no more than 100 people ashore at any site at the same time, this IAATO bylaw depends on the honor system, and even member companies violate it when it suits them. With a smaller ship, you will not have such overcrowding. There is a different atmosphere aboard larger ships, too. An expedition on a large ship can feel like a Caribbean or Mediterranean cruise, with glitzy nightclubs, marble bathtubs, six-course dinners, and chocolates on your pillow every night. Indeed, many passengers on these liners have little interest in Antarctica and do not even leave the ship.

What are the other passengers like? Special interest groups such as birdwatchers or alumni groups sometimes buy a large proportion of a ship's cabins for one or two cruises. Occasionally, a tour operator may try to sell the remaining cabins to unsuspecting people with different interests (or alma maters). Divergent agendas can cause tensions on a voyage. Also, you may want to know where most of the other passengers come from. Although meeting people from other countries can be one of travel's chief joys, language can be a problem on some cruises. While most Antarctic cruise passengers speak English, many do not. If there is a large group of non-English speakers aboard, lectures and briefings may be cut short or skipped, meaning that some passengers miss important information.

Who are the lecturers aboard? The quality and enthusiasm of the lecture staff vary from ship to ship – and even from cruise to cruise. Ask to see the résumés of the lecturers for the cruise you've chosen. The better cruise companies arrange this well in advance of sailing. Most importantly, ask about each lecturer's previous experience in lecturing aboard cruise ships, especially *polar* cruise ships. Many eminent scientists are poor lecturers. Delivering a top-quality talk is a special skill, blending knowledge, entertainment and good humor. Is there a dedicated lecture hall aboard? On some ships, lectures appear to be an afterthought, with slide projectors and screens set up in the dining room or a drafty equipment room. What is the capacity of the lecture theater? Are there seats for all passengers, or is it standing room only for latecomers?

What are the credentials of the physician on board? Some cruise lines use the ship's physician, while others have a special doctor for the cruise. You may feel more comfortable having a doctor whose first language is English.

Does the ship carry helicopters? These can be invaluable for getting to places inaccessible by Zodiac. With their aerial reconnaissance capabilities, helicopters can also help prevent the ship from getting stuck in ice and wasting valuable time. Helicopters can also be used for evacuation in the case of a medical emergency, if the ship is close enough to an inhabited area. There is one disadvantage to helicopters, however: it's difficult to move large groups of people with them, since many models carried on Antarctic cruise ships can accommodate only 6 to 8 passengers at a time.

Is the tour operator an IAATO member? This self-regulating industry group has banded together to promote responsible travel to Antarctica and can pressure its members to maintain high standards of ship, staff and passenger behavior in the delicate Antarctic ecosystem. (For more information, see the Useful Organizations section in this chapter.)

How experienced are the expedition leader and the assistant expedition leader? To heighten customers' sense of adventure, Antarctic tour operators refrain from calling these people 'tour leaders' or 'cruise directors.' Since the expedition leader and the ship's captain make all on-the-spot decisions about landings and itinerary choices, they are an important factor in your cruise. Inexperienced leaders may be overly ambitious in their planning, or they may fail to conduct as many landings as might be possible.

Maps
Although most map stores do not carry a large selection of Antarctic maps, good shops can usually order maps or navigation charts for you, or put you in touch with a

national mapping agency from which maps can be ordered.

Probably the best general map of the continent is the Antarctica map (item £20015C) produced by the National Geographic Society (National Geographic Society Store, ☎ 515-362-3353, toll-free 800-437-5521, fax 515-362-3345, PO Box 11303, Des Moines, IA 50340 USA, www.ngstore.com). Measuring 74cm by 56cm, the map has great information and is a good value at US$8.95.

Also very useful is the 1:10,000,000 scale map published by the British Antarctic Survey, *Antarctica – a topographic database*, available for £6.25, including postage. Send a check payable to University of Cambridge

Antarctic Museums

With the exception of the former British base turned museum at Port Lockroy, there are no permanent museums in Antarctica. But many scientific stations maintain at least a small 'cabinet of curiosities.' The Antarctic Treaty, meanwhile, has designated 72 'historic sites and monuments.' A proportion of these mark sites of genuine international importance (though many important sites remain unmarked). Others, including statues of recent national leaders, are of dubious interest.

The following museums display Antarctic material. Many other museums have smaller exhibits, and temporary exhibitions on Antarctica circulate frequently. (See also the Antarctic Gateways chapter for museums in those cities.)

Australia The Queen Victoria Museum in Launceston, the Power House Museum in Sydney and the Victorian National Museum in Melbourne all have small Antarctic displays.

Germany The sealer *Grönland* is docked at Bremerhaven, and includes a display about her 1872 Antarctic voyage.

Japan The icebreaker *Fuji* has a permanent exhibition aboard; she is moored in Nagoya City. The Shirase Antarctic Expedition Museum near Konoura includes much material on the expedition of 1910-12.

New Zealand The Southland Museum in Invercargill includes an interesting display on New Zealand's sub-Antarctic islands. In Auckland, Kelly Tarlton's Antarctic Encounter includes a replica of Scott's Cape Evans hut, an Antarctic aquarium and displays on the history of Antarctica.

Norway Sandefjord and Tønsberg both have excellent whaling museums with a lot of Antarctic material (they are particularly strong on South Georgia). Oslo has three sites: the famous polar ship *Fram*, used by Amundsen; Amundsen's home 'Uranienborg'; and some additional Amundsen material in the Ski Museum.

Russia St Petersburg is home to the Arctic and Antarctic Museum, located in a former church at Ul Marata 24A.

United Kingdom The Scott Polar Research Institute in Cambridge, England, is a major polar center, with a public museum featuring many artifacts from the expeditions of Scott and Shackleton as well as from more recent research activities. Scott's ship *Discovery* is moored in Dundee, Scotland.

United States The many New England whaling and sealing museums often have Antarctic material, particularly where it refers to the early sealing industry. New York City's American Museum of Natural History includes a large but often-overlooked display on Lincoln Ellsworth.

– Robert Headland

with your order to: Museum Shop, Scott Polar Research Institute, University of Cambridge, Lensfield Rd, Cambridge CB2 1ER, England.

In the United States, the US Geological Survey has topographic, geologic and reconnaissance maps of portions of Antarctica at various scales. *An Index to United States Topographic and Other Map Coverage of Antarctica* is available free of charge from the US Geological Survey Information Services (☎ 303-202-4200, toll-free 888-275-8747, fax 303-202-4693, esicmail@usgs .gov), Box 25286, Denver, CO 80225 USA. For a complete list of USGS maps of Antarctica, check the Web: http://mapping .usgs.gov/mac/isb/pubs/forms/anarctic.html (yes, Antarctic is misspelled). Most of them cost US$4 each. One very nice map is the USGS *Satellite Image Map of Antarctica* (number I-2284 in the Miscellaneous Investigations Series), which shows that the continent is hardly a monochromatic mass of white.

For aeronautic and nautical charts, contact the National Ocean and Atmospheric Administration's Distribution Division, National Ocean Service (☎ 301-436-8301, toll-free 800-638-8972, fax 301-436-6829), 6501 Lafayette Ave, Riverdale, MD 20737-1199 USA. One particularly good map they sell is the large (105cm by 146cm) and detailed *Global Navigation and Planning Chart of Antarctica* (1:5,000,000 scale; code number GNC26). At US$3.55, it's a bargain. You can also ask for a free catalog of other maps: either the Aeronautical Charts catalog (covers the whole world, including Antarctica) or the Nautical Charts catalog for Region 2: Central and South America and Antarctica.

The Smithsonian's National Museum of Natural History in Washington, DC offers another good, big (104cm by 140cm) map of Antarctica on the same scale for US$7. It shows the routes of many traverses of the polar plateau, which look like ant tracks across a vast white desert. Send a check to Smithsonian Institution, Department of Invertebrate Zoology, Attn: Valorie Barnes – MRC: 543, Washington, DC 20560 USA. For more information, email barnes.valorie@ nmnh.si.edu or visit www.nmnh.si.edu/iz/ usap/usapmap.html.

The British Admiralty charts of Antarctica are also excellent. They can be purchased from many firms; one of the best is Kelvin Hughes (☎ 44-171-709-9076, fax 44-171-481-1298), Charts Department, 142 Minories, London, EC3N 1NH, UK, www .kelvinhughes.co.uk). All charts are £15.30 each.

A catalog of Australian mapping of the Antarctic is available from the Australian Surveying and Land Information Group (AUSLIG). Particularly useful is the map of the Australian National Antarctic Research Expeditions 1947-1966 (A$15.95) and the Cape Denison Historic Site-Commonwealth Bay 1:3300 map, which serves as a visitor's guide to Mawson's Huts (A$15.95). Contact AUSLIG Map Sales (☎ 61-2-6201-4300, toll-free 800-800-173, fax 61-2-6201-4381, mapsales@auslig.gov.au, www.auslig.gov.au), PO Box 2, Belconnen, Australian Capital Territory, 2616 Australia.

One of the best atlases of Antarctic maps was produced, not surprisingly, by the US Central Intelligence Agency. The oversize paperback, entitled simply *Polar Regions Atlas*, was published in Washington, DC in 1981. There's no spy stuff, just a comprehensive, chart-filled look at both the Arctic and the Antarctic, with an eye to the resources of each region. It's out of print, but can sometimes be found in the catalogs of Antarctic book dealers (see the Books section in this chapter).

Besides the excellent topographic maps and navigation charts available, three tourist maps of Antarctica are also available. The *Antarctica Info Map* was produced by the International Antarctic Centre in Christchurch (see the Antarctic Gateways chapter) in conjunction with New Zealand's Department of Survey and Land Information. One side offers a large and detailed map of the continent (with an inset of Ross Island), while the other gives basic information on Gondwana, the ozone hole, exploration, ice, plants and animals, geology and the Antarctic Treaty. The other two maps are not as good; the first is the English-

Spanish 'ecomapa' of the Antarctic Peninsula produced by Zagier & Urruty publications of Buenos Aires and Miami, Florida, and sold at the Oficina Antártica in Ushuaia (see the Antarctic Gateways chapter) and at the Ushuaia airport. Although the ecomapa has some handsome illustrations of whales and penguins, its detailed maps of the Peninsula are labeled almost exclusively in Spanish, despite its claim of being bilingual. International Travel Maps (☎ 604-879-3621, fax 604-879-4521, travelmaps@nas.com, www.nas.com/travelmaps/list.html), 345 W Broadway, Vancouver, British Columbia, Canada V5Y 1P8, produces a 1:8,000,000 map of Antarctica that costs the same as the National Geographic map (US$8.95) but is not as detailed.

Anyone visiting the Ross Sea – or merely reading an account of one of Scott or Shackleton's expeditions – would benefit greatly by purchasing the excellent *McMurdo Sound, Antarctica* map produced by Molenaar Maps in 1985. Available from the Antarctic Connection (see the Shopping section in this chapter) for US$9.95, this 60cm by 90cm map gives a detailed view of the entire region and includes illustrations of area landmarks in the margins. On the reverse in densely packed type is a comprehensive discussion of Antarctica's history, geology, climate and scientific research.

The Antarctica Project (see the Useful Organizations section in this chapter) has a newly updated *Antarctic Habitat* poster map, which is large (63cm by 102cm) and attractively illustrated. It identifies and describes the major breeding sites where Antarctic and sub-Antarctic wildlife are found, and sells for US$15.

What to Bring

Along the coast, Antarctic summers are less cold than you might imagine. Anyone who has lived through a reasonably tough winter in the northern part of the Northern Hemisphere should be fine without buying a lot of expensive clothing. Dressing for the cold is best accomplished by wearing several layers of lighter clothing rather than a single heavy garment, since air is trapped and warmed between layers. As an outer layer, a windproof and waterproof jacket is preferable to a heavy, bulky coat.

For shipboard dress – which is very casual on most ships – a pair of jeans and a sweatshirt or sweater will be most comfortable, since the ship's interior is heated to room temperature. The ship's bridge, a favorite spot for passengers while underway, is also heated, although it often provides access to an outside deck for those who want to take a quick photo or two.

Remember, too, you'll be sailing from a Southern Hemisphere port in the summertime, so you'll need warm weather clothing before and after the cruise.

For footwear, the single most important item is a pair of knee-high waterproof rubber boots (ie, Wellingtons) for landings. For shipboard wear, a comfortable pair of sneakers or even sandals will suit perfectly. Hiking boots can be useful for long walking trips ashore on sub-Antarctic or Southern Ocean islands, but they may be more weight and trouble than they're worth.

Following is a suggested packing list for a two-week Antarctic cruise; it assumes a certain number of repeated wearings and perhaps one laundering en route: waterproof pants and jacket; two or three pairs wool pants or jeans; two wool sweaters or polar-fleece pullovers; three or four flannel or wool shirts; two pairs long underwear pants; three or four pairs of thick wool socks; five pairs of cotton socks to wear underneath wool socks; three or four cotton turtleneck shirts; warm, waterproof, ski-style gloves (invest in good ones!); silk gloves to wear beneath ski gloves; and a thick wool or even fur hat.

High-tech synthetic fabrics are readily available and are in many ways superior to wool and cotton. Polartec, famous for being the cloth made from recycled plastic bottles, is especially good: it's lightweight and fast drying. Brightly colored Polartec pullovers are de rigueur for expedition staff. Also good, especially for underwear, are such fabrics as Capilene and polypropylene, which wick perspiration away from the skin, wash easily and dry overnight.

Choosing and Using Binoculars

Binoculars are indispensable for identifying distant objects, and their usefulness is not restricted to keen birders. Because optical quality and design have improved enormously in recent years, old binoculars are not necessarily better than modern ones.

Choosing Before you buy, check the following:

• SPECIFICATION: this is indicated on the binocular, eg 8x30 (8x is the magnification; 30 is the diameter in millimeters of the objective, or end, lenses). Bigger magnification is not better – a low magnification (7x or 8x) is best. Otherwise, you'll have difficulty obtaining a steady, bright, clear image. By contrast, the diameter of the objective lenses should be big (at least 30mm) to let in as much light as possible and give a wide field of view.

• WEIGHT: anything heavier than 750g will be like a millstone around your neck. But beware of mini 'compact' models because they give far too small a field of vision.

• EYECUPS: choose a pair with fold-back or snap-up-and-down rubber eyecups. If you wear eyeglasses for distance, keep your glasses on and fold back (or snap down) the cups so that the binocular is flush with your eyeglass lenses. If you don't wear glasses, pull or snap out the cups. A good model will give you the same field of view either way.

• RIGHT EYEPIECE ADJUSTMENT: most models have a calibrated scale (-, 0, +) on the right lens nearest the eye. You cannot judge the binoculars until you adjust this for your own eye, as follows: focus on some sharply defined object (ideally, a sign) at a medium distance. Using your left eye only, focus on the object using the center focusing wheel. Then, using your right eye only, focus on the same object using *not* the center focusing wheel but the right eyepiece, which twists to focus. Now, using both eyes, you will have the best view through those binoculars.

Using Just as with a camera, getting the most out of your purchase of binoculars requires some instruction:

• LENS CAPS: discard them or save them at home in case you need to mail the binoculars (for repair). They protect lenses in transit but are otherwise unnecessary.

• STRAP: the longer the strap, the more your binoculars will swing about, so shorten it. Always keep the strap around your neck, and put it around the neck of anyone borrowing your pair.

• STEADINESS: to hold the binoculars steady, seat them firmly in your hands (not fingertips) and keep your elbows in toward your body. You can also lean against a wall or rail for support.

• CLEANING: avoid abrasion – don't keep cleaning the lenses! When you do, use a clean soft cloth kept in a pouch – not just the corner of a handkerchief or a paper tissue, which can contain minute particles of aluminum. To provide a touch of moisture, blow (don't breathe) on the lenses – this is also more likely to remove any speck of dust or grit which might otherwise be ground into the lens. Check the cloth for dust or grit as well.

• MICROSCOPE: if you use your binoculars wrong way round and up close, they make an excellent microscope – a real bonus.

– **Graham Bell,**
a well-known British ornithologist, who regularly accompanies
voyages all over the world as a guest lecturer

❄ ❄

Other essentials include: UV-filtering sunglasses – absolutely necessary with sun reflecting off ice, snow and water; a nice dress for women and sport jacket and tie for men (for Captain's welcome and farewell dinners); lip balm and sunscreen (remember the thinning of the ozone layer), as well as moisturizing lotion, since the extremely low humidity can dry and even crack the skin; shampoo and conditioner, which most Antarctic tour companies do not supply; and, of course, camera equipment. Nobody visits Antarctica without a camera, even the most jaded ship staff member.

Be sure also to bring a guidebook (preferably this one) and perhaps some kind of wildlife identification guide or chart (see the sections on Shopping and Books in this chapter).

Among the optional items are a small backpack or fanny pack for carrying things ashore; a bathing suit (for shipboard pools and saunas, the Deception Island thermal springs and perhaps even an icy dip in the Southern Ocean); binoculars (see the boxed text 'Choosing and Using Binoculars' in this chapter); flashlight (especially useful inside dark historic huts); extra eyeglasses or contact lenses; aspirin; seasickness pills (though the ship's doctor will also have a supply); and a travel alarm clock. Avid exercisers may wish to bring workout gear, though shipboard exercise equipment tends to be limited to basic barbells tucked away on a lower deck.

If you're so inclined, current magazines or newspapers make good gifts for members of Antarctic stations, but don't overdo it; a little news of the world goes a long way.

TOURIST OFFICES

The only Antarctic tourist office is in Ushuaia, Argentina: the Oficina Antártica (Antarctic Unit) of Infuetur, the Tourism Board of Tierra del Fuego, at Avenida Maipú 505 (☎ 54-29014-24431, fax 54-29014-30694, antartida@tierradelfuego.org.ar.tier-radelfuego.org.ar/antartida/indexeng.htm).

The staffers, Andrea Barrio and María Gabriela Roldán, are very friendly and helpful, and part of their role is to collect information about the tourists who pass through Ushuaia on the way to The Ice. They sell an 'ecomapa' of the Antarctic Peninsula, postcards and a small selection of other Antarctic-related books and trinkets. They also have a small display of relics left behind in the Antarctic by Otto Nordenskjöld's expedition.

For information about Antarctica tour companies see the Getting There & Away chapter, or contact IAATO (see the Useful Organizations section in this chapter).

VISAS & DOCUMENTS
Passports & Visas

Because of the Antarctic Treaty, no visas are necessary to visit Antarctica. For environmental reasons, however, some countries are beginning to require their citizens to obtain a permit before visiting Antarctica (see the boxed text 'Antarctic Visas.').

Even people traveling from their home country directly to Antarctica and back need their passports, because Antarctica's difficult weather and ice could force a change in itinerary. You just might find your ship returning to a different port – and country – than originally planned, though it's very unlikely.

When you come aboard your Antarctic ship the expedition staff will probably collect your passport and keep it until the end of your cruise. This is to enable staff to handle all passports as a group if, for instance, you visit an Antarctic research station and they stamp passports with the station's stamp. (This is for 'vanity' purposes only, and you may request that your passport not be stamped, though you may find that an Antarctic stamp can be a real conversation-starter, even with blasé immigration officials.)

Visas are often required for the country from which your Antarctic cruise departs. Check with the tour operator or your travel agent for details. But don't get sucked into the expensive visa services offered by some cruise lines, which can cost up to US$30 for a visa that is often free for the asking from the issuing country.

Antarctic 'Visas'

Since no single government controls Antarctica, visitors need no visas to go there. But with the ratification of the Antarctic Treaty's Protocol on Environmental Protection in 1998, several countries now require their citizens to obtain permits to go to Antarctica – even as tourists.

Any Japanese citizen who visits Antarctica, for example, whether scientist, explorer, worker or tourist, must obtain a 'Certificate for Antarctic Activities' from Japan's Director General of the Environmental Agency. As part of the certification process, applicants are briefed on the regulations of the Antarctic Treaty, the Protocol on Environmental Protection and the Agreed Measures for the Conservation of Antarctic Flora and Fauna. The certificate, when issued, lists the purpose of the visit; dates, location and means of permitted travel; and regulations by which the visitor must abide.

Norwegian citizens must provide advance notice to the Norwegian Polar Institute at least a full year before any visit to Antarctica. The notice must describe who is responsible for the proposed activity, the scope of the activity – including an initial environmental evaluation – and the technology and measures that will be adopted to limit any harmful effects. The Norwegian Polar Institute has separate forms for sea-based tourism, land-based tourism (such as skiing and mountain-climbing expeditions) and research.

Sweden's Antarctica Act requires all Swedes staying or conducting activities in Antarctica to apply for a permit. A 12-page fact sheet, entitled *Antarctica is Unique!*, explains how to acquire a permit.

Although these three countries were the only ones at press time that required their citizens to obtain a permit to visit Antarctica, other countries may add such a requirement. Your tour operator should be able to help you determine whether or not you must get one.

Travel Insurance

Most tour operators recommend travel insurance to 'insure' you against their trip-cancellation penalties, which in most cases are severe. For relatively early cancellations penalties vary widely, but typically, if you cancel less than 60 days before sailing, you forfeit 100% of the cruise price. On the other hand, travel insurance for a US$13,000 cruise costs nearly US$1000, so if you're sure that you'll be able to go on the trip, you're better off without it.

Photocopies

Losing your passport is bad news, since getting a new one takes time and money. It's a good idea to carry a driver's license, ID card, birth certificate or some other form of photo identification to make replacing a lost passport a little easier. Having an expired passport can be very useful. It also helps to have a separate record of your passport number and issue date, as well as a photo-copy of the ID pages. While you're compiling that information, add the serial numbers of your traveler's checks, details of your health insurance and about US$100 cash for emergencies.

CUSTOMS

Some countries allow travelers to the Antarctic to purchase goods duty-free, since technically you leave all national territory by going to Antarctica. Make sure to save any duty-free receipts, however, since customs officials may board your ship upon return to port. Even if the tour operator tells you that customs does not plan to do an inspection, bureaucrats can always change their minds while you're away.

Remember also that citizens of many countries are subject to national laws that prohibit taking any animal, mineral or plant 'souvenirs' from Antarctica. The Antarctic Treaty's Protocol on Environmental Protection also prohibits such taking. Customs agents inspecting your bags upon your return from The Ice may seize such items – and impose heavy fines for violating these laws. At its headquarters in Hobart, the Australian Antarctic Division has a display of seals' teeth confiscated from the luggage of tourists. Don't take souvenirs; it's against the ethic of what Antarctica is about. And if that argument doesn't convince you, just remember that it's not worth getting caught.

MONEY
Costs

Most Antarctic tour brochures carefully spell out what is not included in the price of the cruise, although some try to make their trips appear cheaper by separating the port taxes (which can add nearly US$600 to the price of the cruise) from the price. More typically, the additional costs of a cruise are for optional items including alcohol, laundry, faxes, satellite phone calls, tips, souvenirs, extra helicopter time and massages.

Cash, Traveler's Checks & Credit Cards

Each ship runs its onboard economy in a slightly different manner, but generally a chit system is used, whereby passengers merely sign for items. Often no prices are listed for items in the shop or at the bar, which can be hazardous for spendthrifts. On the penultimate day of the voyage, the ship's purser or hotel manager distributes bills. These can usually be settled with cash, traveler's checks or credit cards (some ships take an imprint of your credit card early in the trip so you merely have to sign off on your accumulated charges at the end of the voyage). Most ships, regardless of country of origin, accept only US dollars for cash transactions.

Antarctican Dollars: The Coolest Cash

Although Antarctica has no national government, it does have one of the world's most beautiful 'currencies.' Antarctican dollars began circulating on March 1, 1996, the brainchild of Canadian numismatist David J Hamilton, 'comptroller of currency' at the Antarctica Overseas Exchange Office Ltd.

Hamilton sells his banknotes – $1, $5, $10, $20, $50 and $100 – for their face value in US dollars. Until their expiration on December 31, 2001, the Antarctican notes can be redeemed for their purchase price, less shipping and handling. After that, any unsold notes will be destroyed, making those that remain collector's items.

The goal of the Antarctica Overseas Exchange Office is to raise funds for Antarctican research and humanitarian projects, Hamilton says, with preference given to work contributing to what he calls 'the assertion of Antarctican self-determination.' A local currency, he declares, is 'precisely what Antarctica needs to generate capital needed to perform valuable scientific and humanitarian research within her borders.' Upon the expiration of the outstanding notes, fully 80% of all proceeds from the sale of Antarctican dollars will be given to organizations seeking funding for such projects. Hamilton will retain 20% to cover production, marketing and administration expenses.

Despite their beauty, the notes are not legal tender and are not money. 'Representatives of the territorial governments now in Antarctica may not recognize these notes, even in Antarctica,' Hamilton says, 'so please ask first before attempting to use them in a transaction.' On the other hand, personnel at Antarctic stations would most likely be quite happy to accept Antarctic $1 notes as small gifts.

A total of 89,103 Antarctican dollars were in circulation worldwide as of January 1, 2000. For more information, call David J Hamilton at ☎ 604-431-8017. The notes can be seen at the Antarctica Overseas Exchange Office website, www2.portal.ca/~ntarctic.

No matter what country is operating them, most bases expect tourists to pay in either the national currency or in US dollars – and sometimes only in US dollars, even at non-US stations. But some are more flexible. The shop at New Zealand's accommodating Scott Base, for example, accepts NZ and US dollars, as well as Visa, Mastercard and American Express.

Tipping

Tipping is not included in the cruise fare and so is an additional (though optional) cost. While tipping is always at your discretion, it is considered an appropriate supplement to crew and staff wages for service. Near the end of the voyage most tour operators distribute tipping guidelines, which are just that: suggestions only and not in any way requirements. Generally US$10 a day from each passenger is considered appropriate. Depending on the tour company, this sum may be divided evenly among all the cruise staff (including chefs, sous chefs, bartenders and cabin attendants) as well as the ship's crew, from the captain on down to the lowliest deckhand. Other companies choose to divide the tipping groups into two categories, distinguishing the staff from the crew. Sometimes expedition leaders and lecturers are included in the tip pool, although often they are not. Of course, if you wish to reward particularly good service from an individual the best way is the most direct: simply slip them an envelope with your cash gratuity enclosed. Personal gifts can also be a nice gesture for showing appreciation. Depending on the tour company, gratuities may be paid by any combination of credit card, traveler's checks or cash.

POST & COMMUNICATIONS
Postal Rates & Sending Mail

In general, you should only send letters or postcards from Antarctica for the novelty of doing so, since service is understandably slow (often as long as two or three months). Many Antarctic stations send tourists' mail back to their program's home country for forwarding to the recipient, while others send the mail from the relief ship's first port of call on the voyage home. Other stations (US ones in particular) do not handle tourist mail, although arrangements are sometimes made so that tour ship staff can stamp postcards and letters with a station stamp. The rate for a postcard from Antarctica is usually US$1, probably because this is a round number requiring no change. For that you'll get a (sometimes surprising) postmark, and – if you send one to yourself – a happy reminder of your trip right around the time your memory of it is starting to fade.

Telephone & Fax

Sure, modern satellite technology makes it possible to call your mom from Antarctica – but it'll cost you. Ship communications (fax, telephone and, in some cases, email) use the INMARSAT (International Maritime Satellite), which provides reliable connections. However, there is often a significant time lag (two or three seconds) from transmission to reception, so until you get the rhythm of the delay you'll find yourself speaking over your answering party. All this can be a bit frustrating, as the meter is running at a rate of anywhere from US$12 a minute on up. Much of this charge is in fact pure profit for the ship, since the normal cost for INMARSAT is less than US$5 per minute.

Some ships offer INMARSAT service in individual cabins, while others require passengers to visit the radio room to make or receive calls. Receiving calls, by the way, is relatively easy, since the ship's radio officer can simply page a requested passenger. Typically, the radio officer will ask the outside caller to ring back in five minutes, allowing the receiving party enough time to get to the radio room, thereby saving five minutes of expensive dead time.

Remember to calculate carefully the time difference between your ship and the recipient of your call, who will surely appreciate it if they are not awakened at 3 am to hear about the enchanting antics of the penguins you just saw. The ship's radio officer can help you to determine this.

The code used for international dialing in Antarctica is ☎ 672.

INTERNET RESOURCES

There are several Internet sites of interest to Antarcticophiles. See below for an alphabetical list.

Antarctica's Internet suffix is .aq.

The Australian Antarctic Division's website includes such highlights as video views of Mawson station, a map showing the location of Australia's research ship *Aurora Australis*, and stacks of information on Australian Antarctic science, stations and history.

The US program is represented by the National Science Foundation home page. For an 'inside' view of life at US stations, visit either The Ice (www.theice.org) or Antarctica Online (www.antarcticaonline.com), pages privately designed by veterans of the US Antarctic Program.

Many other national Antarctic programs are represented on the Web, including the Belgian Antarctic Research Program, the British Antarctic Survey, the Italian Antarctic Program, the South African National Antarctic Program, and Germany's polar research center, the Alfred Wegener Institute.

The CIA's page devoted to Antarctica is outdated, but contains the little-known fact that the continent's international digraph is AY.

The *New South Polar Times* is an online newspaper produced by the staff of the US Amundsen-Scott South Pole station, while the *Antarctic Sun* is published by staff at the US McMurdo station. Also check out the reports produced by Antarctic Heritage Trust (see the Useful Organizations section).

The *Antarctican* is an independent, international news service devoted strictly to news about Antarctica, edited by veteran Antarctic journalist Andrew Darby of Tasmania, Australia. It is available only on the Web.

There are several good websites devoted to Antarctic philately:

www.newzeal.com/steve/antarctica.htm;
www.south-pole.com;
www-mo.enst-bretagne.fr/~duflot/philadelie/ (French Antarctic postal history – in French); and http://Antarktis.here.de/ (Antarctic postal history – in German).

Internet Addresses

Alfred Wegener Institute (Germany) www.awi-bremerhaven.de/

Antarctic Sun www.asa.org/antsun/index.htm

Antarctic Support Associates www.asa.org

Antarctica New Zealand www.antarcticanz.govt.nz

The Antarctican www.antarctican.com

Argentine Antarctic Institute www.dna.gov.ar

Australian Antarctic Division www.antdiv.gov.au

Belgian Scientific Research Programme on the Antarctic www.belspo.be/antar

British Antarctic Survey www.nerc-bas.ac.uk

Chilean Antarctic Institute www.inach.cl

CIA's Antarctica page www.cia.gov/cia/publications/factbook/ay.html

Council of Managers of National Antarctic Programs www.comnap.aq

French Polar Institute www.ifremer.fr/ifrtp/wwwenglish/index.html

Heritage Antarctica www.heritage-antarctica.org

Italian Antarctic Program www.pnra.it/index_inglese.html

Japan's National Institute of Polar Research www.nipr.ac.jp

US National Science Foundation www.nsf.gov/od/opp/

The New South Polar Times 205.174.118.254/nspt/home.htm

Norwegian Polar Institute www.npolar.no

South African National Antarctic Program www.sanap.org.za

Swedish Polar Research Secretariat www.polar.kva.se/eng/index.html

'virtual tour' of McMurdo station astro.uchicago.edu/cara/vtour/mcmurdo/

'virtual tour' of South Pole station astro.uchicago.edu/cara/vtour/pole/

BOOKS

Some of the most interesting books on Antarctica are out of print. To find them you can either haunt secondhand bookshops, or if you prefer the easy way, contact one of the following specialists, who will probably be happy to send you a free catalog. Unfortunately, interest in collecting Antarctic titles has greatly increased over the past two decades, driving up prices.

Adventurous Traveler.com (☎ 802-860-6776, toll-free 800-707-0892, fax 802-860-6667, toll-free fax 800-677-1821, gglade@atbook.com, www.adventuroustraveler.com), PO Box 64769, Burlington, VT 05406 USA

Antipodean Books (☎ 914-424-3867, fax 914-424-3617, antipbooks@highlands.com), PO Box 189, Cold Spring, NY 10516 USA

Arnold Books (☎ 64-3-365-7188, 64-3-365-2630, arnold@netaccess.co.nz), 11 New Regent St, Christchurch, New Zealand

Astrolabe Books (☎/fax 61-3-6223-8644, astrobks@anzaab.com.au), 81 Salamanca Place, Hobart, Tasmania, Australia (mailing address: PO Box 475, Sandy Bay, Tasmania 7006 Australia)

Blue Dragon Book Shop (☎ 541-482-2142), 293 E Main St, Ashland, OR 97520 USA

Bluntisham Books Oak House (☎ 44-1487-840-449, fax 44-1487-840-894), East St, Bluntisham, Cambridgeshire, England PE17 3LS UK

Cavendish Rare Books (☎ 831-375-6671, fax 831-375-3459, grigorbook@aol.com)

Charles D Dyer Books (☎ 937-644-0285), 13904 Fairway Dr, Marysville, OH 43040 USA

Chessler Books (☎ 303-670-0093, toll-free 800-654-8502, fax 303-670-9727, chesslerbk@aol.com, www.chesslerbooks.com), PO Box 4359, 29723 Troutdale Scenic Dr, Evergreen, CO 80437 USA

Colin Bull's Polar Books (☎ 206-842-9660, gbull@krl.org), Box 4675, Rolling Bay, WA 98061 USA

Explorer Books Fallow Chase (☎/fax 44-1-483-200-286, explbooks@aol.com), Durfold Wood, Plaistow, West Sussex, England RH14 0PL UK

Gaston Renard (☎ 61-3-9417-1044, fax 61-3-9417-3025, booksaus@anzaab.com.au), 51 Sackville St, Collingwood, Victoria, Australia 3066 (mailing address: GPO Box 5235BB, Melbourne, Victoria 3001, Australia)

High Latitude Books (☎ 206-842-0202, fax 206-842-6101, highlatitude@cwix.com), PO Box 11254, Bainbridge Island, WA 98110 USA

Longitude Books (☎ 212-463-8464, toll-free 800-342-2164, fax 212-691-5295, info@longitudebooks.com, www.longitudebooks.com), 27 West 20th Street, Suite 1101, New York, NY 10011 USA

McEwan Fine Books (☎ 44-1-3397-55429, fax 44-1-3397-55995 pjmm@easynet.co.uk), Ballater, Aberdeenshire AB35 5UB Scotland UK

Nimue Books (☎ 207-947-8016, fax 207-581-2323, nimue@mint.net), PO Box 325, Orono, ME 04473 USA

Patrick Walcot (☎ 44-21-382-6381, fax 44-21-386-1251, patrick@walcot.demon.co.uk), 60 Sunnybank Rd, Sutton Coldfield, West Midlands, B73 5RJ UK

Parmer Books (☎ 619-287-0693, fax 619-287-6135, parmerbook@aol.com), 7644 Forrestal Rd, San Diego, CA 92120-2203 USA

Rainy Day Books (☎ 603-585-3448, fax 603-585-9108, rainyday@cheshire.net), PO Box 775, Fitzwilliam, NH 03447-0775 USA

Terra Incognita Books (☎ 212-362-2849), 244 West 74th St, New York, NY 10023 USA (mail and phone orders only)

West Side Book Shop (☎ 734-995-1891), 113 West Liberty, Ann Arbor, MI 48104 USA

Lonely Planet

Lonely Planet publishes guides covering every country in the world, including every country that has an Antarctic Gateway: *Australia* (see also the *Tasmania* state guide); *Argentina, Uruguay & Paraguay* (including the Falkland Islands); *Chile & Easter Island*; *New Zealand*; and *South Africa, Lesotho & Swaziland*. Also look for the *Cape Town City Guide*. When accompanying younger travelers, consider Lonely Planet's *Travel with Children*.

Guidebooks

With three exceptions, other Antarctic guidebooks to date have been rather thin. First, the exceptions: Ron Naveen's *The Oceanites Site Guide to the Antarctic Peninsula* (Chevy Chase: Oceanites, 1997), available through

Longitude Books (mentioned earlier), is a beautiful and informative book with wonderful photography, highly detailed maps and descriptions of 39 sites in the Peninsula region. Also very good is Bernard Stonehouse's *The Last Continent: Discovering Antarctica* (Burgh Castle, Norfolk: Shuttlewood Collinson Publishers, 2000), with its many color photographs and useful information handsomely presented. If you're interested in the historic explorers' huts, David L Harrowfield's excellent *Icy Heritage: Historic Sites of the Ross Sea Region* (Christchurch: Antarctic Heritage Trust, 1995) is indispensable. Harrowfield, who has been helping to restore the huts since 1977, has put together fascinating and detailed accounts of 34 historic places, from major attractions such as Shackleton's Hut to more obscure supply depots and message posts of early-20th-century explorers.

The others: Diana Galimberti's *Antarctica: An Introductory Guide* (Miami Beach: Zagier & Urruty Publications, 1991) is just what it says it is, a good first look at the continent, but it has no photos and only rudimentary maps. Marco Polo's 96-page *Antarktis* (Ostfildern, Germany: Mairs Geographischer Verlag/Hachette, 1993), written by Diana Galimberti and Rolf Erdorf, is a great little pocket-size guide if you can read German. *Antarctica* (London: Cadogan, 1997), by Sara Wheeler, is of little use to tourists as it is written by a journalist who merely visited a few Antarctic stations.

Adventure

Many of the adventurers who have skied, walked or mushed dogsleds across sections of Antarctica, or sailed around it, have written memoirs.

New Zealand yachtsman-physician David Lewis describes circumnavigating Antarctica single-handedly in his 10m sloop *Ice Bird* in his book of the same name (New York: Norton, 1976). In *Icebound in Antarctica* (New York: Norton, 1987), he tells of research done in *Explorer* along the coast west of Australia's Davis station. Deborah Shapiro and Rolf Bjelke wrote *Time on Ice: A Winter Voyage to Antarctica* (Camden,

ME: International Marine, 1998) about their yachting adventures in Antarctica.

Mountain climbing is covered in three handsome books, Lincoln Hall's *The Loneliest Mountain* (Brookvale: Simon & Schuster Australia, 1979) and Ivar Erik Tollefsen's *Queen Maud Land Antarctica* (Larvik, Norway: Østlands-Postens Press, 1994) and *Antarctica: The Ronde Spire* (Norway: A.s. Joh. Nordahls Tyrkkeri, 1997).

Britain's Sir Ranulph Fiennes accomplishes the first pole-to-pole circumnavigation of the globe in *To the Ends of the Earth: The Transglobe Expedition* (New York: Arbor House, 1983). Not content with one pass at the South Pole, Sir Ran was back in 1992 to ski across Antarctica with Dr Mike Stroud. Fiennes' *Mind Over Matter* (New York: Delacorte Press, 1993) and Stroud's *Shadows on the Wasteland* (Woodstock, NY: Overlook Press, 1994) offer complementary views of their two-man, unsupported race against starvation and cold.

Britons Roger Mear and Robert Swan's book *In the Footsteps of Scott* (London: Jonathan Cape, 1987) chronicles their recreation of the British explorer's polar journey with a third companion, Gareth Wood, who tells his side of the story in *South Pole: 900 Miles on Foot* (London: Horsdal and Schubart, 1996).

Norwegian Børge Ousland's startlingly fast solo crossing of the continent, the first ever, is chronicled in the beautifully illustrated *Alone Across Antarctica* (Oslo: Tangen Grafiske, 1997). Ousland, who only accomplished the feat on his second attempt, was meticulously prepared, having even asked his young son to paint his skis with drawings to remind him not to take unnecessary risks so he could return unhurt to his family.

Reinhold Messner, the world's greatest mountain climber, crossed the continent on skis with Arved Fuchs in 1989-90. His *Antarctica: Both Heaven and Hell* (Seattle, WA: The Mountaineers, 1991) offers a unique perspective on adventure in Antarctica. American Will Steger and a five-man international team mushed dogsleds across the continent, a story told in *Crossing Antarctica* (New York: Knopf, 1982).

The most disgusting Antarctic book title is Jerry Corr's *The Snotsicle Traverse* (E Lansing, MI: Frandorson Publications, 1993), about a ski trip he made with two fellow adventurers from the South Pole to the Ross Ice Shelf. Joseph E Murphy and his friends went in the opposite direction in *South to the Pole by Ski* (St Paul, MN: Marlor Press, 1990).

Antarctica in Fiction

We are now beginning the fifth century of Antarctic fiction, which started in 1605 with the publication of a Utopian story, *Mundes Alter et Idem* ('Another World and Yet the Same'), by Bishop Joseph Hall of England, in which a traveler to Antarctica finds it inhabited by gluttons, drunkards and eccentrics. The genre has been enriched by such celebrated writers as Samuel Taylor Coleridge, James Fenimore Cooper, Rudyard Kipling, Edgar Allan Poe and Jules Verne (in *20,000 Leagues Under the Sea*).

Coleridge, of course, wrote the most famous polar poem, *The Rime of the Ancient Mariner* (1798), in which an Antarctic ship is cursed when a sailor kills an albatross. In Cooper's fantasy, *The Monikins* (1835), a British baronet rescues four South Polar Monikins (simian-like beings) and returns them to their home. Another novel by Cooper, *The Sea Lions* (1849), draws on his personal experience as a major owner of a whaling ship to tell the story of two rival schooners searching for a mysterious sealing ground in the Antarctic. Kipling's *The Jungle Book* (1893) includes the story of Kotick, the white seal, who visits several sub-Antarctic islands.

Poe's novella *The Narrative of Arthur Gordon Pym* (1837) has been the most influential Antarctic story. It so inspired Verne that he wrote a sequel, *Le Sphinx des Glaces*, in 1897. Other authors who took up Poe's story line were Charles Romyn Dake in *A Strange Discovery* (1899), Steven Utley and Howard Waldrop in the short story 'Black as the Pit, From Pole to Pole,' (in *The Year's Finest Fantasy*, 1978) and Rudy Rucker in *The Hollow Earth* (1990). Echoing from Pym through all these works is the eerie cry *Tekeli-li*, the call of the white birds in the South Polar region. (Poe wrote another story about a whirlpool at the South Pole, the shorter and more mysterious 'Ms Found in a Bottle' of 1833.)

Antarctic fiction over the last century has tended toward adventure stories and 'thrillers.' It can be classified by themes, which have remained consistent.

Adventure Stories George Griffith's *Olga Romanoff or the Syren of the Skies* (1894) envisions Kerguelen Island as a submarine and aircraft base. In *Mary of Marion Island* (1929), H Rider Haggard maroons Mary on the island with a young British lord.

Natural Disasters Volcanic activity destroys part of Antarctica in Godfrey Sweven's *Limanora, the Island of Progress* (1903), while in the title story of Valery Brussof's *The Republic of the Southern Cross and Other Stories* (1977), an epidemic wipes out most of Antarctica's human population. A huge section of the ice cap breaks away in James Follett's *Ice* (1977), while in Richard Moran's *Cold Sea Rising* (1986), an undersea volcanic plume severs the Ross Ice Shelf and sets it adrift. Solar flares cause a surge of the ice sheet in Crawford Killian's *Icequake* (1979), and Antarctica is about to heat up after nuclear war tilts the Earth's axis in David Graham's *Down to a Sunless Sea* (1981).

Nazi Thrillers Captain WE Johns' *Biggles' Second Case* (1951) tracks a Nazi U-boat carrying stolen British gold near Kerguelen. Marion Morris' *The Icemen* (1988) sees a remnant group of Nazis taking over an Argentine Antarctic station. In Richard Henrick's *Ice Wolf* (1994), Nazis try to retrieve the Holy Grail from an Antarctic cave, while in *Ice Reich* (1998) by William Dietrich, an American pilot is hired by Hermann Göring to sail to Antarctica.

History

Robert K Headland's *Chronological List of Antarctic Expeditions and Related Historical Events* (Cambridge: Cambridge University Press, 1993) is *the* standard work on the subject, an invaluable resource for all authors (including this one) who write about Antarctic history. A new version is due out soon.

Antarctica in Fiction

Terrorism & Espionage Eco-terrorists try to blow up a Russian whaling factory ship in John Gordon Davis' *Leviathan* (1976), and an oil-cartel-backed group seizes control of Antarctica in DC Poyer's *White Continent* (1980). In David Smith's *Freeze Frame* (1992), French adventurers develop a secret uranium mine at Dumont d'Urville. In Kim Stanley Robinson's *Antarctica* (1998), Marxist 'ecoteurs' blow up Antarctic stations established by corporations to exploit the continent's resources. The British, French and Americans are involved in a high-tech battle in Matthew Reilly's *Ice Station* (1998). *Icefire* (1998) by Judith and Garfield Reeves-Stevens, has rogue Chinese generals setting off nuclear weapons beneath the Ross Ice Shelf.

Plane Crashes Paralee Sweeten Sutton's *White City* (1949) describes a young couple lost in a small plane who discover an Antarctic civilization whose members communicate by thought transference. In David Burke's *Monday at McMurdo* (1967), a plane carrying a US congressman crashes on a glacier. John Gordon Davis' *Seize the Wind* (1985) has an Australian DC-10 filled with sightseers crashing on the Beardmore Glacier while Charles Neider's *Overflight* (1986) slams a DC-10 tourist flight into Mt Erebus.

Yachting An American plane is looking for a missing yacht in Clive Cussler's *Treasure* (1988). A yacht crew searches for a 19th-century sailing ship in Hammond Innes' *Isvik* (1991), while the vessel in Charles McCarry's *The Better Angels* (1979) is simply carrying its owner on a vacation. In *158 Vuorokautto* ('158 Days,' published in 1983), by Alpo Ruuth, a Finnish yacht sails into a blizzard near the Antarctic Peninsula during a round-the-world race, while a chilling regatta ends near the South Sandwich Islands in Robert Stone's *Outerbridge Reach* (1998).

Tourist Cruises In Edwin Woodard and Heather Woodard Bischoff's *Storehouses of the Snow* (1980), a cruise ship gets trapped in the Lemaire Channel after a sudden tilt of the Earth's axis, while another tour vessel runs aground in Wilbur Smith's *Hungry As the Sea* (1978). A tourist gets stranded on an iceberg in Madeleine L'Engle's *Troubling a Star* (1994). Another is abandoned on Seymour Island in Clive Cussler's *Shock Wave* (1996).

Mysteries Agatha Christie weaves a good yarn about a geophysicist who returns from the Antarctic to discover that he was the alibi for a late murder suspect, in *Ordeal by Innocence* (1958). Thomas Keneally tells an eerie tale about the killing of a newsman during the dark Antarctic winter in *Victim of the Aurora* (1977). An Antarctic murder is solved by a policeman working as a research assistant for his son in Emmy Lou Schenk's 'Ice Cave' (in *Alfred Hitchcock Mystery Magazine*, August 1987). In Bob Reiss' *Purgatory Road* (1996), members of an Antarctic station are plagued by madness and murder.

Other An East Hollywood chef builds a summer home on Ross Island in Crispin Kitto's *The Antarctica Cookbook* (1984). Nikki Gemmell's *Shiver* (1997) sends a young woman journalist to the Antarctic, where she falls in love, while Liane Shavian's *Surfing Antarctica* (1999) promises 'a wild roller-coaster ride of eco-heroics and hot lust.'

– Fauno Cordes,
world's foremost authority on Antarctic fiction whose bibliography
on the subject can be found at www.antarctic-circle.org/fauno.htm

Two other books build from Headland's work and expand it in differing directions. LJ Conrad's *Bibliography of Antarctic Exploration: Expedition Accounts from 1768 to 1960* (privately published, 1999; available through Parmer Books) gives a succinct but thorough account of all the major expeditions and of the published works about them. Damien Gildea's *Antarctic Mountaineering Chronology* (Fyshwick, Australia: Paragon, 1998), is likewise a useful work, giving details of first ascents and the continent's nascent climbing history.

Nearly every early explorer wrote a first-hand account of his expedition, and many of them have been reprinted during the past decade. The major ones include: Amundsen, *The South Pole*; Borchgrevink, *First on the Antarctic Continent*; Byrd, *Alone*, *Discovery*, *Little America* and *Skyward*; Frederick Cook, *Through the First Antarctic Night*; Mawson, *The Home of the Blizzard*; Nordenskjöld, *Antarctica*; Scott, *The Voyage of the Discovery* and *Scott's Last Expedition*; and Shackleton, *Heart of the Antarctic* and *South*.

In *The Myth of the Explorer* (Oxford: Oxford University Press, 1994), Beau Riffenburgh, editor of the journal *Polar Record*, examines the role that newspapers have played in 'creating' both Arctic and Antarctic

Antarctica: A Discography

Some currently available CDs about Antarctica:

Antarctica, Vangelis (1983; Polygram 815732-2) – synthesizer music from Koreyoshi Kurahara's film of the same name; title track is the definitive Antarctic mood music

Antarctica: Suite for Guitar and Orchestra, Nigel Westlake (1992; Sony Classical SK53361) – Westlake wrote the score for the IMAX film *Antarctica*, then reworked it into this; guitar playing by John Williams

Antarctica: The Last Wilderness, Medwyn Goodall (1993; Mar 3812) – dreamy, peaceful instrumental pieces, including 'All White,' 'Endless Emptiness' and 'Snow Kingdom Forever'

Antarctica, Richie Beirach (1994; ECD 22086-2) – jazz piano solos; titles include 'The Ice Shelf,' 'Deception Island' and 'Neptunes Bellows'

Antarctica, Ian Tamblyn (1994; North Track NTCD3; In the US, NorthSound NSCD 29532) – New Age/folk-rock/jazz supplemented by Adélie penguin brays and Weddell seal trills; most memorable title: 'The Penguin came from Pittsburgh'

Antarctica, Douglas Quin (1998; Miramar 09006-23113-2) – natural recordings of Weddell and leopard seals, of orcas and of emperor and Adélie penguins; of special note are the creaks and groans of the Canada Glacier

Antarctic Arrival: A Tribute to a Frozen Land, Valmar Kurol and Marc-André Bourbonnais (1999; available from the Montreal Antarctic Society, which is listed in the Useful Organizations section of this chapter) – New Age/light rock/classical; titles include 'Antarctic Arrival,' 'Never Mind the Icebergs,' 'Flight of the Albatross,' 'Seekers of the Pole' and 'Aurora Australis'

Antartida, John Cale (1995; Les Disques du Crépuscule TWI-1008) – soundtrack from the Manuel Huerga film, *Antarctica as a State of Mind*; Cale is a former member of the Velvet Underground; theme song from *Antarctica Starts Here*, from his 1973 solo album *Paris 1919* (Reprise/Warner Bros 2131-2)

Lulie the Iceberg, music by Jeffrey Stock, story by Her Imperial Highness Princess Hisako of Takamado of Japan (1999; Sony Classical SK 61665) – based on the Princess' children's book, written

explorers. Robert E Feeney's *Polar Journeys: The Role of Food and Nutrition in Early Exploration* (Fairbanks: University of Alaska Press, 1997) focuses on the rations carried by explorers of both polar regions.

Apsley Cherry-Garrard's *The Worst Journey in the World* (London: Constable, 1922), which has been republished several times, is regarded by many as the single best Antarctic book ever written. His highly readable account of Scott's fatal *Terra Nova* expedition details the incredible suffering endured on the hellish midwinter manhaul to the emperor penguin rookery at Cape Crozier. Also covered is the discovery of the remains

of the ill-fated polar party the spring after they perished.

There are several good general histories of Antarctica. LP Kirwan, who wrote *The White Road* (London: Hollis and Carter, 1959), never visited Antarctica, but spoke with many of the 20th-century explorers who mapped the continent. Also highly readable is Alan Gurney's terrific *Below the Convergence: Voyages Toward Antarctica, 1699-1839* (New York: Norton, 1997), which is to be followed – soon, one hopes – by a second volume. Stephen Martin's *A History of Antarctica* (Sydney: State Library of NSW Press, 1996) gives a lively presentation of the

Antarctica: A Discography

after she saw a lone iceberg drifting off Greenland; recorded live at New York's Carnegie Hall; one of the movements is 'South Pole'

On the Last Frontier, Einojuhani Rautavaara (1999; Ondine ODE 921-2) – spawned by this Finnish classical composer's lifelong interest in author Edgar Allan Poe's *Narrative of Arthur Gordon Pym*

Polar Shift: A Benefit for Antarctica, various artists (1991; Private Music BMG2083-2-P) – compilation of New Age instrumental and vocal music by Vangelis, Yanni, Enya, Kitaro, John Tesh et al

Sinfonia Antarctica, Ralph Vaughan Williams' Symphony No 7 – the mother of all Antarctic music, originated as the sound track for the film *Scott of the Antarctic* (1949); many versions exist, notably the Raymond Leppard version (1993; Koss KC 2214) with narrated excerpts from Scott's journals

The Thing, Ennio Morricone (1982; Varèse Sarabande VSD-5278) – sound track from the popular Antarctic sci-fi movie

Individual songs entitled 'Antarctica' or about The Ice also appear on these discs:

Across the White Plains, Deborah Liv Johnson (1995); *Blue Sky Mining*, Midnight Oil (1990); *Bonzai Germany Compilation – Vol 1*, various (1998); *Carnival of Chaos*, GWAR (1997); *Cinematic*, Adrian Borland (1996); *Descanso Dominical*, Mecano (1988); *Earth: Voices of a Planet*, Paul Winter (1990); *Games People Play*, Peechees (1997); *Greatest Hits*, Men Without Hats (1996); *I'm in Love*, The Jackie Papers (1999); *'Jungle' Jack Hanna's World*, (1996); *Last Days of the Century*, Al Stewart (1988, reissued 1997); *Liberty*, Duran Duran (1990); *Music for the Friends of the Whales*, Gregor Theelen (1995); *Not We But One*, Mike Nock Trio (1997); *Oceanscape*, William Goldstein (1986); *Same River, Same Song*, Kym Pitman with IBIS (1993); *Sea Power: A Global Journey*, Michael Whalen (1993); *Sound of the Whales: Music for Relaxation*, (1997); *The Body Needs to Travel*, Ian Tamblyn (1997); *Three Day Weekend*, Evan Marks (1998); *Walking with Dinosaurs*, Benjamin Bartlett (1999)

– Valmar Kurol,
President of the Montreal Antarctic Society

continent's brief human history. David Mountfield's *A History of Polar Exploration* (New York: Dial, 1974), like Kirwin's book, includes information about both ends of the Earth, and is well illustrated. GE Fogg's *The Explorations of Antarctica* (London: Cassell, 1990) includes interesting paintings by David Smith.

History from a different viewpoint is available in *Postcards of Antarctic Expeditions – A Catalogue: 1898 – 1958*, published privately in 1998 by Margery Wharton, 18 Millfield Rise, Bexhill-on-Sea, East Sussex TN40 1QY, England. It offers a fascinating look at expeditions through the postcards printed by the expeditions themselves.

Philip I Mitterling's *America in the Antarctic to 1840* (Urbana, IL: University of Illinois Press, 1959) and Kenneth J Bertrand's *Americans in Antarctica, 1775-1948* (Burlington, VT: American Geographical Society, 1971) are two of the more scholarly works about US exploration of the continent. Two recent books describe the US Antarctic Program's work during the International Geophysical Year: John Behrendt's *Innocents on the Ice: A Memoir of Antarctic Exploration, 1957* (Niwot: University Press of Colorado, 1998) and George Doumani's wonderfully titled (but less interesting) *The Frigid Mistress* (Baltimore: American Literary Press, 1999). In *Flying Upside Down: True Tales of an Antarctic Pilot* (Annapolis, MD: Naval Institute Press, 1999) Mark A Hinebaugh writes well about his years flying planes for the US Antarctic Program.

The Endurance: Shackleton's Legendary Antarctic Expedition by Caroline Alexander (New York: HarperCollins, 1997) retells the story previously told by Alfred Lansing in *Endurance* (New York: McGraw-Hill, 1959), by Frank A Worsley in *Endurance: An Epic of Polar Adventure* (London: Philip Allan & Co, 1931) and of course best of all by Shackleton himself in *South* (London: William Heinemann, 1919). Alexander's book, however, adds most of the terrific photographs taken by expedition photographer Frank Hurley.

Shackleton's leadership style is carefully examined in *Shackleton's Way* (New York:

Viking, 2000) by Margot Morrell and Stephanie Capparell, who offer lessons that can be taken from the methods Shackleton used in leading his expedition members to survival against enormous odds.

Janet Crawford's *That First Antarctic Winter: The Story of the Southern Cross Expedition of 1898-1900* (Christchurch: South Latitude Research Ltd, 1998) is a welcome addition to early Antarctic history.

Britain's establishment of its first Antarctic bases during the closing years of World War II is described in Harold W Squires' memoir, *SS Eagle: The Secret Mission, 1944-45* (St Johns, Newfoundland: Jesperson Press, 1992). Sir Charles Swithinbank, who has perhaps more Antarctic seasons to his credit than anyone else, has written three fascinating reminiscences: *An Alien in Antarctica* (Blacksburg, VA: McDonald and Woodward, 1997), *Forty Years on Ice* (Sussex, England: The Book Guild, 1998) and *Foothold on Antarctica* (Sussex, England: The Book Guild, 1999).

The definitive study of worldwide whalehunting, *The History of Modern Whaling* (London: C Hurst & Co, 1982) by JN Tönnesen and AO Johnsen, includes Antarctica.

G Barnett Smith's *The Romance of the South Pole* (London: Thomas Nelson, 1902), describes early expeditions by Cook, Weddell, Ross, Wilkes, Nares and Bruce – and is illustrated with fine engravings. Oddly reflecting the limited knowledge about Antarctica of the time, it features a parade of polar bears marching across the cover. This early book is hard to find.

Antarctic aviation, from Scott's early balloon trials to the US Navy's ski-equipped Hercules flights, is covered in David Burke's excellent *Moments of Terror* (Kensington, Australia: New South Wales University Press, 1994).

Politics

Tomes on Antarctic politics tend to be scholarly and legalistic. Among the more readerfriendly are Keith Suter's *Antarctica: Private Property or Public Heritage?* (Leichardt, NSW: Pluto Press Australia, 1991) and Deborah Shapley's *The Seventh Continent:*

Antarctica in a Resource Age (Washington, DC: Resources for the Future, 1985). Both are a bit out of date, but offer good background for current issues.

Biography

So many good biographies of Antarctic explorers have been written that only some of them can be described here. Most famous – or infamous – of the recent titles is Roland Huntford's *Scott and Amundsen* (London: Hodder and Stoughton, 1979), which argues (not without reason) that Scott's tragedy was due to incompetence. But Huntford's anti-Scott bias is so strong that one cannot help wondering what drives it. His *Shackleton* (New York: Fawcett Columbine, 1985) is a well-researched and more balanced biography of the most heroic Antarctic explorer. Huntford also wrote a book showcasing a trove of rare lantern slides used by Amundsen for his lectures, found by one of his descendants in a Norwegian attic in 1986, *The Amundsen Photographs* (New York: Atlantic Monthly Press, 1987).

Philip Ayres' *Mawson: A Life* (Melbourne: Melbourne University Press, 1999) reveals new information about the expeditions of the Australian explorer and includes terrific photographs.

James and Margery Fisher's *Shackleton and the Antarctic* (Boston, MA: Houghton Mifflin, 1958) is a thorough biography, sympathetically written, with a unique appendix of Shackleton's poetry and prose. *Sir Hubert Wilkins* (New York: Times Books, 1983) is a detailed biography about the Australian adventurer written by his friend, Lowell Thomas. Finally, Lars-Eric Lindblad's *Passport to Anywhere* (New York: Times Books, 1983) is a ghostwritten autobiography of the free spirit who pioneered mass-market Antarctic tourism in 1965-66.

The Rarest Book

The first – and only – book ever published in Antarctica is Ernest Shackleton's *Aurora Australis*, hand-printed in 1908-09 by four of his men at Cape Royds on Ross Island. The 80 copies they created were bound into a leather spine and covered with boards taken from provision crates. Thus the various copies are known as the 'Butter' edition or the 'Bottled Fruit' copy or the 'Irish Stew' edition. The book was intended as a souvenir for expedition members and as a gift for expedition patrons. Today, many can be found in institutional libraries. Only one or two copies come up for sale each decade; at an auction in late 1999, an especially fine copy sold for US$55,000. Fortunately, *Aurora Australis* was reprinted by Bay Books of Kensington, Australia in 1988, giving average folks a chance to read this rare behind-the-scenes look at the expedition.

Controversial American Lieutenant Charles Wilkes' report on the United States Exploring Expedition was limited by the US Congress to just 100 copies, making the five-volume *Narrative* published in 1844 one of the rarest Antarctic books (although it is not exclusively about Antarctica). The complete set of the expedition's reports, comprising 26 volumes including many books of plates, was published over a 30-year period. If a complete set were to find its way to the market today – an unlikely possibility – one knowledgeable dealer estimates it would fetch a cool US$200,000.

Wildlife

There are many excellent books about Antarctic wildlife, but few are portable enough to take along. Tony Soper's small book *Antarctica: A Guide to the Wildlife* (Old Saybrook, CT: Globe Pequot Press, 1994) is an exception, and its handsome drawings by Dafila Scott (granddaughter of Robert F Scott) offer a different perspective from the usual photographs. Sanford Moss' *Natural History of the Antarctic Peninsula* (New York: Columbia University Press, 1988) has no color illustrations but includes much good biological data.

Peter Harrison's *Seabirds: An Identification Guide* (Boston, MA: Houghton Mifflin, 1985), the definitive volume, is often found on the bridge of Antarctic tourist vessels. It's excellent.

Among the large volumes, Eric Hosking's *Antarctic Wildlife* (Beckenham, Kent: Croom Helm, 1982) is primarily a photographic book, but the text by Bryan Sage is informative. Bernard Stonehouse's *Animals of the Antarctic* (New York: Holt, Rinehart & Winston, 1972) is dated, but the photos are quite good; his *North Pole, South Pole* (London: Multimedia Books, 1990) is more current, but deals with both the Arctic and the Antarctic. Best of the lot is Alastair Fothergill's *Life in the Freezer* (London: BBC Books, 1993), associated with the excellent video series by the British Broadcasting Corporation. The photographs are superb and the book is unusually well written.

Beautiful, detailed sketches and watercolors of Edward Wilson, chief scientific officer on both of Scott's expeditions, illustrate *Birds of the Antarctic* (Poole, Dorset: Blandford Press, 1967). Two other excellent bird guides are David F Parmelee's *Antarctic Birds* (Minneapolis, MN: University of Minnesota Press, 1992) and George E Watson's classic *Birds of the Antarctic and Sub-Antarctic* (Washington, DC: American Geophysical Union, 1975). Pauline Reilly's *Penguins of the World* (South Melbourne: Oxford University Press Australia, 1994) is a serious guide, with few color illustrations (many black and whites, however), and good data on feeding, breeding, distribution and population.

Whales of the World, by Lyall Watson (London: Hutchinson & Co, 1981), is detailed and scholarly, with many excellent photographs and illustrations. A heavy 302-page hardcover, it's not highly portable.

Science

There are several good books about Antarctic science. David Walton, author of this book's Antarctic Science chapter, has edited an excellent book with the same title, *Antarctic Science* (Cambridge: Cambridge University Press, 1987). GE Fogg's *A History of Antarctic Science* (Cambridge: Cambridge University Press, 1992) is similarly comprehensive. Richard S Lewis' *A Continent for Science* (New York: Viking Press, 1966) is dated, but very readable and has many excellent photos. AJW Taylor's *Antarctic Psychology* (Wellington: Science Information Publishing Centre, 1987) tends toward the

scholarly, but contains an interesting discussion of psychological research and testing done in Antarctica.

Children's Books

During the past decade there has been an explosion of children's books about Antarctica, especially the wildlife. Jonathan Chester's *A for Antarctica* (Hunters Hill, Australia: Margaret Hamilton Books, 1994) is a photo alphabet book with a polar twist. Mark Cawardine's *Whales, Dolphins and Porpoises* (London: Dorling Kindersley, 1992) is a children's version of his excellent cetacean guide for adults. Alastair Fothergill's *Life in the Freezer* (London: BBC Children's Books, 1994) is another elementary- and middle-school children's version of an adult guide to Antarctic wildlife; both are associated with the video series by the British Broadcasting Corporation. Laurence Pringle's *Antarctica, the Last Unspoiled Continent* (New York: Simon & Schuster, 1992) is a survey of Antarctic plants and animals for middle-school children. Barbara Taylor's *Arctic and Antarctic* (London: Dorling Kindersley, 1995) compares the regions; it's part of the excellent Eyewitness Guides series for elementary- and middle-school children. Trish Hart's aptly titled *There Are No Polar Bears Down There* (Sydney: Nelson Australia, 1994) includes handsome illustrations.

The best series of children's books about Antarctica is the Antarctica Discovery Library (Vero Beach, FL: Rourke Publishing, 1995). Each of the six 24-page titles (*Antarctica: The Land, The Antarctic Ocean, Birds of Antarctica, Life in the Antarctic, Mammals of Antarctica* and *People in Antarctica*) is beautifully illustrated and sturdily bound. Michael Woods' *Science on Ice: Research in the Antarctic* (Brookfield, CT: Millbrook Press, 1995) and Sandra Markle's *Super Cool Science: South Pole Stations, Past, Present and Future* (New York: Walker and Co, 1998) are also excellent.

Louis Darling's *Penguins* (London: Angus & Robertson, 1961) is older, but it contains such useful information that it's appropriate for adults. Jenny Woods' *Icebergs* (New York: Penguin Books, 1990) provides factual information for elementary- and middle-school children about Antarctica's most beautiful feature.

Antarctic Encounter: Destination South Georgia (New York: Simon & Schuster, 1995) by Sally Poncet describes the wildlife and history of South Georgia through the eyes of three young boys who explore it with their parents by yacht.

Many titles cover Antarctic exploration and research. Ian Cameron's *Exploring Antarctica* (Burnt Mill, Harlow, Essex: Longman, 1984) is another children's version of an adult book, part of the Royal Geographical Society's Exploring Series for elementary- and middle-school students. Leo Flaherty's *Roald Amundsen and the Quest for the South Pole* (New York: Chelsea House, 1992) is part of the World Explorers series, which also includes *Lieut Charles Wilkes and the US Exploring Expedition*; both are for middle-school children.

No fewer than three recent children's books tell the story of the star-crossed *Endurance* expedition: Michael McCurdy's *Shackleton's Amazing Antarctic Adventure: Trapped by the Ice!* (New York: Walker and Company, 1997), Jennifer Armstrong's *Shipwreck at the Bottom of the World* (New York: Crown Publishers, 1998) and Elizabeth Cody Kimmel's *Ice Story: Shackleton's Lost Expedition* (New York: Clarion Books, 1999). Robert Burleigh's *Black Whiteness: Admiral Byrd in the Antarctic* (New York: Atheneum Books for Young Readers, 1998) describes the American explorer's solo winter at Advance Base.

Meredith Hooper may be the most prolific author of Antarctic children's books. Her best is *A for Antarctica* (London: Pan Books, 1991), a mini-encyclopedia of facts about The Ice (not to be confused with Jonathan Chester's book of the same title), but a close second is *Tom's Rabbit* (London: Frances Lincoln, 1998), the charming and beautifully illustrated true tale of a rabbit that accompanied Scott's *Terra Nova* expedition. Hooper's other books include *Journey to Antarctica* (Gosford: Scholastic Australia, 1997) and *Seal* (Cambridge: Cambridge University Press, 1996).

At least two contemporary authors offer fictional fun (for more about fiction see the boxed text 'Antarctica in Fiction' in this chapter). Geoffrey T Williams' *The Last Frontier: Antarctica* (Los Angeles: Price, Stern, Sloan, 1992) is an adventure story for elementary- and middle-school children, while Helen Cowcher's *Antarctica* (New York: Farrar, Straus & Giroux, 1990) is a story of penguins for elementary-school children.

For additional ideas, contact The Antarctica Project (see the Useful Organizations section), which publishes excellent 'Antarctica Resource Lists' of suggested reading for elementary-, middle- and high-school students.

General

Unquestionably the single best book on the subject, Readers Digest's *Antarctica: The Extraordinary History of Man's Conquest of the Frozen Continent* (Sydney: Readers Digest, 1990) is packed with photos, charts and facts.

Other very good general works about Antarctica are *The Greenpeace Book of Antarctica* (New York: Doubleday, 1988) by John May and *The Australian Geographic Book of Antarctica* (Terrey Hills, New South Wales: Australian Geographic, 1993) by Keith Scott. Louise Crossley's *Explore Antarctica* (Melbourne: Cambridge University Press, 1995) with lots of charts and graphics, is also a valuable reference.

Those willing to work a bit harder at their reading – and thus earn greater knowledge – should seek out *Antarctic Environments and Resources: a Geographical Perspective* (New York: Addison Wesley Longman, 1998) by James D Hansom and John E Gordon. This book, which goes into greater depth and uses more scientific language, covers everything from Antarctica's geology and climate to the biology of the Southern Ocean and Antarctic geopolitics in a clear, interesting style.

The National Geographic Society in Washington, DC, US published Kim Heacox's *Antarctica: The Last Continent* (1998) but it's a disappointment, a once-over-lightly look at The Ice with neither substance nor much style.

Of the many photographic books produced about the most photogenic continent of all, three stand out. The best, *Wild Ice* (Washington, DC: Smithsonian Institution Press, 1990), includes the work of four photographers – Ron Naveen, Colin Monteath (author of this book's Private Expeditions chapter), Tui de Roy and Mark Jones – who among them have made more than 100 voyages to Antarctica. Their beautiful

Collecting Antarcticana

For some, a fascination with Antarctica goes beyond the desire to acquire knowledge about the continent and becomes an interest in collecting published accounts and other material related to its history. If you're an aspiring collector of 'Antarcticana,' here are some things to consider before starting out.

The foundation of your collection will be the principal accounts written by those who actually participated in the first expeditions carried out during the Heroic Age of Antarctic exploration: Amundsen, Borchgrevink, Nordenskjöld, Scott, Shackleton. Many of these accounts were published in a number of different editions and have been reprinted many times, so with a little perseverance, they're fairly easy to acquire. Finding a first edition, or a numbered copy in a limited edition, however, will require some patience.

Next in significance are the secondary accounts written by observers of events, rather than by the participants themselves. A good example is HR Mill's *An Autobiography* (1951). Although he himself did not go to the Antarctic, Mill was the consummate Antarctic historian of his day and, as the secretary of the Royal Geographical Society in London, knew all the important players. Another important work is Janet Crawford's *That First Antarctic Winter* (1998), the story of Borchgrevink's *Southern Cross* expedition as related in the diary of Louis Bernacchi. Margaret E David, the daughter of Edgeworth David, one of the two men who accompanied Shackleton to the South Magnetic Pole, wrote a memoir of her father entitled *Professor David: The Life of Sir Edgeworth David* (1937), another notable work to consider.

One final group of publications consists of what might be called 'tertiary' works, such as histories of Antarctic whaling, accounts of scientific expeditions, biographies of the early participants and records of visits to the continent by interested observers. Some more recent books take a 'revisionist' approach to the early explorations – for example, Diana Preston's *A First Rate Tragedy* (1998), a re-examination of Scott's ill-fated *Terra Nova* expedition.

Every serious Antarctic collector also needs to be familiar with some of the more unusual and even unique items. Most of these are not so much *about* the Antarctic as actually part of the history itself.

The South Polar Times was a monthly newsletter put out by the members of Scott's 1901-04 *Discovery* expedition – a single manuscript copy was produced. In 1907, Smith, Elder & Co of London published an exact reproduction of the newsletter in a two-volume edition limited to 250 copies. Scott's 1910-13 *Terra Nova* expedition produced its own two volumes of *The South Polar Times*, but only the first volume, which is Volume III of the complete run, was published in 1914 in facsimile, again by Smith, Elder & Co in an edition of 350. But collectors take note: Volume IV, the original of which is in the archives of the Scott Polar Research Institute, will be published this year in an edition of 350 and a format matching Volume III.

Another work of historical interest, and a unique one, is *The Blizzard*, a supplementary journal consisting of the overflow of contributions to *The South Polar Times*. *The Blizzard* was the first item to be printed and published in Antarctica, and only 50 copies were produced. In his book *Two Years in the Antarctic* (1905), Albert B Armitage characterized the contents of *The Blizzard*

photos are the best of a rich harvest. Eliot Porter's *Antarctica* (New York: Arch Cape Press, 1978) is an unusual collection of shots by the veteran photographer, who visited The Ice at age 73. *Antarctica: Beyond the Southern Ocean* (Auckland: David Bateman, 1996) by Colin Monteath shows off photos that are the envy of many other professionals. Mike Lucas' *Antarctica* (New York: Abbeville, 1996) is also quite good.

Collecting Antarcticana

as 'poetical effusions rejected by *The South Polar Times.*' Also of note is *Aurora Australis*, which was written, printed and bound at Cape Royds, the winter quarters for Shackleton's *Nimrod* expedition. This required the transport of a press and the setting up of a printing shop at Cape Royds, as well as training expedition members to typeset the manuscript, operate the press and bind the finished work. Fewer than 100 copies were produced, and most of the surviving 70 or so are in institutional libraries.

Another kind of publication that is part of Antarctica's history is the promotional material or prospectus produced to raise funds for an expedition. This is a type of ephemera, produced for a specific occasion, and therefore not intended to last. Although the prospectus sent by Shackleton to potential contributors to promote his *Endurance* expedition was a high-quality production by ephemera standards, only about 200 copies were produced, and only 100 or so probably survive.

Now that you have an idea of what's out there, you need to choose a focus. In most cases this is not really a deliberate choice, because wanting to be a collector is probably the result of an existing interest in some aspect of Antarctic history. However, the beginning collector has to make some important decisions, not just about subject matter, but also about condition. Do you want to acquire only first editions, or multiple editions, including foreign-language first editions? With or without dust jackets? Condition not less than 'very good,' or a complete copy in merely decent condition, in order to acquire a particular title, with an eye to upgrading as you go along? Copies signed and/or inscribed by the author, or association copies – for example, a copy of a Shackleton title from the library of another member of the expedition, or with an inscription by Lady Shackleton?

Next, the aspiring collector needs a good Antarctic bibliography. Because a bibliography is a basic guide to what exists in a given field – all known editions of the works of a particular author, for example – it is also a help in knowing what there is to collect. The standard work in the field of Antarctic publication is Spence's *Antarctic Miscellany* (1980).

Now that you know what to look for, where do you find it? First, find the booksellers who specialize in polar material. (See Books in this chapter.) One way to do this is through the Internet: browse through the online bookselling services in search of Antarctic titles and you'll soon identify the specialists. Some of these booksellers issue catalogs. Book auctions and antiquarian book fairs are another potential source of material. Don't forget your local bookstores: treasures can still be found in unexpected places.

It's certainly true that some of the finer Antarctic material is quite difficult for today's collector to acquire, as more and more people have become interested in the continent's history. However, it's also true that the past 50 years have seen the publication of a large number and variety of Antarctic-related books. Unlike some other areas of collecting, it's still possible that with only 500 well-chosen Antarctic titles, a relatively small number, you'll have a library you can be proud of.

– J Bugayer,
who has a long-standing fascination with Antarctica and its history

John Stewart's two-volume *Antarctica: An Encyclopedia* (Jefferson, NC: McFarland & Co, 1990) is a comprehensive reference with thousands of entries but, unfortunately, no illustrations.

For geography and natural history essays, Michael Parfit's *South Light* (New York: Macmillan, 1985), David G Campbell's *The Crystal Desert* (Boston, MA: Houghton Mifflin Co, 1992) and Bill Green's *Water, Ice & Stone* (New York: Crown, 1995) are all excellent. Stephen J Pyne's *The Ice: A Journey to Antarctica* (Iowa City: University of Iowa Press, 1986) may be the best of the genre, though its dense prose can be slow going.

Ron Naveen's wonderful *Waiting to Fly: My Escapades with the Penguins of Antarctica* (New York: William Morrow, 1999) is the personal memoir of a researcher who has spent the better part of two decades studying the short-feathered, oft-anthropomorphized creatures – and it's clear that he knows his subjects well and loves his work.

National scientific programs in Antarctica are well covered. Australia's research is chronicled in at least four books: Philip Law and John Bechervaise's *ANARE: Australia's Antarctic Outposts* (Melbourne: Oxford University Press, 1957); RA Swan's *Australia in the Antarctic* (Parkville, Victoria: Melbourne University Press, 1961); Elizabeth Chipman's *Australians in the Frozen South* (West Melbourne: Thomas Nelson, 1978) and Tim Bowden's near-encyclopedic *The Silence Calling: Australians in Antarctica, 1947-97* (Sydney: Allen & Unwin, 1997). Canada's underecognized Antarctic work is documented in Dean Beeby's book *In a Crystal Land: Canadian Explorers in Antarctica* (Toronto: University of Toronto Press, 1994).

Unquestionably the most poetic title, Sir Vivian Fuchs' *Of Ice and Men* (London: Anthony Nelson, 1982), describes Antarctic exploration, British government-style, specifically the work of the British Antarctic Survey (BAS) from 1943 to '73. Wags now sometimes honor Sir Vivian's title by referring to BAS as 'Office and Men.'

Women's role in Antarctic research is covered in only a few books. Barbara Land's *The New Explorers: Women in Antarctica* (New York: Dodd, Mead, 1981) chronicles the work of American women researchers, and Elizabeth Chipman's *Women on the Ice* (Carlton, Victoria: Melbourne University Press, 1986) discusses work done by women from many different countries. Jennie Darlington offers a unique perspective on personality conflicts during a mid-20th- century American expedition to The Ice in *My Antarctic Honeymoon* (London: Frederick Muller, 1957), while Nan Brown's *Antarctic Housewife* (London: Hutchinson & Co, 1971) describes 30 months at South Georgia in the 1950s.

FILM & VIDEO

Starting with motion pictures recorded by William Spiers Bruce on the Scottish National Antarctic Expedition of 1902-04, The Ice boasts a rich, if spare, legacy of films.

Three recently restored movies of early expeditions offer a fascinating look at Antarctic exploration:

'Camera-artist' Herbert Ponting's *90° South: With Scott to the Antarctic* (1933) was restored by the British Film Institute's National Film Archive. Ponting's tribute to his lost companions is deeply moving, but the first half of the film is by far the more interesting, with superb cinematography of wildlife and the expedition's daily activities, all narrated by Ponting. Watch for the politically incorrect penguin chase, as well as the expedition's amazing jumping cat.

Joseph Rucker and Willard Van der Veer's *With Byrd at the South Pole: The Story of Little America* (1930), a record of Richard Byrd's flight to the Pole in 1929, actually won the Academy Award for Best Cinematography in 1930. It begins with a remarkably stilted introduction by Byrd himself, but the images that follow are spectacular. The gung-ho narration is corny but amusing ('Oh, for a chance to slap those plucky devils on the back!' goes a typical line). Watch for the politically incorrect penguin outfitted with a black bow tie, as well as Byrd's dog Igloo.

The British Film Institute has also beautifully restored Frank Hurley's *South* (1998), which includes very good footage of Shackleton's men and dogs working on *Endurance* and of the ship beset. Of course there's no footage of the boat journey or the South Georgia crossing, but the shots of the doomed ship's rigging collapsing are chilling, and the accompanying piano music is terrific. Much of the final 30 minutes is devoted to Antarctic wildlife.

All of these movies are sold by Milestone Film & Video (☎ 212-865-7449, toll-free in the US 800-603-1104, fax 212-222-8952, milefilms@aol.com), 275 West 96th St, Suite 28-C, New York, NY 10025. Cost: US$29.95 each or all three for US$74.95.

Charles Frend's *Scott of the Antarctic* (1948) is a popular classic. This melodramatic British film perhaps not surprisingly takes a near-worshipful view of Captain Robert Scott, who is played by John Mills.

Richard Byrd: Alone in Antarctica (1997) chronicles the US explorer's solo winter at 'Advance Base' on the Ross Ice Shelf in 1934, when he nearly died of carbon monoxide poisoning. To examine Byrd's controversial exploit, the video uses original expedition footage, dramatic reenactments and interviews with fellow explorers. Produced by Café Productions Ltd, it's available for US$59.98 – only in the US and Canada – from PBS Home Video (☎ toll-free 800-645-4727, fax 703-739-8131, shop.pbs.org), PO Box 751089, Charlotte, NC 28275 USA as part of a five-hour, five-part series called *The Adventurers* (item number A2763-WEBHV). The other profiles in this set are of non-Antarctic explorers. Byrd's story can be purchased as a single cassette from The Antarctic Connection (see the Shopping section in this chapter) for US$19.98.

While not strictly about Antarctica, Irving Johnson's film of his 1929 voyage around Cape Horn in the square-rigger *Peking* gives an eyewitness view of the Southern Ocean's ferocity – and life aboard a 19th-century wooden sailing ship. Though he shot the film in 1929, Johnson narrated it a half-century later. By then he was a captain with a lifetime of ocean-going experience, and his matter-of-fact descriptions add to the realism of the spectacular footage. *Around Cape Horn* (1929) is a production of Mystic Seaport

Museum (☎ 860-572-5386, fax 860-572-5324, store@mysticseaport.org, mysticseaport.org), 47 Greenmanville Ave, Mystic, CT 06355-9947 USA). Price: US$29.95.

The aurora is featured in two videos, *The Aurora Explained* and *The Aurora Color Television Project*, which are about the aurora borealis rather than the aurora australis. Nevertheless, they're interesting and informative, and feature spectacular images. Both were produced by the Geophysical Institute of the University of Alaska. Order from the University of Alaska Press (☎ 907-474-5831, fax 907-474-5502, fypress@aurora.alaska.edu), PO Box 756240, Fairbanks, AK 99775-6240 USA. Price: US$20 each.

Ironically, a movie somehow more genuinely heartrending than *Scott of the Antarctic* chronicles the fate not of men on a historic British expedition, but of sledge dogs on a 1958 Japanese expedition: Koreyoshi Kurahara's *Antarctica* (1984). The eerie soundtrack of the same name by *Chariots of Fire* composer Vangelis is highly regarded among Antarctic audiophiles.

Another Japanese film, Harushi Kadokama's gloriously awful nuclear holocaust thriller, *Virus* (1980), partially filmed on location in Antarctica, has achieved cult status aboard some Antarctic tour ships. After a deadly germ wipes out the Earth's human population, 858 men – and eight anxious women – struggle to survive in Antarctica.

Two other sci-fi movies, *The Thing from Another World* (1951) and its remake, *The Thing* (1982), star an extraterrestrial that terrorizes polar research stations. Among serious sci-fi buffs, the 1951 film, directed by Howard Hawks, is widely regarded as one of the best science-fiction films ever made, but it's set in the Arctic, not the Antarctic. The much-too-gory remake is a bona fide Antarctic movie. Starring Kurt Russell, it feels a lot like a version of *The Alien*. A naval expedition sent to explore Antarctica discovers a tropical region filled with clunky-looking dinosaurs in *The Land Unknown* (1957), while an investigation among Antarctic whalers turns deadly in *Hell Below Zero* (1953).

There are even a couple of dopey Antarctic comedies. *Quick Before It Melts* (1965)

features a magazine reporter sent to cover a naval expedition to the Little America base who tries to engineer the defection of a Russian scientist in order to obtain a 'scoop.' *Cry of the Penguins* (1972) stars John Hurt as a blasé young scientist who volunteers for Antarctic duty to impress a girlfriend. He orders the finest equipment and provisions from London's fanciest shops, and finds the expedition quite boring until he begins to identify with the Adélies he's studying.

IMAX's *Antarctica* (1991) offers magnificent scenery but leaves many people cold. First-timers may be blown away by the spectacular images, but some Antarctic connoisseurs feel disappointed that the unique medium wasn't more effectively exploited – outside of some terrific underwater shots of penguins and seals. The Swiss Hans-Ulrich Schlumpf's *Der Kongress der Pinguine* (The Congress of the Penguins) of 1994 stars gentoo penguins in a bizarre morality tale of alleged environmental destruction in Antarctica and at South Georgia. It's definitely weird.

Antarctica starred in the finale of *The X-Files* (1998). The collapsing ice shelf scene was dramatic but definitely not realistic.

In recent years TV documentaries about Antarctica – and especially its wildlife – have proliferated, and many are available on video. The best may be David Attenborough's *Life in the Freezer* series produced by the BBC; It has some amazing underwater footage of a leopard seal devouring a penguin, toying with it just as a cat does with a mouse. *The Last Place on Earth* is a seven-part, 6½-hour made-for-TV series describing Amundsen and Scott's race to reach the South Pole. Made in 1985 by Central Independent Television and based on Roland Huntford's book, it takes some annoying narrative liberties. It includes some ridiculous scenes, one showing Scott crying at the South Pole after seeing Amundsen's tent. But overall it's well made and interesting.

Natural History New Zealand (☎ 64-3-479-9799, freephone in NZ only 0800-4-94537, fax 64-3-479-9917, www.naturalhistory .co.nz) PO Box 474, Dunedin, New Zealand, one of the world's largest producers of wildlife television programs, has made more films in Antarctica than any other company. It has put together a terrific collection of 18 different titles covering Antarctica and the sub-Antarctic islands. Among the best is *The Longest Night*, which chronicles the lives of a small group wintering at Scott Base – watch for the courageous skinny-dippers! Another gem is *Solid Water, Liquid Rock*, a unique look at Mt Erebus, from its undersea foundation to its lava-showering summit. Other titles cover everything from Ralph Vaughan Williams' *Sinfonia Antartica* to katabatic winds and artists in Antarctica.

CD-ROMS

Five CD-ROMs about Antarctica are currently available. Most are very good, especially as educational tools, though even a multimedia experience can't compete with being there.

Aoraki Corp's *Antarctica* (1994) was produced in conjunction with the International Antarctic Centre of Christchurch. Price: NZ$79.95 from The Antarctic Shop at the International Antarctic Centre in Christchurch (☎ 64-3-358-9896, fax 64-3-353-7799, info@antarcticshop.co.nz).

Virtual Antarctica (1996), produced in partnership with Antarctic tour operator Mountain Travel-Sobek and WorldTravel Partners, features the excellent photography of Jonathan Chester. Price: US$24.95 from Extreme Images Inc (☎ 510-524-6336, fax 510-525-4961, jchester@extremeimages.com, www.extremeimages.com), PO Box 7398, Berkeley, CA 94707 USA.

Best of all is *Attenborough's Antarctic* (1997), a personal tour of The Ice led by famed TV naturalist Sir David Attenborough and produced by BBC Multimedia. As you would expect, it is professionally done, with the sharpest photographs (more than 1000), smoothest video and most information. There's so much here, it's a little overwhelming at first. Still, there are a few of the dead ends common to this medium: the South Pole 'section' is just a couple of tiny photos. Price: £29.99 from JEM Marketing, JEM House (☎ 44-1483-268-888, fax 44-1483-268-889, jem@dircon.co.uk, www

.j-e-m.com), Littlemead, Cranleigh, Surrey GU6 8ND UK.

Voyage to Antarctica: A Celebration of Beauty (1998), produced by Dr Thomas Bauer, presents a tourist-eye view of the Antarctic Peninsula and nearby islands. Unique are some wonderful aerial views. Be sure to catch the short video of the mating king penguins. Price: A\$59.95 from CALC Multimedia (☎ 61-3-9248-1090, fax 61-3-9248-1091, info@calc.com.au, www.calc.com.au/antarctica.html), Victoria University of Technology, PO Box 14428 Melbourne City, Victoria 8001 Australia.

Wildlife of the Deep Antarctic (1998), produced by MastroMedia Interactive, highlights emperor and Adélie penguins, Weddell seals, orcas and skuas. Each is covered by text, video (some underwater), a slideshow and an audio file. In addition, there's an overview of Antarctica. The price is US\$24.95 from MastroMedia (☎ 760-434-6110, fax 760-434-7174, info@mastromedia.com, www.mastromedia.com), 3597 Roosevelt St, No 201, Carlsbad, CA 92008 USA.

MAGAZINES & JOURNALS

Although there are no general-interest magazines devoted strictly to Antarctica, *Australian Geographic*, Germany's *Geo* and the US's *National Geographic* all run occasional features on the southern continent.

The quarterly *Polar Record*, published by Cambridge University Press, contains mainly academic research papers, but it also includes reports on Antarctic logistics, books and history. Subscriptions cost £52 or US\$88 per year, and are available from Cambridge University Press (☎ 44-1223-312-393, fax 44-1223-315-052, information@cup.cam.ac.uk, www.cup.cam.ac.uk), Edinburgh Building, Shaftesbury Rd, Cambridge, England CB2 2RU UK.

The *Antarctic Journal of the United States* describes US research and activities. There's an annual issue reviewing the US Antarctic Program. It's available from: New Orders (☎ 202-512-1800, fax 202-512-2233), Superintendent of Documents, PO Box 371954, Pittsburgh, PA 15250-7954 USA. Several complete issues are available online at www.nsf.gov/od/opp/antarct/journal/start.htm.

The Antarctican Society newsletter, written in an inimitable style by Paul Dalrymple, is a lively compendium of information about US activities on the continent as well as a good deal of news about the way things once were in Antarctica (see the Useful Organizations section).

The *Polar Times*, published by the American Polar Society, is a collection of news clippings about Antarctica from US newspapers, along with articles written by members. The Montreal Antarctic Society publishes a quarterly newsletter, *The Seventh Continent*, about Canadian work in Antarctica. *Aurora* (www.anareclub.org.au/aurora.html), published by Australia's ANARE Club, gives one view of Australian Antarctic activities, while the Antarctic Society of Australia presents another in its quarterly newsletter, *Antarctic News and Views*. The New Zealand Antarctic Society's quarterly, *Antarctic*, covers activities by all countries operating in Antarctica. *Heritage Hearsay*, published by the Antarctic Heritage Trust, includes information about the restoration of Antarctic historic sites. (For information on all of these societies, see the Useful Organizations section.)

Polar News Notizie Polari is a bilingual English/Italian newsletter devoted to the polar regions. Subscriptions are available for US\$27 per year (11 issues) from Alberto Marenga, Polar Documentation Center (☎ 39-6657-1173, amarenga@pelagus.it), PO Box 14302, 00149-Roma (Trullo), Italy.

Expedition News is a monthly review of significant expeditions and adventures, many of them in Antarctica. It's available either by email or regular mail for US\$36 per year from Blumenfeld and Associates (☎ 203-855-9400, fax 203-855-9433, blumassoc@aol.com, www.expeditionnews.com), 137 Rowayton Ave, Suite 210, Rowayton, CT 06853 USA.

The *Antarctic Sun* is published during summer at McMurdo station. It includes a popular 'Around the Continent' section as well as articles about life in Antarctica's biggest town. Outside Antarctica you can get this via the Internet (see the list of Internet addresses in this chapter).

PHOTOGRAPHY & VIDEO

Nearly all cameras are suitable for Antarctica. Pocket-size autofocus cameras with their built-in flash units are perfect for recording shipboard life and the dark interiors of historic huts, which often have boarded-over windows to protect against drifting snow. For most other situations, single-lens reflex (SLR) cameras with their interchangeable, high-quality lenses produce sharper images. Disposable cameras – especially the panoramic types – can be useful for shots in rugged conditions, ie, aboard a spray-soaked Zodiac, in a kayak or during a snowstorm.

Don't think black-and-white film will do justice to Antarctica's phenomenal beauty, unless you're aiming for an artistic or historical look. Bring it only *in addition to* your supply of color film.

It cannot be repeated too many times: bring more film than you think you will need. You can always carry it home, or sell it to film-starved fellow passengers. You'll be sorry if you run out of film before that magnificent sunset or amazing encounter with humpback whales or ... whatever!

Remember a good case to protect your camera from salt spray, rain, snow and dust. Helicopters create powerful downblasts full of grit and gravel that can ruin a lens in seconds. A plastic bag will work in a pinch, but you run the risk of a strong gust ripping it away from you to pollute either Antarctica or the sea. A camera bag with a shoulder strap offers the best protection and leaves hands free for climbing steep ship gangways.

Technical Tips

Many photography principles detailed here and in Ron Naveen's boxed text 'Taking Photos in the Antarctic' (in this chapter) hold true in general for movie and video

Taking Photos in the Antarctic

Equipment Antarctic photography is made considerably easier by modern, computer-chip-driven cameras. It is difficult not to take great shots, if a few simple rules are followed:

Take lots of color slide or color print film – perhaps twice as much as you might ordinarily carry. Slower speed film (ASA 64, 100 and 125) is usually quite adequate because of the high reflectivity of light during the austral summer. And slower speed film produces much snappier results because it is finer-grained than the ASA 200 and 400 speed films. A few higher speed rolls may be useful on the very cloudy, murky days that do occur, or to assist your efforts to capture fast-flying seabirds on film.

Wide-angle lenses (24-28mm) and 70- or 80-200mm zoom lenses are extraordinarily useful. The wide angles allow you to capture all of the breathtaking scenery you'll encounter, and the zoom allows you some alternatives for framing and capturing shots of the many penguins, seals and flying birds you'll see – and at relatively close distances. Antarctic animals are, generally speaking, quite relaxed about human visitors. You'll encounter numerous situations where you, the photographer, have plenty of time to frame your picture and take excellent shots. Longer lenses, 300mm and 400mm, are very bulky, but useful when trying to capture distant seabirds at sea.

Don't hesitate to rely on your camera's built-in, sophisticated metering systems. The matrix metering systems in new cameras do a great job of sorting through light imbalances.

Technique Antarctic scenery and animals are so spectacular that it's quite natural to worry whether one's trophy shots will actually come out, but by observing the following suggestions, you should experience no difficulty.

Take a millisecond before each shot to ask: Is there too much white or black in the viewfinder? Remember that the camera's meter wants to turn everything to what is called

photography, but shooting in Antarctica requires some additional special knowledge. Light meters, particularly on video cameras, can be fooled by the bright polar light; framing your composition so less sky is visible should prevent overexposure. Try to limit the amount of automatic panning, zooming and fading you do, despite the sophisticated capabilities of many cameras. Not only will limiting the camera's movement prevent dizziness in those who eventually view the footage, it will also save precious battery life, which cold will shorten by as much as 50%. When possible, it's best to shut off the autofocus and automatic zoom features on the camera to save battery time.

Try to let your shots run for at least 10 or 15 seconds before you change subjects; otherwise, your video will appear jerky and too much like a music video (unless that's the effect you intend). It's best to shoot your footage and then pause or stop the camera before setting up the next shot. Also, be mindful of others when filming. Don't get so involved in looking through your viewfinder (or narrating your shot aloud to your microphone) that you step on an animal or intrude on a fellow visitor's photography.

Politeness dictates that whenever you're inside a scientific station, you ask the residents for permission to use your camera. The station is their home, and you should treat it that way.

Photographing Wildlife

Although Antarctic animals may appear to be unconcerned about humans nearby, they may in fact be under considerable stress caused by your activity. People as far as 30m from a penguin rookery have been shown to increase the birds' heart rates significantly. And penguins may deviate from their usual

Taking Photos in the Antarctic

'18% grey,' which is like photographically mixing together the black and white on a checkerboard. If your intended shot has too much white (snow or ice), the picture will come out grey unless you 'open up' at least one stop and add a little extra exposure. This is done by reducing the shutter speed to the next slowest speed, using the next larger aperture (f-stop), or by turning your camera's exposure compensation dial to +1. Conversely, if there's too much dark color in the viewfinder (black hillsides, volcanic ash) you need to 'stop down' by at least one stop to prevent the black from being turned into a grey wash. This is done by increasing the shutter speed to the next fastest speed, using the next smallest aperture (f-stop), or by turning your camera's exposure compensation dial to -1. There may be up to a three-stop difference between a proper exposure and a stark white or stark black subject; thus, you might even extend your exposure adjustment to +2 or -2, but the recommendation is not to go all the way to +3 or -3 because the definition in your intended subject is likely to be lost. When you really want to make sure you've nailed a particularly wonderful composition, consider bracketing, which means taking a few shots at different exposures: With close-to-average shots, follow your camera's recommendation, then shoot down one stop (-1) and open up one stop (+1); with shots having much white, follow your camera's recommendation, then open up by one (+1) and two (+2) stops.

A UV filter on the end of your lens keeps it from being scratched and cuts off the blue cast that might creep into your shots. Polarizing filters cut through glare in the water and darken skies, and can lead to nice shots, but they also cost about two stops of light, meaning that you'll have to use a slower shutter speed or wider aperture to get your shot.

Finally, don't forget to bring lots of spare batteries. The ship you're on probably won't have what you need, and if it does, the stock is likely to be outdated.

– Ron Naveen

path when approaching or leaving a colony for as long as three days after people visit.

Always remember to keep the required distances from animals: *at least* 5m from penguins, seabirds and seals – except fur seals, which should not be approached closer than 15m. Never block an animal's path to the sea or its young. When approaching, remember to stay low. Don't move suddenly or speak loudly. When you're finished photographing, back out quietly, the same way you moved in. If an animal starts to move, you're too close. If an animal changes its behavior, you're too close. The farther you stay from an animal, the more natural its behavior will be. For this reason, many biologists and naturalists prefer to view wildlife through binoculars or telephoto lenses even when ashore.

It is much better to get animals to come to you, which they often will do if you merely sit down, stay quiet and be patient.

TIME

Time is all but irrelevant to most visitors to the Antarctic, since the tourist season occurs during summer, when the sun stays up as long as 20 hours a day. Most Antarctic ships' clocks remain at their port of departure time (if they are returning to the same port). Or they keep 'ship time' day by day based on the port of disembarkation as they cross the Southern Ocean on the return voyage. Life aboard ship is often ruled by landing opportunities, with meals delayed or advanced according to possibilities for getting ashore.

Most Antarctic stations run on the same time as their home countries or logistics bases, so that communications are coordinated. But others adjust their times slightly to account for their geographic location. Australia's Antarctic stations, for instance, are managed from headquarters in Hobart. But when it's noon in Hobart, it's 9 am at Casey station, 8 am at Davis station and 7 am at Mawson station. Scientists working in the field generally develop their own time schedules, often working in midnight 'day'-light and sleeping late into the 'morning.'

Your main concern with time will be to make sure that when you telephone someone in the civilized world, you won't be waking them up. The ship's radio officers can help you calculate the time difference (see the Post & Communications section earlier in this chapter).

ELECTRICITY

Each ship has its own type of electricity, based on its country of origin, so you should check with the tour operator before buying converters. Many of the ships are from Russia, and use 220 volts, 50 hertz, with electrical sockets accommodating the standard European two round-pin plug.

LAUNDRY

Every Antarctic tourist ship has a laundry, and service is generally excellent. You simply leave your laundry in a bag in your cabin, and the attendant picks it up and returns it to you. Shipboard laundry prices are not cheap, but they're also not so expensive as to discourage occasional use. Shipboard laundries can actually deliver good value, since they allow you not to pack – and carry – so many clothes from home. Service is usually within two days.

Hand-laundering items like socks (polypropylene sock liners are especially fast-drying) will allow you to pack less and still not become a social outcast. To make hand-washed items dry faster, roll them in a towel and squeeze before hanging them up.

HEALTH

Antarctica is largely a clean, healthy, disease-free place, but medical resources are limited. While the ship's doctor stands ready to treat any problems arising *en voyage*, he or she is not available for general consultation.

Tap water is fine to drink aboard all Antarctic tour ships.

For a detailed examination of the health issues of Antarctic tourism, consult *Safe Passage Questioned: Medical Care and Safety for the Polar Tourist* (Centreville, MD USA: Cornell Maritime Press, 1998), by Dr John M Levinson and Errol Ger.

Predeparture Preparations

Health Insurance A travel insurance policy to cover theft, loss and medical problems is a good idea. There is a wide variety of policies, and your travel agent will have recommendations. Check the small print, since some policies specifically exclude 'dangerous activities,' which can include scuba diving and hiking. You might want to check if they include travel to Antarctica in that category!

Immunizations No vaccinations are needed to visit Antarctica. It's always a good idea to keep your tetanus immunization up-to-date no matter where you are – but even this is not required.

Sunburn
In Antarctica, you can get sunburned quickly, even on overcast days. The sun is particularly dangerous here, because it reflects off of snow, ice and the sea. Use sunscreen! Calamine lotion is good for mild sunburn.

Eye Hazards
Antarctica's reflected sunlight produces a powerful glare, so sunglasses are essential. Be sure to buy UV-filtering glasses and not just untreated dark lenses, which cause your pupils to dilate while offering no protection from UV rays. Your best bet is glacier glasses, which come equipped with leather flaps to block light coming in from the sides. Snow blindness, an extremely painful – though rare – inflammation that causes headaches and temporary loss of sight, is preventable.

Hypothermia
Although shore visits are not conducted in severe weather, and most are not long enough to induce hypothermia, it is still possible. Hypothermia occurs when the body loses heat faster than it can produce it, and the core temperature falls. It is surprisingly easy, even if the air temperature is above freezing, to progress from very cold to dangerously cold due to a combination of wind, wet clothing, fatigue and hunger. It is best to dress in layers: silk, wool and some of the new artificial fibers are all good insulating materials. Keeping dry is critical, so a strong, waterproof outer layer is essential. A hat is

very important, as a lot of heat is lost through the head.

Symptoms of hypothermia are exhaustion, numb skin (particularly fingers and toes), shivering, slurred speech, irrational or violent behavior, lethargy, stumbling, dizzy spells, muscle cramps and violent bursts of energy. Sufferers who become irrational may claim they are warm and try to take off their clothes.

To treat hypothermia, first get the patient out of the wind and rain, remove any wet clothing and replace it with dry. Give the person hot liquids – not alcohol – and some high-calorie, easily digestible food. This should be enough for the early stages of hypothermia, but if it has gone further it may be necessary to consult the ship's doctor. If possible, place the sufferer in a warm (not hot) shower.

Dehydration
The extremely dry Antarctic environment can lead to mild dehydration, so it is good to drink at least 4 liters of water a day. Signs of dehydration include dark yellow urine and/or a feeling of fatigue. Coffee and tea are diuretics and as such are counterproductive when trying to combat dehydration.

Insomnia
Sleeplessness can be a problem in the Antarctic, with its extended hours of sunlight in summer and darkness in winter. There's even a special Antarctic term coined for the problem – 'Big Eye.' Caused by a disruption in the body's normal circadian rhythm, this insomnia usually cures itself after a few days.

In fact, many people experience some type of insomnia during the first day or two aboard ship. It may be compounded by jet lag, thanks to your long journey from home. The singular motion of a ship underway also may take some getting used to. If you're feeling sleepless, you might try going up on the bridge or out on deck for a look at the scenery – you can always sleep at home.

Seasickness
The bane of many a traveler, seasickness (or, in French, the more poetic *mal de mer*) can

be one of the prices exacted by King Neptune for passage through his oft-stormy Southern Ocean. One cynical suggestion for alleviating this uniquely horrible feeling is to sit down under a tree and wait for it to go away. In fact, seasickness is simply a natural response to the abnormal motion of the sea. If you've never been seasick, sailors say, you just haven't sailed enough. You may not be seasick en route to The Ice; there's a very

Antarctic Medicine

The chief work of the surgeon of a polar expedition is done before the ship leaves...if it has been properly carried out there should be little to do during the actual journey...casualties are excepted, for...they cannot be foreseen...ordinary sickness can be largely ruled out by careful examination....

Thus wrote Dr AH Macklin at the conclusion of Shackleton's *Quest* expedition, on which the leader died of a heart attack, a pre-existing condition. Macklin's words are still relevant for anyone journeying to Antarctica, where health care services are limited. All persons, whether tourists, scientists or support staff, should be physically fit and free of significant disease. National operators as well as tourist groups and private expeditions have varying standards of medical screening and provision of health care services. All, however, must be self sufficient.

Most wintering expeditions have a rigorous screening program, and some include psychological testing. Despite this, doctors selected for Antarctic service must have the skills to cope with any eventuality. Since it's unrealistic to expect any doctor to have all the specialist skills necessary, predeparture training is organized in environmental and occupational medicine, anesthetics, surgery, laboratory techniques, radiography, dentistry, physiotherapy and medical communications so that specialist advice can be obtained from outside Antarctica. As there has been a high rate of appendicitis in Antarctica, some nations require their doctors to undergo a prophylactic appendectomy. Lay personnel are given basic first aid training, and some are trained in anesthetics and sterile operating theater techniques in order to assist a doctor if necessary.

The lack of all-weather airfields or permanently based aircraft in Antarctica and the inability of all but a few nations to make direct intercontinental flights during most of the year mean that many stations and bases remain largely inaccessible. Most wintering groups are accompanied by one doctor (some national expeditions have two doctors; others have paramedics). This doctor works on the principle that he or she must handle any medical, surgical or dental emergency without the assistance of medical evacuation.

There is no Antarctic-specific disease or ailment. Cold injury, snow blindness and other environmental conditions are always a threat, but serious cases occur infrequently. Trauma resulting from accidents is most common, along with resultant lacerations, broken bones, burns or death.

Nearly 1200 people have died in Antarctica since humans first went to the southern continent (three-quarters of them in the wreck of *San Telmo* and the Air New Zealand crash on Mt Erebus), but the mortality in this relatively young and fit population is still low compared with more densely populated regions. Antarctica travelers are not spared from such conditions as heart attacks, ulcers, intracranial bleeding, psychiatric ailments, carbon monoxide poisoning and infectious diseases (malaria, sexually transmitted diseases, amoebiasis, polio) brought from the outside world.

Antarctic doctors must be masters of improvisation. In 1961, the physician to the Soviet expedition was forced to operate on himself for acute appendicitis. He was assisted by two

good chance the waters will be calm and you'll be just fine.

Eat lightly during your trip to reduce your chances of seasickness. Try to find a cabin that minimizes motion – close to midship can be slightly more comfortable. Fresh air and a view of the horizon usually help. Things that definitely won't help you feel better include reading, cigarette smoke, alcohol and diesel fumes.

Antarctic Medicine

coworkers, who held the retractors and a mirror. The operation was successful. In the same year, a ruptured intracranial aneurysm was operated on at an Australian station. The doctor had neither previous neurosurgical experience nor sufficient instruments, but a brain cannula and sucker were improvised based on illustrations from a surgical catalog. A neurosurgeon in Melbourne provided advice via radio telegrams for the operation, which also was successful.

The records of most expeditions highlight ingenuity: dentures have been repaired with parts made from a seal's tooth, and intricate equipment has frequently been repaired and fabricated. One scientist lost both glasses and contact lenses, so new ones had to be ground out of Perspex in the station workshop to conform to a prescription provided by an eye specialist outside Antarctica.

Primitive Antarctic medical offices, however, are now being replaced. Modern facilities contain a consulting room, dental and examination room, operating theater, laboratory, medical ward, storeroom and area for treatment of hypothermia. Equipment includes X-ray machines, electrocardiograph monitors and defibrillators, anesthetic machines, pulse oximeters, electrosurgical units, dry chemistry laboratory analyzers, dental equipment, autoclave and gas sterilization and therapeutic ultrasound. The doctor's work includes all the practical tasks of lab tests, radiology, nursing, cleaning the surgery, sterilizing instruments and even bed-making. A wide range of pharmaceuticals is supplied, and as with the equipment, the selection is continually reviewed and upgraded.

Many doctors also perform research. Particular emphasis has been placed on research in the applied areas such as health and behavioral studies, nutrition, epidemiology, thermal adaptation, hormone adaptation, cardiovascular studies, photobiology (especially ultraviolet radiation) and diving medicine. Research into the capacity of winterers to resist infection has indicated that living for long periods in Antarctic isolation causes reduced immunity.

International cooperation has always been excellent in the Antarctic, especially in dealing with operational problems. Although polar human biology research was carried out on early Antarctic expeditions, it was ad hoc and had little continuity or coordination. The advent of the Scientific Committee on Antarctic Research (SCAR), and coordination by subsidiary groups such as the SCAR Working Group on Human Biology and Medicine, have had a great impact on research and Antarctic health care. The International Biomedical Expedition to the Antarctic 1980-81 (IBEA), the first Antarctic expedition solely for human studies, was organized by the Working Group.

Collaborative research is now taking place between Antarctic and space agencies. Much of the research has relevance beyond Antarctica. The problems faced by personnel in polar regions, including those related to isolation and living and working in confined environments, are also experienced by space crews. Mutual studies have enormous potential to enhance the performance, health and safety of people in both settings.

– Dr Des Lugg,
Head of Polar Medicine at the Australian Antarctic Division

Over the years, many bizarre methods have been tried to alleviate seasickness. One remedy, formerly used on ore boats in the Great Lakes of North America, was to cinch a belt or a length of rope tightly around one's midsection. Other remedies include placing an aspirin tablet in one's navel (truly!) or wearing a paper bag inside one's shirtfront. None of these has proved successful, though the latter may have made the wearer feel ready in case of emergency.

In fact, no method works for everyone. There are many commercial motion sickness remedies, and the ship's doctor will dispense at least one or two types. On some ships, seasick pills are placed in bowls in public areas, like candy. If you're concerned about seasickness, consider bringing several remedies in case one is ineffective. Many pills can cause drowsiness, and all must be taken before heavy seas start the ship rolling. By the time you're feeling sick, it's too late.

Ginger is supposed to be a natural preventative for seasickness and is available in capsule form. Other nontraditional methods include acupressure wristbands and specially recorded music.

Even if you do get sick, once you get to Antarctica you'll be fine. The protected waters of its bays and channels experience almost no wave action, and pack ice dampens the ocean's motion almost completely.

For humorous – and fascinating – reading on the subject, pick up Charles Mazel's wonderful *Heave Ho! My Little Green Book of Seasickness* (Camden, ME USA: International Marine, 1992), a slim volume packed with historical notes, interesting quotes and loony 'remedies,' as well as some serious advice on dealing with what is sometimes called 'the liquid laugh.'

DISABLED TRAVELERS

The physical challenges of shipboard life, Zodiac boats and icy landing sites can make Antarctica difficult and dangerous for able-bodied as well as disabled travelers. However, it may be possible for a disabled tourist to make special arrangements with a tour operator, especially if an able-bodied traveler accompanies him or her. Although

Antarctica is spectacular when seen from the deck of a ship, helicopters can also be employed to reach otherwise inaccessible sites. So a ship equipped with helicopters can offer advantages (as does a ship with elevators). Mobility-impaired visitors have been able to enjoy Zodiac rides on calm days, thanks to willing cruise staff members who have carried wheelchairs down the gangway. Check with tour operators to see how flexible they are and how well-equipped the ship is to handle wheelchairs.

Some travel agencies specialize in helping disabled clients plan their adventures. One such company that has been helpful to clients booking Antarctic cruises is Flying Wheels Travel (☎ 507-451-5005, toll-free 800-535-6790, fax 507-451-1685, thq@ll.net; www.flyingwheels.com), PO Box 382 Owatonna, MN 55060 USA. Ask for Barbara Jacobson.

SENIOR TRAVELERS

The majority of passengers on most Antarctic cruises are senior citizens, since they often have the time and money to spend on travel. There's no reason advanced age should present insurmountable difficulties for visiting Antarctica. Norman Vaughan, who first set foot on the continent in 1928 with American aviator Richard E Byrd, reached the summit of the 3139m mountain in Antarctica that Byrd named for him – three days before his 89th birthday in 1994. Vaughan's personal motto: 'The only death you die is the death you die every day by not living.'

On the other hand, you don't want to die in Antarctica. Some of the more strenuous walks may be too difficult. Know your limits. Enjoy what you can do, but don't overexert. Antarctica's beauty and wildlife are often best experienced by standing still or even sitting down. Too many people of all ages rush around while ashore, snapping photos and marching from one end of a landing site to another. Slow down and enjoy.

TRAVEL WITH CHILDREN

Children are still relatively rare visitors to Antarctica, which is a shame. Antarctica's amazing landscapes and abundant wildlife are especially exciting for young people. But if your kids can't go for more than an hour without playing with a Game Boy, leave them at home; they won't be able to handle the long sea time, which can be tedious even for adults. If it is financially possible, try to get a suite so children have enough room to spread out on the floor and play with toys and books. Also, check to see if an in-cabin video player is available, so children can screen their favorite videos as well as educational tapes about Antarctica. You should probably count on there being no other children aboard ship for your kids to play with.

Unfortunately, you should also be prepared to encounter resentment from other passengers – especially older travelers – until they see that your children can behave in a civilized manner. 'No one talks to you for the first three days,' said a perfectly behaved young girl on a recent Antarctic voyage. People will even sometimes tell parents later in the trip that they weren't happy to see the children aboard the ship – at first. But often youngsters find themselves becoming the object of grandparent-like attention from other travelers, especially in the dining room, where seating is usually open.

Children traveling to Antarctica (like grown-ups) will get more out of the experience if they're prepared for it. Watching videos and reading about Antarctica (see the Children's Books section in this chapter) before sailing can help build excitement and knowledge. Giving children 'assignments' to learn about particular Antarctic topics while on the voyage – and encouraging them to ask the ship's staff to help them with research – can enrich their experience. Remember to bring plenty of materials such as drawing paper, pencils, crayons, markers, scissors, Scotch tape and glue for arts and crafts projects.

USEFUL ORGANIZATIONS

Several organizations concern themselves with Antarctica, especially its environment and history.

American Polar Society This society was founded in 1934 as a forum for people involved or interested in polar exploration and research. Annual membership dues are US$15 (US$17 for foreign memberships). Members receive the *Polar Times* twice a year. The contact is Captain Brian Shoemaker, the society's secretary (☎ 541-756-9013; apolars@presys.com), at PO Box 591, North Bend, OR 97459 USA.

ANARE Club The club has various categories of membership for those who have served with the Australian National Antarctic Research Expeditions (ANARE), and also a category called 'subscriber' (annual dues: A$25 within Australia; otherwise A$30), which entitles one to receive the Club's quarterly magazine *Aurora*. Contact the club's secretary at GPO Box 2534 W, Melbourne 3001 Australia (www.anareclub.org.au).

Antarctic Society of Australia This group promotes interest in all matters relating to Antarctica and the sub-Antarctic islands. Annual dues are A$30 and include a quarterly newsletter, *Antarctic News and Views*. Contact the society (☎ 61-2-9981-5809, dgore@laurel.ocs.mq.edu.au, www.es.mq.edu.au/physgeog/antsoc.htm) at PO Box 243, Pymble, New South Wales 2073 Australia.

Antarctica Project The only environmental organization in the world devoted exclusively to protecting Antarctica, this group is also a cofounder and supporter of the Antarctic and Southern Ocean Coalition (ASOC), which has nearly 230 member conservation organizations in 49 countries. The Antarctica Project lobbies national governments on behalf of conservation issues and attends Antarctic Treaty System meetings as a certified Non-Governmental Observer (NGO). Membership is US$30 per year (tax deductible in the US), and contributing members receive quarterly newsletters. The Antarctica Project publishes three valuable 'Antarctica Resource Lists' for elementary-, middle- and high-school students listing appropriate books, films, CD-ROMs, study aids, teacher packets and also magazines. The Antarctica Project (☎ 202-234-2480,

Antarctica – The Bar

Kevin Barry named his New York City bar after the ice continent because, he says, 'We're in an underappreciated part of Manhattan, and Antarctica is an underappreciated part of the world.' I don't know about that, but the bar – which opened in 1997 – is certainly in a lesser-traveled part of town: the 'Hudson Square' neighborhood south of the West Village, north of Tribeca and west of Soho. Though it has no connection to Antarctica beyond its name, it's a fine spot for a drink, with a handsome wood bar and a pool table in back. Antarctica's T-shirts, featuring a stylized emperor penguin, are terrific and cheap (US$10). Antarctica (☎ 212-352-1666, fax 212-627-5923) is located at 287 Hudson Street at Spring Street.

❉ ❉ ❉ ❉ ❉ ❉ ❉ ❉ ❉ ❉

fax 202-234-2482, www.asoc.org) is at PO Box 76920, Washington, DC 20013 USA.

Antarctican Society This association was organized to unite 'persons interested in Antarctica to facilitate friendly and informal exchanges of information and views on Antarctica.' Founded in 1959, it holds several meetings a year, many of them with distinguished Antarctic scientists as speakers. Most take place in the Washington, DC, area, where a quarter of the members live. One of the best reasons to join is the lively Antarctican Society newsletter, written and edited by Paul Dalrymple from his redoubt in Maine. It's larded with inside dope on the US Antarctic Program, as well as a strong measure of Antarctic history covering the past half-century. Dues start at US$10 a year. The Antarctican Society's address is c/o Ruth Siple, 7338 Wayfarer Dr, Fairfax Station, VA 22039 USA.

Heritage Antarctica This organization coordinates the preservation and protection of the historic sites of the Ross Sea region. Contrary to popular belief, the sites and their relics are not permanently preserved by the Antarctic climate, but in fact are being deteriorated by time and the elements. Heritage Antarctica has established a database of the artifacts in the Ross Sea huts and has done extensive repair and protection work on the huts. All tourist visits to the huts are chaperoned by designated representatives of the Antarctic Heritage Trust, the New Zealand branch of the organization. Membership in the Trust, which was established in 1987, costs NZ$20 for New Zealanders; NZ$25 for people living overseas; the difference is due to the costs of mailing out the Trust's newsletter, *Heritage Hearsay*, published two or three times annually. The Trust also published David Harrowfield's excellent book, *Icy Heritage: Historic Sites of the Ross Sea Region*. The address for AHT (☎ 64-3-358-0200, fax 64-3-358-0211) is PO Box 14-091, Christchurch Airport, New Zealand. The Trust has a British sister organization, the United Kingdom Antarctic Heritage Trust (☎ 44-1243-535-256), which is developing a protection program for historic sites outside the Ross Sea area. UKAHT's address is: c/o Captain Pat McLaren, RN, UK AHT, The Blue House, East Marden, Chichester, W Sussex, PO18 9JE, UK. For more information on both groups, you can visit www .heritage-antarctica.org.

International Association of Antarctica Tour Operators This trade association was formed in 1991 by seven private tour operators to create a set of visitors' guidelines for tourists in Antarctica and to lobby the Antarctic Treaty countries on tourism issues. Now grown to include 32 Antarctic tour companies from 11 countries, IAATO is dedicated to responsible private-sector travel in the Antarctic. It can't make any specific travel recommendations (other than suggesting that you use a member company), but can send you a copy of the IAATO directory (also available on its website), which describes the organization's objectives and members. IAATO (☎ 970-704-1047, fax 970-704-9660, iaato@iaato.org, www.iaato.org) can be reached at PO Box 2178, Basalt, CO 81621 USA.

James Caird Society Named for the open boat in which Ernest Shackleton sailed across the Southern Ocean on his epic 1916 journey from Elephant Island to South Georgia, the society was formed in 1994 to educate the general public about all of Shackleton's Antarctic expeditions and related aspects of Antarctic history. For information contact chairman Harding Dunnett, The James Caird Society (☎ 44-181-852-0302, fax 44-181-318-5829), c/o Dulwich College, London SE21 7LD, UK.

Montreal Antarctic Society Dedicated to providing a Canadian perspective on Antarctica, the society was founded in 1994. It publishes a quarterly newsletter, *The Seventh Continent*. Contact its president, Valmar Kurol, at 4633 Harvard, Montreal, Quebec, H4A 2X3 Canada (mtl.ant.soc@sympatico.ca).

New Zealand Antarctic Society This organization was founded in 1933 and includes a large number of overseas members. Its journal, *Antarctic*, is published quarterly; subscriptions begin at NZ$45. You can contact the Society's secretary (☎ 64-3-377-3173, fax 64-3-365-2252, marga@chch.planet.org.nz) at PO Box 404, Christchurch 8000, New Zealand.

Polar Philatelic Organizations For those interested in collecting stamps from or about Antarctica, there are several organizations of interest. All publish newsletters or journals.

American Society of Polar Philatelists, Secretary, Richard A Julian, 1153 Fairview Dr, York, PA 17403-3611 USA (rajulian@netrax.net)

Union Française de Philatelie Polaire – SATA c/o Gerald Brandel, 17 route de Flanville, F 57645 Montoy – Flanville, France (newsletter in French)

Sociedad Espanola de Filatelia Polar – SEFP Apartado de Correos 7, 43530 Alcanar (Tarragona), Spain (newsletter in Spanish)

Polar Postal History Society of Great Britain c/o Margery Wharton, 18 Millfield Rise, Bexhill-on-Sea, East Sussex TN40 1QY, UK

Polarphilatelie e.V. Dieter Querndt, Postfach 20-01-12, 99040 Erfurt, Germany (newsletter in German).

DANGERS & ANNOYANCES

While tourists are largely shielded from Antarctica's worst dangers such as blizzards and crevasses, life aboard ship has its own unique hazards. Always keep 'one hand for the ship' in case you suddenly need support as the ship rolls. Take care not just when climbing ladders and stairs, but anywhere that a sudden slam into furniture could result in a fractured limb or skull – yes, it happens nearly every year. A vessel pushing through ice can lurch suddenly, pitching an unaware passenger onto his or her nose. Doors likewise can swing dangerously, so don't curl your fingers around door jambs. Wide-open decks can be slippery with rain, snow or oil, so take it easy when moving about. Beware of raised doorsills, stanchions and other shipboard hardware which can easily trip you.

Shipboard theft is so unusual that many passengers on Antarctic cruises don't even lock their cabin doors. In fact, a greater annoyance usually is dealing with balky or lost cabin keys.

A hangover plus seasickness is a unique recipe for misery, so be careful not to overdo it in the cozy shipboard bar.

If you fall overboard, you will die. Although this may not be true in every case, it is almost certain, for human survival in the 4°C water of the Southern Ocean is calculated in minutes. Since drowning is thought by some to be preferable to freezing to death, one bit of only half-cynical advice for those who fall overboard is to swim as hard as you can for the bottom.

Cold and exposure on land can also be dangerous, so be sure you're properly clad before leaving the ship. The infamous windchill factor is a scientific way of measuring the intensifying effect of moving air upon heat loss. Since Antarctica is the windiest continent on Earth, it pays to have a windproof (and waterproof) outer garment. Remember that the intense rays of the sun more easily penetrate the ozone-depleted Antarctic atmosphere, so you should wear sunscreen and sunglasses even on overcast days when the sun doesn't shine.

One often overlooked aspect of shipboard travel is the common feeling of claustrophobia that comes from being stuck in close quarters with people you can't escape from. The best way to keep this in perspective is to remind yourself that it will all be over with shortly – and to consider that your shipmates just might feel the same way about you. Showing a little consideration goes a long way in matters of snoring (bring earplugs for unsuspecting cabinmates), smoking (most tour operators only allow it if your cabinmates agree) and personal hygiene (fastidiousness in this matter is always appreciated).

LEGAL MATTERS

Many countries apply their national laws to their citizens in Antarctica, so despite its extralegal status, the continent is not somewhere you can rob or kill with impunity.

Marriages are among the most common of Antarctica's few legal ceremonies. In February 1978, at Argentina's Esperanza station, what is believed to be the first wedding in Antarctica took place when Julia Beatriz Buonamio and First Sergeant Carlos Alberto Sugliano were married by a military chaplain.

Since then, many more have been celebrated. In 1985, the chaplain at the US McMurdo station flew to the South Pole to officiate at a wedding there – the bride carried a bouquet of fresh vegetables. On New Year's Day, 1999, another couple got married at the Pole station, with their fellow station residents standing hand in hand in a circle around them at the Ceremonial Pole. The lucky pair spent their wedding night in a heated tent. Shipboard weddings, with the captain presiding, are not unusual. On one recent voyage, the ship's hotel manager and a senior lecturer tied the knot, and the bride wore a hand-sewn wedding dress made from white polar fleece!

Spur-of-the-moment newlyweds should check the validity of their Antarctic weddings to be sure they're legally recognized by their local authorities.

SPECIAL EVENTS

Antarctica's biggest endemic holiday is the winter solstice, or Midwinter's Day (June 21 or 22, depending on the year), when the long polar night is half over. It's traditionally celebrated in fancy dress with, among other things, feasting, gift-giving, games, barbecuing, karaoke, magazine publishing, wine tasting, songs, showing of old film footage from the station library and theatrical performances. Winter stations exchange radio messages, and national leaders usually find it convenient to send congratulatory and encouraging messages to the polar denizens.

The last day of the sun and the return of the sun are also, understandably, very important dates on the Antarctic calendar; they occur on different dates at different latitudes.

Tourists won't experience any of these holidays, since they occur during winter, but Christmas and New Year's Eve are celebrated in unique Antarctic style aboard ship.

ACTIVITIES

By and large, tourist activity in Antarctica is limited to trooping around ashore during Zodiac landings from the ship. Visitors with fat wallets can fly into the continent's interior with Adventure Network International for mountain climbing, skiing, camping and trekking.

Scuba diving for advanced divers is now being offered as an option on a few Antarctic cruises. Short camping and mountain-climbing trips have also recently become available for cruise passengers, as has sea kayaking. Mountaineers foresee Antarctica becoming a climbing mecca. See the Getting There & Away chapter for more about these activities.

WORK

Unless you're a scientist (and even then), landing a job with one of the national programs in Antarctica is very difficult. Anyone working in Antarctica has to submit to a battery of physical and psychological tests – and most important, must possess advanced skills in one or probably several areas.

Length of service varies from three to 24 months.

National programs usually hire only citizens of their own country. For this reason you should write to your country's national Antarctic program to inquire about employment (see below for some addresses; see also the boxed text 'Internet Addresses'). Scientists are usually sent to Antarctica as the result of specific research proposals approved by peer review, but support personnel are selected by the national programs themselves, or, in the case of the US, Antarctica's largest employer, by a private contractor.

Antarctica New Zealand (☎ 64-3-358-0200, fax 64-3358-0211), International Antarctic Centre, Orchard Rd, Private Bag 4745, Christchurch, New Zealand

Australian Antarctic Division (☎ 61-3-6232-3209, fax 61-3-6232-3288), Channel Highway Kingston, Tasmania 7050 Australia

British Antarctic Survey (☎ 44-1223-361188), High Cross, Madingley Rd, Cambridge, England CB3 0ET, UK

French Institute for Polar Research and Technology (☎ 44-1223-361188), (Institut Français pour la Recherche et la Technologie Polaires), Technopôle Brest-lroise BP 75 - 29280 Plouzané, France

Japanese National Institute of Polar Research (☎ 81-3-3962-4711, fax 81-3-3962-2529), Kaga 1-9-10, Itabashi-ku, Tokyo 165, Japan

Raytheon Polar Services Company (☎ 303-306-8822, fax 303-306-8252, jrpetrarca@west.raytheon .com, http://rpsc.raytheon.com) recruits about 600 people a year to work at US Antarctic stations. Proof of US citizenship or permanent residency is required, and candidates must pass stringent physical and dental examinations after receiving an offer of employment. Positions . range from chefs and clerks to hair stylists and physicians, but the hot jobs – those for which openings are most often available – are usually in the trades or construction. A five- to 13-month contract is usual. Raytheon Polar Services Company, 16800 East CentreTech Parkway, Mail Stop DN/485/5M86, Aurora, CO 80011-9046 USA

South African National Antarctic Programme (☎ 27-12-310-3560), Dept of Environmental Affairs and Tourism, 315 Pretorius St, Private Bag X447, Pretoria 0002, South Africa

ACCOMMODATIONS

Nearly all Antarctic tourism involves ship-based visits, although a couple of tour operators offer camping on the continent; a polar-rated sleeping bag is highly recommended. See the Getting There & Away chapter for more camping information.

FOOD

The food on Antarctic cruises varies somewhat from ship to ship (in pretty direct proportion to the price of the cruise). Most is quite satisfying, though vegetarians may find it rough going at times. On longer cruises especially, fresh fruits and vegetables are eventually exhausted. Gourmet cooking is simply not the emphasis in Antarctic tourism. If five-star dining is critical to you, you'd be better off taking *QEII* across the Atlantic.

At least once during the cruise, you'll probably experience the de rigueur 'Antarctic barbecue,' in which grills are set up out on deck or even down on the fast ice and everyone bundles up for chicken, hamburgers, sausages and the like. It's a bit clichéd but fun nevertheless and a change from the dining room.

If you have your own favorite 'national' foods – peanut butter, Vegemite, Marmite, Promite, orange marmalade, miso soup – you might want to bring them with you.

DRINKS

It is fair to say that alcohol is available almost everywhere on the continent you find humans, with the possible exception of a remote field camp or two. Champagne is a popular tourist drink, especially in Antarctic cruise set pieces such as Champagne On The Ross Ice Shelf and Champagne On The Sea Ice. You should also have little trouble finding some glacier ice for your whiskey; many Antarcticans enjoy sipping their Scotch on *very* old rocks!

One of the few 'native' Antarctic drinks is a concoction called the Antarctic Old Fashion, invented by the crew at the US Little America V base from 1956 to 1958, and perfected at Camp Michigan on the Ross Ice Shelf. Here's the recipe, as described by

James 'Gentleman Jim' Zumberge in the Antarctican Society newsletter (reprinted by permission):

This is a long way around to telling the recipe (formula is a better word) for an Antarctic Old Fashion. It is impossible to make a simple Antarctic Old Fashion. All the research at Little America V was based on a batch quantity. Here are the ingredients: one fifth of Old Methusala (100 proof Navy 'bourbon') and seven packages of multifla-vored Life Savers. Pour the Old Methusala into another container and fill the empty bottle half full with freshly melted snow. Then force the Life Savers, one by one, into the mouth of the Methusala bottle and shake until all are dissolved. (Here it should be noted that painstaking research on the formula by the originators revealed that the final product was vastly improved if only two of the red Life Savers were used. All of our Camp Michigan Antarctic Old Fashions were made accordingly.) The final step in the process is to pour

Guidance for Visitors to the Antarctic

Activities in the Antarctic are governed by the Antarctic Treaty of 1959 and associated agreements, referred to collectively as the Antarctic Treaty system. The Treaty established Antarctica as a zone of peace and science.

In 1991 the Antarctic Treaty Consultative Parties adopted the Protocol on Environmental Protection to the Antarctic Treaty, which designates the Antarctic as a natural reserve. The Protocol sets out environmental principles, procedures and obligations for the comprehensive protection of the Antarctic environment and its dependent and associated ecosystems.

The Environmental Protocol applies to tourism and nongovernmental activities as well as governmental activities in the Antarctic Treaty area. It is intended to ensure that these activities do not have adverse impacts on the Antarctic environment or on its scientific and aesthetic values.

This *Guidance for Visitors to the Antarctic* is intended to make visitors aware of, and therefore able to comply with, the Treaty and the Protocol. Visitors are, of course, bound by national laws and regulations applicable to activities in the Antarctic.

Respect Protected Areas A variety of areas in the Antarctic have been afforded special protection because of their particular ecological, scientific, historic or other values. Entry into certain areas may be prohibited except in accordance with a permit issued by an appropriate national authority. Activities in or near designated historic sites and monuments and certain other areas may be subject to special restrictions.
• Know the locations of areas that have been afforded special protection, and any restrictions on entry or on activities that can be carried out in and near them.
• Observe applicable restrictions.
• Do not damage, remove or destroy historic sites or monuments, or any artifacts associated with them.

Respect Scientific Research
• Do not interfere with scientific research, facilities or equipment.
• Obtain permission before visiting Antarctic science and logistic support facilities; confirm arrangements 24 to 72 hours before arriving, and comply strictly with the rules regarding such visits.
• Do not interfere with or remove scientific equipment or marker posts, and do not disturb experimental study sites, field camps or supplies.

Be Safe Be prepared for severe and changeable weather. Be sure that your equipment and clothing meet Antarctic standards. Remember that the Antarctic environment is inhospitable, unpredictable and potentially dangerous.

the Old Methusala, stir well, and serve over Antarctic glacier ice. No fruit or other garbage is needed since those flavors are all embodied in the mixture.

Zumberge also recalled the utility of 60ml bottles of Navy brandy in coping with the cold: 'Our usual practice [was to drink] half before getting into our sleeping bags and the other half the next morning when rising. Because we slept in unheated tents, an ounce

of brandy gave one the feeling of warmth before crawling into a cold sack, and in the morning it gave you the courage to get out.'

SHOPPING

Antarctic souvenirs, once relatively rare, now run the typical full range from cheesy sweatshirts, baseball caps, coffee mugs, refrigerator magnets, ceramic 'sculptures' and postcards all the way to high-quality coffee-

---

Guidance for Visitors to the Antarctic

- Know your capabilities and the dangers posed by the Antarctic environment, and act accordingly. Plan activities with safety in mind at all times.
- Keep a safe distance from all wildlife, both on land and at sea.
- Take note of, and act on, advice and instructions from your leaders; do not stray from your group.
- Do not walk onto glaciers or large snowfields without proper equipment and experience; there is a real danger of falling into hidden crevasses.
- Do not expect a rescue service; self-sufficiency is increased and risks reduced by sound planning, quality equipment and trained personnel.
- Do not enter emergency refuges (except in emergencies). If you use equipment or food from a refuge, inform the nearest research station or national authority once the emergency is over.
- Respect any smoking restrictions, particularly around buildings, and take great care to safeguard against the danger of fire. This is a real hazard in the dry environment of Antarctica.

Protect Antarctic Wildlife Taking or harmfully interfering with Antarctic wildlife is prohibited except in accordance with a permit issued by a national authority.

- Do not feed, touch or handle birds or seals, or approach or photograph them in ways that cause them to alter their behavior. Special care is needed when animals are breeding or molting.
- Do not harm plants; damage can be caused by walking, driving or landing on extensive moss beds or lichen-covered scree slopes.
- Do not use guns or explosives. Keep noise to a minimum to avoid frightening wildlife.
- Do not bring non-native plants or animals (including house plants, pet dogs and cats) into the Antarctic.
- Do not use aircraft, vessels, small boats or other means of transportation in ways that disturb wildlife, either at sea or on land.

Keep Antarctica Pristine Antarctica remains relatively pristine, and has not yet been subjected to large-scale human perturbations. It is the largest wilderness area on Earth. Please keep it that way.

- Do not dispose of litter or garbage on land. Open burning is prohibited.
- Do not disturb or pollute lakes or streams. Any materials discarded at sea must be disposed of properly.
- Do not paint or engrave names or graffiti on rocks or buildings.
- Do not collect or take away biological or geological specimens or artifacts as souvenirs, including rocks, bones, eggs, fossils or parts or contents of buildings.
- Do not deface or vandalize buildings or emergency refuges, whether occupied, unoccupied or abandoned.

table books and maps (see the Books section and the Maps section earlier in this chapter). Prices vary widely, but you should expect to pay a premium for these souvenirs. Remember that the items sold at Antarctic bases have come a long way to reach the store shelf. Revenues from sales often go toward recreation for base members – or, more rarely, to support the scientific program. The items in shipboard shops are usually sold via 'chit,' so they sometimes don't even display a price tag since you'll just sign your credit-card slip at the end of the voyage. Often the shipboard shop is run by a separate company from the cruise itself, and the shop's overhead can be quite high.

Aside from the plethora of available books on Antarctic wildlife (see the Book section), another item that can be useful aboard ship is the Selected Wildlife of Antarctica: An Identification Guide. It's a laminated 22cm by 17cm card with handsome color drawings by Conrad Field of Homer, Alaska showing 33 species, including whales, seals, penguins and other seabirds, with the common and Latin name of each. Cost: US$9.25, from The Antarctic Connection (address listed at the end of this chapter).

Among the many handsome posters of Antarctica, a few stand out both for beauty and educational value. The 'Antarctic Habitat' poster produced by the Antarctica Project (see the Useful Organizations section) is large (64cm by 102cm), attractively illustrated and annotated, showing the major Antarctic and sub-Antarctic breeding sites for penguins, whales, seals and seabirds. Two handsome posters featuring the work of photographer Jonathan Chester, 'Penguins of Antarctica' and 'Penguins of the World,' are each 58cm by 89cm and cost US$11 each, or US$16 for the pair. To order, contact Jonathan Chester's Extreme Images Inc (see the CD-ROM section in this chapter).

The most unusual clothes with an Antarctic theme are the splendid, brightly colored tights featuring royal penguins, sold at the International Antarctic Center in Christchurch (see the Gateways chapter). The best T-shirt slogan says simply, 'Ski South Pole: two miles of base, ½ inch of powder.'

A unique gift for Antarcticophiles is a limited edition photographic print made from the original glass plates exposed by Australian photographer Frank Hurley during Ernest Shackleton's British Trans-Antarctic Expedition of 1914-17. Hurley took some 500 photographs, and after *Endurance* was crushed by the pack ice, dove into the flooded and slowly sinking ship to retrieve them. When Shackleton asked him to winnow the heavy glass negatives down to a manageable number, Hurley smashed all but 120 so he'd never regret having left them behind. Of the surviving negatives, which are now in the possession of Britain's Royal Geographical Society, 35 were used to make 400 prints each, including shots of *Endurance* caught in the ice. Each image measures 30cm by 40cm, on paper measuring 40cm by 50cm. Prices range from £140 to £330. Contact: Atlas Limited Editions (☎ 44-171-490-4540, fax 44-171-490-4514, order@atlasgallery.com, www.atlasgallery.com), 55-57 Tabernacle St, London EC2A 4AA UK.

Similarly, 19 limited edition HG Ponting photographs from Scott's last expedition are available from the Discovery Galley (☎ 44-181-543-4238, fax 44-181-543-4258), Suite A, Jubilee House, 10-12 Lombard Rd, London SW19 3TZ UK. They range in price from £160 to £220, with each image measuring 30cm by 40cm, on 40cm by 50cm paper.

Philatelic items are popular items to buy at Antarctic stations. They are suitably embossed or stamped with the station's name and, perhaps, the date of your visit. These are usually beautifully illustrated miniature artworks, and have the advantage of being highly portable. Be prepared to pay, however: one popular station at King George Island charges US$20 for a single envelope covered with postmarked Antarctic stamps from six countries.

Antarctic calendars are perennially popular. The best is the beautiful calendar produced by Colin and Betty Monteath's Hedgehog House New Zealand (☎/fax 64-3-332-8790, www.hedgehoghouse.com), 398 Barrington St, PO Box 33-152, Christchurch, New Zealand. This 23cm by 33cm beauty features unusual photographs of icebergs, wildlife and scenery. Cost: NZ$15; overseas economy post orders, NZ$17.

A fine selection of Antarctic items can be found via the Internet. The first and best place to look is The Antarctic Connection (☎ 603-383-8933, manager@antarcticconnection.com, www.antarcticconnection.com), PO Box 538, Jackson, NH 03846 USA, which declares 'Antarctica is closer than you think!' It carries a wide range of maps, books, videos, photos, posters and gifts.

For those who can't resist penguin kitsch (and it *is* kitschy!), Penguin Place (☎ 718-855-5432, toll-free 877-736-4946, penguin@bway.net, www.penguin-place.com), 220 Water St, Brooklyn, NY 11201 USA, offers penguins on everything: shirts, hats, ties, jewelry, wristwatches, clocks, rugs, shower curtains, showercaps, nightshirts, pillowcases, beach towels, bags, socks, underwear, umbrellas, lunch boxes, bumper stickers, magnets, puzzles, air fresheners, pencils, pens, computer mouse pads, books, greeting cards, coasters, Christmas ornaments, oven mitts, rubber stamps, wrapping paper, coffee mugs, light switch covers, night-lights, bath mats – even 15cm-tall 'wedding cake toppers' (US$27.95) and Limoges porcelain figurines (US$189.95). Penguin Place also has a retail store called Next Stop South Pole (☎/fax 410-659-0860), 301 Light St, Baltimore, MD 21202 USA, in Baltimore's Inner Harbor.

Getting There & Away

Choosing your trip is an individual matter, but there are several general things you should know. First, see the Planning section in the Facts for the Visitor chapter, especially 'Questions to Ask Your Tour Operator.' Second, use the information in this chapter as a guide *only*. Itineraries and destinations change from year to year and from company to company, as each tour operator strives to come up with the best mix of trips for its customers. Ships may also change from year to year, as different companies charter different vessels – though some tour operators either own their own ship or charter the same one year after year.

Obviously, particular details – especially prices – also change, so be sure to call several tour operators for their free brochures – or visit their websites, which in many cases are very good. Read through them carefully – and compare your options. Don't be afraid to ask the tour operator as many questions

as you can think of. As one tour brochure puts it, you are making an 'investment' in your Antarctic cruise – although with some of the prices charged, it's more likely that you might have had to *liquidate* a few investments!

SEA
Cruises

One of the most important factors in the large increase in Antarctic tourist numbers during the late 1980s and early '90s was the collapse of the Soviet Union. Economic hard times increased the Soviet scientific academies' hunger for hard currency, enabling Western companies to lease many ice-strengthened or even ice-breaking research ships for favorable rates. This helps to explain why so many tour vessels visiting the Antarctic today are Russian-flagged ships. Note that the same ship may have different passenger capacities for different cruises, based on the varying staff accommodation requirements on each cruise.

The following companies offer cruises to the Antarctic. Those marked with an asterisk (*) are members of IAATO, the International Association of Antarctica Tour Operators (see the Useful Organizations section in the Facts for the Visitor chapter) – and are most recommended.

Abercrombie & Kent* A&K operates *Explorer*, an ice-strengthened ship commissioned by Antarctic tourism pioneer Lars-Eric Lindblad and originally known as *Lindblad Explorer*. The 100-passenger ship has sailed to Antarctica every year since 1970, making it the grandame of Antarctic cruising. It was refurbished in 1992, with twin cabins all offering outside views, two lower berths, and private shower and toilet facilities. A&K offers voyages to Antarctica, the Falkland Islands and South Georgia each season.

Itineraries offered include 'Antarctica' (14 days, with five days in Antarctica), with fares beginning at US$5995; 'Antarctica and the

Falkland Islands' (16 days, with six in Antarctica), beginning at US$6995; 'An Adventurer's Ice Cruise' (17 days, with seven days in Antarctica, plus the Falklands), beginning at US$7595; and 'Antarctica, the Falklands and South Georgia,' including the South Orkney Islands (19 days, 15 nights aboard ship) with fares beginning at US$8995.

The 35-day 'Lost Islands of the Atlantic' cruise departs from the Canary Islands, visiting the Cape Verde Islands, Ascension Island, St Helena, Tristan da Cunha, Nightingale Island, Gough Island, South Georgia and the Falklands, with disembarkation in Stanley. Fares begin at US$4950.

Abercrombie & Kent (☎ 630-954-2944, toll-free 800-323-7308, fax 630-572-1833, www.abercrombiekent.com) is at 1520 Kensington Rd, Oak Brook, IL 60523-2156 USA.

Adventure Associates* Adventure Associates operates a limited number of voyages each season from Tasmania to Macquarie Island and the Ross Sea region, as well as several voyages in the Antarctic Peninsula region. Its ships include the 78-passenger *Akademik Sergey Vavilov*, the 49-passenger *Professor Multanovskiy* and the 114-passenger icebreaker *Kapitan Khlebnikov*.

Sample itineraries include 'Antarctic Peninsula' for either nine nights (beginning at US$3950) or 12 nights (US$5250), both on *Vavilov*; or 9 nights on *Multanovskiy*, with prices beginning at US$3050. Eleven-night voyages are also available.

'Antarctic Peninsula, South Georgia & the Falklands' offers 18 nights for US$7650 on *Vavilov*, or aboard *Multanovskiy*, with prices beginning at US$6450. Voyages lasting 19 nights are also available.

Three trips are offered aboard the icebreaker *Khlebnikov*, which also uses onboard helicopters for flightseeing and excursions to the Dry Valleys. All cabins include bathrooms. 'Lords of Antarctica – Emperor Penguin Adventure' is a 25-day trip visiting the Ross Sea region, Macquarie Island and New Zealand's sub-Antarctic islands; prices begin at US$11,250. 'Voyage to the Farthest South – Bay of Whales, Ross Ice Shelf and McMurdo Sound' is a 24-day trip to the Ross Sea region, Macquarie Island and New Zealand's sub-Antarctic islands; prices begin at US$9950. 'The Great Explorers – Mawson, Shackleton and Scott' is a 25-day trip to the Ross Sea region, Commonwealth Bay, Macquarie Island and New Zealand's sub-Antarctic islands; prices start at US$11,250.

Adventure Assoc (☎ 61-2-9389-7466, fax 61-2-9369-1853, mail@adventureassociates .com, www.adventureassociates.com) is at 197 Oxford St Mall (PO Box 612), Bondi Junction, New South Wales 2022 Australia.

Adventure Network International While its main business is air travel to the interior of the Antarctic continent, ANI also offers two unique ship-based trips. A 14-day 'Peninsula Cruise & Climb' aboard the 50-passenger *Akademik Shuleykin* stops in two places along the Antarctic Peninsula, spending two days at each to allow mountain climbing, skiing and camping. Prices begin at US$7500 per person. A 20-day 'Shackleton/South Georgia Cruise' (from US$8600) on *Shuleykin* allows qualified participants to attempt to retrace Shackleton's crossing of the island. Meanwhile, the other passengers visit the numerous South Georgia sites associated with Shackleton's *Endurance* expedition.

Adventure Network (☎ 44-1494-671-808, fax 44-1494-671-725, adventurenetwork@ compuserve.com, www.adventure-network .com) is based at Canon House, 27 London End, Beaconsfield, Buckinghamshire HP9 2HN, UK or, from October until the end of January only, at 935 Arauco, Punta Arenas, Chile (☎ 56-61-247-735, fax 56-61-226-167).

Aurora Expeditions* Aurora offers a much wider range of activities in Antarctica than most other sea-based Antarctic tour operators: scuba diving, sea kayaking, mountain climbing and camping. Since 1996, mountaineers and trekkers on the company's 'Climbers and Photographers' expeditions to the Peninsula have climbed nine peaks, making several first ascents. In 1998 Aurora offered the first Antarctic scuba diving trips for tourists, giving visitors exquisite views of sea spiders, brilliantly colored starfish and the iridescent white undersides of icebergs, among other sights previously seen only by scientists.

The 13-day 'Spring Explosion – Falkland Islands & Antarctic Peninsula' trip on 52-passenger *Professor Molchanov* offers optional scuba diving and sea kayaking. Up to 12 paddlers can be accommodated each voyage. The number of divers is also limited for safety. An ice dive master oversees the diving, which takes place in the West Falklands, the Peninsula and the South Shetlands. Prices begin at US$3790, with a US$500 diving surcharge and a US$600 kayaking surcharge.

Divers must have extensive experience and at least advanced open water qualifications or equivalent. They must have dived actively within the last 12 months and completed a dry suit diving course. All divers will be interviewed to ensure that they have the necessary skills for Antarctic diving. Before diving in Antarctica, all will undergo a check-out dive in the Falklands with the company's dive master. All equipment except tanks must be supplied by the diver.

Paddlers must have at least five years open water sea kayaking experience and must be competent with their rolling techniques. Plastic double kayaks, paddles, life jackets, safety equipment, dry bags and pogies (insulated mitts that attach to the paddles and keep hands warm) are supplied. Dry suits are required and will be available for rental aboard ship. A guide accompanies the paddlers and radio contact is maintained with the ship.

Other itineraries on *Molchanov* include the 19-day 'South Georgia and the Antarctic Peninsula,' which also visits the Falklands and the South Orkneys; prices begin at US$6190. 'Antarctic Peninsula' trips, lasting

Life Aboard a Polar Ship

Voyages to polar seas are different from other sorts of travel, and even seasoned 'cruisers' may need to make some adjustments. Some people find shipboard life difficult to handle at first, feeling a bit claustrophobic. This can be heightened in Antarctica, since the cruise ships are small and relatively spartan compared to the lavish floating palaces that ply the Caribbean, Mediterranean and other seas. It's also completely normal to feel lethargic and sluggish during the several days of sailing required to reach Antarctica.

Typically, a printed bulletin listing the day's planned activities is distributed the night before to let you know what's ahead. It helps to attend the educational lectures and video screenings, which are given, in part, to relieve the monotony of long ocean crossings. Enterprising passengers will find activities to occupy themselves – seabird watching, iceberg spotting, visits to the bridge or engine room, diary writing, reading – but even these can get stale after three or four days. Don't worry: Antarctica is worth the wait.

International law requires that every ship hold a lifeboat drill within 24 hours of sailing. These drills are serious and are mandatory for all passengers. Each cabin should contain a sign or card telling which lifeboat station the occupants should use. There will also be a life vest for each person in the cabin; these are usually equipped with a whistle, reflective patches and a battery-powered beacon light, which starts flashing automatically upon contact with saltwater. The universal signal to proceed to lifeboat stations is seven short blasts on the ship's bell or horn, followed by a long blast. This signal may be repeated several times for the lifeboat drill. Since there is only one such drill held during each voyage, if you ever hear the signal a second time during your voyage, it is the *real thing*. You should go immediately to your cabin to pick up your life vest and warm clothing and then straight to your lifeboat station to await instructions from the crew.

Extra care is needed when moving about any ship, but passengers on Antarctic cruises especially should keep in mind the rule of 'one hand for the ship,' always keeping one hand free to

11 days, begin at US$3490, with options for kayaking and camping.

Camping is offered, for one night only, on each of the Peninsula trips. There is no surcharge for camping, but passengers are encouraged to bring their own sleeping bags. Because Aurora's environmental impact statement is scrutinized by the Australian Antarctic Division, the company has developed guidelines for this relatively new tourist activity in the Antarctic. A portable toilet is brought to the campsite and toilet waste is taken back to the ship at the end of each camp. No food is taken ashore – passengers eat dinner aboard ship beforehand. Small two/three-person tents are brought ashore, along with sleeping bags and mats. Very often people choose to sleep in the open air. Staff members who join the camping party maintain all-night radio contact with the ship, which moves away from the site. Most campsites do not have wildlife, but camping at those that do always takes place at least 200m away from any nesting birds. Camping is only done on snow or bare rock, never on gravelly ground that could show signs of tent sites. Each site is used only once per season.

The 12-day 'Expedition for Climbers and Photographers,' also on *Molchanov*, includes climbing and camping options, with extra time at each location for photographers and climbers, who are accompanied by three experienced guides. Prices begin at US$3790.

Aurora (☎ 61-2 -9252-1033, fax 61-2-9252-1373, toll-free in Australia 800-637-688, auroraex@auroraexpeditions.com.au, www.auroraexpeditions.com.au) is at Level 1, 37 George St, Sydney, New South Wales 2000 Australia.

Clipper Cruise Line* Clipper operates the 122-passenger *Clipper Adventurer* (formerly

---

Life Aboard a Polar Ship

grab a railing or other support should the ship roll suddenly. You may notice that even some berths on the ship (usually those running fore-and-aft) are equipped with airline-style seat belts for use when seas get a bit heavy. Take care not only when climbing steep ladders and stairs, but when in wide-open 'flat' areas such as the bridge, dining room or lecture hall, where a sudden slam into a chair or table could result in a broken arm or leg. Although the rolling motion of a ship on the open ocean tends to be fairly regular and predictable, a vessel pushing through ice can lurch suddenly, pitching unaware passengers onto their noses. Closet and bathroom doors likewise can become dangerous swinging projectiles in high seas. You should also take care not to accidentally curl your fingers around doorjambs, as a fractured finger can result if the door closes suddenly. Decks can be slippery with rain, snow or oil, and you can easily trip on raised doorsills, stanchions and other shipboard tackle.

Cameras or video equipment should be securely stowed in the cabin. The best place to put such valuables, especially at night, is either on the floor or closet-bottom. You don't want the sound of your Leica shattering as it hits the floor after flying off your desk to be the first noise that alerts you to the onset of a sudden storm.

Antarctic tourist ships generally maintain an 'open bridge,' welcoming passengers to the navigation and steering area. The bridge will be closed during tricky navigation and whenever the pilot is aboard or the ship is in port. Etiquette demands that no food or drink be brought to the bridge, especially alcohol, and going barefoot on the bridge is also not appreciated. Keep your voice down; excessive noise interferes with communication between the navigator and helmsman. The low humming sound audible on the bridge is the ship's gyrocompass. Of course, it's always unwise to touch any equipment without being invited to do so by an officer of the watch. One further warning: Sailors are a superstitious lot, and whistling anywhere on a ship is considered bad luck – seriously. Tradition says that a person whistling is calling up the wind, and that a storm will result.

Alla Tarasova), which in 1998 underwent a US$13 million conversion in a Danish shipyard. All cabins include private bathrooms.

Three itineraries are offered: the 15-day 'Antarctic Peninsula,' beginning at US$7330; the 17-day 'Antarctic Peninsula and the Falkland Islands,' beginning at US$7780; and the 23-day 'Antarctic Peninsula, South Georgia, Shag Rocks and South Orkney Islands' beginning at US$10,580. Airfare is included in these prices.

Clipper (☎ 314-727-2929, toll-free 800-325-0010, fax 314-727-6576, smallship@aol.com, www.clippercruise.com) is at 7711 Bonhomme Ave, St Louis, MO 63105-1956 USA.

Expeditions Inc* Expeditions Inc is a provisional (new) member of IAATO. It operates two ships, the 36-passenger *Alexey Maryshev* and the 36-passenger *Gregoriy Mikheev*.

Sample itineraries include an 11-day (10 nights aboard ship) Peninsula trip, beginning at US$4390. A 19-day (18 nights aboard)

'Antarctica, South Georgia and the Falkland Islands' trip begins at US$7295. The ships themselves are available for charter for US$8000 per day including crew, Zodiacs, chef and food.

Expeditions Inc (☎ 541-330-2454, toll-free 888-484-2244, fax 541-330-2456, expeditions@exp-usa.com, www.expeditioncruises.com) is at 133 SW Century Dr, Suite 100, Bend, OR 97702-1021 USA.

Hapag-Lloyd Kreuzfahrten* Hapag-Lloyd merged with Hanseatic Tours/Cruises in 1997. Hapag-Lloyd operates two ice-strengthened ships: the 184-passenger *Hanseatic* and the 164-passenger *Bremen* (formerly *Frontier Spirit)*. Both offer more luxurious accommodations than most other Antarctic ships. All staterooms and suites have closed-circuit color TV, minibars and minirefrigerators, marble bathrooms with full-size tub and shower, built-in hair dryers, in-cabin satellite telephones, and either two

Helicopter Safety

Some ships that visit Antarctica carry helicopters, both for reconnoitering the pack ice and, of course, for carrying passengers ashore and on sightseeing flights. This is a spectacular way to view Antarctica and to get to less accessible places farther inland such as the Dry Valleys.

The cruise staff will hold a briefing before your first helicopter flight to alert you to safety regulations. The rules are simple:

• Wear a lifejacket in case of a forced water landing.

• Listen to directions from staff regarding entry and exit from the helicopter landing area. Pilots are justifiably concerned about people accidentally wandering into the landing zone.

• Keep away from the rear of the helicopter, where the rapidly spinning (and deadly) tail rotor can be hard to see. Always approach the helicopter from the front or side.

• Stay low when entering or exiting, because a sudden windshift could force the rotor down. For the same reason, never raise your hands or arms above your head.

• Fasten clothing, hair, jewelry and bags securely before entering the landing zone; the rotor's powerful downblast will blow away any loose items.

• Protect your eyes and cameras from dust, sand and gravel that are blown by the rotor downblast.

lower beds or – a rare luxury among expedition ships – a double bed. Certain cabins and suites also feature queen-size beds and their own private veranda; private butler service is available for deluxe suites and staterooms. Among public amenities aboard, an indoor jacuzzi might be especially appreciated on the Antarctic trips.

Sample itineraries include the 16-day (11 nights aboard ship) 'Antarctica and the Weddell Sea,' with prices beginning at DM10,900 (deutsche marks), with a 15-day version offered at DM10,500. The 14-day (10 nights aboard ship) 'Antarctica' begins at DM9950. The 16-day (11 nights aboard) 'Antarctica and the Falkland Islands' begins at DM12,300, while a 15-day version begins at DM11,310. 'Antarctica and South Georgia,' a 20-day trip (16 nights aboard) begins at DM13,450, and a 22-day trip visiting Antarctica, the South Orkneys, South Georgia and the Falklands with 19 nights aboard, begins at DM16,490.

Hapag-Lloyd (☎ 49-40-3001-4600, fax 49-40-3001-4601, info@hapag-lloyd.com, www .hapag-lloyd.com) is at Ballindamm 25, 20095 Hamburg, Germany.

Heritage Expeditions* Heritage Expeditions operates the 46-passenger, ice-reinforced (not icebreaker) *Akademik Shokalskiy*, which was refurbished in November 1998. It also offers scuba diving as an option.

Among the itineraries offered is a 13-day 'Sub-Antarctic Islands' trip, which visits Campbell Island, Macquarie Island, Auckland Islands and The Snares, beginning at US$4460. A six-night 'Sub-Antarctic Islands' trip visiting Campbell Island, the Auckland Islands and The Snares begins at US$1933.

A 16-night 'Ultimate Down Under Birding Expedition' visits The Snares, Auckland Islands, Macquarie Island, Campbell Island, Antipodes Islands, Bounty Islands and the Chatham Islands. Prices begin at US$6303. A 22-night 'In the Footsteps of Scott and Shackleton' expedition visits Campbell Island, Ross Sea region, the very rarely visited Scott Island, and the Auckland Islands, beginning at US$8669. A 29-night 'South to Antarctica – In the Footsteps of Sir James Clark Ross' expedition visits Campbell Island, the Ross Sea region, the Auckland Islands and Macquarie Island, and begins at US$10,114.

Diving is an option on both the 'Sub-Antarctic Islands' and the 'South to Antarctica' voyages. Diving on the Sub-Antarctic Islands trip will cost an additional US$250, with nine dives planned, including night dives and wreck dives. All dives will be less than 39m. All divers must have a minimum of 100 logged dives and be certified as a PADI Rescue Diver or higher (equivalent qualifications accepted). Heritage will provide air tanks; divers must bring their own gauges, regulator, octopus, wet suit (for the hardy) or dry suit, mask, snorkel, fins, gloves, booties, dive knife, flashlights, cyalume light sticks and buoyancy control device with whistle attached. For calculating the time one can safely remain underwater without requiring decompression, a dive computer is highly recommended.

For the 'South to Antarctica' trip, diving will cost an extra US$450, with 10 dives planned, including under-ice diving in McMurdo Sound, as well as in open water and offshore from historic huts at Cape Evans. All dives will be made from an open inflatable boat, and only during perfectly calm conditions. Divers (two down at a time, each on a lifeline) will be assisted by a tender, dive master and boatman. Diving will be terminated if dangerous marine mammals (eg, killer whales) are active in the area. The same visitor rules apply as when ashore anywhere in Antarctica, meaning no artifacts or natural history specimens can be removed. Divers must be certified at least as a PADI Rescue Diver or equivalent and must have completed a diving medical examination in the past 12 months. Twin valve air cylinders, air fills, lifelines, weight belts and weights will be supplied by Heritage. Divers must bring their own full-length dry suit, gloves, two separate first- and second-stage regulators, cylinder contents gauge, depth gauge, watch, fins, mask, snorkel and knife. Because the sea temperature will be -2°C, all equipment should be mechanical, and dry suits should be completely checked out. Divers should

Air Travel Glossary

Cancellation Penalties If you have to cancel or change a discounted ticket, there are often heavy penalties involved; insurance can sometimes be taken out against these penalties. Some airlines impose penalties on regular tickets as well, particularly against 'no-show' passengers.

Courier Fares Businesses often need to send urgent documents or freight securely and quickly. Courier companies hire people to accompany the package through customs and, in return, offer a discount ticket which is sometimes a phenomenal bargain. However, you may have to surrender all your baggage allowance and take only carry-on luggage.

Full Fares Airlines traditionally offer 1st class (coded F), business class (coded J) and economy class (coded Y) tickets. These days there are so many promotional and discounted fares available that few passengers pay full economy fare.

Lost Tickets If you lose your airline ticket an airline will usually treat it like a traveler's check and, after inquiries, issue you another one. Legally, however, an airline is entitled to treat it like cash and if you lose it then it's gone forever. Take good care of your tickets.

Onward Tickets An entry requirement for many countries is that you have a ticket out of the country. If you're unsure of your next move, the easiest solution is to buy the cheapest onward ticket to a neighboring country or a ticket from a reliable airline which can later be refunded if you do not use it.

Open-Jaw Tickets These are return tickets where you fly out to one place but return from another. If available, this can save you backtracking to your arrival point.

Overbooking Since every flight has some passengers who fail to show up, airlines often book more passengers than they have seats. Usually excess passengers make up for the no-shows, but occasionally somebody gets 'bumped' onto the next available flight. Guess who it is most likely to be? The passengers who check in late.

Promotional Fares These are officially discounted fares, available from travel agencies or direct from the airline.

Reconfirmation If you don't reconfirm your flight at least 72 hours prior to departure, the airline may delete your name from the passenger list. Call to find out if your airline requires reconfirmation.

Restrictions Discounted tickets often have various restrictions on them – such as needing to be paid for in advance and incurring a penalty to be altered. Others are restrictions on the minimum and maximum period you must be away.

Round-the-World Tickets RTW tickets give you a limited period (usually a year) in which to circumnavigate the globe. You can go anywhere the carrying airlines go, as long as you don't backtrack. The number of stopovers or total number of separate flights is decided before you set off and they usually cost a bit more than a basic return flight.

Transferred Tickets Airline tickets cannot be transferred from one person to another. Travelers sometimes try to sell the return half of their ticket, but officials can ask you to prove that you are the person named on the ticket. On an international flight tickets are compared with passports.

Travel Periods Ticket prices vary with the time of year. There is a low (off-peak) season and a high (peak) season, and often a low-shoulder season and a high-shoulder season as well. Usually the fare depends on your outward flight – if you depart in the high season and return in the low season, you pay the high-season fare.

have completed two dives using all of the above equipment within the two months previous to the voyage.

Heritage Expeditions (☎ 64-3-338-9944, toll-free in NZ 0800-262-8873, toll-free in Australia 800-143-585, or fax 64-3-338-3311, info@heritage-expeditions.com, www.heritage-expeditions.com) is at PO Box 6282, Christchurch, New Zealand.

Lindblad Special Expeditions* Special Expeditions' inaugural Antarctic voyages took place in 1998, aboard the 120-passenger *Caledonian Star.*

A 15-day 'Antarctica' trip visits the Peninsula, with prices beginning at US$6890. 'Antarctica and the Falkland Islands,' a 19-day trip, starts at US$8980, while the 25-day 'Antarctica, the Falkland Islands & South Georgia,' which also visits the South Orkney Islands starts at US$11,980.

Lindblad Special Expeditions (☎ 212-765-7740, toll-free 800-397-3348, fax 212-265-3770, explore@specialexpeditions.com, www.expeditions.com) is at 720 Fifth Ave, New York, NY 10019 USA.

Marine Expeditions* Marine Expeditions operates a variety of vessels on voyages from Ushuaia to Antarctica, the Falkland Islands and South Georgia, including a number of nine-day Peninsula voyages.

Marine boasts that it offers 'the best prices available anywhere,' and this is true. For one thing, airfare from North America is included in the price of its programs, which is not usual with Antarctic tours.

Sample itineraries include a 14-day (eight nights aboard ship) 'Antarctic Peninsula' trip, beginning at US$2645. 'Extended Antarctica' trips last 16 days (10 nights aboard) and begin at US$2995. 'Antarctic Peninsula and the Falkland Islands,' 20 days (14 nights aboard ship), begins at US$3995, while a 'Falklands, South Georgia & Antarctic Peninsula' voyage lasts 24 days (18 nights aboard) and begins at US$6315.

Marine's 49-day (45 nights aboard) 'Remote Islands of the Southern Atlantic' cruises stop at Gibraltar, Madeira, Canary Islands, Cape Verde, Ascension Island, St

Helena, Tristan Da Cunha, Nightingale and Inaccessible Islands, South Georgia, the Falkland Islands and Ushuaia. Prices begin at US$2995. These long voyages up or down the Atlantic are actually 'repositioning cruises' at the beginning or end of the season, when the ships are making their way to or from the Arctic, where they are used during the Antarctic winter. Since the ships have to travel these routes anyway, whether or not they have passengers, companies can offer low fares. Indeed, they have to offer low fares to lure people aboard for such long voyages, with so few landfalls.

Marine also offers a standby rate for travelers joining a voyage in Ushuaia. For the eight-night Antarctic trip, the standby fare is US$1995; for the 10-night trip, US$2295; and for the 14-night trip, US$2595. The fares can be purchased up to 21 days before sailing, either by applying dockside or at Rumbo Sur (☎ 21139 or 22275 or 22441, fax 34788 or 30699, Av San Martín 342), Marine's agent in Ushuaia (see the map in the Antarctic Gateways chapter).

Marine Expeditions (☎ 416-964-5751, toll-free 800-263-9147, fax 416-964-2366, info@marineex.com, www.marineex.com) is at 890 Yonge St, 3rd Fl, Toronto, Ontario M4W 3P4 Canada.

Mountain Travel-Sobek* This company offers cruises of various lengths, on both the 117-passenger *Ioffe* and the 52-passenger *Akademik Shuleykin* (which the company calls MTS *Quest*). The 15-day 'Explore Antarctica' program takes in the Peninsula, with 10 nights aboard ship, beginning at US$5295. The 19-day (14 nights aboard) 'Antarctic Circle and Beyond' visits the Peninsula and attempts to cross 66°33'S; prices begin at US$7195. 'In the Realm of Shackleton' visits the Peninsula, South Georgia and the South Orkneys on a 26-day trip (21 nights aboard), beginning at US$6945.

Mountain Travel-Sobek (☎ 510-527-8100, toll-free 888-687-6235, fax 510-525-7710, info@mtsobek.com, www.mtsobek.com) is one of the founding members of IAATO. It's at 6420 Fairmount Ave, El Cerrito, CA 94530-3606 USA.

Oceanwide Expeditions* Oceanwide, a provisional (new) member of IAATO, operates the 30-passenger *Victor Buynitskiy* and the 52-passenger *Professor Molchanov*, with some voyages including a scuba diving option.

A 12-night 'Falklands and Antarctic' trip on *Molchanov* begins at US$4390. A 10-day 'Antarctic Peninsula' trip on *Molchanov* begins at US$3690. An 11-day Peninsula trip is also available.

A 19-night 'South Georgia and Antarctic' trip on *Buynitskiy* begins at US$5970, while an 11-night 'Antarctic Peninsula' trip on *Buynitskiy* begins at US$3780. A 12-night 'Polar Circle' trip on *Buynitskiy* begins at US$4720.

A maximum of 20 scuba divers can be accommodated on selected voyages for a surcharge of US$500 each. Divers must be at the Advanced level, be familiar with ice diving and dry suit diving (at least 20 dives) and supply a doctor's statement confirming their health for diving. Divers supply their own dry suit, mask, underwater garments, dry gloves or extra under gloves, two freeze-protected regulators, pressure gauge, buoyancy control device, depth gauge, watch or dive computer, knife, fins, snorkel and weight belt.

Oceanwide Expeditions (☎ 31-118-410410, fax 31-118-410417, expeditions@ocnwide.com, www.ocnwide.com) is at Bellamypark 9, 4381 CG Vlissingen, The Netherlands.

Orient Lines Orient operates the Bahamas-flagged luxury liner *Marco Polo*, formerly known as *Alexandr Pushkin*, built in 1965 in the former East Germany and refurbished in 1991-92. Its capacity is 845 passengers (plus 340 crew members), although it 'only' takes 550 to 600 passengers on Antarctic cruises. Because these numbers exceed the limit of 400 passengers set by IAATO, Orient Lines is not an IAATO member.

Alone among the vessels visiting the Far South, *Marco Polo* has a casino, piano bar and nightly entertainment, including cabaret shows. Cabin amenities include TVs, hair dryers, international direct-dial telephones and, in some cabins, personal refrigerators. 'Shipboard delights,' one recent passenger writes, 'included bridge lessons, tango danc-

ing with Armando and Jeanette, and slot machines – to my amazement, there were people on board only for the cruise, who never bothered to go ashore at all!'

It's just as well that not all *Marco Polo* passengers want to go on landings, since only 100 people are allowed ashore at one time, to comply with IAATO guidelines. Because of the large amounts of time required to land so many passengers in groups limited to 100 people, *Marco Polo*'s itineraries are designed with few landings.

Eleven-day 'Antarctic Peninsula' programs include eight nights aboard, beginning at US$3562. The misnamed 'Grand Antarctic Circumnavigation' (26 days; 23 nights aboard) visits only the Peninsula and the Ross Sea, beginning at US$6887. 'Antarctica and New Zealand' visits the Peninsula, Ross Sea region and New Zealand during a 37-day trip (34 nights aboard ship), starting at US$8407.

Orient Lines (☎ 954-527-6660, toll-free 800-333-7300, fax 954-527-6657, info@orientlines .com, www.orientlines.com) is at 1510 SE 17 St, Ft Lauderdale, FL 33316 USA.

Peregrine Expeditions* Peregrine, a provisional (new) member of IAATO, operates the 52-passenger *Akademik Boris Petrov* and also offers camping and kayaking.

Sample itineraries include an 11-day 'Antarctic Encounter,' beginning at US$4050; a 10-day 'Antarctic Expedition' beginning at US$4090; and a nine-day 'Antarctic Adventure' beginning at US$3190. A 19-day 'Antarctica, the Falklands and South Georgia' trip begins at US$6990.

Optional overnight camping and kayaking cost nothing extra, with all gear provided by Peregrine. Paddlers must have previous experience.

Peregrine (☎ 61-3-9662-2700, fax 61-3-9662-2422, travelcentre@peregrine.net.au, www.peregrine.net.au) is at 258 Lonsdale St, Melbourne, Victoria 3000 Australia.

Quark Expeditions Using some of the world's most powerful (Russian-flagged) ice-breakers, Quark has made several pioneering tourist cruises, including the first to the emperor penguin rookeries of the Weddell

Sea and, in 1996-97, the first tourist circumnavigation of Antarctica, a 66-day, 19,300km odyssey aboard *Kapitan Khlebnikov*, the cost of which began at US$29,900 per person for a shared triple room. *(Kapitan Khlebnikov* boasts 24,000 horsepower and a 45mm-thick hull; it also carries two helicopters.) Alas, Quark has no immediate plans to repeat the circumnavigation.

Sample itineraries include 'Classic Antarctica,' which visits the Peninsula and lasts either 11 days (starting at US$3795 on the 80-passenger *Akademik Sergey Vavilov)* or 12 days (starting at US$4195 on *Vavilov* or at US$3295 on the 49-passenger *Professor Multanovskiy).* The 13-day (10 nights aboard) 'Antarctica and the Falklands' begins at US$4595 on *Vavilov*, while the 20-day (18 nights aboard) 'Antarctica, South Georgia and the Falklands' begins at US$7295 on *Vavilov* or at US$6195 on *Multanovskiy.*

The 'Connoisseurs Cruise to Antarctica and Islands of the South Atlantic,' a 20-day trip with 18 nights aboard *Vavilov*, includes the Peninsula, South Georgia, South Orkneys and the Falklands. Prices start at US$7295.

'In the Footsteps of Scott and Shackleton,' aboard the icebreaker *Khlebnikov*, visits Macquarie Island, the Balleny Islands, the Ross Sea region, Campbell Island and the Auckland Islands, beginning at US$10,995.

Quark Expeditions has two offices. In the US (☎ 203-656-0499, toll-free 800-356-5699, fax 203-655-6623, quarkexpeditions@compuserve.com, www.quark-expeditions.com), the address is 980 Post Rd, Darien, CT 06820-4509 USA. Quark in the UK (☎ 44-1494-464-080, fax 44-1494-449-739, enquiry@quarkexpeditions.co.uk, www.quark-expeditions.com) is at Crendon St 19A, High Wycombe, Bucks, HP13 6LJ England.

Society Expeditions* Society operates the 138-passenger *World Discoverer*, veteran of nearly 300 Antarctic voyages since 1977.

Sample itineraries include 'The Great White Continent,' which lasts 14 days (10 nights aboard) and visits the Peninsula, beginning at US$3990.

A 22-day (17 nights aboard) 'Antarctica, South Georgia, South Orkneys and Falklands' voyage begins at US$5870, while an 18-night version begins at US$6110.

Society Expeditions (☎ 206-728-9400, toll-free 800-548-8669, fax 206-728-2301, societyexp@aol.com, www.societyexpeditions.com), one of the seven founding members of IAATO, is at 2001 Western Ave, Suite 300, Seattle, WA 98121-2114 USA.

WildWings* This company has operated many bird and wildlife tours to Antarctica since 1991.

Sample itineraries include 'Antarctic Peninsula' cruises lasting from eight to 11 days (starting at £2579) aboard ships including the 52-passenger *Professor Molchanov*, the 78-passenger *Akademik Sergey Vavilov* and the 138-passenger *World Discoverer*. 'Antarctica & The Falklands' itineraries (11-15 days) start from £2869. 'Antarctica, The Falklands and South Georgia' trips (15-19 days) start at £3049, while 'Sub-Antarctic Islands of New Zealand & Australia' (15 days) on the 46-passenger *Akademik Shokalskiy*, starts at £3649. The 'Atlantic Odyssey' is a repositioning trip for *Mochanov*, returning to Europe via Tristan da Cunha, St Helena and Ascension Islands, beginning at £2800. 'Far Side' and 'Ross Sea' voyages (20-24 days) on the 114-passenger icebreaker *Kapitan Khlebnikov*, begin at £5929.

WildWings (☎ 44-117-984-8040, fax 44-117-961-0200, wildinfo@wildwings.co.uk, www.wildwings.co.uk) is at International House, Bank Rd, Kingswood, Bristol BS15 8LX, UK.

Zegrahm Expeditions* Zegrahm offers cruises on several different vessels.

Sample itineraries include a 21-day 'Antarctica, South Georgia, and The Falkland Islands,' which also covers the South Orkneys, on either the 138-passenger *World Discoverer* or the 120-passenger *Clipper Adventurer*, starting at US$11,490.

The 20-day 'Circumnavigation of South Georgia & the Falkland Islands' aboard the 100-passenger *Explorer* includes the rare opportunity to spend a full week at South Georgia, with stops at Grytviken, King Haakon Bay, Cape Rosa (where Shackleton and his men arrived after their voyage from Elephant Island in *James Caird*), Peggotty Camp (from which Shackleton and his two companions set out to cross the island) and Stromness whaling station (where they finally received aid). Prices start at US$7990.

Zegrahm (☎ 206-285-4000, toll-free 800-628-8747, fax 206-285-5037, zoe@zeco.com, www.zeco.com), a founding member of IAATO, is at 192 Nickerson St, Suite 200, Seattle, WA 98109-1632 USA.

Yacht Voyages

A small but growing handful of visitors reach Antarctica aboard private vessels. All are sailboats (though obviously equipped with auxiliary engines), and some have even wintered in sheltered anchorages such as Yankee Harbor at Greenwich Island or near Palmer Station on the Peninsula. In three decades of Antarctic cruising, there have been about 150 yacht voyages to The Ice. For some reason, this type of travel particularly seems to appeal to the French, who have made up the majority of yacht visitors to Antarctica. About 125 fare-paying passengers visit Antarctica by yacht each year.

Although the national Antarctic programs cannot regulate yacht tourism, since Antarctica is open to everyone, research stations are no longer instantly hospitable whenever a yacht turns up on their doorstep. Where once they welcomed the rare visitors from the outside, these days traffic is so heavy at most stations that advance notice of several weeks or even months is required for a station tour, though there are some exceptions, mainly among the smaller countries operating in Antarctica.

Sailing a yacht to Antarctica is obviously not something one undertakes lightly. An old sailor's adage has it that 'Beyond 40° S, there is no law . . . Beyond 50° S, there is no God.' And, by tradition, writes Alan Gurney in *Below the Convergence* (see the Books section in the Facts for the Visitor chapter): 'Those who have rounded Cape Horn under sail can take their after-dinner drink with

one foot upon the table; those who have sailed across the polar circles can drink with both feet upon the table.'

It would be foolish to attempt to sail to Antarctica without taking one – or, preferably, both – of the following: *The Antarctic Pilot*, fifth edition (1997), published by Britain's Hydrographer of the Navy; and *Sailing Directions (Planning Guide & Enroute) for Antarctica*, third edition, 1997, published by the US National Imagery and Mapping Center (NIMA reference number SDPUB200). *The Antarctic Pilot* (US$70) is much superior, with more comprehensive entries, as well as a hardcover binding and an index, both of which *Sailing Directions for Antarctica* (US$21.25) unfortunately lacks. Both are available from New York Nautical, 140 West Broadway, New York, NY 10013 USA (☎ 212-962-4522, fax 212-406-8420).

Anyone considering a yacht voyage to Antarctica should also read Sally and Jérôme Poncet's excellent 60-page *Southern Ocean Cruising*. This guide, published privately in 1991, is available from the Poncets at Beaver Island (☎ 500-42316, fax 500-22659, sallyponcet@yahoo.com), c/o Post Office Stanley, Falkland Islands via UK. (See also the boxed text 'Southern Ocean Yachting,' by Sally Poncet.)

For those who don't own a yacht, or prefer to have someone else do the skippering, an increasing number of private yachts take fare-paying passengers, who are generally expected to lend a hand with the sailing and watch-keeping. All but one of the yachts sail from Ushuaia or Stanley to the Peninsula, the exception being *Spirit of Sydney*, which sails from her namesake city to Commonwealth Bay.

Two agencies act as clearinghouses for Antarctic yachts; several more yachts work independently.

Six yachts are managed by Eric Leyes of Croisieres Australes. Each offers 28-day (29 nights aboard) voyages to the Peninsula from and returning to Ushuaia for 37,000FF (French francs) per person, while 21-day (22 nights aboard) trips cost 30,000FF. A 35-day (36 nights aboard) trip to South Georgia costs 37,500FF, while a 42-day (43 nights on board) trip costs 45,000FF. Croisieres Australes' member yachts include:

Baltazar, a 16m schooner; skipper: Bertrand Dubois; six participants

Le Boulard, a 14m aluminum sloop; skipper: Jean Monzo; six participants

Fernande, a 21.5m aluminum ketch; skipper: Pascal Grinberg; 10 participants

Kekilistrion, a 12m sloop; skipper: Olivier Pauffin; four participants

Kotick I, a 15m steel schooner; skipper: Alain Caradec; five participants

Valhalla, a 20m steel schooner; skipper: Pascal Boimard; eight participants

Croisieres Australes (☎ 33-2-9923-6741, fax: 33-2-9923-6739, croisieresaustrales@nature-sailing.com, www.nature-sailing.com) is at 3 allée de l'Oseraie, F 35760 St Grégoire, France.

The other agency is Ben Garrett's Victory Yacht Cruises, which manages several yachts. Voyages cost between US$6500 and US$7000 per guest for 28 to 30 days, with everything included. Victory 's member yachts include:

Fernande, a 21.5m aluminum ketch; skipper: Pascal Grinberg; 10 participants

Kotic II, a 19m steel schooner; skipper: Frenchman Oleg Bely; 10 participants

Mago II, a 13m cutter-rig sailboat; skipper: Argentine Alejandro Jorge Da Milano; six participants

Santa Maria, a 14.7m steel sloop; skipper: German Wolf Kloss; five participants

Tiama, a 15m steel sloop; skipper: New Zealander Henk Haazen; six participants

Victory Yacht Cruises (☎ 56-61-621-010, fax: 56-61-621-092, sailing@victory-cruises.com, www.victory-cruises.com) can be contacted at PO Box 70, Puerto Williams, Tierra del Fuego, Chile.

A number of other independent yachts also sail to the Antarctic regularly, again mostly from Ushuaia or Stanley, though they primarily charter out to private expeditions and commercial groups such as film crews.

Croix St Paul II is an 18m aluminum sloop skippered by Alex Foucard. It accommodates eight participants. A 29-day Antarctic Peninsula trip costs 37,000FF per person, while a 42-day South Georgia trip costs 46,000FF. Contact Marie Foucard (☎/fax 33-1-4354-7179, mfoucard@club-internet.fr) at 15 rue du Cardinal Lemoine, 75005 Paris, France.

Dove, a 16.5m sloop, skippered by Larry Tyler, accommodates four guests. Antarctic Peninsula voyages cost $US1700 per day; prices for voyages of more than 40 days are negotiable. Contact Dove (thedove88@iname.com) through agent Frances David (caribcon@candwbvi.net) at CC PO Box 3069 Road Town, British Virgin Islands.

Golden Fleece, a 19.5m steel schooner accommodating eight passengers, and *Damien II*, a 15m steel schooner accommodating six passengers, are both skippered by Jérôme Poncet, who has sailed in Antarctic waters for 25 years, making him the world's most experienced Antarctic yachtsman. Charter rates start at US$1000 per day and vary with the length and destinations of the trip. Contact Jérôme Poncet (☎/fax 500-42316, fax 500-22659, www.tourism.org.fk/pages/fleece.htm) at Beaver Island, c/o PO Stanley, Falkland Islands via UK.

Meander is a 25.2m steel schooner skippered by Eef Willems. It accommodates 12 guests. A 29-day trip to South Georgia from and returning to Stanley costs f7000 (Dutch guilders) per person, while a 27-day trip to the Peninsula costs f8500 per person. Contact Eef Willems or Gerrit van der Veer and Ingela Abbing (☎/fax 31-228-319-230, mobile 31-655-325-898, ☎/fax 31-38-332-6311, Inmarsat-C 'Meander' 424-629-110, alida@wxs.nl), Zuider Havendijk 72 a.b. 'Spes,' 1601 JD Enkhuizen IJsselkade to. 84, 8261 AH Kampen, The Netherlands.

Northanger, a 15.6m steel ketch, skippered by Greg Landreth and Keri Pashuk, accommodates six participants. Contact Northanger (☎ 250-920-6753, ☎/fax 250-658-2432, seamount@islandnet.com, www.islandnet.com/~seamount/northanger.html) at 5095 Cordova Bay Rd, Victoria, British Columbia V8Y 2K1 Canada.

Pelagic is a 16.5m steel sloop specially built in 1987 for polar expeditions. Owned by Skip Novak, it has sailed to the Antarctic seven seasons and accommodates six participants and two crew. Antarctica and South

Georgia voyages cost $US1750 per day for the six-person group. Prices for voyages of more than 42 days are negotiable. Pelagic Expeditions (☎/fax 44-1703-454-120, skipno-vak@compuserve.com, www.pelagic.co.uk), a member of IAATO, is at 92 Satchell Ln, Hamble, Hants. S03 14HL UK.

Philos is a 15m steel schooner skippered by Swiss Erich Barde. It accommodates five participants. A four-week Antarctic Penin-sula cruise costs US$6470 per person and a two-week trip down the Beagle Channel to Cape Horn costs US$2450. Contact Sophie Losey at JPB-Albertsen (☎ 41-21-320-63-21, slosey@albertsen.ch, www.albertsen.ch) 7 Av Benjamin-Constant, CH-1002 Lausanne, Switzerland, or email *Philos* at: philosexp@ hotmail.com.

Southern Ocean Yachting

Yachts have visited the Antarctic since 1966, when Bill Tilman in *Mischief* called at Deception Island. Since then, hundreds of yacht voyages have been made south to The Ice, in vessels ranging from luxurious 30m motor-sailors with professional crews and the latest in electronic wizardry to more modest 10m cruising yachts equally well prepared but crewed by husband-and-wife teams. These yachts and their crews and passengers go to Antarctica primarily to experience the beauty of the White Continent. Some are on expeditionary, sporting or scientific missions, while others carry small numbers of tourists. All share a common awe for Antarctica.

In recent years, an average of 15 yachts have visited the Antarctic Peninsula each summer, a re-markably small number, given the popularity of cruising. The widespread use of radar, GPS naviga-tion devices, radio, satellite communications and weather fax – together with the availability of strong, reliable hull materials and improved navigation charts – may tempt some sailors to rely less on experience and skill and increasingly on modern technology. It is far easier to sail to the Antarc-tic today than it was 35 years ago – but the rules remain the same.

Whatever the size of the yacht and its budget and goals, there are a few essential points to re-member when preparing for a cruise to the Antarctic. The first is autonomy: you must make sure to carry enough of everything – food, fuel, clothing and spare parts – to be completely self-sufficient for the duration of your cruise. A reliable engine, a cabin heater, a hull strong enough to withstand collision with ice and rocks and a generously dimensioned anchor and chain – together with an ex-perienced crew – will increase the odds for a trouble-free cruise. It's also important to be certain you are physically and mentally capable of coping with several weeks of isolation under often strenuous conditions.

Familiarize yourself and your crew with the latest Antarctic Treaty regulations for visitors. (See the boxed text 'Guidance for Visitors to the Antarctic' in the Facts about Antarctica chapter.)

When planning your itinerary, bear in mind that there are a number of protected areas, which may not be entered. Also, most stations maintain long-term scientific research programs on nearby islands or ice-free areas, to which access is restricted. Visits to stations require advance notice so they can be scheduled around the station's work program and its resupplying. Even if you are simply anchoring in the vicinity of a station, courtesy requires that you inform the station manager by VHF radio of your intentions while in the area.

Typically, a voyage to Antarctica commences in Tierra del Fuego. This is the shortest ocean cross-ing, taking around four days, depending on the weather and the yacht. Formal clearance for Antarc-tica is carried out at Puerto Williams, 50km east of Ushuaia along the Beagle Channel, by Chilean Navy personnel, who follow yacht movements with administrative zeal and friendly interest.

Actual departure time may depend on the succession of low-pressure systems coming in from the west and funneling through the Drake Passage. A deep front and its usual attendant gale-force winds can transform the crossing from an exhilarating three-day cruise into six days of headwinds,

Santa Maria, a 14.7m steel sloop owned and skippered by German Wolf Kloss, carries five participants and two crew. Four-week trips to the Peninsula cost US$6500. Contact Turismo SIM (stands for Sea, Ice & Mountain Adventures) Ltd (☎ 56-61-621-225, fax 56-61-621-227, sim@entelchile.net, www.simltd.com), PO Box 6, c/o 'Backpacker's Lodge,' calle Ricardo Maragano 168, Puerto Williams, Tierra del Fuego, Chile.

Sarah W Vorwerk, a 16m steel sloop, skippered by Dutchman Henk Boersma, accommodates seven guests. A 28-day voyage to the Peninsula costs US$6085 and a 42-day voyage to South Georgia costs US$8215. You can contact Bettina Boersma (☎ 49-4488-85-95-77, fax: 49-4488-73291,

Southern Ocean Yachting

huge seas and much discomfort. Yachts with weather fax plan their departure accordingly, seeking shelter among the islands near Cape Horn while waiting for fronts to pass through.

Once at sea, life on board quickly settles into a routine of watch-keeping, with crew members sharing the cold hours on deck, keeping watch for fishing boats, freighters and icebergs. Although most yachts are equipped with self-steering, which obviates the need for a helmsman, crew and passengers alike benefit from being outside each day. Astern, the wake spins out a voyager's tale to the ocean and its seabirds as the yacht heads south at 6 or 7 knots, covering 300km every 24 hours.

During a four-week voyage to the Antarctic, a yacht will probably experience extremes. Cruising the Southern Ocean is as much a feat of mental strength as of practical physical preparation.

There is nothing quite like an ocean passage in the southern latitudes; it can be cold, uncomfortable and frightening. Yet the miseries of yesterday are quickly forgotten after a few hours of fair winds, sailing along at 8 knots in a white-crested sea, with a cape petrel keeping pace at the stern rail.

On a clear day the white peaks of Brabant and Anvers islands are visible more than 80km away. Tucked between them are the Melchior Islands, a popular landfall for yachts, with seaward approaches clear of dangers. There's also an excellent anchorage within the island group, which is only a few hours' sail from one of the most beautiful – and most visited – areas of the Antarctic: the Gerlache Strait, with its 100km of sheltered waterways, its bays, coves, islands and glaciers, all dominated by the mainland plateau and mountain peaks, which rise 1800m above the sea.

Exploring this coastline by boat is a constant challenge, but it has its daily rewards. Working with incomplete – and in some cases, inaccurate – marine charts means that constant vigilance is required when close inshore; the danger of uncharted rocks is very real.

There is a handful of all-weather anchorages – among them, Dorian Cove at Port Lockroy, the Argentine Islands and Pléneau Island, while Cuverville, Enterprise and Booth islands and Paradise Harbor offer temporary shelter in certain conditions. Thus, a day's cruising can be planned around reaching safe anchorage by nightfall – and hopefully before the worst of a gale arrives.

Sea ice is rarely a problem in this area during the height of austral summer. There is little risk of becoming beset if extensive fields of sea ice are avoided and a careful eye is kept on the weather. A healthy respect for bergs and pack ice is essential, however, particularly in areas where current and wind could jeopardize a yacht's attempts to reach the safety of open water.

But there will be moments when the sea and the sky could not be more tranquil, when the high plateaus of the Antarctic Peninsula reflect in waters of perfect silence and utter stillness, peaks aglow in evening gold tinged with pink and lilac. From a nearby Adélie colony you may hear a distant clamor of hungry chicks and harassed parents, with the occasional raucous call of a passing skua. To glimpse the Antarctic on such a day is incomparable.

– **Sally Poncet,**
coauthor of *Southern Ocean Cruising*

boersma@t-online.de, www.dive-info.com/ antarctica/antarctica.htm) at Ringelmanns-damm 33, D-26655 Westerstede, Germany.

Spirit of Sydney is an 18m aluminum cutter skippered by Australian Don Mc-Intyre. It visits Commonwealth Bay, a 4000km voyage from Sydney. Up to nine 'working crew' positions are available for A$12,000 each. Contact McIntyre Marine Services (☎ 61-2-9979-8525, fax 61-2-9979-8535, mcintyremarine@ozemail.com.au, www .oceanfrontiers.com.au), PO Box 404, Mona Vale, New South Wales 1660 Australia.

Tiama, a 15m steel sloop owned and skip-pered by New Zealander Henk Haazen, ac-commodates six participants and two crew on voyages to Antarctica or South Georgia. Charter costs are US$1400 per day, with a 28-day minimum. Contact Waterline Yachts (☎ 64-9-815-1640, fax 64-9-846-4180, tiama@ clear.net.nz, home.clear.net.nz/pages/tiama), PO Box 56-403, Dominion Rd, Auckland, New Zealand.

Tooluka is a 14.5m steel sloop owned and skippered by Australian Roger Wallis. It has a crew of two and accommodates six partic-ipants. For itineraries and costs, contact Ani Wallis (☎ 61-3-5155-2814, wallis@net-tech .com.au), PO Box 689, Lakes Entrance, Vic-toria, 3909 Australia.

Resupply Vessels

The 110-passenger French resupply ship *Marion Dufresne II* visits France's Terres Australes et Antarctiques Françaises to deliver personnel and provisions to the three research stations there. Since 1994, the territory's administration has allowed a very limited number of tourists to travel on the quarterly resupply voyage. About 30 people

Zodiacs

Without Zodiacs, Antarctic tourism would be much more difficult and much less pleasurable. Popularized by the late French oceanographer Jacques Cousteau, Zodiacs are small, inflatable boats powered by outboard engines. Their shallow draft makes them ideal for cruising among icebergs and ice floes and for landing in otherwise inaccessible areas. They are made of a synthetic, rubber-like material forming a pontoon in a roughly wishbone shape, with a wooden transom on the back holding the engine. The deck (floor) is made of sections of aluminum. Zodiacs are very safe and sta-ble in the water and are designed to stay afloat even if one or more of their six separate air-filled compartments are punctured. Zodiacs come in a variety of sizes, but on most trips you can expect to share your boat with nine to 14 other passengers, a driver and one other cruise staff member.

Smoking anywhere near Zodiacs is prohibited – and dangerous – since the fuel tanks are exposed. Safety vests must be worn during Zodiac trips. Wet weather jackets and pants are also critical, because even in fine weather the boat's flying spray will give you a good shower. Personal items should be carried in a waterproof backpack (or in a waterproof bag inside the backpack); you can also tuck cameras, binoculars or bags inside your foul-weather jacket or parka to keep them dry. Remember, there are no toilets ashore, so go before you leave the ship.

To ensure that no one gets left behind in Antarctica, tours maintain a system for keeping track of passengers. On some ships, a staff member checks your name off of a list when you leave the ship, and again when you leave the shore. On others, you are responsible for turning over a colored tag on a large notice board inside the ship, indicating your departure and return.

Entering and exiting Zodiacs are probably the most hazardous activities a tourist in Antarctica will undertake – but with a little care, there is no need for anyone to get hurt. Passengers descend the ship's gangway to the Zodiac, which is held to the landing at the bottom of the gangway by a crew member and/or several lines. Since the Zodiac will be rising and falling with the swell, it's important to have both hands free. If you have a camera or a bag, the Zodiac crew will ask you to hand it to them. They will then take hold of your wrist (you should likewise seize theirs) in a hold known as the

see the French sub-Antarctic this way each year. The voyages last 21 to 29 days and sail from Réunion in the western Indian Ocean. After a 2860km journey, the ship arrives at Alfred-Faure station in Îles Crozet, spends about half a day there, then sails another 1420km to Îles Kerguelen's Port-aux-Français station, staying four to seven days. After another 1480km, about half a day is spent at Martin-de-Viviès station on Île Amsterdam. Visits are also sometimes made to Île St Paul for a few hours maximum. The amount of time spent at the other islands depends on how long is required to load and unload goods and people at the station. To safeguard the islands' environments, naturalist guides from different scientific laboratories accompany each group of tourists on landings. At Kerguelen, tourists can stay overnight at Port-aux-Français station. They can also go on hikes of up to several days' duration, staying overnight in small refuges built to allow easier and controlled access to different sites, including Port-Jeanne d'Arc. Cost: 28,200FF for a double cabin, 36,000FF for a single. The fare is the same no matter how long the voyage. Bookings are handled by a travel agency, Mer et Voyage (☎ 33-1-4926-9444, fax 33-1-4926-2939, mer.et .voyages@wanadoo.fr), c/o Explorator, 16 rue de la Banque, 75002 Paris, France.

During the 1980s, Chilean and Argentine military ships resupplying scientific bases commonly took tourists along. Although the Argentine navy has largely stopped the practice since the *Bahía Paraíso* oil spill in 1989, it's still possible to get a berth aboard a Chilean naval vessel if space is available. This type of cruise to Antarctica does not offer the educational lecture and slide programs

Zodiacs

'sailor's grip.' This is much safer than a mere handshake grip, since if one party accidentally lets go, the other still has a firm hold. Move slowly: step onto the pontoon of the Zodiac and then down onto the deck or floor, before moving to your seat, a spot along the pontoon. Sit facing the inside of the boat, and hold onto the ropes tied to the pontoon behind you, since the ride can be quite bumpy.

Only one passenger at a time should stand in a Zodiac. You should never stand while the boat is moving; ask the driver to slow the Zodiac down before you do.

Exiting is as simple as entering. Most landings are made bow-first, and tour staff will be on hand to help you get out of the boat. Passengers sitting in the bow should swing their legs toward the *stern* of the Zodiac (naturally taking care not to kick their neighbor), then over the side and down onto the beach. Swinging your legs to the front of the Zodiac would be more difficult, since the pon-

toon is higher in the bow, and you might well fall back into the Zodiac, presenting a great photo opportunity for your fellow passengers. If there's a large swell, landings may be made stern-first. In this case, passengers in the stern disembark first. Never try to exit over the transom, since a surging wave could knock you over or lift and drop the heavy engine or even the entire Zodiac onto you.

Zodiac landings are either 'wet,' meaning you have to step into a bit of water before getting to the dry beach, or 'dry,' in which case you can step directly onto a rock, jetty, dock or other piece of dry land. No matter what anyone may tell you, *all* landings in Antarctica can be classified as 'wet.'

❋❋❋❋❋❋❋❋❋❋❋❋❋❋❋❋❋❋

found on commercial cruises, however, and non-Spanish speakers may have difficulty communicating. Still, this can be a cost-effective option for the independent and flexible traveler.

One group – an American, an Englishman and a Dutchman – recently went on a 10-day trip to the Peninsula aboard a Chilean tug transporting a group of marines to Antarctica. The passengers, who had little to eat besides bread, chocolate and flan (though it didn't much matter since the rough seas dampened their appetites), slept with 18 marines in a cramped, unheated bunkhouse, which was chained to the ship's deck. The trip, according to one of the participants, was 'absolutely fantastic.' They visited several Chilean bases and had a Zodiac tour around a group of icebergs.

The only way to find out about these trips is to go down to the pier in Punta Arenas and ask a lot of questions (this is where Spanish helps). Because the tourist trips are 'unofficial,' you'll have to be persistent to find out about them. It may take a week – or several – before a vessel that is headed to Antarctica shows up in port. Getting useful information from the Tercera Zona Naval in Punta Arenas, located at Lautaro Navarro 1150, between Roca and Errázuriz (see the Punta Arenas map in the Antarctic Gateways chapter), is very difficult. Go down to the pier instead.

Talking to an officer aboard the vessel is the only way to secure passage, since that officer will be the one collecting your money. The current rate – you do not bargain – is about US$70 per day, US dollars, cash only. Because the length of the trip will vary according to the vessel's resupply mission, you may only be able to find a ship making long cruises. You have no choice in the length of the voyage, so if you can't afford the US$2800 that a 40-day trip costs, you're out of luck. Payment is made upon return to Punta Arenas. The ship's officer with whom you negotiated your trip holds your passport as collateral during the voyage. No doubt due to historical differences between the two countries, Argentines are unwelcome on the Chilean naval vessels. One other thing: bring your own sleeping bag.

AIR

Although several countries in Antarctica operate airstrips, only the Chileans at Teniente Marsh station on King George Island provide facilities for commercial aviation. All private flights to one of these fields require advance permission, which is difficult, if not impossible, to secure. Antarctic aviation can also be dangerous: more than 50 wrecked aircraft litter the Antarctic ice.

The first Antarctic tourist flight occurred on December 22, 1956, when a LAN Chile DC-6B flew from Chacabuco, Chile, over the South Shetlands and the Antarctic Peninsula with 66 passengers. Regular flights over the continent, however, did not begin until February 1977, when Air New Zealand and Australia's Qantas began regular schedules.

Those overflights came to an abrupt halt after all 257 people aboard Air New Zealand flight 901 died when their DC-10 slammed into Mt Erebus on November 28, 1979. Peter Mahon's book *Verdict on Erebus* is a thorough examination of the disaster; Mahon was New Zealand's Royal Commissioner of Inquiry for the crash.

Flightseeing

Qantas resumed Antarctic overflights in 1994, and the new program quickly proved just as popular as the earlier one. For those who can't afford an Antarctic cruise – or who don't want to take the week or more it takes to visit The Ice – flightseeing is a good alternative. You travel in relative comfort (the plane never touches down in Antarctica) and you get a good glimpse of the continent's spectacular glaciers, mountains and icebergs. The flights also offer a way for a large number of people – about 15,000 to date – to see Antarctica without significantly impacting the continent.

For safety, no smoking is allowed during the flights, and no cargo is carried in the hold. The Boeing 747-400 aircraft do not descend below 3050m – or 610m above the highest terrain within 185km, whichever is higher. While over Antarctica, jet engines are operated at less than a third of their full throttle, giving a slower airspeed as well as reducing noise and exhaust. Each Antarctic flight carries a management captain with at least 25 years' flying experience as well as previous Antarctic flight experience.

Croydon Travel, of Melbourne, lobbied Qantas for several years to resume the overflights. Croydon is the primary booking agency for the flights, which depart from Melbourne, Sydney and Adelaide. No passport is required, since the roughly 12-hour flights are considered domestic Australian travel. Lunch and dinner are served in flight. Just as on Antarctic cruises, there are onboard lecturers and Antarctic-themed videos. A nose-mounted video camera captures the view beneath the aircraft, which gets projected onto the plane's movie screen. This is especially interesting during takeoff and landing. Over Antarctica, the pilots fly figure-eight patterns over points of interest, so both sides of the plane get a good view. The beauty of traveling 800km/h is that if one part of Antarctica is clouded over, you simply fly on to a part of the continent where skies are clear.

There are five fare categories: first class, A$3399; business, A$2799; economy premium (not over a wing), A$1699; economy standard (over a wing), A$1149; and economy center, A$799. (A surcharge of A$150 applies to the Adelaide flights.) All passengers except those in economy center are required to rotate seating, which is accomplished without too much fuss – after all, the flights spend three to four hours over The Ice. No center seats are sold in the first class or business cabins. Although some passengers have reported that economy center passengers seem to get a chance to see out the window as much as anyone else, it might be a false economy not to spend the extra money. For those contemplating using the trip to rack up significant 'frequent flier' points, be forewarned: unfortunately, these flights don't qualify for them.

Croydon Travel (☎ 61-3-9725-8555, toll-free 800-633-449, fax 61-3-9723-9560) is at 34 Main St, Croydon, Victoria 3136 Australia.

Flights to Chile's Frei Station

Chilean regional airline Aerovías DAP offers tourist flights four times a year from Punta Arenas to Chile's Presidente Eduardo Frei Montalva station on King George Island in the South Shetlands. The flights, aboard a Twin Otter, depart from the Punta Arenas airport at 7 am. They cruise over the southern end of the Andes, numerous glaciers, Cape Horn and the Drake Passage before arriving at Frei station after four or five hours. At Frei, passengers are able to walk around the Villa de las Estrellas, the residential section of the sprawling base. Passengers are lodged in shelters and all meals are included. The flights return after staying overnight at the station. DAP provides passengers with special suits and accessories necessary to stay overnight in the Antarctic. 'This singular experience,' boasts DAP's website, 'will make you feel lucky and unique.' Cost: US$4300, with a maximum of nine passengers per flight, and a minimum of six passengers required to make the trip. It is possible to charter the Twin Otter and its crew for a flight to Frei, at a cost of US$23,000 per planeload. It's also possible to arrange longer stays at Frei. Aerovías DAP (☎ 56-61-223-340, fax 56-61-221-693, aeroviasdap@ctcinternet.cl, www .aeroviasdap.web.cl) is at O'Higgins 891, Punta Arenas, Chile (see the Punta Arenas map in the Antarctic Gateways chapter).

The flights stop for refueling in Puerto Williams, Chile (see the last part of the Ushuaia section in the Antarctic Gateways chapter). Victory Yacht Cruises can book your flight if you only want to fly from Puerto Williams to Frei and then fly back. Contact Victory (☎ 56-61-621-010, fax 56-61-621-092, sailing@victory-cruises.com, www .victory-cruises.com) at PO Box 70, Puerto Williams, Tierra del Fuego, Chile.

The Interior by Air

Adventure Network International, also known as Antarctic Airways, is the first and only private company offering flights to the Antarctic interior. ANI, a Canadian company, began operating in Antarctica during the 1985-86 season, with one De Havilland Twin Otter aircraft.

Since then, ANI has flown more than 800 passengers on at least 150 round-trips to

Antarctica, covering a total of 1.6 million km. The company has supported every private expedition to the Antarctic interior since 1986, including mountain climbing, skiing and manhauling expeditions across the continent. In 1991, ANI began offering the first-ever tourist flights to an emperor penguin rookery. ANI was also one of the seven founding members of IAATO.

ANI owns and operates a ski-equipped Cessna C-185 and a Basler Turbine DC-3, and contracts with high-latitude aircraft operators for both ski-equipped Twin Otter aircraft and larger planes (such as a wheeled Hercules, capable of carrying 45 passengers and a total payload of two tonnes).

ANI flies passengers six hours (3100km) south from Punta Arenas, Chile, to its camp at Patriot Hills, between the Ellsworth Mountains and the Ronne Ice Shelf. The Patriot Hills area, discovered in 1986 by one of ANI's co-founders, Giles Kershaw, along with British glaciologist Dr Charles Swithinbank, has a natural blue-ice runway, making it one of the few places in the continent's interior where wheeled aircraft can land.

The Continent in a Day

Overflights are the quickest and least expensive way to see Antarctica. Although no landings are made, observing the continent from altitude provides a unique perspective – unavailable to those who remain at sea level.

Some preparation hints: checked baggage is not permitted, so limit yourself to a small bag. Wear loose-fitting clothes, a light baggy sweater (this is not a fashion contest) and shoes you can easily kick off during the 13- to 14-hour, 10,000km round-trip. Sunglasses are a must, since the glare over the ice can be blinding. If you have small, lightweight binoculars, take them as well. If you smoke, bring some nicotine substitute, as these are strictly no-smoking flights.

Remember your camera and plenty of film. Your preflight package contains advice on photography, but you should still test your camera well before your trip. Also, a commercial photographer records the flight on video, and you can buy a copy after the flight.

Interestingly, you'll receive two boarding passes: one for the journey south until midway through the viewing period, the other from then until the flight's conclusion. Don't worry if you're not close to a window. Seats are rotated during the flight, and there's a friendly, cooperative spirit on board. Passengers move about the plane more freely than normal, and people like to get the view from several vantage points, including the exit zones. But remember, you get what you pay for: some tickets do not provide you with direct window access at any time in the flight, and you may have to look over someone's shoulder. Make sure to read the fine print when booking your tickets.

Upon boarding, you'll find on your seat a package of information on Antarctica, its history and current research work there, along with maps showing the flight route. In addition to the usual safety video shown at the beginning of all airline flights, a special video gives instructions in the unlikely event an emergency landing is required in Antarctica.

People with considerable Antarctic field knowledge and expertise will also be aboard, and they'll be keen to answer your questions. During the first few hours of the flight, they wear brightly colored, heavily insulated Antarctic clothing, thus subjecting themselves to the flight's only real danger: heatstroke from the cabin's constant 22°C temperature. The experts provide continuing commentary – and also try to leave some time for silence, so people can absorb what they're seeing.

Food served is standard aircraft fare. A meal is served en route south, and another soon after the aircraft commences its northward journey. Plenty of complimentary liquid refreshment, including bar service, is also on hand. For New Year's Eve flights, it flows in particular abundance.

About four hours into the flight, the first icebergs and sea ice are often spotted, depending on the location and weather conditions. Generally, a maximum of three hours is spent viewing the

From Patriot Hills, ANI flies ski-equipped Twin Otters 1100km to the South Pole, to Vinson Massif (see the boxed text 'Patriot Hills, Antarctica'), to an emperor penguin colony at the Dawson-Lambton Glacier in the Weddell Sea, to the mountains of Dronning Maud Land – indeed, to just about anywhere in Antarctica.

'Fly to the South Pole' trips last about 14 days. They include a week's stay at Patriot Hills and cost US$25,000. The highlight: a five-hour flight to the Pole (then six hours back to Patriot Hills).

For the more adventurous, there are two other ways to get to 90° S. The 60-day 'Ski to the South Pole' trip (US$45,000) leaves from Hercules Inlet 40km from Patriot Hills on the edge of the Ronne Ice Shelf. Two guides accompany the skiers, and minimum group size is six people.

All equipment – tents, sleeping bags, sledges, skis – is supplied. If that sounds too tough or you don't have the luxury of 60 available days, you can always try the 10-day 'Ski to the South Pole, Last Degree' trip (US$29,500), which departs from one degree

The Continent in a Day

continent, and another five are spent flying home. When the weather is right, viewing is spectacular, the clear air of Antarctica allowing objects 100km or more away to be seen. Over points of interest, the aircraft flies long figure eights to ensure that both sides of the plane have good views. While enjoying the ice cream that is served while your warm, snug airplane flies over The Ice, with a single glance you can take in entire routes of famous, back-breaking journeys that took many months to complete. Seeing the rugged terrain below inspires many to marvel at the pioneer expeditions, and to realize what formidable difficulties still confront modern operations in Antarctica.

Individual buildings can be seen clearly when stations are overflown. But it is impossible to observe individual animals such as penguins, even with binoculars. Those wanting more detail will need to land on the continent, arriving there by ship or by aircraft.

Several times during the flight, the plane makes radio contact with some of the stations in the region, and the conversations are relayed into the cabin for everyone to hear. These chats with overwintering personnel provide a feel for what it's like to be on The Ice for an extended period.

Although little physical effort is required during the flight, you may start to feel the excitement and length of the day as the plane turns homeward and weariness sets in. Now is the time to eat a leisurely dinner, to watch Antarctic films and to purchase memorabilia such as T-shirts and books.

A few hours before touchdown, an auction is held for the right to occupy the seat behind the pilots. Four-figure sums are often paid, the money going to a nominated charity. Those interested in bidding must remember to take with them that modern survival tool: a credit card.

Upon landing, the experts gather at the exit door to wish everyone well. People usually leave with a faraway look in their eyes. Partly this is from the long journey, but mostly it is from the experience of seeing Antarctica for the first time. The reaction of those who see the continent this way is the same as those who actually step ashore: wonder – coupled with a desire to return soon.

– **Martin Betts,**
Senior Policy Officer at the Australian Antarctic
Division, who has been on four overflights

TONY WHEELER

Patriot Hills, Antarctica

Adventure Network's clients generally spend a few days at the company's Patriot Hills base camp to get acclimated to Antarctica's altitude and cold before heading off on flights to their climbing, skiing or photographic destinations. Weather may delay takeoff, but Patriot Hills – just 1100km from the South Pole – is a reasonably comfortable place to wait out a blizzard.

As the only private semipermanent camp in Antarctica, it offers accommodations for 60 guests in large insulated tents (bring your own polar-rated sleeping bag). The tents are so well insulated, an ANI official says, 'we find that most tents are naturally heated by the midnight sun.' This despite the air temperature, which in early October can be around -30°C , rising to a high of -5°C in mid-December, with steady 20 to 30km/h winds.

Cooking and kitchen facilities (which turn out such delicate meals as smoked salmon, chocolate mousse and Welsh rarebit, accompanied by fresh fruit, vegetables and wine flown in from Chile) are in one tent, while the staff of 20 sleeps in several others. (The Chilean military posts a small contingent of personnel here each summer as well.) There's even a library tent. Primitive hot-water showers are also available, though most guests prefer sponge baths or even 'snow baths.' A physician is on the camp staff for the entire season.

Despite its remote location, Patriot Hills is far from isolated, thanks to technology. Nearly every expedition or group visiting the camp these days seems to carry an Iridium satellite telephone. 'It is commonplace for the phone to ring in the dining tent and for people to chat to friends and relatives across the world,' says one recent visitor. 'The woman running the meteorology reports in the radio tent complained that she felt like a receptionist answering telephone calls all day long.'

Among recreational activities available at Patriot Hills are snowmobiling, bowling, hiking or zipping along on skis over the smooth, flat ice while being towed by a wind-borne 'Skygrazer' kite!

In keeping with ANI's philosophy of leaving little impact on the Antarctic environment, a wind generator and solar panels produce enough power to operate all the camp equipment on a daily basis, a commendable achievement – and one which doubtless also greatly helps the company's bottom line, given the enormous cost of transporting fuel to Patriot Hills.

ANI also has a strict carry-in-carry-out policy at Patriot Hills. All refuse, including human waste, is removed from Antarctica, and no incineration takes place. All fuel drums are inventoried and either reused or removed from Antarctica. Even climbing expeditions on Vinson Massif are expected to pack out all their waste. Only grey water from Patriot Hills' kitchen and showers is disposed of in Antarctica.

❄ ❄ ❄ ❄ ❄ ❄ ❄ ❄ ❄ ❄ ❄ ❄ ❄ ❄ ❄ ❄ ❄ ❄ ❄ ❄

of latitude (60 nautical miles, or 110km) from the Pole; again, all equipment is supplied.

A 17-day trip to see the emperor penguins at the Dawson-Lambton Glacier rookery costs US$22,000 and includes seven to 10 days' camping at the rookery. A two-week trip to both the emperor rookery and the Pole costs US$42,000.

Fifteen-day 'Heart of Antarctica' trips to Patriot Hills (US$14,000) emphasize opportunities to camp and to learn celestial navigation. They include a 45-minute local sightseeing flight.

Trips to climb Antarctica's highest mountain Vinson Massif (see the boxed text 'On Top of the Bottom of the World' in the Private Expeditions chapter), last an average of 12 to 14 days and cost US$26,000.

Adventure Network also now offers a limited range of interesting ship-based trips (see the Cruises section earlier in this chapter).

Adventure Network (☎ 44-1494-671-808, fax 44-1494-671-725, adventurenetwork@ compuserve.com, www.adventure-network .com) is based at Canon House, 27 London End, Beaconsfield, Buckinghamshire HP9 2HN, UK or, from October until the end of January only, at 935 Arauco, Punta Arenas, Chile (☎ 56-61-247-735, fax 56-61-226-167).

Wildlife Guide

WILDLIFE GUIDE

By Dr John Cooper

Humpback Whale

Humpbacks *(Megaptera novaeangliae)* may be recognized by their enormous flippers, which can reach one-third of their total body length. They are normally black, but undersides of flippers and flukes have varying amounts of white and can be used as aids for recognizing individuals. Maximum lengths recorded are 17.5m for a male and 19m for a female.

Humpbacks occur in all oceans. They migrate seasonally from their Southern Ocean summer feeding grounds toward the equator, where they breed during the southern winter, generally in shallow waters close to land. Humpbacks are highly vocal on their breeding grounds. Their songs, which last up to 20 minutes, are thought to be mainly produced by adult males to advertise their presence. They eat primarily Antarctic krill *(Euphausia superba)* – more than a tonne a day may be taken. Humpbacks were grossly overexploited by whalers in the past, but since 1963 they have been fully protected in the Southern Hemisphere.

Southern Right Whale

Whalers named the slow-moving, inshore-visiting *Balaena glacialis* 'right' because it could be relatively easily rowed down and harpooned – and then it obligingly stayed afloat to yield its long baleen plates and much oil. Southern rights go up to 16m in length and can attain 74 tonnes. The whitish callosities on the jaws and forehead can be used to identify individuals. Southern right whales occur in the southern oceans between 20°S and 50°S and have been recorded around the more northerly of the southern islands. They are seasonally common (May to September) and easily seen from the shore in bays on the southern coast of South Africa, where calving and mating occur. Southern right whales are lucky not to be extinct; they were overexploited to 'commercial extinction' as early as the mid-19th century, although full protection came only in 1935. Numbers are now slowly recovering at a rate of 7% a year, based on South African long-term studies. Watching southern rights court within 100m of the shore is an experience not to be forgotten.

Above: Humpback wha

Below: Southern right whale

Sperm Whale

The sperm whale *(Physeter macrocephalus)* is an unmistakable species, of *Moby Dick* fame, with its enormous head and narrow tooth-filled jaws. At sea, the low 'bushy' forward-directed blow and small fleshy dorsal fin are important identifying features. Males can reach 19m in length, females 12m.

Sperm whales occur in all the world's oceans, but rarely in shallow seas. Most sperm whales south of 40°S are adult males. Schools (20 to 25 individuals) are made up of females and their young, joined by males during the breeding season from October to December. A 4m calf is born after a gestation period of 15 to 16 months. They eat mid- to deep-water squid, some of which reach 200kg: veritable krakens of the deep, caught in absolute darkness at depths of nearly 3km.

Sperm whales were much exploited in the past for their oil, ambergris and teeth. Now they are fully protected in the Southern Ocean. It can only be hoped that their numbers will build up to pre-exploitation levels.

Killer Whale

Killer whales *(Orcinus orca)* are the largest of the dolphin family. Also known as orcas, their black and white markings and tall dorsal fins (especially in the adult male) are distinctive. Males reach 9m, females nearly 8m. Large specimens can weigh nearly 9 tonnes.

Orcas occur in all seas, but are more abundant in colder waters. They travel in schools or pods of up to 50 individuals. Pods have their own 'dialect' of discrete calls and are presumably made up of closely related animals. Maturity is reached from 12 years of age in females and 14 years in males. They feed on squid, fish, birds and marine mammals. Resident killer whales have been seen at sub-Antarctic Marion Island swallowing king penguins whole. Orcas will also tip up small ice floes to get at resting seals.

There are still many killer whales in the Southern Ocean. They have not been caught commercially since 1979-80 when Soviet whalers killed 916 of them. Catching orcas for captive display is an emotive issue, but can hardly be said to be of conservation significance based on the small numbers taken. There is no reason to believe that this splendid animal will not continue to grace southern seas.

Above: Sperm whale

Below: Killer whale

Sei Whale

Sei whales *(Balaenoptera borealis)* are the third-largest whales in the Southern Ocean. Average size is 14.5m in males and 15.5m in females. A 16.4m female was weighed at 37.75 tonnes. The blow is similar to that of the fin whale but not so high. Seis can achieve speeds up to 55 km/h over short distances.

The species can be found in all oceans, but only larger individuals have been recorded south of the Antarctic Convergence. Seis occur in small schools of three to eight animals. Some sexual segregation seems to occur, based on harpooners' records. The calf is 4.5m long at birth and is weaned after six months, when it has grown to 8m. In the Southern Hemisphere, sei whales feed on copepods and euphausiids, with the former thought to be the more important. Their finely fringed baleen plates help them feed on such small prey.

Like humpback, blue and fin whales, seis were overexploited through greed to the point of 'commercial extinction.' Over 20,000 were harpooned in the 1964-65 season, immediately after which the population collapsed. They've been completely protected since 1979.

Fin Whale

Female fin whales *(Balaenoptera physalus)* attain 27m in length; males reach 25m. They are the second-largest whales, after the blue. Unusually, the anterior part of the animal is asymmetrically colored: The left mandible is bluish-grey, the right is white. The reason for this peculiar patterning is unclear but may be related to the species feeding in a tilted position. Fins' maximum speed may be 37 km/h.

Fin whales occur in all oceans. In Antarctic waters, they have a circumpolar distribution in summer, moving to lower latitudes in winter. Calves are born at about 6.5m in length in temperate or subtropical waters. While their principal food in southern seas is euphausiid crustaceans, fin whales may not feed at all in winter, relying on their accumulated blubber for energy as do other baleen whales.

Above: Sei whale

Fins formed the largest part of whalers' catches after World War II, when a maximum 28,761 were taken in 1960-61. Whaling reduced

Below: Fin whale

the population from an estimated 400,000 to about 84,000. The species has been totally protected since 1976. For the fin, like all other baleen whales, protection came only after 'commercial extinction.' Recovery rates are likely to be slow in this species, whose longevity was exemplified when one whaler's identifying mark was recovered from an individual after 37 years.

Blue Whale

Blue whales *(Balaenoptera musculus)* are the largest animals that have ever lived. A female landed at South Georgia reached 33.5m in length. A 27.6m female caught by a Soviet whaling fleet in 1947 weighed 178 tons. Aside from the animal's huge size, characteristics include its habit of showing its flukes on diving (the other rorqual whales do not).

Blue whales can be found in all oceans. In the southern summer they frequent the fringes of the ice shelf, moving to subtropical waters in winter. The larger individuals occur the farthest south. Blues are usually solitary or travel in pairs. Females reach sexual maturity at about 5 years of age. In southern waters, blues prey predominantly on Antarctic krill *(Euphausia superba)*. A single blue can eat as much as 4.5 tonnes of krill in one day, filtering the tiny crustaceans from the water with its 250 to 400 pairs of baleen plates.

It is thought the blue whale population of the Southern Hemisphere once numbered 200,000 animals, but commercial whaling severely reduced the species' numbers and it became fully protected in 1965. Nevertheless, recovery has been slow, and the current population is thought to be just 1% of original numbers.

Minke Whale

The minke whale *(Balaenoptera acutorostrata)* is the smallest of the great baleen whales, although with a maximum length of 10m and a weight up to 8 tonnes, it's still a very large animal. Minkes are fast swimmers and will approach slow-moving and stationary vessels. Their blow reaches 2m.

Above: Blue whale

Below: Minke whale

Minkes are circumpolar in distribution in summer, with highest densities seen at the pack ice edge. In winter, most animals move to lower

latitudes. Sexes and age classes are often segregated, with the largest animals – usually females – occurring farthest south. Pairing and calving take place in the southern winter. Diet consists mainly of krill and copepods.

Minkes are by far the most abundant baleen whales in the Southern Ocean, with a population of possibly half a million. Not targeted by whalers because of their relatively small size, they escaped the slaughter of the first half of the 20th century. However, a few hundred are currently (and controversially) killed by Japanese whalers each year, ostensibly for scientific purposes, although their meat is sold for human consumption in Japan to 'allay costs.'

Antarctic & Sub-Antarctic Fur Seals

Fur seals can be found on most of the circumpolar southern islands – in very large numbers at some of them. Vagrants have reached the southern continents. The Antarctic fur seal *(Arctocephalus gazella)* occurs farther south than its close and slightly smaller relative, the sub-Antarctic fur seal *(A tropicalis)*, with which it sometimes hybridizes. Female Antarctic fur seals are grey to brownish with creamy throats and chests. Adult males are silvery-grey with a mane of longer hair. Sub-Antarctic females are greyish with orange throats and chests. The males are buff to black with cream to orange throats and chests, and have a 'topknot' that helps distinguish them from male Antarctics. About 1 in 800 fur seals are of the 'blonde' variety, with markedly yellow or cream-colored fur. Males, at over 200kg, far outweigh females, which weigh up to 55kg.

Fur seals breed in harems, and males can be formidable opponents to rivals and human visitors alike. Quite a few scientists bear the scars of injudicious approach. Pupping takes place in December. Diet consists of squid, fish and small crustaceans such as krill.

Fur seals are now showing a remarkable recovery in numbers from overexploitation for their coats early in the 19th century – so much so that at some localities, they are displacing breeding albatrosses and killing vegetation, leading to conservation dilemmas. Perhaps some form of carefully controlled exploitation will one day be allowed, but this is certain to be controversial.

SALLY TROY

Southern Elephant Seal

The southern elephant seal *(Mirounga leonina)* is the world's largest seal. Males attain 3.5 tonnes and 5m in length, and females 900kg and 3m. They have a circumpolar distribution, occurring on most of the southern islands and on the Peninsula.

Above: Atlantic fur seal pup

Above: Bull elephant seal

Below: Angry crabeater seal

Breeding follows a seasonal pattern. Males spend the winter at sea and first haul out in August, followed by the females. Fighting then follows among the males to see who will be 'beachmaster,' with mating rights to a 'harem' of females. Pups grow incredibly quickly on their mothers' rich, 50% fat milk. By the time they're weaned at 22 days, they've quadrupled their weight. Adults' diet is predominantly squid, caught during very deep (up to 2km) and long (up to two hours!) dives, when they lower their heart rate to as little as a single beat per minute, separated by remarkably short periods at the surface.

Elephant seals, especially males, were heavily exploited ashore for their oil during the 19th and early 20th centuries by sealers, who called the animals 'sea elephants.' Although this fortunately no longer occurs, numbers are decreasing at some of the southern Indian Ocean islands. The species is being studied in an attempt to explain this alarming trend, which may be linked to climatic change affecting food supplies.

Crabeater Seal

Crabeaters (*Lobodon carcinophagus*) are misnamed, since they actually eat krill, not crabs. They are slim seals reaching about 3m in length. Their distribution is circumpolar, though they prefer pack ice to open sea. Although considered to be the world's most abundant seal (by one estimate, they may number 30 million), the species' habit of occurring in small family groups suggests smaller numbers when compared with the teeming breeding beaches occupied by fur seals.

Not much is known about crabeaters' breeding, which occurs among the pack ice during the austral spring. Like southern elephant seal pups, crabeater pups grow very quickly and are weaned within two to three weeks. Adult crabeaters have teeth that form a sieve to strain out Antarctic krill, their almost exclusive diet.

Very little is known about this abundant animal (for example, copulation has never been observed), as pack ice is a difficult place for scientists to work. It seems to be under no conservation threat.

Leopard Seal

Adult male leopard seals *(Hydrurga leptonyx)* reach a length of 3m and weigh up to 300kg. Females are larger, at 4m and 450kg. Leopard seals have a large head with a huge gape, making them fearsome predators. They're found among the pack ice in summer and on the more southerly sub-Antarctic islands in winter.

Little is known about their breeding behavior. Pups are born on the ice during summer. Except during the breeding season, they are solitary. Their diet includes penguins and seals.

There is much folklore about the dangers of leopard seals, perhaps mostly untrue, although a few attacks by 'sea leopards' on humans have been documented. Given their size and formidable jaws, caution is recommended.

Weddell Seal

Weddell seals *(Leptonychotes weddellii)* are fat animals, not so streamlined as crabeater and leopard seals. They reach 3m in length and a weight of 400kg. Females are a little larger than males. Weddell seals have a circumpolar distribution, living farther south than any other mammal (other than Antarctic explorers!). Fast shelf ice is their main home year-round, but sightings have been recorded in pack ice.

Pups are born in colonies in September and October, on fast ice near cracks and holes that allow their mothers access to the water. Extensive tooth wear occurs as animals use their incisors and canines to scrape away at the ice to keep their

Above: Leopard seal

Below: Crabeater seals

breathing holes open. Weddells are the best studied of the Antarctic seals, because they can be more easily approached over fast ice than can the pack-ice species. Studies have shown Weddells can dive to 600m and stay underwater for more than an hour. They eat fish, squid and crustaceans. Weddells have been observed blowing air bubbles into cracks under the sea ice to flush out prey. They are the archetypical Antarctic seal, and along with the Adélie penguin are fixed in the public consciousness as animals of the far south.

Ross Seal

The Ross seal *(Ommatophoca rossii)* is the least-often seen of the Antarctic seals. Until the 1970s, it had been observed by fewer than 100 people, because although it has a circumpolar distribution, the Ross seal lives only in heavy pack ice. A solitary animal, it is usually found hauled out onto large floes, alone or in pairs.

Ross seals have dark grey to chestnut backs and lighter undersides. They have very large eyes, a short snout and a wide, short head. The characteristic broad dark streaks on the lighter colored throat and chest are clearly visible when the animal is disturbed, for then it rears back almost vertically, with its mouth open and its throat inflated. The seal is also known for its distinctive vocalizations: trilling, warbling or 'chugging.' Males reach 2m and 180kg; females are slightly larger.

They eat mainly squid and fish. Pups are rarely observed. Much remains to be learned about this species, which is named for its discoverer James Clark Ross, leader of the British Antarctic Expedition of 1839-43, but it is becoming better studied as icebreakers more frequently penetrate the densest regions of pack ice.

Below: Emperor penguin and chick

KEVIN SCHAFER

Emperor Penguin

The emperor penguin *(Aptenodytes forsteri)* is the world's largest penguin, although some fossil penguins were even larger. It stands more than 1m tall and can weigh 40kg. The emperor can only be confused with its close relative, the sub-Antarctic king penguin, which is smaller and more brightly marked. Emperor chicks are silvery-grey with a white face mask and blackish head.

About 45 breeding localities are known, concentrated in the Weddell Sea and Dronning Maud Land, Enderby and Princess Elizabeth Lands, and the Ross Sea. The emperors' at-sea distribution does not extend north of the Antarctic Convergence, except for vagrants. The known population is a little under 200,000 breeding pairs.

The emperor is the only Antarctic bird that breeds in winter. A single egg is incubated on the feet of the males, which then huddle in the winter cold to reduce heat loss. Incubation averages 66 days, and chicks become independent during November to January. Emperors eat fish such as the Antarctic silver fish *(Pleurogramma antarcticum)*, krill and squid. Breeding birds may travel long distances across the ice to find open water to feed. Prey is captured by pursuit-diving, often to amazing depths and durations: the records stand at 535m and 22 minutes, by far the deepest and longest dives for any bird.

Emperors are not globally threatened, although human disturbance has been implicated at the Pointe Géologie colony in Terre Adélie, which decreased from 6000 pairs to 2000 pairs between 1952 and 1987.

King Penguin

The king penguin *(Aptenodytes patagonicus)* is the world's second largest penguin, standing 20cm shorter than the closely related emperor, but it's much lighter at 9kg to 15kg. The downy chick is uniform dark brown – and was once described as the 'woolly penguin,' a species of its own! Kings breed on seven sub-Antarctic island groups, with a breeding population estimated at between 1 million and 1.5 million pairs.

Breeding occurs in often very large colonies close to the shore on rocky terrain. A single egg is incubated during summer on the feet of both parents, taking turns. It takes 55 days to hatch. Incubating birds can shuffle along slowly with their eggs – to avoid lumbering southern elephant seals, for instance. Chicks are reared right through the winter (huddling in crèches to keep warm) and only fledge the following summer, making annual breeding impossible. Scientists have worked hard to unravel the species' breeding interval: Is it every second year, or two years in three? Diet includes fish and squid, caught by deep (several hundred meter) dives lasting as long as 15 minutes.

Kings have been exploited in the past, but thankfully their numbers have subsequently increased at several breeding localities. Their conservation status seems secure.

MARK NORMAN

Above: King penguin

Adélie Penguin

The Adélie *(Pygoscelis adeliae)* is the archetypical penguin, named after French explorer Dumont d'Urville's wife. They're purely black and white, with a distinctive white eye ring. Like all penguins, the sexes are similarly marked, although Adélie females are smaller. The downy chick is uniformly brown. Breeding occurs all around the Antarctic continent and Peninsula and at some of the more southerly sub-Antarctic islands.

GORDON COURT (HEDGEHOG HOUSE)

There are about 2.5 million breeding pairs known for 177 localities, although there are very likely new colonies yet to be discovered in little-explored sections of the Antarctic coast.

Breeding occurs during summer in large colonies. Comical chases of adults by chicks ensure that meals are not fed to weak or unhealthy chicks. Diet is mainly Antarctic and ice krill *(Euphausia superba* and *E crystallarophias)*. Deep dives for prey (reaching depths of nearly 150m) may be undertaken, but usually dives are much shallower. In winter, Adélies stay at sea, resting on pack ice and icebergs in groups.

Adélie penguins are well studied. Their breeding success, numbers and diets are monitored as part of international studies conducted under the auspices of the Convention for the Conservation of Antarctic Marine Living Resources (CCAMLR). Some colonies near Antarctic stations have decreased in size, a change thought to be due to human disturbance. Elsewhere, however, colonies have grown, so the species is not in danger.

Chinstrap Penguin

Chinstraps *(Pygoscelis antarctica)* are superficially similar to Adélies, being black and white, but they have a distinctive black line connecting the black cap to below the chin – hence the name. Breeding occurs around the Peninsula and on islands south of the Antarctic Polar Front. With an estimated 4 million pairs, the chinstrap is the second most abundant Antarctic/sub-Antarctic penguin, after the macaroni. On the little-visited South Sandwich Islands, 1.5 million pairs of chinstraps have recently been reported breeding.

KEVIN SCHAFER

Two eggs are laid in November or December and chicks fledge in late February and early March. Pursuit dives for prey – almost entirely krill – are usually less then 100m deep. Chinstraps forage among the pack ice, although vagrants may be seen in the open sea.

Although population changes have been detected among colonies on the Peninsula studied by a number of nations, chinstraps' overall population seems stable.

Gentoo Penguin

An orange bill and a white flash above and behind its eye distinguish the black and white gentoos *(Pygoscelis papua)* from the slightly smaller Adélies and chinstraps. Breeding distribution is circumpolar on the sub-Antarctic islands and on the Antarctic Peninsula. There are an estimated 300,000 breeding pairs. Large populations occur at South Georgia (100,000 pairs), the Falkland Islands (70,000 pairs) and Îles Kerguelen (30,000 pairs).

Above: Adélie penguins

Right: Chinstrap penguin

At the more northerly sub-Antarctic islands, gentoos breed in winter, laying two eggs as early as July. On the more southerly islands and the Antarctic Peninsula, laying occurs from October to December. Pursuit dives for prey can go deeper than 100m, reaching the bottom in inshore waters, but most dives are probably shallower. Diet includes crustaceans (mainly euphausiids), fish (mainly lantern fish, *Myctophidae*) and squid.

Gentoo populations are showing some alarming decreases at their sub-Antarctic breeding localities, suggesting a conservation problem, although other populations on the Peninsula are increasing in size.

Macaroni Penguin

Orange tassels meeting between the eyes distinguish the macaroni *(Eudyptes chrysolophus)* from the slightly smaller (and lighter-billed) rockhopper. 'Maccies' breed on sub-Antarctic islands near the Antarctic Convergence from South America eastwards to Heard Island and off the Peninsula. The macaroni is the most abundant of the sub-Antarctic/Antarctic penguins, with a minimum breeding population of 11.8 million pairs. Major concentrations are at South Georgia (5.4 million pairs), Îles Crozet (2.2 million), Îles Kerguelen (1.8 million) and Heard and McDonald Islands (2 million).

WAYNE BERNHARDSON

Macaronis breed in summer. Breeding colonies, which can be immense, are deserted in winter. Two eggs are laid, the first smaller than the second (extremely unusual for birds). The first-laid ('A') egg is usually kicked out of the nest soon after the 'B' egg is laid and only one egg ever hatches. This odd system has prompted many studies. Macaronis eat lantern fish and euphausiid crustaceans, caught by pursuit-diving.

Above: Macaroni penguin (left) talking to a rockhopper penguin (right)

Like the pygoscelid penguins, 'maccies' are monitored for CCAMLR purposes. They have decreased at some sub-Antarctic breeding localities recently, arousing conservation concern. More accurate censuses are required at the major breeding localities – easier said than done in a million-strong colony.

Below: Rockhopper penguin

Rockhopper Penguin

'Rockies' *(Eudyptes chrysocome)* are smaller than macaronis and have yellow tassels that do not meet between the eyes. Although there is as yet no consensus of opinion, three subspecies have been recognized. Rockhoppers are sub-Antarctic and southern, cool, temperate island breeders, found as far north as Tristan da Cunha. There are an estimated 3.7 million pairs. The largest population (1 million pairs) is at the Falklands.

Rockhoppers breed in summer, laying two dimorphic eggs. The smaller, first-laid 'A' egg is often lost during incubation and even if retained,

K HANDASYDE

does not always hatch. Rockhopper rookeries are smaller than those of macaronis, and rockhoppers are able to breed among tumbled boulders on exposed shores, where their hopping and swimming abilities are required to enter and emerge from the sea and to reach their nest sites. Rockhoppers prey upon lantern fish and small euphausiid crustaceans.

Rockhoppers have decreased alarmingly at islands south of New Zealand and in the southern Indian Ocean. Disease, introduced rats and sea temperature rises have all been implicated. With a well-scattered population in the millions, the rockhopper is not at any immediate risk of extinction, but the continuing downward population trends are indeed worrying, earning the bird a World Conservation Union 'vulnerable' status.

MARK NORMAN

Above: Royal penguin

Royal Penguin

Royals *(Eudyptes schlegeli)* are found only at sub-Antarctic Macquarie Island. Essentially, they look like white-faced macaronis, although some dark faces do occur. The most recent census, in 1984-85, found 848,700 breeding pairs, which is now regarded as an underestimate.

Two eggs are laid in often huge coastal colonies in October. As usual in *Eudyptes* penguins, the smaller, first-laid 'A' egg is ejected from the nest and usually does not hatch; the reason for this is still unclear, despite a number of studies. Chicks fledge in late January or early February. Colonies are deserted by May, after adults complete their molt ashore. Royals eat mainly small euphausiid crustaceans and lantern fish, caught by pursuit-diving.

Royals have been well studied in recent years, and much is now known about their foraging ecology and breeding biology. There appear to be no serious imminent conservation threats to the species. Years ago, they were exploited for their oil, but protest against this led to Macquarie Island being made the first sub-Antarctic island nature reserve.

Amsterdam Albatross

Confined to Île Amsterdam in the South Indian Ocean, with a tiny population of fewer than 100 birds and only 13 pairs breeding in 1995, the Amsterdam albatross *(Diomedea amsterdamensis)* was described as a separate species only in 1983. It's the rarest Southern Ocean seabird – indeed, one of the world's rarest birds. Looking for one at sea is thus likely to be a forlorn task. The good news is that ornithologists think its numbers are slowly increasing, perhaps due to the removal of feral cattle from its breeding habitat 600m up on the central plateau.

Wandering Albatross

The wandering albatross *(Diomedea exulans)* is a bird of superlatives –
for many travelers, it is *the* bird of the Southern Ocean. To see one glide
past your vantage place on a ship, just a few meters away as it watch-
es you with its soft brown eyes, is to experience a thrill not for 'lesser
mortals.' The species is distinguished from the smaller 'mollymawk'
albatross by its huge size (wingspan up to 3.5m), but telling it at sea
from the closely related (but less widespread) royal and Amsterdam
albatrosses is not easy and requires recourse to a specialized field guide
or friendly marine ornithologist. In fact, recent genetic studies have proposed splitting the wanderer into four species.

The latest population estimates are 21,000 annual breeding pairs at
10 island groups in the Southern Ocean. But the bird's more than year-
long breeding season means it breeds (if successful) only every second
year, so the total breeding population is nearly twice this figure. At several localities, populations have decreased because the bird is at serious
risk from being caught by longline vessels fishing for tuna – an ignoble
death by drowning for such a splendid animal. Much research is currently being done into ways of reducing this mortality, and some populations have stabilized, perhaps as a result.

Diet is mainly squid and fish caught, it is thought, by predation at
night and scavenging by day. Satellite tracking has recently revealed
that wanderers can cover vast tracts of the Southern Ocean, flying up
to several thousand kilometers on a single foraging trip, so they are

Below: Wandering
albatrosses

COLIN MONTEATH (HEDGEHOG HOUSE)

aptly named. Indeed, young birds may not return to land for five years or more, staying at sea the whole time.

Royal Albatross

The royal albatross *(Diomedea epomophora)* is one of the three 'great' albatrosses of the Southern Ocean. It is primarily recognized at sea by its huge size and its combination, when adult, of an all-white tail with mostly black upper wings and a dark edge to the upper mandible. It breeds on islands off New Zealand (Chathams, Campbell and Aucklands), with a small population on Taiaroa Head near Dunedin on New Zealand's South Island. This is the most accessible breeding locality of a southern albatross and is a famous tourist attraction. Total annual breeding population is about 11,000 pairs, but biennial breeding means there are about twice this number of breeders. As with the

wandering and Amsterdam albatrosses, the very long breeding season means royals, if successful, can only breed every second year. There are two subspecies, considered by some ornithologists to be worthy of specific status, but interbreeding has occurred at Taiaroa Head.

MARK NORMAN

Royals eat squid, fish and crustaceans caught at the sea surface. Like wanderers, they are accidentally caught by tuna longlines. It is hoped that recent regulations and new practices, such as only setting lines at night and using 'tori' poles with attached streamers to scare birds away from baited hooks, will protect this splendid bird.

Black-browed Albatross

The black-browed albatross *(Diomedea melanophris)* is one of the smaller mollymawks, but with a 2.5m wingspan and a mass up to 5kg, it's still a big bird. It can be identified at a distance by its underwing pattern featuring a wide, dark leading edge. At close range, the adult bird's yellow bill with orange-red tip and dark line through the eye makes identification easy.

Right: Royal albatross

Below: Black-browed albatrosses

WAYNE BERNHARDSON

The species is widespread in southern seas, and numbers may be seen accompanying fishing trawlers off Australasia, southern Africa and South America. Breeding occurs at nine island groups, spread from South Georgia to the Antipodes Islands, as well as at Cape Horn. There are many black-brows – probably more than 500,000 breeding pairs – so with nonbreeding birds the species' population is over 2 million. An annual breeder, the bird builds a cone nest out of mud and vegetation and lays a single egg. It often breeds in vast numbers: Beauchene Island, off the Falklands, has a colony estimated in 1991 at 135,000 pairs.

Black-brows eat squid, fish and crustaceans, caught at the sea surface or by shallow dives. Interactions with fisheries, especially long-liners fishing for tuna and toothfish, are a cause for concern. The species is still abundant and new measures being adopted by the fisheries should help with its conservation.

Shy Albatross

The shy albatross *(Diomedea cauta)* is the largest of the southern mollymawks, with a wingspan of up to 2.6m. Its distinguishing features are a hump-backed appearance in flight, dark upperwings which are not as black as other mollymawks' and a narrow dark leading edge to the underwing in both adults and juveniles. The shy albatross is misnamed, since it approaches and follows ships. It breeds on islands south of New Zealand and around Tasmania, with a tiny population of only four pairs recently found breeding on Îles Crozet. However, the bird (perhaps as many as four species) has a widespread at-sea distribution and can be seen anywhere in the Southern Ocean in the Roaring Forties and Furious Fifties. Total estimated population is 1 million birds, including juveniles. The largest breeding colonies are on the Bounty and Auckland groups.

Shy albatrosses lay single eggs in mud and vegetation nests in colonies on cliffs. They eat fish, squid and crustaceans. Interactions with fishing vessels are a serious cause for concern, but during this century, some colonies have increased in size as exploitation of the birds' feathers and eggs has greatly diminished.

Yellow-nosed Albatross

The yellow-nosed *Diomedea chlororhychos* is the smallest of the southern mollymawks, weighing up to 3kg. Viewed up close, the black bill with its striking orange streak on the upper mandible is a distinguishing feature. They breed on the northerly islands of the Southern Ocean: Tristan da Cunha, the French sub-Antarctic islands and Prince Edward Island. The Atlantic and Indian ocean populations are sub-specifically distinct, and may even be separate species: the Atlantic birds have noticeably greyer heads.

Below: Yellow-nosed albatross

The population is about 100,000 breeding pairs. At sea, they can be seen in the South Atlantic and Indian, but not Pacific, oceans. They breed annually, laying a single egg in summer in mud and vegetation nests. At some localities, such as Tristan da Cunha, they nest in a widely scattered pattern among dense fern vegetation. At Prince Edward Island, they nest on cliff ledges in a mixed colony with grey-headed albatrosses.

Their diet is similar to that of the other mollymawks. Among the yellow-nosed albatrosses nesting at Îles Crozet, fish

P PRINCE (BAS)

forms the bulk of the diet. Off southern Africa, yellow-noses scavenge from trawler discards. They were exploited for their eggs and flesh by the Tristan Islanders in the past, but are now fully protected. Interaction with fishing boats is a cause for concern, as some population decreases have been noted.

Grey-headed Albatross

Below: Grey-headed albatross

The grey-headed *Diomedea chrysostoma* is identifiable by its greyish head, broad, dark leading edge to the underwing and orange stripes on both upper and lower mandibles. A more southerly breeding species than the yellow-nosed albatross, with colonies on South Georgia, the Prince Edwards, Îles Crozet and Kerguelen, Campbell and Macquarie, the grey-head has a circumpolar breeding distribution. The most recent population estimate is 106,000 breeding pairs, which can be doubled since the bird normally breeds only every second year.

JIM HENDERSON (HEDGEHOG HOUSE)

Grey-heads breed in colonies on cliff ledges, sometimes alongside black-browed or yellow-nosed albatrosses. Like all albatrosses, they lay only one egg. Both parents share incubation and chick-feeding.

Diet has been studied at three breeding localities and appears to consist of fish, cephalopods and crustaceans, including Antarctic krill *(Euphausia superba)* off South Georgia. Interactions with longline fishing vessels remain its most serious conservation problem.

Darkmantled Sooty & Lightmantled Sooty Albatrosses

Below: Lightmantled sooty albatross

With care, it is possible to distinguish between the two species of sooty albatrosses at sea. The darkmantled *Phoebetria fusca* is uniformly chocolate brown, whereas the lightmantled *P palpebrata* has a contrasting pale back. When viewed close-up (impossible at sea unless the bird flies right alongside your vessel), the darkmantled sooty has a yellow stripe 'sulcus' along its lower mandible, whereas the lightmantled has a blue one. Their long, pointed tails and narrow wings make these two species easily distinguishable at sea from giant petrels, which have broader, shorter wings. The flight of the sooty albatross is most graceful, and many a happy hour can be spent watching them fly behind and alongside vessels traversing the Southern Ocean.

JIM HENDERSON (HEDGEHOG HOUSE)

Both species have circumpolar at-sea distributions, but lightmantles tend to occur farther south, reaching the edge of the pack ice. This is mirrored by their breeding distribution, with the darkmantle generally breeding farther to the north, such as in the Tristan group. In contrast, only lightmantles breed at South Georgia. Both species occur on sub-Antarctic islands in the Indian Ocean, making for interesting comparative studies of breeding biology and feeding ecology. Both nest in small colonies on cliffs. Their paired courtship flights and haunting calls around misty cliffs make up one of the quintessential experiences for visitors to Southern Ocean islands.

Annual breeding populations are about 16,000 pairs for darkmantles and 23,000 pairs for lightmantles. They eat squid, fish, crustaceans and small seabirds such as prions and diving petrels. Exactly how these last are caught remains unknown, but the species' agile flight and dark coloration suggests predation at night. Darkmantles were once heavily exploited in the Tristan group by the inhabitants (where they are called 'Peeoos' because of their haunting call), but fortunately no longer. *Phoebetria* albatrosses do not seem to get caught as often on longlines as do the great albatrosses and mollymawks, although a population decrease in the darkmantle at Îles Crozet may be due to being caught on fishing hooks. Sooty albatrosses are very special birds, admired by all fortunate enough to see them.

Giant Petrels

Giant petrels are the largest of the petrel family, which goes to make up the order of tubenose or procellariiform seabirds, along with albatrosses, storm petrels and diving petrels. The crucial feature used to distinguish the northern giant petrel (*Macronectes halli*) from the closely related southern giant petrel (*M giganteus*) is the color of the bill tip: greenish in northerns, reddish-brown in southerns. This characteristic is not easy to spot at sea. Some southerns are all white, except for the odd dark feather. This color phase does not occur in northerns, helping with specific identification. White-phase southerns are more common at southerly breeding sites, and absent at the northerly ones, such as Gough and Marion Islands.

COLIN MONTEATH (HEDGEHOG HOUSE)

Giant petrels can be seen in all parts of the Southern Ocean, with southerns occurring farther south – indeed, some breed on the Peninsula and in Terre Adélie. At New Zealand's sub-Antarctic islands, only northerns occur, whereas the birds that breed at the most northerly island, Gough, are southerns, not northerns as might be expected. Genetic studies should lead to a clearer understanding of these patterns. There are an estimated 12,000 breeding pairs of northerns and 36,000 pairs of southerns.

Southerns breed in colonies, while northerns breed singly or in scattered groups. Genetic isolation is helped by the fact that northerns commence breeding earlier. Both species are annual breeders.

Unlike albatrosses, giant petrels forage on both land and sea. On land, they kill birds as large as king penguins and scavenge in seal colonies. At sea, they eat fish, squid and crustaceans, and scavenge dead cetaceans and seabirds. Watching blood-stained giant petrels (nicknamed 'Nellies' or 'stinkers') squalling and fighting over a seal car-

Above: Southern giant petrel

Right: Antarctic petrel

cass is not for the faint-hearted. Indeed, old-time whalers used to call them 'breakbones.' But the birds have a raffish charm that appeals to some, and they are undeniably magnificent fliers.

Giant petrels are caught by tuna and toothfish longline fishing vessels in the Southern Ocean. Several populations of the southern species are decreasing, probably as a result. Northerns are faring better, with some increases recorded, perhaps due to increasing seal populations giving more opportunity for scavenging.

Antarctic Fulmar

A medium-sized petrel (800g, 1.2m wingspan), the Antarctic fulmar *(Fulmarus glacialoides)* is readily identified by its pale grey plumage with white head and black flight feathers. The bill is pink with a dark tip and the dark eye is a distinguishing feature. Antarctic fulmars are a southerly species with a circumpolar distribution at sea and are commonly found on pack ice fringes. They breed in large colonies on the islands off the Peninsula, the South Orkneys and South Sandwiches, and along the Antarctic coastline and on Bouvetøya. There are no good population estimates yet, but the bird is very abundant.

They breed from December to April on rock ledges on coastal cliffs, often in large and dense colonies. They feed on Antarctic krill and other crustaceans, fish and squid, as well as carrion. Food is caught by surface-seizing and occasionally by shallow dives.

Antarctic Petrel

The Antarctic petrel *(Thalassoica antarctica)* is a boldly marked dark brown and white petrel, a little smaller than the Antarctic fulmar. It is bigger but less speckled than a cape petrel, which is also dark brown

MARK NORMAN

and white. This species breeds only on the Antarctic continent, but not many colonies are known, and more may still be found. The largest known colony, at Svarthamaren in Dronning Maud Land, supports about 250,000 pairs. There is no good estimate for the breeding population, since many colonies have never been properly surveyed.

They breed in dense colonies on cliffs and steep rocky slopes, some of them 100km or more from the open sea on inland nunataks and mountain ranges. Eggs are laid in November after the adults arrive at their nest sites the previous month. Chicks fledge in March. The rest of the year, the colonies are deserted while the birds stay at sea among and just north of the pack ice. They eat Antarctic krill, fish such as *Pleuragramma antarcticum* and small squid taken by surface-seizing, dipping and shallow diving.

Snow Petrel

Snow petrels *(Pagodroma nivea)* are unmistakable. With their all-white plumage, black bill and small black eyes, they are truly creatures of the ice. Their flight is more fluttering than most petrels. They breed on the Antarctic continent and Peninsula, and also at Bouvetøya on rocky slopes and in crevices among boulders on nunataks and sea cliffs. No fewer than 298 breeding sites are known. The birds' at-sea distribution does not extend far north; they are very much denizens of the pack-ice zone, where they roost on icebergs.

They lay a single egg in late November or early December, and chicks fledge in March or April. Snow petrels are nervous at the nest and will desert their eggs if overly disturbed. This is in contrast to most of the petrel family, which are not too concerned about the presence of humans.

STEFAN LUNDGREN (HEDGEHOG HOUSE)

Snow petrels eat primarily krill, fish and squid, caught mainly by surface-dipping while on the wing. They can regurgitate their stomach oil as a defense mechanism. Deposits of this substance, called 'mumiyo,' have built up around nest sites over thousands of years and can be radiocarbon-dated. The oldest known colony dates back an astounding 34,000 years. No immediate conservation problems are known for the snow petrel.

Cape Petrel

The cape petrel *(Daption capense)* is a dark brown-black and white petrel smaller than the Antarctic petrel. Its speckled appearance gives it its other common name, pintado, which means 'painted' in Spanish. Interestingly its generic name *Daption* is an anagram of pintado and has no meaning otherwise. Some ornithologists think 'pintado' a far better name than the dull 'cape.' The old name 'Cape pigeon' is singularly unhelpful and has thankfully gone out of use: no pigeon can fly the oceans the way a petrel can.

Cape petrels have a circumpolar at-sea distribution, which extends much farther north than does the Antarctic petrel. In fact, they can be quite common off Africa, South America and Australia, especially in winter. They also have a wide breeding range: from the Antarctic continent to the more southerly sub-Antarctic islands, where they breed on cliff ledges. As an assiduous ship-follower, the cape petrel eats just about anything edible thrown overboard. In the days of whaling, it was seen in vast noisy numbers around South Georgia's whaling stations. There is no good information on population size and trends yet. There currently seem to be no conservation problems of note.

Great-winged Petrel

The great-winged petrel *(Pterodroma macroptera)* is an all dark-brown gadfly petrel found in the Roaring Forties. Separating it from the slightly smaller Kerguelen petrel is tricky and requires guidance from an expert or a good field guide. In New Zealand, a clearly differentiated subspecies is known as the grey-faced petrel. Great-wings breed on the sub-Antarctic islands of the South Indian Ocean, and also on islands around southern Australia and New Zealand.

They breed in winter and lay a single egg in May to July in burrows excavated in vegetated peat slopes. Chicks fledge in November and December, just when the summer-breeding burrowing petrels are getting started. Like most burrowing petrels, great-wings arrive at their burrows after dark, to reduce their chances of being caught by predatory Antarctic skuas. Breeding in winter may thus be an advantage, since most skuas leave the islands to winter at sea.

Above: Cape petrel

Left: Snow petrel

MARK NORMAN

Great-wings eat primarily squid, which is caught at night. They are numerous and not globally threatened. At some islands, however, introduced cats have reduced populations and caused nearly complete breeding failure, as at Marion Island in the 1970s and 1980s. Happily, Marion Island is now cat-free after a long and expensive eradication program, and the great-wings are breeding successfully again.

White-headed Petrel

A distinctive burrowing petrel of the sub-Antarctic, the white-headed petrel *(Pterodroma lessonii)* has a pale body and tail, dark wings and a white head with a dark eye. Thanks to its whiteness, it can be seen at great distances at sea, which is helpful to bird-watchers, since it seems to be unattracted to ships. White-heads have a circumpolar distribution at sea in the 40 to 60°S latitudes. They breed on Îles Crozet and Kerguelen, Macquarie Island, the Aucklands and the Antipodes.

They breed in summer, laying a single egg in burrows they excavate in the soft peat of tussock grassland. Their diet is not well known, but includes squid, crustaceans and lantern fish, caught by surface-seizing.

White-heads are not rare and their population probably numbers in the low hundred thousands. As is the case with many burrowing petrels of the sub-Antarctic islands, introduced cats have reduced populations, especially at Macquarie Island. Australia has instituted a cat-eradication program at Macquarie, so let us hope, in due course, for a success story similar to the revival of the great-winged petrels on Marion Island, which is now cat-free.

Atlantic Petrel

The Atlantic petrel *(Pterodroma incerta)* is one of the largest gadfly petrels, recognized by its white breast and belly, which are clearly demarcated from the rest of its uniformly brown plumage. They breed only on the Tristan da Cunha-Gough group. Their at-sea distribution hardly extends out of the Atlantic Ocean.

Practically nothing is known of the Atlantic petrel's population size, but it must be in the low tens of thousands at least. They breed in excavated burrows in winter, with chicks on Gough Island being fed in October. Their diet appears to be mainly squid, with fish a minor component.

In the past, Atlantic petrels – like other burrowing petrels – were exploited for meat and eggs by the Tristan Islanders. Fortunately, they are now legally protected, so they face no serious conservation problems.

Soft-plumaged Petrel

The soft-plumaged petrel *(Pterodroma mollis)* is a dark-brown and white, medium-size gadfly petrel. In flight, the back and upperwings carry a dark 'M' shape.

Soft-plumes occur at sea from South American waters east to New Zealand, mainly in sub-Antarctic latitudes, but they are absent from the South Pacific. They breed on the Tristan-Gough islands, the Prince Edwards, Îles Crozet, Kerguelen and the Antipodes. There are no good estimates of total population, since burrowing petrels are notoriously difficult to count, but they are abundant at many breeding localities and are commonly seen at sea within their normal range.

They eat primarily squid, caught by surface-seizing thought to occur mostly at night. Exploitation of the soft-plumaged petrel at Tristan da Cunha has halted, and the recent removal of feral cats from Marion Island should eventually lead the species to a recovery there. Cat abatement at other islands where they occur (such as Îles Crozet and Kerguelen) would further improve soft-plumes' conservation status.

Kerguelen Petrel

Kerguelen petrels *(Lugensa brevirostris)* are uniformly dark brown, except for their silvery underwings. Their smaller size and proportionally large head distinguishes them from the great-winged petrel. Their distinctive and fast soaring flight is also helpful in identification at sea.

Kerguelen petrels breed on the Tristan-Gough islands in the south Atlantic and on the Prince Edwards, Îles Crozet and Kerguelen. At-sea distribution is circumpolar, with irregular irruptions, linked to adverse weather conditions, bringing sometimes large numbers of birds to the waters off southern Africa and Australasia. Such birds are often then 'wrecked,' and their dead bodies may be found washed up on beaches.

They eat mainly squid, fish and crustaceans caught by surface-seizing at night. They breed in burrows in summer. There are probably several hundred thousand birds, so the species is in no danger of extinction, but eradication of introduced cats and rats at its breeding islands will help its conservation status.

Blue Petrel

The small (65cm wingspan) blue petrel *(Halobaena caerulea)* superficially resembles a prion, but look for the white – not black – terminal band to the tail. Blue petrels have a prominent dark 'M' shape on their upper wings and back. They breed at the Diego Ramirez Islands off Cape Horn, South Georgia, the Prince Edwards, Îles Crozet, Kerguelen, Heard and Macquarie. Their at-sea distribution is circumpolar, from far south to the more southern parts of the South American, African and Australian continents (where irregular irruptions following bad weather may bring large numbers to be 'wrecked' on shorelines).

Blue petrels are abundant and breed in large, dense colonies in thick tussock. One rough estimate puts the total population at 'several million.' No information is available on population trends, except that breeding success has improved with

Above: Kerguelen petrel

Below: Blue petrel

the removal of feral cats from Marion Island. This program, implemented by the South Africans, is probably the greatest conservation success at any sub-Antarctic island since the halt of the exploitation of royal penguins for their oil at Macquarie Island many years ago.

Blue petrels eat primarily small crustaceans, such as krill and amphipods.

Prions

Prions or whalebirds *(Pachyptila spp)* are small grey-blue and white birds. They can be distinguished from blue petrels by their black terminal band to the upper tail. All have a vague 'M' shape visible on their upper parts in flight. Their taxonomy is still a matter for debate – there may be as many as six species, which vary subtly in their markings and also by the width of their bills. Broadbilled prions *(P vittata)*, affectionately known as 'Donald Ducks' in some quarters, have the broadest bills, with lamellae for straining out food, analogous to the baleen plates of the great whales. The fairy prion *(P turtur)* and thin-billed prion *(P belcheri)* have narrow bills. At-sea identification of species can stump the very best experts in all but excellent (and close-up) viewing conditions.

Breeding takes place at many southern islands, with one or two species occurring together. Prions may burrow, or they may breed in crevices among boulders and at the base of cliffs in scree slopes. They can be seen in all areas of the Southern Ocean north of the pack ice to continental waters, often in very large flocks.

Their diet varies with species and bill width, as does their method of foraging, but small crustaceans, especially amphipods, taken by filtering or surface-seizing, are their main prey. Like most burrowing petrels of the southern islands, prions have suffered from predation by introduced cats and rats. Removal of these should eventually lead to population recoveries.

Grey Petrel

Grey Petrels *(Procellaria cinerea)* breed at the Tristan-Gough Islands, the South Indian sub-Antarctic islands, Campbell Island and the Antipodes. Their at-sea distribution is circumpolar, extending south past 60°S and north to continental coasts. Little is known of their numbers, because like all burrowing petrels they're incredibly difficult to count accurately.

They breed in winter and in March lay a single egg in burrows in peat or in rock crevices. Chicks fledge in October. Their diet is poorly known, but at Îles Crozet it is mainly squid and fish.

Introduced cats have severely diminished some populations, such as at Marion Island, where the grey petrel is now a rarity. Rats also take chicks at Îles Crozet and Campbell Island. Eradication of cats and rats from breeding sites is required for this species – and for a number of

Above: Fairy prion

Right: White-chinned petrel

other burrowing petrels – to ensure a healthy conservation status. Grey petrels are also caught on longline hooks, so they face threats both on land and at sea.

White-chinned Petrel

The white-chinned petrel *(Procellaria aequinoctialis)* is the largest burrowing petrel, with a wingspan reaching nearly 1.5m. The clearly marked spectacled form *(conspicillata)* may be a distinct species. In the past, white-chinned petrels have been called 'cape hens' and also 'shoemakers,' the latter based on their call, which resembles that of a cobbler hammering shoes. White-chins are bigger than the all-dark gadfly petrel species such as the great-winged and the Kerguelen, and their wings are held unbent in a 'stiff' manner, making them look like small giant petrels as they follow ships.

They breed at the Falkland Islands, South Georgia, Prince Edwards, Îles Crozet, Kerguelen and on New Zealand's sub-Antarctic islands. At-sea distribution is circumpolar, with a wide latitudinal range. They breed in summer, and their burrows are recognizable by their large size and the presence of a pool of muddy water at their entrance.

C DUCK (BAS)

They eat fish, squid and crustaceans, with the proportions of each varying at different localities. On the fishing grounds off South Africa's west coast, they often scavenge from discards left by trawlers.

Introduced cats have reduced breeding success at islands where they occur. The eradication of cats at Marion is helping to secure the white-chinned petrel's future, although the birds continue to be caught on longline hooks.

Great Shearwater

The great shearwater *(Puffinus gravis)* is handsomely marked. Its dark cap and white band at the base of the upper tail are very noticeable. They breed only in the Tristan-Gough group of islands and are not seen to any great extent outside the Atlantic (except off the east coast of South Africa). The species is a transequatorial migrant and is better known from its winter quarters in the North Atlantic than at its Southern Hemisphere breeding grounds, where it awaits detailed study.

The Tristan-Gough population is huge, and could number more than 5 million breeding pairs. The population appears stable, although it has been brought to very low numbers by past exploitation and habitat loss on Tristan da Cunha. Tristan Islanders on nearby Nightingale Island still legally take eggs and chicks (for their fat).

They breed in summer and lay a single large egg in short burrows among tussock and under trees. They often forage by plunge-diving and so can exploit more of the ocean than the surface-seizing gadfly petrels. Conservation threats include ingestion of plastic particles and pesticides.

Little Shearwater

The small (wingspan up to 27cm) black and white little shearwater *(Puffinus assimilis)* is recognizable by its low flight, which alternates glides with a few rapid wing beats. It is often seen in groups of two or three, usually close to breeding localities. It has a circumpolar at-sea distribution in the Southern Ocean.

They breed in summer, nesting in burrows, among tussock and in rock crevices on the more northerly islands of the Tristan-Gough group, on Île St Paul and on islands around Australia and New Zealand. They eat fish and squid, caught both by pursuit-plunging and surface-diving.

More studies are needed on this little-known bird, and the effect of introduced cats and rats at some breeding localities needs to be assessed.

Sooty Shearwater

The sooty shearwater *(Puffinus griseus)* is all brown, apart from its silvery underwings obvious in flight. Three characteristics distinguish it from the noticeably larger white-chinned petrel and the more solitary gadfly petrels: its distinctive, swift flight; its long, narrow wings; and its habit of occurring in large-to-huge flocks.

Sooty shearwaters have a circumpolar at-sea distribution. Their range crosses the equator in both the Atlantic and Pacific oceans, and extends south to the pack ice fringe. They breed in often vast colonies on islands off New Zealand and Cape Horn, and lay a single egg in burrows in November. Chicks depart in April or May. They eat fish (such as anchovies), squid and crustaceans, with proportions of prey varying with place and time.

DON HADDEN (HEDGEHOG HOUSE)

Sooty shearwaters face several pressures. Exploitation continues in New Zealand as part of traditional rites and customs, with perhaps 250,000 young taken annually by Maoris, who call them mutton birds. The birds also drown in gill nets in the North Pacific, and on some islands predatory species have been introduced. But with one estimate putting the Snares' population alone at 2.75 million breeding pairs, there seems no reason to be concerned about this species' conservation status.

Wilson's Storm Petrel

Storm petrels are the smallest and lightest seabirds in the world. The Wilson's storm petrel *(Oceanites oceanicus)* weighs only 35g to 45g. 'Willies' have a circumpolar distribution and cross into the Northern Hemisphere in the Atlantic, Indian and Pacific oceans. They breed on the more southerly sub-Antarctic islands, such as South Georgia, and on the Peninsula and continent, as well as on islands near Cape Horn and in the Falklands. They have been regarded as the world's most abundant seabird; there are certainly several million of them. They are regular ship followers and associate with whales.

They lay a single egg in December in burrows and rock crevices in cliffs, rocky slopes and scree banks. They eat mainly planktonic crustaceans, including copepods, krill and amphipods, as well as small squid

Above: Sooty shearwater

and fish, feeding while on the wing, skimming and pattering with their feet over the sea surface. Indeed, this behavior earned them their name, for 'petrel' means 'little Peter,' the Apostle who walked on the water with Christ on the Sea of Galilee.

Superstitious sealers and whalers called Wilson's storm petrels 'Mother Carey's chickens,' from 'Mater Cara,' the Virgin Mary, because they believed that the birds came to collect the souls of dead sailors: possibly too heavy a burden for such diminutive creatures?

Grey-backed Storm Petrel

The small grey-backed storm petrel *(Garrodia nereis)* is distinctively marked with white underparts, dark brown head and back and a grey rump. Grey-backs have a discontinuous distribution in the Southern Ocean, with three centers near breeding localities in the South Atlantic Ocean, South Indian Ocean and south of Australasia.

There are no accurate censuses, but the species probably numbers in the tens of thousands of pairs. They breed in summer and lay eggs in December, nesting in coastal grassland among tussocks and in hollows among rocks. Their diet has been little studied, but at Îles Crozet it comprises almost exclusively immature and planktonic *Lepas* barnacle larvae. They feed by pattering over the sea surface, and by dipping and shallow-plunging.

White-faced Storm Petrel

The white-faced storm petrel *(Pelagodroma marina)* has a distinctively marked head with a white line above the eye (the supercilium). The projecting feet on very long legs have yellow webs. They breed on islands around Australia and New Zealand, at the Tristan-Gough group in the South Atlantic and across the Equator in the North Atlantic. They must number in the low millions.

White-faces breed in summer, lay eggs in burrows in colonies in November and fledge in February. They eat planktonic crustaceans and small fish and squid, which they catch by pattering and dipping, probably at night. They sometimes get their legs entangled with free-living trematode larvae, which later can cause them to become snared in vegetation at their nest sites. An estimated 200,000 were found dead from this unusual cause in the Chatham Islands off New Zealand in 1970.

Black-bellied & White-bellied Storm Petrels

Black-bellied *Fregetta tropica* and white-bellied *F grallaria* storm petrels are medium-sized storm petrels. Closely related, they are separated by the presence or absence of a black line down the center of an otherwise white underbody.

White-bellies breed on the more northerly islands of the Southern Ocean, such as Tristan and Gough. Black-bellies breed on South Georgia, Îles Crozet, Kerguelen, and on islands along the Peninsula.

Both species breed in summer and nest in burrows in loose colonies. Diet, based on a study of black-bellies at Îles Crozet, includes free-living barnacle larvae, amphipods and small euphausiids, with fish occasionally taken. Foraging is by pattering and dipping.

Diving Petrels

Diving petrels are small seabirds with stubby wings that seem to whir like wind-up toys as they fly fast and low above the sea. Two species, the South Georgian *(Pelecanoides georgicus)* and the common *(P urinatrix)*, are difficult to tell apart, even in the hand. Most ornithologists do not even attempt to distinguish between them at sea.

Diving petrels are not seen at great distances from their breeding sites. South Georgians breed at South Georgia, and on islands in the South Indian Ocean and off New Zealand. Commons breed at a number of southern islands, from South Georgia to Tristan da Cunha and south of New Zealand. Populations are estimated in the millions.

Both species breed in summer in burrows in bare ground or in vegetated peat. They eat planktonic crustaceans, such as krill, copepods and amphipods, as well as small fish and squid. Prey is caught underwater by pursuit-diving, the birds using their half-open wings to 'fly' through the water like the diminutive auks of the Northern Hemisphere.

As with practically all the burrowing petrels, introduced cats and rats have severely reduced some populations of diving petrels. Both species appear to be extinct at South Africa's Marion Island, for example, most likely due to predation by the now-eliminated feral cat population.

Cormorants

There is not yet agreement on how many species of cormorants (or shags, to give them their other commonly used name) *(Phalacrocorax)* inhabit the southern islands and the Peninsula. There could be as many as seven or as few as two, depending on what taxonomic levels are used. All are reasonably similar.

Cormorants are inshore-feeding birds and are not normally seen out of sight of land. Their presence alongside a ship in the mist is a sure sign of approaching land, which must have been a comfort to sailors of the past.

DON HADDEN (HEDGEHOG HOUSE)

Cormorants breed on the Peninsula, on all the sub-Antarctic islands and on the islands south of New Zealand. Interestingly, the more northerly islands of Tristan da Cunha, Gough, St Paul and Amsterdam do not have resident cormorant populations. They breed in summer. Nests in colonies are made of seaweed and terrestrial vegetation on cliff tops and ledges directly above the sea. Up to three eggs are laid, and the young hatch naked, unique for a southern seabird. They eat mainly benthic fish, caught by deep and long dives from the surface.

Cormorants do not seem to be under any current threat, but some populations are so small (a few hundred pairs) that their status needs monitoring. Development of new fisheries, for example, could have adverse effects.

Sheathbills

Sheathbills are odd birds in a number of ways. They're not seabirds (for example, their feet are not webbed) but are in their own family, allied to waders. They cannot be mistaken for anything else as they strut and

Above: Imperial shag

squabble around penguin colonies. The greater, American, snowy or pink-faced sheathbill *(Chionis alba)* occurs at South Georgia, the South Shetlands, the South Orkneys and on the Peninsula. It migrates north to South America and the Falklands in winter. Lesser or black-faced sheathbills *(C minor)* are somewhat smaller, with noticeably shorter wings, and are strict residents of the four sub-Antarctic island groups of the South Indian Ocean, each with its own subspecies.

Sealers called sheathbills 'paddies' because of their thieving (really just honest scavenging) – undoubtedly a slur on both the birds and the Irish. They also called them 'sore-eyed pigeons,' a name which seems quite apt when one sees them.

Sheathbills nest in crevices in summer, usually near penguin colonies, where they scavenge widely on eggs, spilled food being fed to chicks, and carcasses killed by giant petrels. They also feed on intertidal life and on invertebrates in the peat.

At Marion Island, the lesser sheathbill population has decreased in the last two decades. This may be due to competition for terrestrial invertebrates from an increasing house mouse population. Further research is needed to see if the species is at any real risk. Elsewhere, no conservation problems have been described.

Kelp Gull

The kelp, or Dominican, gull *(Larus dominicanus)* is the only gull of the Southern Ocean. It lives on the Peninsula and at most sub-Antarctic islands, where it is resident year-round, generally in small numbers.

Like most southern seabirds, kelp gulls breed in summer. They lay up

to three (though usually only two) mottled eggs in an open nest lined with vegetation. Chicks can leave the nest soon after hatching, but are still fed by their parents until after they can fly. Diet includes scraps scavenged from giant petrel kills, and in penguin colonies, terrestrial invertebrates such as earthworms and moth larvae and intertidal shellfish such as limpets.

No conservation problems are known for this species, which also breeds in southern Africa, Australasia and South America.

Terns

Top: Sheathbills

Above: Kelp gulls & female elephant seals

Several species of tern *(Sterna spp)* may be seen in the Southern Ocean. The Antarctic *(S vittata)* and the rarer Kerguelen *(S virgata)* terns are breeding residents of a number of southern islands, the former being more widespread and occurring on the Peninsula as well. Away from land, terns seen at sea are most likely to be Arctic terns *(S paradisaea)*, long-distance migrants from the Northern Hemisphere.

All three species are similarly sized, slender, long-winged grey and white birds. Arctic terns in nonbreeding plumage have white foreheads and dark bills. The two breeding species are red-billed and have conspicuous black caps. Distinguishing Antarctic from Kerguelen terns, however, can confound even the experts. Kerguelens are probably resident on the few islands where they occur, whereas Antarctic terns migrate, several thousand reaching South African waters to spend the winter.

Antarctic and Kerguelen terns breed in summer, laying mottled eggs in open nests in loose colonies. They eat mainly small fish caught at the surface or by shallow dives within sight of land, often within the kelp bed zone.

Skuas

Skuas are large, heavily built gull-like birds, mainly brown but with conspicuous white flashes in their wings. South Polar skuas *(Catharacta maccormicki)* are marginally smaller than Antarctic or brown skuas *(C antarctica)* and have a paler plumage. Their flight is heavy, with relatively little gliding and much flapping.

Antarctic skuas breed on most of the southern islands, whereas South Polars occur on the Antarctic continent. On the Peninsula, both species occur, and hybrid pairs are regularly recorded. The South Polar skua has the distinction of being the world's most southerly bird: several have turned up at the South Pole.

In winter, both species leave their breeding localities and spend time at sea, occasionally even reaching the Northern Hemisphere. Both breed in summer, generally laying two mottled eggs in open nests on the ground. Breeding birds are strictly territorial and will quickly chase off intruders, not hesitating to fly – claws outstretched – right at the head of an unwelcome human who comes too near their nest.

South Polar skuas prey upon the eggs and chicks of penguins and other colonial seabirds (including adults of the smaller species) but also clean up any carrion. They also feed on Antarctic krill, squid and fish. At sea, they chase smaller seabirds to force them to regurgitate or drop their prey (kleptoparasitism), often retrieving it spectacularly before it reaches the water.

Above: Tern

Below: Antarctic skua

Skuas number in the thousands and seem to be at no particular conservation risk, although it has been postulated that decreases in burrowing petrel numbers (important prey) could have led to decreases in Antarctic skua populations at islands with cats. Because of the lack of pre-cat censuses, this is hard to prove.

Fishes of the Southern Ocean

The Southern Ocean supports more than 270 species of fish. Several are interesting because of their ability to survive in subzero waters without freezing. They actually have 'antifreeze' glycopeptides in their

blood. Members of the family Channichthidae, ice fishes such as the mackerel ice fish (Champsocephalus gunnari), have no hemoglobin and are 'white-blooded.'

Some finfish are now the target of commercial fisheries. As a consequence of initially uncontrolled fishing, several species are now 'commercially extinct,' such as the marbled notothon (Notothenia rossii) and the mackerel ice fish (Champsocephalus gunnari). Fisheries have targeted new species, which in turn have been overexploited. CCAMLR attempts to control the fisheries with a system of annual quotas and inspections.

One recently opened fishery is longlining for Patagonian toothfish (Dissostichus eleginoides). This continues to cause serious rates of death to seabirds that become hooked as lines are set around many islands and sea mounts in the Southern Ocean. This problem has led to the adoption by CCAMLR of a number of measures (such as only setting lines in the hours of darkness) in an attempt to reduce such mortality, but many fishing vessels operate unlicensed and unchecked in the vastness of the Southern Ocean, which makes enforcement difficult.

Unregulated fishing for and trade in toothfish (known as 'Chilean sea bass' or 'black hake' in the US, 'austro merluza negra' in Chile and Argentina, 'légine australe' in France, 'mero' in Japan and 'patagonsky klykach' in Russia) makes this fish a decidedly seabird-unfriendly product. Conservation-minded people should avoid buying it at the market or ordering it in restaurants. Concerted efforts to control this latter-day gold rush are trying to avoid both the fish's commercial extinction and the extinction of the seabirds of the Southern Ocean.

Antarctic Krill

Antarctic krill (Euphausia superba) is a 6cm-long planktonic crustacean that occurs in what at times are enormous swarms south of the Antarctic Convergence. Krill is sifted out of the water by the baleen whales, and eaten by many species of southern seabirds (especially penguins), squid, fish and crabeater seals, which have specially adapted teeth for this purpose. Without krill, the ecosystem of the Southern Ocean would collapse.

Antarctic krill (there is also a smaller species, the ice krill E crystallarophias) has been the target of a fishery for a number of years. Krill is difficult to process for human consumption. Catches peaked in the early 1980s at over 400,000 tonnes a summer season, but have subsequently dropped to much lower levels. Quotas are now set by CCAMLR, which also encourages research on krill and its predators.

Below: Antarctic krill

Terrestrial Invertebrates

The sub-Antarctic islands and the Antarctic continent are populated with specialized terrestrial invertebrates. On the islands, the often strong winds make flight maladaptive (too risky to be blown out to sea), so some flies and moths have become flightless. On the continent, tiny free-living mites inhabit the exposed soil and somehow survive the extreme cold and also the dryness, since liquid water is at a premium.

Inadvertently introduced invertebrates can become a problem on the islands. Slugs, snails, earthworms, spiders and aphids have all arrived, some changing the ecosystem balance in subtle ways. The cabbage moth *(Plutella xylostella)*, for example, has attacked the Kerguelen cabbage on Marion Island.

On the Antarctic continent, which supports no native terrestrial vertebrate life, studies have concentrated on the microbiota: ciliates, rotifers, tardigrades (also charmingly called 'water bears') and free-living nematodes. Most of these are only visible under a microscope, but their unseen presence does bring life to the continent's seemingly sterile nunataks and mountains.

Terrestrial Plants

Antarctica's plants differ greatly from those found on the sub-Antarctic islands. The high rainfall and long hours of summer sunshine allow the islands to support an at-times lush vegetation, epitomized by tussock grassland, fertilized by thousands of burrowing petrels. The continent, by contrast, supports only mosses, lichens and algae, along with two flowering plants, a grass *(Deschampsia antarctica)*, and a cushion plant *(Colobanthus quitensis)*, which have footholds on the comparatively milder Peninsula. Interestingly, global warming is believed to be the cause for the observed spread of this grass.

The true sub-Antarctic islands have many vascular ('higher') plants, but no woody species, so trees are absent. The more northerly cool temperate islands, such as Tristan da Cunha and Gough, support a few native tree species. One of the most intriguing plants of the South Indian Ocean islands is Kerguelen cabbage *(Pringlea antiscorbutica)*. As its scientific name suggests, it was used by shipwrecked 19th-century sealers to ward off scurvy. The early accounts differed in their opinion of its tastiness (and how to cook it), but it can be imagined that necessity came before flavor.

Marine Plants

The intertidal and subtidal areas of the southern islands support giant kelps such as *Durvillea antarctica*, which form thick bands around many of the islands and protect their shores from rough seas. The kelp 'forests' offer an environment that supports fish, shellfish, octopus and crustaceans, which in turn provide food for inshore-foraging birds such as cormorants and terns.

Kelps have a phenomenal rate of growth and constantly replace fronds as they are worn away by waves. Plants break free during storms and wash ashore, where they contribute to a new environment by fertilizing shore vegetation and providing soft 'beds' for resting elephant seals.

Other types of marine plants make up the phytoplankton, tiny single-celled plants at the bottom of the pelagic food chain. There are even ice algae, which stain pack ice pink or brown. During algal blooms at sea, the sheer density of phytoplankton is so great that they actually color the ocean.

ENVIRONMENTAL ISSUES

By Dr Maj De Poorter

Antarctica is often called the 'last paradise on Earth.' That may be a clichéd description, but it's also a good one. Where else can snow glow with so much deep, pink warmth? Where else can silence be so pervasive, accentuated only by a distant penguin squawk? Where else will a penguin be so curious as to waddle up to pick your shoelace, or a seal be so unafraid that it barely even lifts its head to look at you before snoozing on?

As in that other paradise, it was the human species that brought discord. Antarctica has a history of human folly to rival its history of intrepid endeavor.

The contemporary era has brought more modern and enlightened views about environmental protection, including an appreciation of Antarctica's intrinsic value as 'wilderness.' However, this modern outlook has not been achieved without significant pressure from the public.

Modern technology has also brought with it new problems and new threats to the Antarctic environment – including fishing, tourism and the potential for deep-sea mining. Some of these developments await satisfactory resolutions.

Antarctica is also impacted by human activities and pollution from often-distant parts of the globe. Radioactive fallout from atmospheric nuclear tests has been traced in snow cores, and birds and seals have been found to have pesticides and other toxins in their tissues. However, with the exception of the effects from global warming and the 'ozone hole,' which also have their root causes half a world away, this chapter focuses on impacts created within the Antarctic itself.

Exploitation of Marine Life
The Past
Sealers were the first to follow the explorers – and in many cases actually preceded them. For instance, the South Shetland Islands were discovered in 1819, and in the 1820-21 season, more than 50 British and American sealing vessels arrived. Their catch exceeded 42,000 skins. By 1823-24, the fur sealing was over, owing to the virtual extinction of the seals. Imagine the present-day fur seal colony at Bird Island, South Georgia (hundreds of thousands of seals), and then imagine the level of butchery it must have taken to wipe out such teeming life in a mere four summers. The sad pattern started with seals and repeated itself with whales and then fish.

The first Antarctic whaling station was established in 1904 by an Argentine-Norwegian company, which took 183 whales in its first season. An exploitation explosion followed. In 1912-13 six land stations, 21 factory ships and 62 catcher boats killed and processed 10,760 whales. By 1930-31, the kill had increased to 40,000. With the exception of the years during WWII, the killing continued at this level for the next 20 years. Targeted species had to be switched, as one after another they were driven to near extinction. Of the large whales, only the minke is still abundant. The other species – including the humpback whales seen frolicking in the Gerlache Strait – have been reduced to a small percentage of their original number.

Next to be exploited, in the 1970s, were fish (finfish, as they are called, to distinguish them from shellfish): commercially interesting species (Antarctic cods and ice fish) in the South Georgia area were 'vacuumed up' with great enthusiasm, mostly by the Soviet Union's fishing fleet. Commercial extinction (a condition in which there are so few individuals of a species remaining that it is no longer economically worthwhile to continue catching or hunting them) followed, from which these species have never recovered.

At the same time, world interest turned to krill. It was postulated that millions of tonnes might be harvested each year, solving the world's famines. Unfortunately, the optimistic estimates of huge sustainable catches were based on a lack of knowledge. For example, the small-sized krill present in wintertime were not juveniles (which would have pointed towards high productivity) but adults shrinking to reduce their need for food. Krill-fishing took off before this was discovered, and krill would probably have been added to the infamous list of mismanagement but for the natural restriction on its use as human food. Fluoride from the krill's carapace starts to move into its meat after the catch, making it unsuitable for human consumption unless it is processed very quickly, which is technologically difficult. The bulk of the annual catch is therefore used as fertilizer or food for fish or cattle – quite an irony after the high hopes that it might solve the world's hunger problems.

The Present
Seals Seals are officially protected on land and ice shelves, where they can only be killed for scientific purposes, provided a permit has been obtained. The Convention for the Conservation of Antarctic Seals extends this protection to the sea, the sea ice and the pack ice. It prohibits commercial culling of fur, elephant and Ross seals and establishes closed areas and closed seasons for the other species.

As recently as the 1986-87 season, a total of 4804 seals, mostly crabeaters, were killed by a Soviet expedition near the Balleny Islands. A certain amount of research was done on teeth from these catches, but environmental groups questioned what kind of 'science' could be the motivation for the kill. One of Russia's official explanations was that many schools wanted to have a seal specimen for educational purposes. The fact that no significant catches have taken place since then could indeed be due to the mind-boggling possibility that every school that wanted one now has its own stuffed seal. More likely, however, it is thanks to the large scars from orca or leopard seal attacks on many crabeater seals. The crabeater skins fall apart along these scars, making them commercially worthless. Talk about being saved by the enemy!

In theory, commercial sealing could occur at any time – the Convention still contains catch limits for crabeater (175,000), leopard (12,000) and Weddell seals (5000) – but the public outcry it would generate makes this unlikely.

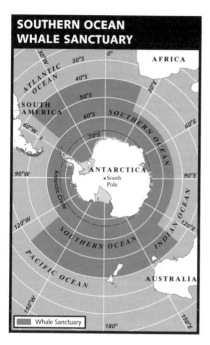

SOUTHERN OCEAN WHALE SANCTUARY

Whale Sanctuary

Whales The International Whaling Commission (IWC) was established in 1946 to regulate the 'orderly development of the whaling industry' worldwide. It agreed to a moratorium, which came into force in 1986, on all commercial catches, but that agreement has lately come under pressure from whaling nations. Additionally, in May 1994 the IWC established the Southern Ocean Whaling Sanctuary to protect the primary feeding grounds of the majority of great whales and to provide an opportunity for depleted species to recover. The sanctuary does not allow commercial whaling, even if the worldwide moratorium were to be lifted again. However, 'science' is used as a loophole; Japan kills 300 to 400 minke whales a year in the Southern Ocean and calls it 'research,' even though the program has not been endorsed by the IWC Scientific Committee and the meat still ends up in restaurants.

Finfish, Krill & Squid The Convention for the Conservation of Antarctic Marine Living Resources (CCAMLR) went into effect in 1982. CCAMLR represents a major breakthrough in marine conservation because, instead of considering each species separately, decisions on harvesting take into account the effects on other species (ie, predators). Its area of application is south of the Antarctic Convergence, a zone much larger than the Antarctic Treaty area, and this makes more sense ecologically.

The principles of CCAMLR are:

• prevention of a decrease in the size of any harvested population to levels below those which ensure stable recruitment (a fisheries term referring the new animals that are born each year)

• maintenance of ecological relationships between harvested, dependent and related species, and the restoration of depleted species to the level at which recruitment is stable

• prevention of changes or minimization of the risks of changes in the marine ecosystem that are not potentially reversible over two or four decades.

CCAMLR is one of the most ecologically enlightened international fisheries agreements to date.

Unfortunately, CCAMLR came too late to save many finfish species that had already gone into commercial extinction during the 1970s. Initially, too, CCAMLR could not make much headway toward establishing its innovative principles at all: consensus decision making was used by the fishing nations to block any regulations they didn't like.

Moreover, the fishing nations tended not to provide sufficient fishing data, and then insisted that in the absence of such data, there was no scientific basis to the catch limits.

Since those early days, however, the tide has turned and the burden of proof has been reversed: fishing tends to be limited unless there are scientific data to show that catches can be increased. Inspection and scientific observer schemes have also been put in place. This evolution has been due in part to the pressure of environmental nongovernmental organizations (NGOs) and in part to increased environmental awareness worldwide, and, to be honest, has been facilitated to a large extent by the collapse of the former Soviet Union. The change from a communist economy to one where the fleets have to pay market prices for fuel has meant that the pressure to keep chasing uneconomical catches has dropped dramatically. Moreover, with détente, the need for a Soviet 'presence' in the Southern Ocean was lessened (some of the fishing vessels used to bristle with an amazing array of unusual radio antennae).

However, at present, many environmental concerns remain unresolved by CCAMLR. Massive illegal catches of Patagonian toothfish in the South Georgia area (estimated to equal or surpass the legal harvest itself), for example, dramatically increase the risk of overfishing. Chilean and Argentine vessels are sometimes reported in contravention, Spanish and Norwegian commercial interests are 'disguised' through re-flagging of vessels, and ships registered in non-CCAMLR states are increasingly seen in the Southern Ocean. So far, in spite of widespread concern, no effective measures have been adopted, and the future looks bleak. In addition, the situation has created a flare-up of international political tension in this region of already disputed sovereignty.

Another current issue is the killing of albatrosses and petrels in the CCAMLR longline fisheries. The wandering albatross has been declining in number for decades. True to their name, they roam the oceans, and birds banded at South Georgia have been killed as far away as the Brazilian fishing grounds. The birds drown after they get hooked on the longlines when diving for the bait on them. Most casualties occur outside the CCAMLR area, but birds are also killed by the South Georgia longline fleets. CCAMLR has acted to address this problem in its own area by requiring the use of streamers to scare birds away from the bait and by taking measures to ensure that the baited hooks sink faster. In addition, CCAMLR has shifted the remaining mortality away from albatrosses by prohibiting long-lining during daylight hours. However, as a result of this change, more nocturnal petrels are being killed instead, which is no solution.

Exploitation of Minerals

Throughout the 1980s, Antarctic Treaty nations held closed-door negotiations for an Antarctic minerals regime. According to some, a regime would provide at least some protection when the 'inevitable' mining began. But to environmentalists, the wrong question was being asked. Rather than 'How should we mine?' they felt the question should be 'Should we touch Antarctic minerals at all?' Convinced that global opinion would answer that question with a resounding 'No,' the NGO community set out to make sure that the world at large knew about the negotiations and about the threat of mining to the environment, peace and science. Petitions were circulated (and millions of signatures collected) and secret documents from the governmental meetings were leaked and distributed. The public movement against the minerals exploitation in Antarctica built up and gained momentum. Despite this, governments signed the Convention for the Regulation of Antarctic Mineral Resources Activities (CRAMRA) in 1988.

CRAMRA was never ratified, though. The *Exxon Valdez* spill in Alaska, and the resulting images of oiled birds, sea otters and beaches on TV every night, followed in January 1989 by the sinking of *Bahía Paraíso*, which spilled refined fuel in the Antarctic itself, brought home to decision makers what environmentalists had been stressing all along: accidents would happen and the results would be devastating. Shortly after, the Belgian parliament, against its government's position, passed a law prohibiting Belgian nationals from taking part in Antarctic minerals activities. Then the French and Australian governments decided not to ratify CRAMRA, stopping it from ever coming into force. The Protocol on Environmental Protection, including a ban on mining, was negotiated and signed instead. The ban will continue indefinitely. In 50 years' time, the criteria required to lift it become less stringent, but if no action is taken, the ban goes on. It came into force in 1998, a clear example of people-power overturning government plans.

Global Changes Affecting Antarctica

Possibly the most spectacular discoveries in Antarctica have been those regarding the global effects of pollution, and the dramatic and disastrous effects that may follow. The issues of ozone depletion and global climate change are of relevance to everyone (not to mention plants and animals).

Ozone Depletion

Since its discovery in 1985, the spring ozone 'hole' over the Antarctic continent has continued to grow. This stratospheric ozone depletion is caused by various artificial chemicals such as chlorofluorocarbons (CFCs) and halons, mostly created in the Northern Hemisphere, half a world away from the Antarctic. This depletion is significant because stratospheric ozone restricts the amount of ultraviolet-B (UV-B) radiation reaching the Earth's surface. The hole allows substantially higher levels of UV-B to reach Antarctica and the Southern Ocean in spring and early summer, the peak period of biological activity. These increased UV levels threaten the plankton at the base of the Antarctic marine ecosystem, upon which all life – from fish to seabirds, penguins, seals and great whales – ultimately depends. Researchers have found a 6% to 12% reduction in marine primary productivity during the period of the 'hole,' and there are indications that the composition of planktonic communities may also be altered. In addition, Antarctic animals and the continent's sparse vegetation may become directly damaged by increased UV-B, or the even more worrying appearance of a band of shorter wavelength UV-C, by far the most damaging form of this radiation. Nobody knows yet to what degree Antarctic life can adapt to withstand this increasing stress.

Global Climate Change

The world's top climate scientists (members of the Intergovernmental Panel on Climate Change, or IPCC) suggest that global warming, resulting from the production of 'greenhouse gases' such as carbon dioxide, will be greatest in the polar regions. Recent British data shows a sustained atmospheric temperature increase of around 2.5°C in the Peninsula region since the 1940s. This rate is a tenfold increase over the last century in the global warming average.

Also consistent with the predictions of global climate change is the rapid disintegration of vast areas of ice shelves. In February 1995, an iceberg the size of Luxembourg calved off the Larsen Ice Shelf. At the same time, a large tongue of ice connecting James Ross Island to the northeast coast of the Peninsula also disappeared, together with a section of the northern part of the Larsen Ice Shelf. While the formation of icebergs is a regular occurrence in Antarctica, this one was unusual in that it had not been foreseen and was accompanied by large-scale disintegration of the ice shelf, including a 60km-long crack.

Some researchers suspect that winter sea ice is contracting. It is postulated that this will result in fewer associated sea algae. The extent of sea ice is known to influence penguin breeding success, and contracting of the sea ice cover is thought by some to have negatively affected Adélies in the Peninsula.

To make matters worse, ozone depletion over the Antarctic might exacerbate climate change even further by allowing greenhouse gases to persist longer in the troposphere and by killing off plants and phytoplankton, which remove carbon dioxide from the atmosphere. Disturbances caused by ozone depletion and/or global warming may therefore have major disruptive effects on the Southern Ocean ecosystems. Due to human disturbance, Antarctica, set aside for its environmental and scientific value, could still be lost.

What effect would a warming of Antarctica have on the rest of the world? In 1990, the IPCC calculated that warming in Antarctica would actually *decrease* sea level because the increase in snowfall was expected to be bigger than the increase in melting. Thus, more water would be frozen into the ice sheet through snowfall than would be released by melting. Now, scientific opinion has changed, and it is thought that warming in Antarctica would melt ice sheets and contribute to a rise in sea level. A rise of 30cm or 50cm, for instance, would spell the disappearance of entire Polynesian island-states. An alarming possibility is that the additional loss of West Antarctica's ice sheet, grounded ice that is thought to be unstable, could contribute to a sea level rise of up to 6m.

Environmental Impact of Science

There is no doubt that much Antarctic science is of global importance, while other subjects are more local in focus but nevertheless of intense interest. One doesn't have to be a scientist to be intrigued by polar summers with 24 hours of daylight, by ice cores several thousands of meters deep revealing the Earth's past climate, by fish with antifreezing agents in their blood, or by emperor penguins fasting for several months in winter while incubating a single egg on their feet.

Most humans on the Antarctic continent and islands are involved in some scientific endeavor, either research or related logistic operations. However, political motivations have always played a role in a nation's decision to establish scientific stations in Antarctica, from the seven nations with territorial claims and the US's establishment of a station at the South Pole itself (cleverly acquiring a presence in every claimed portion) to the rush of Antarctic scientific bases established during the 1980s – coinciding with the negotiations for mineral exploitation. Scientific activity, genuine or pretended, gives a country Consultative Party status in the Antarctic Treaty System, putting it 'inside' the decision-making circle.

The apparent lack of environmental awareness at some scientific bases has been criticized. This is not an argument against science, but one proposing that scientific research – and all other Antarctic activities – be carried out in such a way that the ecological, wilderness and aesthetic values are protected, along with the continent's value for future science. A clean Antarctic has great scientific value; a contaminated one doesn't.

Stations and some field activities have undoubtedly had a negative impact on the environment. Hallett, for example, was established in 1956-57 as a joint US-New Zealand station. The site, on the edge of the Ross Sea, was in the middle of a penguin rookery. To make room for it, more than 6000 birds were 'relocated.' Penguins that tried to return to their former nesting site were kept out with barricades of fuel drums.

The US's McMurdo station on Ross Island installed a nuclear reactor in 1961. It was shut down in 1972 and shipped back to the US – along with 101 large drums of earth made radioactive by 'normal discharge of effluent.' Later, another 11,000 cubic meters of soil were removed, and the site – still visible as the 'bite' taken out of Observation Hill – was not released for unrestricted use again until May 1979. The seafloor offshore from McMurdo station, meanwhile, holds a most extraordinary collection of rubbish, and toxic waste (including PCBs) pollutes its sediments.

Meanwhile, the Fildes Peninsula on King George Island, recommended as a Specially Protected Area (SPA) by the 1966 Antarctic Treaty meeting because of the biological value of its melt lakes, was largely turned into a construction site by the USSR and Chile in 1968 and '69, respectively, when they built stations there. The area's protected status had to be abandoned because its biological value was so diminished. China and Uruguay added bases later, within walking distance of each other. The once-protected melt lakes have been used both for drinking water and, ironically, for rubbish dumps. Today, only a very small Site of Special Scientific Interest (SSSI) remains protected on the Fildes Peninsula – protecting fossils, not lakes.

Other scientist-imposed damage on the Antarctic environment includes Argentina's Marambio station, which for decades threw thousands of empty, full or partially filled barrels containing fuel, chemical waste and ordinary rubbish over a bank, blanketing a vast slope to the sea and leaking toxins into soil and streams. At Australia's Casey station, a visiting scientist in 1986 found that an SSSI had been partially bulldozed, and that cement from nearby construction was killing mosses and lichens. More famously, in 1982-83, France started the construction of a hard-rock airstrip at its Dumont d'Urville station, thereby destroying the habitat of thousands of birds, including cape pigeons, snow petrels, Wilson's storm petrels and Adélie penguins, which, ironically, were named by French explorer (and station namesake) Dumont d'Urville for his wife. Explosives used to construct the airstrip killed many birds with rock shrapnel.

Even into the 1980s, many practices that were standard in the rest of the world had not yet caught on in Antarctica. Environmental impact assessments, for instance, were commonplace in many parts of the world, but not in Antarctica, the most pristine place on Earth.

Two common methods of waste disposal – open burning and discarding large pieces of equipment on the sea ice until it melted – would not have been acceptable at home in many Antarctic Treaty countries. 'So why in Antarctica?' NGOs asked. Military personnel, logistical restraints and financial considerations had all contributed to the situation in the past, but one of the main reasons for the careless behavior was that there were no independent eyes and ears to see 'down there.'

In the 1980s that changed. Tourists on ships were the first independent visitors. They also were the first to comment. Abandoned Hallett station, for instance, was cleaned up after tourists complained about the mess. Then came expeditions by NGOs such as Greenpeace.

They took pictures, wrote reports, brought independent journalists and generally poked their noses where no one had done so before. And the results showed. Station personnel, after initial suspiciousness, actually welcomed these environmental 'inspections' from Greenpeace, because they created pressure on the politicians at home to provide the bases with resources to operate in a more environmentally sound manner. The personnel on The Ice quite often had wanted to 'do the right thing,' but hadn't been able to convince headquarters of the need.

What has been the result? Hallett station (abandoned after two decades) has been cleaned up, and the penguins have reclaimed their territory. McMurdo is now running in a much more environmentally acceptable way. It now recycles materials, returns wastes to the US and no longer burns, incinerates or 'ice stages' rubbish (though NGOs still question the need for the base to be so big and point to the irreversible changes in landscape and soils). Bases on the Fildes Peninsula have emptied the lakes of rubbish (though it appears that some merely bulldozed the rubbish under soil and loose rock). They are also collecting and storing wastes for return to the country of origin. Marambio has undergone vast cleanups and regular environmental audits. The Australians had a big cleanup of their stations and old rubbish dumps and initiated stringent training of personnel. The French airstrip created so much controversy that 'mitigative measures' were put in place, at least preventing birds from being blown up during the dynamiting, and artificial breeding burrows for petrels were established. In spite of widespread protest, the construction continued until January 1994, when a tidal wave caused by a calving iceberg resulted in such destruction that the runway was abandoned (a case of natural justice, according to some).

Many governments now have environmental officers and waste management programs with environmental awareness training for all staff. The programs have cleaned up several old sites and abandoned buildings and, in some cases, have begun to audit the environmental impact of their activities.

The major international change in attitude, though, was the abandonment of CRAMRA and the 1991 signing of the Protocol on Environmental Protection instead. The Protocol designates Antarctica a special conservation area dedicated to peace and science. Its main principle states that the protection of the Antarctic environment and dependent and associated ecosystems, and the intrinsic values of Antarctica (including wilderness, aesthetic and scientific values) shall be fundamental considerations in the planning and conduct of all activities in the Antarctic Treaty Area. The Protocol also contains provisions on environmental impact assessments (EIAs), monitoring of environmental impacts, protection of flora and fauna, waste disposal, avoidance of marine pollution, and protected areas. The Protocol came into force in 1998, except for the Annex on Protected Areas, which requires separate ratification (expected in 2000).

While attitudes toward the environment have changed dramatically in the last decade, not all problems have been solved. To minimize cumulative impact, joint regional planning will be necessary. A first step would be the production of joint EIAs in a cooperative effort by all nations and tour operators active in a particular area – for example, the Dry Valleys.

Increased efforts to avoid the introduction of non-native species, including pathogens, to Antarctica are also urgently required. This urgency was highlighted by Australian research, presented at the Antarctic Treaty meeting in 1998, which indicated that some penguin colonies had been in contact with potentially lethal poultry disease pathogens, presumably transported by human visitors.

Both environmental groups and SCAR (the Scientific Committee on Antarctic Research) are concerned about the increased interest in 'bio-prospecting' of organisms by the pharmaceutical industry. It seems that the Protocol may not be well equipped to deal with this issue, since it doesn't specifically include micro-organisms in its protection. Nor are deep-sea organisms such as sponges adequately protected, as CCAMLR does not apply to them, and the Protocol only covers the area south of 60°S.

Another worrying global trend is the increasing commercialization of ownership of scientific data. This trend eventually results in restricted availability of knowledge – limited to those who can pay for it. Antarctic scientific research (including the history of global climate change, ozone depletion, monsoon research, and biodiversity) is of great value to all, and if this global trend were to reach the Antarctic, both science and the human race as a whole would suffer. Fortunately, the concept of freedom of access to scientific data and results is enshrined in the Antarctic Treaty. The challenge will be to safeguard this.

Environmental Impact of Tourism

Antarctica is an increasingly popular tourist destination. In fact, tourists visiting Antarctica greatly outnumber scientists and support personnel working on the continent. While the number of person-days is higher for scientists than tourists, tourists mainly visit areas where wildlife is concentrated, which increases the risk to plants and animals. Large numbers of people making frequent visits to a few popular sites intensifies cumulative long-term effects.

Some damage from tourism is obvious. Graffiti certainly does not benefit the historic relics on Deception Island, for instance. A more serious possibility is the introduction of non-native organisms to Antarctica. Cockroaches and house plants have been found aboard tourist ships. On sub-Antarctic islands especially, these species could create ecological havoc if they were to 'escape' into the environment. In East Antarctica's Larsemann Hills, non-native grasses have been found surviving after their inadvertent introduction by scientific personnel. Incidents of such accidental introduction, reported more and more frequently, are a growing concern.

An older example of environmental impact is Cape Royds, the southernmost Adélie rookery and home of Shackleton's Hut. Between 1956 and 1975, the number of penguins at Cape Royds declined sharply because of the steady flow of base personnel and VIPs and their accompanying helicopter traffic. The site was declared an SSSI, access to the actual breeding colony was restricted, and the penguin numbers have recovered.

On the other hand, recent results from a long-term study near Palmer station that compared changes in the population sizes of Adélie penguins at Torgerson Island (visited regularly) and Litchfield Island (a protected area) suggest that environmental variability rather than human disturbance was the key factor in changes to the penguin populations studied. However, one or two studies cannot – and should not – be extrapolated to other sites, other populations, other species or other local circumstances. Many more long-term, scientifically structured research programs are needed. In general, the absence of data does not equal the absence of deleterious effect. In other words, even if no damaging effect has been shown, it does not mean that there's no impact at all. It could simply mean that the damage has not been noticed, that only under specific circumstances is there no damage, or that not enough research has been done yet. Tourism in particular, with its many repeated visits to breeding colonies, carries numerous questions about its impact on populations.

We do know about specific cases in which human presence in the Antarctic has an impact. The classic example is a footprint in a moss bed, still visible a decade or two after it was made. Less obvious is the impact on 'invisible' wildlife, such as the algae species living inside rocks or flora underneath snow that may get trampled, or the damage done to ancient geological formations simply by walking over them (in the Dry Valleys, for example). Animals, too, can be affected even when they do not show it in their behavior, or at least not in a way that humans can easily notice. German researchers, for instance, found that heart rates of incubating Adélies increased markedly when they were approached by a human still 30m away, even though the birds showed no visible response.

Other effects of human presence can be very unexpected. The same German researchers found that a single human being, standing at a 20m distance from penguins 'commuting' on a well-used 'pathway' to the sea, caused the birds to deviate from their path by 70m, even hours after the person had gone. In one case, the single observer caused an estimated 11,934 birds to deviate during 10 hours (resulting in an extra 835 penguin km walked). Not surprisingly, the disturbance from helicopters was even more pronounced.

Does it matter? The assumption has to be that it does. Energy expenditure can be a crucial factor in breeding success. While one disturbance may not matter much, the combined effect of several disturbances could very well be detrimental.

This research concluded with a recommendation that nesting birds should not be approached closer than 30m unless absolutely necessary, that penguins walking between the colony and the sea should not be approached closer than 100m by humans on foot, that aircraft should use the same paths each time, and that very noisy aircraft (Puma helicopters, for instance) should not approach colonies closer than 1000m horizontally or 200m vertically.

In the past, Antarctic Treaty regulations included 'safe' distances to approach wildlife, but the 1991 Special Consultative Meeting decided to abandon these because they were probably too liberal and because it was very hard to reach agreement on what they should be. Where tour companies have rules about approaching wildlife, the recommended distances tend to be based on the former regulations and allow far closer approaches than the distances suggested by the German research. Of course, that study was only performed on one species (Adélies), and on a limited number of birds. But who should carry the risk caused by our ignorance about the exact effects of human beings on wildlife? Should the risk be that animals are disturbed? Or that people may be unduly restricted and miss a particular photo opportunity? The precautionary approach demands the latter option.

One problem very specific to the tourist industry is the number of different operators involved, all with their own commercial interests to protect. While most individual IAATO (International Association of Antarctica Tour Operators) members produce reasonable EIAs, this does not properly deal with their impact. Instead, operators need to produce joint EIAs, sitting down with each other prior to each season to work out how their activities are going to affect each other and the environment, and how they can limit the combined impact. One shore visit by one vessel to a particular colony may have a negligible impact, but what about several ships a day, several days in row? In practice, this will almost certainly require limits on where to visit, and on the number of ships or people allowed into a particular region or site during a particular season.

Land-based tourism, including the building of hotels and hard-rock airstrips, is opposed by all environmental NGOs, on the basis that the environmental impact cannot be justified. Some environmental groups are opposed to all tourism in Antarctica, but many environmental NGOs, including Greenpeace, the Worldwide Fund for Nature (WWF) and the Antarctic and Southern Ocean Coalition (ASOC) are not opposed to most ship-based, yacht-based or small adventure tourism groups per se, provided their environmental management is, as a minimum, in accordance with the Protocol.

However, the continued growth of tourism, the lack of sufficient knowledge about the environmental impact of visitors and the desire of some to go to ever 'new' places has led these environmental groups to ask for limits on the number of tourists visiting Antarctica and the number of sites they visit.

The recent appearance of very large tourist ships (those carrying more than 400 passengers) with their associated increased risks – and without a discussion on the philosophical or ethical desirability of such developments in Antarctica – has raised the level of concern. If these issues are not satisfactorily addressed, it wouldn't be surprising if environmental concerns focus increasingly on all commercial tourism as a problem activity. The tour industry's attitude toward the Antarctic environment will determine its fate.

Your Own Presence

Before undertaking a trip to the Antarctic, you should ask yourself: Would I be just as happy going somewhere else or watching a documentary? Or is visiting Antarctica truly a dream come true?

While you're on The Ice, there are further aspects to consider. As a minimum, stick to the guidelines that you are given by your operator – but don't hesitate to apply your own more stringent rules, especially about approaching wildlife. Don't be afraid to speak up if there are aspects that you particularly like or dislike about the tour operator, ship or voyage, or about your fellow passengers' environmental attitudes – do it *at the time, not later*. If you have comments, tell the captain, the expedition leader, the organizing company, IAATO, environmental watchdog organizations and your department or ministry of foreign affairs. Remember, your comments don't have to be limited to the tour you were on. If you feel positive or negative about anything you witnessed, whether by commercial or government programs, tell people about it. Antarctica is still a remote place, and its native inhabitants cannot speak for themselves. You can – and must – do it for them.

Antarctica is a continent of beauty and nature, a place to be in awe of – not an amusement park. Just as bungee jumping would be inappropriate in a cathedral, it (and similar activities) are inappropriate in Antarctica. Every human presence in the Antarctic has an environmental impact. Depending on the activity, the impact will be small or large, direct, secondary or cumulative. There are cases where the impact can be justified, and there are cases where it cannot. If you are visiting Antarctica, you have a responsibility to treat this subject seriously.

ANTARCTIC SCIENCE

By Dr David Walton

Introduction

From Exploration to Science

Captain James Cook was not impressed by Antarctica in 1775. He had been looking for a fabled continent rich in resources that he could claim for the British Empire. Instead, he found foul weather and endless ice. Cook, who qualified his failure to reach the continent of Antarctica by stating that the world would not 'be profited' by the discovery, would have been surprised to see just how important Antarctica has become for science.

But how could he have known about the importance of the Antarctic ice sheet to world climate and sea level, the special features of the high atmosphere that produce the southern lights, the remarkable food chains in the Southern Ocean, or the key role played by Antarctica in the origin of all the southern continents? Particularly in the last 40 years, Antarctica has come to play a central role in many scientific disciplines.

Why Do Science in Antarctica?

Antarctic science is expensive science. So why do science in Antarctica? The answers are slightly different for each discipline, but all have three principles in common: only undertake the kind of science in Antarctica that cannot be done elsewhere in the world; only undertake the highest quality science; and if possible make sure it contributes to solving a global problem. Despite the remoteness of Antarctica, some of the research done there is immediately relevant to the more populated areas of the world. The most obvious example is the study of the increase in ultraviolet radiation – but there are others, such as research on the world sea level and on satellite communications.

Two important features of all science in Antarctica are (1) that the research findings are freely available to everyone and (2) that many of the projects are internationally coordinated and supported. This coordination has been organized since 1957 through the Scientific Committee for Antarctic Research (SCAR). Each year, every country active in Antarctic science makes a report on its projects to SCAR, and every two years SCAR organizes a two-week international meeting to report on progress and plan for the future.

The extent and quality of science undertaken by any nation in Antarctica depends not only on the excellence of the scientists themselves but also on the logistics the facilities provide. In many fields, state-of-the-art science can now be carried out in Antarctica. The installation within the last 20 years of research aquariums at Jubany, McMurdo, Palmer, Rothera and Terra Nova Bay stations has been as important to marine biologists as the expansion of automatic weather stations on the polar plateau has been to climatologists.

When visiting scientific stations or field camps in Antarctica, you will only be able to gain a glimpse of the complex facilities required to support modern science. Many of the most exciting developments are too remote to be easily accessible to tourists, yet you should see and hear enough from scientists that you meet to capture something of the excitement and importance of Antarctic science.

Living on a Scientific Station

There is a wide range of sophistication among the various stations. Some are little more than storage containers or primitive huts, providing only the most basic protection for short visits. Others are the height of modern convenience, with private rooms, showers and a range of sports facilities. Some have email facilities available to all, while others have limited communication capabilities. Each one in its own way reflects the culture of the nation that established it – visiting Antarctic research stations is seeing a distillation of national characteristics.

Many of the scientists and support staff are there only for the summer, or part of it. They come from a wide range of backgrounds, and there are major differences in the way each country organizes its programs. The UK, Germany, Russia and Japan all have major polar research institutes, which provide most of the scientists and the support staff. Other countries such as the US, Italy, New Zealand, Sweden, Argentina, Chile and Brazil draw most of their scientists from universities, and contract the support systems either from civilian or military operators. Australia and Norway have a hybrid system, with a research institute that runs the logistics and provides a limited number of scientists, with the balance of the researchers coming from universities. Two countries, the Netherlands and Belgium, possess neither stations nor ships, but instead buy places for their scientists on the expeditions organized by other countries.

While some scientists using the air link to McMurdo or Rothera spend as little as a month in Antarctica, personnel at British and Russian stations

'Apple' huts – field camp lodgings

may spend up to 2½ years there without a break. Wintering in a small community, completely cut off from the rest of the world, can be a profound experience and often produces lifelong friendships.

For a long time, Antarctic stations were seen as a male preserve, a historical hangover from the days of Amundsen, Scott and Byrd. All that has changed, with women assuming increasingly important roles at all levels in the organization of stations, including base commander and the leadership of scientific teams. Most stations are still predominantly staffed by men, especially where the support personnel are supplied by the military, but women have comprised nearly half the population of McMurdo in recent years.

For those who are in Antarctica for a long period, especially over winter, a variety of activities occupies their time. Quite apart from the work programs, there are opportunities to develop hobbies, acquire new skills (have you ever wanted to operate a radio or overhaul a generator?), and learn to ski and travel over snow. Midwinter is a special time for all overwintering staff, when social life and parties take precedence over work. The sun is below the horizon for many stations and all of the encampments have been cut off from the rest of the world for months. Some stations even continue the tradition started by Scott and Shackleton of preparing a Midwinter Book, with poems, paintings and photographs contributed by station members.

For many people, going to Antarctica is an opportunity to visit what is perhaps the least disturbed part of the world, to take part in their own adventure, to go where few have gone before. Others are motivated by their interest in science and by the unique features of Antarctica and its surrounding seas. And some are attracted by the extra pay that they get while in Antarctica. Regardless of their reasons, they all experience the same magic that draws you.

The Southern Ocean

The stormy waters of the Southern Ocean encircle Antarctica in a continuous ring of mainly eastward-flowing water. This water comprises 10% of the world's oceans; as well as connecting the Atlantic, Pacific and Indian oceans, it also isolates the continent from warmer waters. The Antarctic Circumpolar Current has an average rate of flow four times greater than the Gulf Stream.

One of our major interests in the Southern Ocean arises from its influence on global climate. The region where the cold Antarctic water meets the warmer waters of the northern oceans is called the Antarctic Convergence, or Polar Front. The seas south of the Antarctic Convergence contain the coldest and densest water in the world. This water, called Antarctic bottom water, is formed as seawater sinks to the ocean floor when ice shelves melt. It then moves along the ocean floor into the Northern Hemisphere, where it adds oxygen and reduces the temperature of these seas to less than 2°C. This cooling effect on tropical and temperate seas is an important feature of the world's heat balance.

Several countries have put current meters on the seafloor around Antarctica to provide data on these deep water movements. This is part of the World Ocean Current Experiment, which is attempting to measure current patterns for all the oceans in order to improve existing computer models for predicting climate change.

Tides are another focus of oceanographic research. In the late 19th century, oceanographers realized that tides were different in different oceans. It has always been more difficult to measure tides in icy waters because the ice destroys the gauges. However, a network of robust gauges, which often report their data via satellite, has been installed at various Antarctic stations. This provides information on how the world ocean level is changing, which is of great interest to those living in coastal communities all over the world.

Three circumstances would result in sea level changes: expansion of the volume of the world's oceans as they warm up, melting of valley glaciers and changes in Antarctic and Greenlandic ice sheets. Existing data suggest that the average world sea level has risen by 10cm in the last century. During that time, the Antarctic ice sheet is believed to have remained roughly stable. It appears that sea level will continue rising by 1 to 2mm per year, without any extra contribution from the Antarctic. Even minor melting of the Antarctic ice cap will significantly increase the rate of rise.

Antarctic Marine Life

The Southern Ocean's very cold water allows more oxygen to dissolve in the sea, which is advantageous for marine life. This, with the upwelling of currents which bring nutrients from the seabed to feed microscopic algae at the surface, is the key factor of all life in the Southern Ocean.

In this marine food chain, the microscopic algae (or plankton) provide food for krill, which in turn are eaten by fish, whales, seals and birds. There are some other diet preferences – for example, leopard seals eat penguins, sperm whales eat squid, and seals eat fish – but despite this, the food web remains remarkably simple when compared with other oceans. Although a tremendous diversity of organisms lives on the Southern Ocean seabed (benthic species), only a limited range of fish inhabit the water column (pelagic species).

A great deal of research is being carried out on seals, birds and terrestrial plants, but the major focus of current study is the marine ecosystem. To undertake such research requires expensive infrastructure: icebreaking research vessels, scuba diving facilities, labs at research stations and access to satellite data. This high cost has helped to promote international research cruises, such as those by the German vessel *Polarstern*, in which expenses are shared among several countries.

The importance of being able to work anywhere in the Southern Ocean has prompted several countries to make huge investments in modern research vessels capable of operating in heavy ice. Some examples that you might see around the Antarctic – besides *Polarstern* – include the US's *Nathaniel B Palmer*, Britain's *James Clark Ross*, Australia's *Aurora Australis*, Japan's *Shirase* and Russia's *Akademik Federov*.

Warm-blooded Animals

Birds Antarctic birds are spectacular – in size, numbers and habits. Many are very tame, making them excellent research subjects. Their total dependence on the sea for food, the bizarre breeding habits of some species and their unusual ecological adaptations are of great interest to ornithologists. Among the birds, penguins and albatrosses are favorite research subjects.

The initial requirements for studying penguins and albatrosses are to record their breeding behavior, rates of growth and diet. All the species return to the same nesting sites each year, so it's easy to mark individual birds with numbered leg rings when they are chicks and follow them through their lives. Analysis of stomach contents of adults when they return to feed their chicks gives information on diet, while daily weighing of the chicks provides growth rates.

More complex questions, such as where are the adults getting the food, when do they find it, and how much energy do they use searching for it, can be answered with the help of modern technology in the form of electronic devices that can be attached to the birds. A tiny satellite transmitter on a bird's back can report on its position, while a small tube on its leg can collect data on the depth and timing of its dives for food. Even the oxygen consumption required for swimming or flying can be measured automatically. Back at the colony, the chick sits on an electronic replica nest, which weighs the little bird automatically every 10 minutes, avoiding the disturbance caused by handling. From this data, the weight of each meal and the growth of the chick can be calculated very accurately. The latest artificial nests are so sensitive that they even detect rain by the increase in the wet chick's weight!

The increasing numbers of banded birds have allowed the calculation of when birds first breed and the success of individuals in raising chicks, as well as pinpointing of the origins of birds found dead. Annual monitoring of the breeding success of penguins is undertaken at a number of sites to measure the effects of fishing on the marine ecosystem. If too many fish or krill are caught, there won't be enough to feed the chicks. This monitoring program is a key contribution to the work of the Convention for the Conservation of Antarctic Marine Living Resources, which sets limits on fish catches for the Southern Ocean to ensure that they don't damage bird and seal populations.

Seals Six species of seals are found in the Antarctic, and another three inhabit the sub-Antarctic islands. Probably no other group of animals has attracted such a wide and detailed range of legislation. There is a special international Convention for the Conservation of Antarctic Seals, and two species – the fur seal and the Ross seal – are the only animals given special protection under the Antarctic Treaty. Such large animals at the top of the marine food chain pose exciting research questions.

Until recently, for example, very little was known about the life of elephant seals at sea, though their mating behavior on land is well understood. Again, the use of satellite transmitters and other electronic equipment has provided remarkable data: while at sea, elephant seals spend almost 90% of the time submerged, making dives of up to two hours' duration and reaching depths of more than 975m. How they manage this is the subject of wide-ranging physiological research, mainly by British scientists at South Georgia and US scientists (working on Weddell seals) at McMurdo.

Harder to determine is the diet of each seal. The latest research analyzes the feces to identify prey from hard parts such as fish bones, or uses unique biochemical markers associated with particular prey types.

Long-term studies by Australian, British, French and US scientists aim to determine if seal populations are increasing or declining. For those species that breed on land, pups can be counted, and for some studies individual animals are marked with flipper tags. For those that breed on ice, such as crabeaters, even pup-counting is difficult. Efforts continue, using helicopters and icebreakers to allow scientists to penetrate the pack ice when the maximum number of animals is likely to be visible.

Sampling of seals' blubber and milk has shown a slow but steady accumulation of pesticides and other organic poisons, transported south from the industries and agriculture of the Northern Hemisphere. As yet, their long-term effects on seals are unknown.

Whales The most productive research period on whales coincided with commercial whaling, and the data collected was used by the International Whaling Commission to set quotas. Since commercial whaling was banned, almost all whale research in the Antarctic has ceased. While there are still occasional attempts to survey areas in order to estimate population numbers, most whale research is now undertaken in more congenial areas such as Baja California. The Japanese and the Norwegians continue to hunt a few whales, usually minkes, each year under a rule that allows limited collection for scientific purposes, though many countries object to this.

Cold-blooded Animals

Fish The first fish from Antarctica were collected in 1840 during Sir James Clark Ross' expedition. Since then, a great deal of research has been undertaken to establish the diversity, life histories and extent of the fish stocks. Commercial fishing began in the Southern Ocean when the first Soviet vessels arrived in the mid-1960s. The fishery is now regulated by the Convention for the Conservation of Antarctic Marine Living Resources (CCAMLR).

About 200 species of fish have been recorded south of the Antarctic Convergence. The main deepwater species are not restricted to the Antarctic, but the coastal species are. Although this latter group has representatives from 15 families, over 60% of the species and over 90% of the individuals belong to just four families, making Antarctic fish very different from those of other oceans.

Most research has concentrated on the two most abundant groups: the Antarctic cod *Nototheniidae* and the ice fish *Channichthyidae*. Initial interest focused on the evolution of the groups, their ability to survive in icy waters, their reproduction and growth rates and their population age structure. These last areas of research naturally also interested commercial fishermen.

These fish resist freezing, thanks to protein-based antifreezes in their blood that prevent ice crystals from forming in their tissues. The studies analyzing this freezing resistance – which were pioneered largely by US scientists – are of great commercial interest, relating to the way in which freezing changes the texture of food – ice cream manufacturers, in particular, have taken notice.

The unusual physiology of the ice fish, which have no hemoglobin in their blood to carry oxygen, has spurred scientists from France, Italy, New Zealand and the US to try to learn what mechanisms evolved to take its place. We now know that oxygen is carried in the ice fish's blood plasma, but this has only 10% of the oxygen-carrying capacity of fish blood containing hemoglobin. To make up for their lack of hemoglobin, ice fish have more blood, a larger heart, larger blood vessels and more gill surface area, and can even exchange oxygen through their tails.

All Antarctic fish grow slowly, with most coastal species requiring five to seven years before they can breed. This is of great importance when deciding sustainable catch limits. Unfortunately, when fishing started in the Southern Ocean, this was not recognized and too many fish were caught, endangering some species. Much current research is concerned with making more accurate estimates of growth and population size.

Squid Little is known about the biology of most species of squid. They seem to grow much faster than Antarctic fish and vary greatly in their adult size – ranging from only 2cm long up to 20m – and most appear to be cannibals. They have several defense mechanisms, the best known being the black 'ink' squirted out to blind or confuse predators.

Because they can move very quickly in the water and have excellent vision, squid are difficult to catch. Therefore, much of our knowledge of them has come from those found in the stomachs of fish, birds, seals and whales. Several researchers are now attempting to collect basic data on squid by fishing for them. Questions of particular interest are when and where squid breed, what they eat, and the population size of each species.

Squid are also being caught commercially, mainly by boats from Japan and Taiwan. Unfortunately, many squid species have only a one-year life cycle, making them sensitive to overfishing. Although most studies so far have been on the squid stocks around the Falkland Islands, there is every reason to suppose that there are significant populations farther south, though this is not yet certain.

Krill Zooplankton are the tiny sea animals that graze on algae, or phytoplankton. In Antarctic waters, zooplankton are dominated by krill, the single most important food of whales, seals and birds – especially penguins.

Hundreds of research papers have reported on every aspect of krill's life cycle and biology. Many of these papers have obvious commercial uses: describing how to find krill, how to estimate the size of a krill swarm using acoustics and how best to process krill for various uses. Though relatively easy to catch once a swarm has been identified, krill have proved costly to process and difficult to market.

Krill possess some of the most powerful protein-digesting enzymes ever found, so they must be processed very rapidly or their tissues begin to break down, turning black and mushy. They become unfit for human consumption after three hours on deck and unfit for cattle feed after 10 hours. Krill also have high levels of fluorine in their outer shell, making them toxic unless the shell is completely removed. Japan and Russia, which now do most of the krill fishing, have perfected equipment for peeling and processing krill rapidly. Frozen blocks of krill meat are made for human consumption, while krill paste is a high-protein additive for pig or cattle feed. The original estimates of the available stock of krill were very large, and some hoped it would provide a cheap, protein-rich food for the world's famine-plagued regions. But catching and processing costs have made krill a first world rather than a third world food.

Interest in krill research continues, with projects being conducted by Australia, Brazil, Chile, Germany, Korea, South Africa, the UK and the US. We still need to know more about krill populations within the winter pack ice – how much of the Southern Ocean algae is eaten by krill, how long krill live (they're difficult to age) and how much krill there actually is in the Southern Ocean. Even krill behavior is inadequately described, although there has been some success recently using video cameras lowered off the side of a ship into a krill swarm.

Algae The productivity of all Antarctic ecosystems rests on the photosynthesis of the microscopic algae (phytoplankton) floating in the upper layers of the Southern Ocean. The upwelling of cold, nutrient-rich water provides ideal conditions for the growth of plankton, which numbers more than 100 species in the Southern Ocean. When a ship is breaking its way through sea ice, the floes often turn over and show brownish bands or discoloration underneath. This is a film of ice algae, grazed during the winter by krill.

Phytoplankton contain chlorophyll, which can be detected by satellite. Recent research shows that the highest concentrations of phytoplankton coincide with high concentrations of nutrients, especially iron. The plankton takes up carbon from carbon dioxide dissolved in the water, and, when it dies, takes the carbon down into the sediments. It can therefore be seen as a 'sink' for carbon. Given the present interest in increasing levels of carbon dioxide and global warming, this finding has prompted considerable research on how much carbon can be taken out of the atmosphere by the phytoplankton and what, if anything, can be done to increase the rate. Some scientists have even suggested that iron is in such short supply that we should consider stimulating carbon uptake by dumping iron in the ocean. So far, experiments have not demonstrated that this would work.

Of equal concern for global warming is the relationship between phytoplankton and a compound called dimethyl sulfide (DMS). This compound is believed to form aerosols when it leaves the sea, and these aerosol droplets promote cloud formation. The subsequent increase in cloudiness increases the amount of radiation reflected back into space and this in turn leads to atmospheric cooling. This mechanism would therefore act to slow down global warming. We know too little about the whole DMS cycle, but what we do know suggests that the Southern Ocean may play a very important role in DMS production.

The annual increase in springtime ultraviolet levels has stimulated research on its effects on phytoplankton. Analysis of historical data arrived at from sediments suggests that there has been no significant change, yet experiments have shown that some species are very sensitive to UV, while others, such as diatoms, are able to protect themselves by making protective pigments.

Many inshore areas of Antarctica have a good covering of seaweeds (macroalgae) below the depth at which the scouring effects of winter ice would remove them. Surprisingly little research has been done on seaweeds, with most of the recent work being done by Dutch and German scientists. Even less is known about giant kelp, a seaweed found around sub-Antarctic islands and the Falkland Islands. The large, brown straplike fronds of the biggest kelp *(Macrocystis pyrifera)* are known to grow at a rate of 30cm per day during the summer, despite the low water temperature.

Seafloor Communities Very little is yet known about the species that inhabit the seafloor around Antarctica. These communities are called the benthos, and are as rich in plants and animals as a tropical coral reef. They comprise Antarctica's true indigenous flora and fauna, adapted to life in a cold ocean over tens of millions of years. Many species are limited to the cold waters south of the Antarctic Convergence – and many are yet to be discovered. Nearly every time a deep-sea sample is brought up, it includes some species new to science, or one that has been collected only once before.

The annual formation of sea ice has a strong effect on much of the benthos, whose food supply consists mainly of algal cells falling to the bottom as they die. In winter, there is only ice at the surface, so seafloor organisms must live for long periods with little food – or use a much wider range of foods than benthos in other oceans. Not surprisingly, this means that they grow slowly and usually reproduce slowly.

Current research increasingly takes place on board ships or in aquariums at stations. The principal efforts in this area are being made by US scientists at Palmer and McMurdo, German and Argentine scientists at Jubany, British scientists at Rothera and Italian scientists at Terra Nova Bay, with ship-based contributions from China and Spain. Video cameras and diving observations are providing details of the structure of the communities on both rocky and muddy bottoms. The greatest potential for research probably lies in studies of the benthos' biochemistry and physiology. Some species, such as sponges, may have the same sorts of antimicrobial defense chemicals that warm-water sponges do, and these could possibly be of pharmaceutical interest. A better understanding of all these fields might also help us to deal with the effects of pollution on benthos.

Antarctica Terrestrial Life
Plants & Microbes

With only 0.4% of Antarctica free of permanent snow and ice, there is not much habitat for plant communities. In addition, any new species spreading to Antarctica must not only cross the Southern Ocean but also hit one of the snow-free patches in order to survive. Under these circumstances, it is surprising that Antarctica is home to at least 200 species of lichens, over 100 species of mosses and liverworts, more than 30 species of macrofungi, two species of flowering plants and many species of algae. The relationships between these plants and those on the surrounding continents have interested botanists for almost 150 years, and it is only now, after a great deal of specimen-collecting and detailed taxonomic study, that the relationships are finally becoming clear.

Within the next few years, definitive guides to both lichen and mosses will be published, based on work by British, Norwegian and Polish botanists. These will not only show the distribution of species in and around the Antarctic, but will also provide data on whether all the species spread to the continent after the last glaciation or whether some survived on isolated mountain peaks. Meanwhile, research continues on how these lichens and mosses survive the extreme cold and desiccation of the Antarctic winter. Scientists from Australia, Britain, Germany, The Netherlands, New Zealand and Spain all have ongoing studies.

One of the most unusual plant habitats on Earth is in Antarctica: in areas formed from large-grained sandstone, most obviously in Victoria Land, the outer skin of the rocks themselves has been colonized by plants. These plants live within the rock, growing between the sand grains and forming separate layers of algae, fungus and lichen. Just enough light penetrates the rock for photosynthesis to occur for a short period each year when melt water is available. Acids excreted by the plants eventually dissolve the rock and the outer skin breaks off, leaving an obvious dark mark where the algal cells remain. The growth rate of these plants is so slow that some may well be many thousands of years old.

Very large specimens of lichens and banks of moss more than a meter deep can be seen in some parts of Antarctica, especially in the Antarctic Peninsula region. Because they grow quite slowly, some of the lichens have been estimated at more than 500 years old, while radiocarbon dates show the base of the large moss banks to be as much as 7000 years old. Both are extremely vulnerable to disturbance.

It has been obvious for a long time that microbial communities are important in Antarctica. In the last 20 years, scientists from Australia, Belgium, New Zealand, the UK and the US have taken increasing interest in how they survive such inhospitable habitats. In several places, glacier margins are retreating, revealing bare rock and soil. This is what happened at the end of the last ice age in the temperate regions, yet we know little about the initial colonization by microbes that eventually developed into the grasslands and forests of today. Using new technologies, it is possible to investigate the earliest stages of colonization of these areas and to develop a better understanding of how complex communities develop.

Considerable effort is also going into a joint program among several countries (Argentina, Australia, Italy, New Zealand, the UK and the US) to study what is being carried to Antarctica by the winds, how these new species establish themselves and what the effects of increased ultraviolet radiation are on survival in terrestrial communities.

Invertebrates

You'll have to look hard to find any insects in Antarctica, but you might see a springtail jumping among vegetation or find a group of tiny mites under a stone. Despite their size, these insects, and the slightly larger ones on the sub-Antarctic islands, are the subject of much research by US, British, French, Italian and South African scientists.

How do they survive extremes of cold, lack of water and oxygen, and high salt levels in the soil? Many are able to make antifreezes which allow them to survive temperatures as low as -28°C. When frozen into ice, some can put their metabolism into a special state to survive the lack of oxygen. They also show a remarkable ability to survive desiccation without long-term damage to their cells. The lack of species diversity makes these invertebrate communities among the simplest anywhere, so they provide ideal models for understanding how ecosystems work.

Lakes & Streams

Most people do not expect to see lakes and streams in Antarctica. Yet there are many ponds and lakes scattered around the ice-free areas, ranging from Don Juan Pond, which contains the saltiest solution on Earth (and does not freeze even at -55°C), to small lakes that have almost no nutrients in them. The lakes are ice-covered for most or all of the year and have very limited flora and fauna. The most developed animal is a small shrimp and the most complex plant is an aquatic moss. Most of the lakes are dominated by microbial communities.

It is the simplicity of the systems that initially attracted scientists, especially since they could choose a lake with just the right chemical characteristics for their studies. Much of the work has concentrated on the lakes in the Taylor and Wright Valleys (mainly by US, Japanese and New Zealand scientists), at the Vestfold Hills (Australian), at the Bunger Hills (Russian) and at Signy Island (British). Some of the saline water bodies are effectively sterile, with just a few bacteria living in them. In other cases, nutrients from the surrounding catchment have allowed a steady development of the aquatic ecosystem.

Lake Vanda in the Wright Valley has been intensively investigated for many years. It consists of two ecosystems: the top 45cm (beneath 4m-thick ice) is nutrient-poor freshwater; below that is saline water four times as salty as seawater, with a lake-bottom temperature of 25°C. The two layers support quite different microbial communities.

In the more nutrient-rich lakes and in those where there is significant melt water running in from the surrounding area, there are new research opportunities. The sediment at the bottom of a lake contains a record of how it has changed over a period perhaps as long as 10,000 years. These lake sediments are a valuable history of Antarctica's recent climate.

Geology, Geomorphology & Paleontology

Even though less than 1% of Antarctica's rock is accessible for direct examination, geologists are very interested in the continent. It forms one of the Earth's seven major rock plates, and its margins are constantly changing, making it one of the best places in the world to study the movements of the Earth's crust. It also contains one of the best climatic archives of the past, with terrestrial sediments covering the last 200,000 years, marine sediments covering millions of years and even older areas of ancient continental rocks.

Minerals

Are there vast deposits of precious metals and ores beneath the Antarctic ice sheet? Are there huge basins of gas and oil under the Weddell and Ross seas? Such ideas were the focus of a great deal of diplomatic activity in the 1980s, as governments struggled to agree how exploitation could be controlled. Now, the Antarctic Treaty's Protocol on Environmental Protection prohibits any mining or drilling for at least 50 years.

In fact, no strong data show that hydrocarbon basins exist in the Antarctic. The geological maps that indicate mineral outcrops merely show where mineral deposits have been identified. None of them are of economic value, since the expense of mining and transporting them to markets would be prohibitive. But Antarctic minerals are still being investigated by geologists, who are not looking for economic value but rather are working to determine how the minerals were formed and what they can tell us about geological processes.

Fossils

Coal beds and plant fossils in the Transantarctic Mountains were reported by both Shackleton and Scott, clearly indicating that the Antarctic was not always covered with ice. Since Shackleton and Scott's time, much more fossil evidence of the preglacial periods has been uncovered. Paleontology has been undertaken by geologists of many countries, with those from Argentina, Australia, Chile, New Zealand, Poland, the UK and the US making especially important contributions.

Fossils provide evidence of the connections between the parts of the ancient supercontinent Gondwana, give indirect information about the changes in Antarctic climate over millions of years and offer an insight into the evolution of present Antarctic species.

Petrified wood is widely distributed in Antarctica, sometimes in pieces as long as 20m. The trunks and leaf impressions show that about 80 million years ago the climate was temperate, and distinct annual growth rings show that it was also seasonal. In some places, ferns and other woodland species are also preserved in great detail.

Many deposits contain fossil plants and fossil pollen, but fossils of land animals are much less common. Material that appears to be from carnivorous dinosaurs about 200 million years old has been found in the Transantarctic Mountains, and parts of Cretaceous plant-eating dinosaurs about 75 million years old have been unearthed on James Ross Island off the northern tip of the Antarctic Peninsula, but no complete fossils have been recovered. Marine deposits containing fish, mollusks and many other types of marine invertebrates provide a great deal of information on the evolution of these groups in the Southern Ocean.

In fossil sequences in various parts of the world, there are sudden, major changes in the species recorded at what is called the Cretaceous/Tertiary boundary (about 65 million years ago). Many theories have been put forward to explain this event, since it appears that it caused mass extinctions. The current theory is that a huge meteorite collided with Earth, producing such massive climate changes that many species could not survive. The evidence cited for this is the occurrence of a high concentration of the rare element iridium, which can be found associated with particular layers in sedimentary rocks. Seymour Island off the east coast of the Antarctic Peninsula is one of the best sites in the world for studying the Cretaceous/Tertiary boundary.

Antarctic Landforms

The study of landforms is called geomorphology. In the Antarctic, geomorphologists have mainly been concerned with the effects of the ice sheet on the underlying rock, as well as the study of glacial deposits, the remains of old beaches left when the sea level fell and the formation of patterned ground.

Glaciers have an important effect on the rock beneath them. As the ice flows slowly toward the sea, it grinds up the rock and produces a suspension of fine yellowish or white particles that flow out of the glacier front with the melt water. This 'glacial flour' runs off into the sea to form sediments. On their way down the valleys, the glaciers may also pick up boulders and weathered rock from the valley sides or outcrops. These, together with glacial flour, are often deposited at the end of the glacier as it melts and retreats, forming mounds called moraines. Where there is a seasonal cycle of melt and retreat of the glacier snout, a series of annual moraines may form, providing clear evidence of the rate of retreat.

Global sea level rises and falls with changes in ice cover. There are relics of previous sea levels all around Antarctica: old beaches of shingle, sand and shells that mark the height of previous wave action. Some of these shells have been dated and mark the timing of major changes in the extent of the ice sheet over the last 5000 years.

Patterned ground is found in polar and mountain regions all over the world. These are the polygons, circles, stripes and sometimes even hummocks that can be seen throughout the Antarctic. They are formed by alternate freezing and thawing of water in the soil, which produces lateral sorting of coarse and fine particles. A stone polygon, with its border of large rocks and center of fine particles, is believed to result from the process of frost heave. This usually happens at night when ice crystals form in the soil and push up the large rocks. When the sun melts the crystals the following morning, the rocks roll down to one side. This, repeated many times over many years, produces the polygons. In extremely dry areas such as the Dry Valleys, a related process called ice wedging produces similar features.

Soils

With less than 1% of Antarctica free of snow and ice, and with very little vegetation, how can there be any soils (mixtures of weathered rock particles, salts and organic matter)? Antarctic soils are almost without organic matter, very dry and with a high salt content. They're primitive soils, and as such have been the subject of detailed research, mainly by New Zealand scientists in Victoria Land, by British scientists on Signy Island and by researchers from several countries working on the sub-Antarctic islands.

On the continent, all soils contain permafrost, which means they're permanently frozen just below the surface. The breakdown of the rocks into soil particles is due to damage caused by ice crystals, and to chemical changes caused by the high salt concentrations. Scientists working on soils in the Dry Valleys have been able to show that some of them are at least five million years old, giving a possible date for the retreat of ice from these valleys.

There are other unusual soils on some of the islands around the Antarctic Peninsula. These are made from accumulations of dead moss and in some places may be nearly 1.5m thick. Because of the permafrost, the dead moss cannot decay, so these peat banks simply keep getting thicker. Radiocarbon analyses of these banks give ages up to 7000 years. On the sub-Antarctic islands, with their much warmer climate, the soils have no permafrost and are better developed, resembling those found in more temperate mountain areas.

There is still a great deal to investigate about Antarctic soils, including their origins and their microbial processes.

Meteorites

Meteorites are a major source of information about the early history of our solar system. Most of our knowledge about meteorites comes from analysis of those found in Antarctica, which acts as a huge meteorite collector and preserver. The first Antarctic meteorite was found by Australians in 1912, but serious collecting did not begin until 1969. Since then, more than 10,000 have been discovered, mainly by Japanese and US scientists. The meteorites are generally found in the 'blue ice' areas of Antarctica, which are expanses of old ice held back by mountains and kept free of snow by constant winds. These areas of sublimating ice allow the meteorites to gradually 'rise' to the surface. The Allan Hills region and the Yamato Mountains have been the most prolific areas so far. (See boxed text 'They Come From Outta Space' in the Facts about Antarctica chapter.)

Ice on Land & Sea
The Ice Sheet

Antarctica's large mass of snow and ice contains about 85% of the world's freshwater and acts as a cold sink for the entire Southern Hemisphere. The Antarctic ice sheet is constantly changing, with snow falling and icebergs breaking off. Small changes in the ice sheet's volume could cause a catastrophic rise of global sea levels. We need to be able to detect small changes to provide adequate warning of any such rise.

Many years of effort by many countries have gone into trying to determine the volume of the ice sheet. The principal method is to record the top and bottom of the ice sheet using airborne radar. There are now maps showing the topography of the underlying rocks, which allow a rough calculation of total volume. The errors, however, are still considerable and are due both to difficulties in deciding the exact thickness of the ice from radar echoes and in mapping the changes in thickness frequently enough at a continental level. This will soon change when new satellite instruments come into use.

Researching the History of Our Climate

Snow is a treasure trove of information to a glaciologist. When a snowflake falls, it brings with it valuable details about the state of the atmosphere at the time it was formed. As it is slowly compressed and recrystallized by snow of later years, it forms a historical record. The present interest in global change makes any information about Earth's past climates valuable for modeling purposes, so a great effort has been made to collect ice cores from some of the oldest and deepest parts of the ice sheet.

Drilling is a difficult and highly skilled activity, which extends over several years. The ice sheet is always moving, so the drill hole is continually being bent and squeezed shut. The major cores have been obtained by Russia, France and the US. The deepest core so far has come from the Russian Vostok station and is 3611m deep – with an estimated age of 420,000 years at the bottom.

Ice cores can reveal patterns of mean air temperature, evidence of major volcanic eruptions and, by analysis of the air trapped in ice bubbles, data on the composition of the atmosphere. To make these useful, the levels in the ice core must be dated. No single method works, so glaciologists count annual layers, date the decay rates of natural isotopes and model the changes in ice flow with age.

Since there is still disagreement about the effects of the present increase in carbon dioxide, the historical record from ice cores is of considerable importance. The data so far indicate that concentrations of carbon dioxide were reduced throughout the last Ice Age and increased sharply as the ice melted, with a 30% increase in just a few thousand years. The carbon dioxide concentration remained stable for the next 10,000 years before beginning to increase again about 200 years ago.

Analysis of the ice cores' microparticles will show if they come from dust storms associated with more arid conditions or from volcanic eruptions. Analysis of the salt types and concentrations can even indicate which volcano erupted.

The Record of Global Pollution

Since industrial development began, there have been increasing amounts of pollutants escaping into the atmosphere. Over the last 200 years, the emissions of toxic heavy metals have increased dramatically. Nuclear tests and accidents have released radioactive fallout that has also spread worldwide. Antarctica is remote from all of these sources, but all of the pollutants can be found in snow and ice cores. The continent thus provides a global baseline against which we can measure the damage inflicted on the rest of the planet.

Research has shown that while lead levels in Greenland snow have increased 100-fold in the last 200 years, there has been little change in Antarctica. Data for other toxic metals, such as cadmium, zinc and mercury, are not yet complete enough to indicate any trends. Nuclear fallout shows up clearly in the ice cores, and is linked to datable events. There is, however, no evidence of sulfur dioxide, which, as 'acid rain,' has caused so much damage in the Northern Hemisphere.

Floating Ice Shelves

Satellite data allow glaciologists to monitor not only when a giant berg breaks off one of Antarctica's ice shelves, but also to measure its slow progress away from the continent. Other research on the ice shelves concentrates on determining flow rates to see how quickly ice is moving off the continent, and how rapidly the shelf ice thins from the melting of its underside. The long-term objective is to provide researchers with a computer model that will allow the loss of ice to the Southern Ocean to be accurately predicted.

Sea Ice

Antarctic sea ice cover varies from a minimum of four million sq km in February to a maximum of 20 million sq km in September. This huge seasonal change has enormous repercussions, since the ice changes the exchange of heat, moisture and momentum between the sea and the air, and the marine ecosystem has to adapt to lower temperatures and a lack of light under the ice. Developing models of the way sea ice affects energy transfers between sea and air is a major concern of several countries, including Finland, the UK and the US.

The ice cover, even at the height of winter in September, is not complete, however. Satellite pictures show that areas of open water, called polynyas, occur in the same places deep in the pack ice each year. We know little about these polynyas, as only the strongest icebreakers can reach them. It seems likely that they play an important role for seals and whales in the winter, providing a breathing space hundreds of kilometers from the open sea.

The sea ice is considered one of the most important research areas, for several reasons. The big General Circulation Models, which attempt to predict the magnitude of global warming, show important discrepancies in their predictions for the Antarctic. To improve the predictions, we need much better data on sea ice, and much of this is now being obtained by special instruments aboard satellites. These also allow us to determine ice movement and ice type deep within the pack ice, and help provide more accurate estimates of the area covered by the ice.

To make sure the satellite data are verified, however, research needs to be undertaken inside the pack ice. In 1992, a very successful drifting ice camp was established in the eastern Weddell Sea to study features of the summer sea ice. Several countries are showing an increased interest in drifting buoys, which will give more information about ice movement within the pack ice, as well as meteorological and oceanographic data, without requiring a ship to enter the pack ice, where it could be crushed and sunk.

Sea ice is also the focus of a major research program called Coastal and Shelf Ecology of the Antarctic Sea Ice Zone. This project brings together biologists, physicists, chemists and oceanographers in an attempt to understand this rapidly changing and fragile habitat. This is a big program, designed to run for 10 years, with contributions from most Antarctic countries. The scientists will be looking at six key questions: What role does ice play in the coastal marine ecosystem? How do Antarctic communities differ from those in other oceans? What factors determine the patterns of production and nutrient cycling in these ecosystems? How are the organisms adapted to low temperatures? What is the interaction between land and sea in the coastal zone? How are these coastal communities impacted by human activities?

Weather Forecasting

The countries surrounding the Southern Ocean have great interest in the meteorology of Antarctica. The weather systems that constantly circle the continent drive storms across the Southern Ocean and beyond, while the seasonal formation and melting of sea ice has a major effect on Southern Hemisphere weather. Since before the International Geophysical Year of 1957-58, all Antarctic stations have tried to collect daily meteorological observations and broadcast them to surrounding countries to help in weather forecasting. At most stations, you will see a small white meteorological screen housing standard instruments.

But stations were not located on the basis of where it would be useful to collect meteorological data, and for a long time there were huge holes in the data maps for Antarctic weather. Now those holes are being filled, as more and more automatic weather stations are carefully positioned. The majority of these stations belong to the US, but they are sited and maintained by the cooperative efforts of several other nations.

Atmospheric Science

Atmospheric science is an expensive and active field of Antarctic research. Global warming and ozone destruction have made the study of atmospheric gases a major discipline, and the Antarctic has an important role to play in this research. There are also unique features of the invisible magnetic fields that surround the Earth that can be most easily investigated in Antarctica.

Atmospheric Chemistry & Ozone Depletion

Probably the most famous science project ever undertaken in Antarctica is the monitoring of stratospheric ozone at Britain's Halley station in the Weddell Sea. A paper published in the international scientific journal *Nature* in 1985 provided such alarming evidence of the increasing rate of ozone destruction that it resulted in a worldwide agreement to ban the principal culprits, chlorofluorocarbons (CFCs). It also stimulated a massive increase in research on polar chemistry.

One of the direct results of this research was the discovery that CFCs are not the only chemicals involved in ozone destruction. The destruction was found to be localized in stratospheric clouds formed from nitric acid and water. Discovering the other chemical reactions involved has been a major concern of many countries, both in the Antarctic and in laboratories elsewhere. While the chemicals involved are now fairly well agreed upon, there is still further work necessary to understand the reactions involved. This is especially important to ensure that whatever chemicals take the place of CFCs in air-conditioning systems and refrigerators do not produce further ozone destruction.

A variety of approaches are now being used to make sure ozone data are as accurate as possible. Satellites stare down on the continent, reporting the concentrations of ozone as seen from above. Looking up from the ground, many countries use Dobson or Brewer spectrophotometers to monitor stratospheric ozone. Upward-pointing laser systems can also detect the formation of the stratospheric clouds in which ozone destruction occurs. There are even direct measurements of ozone obtained by launching hydrogen- or helium-filled balloons with detectors aboard.

For quite some time, the way in which ozone destruction took place was unknown, as the detailed structure of the cloud particles carrying the nitric acid remained only theoretical. Then balloons were sent up, carrying samplers that could not only catch the microscopic particles but photograph them and transmit the images back to a ground station.

Now we have a much clearer picture of the whole complex cycle. During the Antarctic winter, a strong westerly circulation is established, which acts as a vortex, cutting the Antarctic stratosphere off from the rest of the atmosphere. Inside this vortex, the atmosphere cools to temperatures as low as -79°C and thin clouds are formed from aerosols, altering the chemical balance between the chlorine derived from the breakdown of the CFCs and other gases in the stratosphere. During this period it is dark, and it is not until the sun returns in spring that enough energy comes back to the atmosphere to begin the chemical reactions in which the chlorine, together with other chemicals, destroys the ozone. Ozone destruction occurs mainly in the Antarctic, rather than in the Arctic, where no polar vortex forms.

Greenhouse Gases & Global Warming

Carbon dioxide is produced by all animals when they breathe and is taken up by plants during photosynthesis. It has the important property of absorbing heat from the surface of the Earth, thus preventing it from being lost to space and causing the planet to cool. For this reason, carbon dioxide is called a 'greenhouse gas.' Carbon dioxide and water vapor in the Earth's atmosphere together make the planet warm enough for life. Of course, too much of the greenhouse gases can cause too much heating of the atmosphere: 'global warming.' Burning fossil fuels produces a mixture of gases – and the principal one is carbon dioxide.

Agriculture, especially cattle raising and rice growing, produces another greenhouse gas called methane. Because of this, if you want to measure changes in greenhouse gases at a global level, you need a site as far away from industry and with as few animals and plants as possible. For this reason, the US chose the South Pole for global carbon dioxide measurements in 1956. This series of measurements is still running and is perhaps one of the most important monitoring activities in the world.

Concentrations of other gases which may also be involved in global warming are also rising, and these have been added to the analyses at the South Pole. The measurements from the Pole provide the baseline for global changes in greenhouse gases and are extremely important in deciding what needs to be done to reduce global warming. Decisions on the continued unrestricted use of cars, the burning of coal and gas, and the production of waste gases by factories worldwide will all be influenced in large part by projections based on this data. The sampling has now been extended to a large number of other sites all over the world, providing independent checks on the rate of change.

Geomagnetism

For physicists interested in what happens to Earth's magnetic field, Antarctica is a special place. The magnetic field is invisible, but of considerable importance. The sun produces a continuous stream of electrically charged, high-energy particles. This flow is picturesquely termed the 'solar wind,' and when it comes into contact with other particles or enters a magnetic field, its energy becomes channeled and discharged. The only visible signs of this discharge are the spectacular displays of aurora that can be seen at both poles as the particles from the sun collide with gas molecules in the ionosphere.

A less visible – but much more important – sign of the solar wind is interference with communications. Radio, TV, telephones and a variety of navigation systems are all dependent either on bouncing radio waves off charged particles in the atmosphere or on relaying messages via satellites. The crackling, fading or even complete failure of these signals means that there have been changes in the atmosphere, caused by the solar wind, that block the signals.

The peculiar structure of the magnetic field over Antarctica makes it the best place in the world to investigate how the sun's activities affect the ionosphere and to try and model these effects so that they can be predicted. To do this, the UK, Japan and South Africa are setting up three radar systems located at their respective bases, Halley, Syowa and SANAE. The radars are similar to military systems used to look over the horizon to detect incoming missiles. They will utilize the overlap between the beams to create a three-dimensional picture of the ionosphere above the South Pole.

Astronomy

In many parts of the world, air and light pollution makes studying the stars a problem, so astronomers have taken their telescopes to the tops of mountains on remote islands. Still, water vapor in the atmosphere

Davis Station

Hagglunds tracked vehicle, Davis Station

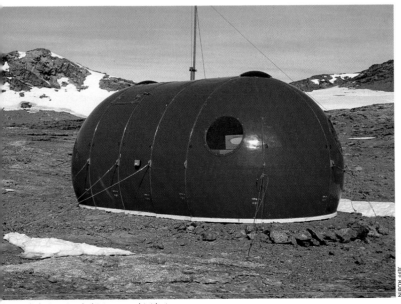

An apple hut, extended into a zucchini hut

Magazines from the 'Wilkes Hilton' at the abandoned Wilkes Station

Shackleton's Hut, Ross Island

Mawson's Hut, Commonwealth Bay

Mawson's Hut, Commonwealth Bay

makes it difficult to see certain types of stars. Telescopes mounted on satellites do not have this problem, but they are horrifyingly expensive. Antarctica provides the next best thing – at a much lower cost.

Some stars produce only infrared radiation, which we usually think of as invisible warmth. The amount of this radiation that reaches Earth is infinitesimally small and, since water vapor absorbs it, even more is lost as it passes through the atmosphere. Antarctica's thin, dry, cold atmosphere makes it the best place on Earth to detect infrared stars.

Another branch of astronomy has also been enthusiastically developed in the Antarctic. Research on the way in which the sun affects the Earth has been going on for centuries. For a long time, it has been known that the sun pulsates, producing plumes of gas that shoot out into space. These events are obviously related to what is happening inside the sun, but it has been difficult to find a way of discovering what exactly this is. A new branch of astronomy called helioseismography is making some progress. Using a special telescope, astronomers monitor the fluctuations in the size of the sun and its relationship to surface changes. Eventually, there will be enough data to extract the frequencies of various types of pulsing, but this is a difficult job since the frequencies produce about 10 million resonations! One scientist has likened the work to 'trying to record the New York Philharmonic from the other side of a concrete wall, while a guy is using a jackhammer on the wall and someone is playing with the volume control; from an analysis of the measured frequencies, you then attempt to determine which instruments are being played!'

Searching for the Origins of the Universe

Antarctica is also playing its part in unraveling the mysteries of where the universe came from. It turns out to be the perfect place to study cosmic microwave background radiation, which is believed to be the remaining echo of the Big Bang. The very dry, cold conditions are ideal for scientists (mainly from Sweden and the US) to make measurements that should show whether there is a spatial structure to the background radiation, as predicted by some theories.

Medical Research

Many people expect medical research in Antarctica to be about cold resistance, but while there is continuing interest in this topic, it's not as important as others. After all, everyone tries hard to stay either in heated buildings or dressed in special clothing to ensure that they keep warm. The real opportunities in Antarctic medical research are the seasonal changes in the climate and the isolation experienced by station personnel during winter, which are similar to conditions on a space station. (See also the boxed text 'Antarctic Medicine' in the Facts for the Visitor chapter.)

Health Care

The length of time that people spend working in Antarctica varies greatly. Several nations staff their stations only during the summer, so the maximum period of duty is around four months. Others have year-round research programs, with some staff spending from one year (Australia) to 2½ years (the UK) in Antarctica.

All Antarctic station members must undergo stringent health checks before they're allowed to go south. Each country undertakes the checks in a different way, largely influenced by cultural attitudes towards health care. Some countries undertake psychological testing (Australia, New Zealand and France), while others require a wide range of chemical and physiological tests (Italy). India is investigating the value of yoga in promoting good health at its Antarctic stations. With increasing movement of scientists between national programs, and the formation of large international teams, this could lead to considerable confusion, so the national programs are trying to agree on a standard minimum health check acceptable to all.

Endocrinology

The hormone melatonin is closely associated with regulating body rhythms. Shift workers and long-distance air travelers have difficulty in resynchronizing their sleeping patterns because their pattern of melatonin secretion becomes disturbed. Obviously, a method for correcting jet lag or sleep disturbance is of great social and industrial importance.

The long Antarctic night removes the normal melatonin secretion trigger – bright sunlight. Research has therefore concentrated on using bright light to suppress melatonin secretion and on using melatonin tablets to increase the hormone. So far, results have been mixed, with some people showing a rapid response to these treatments and others showing none at all. There has also been increasing interest in looking at hormones produced by the thyroid gland and their relationship to the immune responses produced by the white blood cells.

Epidemiology

With such a carefully selected workforce, it's not surprising that statistics show Antarctica to be quite a healthy place to live. However, living far from sources of infection appears to lower natural immunity. Colds or flu often spread rapidly among a station's overwintering population when people on the first ship or aircraft arrive at the end of winter, bringing their germs.

This isolation can be turned to scientific advantage, however. In normal societies, it's difficult to study how a disease spreads among people. To do this scientifically, it is essential to reduce the opportunities for new sources of infection to enter the experimental group. Apart from hermits and members of closed religious orders, there are few people who are willing to live completely cut off from society for long periods to ensure this. Antarctic stations during winter, however, provide just such an opportunity. Using the latest molecular biology techniques, it is possible, on a small station, to characterize every strain of a particular microbe. At the start of the winter, every person has a personal profile made of his or her microbe strains. By monitoring these, it is possible to see which strains become dominant, which are passed on and to whom and which disappear completely. The most recent development of this research has been to use the rate of evolution of Antarctic microbe strains as a baseline against which to assess natural change in microbial populations.

The Psychology of Small Groups

Remote groups have a particular fascination for psychologists. Add to this both a hostile environment and an opportunity to assess changes by testing people before and after their Antarctic experience, and you have an ideal opportunity to study personality characteristics and human interactions. The most detailed and long-running studies in this field have been done by US, French and New Zealand scientists. In general, psychologists are trying to assess three features of behavior: how well a person performs his or her job, how emotionally stable a person remains through the stresses and isolation of the winter and how well a person integrates into a group. A wide range of tests have been used, and in many countries the conclusions have been incorporated into the screening programs for selecting recruits.

Until recently, however, there has been no attempt to standardize the testing to see how different national cultures affect the response of individuals. Now, a project run from Canada is doing just that, with a questionnaire translated into several languages, so the experience of quite different cultures can be compared scientifically.

The Future of Anctarctic Science

With so many countries active in Antarctic science, problems can be tackled on a much larger scale than any single country could manage on its own. Some major new international programs are already underway. In astronomy, there is great interest in constructing some large telescopes at the South Pole for international use. Geophysicists are pooling data to provide a more inclusive picture of the geology of the ocean floor, while an international team of geologists is drilling a deep core at Cape Roberts in the Ross Sea to investigate the history of continental glaciation.

In all these efforts, there is a genuine attempt to utilize the special features of Antarctica to answer our scientific questions. Using the latest tools, we can map the Antarctic more accurately than ever before to assess the changing continent. With geographical information systems, we can synthesize widely differing types of data to gain better understanding of how glaciology interacts with meteorology and geology.

At the same time, scientists are working to protect the continent for the future. Antarctic science is conducted under the rigorous requirements of the Antarctic Treaty's Protocol on Environmental Protection. Great efforts are made to ensure that as little ecological damage as possible is done and that all wastes are removed.

When you see an Antarctic station, remember that its impact is local, its inhabitants are trying hard to be more responsible than most of us are back home, and that the research being done there is likely to benefit us and our children. Antarctic science may be a long way from your backyard, but it is important and relevant science – now and for the future.

PRIVATE EXPEDITIONS

By Colin Monteath

Evolution of Private Expeditions

Joseph Banks, the botanist on James Cook's first voyage of discovery to the southern latitudes in 1769-71, was perhaps the first person to express a desire to stand at the geographic South Pole. 'O, how Glorious would it be,' Banks said, 'to set my heel upon the Pole! and turn myself 360° in a second!'

The drive to reach the South Pole rapidly grew into an obsession for a number of explorers, as the myth of the great southern continent *Terra Australis Incognita* was dispelled – or at least vastly diminished – by Cook's second voyage in 1772-75, and as the coastline of the Antarctic continent was gradually delineated by voyages throughout the 19th century.

Norwegian Roald Amundsen inspired the world with his efficiently organized expedition and use of skis and dogs when he became the first to reach the Pole in 1911. Amundsen's triumph, however, did not stifle the desire to cross the forbidding Polar Plateau in order to stand briefly at 90°S. Just as the first ascent of Everest in 1953 opened the gate for a continuous stream of mountaineers trying to scale the peak, Amundsen's success spawned other attempts to reach the Pole.

A passion for the Pole runs deep in our psyche. Today it has reached fever pitch, since many of the psychological and bureaucratic barriers to Antarctica have been overcome. Traverses to the interior of the continent have become commonplace over the last decade as private air transportation to the Antarctic has become routine.

Antarctica is geographically well endowed for adventure. Not only are its flat ice sheets suitable for skiing and hauling sledges, but the continent is studded with some of the world's great mountain ranges. While not as high as Andean or Himalayan peaks, Antarctic summits have an allure of their own, enhanced by remoteness and extreme cold. Antarctica will certainly be one of the most important mountaineering meccas in the 21st century.

The Early Days

Much of the exploration and science in Antarctica during the early 20th century would not have happened without private initiative and sponsorship under the leadership of famous figures from the heroic era such as Mawson, Scott, Shackleton, Amundsen, de Gerlache and Nordenskjöld. As far back as the 1820s, explorers such as Weddell, Smith, Bransfield, Biscoe and Palmer played a vital exploratory role while working in the sealing industry. During the late 1920s and early '30s, wealthy and influential private aviators such as Lincoln Ellsworth of the US and Hubert Wilkins of Australia dared to make the first long-distance flights in Antarctica. Likewise, American Richard Byrd's two expeditions in 1928 and 1933 at his Little America base on the Ross Ice Shelf were essentially private affairs.

More modest private expeditions on the Antarctic Peninsula in the 1930s and '40s played a significant role in piecing together Antarctica's geographical puzzle. Australian John Rymill led the British Graham Land Expedition in 1934, while American Finn Ronne led an unhappy though productive team from his base on Stonington Island in 1946. Both Rymill and Ronne made skillful use of aircraft and sledging parties, and among Ronne's team were the first two women to winter in Antarctica.

In the 1950s private expeditions took a backseat to the buildup for the International Geophysical Year, or IGY (which ran from July 1, 1957, to December 31, 1958), and a coordinated, multinational drive established government science bases around Antarctica (and in the Arctic, too).

Commonwealth Trans-Antarctic Expedition

The Commonwealth Trans-Antarctic Expedition, inspired and led by Englishman Vivian Fuchs, was associated with the IGY. On his way to complete Shackleton's dream of crossing Antarctica from the Weddell Sea coast to the Ross Sea, Fuchs reached the South Pole with heavy tracked vehicles on January 19, 1958, after a winter at Shackleton base on the Weddell Coast. With Fuchs was a dog team, the first to reach the Pole since Amundsen. Preceding his arrival at the Pole by two weeks was Edmund Hillary's team of New Zealanders. They had driven modified farm tractors to lay fuel depots from Scott Base on Ross Island, New Zealand's newly established IGY station.

Although the expedition was both government sponsored and privately funded, it was never planned that Hillary would go past his last depot to the Pole. His action angered New Zealand's Ross Sea Committee, the organizers of Fuchs' support team. Perhaps this discord foreshadowed misunderstanding and distrust between government departments (which rapidly asserted their control over access to Antarctica) and strong-willed individuals with proven field experience and adventurous spirits.

First Ascents of Vinson Massif & Mt Herschel

The origins of modern Antarctic mountaineering came even later. Although Ellsworth saw the northern part of the Ellsworth Mountains during his trans-Antarctic flight in 1935, he did not see the highest peak in the range, Vinson Massif. Remarkably, Vinson – Antarctica's highest peak – was not even sighted until US Navy pilots made a reconnaissance flight in association with the IGY in 1957.

In 1966, after three years of lobbying by the American Alpine Club, the US National Science Foundation agreed to support a US mountaineering expedition, which had as its prime objective the summitting of Vinson. This granting of semiofficial status to well-known American alpinists with a considerable track record in the Himalaya was in part designed to forestall the efforts of another American, Woodrow Wilson Sayre, who was also trying to reach Vinson Massif.

Sayre's aircraft logistics seemed questionable and the US government probably worried that it would be involved in a costly rescue mission if Sayre actually made it to the continent. Sayre had already fallen from grace in 1962, when he caused a diplomatic incident after his small team of climbers crossed illegally from Nepal into Chinese-occupied Tibet to make a clandestine attempt on Mt Everest. Four years later, Sayre teamed up with American Max Conrad but failed to reach Antarctica when their aircraft 'developed unspecified difficulties in Buenos Aires' (as the journal *Antarctic* reported). In 1970, at the age of 77, Conrad did reach Antarctica. Flying a Piper Aztec from New Zealand to McMurdo station, he made the first solo flight to land at the South Pole. However, on his subsequent takeoff for South America, he crashed, ending the expedition.

On Top of the Bottom of the World

Antarctica's highest peak is 4897m Vinson Massif, a mountain 20km long by 13km wide in the Sentinel Range, discovered only in 1958 by US Navy aircraft. It's named for Congressman Carl G Vinson of Georgia, who influenced the US government to support Antarctic exploration during the period from 1935 to 1961. Thanks to the mountaineering hajj of the 'Seven Summits' (scaling the highest peak on each continent), Vinson is also Antarctica's most climbed mountain.

On December 18, 1966, four members of a private US expedition led by Nicholas B Clinch made the first ascent. Over the next few days, the expedition also reached the summits of Antarctica's second-, third- and fourth-highest peaks, neighboring Tyree (4845m), Shinn (4801m) and Gardner (4686m). You can read all about it in the June 1967 issue of *National Geographic* (vol 131, no 6). Interestingly, this early expedition, sponsored by the American Alpine Club, received not only cooperation but vital help from the US government in the form of the Navy, which flew the climbers through Christchurch and McMurdo. This friendly policy was soon turned around 180°; the US and other governments generally no longer support private expeditions to Antarctica.

Adventure Network International has guided more than 450 climbers to Vinson's summit since 1985. You must be in top physical shape to attempt the climb, since you will carry a load of 27kg at high altitude. You also need several years' alpine experience on peaks above 4300m. ANI must review your climbing résumé before it will accept your participation in one of its guided attempts on Vinson. An ANI brochure advises, 'Technically, Vinson is not a difficult climb….However, climbers should be experienced and in good physical condition to cope with the stresses of altitude and low temperature.' The time required to reach the summit ranges from two to 14 days, varying with the weather, as well as with the climber's experience and fitness level. One successful summiteer has called Vinson 'similar in difficulty, weather and altitude' to the West Buttress of Alaska's Mt McKinley. Vinson's neighbor, Mt Tyree, only 52m lower, is regarded as the continent's most challenging peak – Clinch said that Vinson had been 'a Sunday stroll' by comparison – but dozens of other Antarctic mountains remain virgin.

– Jeff Rubin

The American Alpine Club team, led by Nicholas Clinch, was flown from New Zealand to McMurdo and on to the Sentinel Range in the Ellsworth Mountains, using a US Navy ski-equipped Hercules. After ascending Vinson on December 18, 1966, a climb of little technical consequence, the expedition went on a climbing spree of other major summits, notably Tyree (which may well be Antarctica's most difficult peak), Gardner and Shinn.

In 1967 another group received valuable government assistance. The New Zealand Antarctic Expedition, inspired by Edmund Hillary, was flown by the US Navy from McMurdo Sound in a ski-equipped Hercules, which landed on the sea ice at Cape Hallett. The expedition made the first ascent of the elegant 3300m Mt Herschel in North Victoria Land. For NZ climbers to gain US Navy support was unprecedented; it would not have happened without Hillary's influence on senior NZ government officials. Even so, the NZ team was obliged to take surveyors and geologists with them to add a veneer of respectable science.

Requests Denied

After the American Alpine Club and NZ expeditions, it was clear to US and NZ authorities that providing official support to private teams had created two awkward precedents, which were likely to greatly increase the number of requests for transport and backup logistics from mountaineers and adventurers all over the world.

The US government became the most obvious target for requests of support, thanks to its extensive network of fuel depots around the continent, principally at McMurdo, Byrd, Siple and South Pole stations, and its long-range ski-equipped Hercules aircraft and icebreaking ships. Many applicants thought they should receive assistance as a matter of right, yet they had little idea of just how stretched the Americans were in servicing a complicated science program so far from home. The cost of fuel alone became astronomical after it had been transported by sea from the US to NZ and on to McMurdo, before being flown to inland Antarctic bases. To support private expeditions with aircraft or ships, even in a meager way, would require cancellation of preplanned science programs. It also became evident that some of the aspiring expeditions simply didn't have a proven track record of expedition planning and independent travel in remote regions. The US feared that if these teams were given official support, a percentage of them would require rescue, which would divert scarce resources away from their primary mission, science.

The US and NZ governments drafted a joint policy on private expeditions which effectively ruled out any assistance to private teams in the future. It was much simpler to give all applicants the 'cold shoulder' and ignore or brush off the protests from the growing band of adventurers who were rapidly realizing the recreational potential of Antarctica. In 1969 a well-planned NZ team hoping to climb Mt Minto, the highest peak in North Victoria Land, was the first victim of this policy. While the US-NZ policy of noncooperation was understandable, its interpretation and application soon became overly bureaucratic and unnecessarily obstructive. Resentment toward government 'ownership' of Antarctica grew.

Embarrassingly for US Antarctic administrators, the rug was pulled from under their own policy several times when senior American politicians insisted that their pilot friends attempting 'record-breaking' jaunts across Antarctica receive all-important refueling at McMurdo. In 1971, for example, Elgin Long, who'd already flown solo over the North Pole, flew solo in his twin-engined Piper Navaho from Chile to McMurdo via the South Pole to become the first person to fly solo over both poles. In 1983, pilot Brooke Knapp, whose husband was an associate of US President Ronald Reagan, received similar support at McMurdo after a flight from New Zealand with a crew of three. Knapp then flew over the Pole to South America, claiming no less than 41 aviation records during her speedy round-the-world flight.

British Joint-Services Expeditions

With the US-NZ policy in place, no private expeditions made traverses to the interior of Antarctica during the 1960s and much of the '70s. Instead, Britain allowed several 'Joint Services' expeditions to hold 'adventure training' exercises that made use of Royal Navy transport to reach remote islands such as South Georgia. Several British teams repeated Shackleton's epic crossing of South Georgia, taking the same route the explorer took after his boat journey from Elephant Island in *James Caird* in 1916. The first crossing was under the command of Malcolm Burley in 1964. In 1970, Burley led a British military group which landed on Elephant Island and carried out survey and ornithological work. One member of the team, Chris Furse, returned to Elephant Island in 1976 with 15 others to climb its rugged peaks and experiment with sea kayaks in the ice-choked waters. Furse, with another large military team of mountaineers, returned to the Antarctic in 1983-85 to winterover in tents and snow caves on Brabant Island off the Peninsula.

Major Private Traverses

During the 1960s and '70s many government expeditions crisscrossed the Polar Plateau with large tractor trains supporting glaciological or geophysical research. By this stage Antarctica had also been well mapped and documented by aerial photography. The private traverse parties that have reached Antarctica since 1979, then, can in no way be called explorers. But their journeys can be seen as a valid form of recreation in their own right – tests of spirit and endurance, as well as of many types of new lightweight equipment. As a result of their responsibilities to sponsors, these expeditions have also educated schoolchildren and the public about the need to look after the polar regions.

Transglobe Expedition

The British Transglobe Expedition of 1979-82 did what all of the polar pundits of the day said couldn't be done: completed a crossing of Antarctica using open snowmobiles pulling sledges. Determined to circumnavigate the globe by approximately following the Prime Meridian (0°), Ginnie and Ran Fiennes led a small team to the South African side of Antarctica. They commissioned a ship to transport their equipment to the continent and to pick the expedition up from Ross Island after the crossing. For resupply on the Polar Plateau, the expedition had a ski-equipped Twin Otter, flown by veteran polar pilot Giles Kershaw. The Transglobe team wintered on the edge of the continent in a prefabricated cardboard hut before setting out for the interior the following spring. Later, when at the South Pole, Kershaw flew the Otter to the South African base to help in a major rescue – an example of private adventurers helping government personnel in trouble. Despite concerted efforts by the US, British and NZ governments to block Transglobe, Ran Fiennes and team members Ollie Shepard and Charlie Burton completed the second crossing of Antarctica in only 67 days, reaching NZ's Scott Base in January 1981. Fiennes and Burton went on to cross the Arctic Ocean, becoming the first people to reach both poles by surface means. The Transglobe Expedition proved that, given the determination and ingenuity to bring together a massive pyramid of resources, a small private team could undertake a major traverse in Antarctica.

In the Footsteps of Scott

Determined to retrace Robert F Scott's 1911-12 journey to the South Pole via the Beardmore Glacier, Englishmen Robert Swan and Roger Mear and Canadian Gareth Wood set out from an overwinter base beside Scott's Cape Evans hut in October 1985. Seventy days later, the three manhauled their fiberglass sledges up to the US Amundsen-Scott South Pole station. They received a rather 'frosty' official reception – in tune with the poor relations the expedition had experienced with US leaders at McMurdo. This reaction to private teams has often proved highly embarrassing to junior government support personnel, who naturally wish to extend warmhearted hospitality to anyone who stumbles in out of the wilderness to reach their lonely outpost.

Literally moments after reaching the Pole, the Footsteps of Scott team received the news that their support vessel, the old trawler *Southern Quest*, had been crushed by pack ice and had sunk off Beaufort Island in the Ross Sea. The expedition's aircraft, a modified Cessna 185 flown by Giles Kershaw, had already been off-loaded and was on standby near Ross Island to retrieve the trio from the Pole. US helicopters recovered the ship's crew and flew them to McMurdo, sparking heated debate on both sides. Kershaw reluctantly agreed not to fly to the Pole as long as the US didn't call the retrieval of Swan's group a 'rescue.'

Most of *Southern Quest*'s crew were flown back to New Zealand by US Hercules. However, a team of three stayed for a second winter at Cape Evans to look after the Cessna, with the view of removing the entire base the following summer. The Footsteps of Scott hut was eventually incorporated into Greenpeace's Cape Evans base and removed from Antarctica when the Greenpeace base closed in 1992. The three winterers were picked up at Cape Evans in the spring of 1986 by a Twin Otter again piloted by Kershaw, a remarkable 9600km round-trip flight from Punta Arenas.

The US government charged Swan's expedition US$80,000, a small portion of the costs, for the expedition's 'rescue' from Ross Island and repatriation to NZ. Relations between governments and private expeditions had reached an all-time low.

Norwegian 90° South Expedition

The next private expedition to Antarctica was led by Norwegian glaciologist Monica Kristensen. 'Was it difficult,' she was asked, 'to be a woman and lead a group of men?' Kristensen responded that she had no experience of being anything other than a woman.

The expedition attempted to retrace Amundsen's route to the Pole using dog teams. Sailing from NZ in November 1986 with her own ship, *Aurora*, to transport dogs and equipment, she positioned the vessel near a flat-topped iceberg in the Ross Sea. A Greenland Air Twin Otter then took off from southern NZ and, at the limit of its fuel, landed on the tabular berg. Refueled from *Aurora*, the plane took off and flew to the Bay of Whales on the Ross Ice Shelf. From there, it placed depots across the Ross Ice Shelf and at the head of the Axel Heiberg glacier, Amundsen's gateway through the Transantarctic Mountains.

Kristensen and her three male companions then drove 22 huskies all the way to the Polar Plateau. Slowed down by heavy glaciology gear and having missed one of the depots, the team turned back several hundred kilometers short of the Pole. Not wishing to winter on the continent, Kristensen knew the timing of her decision to turn back was crucial: she needed to arrive back early enough so that *Aurora* would not be trapped by sea ice.

In 1993 she returned to the Antarctic, this time on the Weddell Sea side, for another private expedition that combined science, adventure and the dream of locating Amundsen's dark green tent buried beneath the South Polar snow. This expedition was criticized for poor glacier-travel techniques. One man died in a crevasse accident, sparking a rescue mission by mountaineers from US and NZ bases on Ross Island.

Adventure Network International

It is important to interrupt the chronology of overland traverses to the Pole at this point, because all expeditions after the Norwegian 90° South Expedition – since they did not wish to overwinter or outfit their own ships – have used aircraft to reach Antarctica.

Mountain climbers led the way. The attraction of Vinson Massif and other remote peaks spurred mountaineers to overcome the barriers of aircraft logistics and government bureaucracy in order to reach Antarctica's inland Ellsworth Mountains.

In 1983 American businessmen Frank Wells and Dick Bass wanted to climb Vinson in their quest to ascend the highest peak on each of the seven continents. With pilot Giles Kershaw and mountaineers Chris Bonington and Rick Ridgeway, Bass and Wells flew to Antarctica in an 'experimental' ski-equipped tri-turbo DC-3. Their climb of Vinson, only its third ascent, was the forerunner of dozens of ascents that were to take place every summer over the next decade.

The operation was risky, with no backup should the plane become grounded. In 1984 Canadian Pat Morrow – on his own Seven Summits odyssey – failed to reach Vinson with the tri-turbo after developing engine trouble at Adelaide Island while near Britain's Rothera station. Morrow remained determined to reach Vinson. Pulling together major sponsorship and a landmark deal with the Chilean air force whereby they agreed to airdrop aircraft fuel for the expedition, Morrow, with fellow Canadian guide Martyn Williams and pilot Giles Kershaw, flew to Vinson in a ski-equipped Twin Otter in November 1985. This was the birth of Adventure Network International, which henceforth took paying passengers on other adventures in Antarctica. (See the Getting There & Away chapter for more on ANI.)

By 1986 Kershaw was experimenting with a wheeled DC-4, which could be flown in a single 10-hour flight from Punta Arenas, Chile, to land on natural areas of wind-polished ice. This allowed ANI to set up a base camp at Patriot Hills, not far from the Ellsworth Mountains. With the DC-4, and eventually a DC-6, hauling clients and reserves of fuel from South America, expeditions could then be serviced from the Patriot Hills camp with two Twin Otters. Since 1993, ANI has chartered a South African wheeled Hercules for the Punta Arenas to Patriot Hills flight. This large aircraft has an increased payload; being pressurized, it can fly above bad weather, offering a more predictable flight schedule.

Using its own chartered ship or Quark Expedition's Russian icebreakers to position Twin Otter fuel depots on both sides of the continent, ANI has gradually developed the capability to reach even the remotest locations in Antarctica safely. This has allowed climbers to begin dreaming of vast new mountain playgrounds in the Transantarctic Mountains and in the Queen Maud Mountains. The mountains on the coast of Queen Maud Land were climbed in 1993 on a private Norwegian expedition led by Ivar Tollefsen. This expedition used a Russian government ship to reach Antarctica and achieved by far the hardest mountaineering yet done in Antarctica.

In 1988 ANI director Martyn Williams led a commercial expedition from the inland edge of the Ronne Ice Shelf to the South Pole. This was an especially remarkable piece of guiding, since one of the clients had never been on skis before. The expedition included the first two women to ski overland to the Pole, Tori Murden and Shirley Metz. The group flew back to Patriot Hills, now a commonplace way to end a traverse to the Pole.

Fuchs-Messner Ski Traverse

The austral summer of 1989-90 was a big season in the Antarctic for private expeditions, as both the third and fourth crossings of the continent took place. The third was made by Austro-Italian mountaineer Reinhold Messner, the most celebrated climber in the history of the sport, and German Arved Fuchs (no relation to Vivian Fuchs). The pair teamed up to ski across Antarctica, using depots laid by ANI aircraft.

Although Messner was the first person to ascend all 14 Himalayan 8000m peaks, he had never been to the polar regions. Fuchs was a good choice of partner and navigator, since he had just returned from the North Pole. Towing heavily laden plastic sledges, they reached the South Pole on New Year's Eve, 1989. Fuchs thus achieved the distinction of skiing to both geographic poles within 12 months.

The pair continued on across the continent, striking out for Ross Island on January 3, 1990, and reaching it on February 12 – a total of 92 days since departing the Weddell Sea coast. With no resupply flight on the second half of the trip, they pared everything to a minimum; not even radios were carried. When the wind allowed, parachutes were used to help pull the sledges. The best day with parachutes saw one degree of latitude (60 nautical miles, or about 111km) clatter under their skis.

Messner and Fuchs had arranged a pickup from the Ross Sea coast by a tourist ship scheduled to visit the region. If this rendezvous had failed, they could have elected to summon a costly ANI flight from Patriot Hills. As it turned out, the pair sailed for New Zealand on board an Italian government resupply vessel. Despite external political pressure not to do so, the Italians were probably pleased to assist Messner, who was almost a cult figure at home in Italy.

International Trans-Antarctic Expedition
The 4th crossing of Antarctica turned out to be a truly marathon journey, spanning seven months from July (midwinter) 1989 to March 1990. The international team of six from Japan, UK, China, the Soviet Union, France and the US, led by Jean-Louis Etienne and Will Steger, planned to drive dog teams across the continent. In preparation, the expedition made a 2400km south-to-north traverse of the Greenland ice cap.

In Antarctica, the expedition chose to traverse the longest possible axis: down the continent's spine along the Antarctic Peninsula to the South Pole, then via Vostok to Mirnyy. In all, the trek covered a punishing 6400km. Making use of seven depots laid the year before along the Peninsula by an ANI Twin Otter, the expedition sledged its way into the US base at the South Pole on December 11, 1989, after 137 days and 3187km.

Unlike the last dog team to reach the Pole in 1958 (with the Commonwealth Trans-Antarctic Expedition), which was flown out, Steger's American huskies were still only halfway through their journey: 3212km lay between them at 90°S and Mirnyy. Somewhere in between, across the 'zone of inaccessibility,' was the Soviet Vostok station and a rendezvous with supplies they couldn't afford to miss. By providing aircraft fuel at the South Pole, the Soviets made it possible for an ANI Twin Otter to bring in supplies at the crucial midpoint of the expedition as well as to place two depots between the Pole and Vostok. After nearly losing Japanese team member Keizo Funatsu in a frightful blizzard, the dog teams and their weary drivers finally reached Mirnyy on March 3. From New Zealand, Reinhold Messner sent the message: 'Congratulations on completing one of the great polar journeys of all time. Let us both now fight for a World Park Antarctica.'

Sjur & Simen Mordre
The fifth crossing of Antarctica, in 1990-91, was carried out with efficiency and élan. The Norwegian Mordre brothers, Sjur and Simen, both expert Nordic skiers, used a dog team in their journey to the Pole from the Weddell Sea. An ANI Twin Otter then flew the dogs back to Patriot Hills while the brothers, together with a photographer, skied on toward Ross Island. Pulling sledges and making use of parachutes where possible, the trio used Amundsen's route from the Polar Plateau down the steep Axel Heiberg glacier to the Ross Ice Shelf. They reached the Ross

Sea coast after a 105-day crossing and were picked up on schedule by the tour ship *World Discoverer*.

Ran Fiennes & Mike Stroud
The planned sixth crossing of Antarctica didn't quite make it. Englishman Ran Fiennes returned to Antarctica in 1992, this time with Footsteps of Scott veteran and physician Mike Stroud. The pair planned to haul sledges from the Weddell to the Ross Sea coasts, with no aircraft support or prelaid depots, a 2500km journey. They made it some 2100km to the southern edge of the Ross Ice Shelf before requesting evacuation by ANI aircraft.

Erling Kagge
At the same time that Fiennes and Stroud were walking to the Pole, Norwegian skier Erling Kagge was skiing solo to the Pole. Although some of the media – inaccurately – tried to represent this as a replay of the 'race' between Amundsen and Scott, Kagge never intended to make a complete traverse. He reached the Pole with little fuss after 49 days and flew back to Patriot Hills.

American Women's Expedition
In contrast to the media attention given to Fiennes, Stroud and Kagge, the American Women's Expedition received little notice in the international press. This group, led by Ann Bancroft, successfully reached the South Pole in January 1993, starting from Patriot Hills, 10° inland from the coast. Although the expedition originally planned to make a complete crossing of the continent, the members decided against pushing on past the Pole, primarily due to sickness in the team. Bancroft became the first woman to travel overland to both poles, having reached the North Pole in 1986 on an expedition led by Will Steger.

Other recent traverses to the Pole include Norwegian Liv Arnesen's solo ski trek in 1994, and the journey made by three other Norwegians (including Cato Pederson, who lost one arm and half of the other in an accident at age 14) who also skied to the Pole in 1994. Still another Norwegian, Børge Ousland, gave up an attempt at a solo crossing of Antarctica in 1995-96, but not before he reached the South Pole, thus attaining both poles on skis, solo and without depots.

The sixth crossing of the continent was Børge Ousland's remarkable solo journey. In just 64 days, covering 2845km, he skied from Berkner Island to Ross Island. Learning valuable lessons from his previous attempt in 1995-96, and now highly disciplined in order to maintain a strict routine, Ousland didn't take a break even when he reached the South Pole, immediately heading northward towards the Axel Heiberg Glacier. Unsupported by aircraft-laid depots even at the Pole, he skied on down to the Ross Ice Shelf, covering a staggering 226km in a single parasail-assisted day during his final run to NZ's Scott Base, where he arrived on January 19, 1997.

Belgians Alain Hubert and Dixie Dansercoer completed a 3500km traverse in 1997-98. They started their marathon journey from the coast of Queen Maud Land and 97 days later, with only one ANI resupply flight to replace a broken sledge, reached Ross Island. Their best day's travel with parasails was an astonishing 271km. Significantly, as was Ousland the year before, the Belgians were flown out of Antarctica to New Zealand on a US government aircraft.

Five expeditions hauled sledges to the South Pole over the 1998-99 summer, navigating their way on five different routes. After an ANI Twin Otter flight from Patriot Hills to Hercules Inlet, lone Swede Ola Skinnarmo skied 1000km to the Pole, while a French team of five led by Thierry Bolo traveled 1300km from Berkner Island to the Pole. Both teams flew out with ANI. Reaching the Blue One base camp established in Queen Maud Land by ANI-Polar Logistics and flying aboard an Ilyushin 76 aircraft from South Africa, a two-member Dutch team under Ronald Naar made it to the Pole, a distance of 2250km; the third team member was evacuated early due to injury. Also setting out from Blue One was 46-year-old solo Japanese skier Mitsuro Oba, who covered an audacious 3824km via the Pole, reaching Ellsworth Land before being pulled out by ANI.

In an unusual move by the NZ Antarctic program, a three-person Australian/New Zealand 'Iridium Icetrek' team (Eric Phillips, Jon Muir and Peter Hillary) received air transport and government backing to enable them to set out for the Pole from Ross Island. Their aim was to lay depots across the Ross Ice Shelf and up the Shackleton Glacier, then make a return journey to Ross Island utilizing these depots. By underestimating the severity of the Polar Plateau, the trio ran out of food and fuel, necessitating a US government Twin Otter to make a resupply flight. The team reached the South Pole after 83 days, returning to McMurdo on a routine US Navy flight.

Mountaineering

Australian Bicentennial Antarctic Expedition

On December 31, 1987, the eve of Australia's bicentennial year, the yacht *Alan and Vi Thistlethwayte* (formerly *Dick Smith Explorer*) sailed from Sydney with a team of climbers under Greg Mortimer's leadership that made the first ascent of Mt Minto, at 4163m the highest peak in North Victoria Land. The mountain was reached after manhauling 150km inland from Cape Hallett.

Mt Vaughan Expedition

Alaskan Norman Vaughan was a dog driver with Richard Byrd's 1928 expedition to Antarctica. Since then, he has led a colorful life revolving around huskies and dogsled racing. In 1993 he planned to drive sled dogs across the Ross Ice Shelf and climb the 3140m virgin summit of Mt Vaughan, named after him by Byrd. His motto: 'Dream big, dare to fail.'

Vaughan's big dream was to reach the summit of 'his' mountain on December 19, 1993 – his 88th birthday. His team took the gamble of flying people, dogs and supplies from Punta Arenas to Patriot Hills in an old rented DC-6, flown by a pilot who had worked for Adventure Network in the past. In late November, however, the plane crashed short of the ice runway at Patriot Hills in foul weather, badly injuring one of the four team members on board. Anne Kershaw, Giles' wife and director of ANI, immediately launched a Hercules aircraft stationed in Punta Arenas to evacuate the team from the continent.

After daring to fail, Vaughan was back in Antarctica in 1994, this time with ANI air support and two experienced mountaineering guides, Vernon Tejas and Gordon Wiltsie. Three days short of his 89th birthday, Vaughan and his wife, Carolyn Muegge-Vaughan, reached the summit of their dreams.

Dry Valley Mountaineering Expedition

Until 1990, no cruise vessel had ever been into the Ross Sea twice in a single season. Now, however, it is not uncommon for tour vessels to achieve this. On its maiden voyage, the Antarctic tour ship *Frontier Spirit* (now *Bremen)* dropped off a five-member expedition at Cape Royds under the leadership of Colin Monteath. With their own helicopter to transport them across McMurdo Sound, the climbers were able to ascend several peaks in the Dry Valleys in February and March of 1991. An ascent of Mt Erebus was also made with two members of the Greenpeace Cape Evans overwinter team.

South Georgia Climbs

Climbers have reached South Georgia on expeditions by using their own yachts as bases or by gaining permission for transport aboard British military vessels. A 1984-85 New Zealand expedition led by Ian Turnbull to the peaks above St Andrew's Bay, although delayed by the Falklands War, successfully combined science and mountaineering; participants even made a film of their exploits. In 1989 Stephen Venables led a British expedition that also used military transport. The group made several first ascents, including Mt Carse at the island's southeast end.

Dronning Maud Land Mountaineering

In 1994 Norwegian Ivar Tollefsen led a 13-member private expedition (using Russian government sea transport) to complete Antarctica's first 'big wall' rock climb on the red granite spire Ulvetanna (the Wolf's Fang). This impressive climb involved 11 days of hard climbing with nights spent in hanging bivouacs. Tollefsen was able to fly from the summit using a parapente canopy. Technically Norway's highest point (Queen Maud Land is claimed by Norway), 2965m Jøkulkyrkja (the Glacier Church) also received its first ascent during the expedition, which climbed a total of 36 peaks.

The publishing of Tollefsen's book *Queen Maud Land Antarctica* in 1994 sparked interest in this remote region. In 1997-98 a division of ANI called Polar Logistics began making Hercules flights from South Africa direct to a wind-polished ice runway in Queen Maud Land called 'Blue One.' Two mountaineering groups – another Norwegian team again led by Tollefsen and a six-member US team spearheaded by lead climber Alex Lowe – reached Mt Bergersen and the Filchner Mountains beyond Blue One with the help of an ANI Twin Otter. Another 'big wall' route fell to the Norwegians after a total of 17 days climbing on the stunning north face of Ronde Spire, while the Americans climbed four peaks, including a big wall route on Rakekniven (the Razor).

Airborne Adventures

On November 5, 1988, ANI's Giles Kershaw acted as copilot for Australian aviator Dick Smith, flying a Twin Otter 14 hours from Hobart to Australia's Casey station. Such a flight in a Twin Otter was only possible thanks to auxiliary fuel tanks, which extended its range from 1600km to 3500km. This impressive venture helped pave the way for future cooperation between private expeditions and government science programs in Antarctica.

Kershaw and Smith assisted the Australian government science program for two weeks, completing extended aerial surveys along the coastline to Davis and Mawson stations. They also made goodwill visits to Syowa, Molodezhnaya and Mirnyy stations, with the Japanese and Soviets extending real Antarctic hospitality. The aviators continued on to the South Pole on November 23, having flown from Casey to Ross Island to pick up two Greenpeace members who wanted to inspect the South Pole station. By November 29, they were back at Casey and ready for a flight to South America via Vostok, the South Pole, Patriot Hills and King George Island.

Giles Kershaw's calm and positive manner as a pilot and skillful knowledge of a Twin Otter's capability took the expedition across 41,448km of Antarctica and the Southern Ocean in the space of five weeks (171 hours of flight time). Sadly, on March 5, 1990, Kershaw died in a gyrocopter crash on the Peninsula while he was assisting a film crew on another private expedition led by Mike Hoover. Antarctica lost a great ambassador.

Seaborne Adventures

As early as 1910, the British travel company Thomas Cook advertised that it planned to run a 50-day cruise from New Zealand to McMurdo Sound. It was reported that 'members of the NZ Parliament, a number of ladies and several gentlemen interested in scientific matters' were keen to endure the rigors of the Ross Sea in a wooden vessel, but the voyage never took place.

Today, tourist vessels ply Antarctic waters in large numbers every season. Some ships have carried private expeditions, dropping them off on one cruise and picking them up at a predetermined location during a later voyage. In 1994 an Australian sea kayak expedition led by Wade Fairley spent two weeks paddling along parts of the Peninsula, having been transported by a tour ship.

David Lewis

In 1972, New Zealand physician David Lewis attempted a solo circumnavigation of Antarctica in his 10m *Ice Bird*. The yacht capsized twice on the 14-week voyage from Sydney to the US's Palmer station. After repairs and a winter's delay, Lewis sailed for Cape Town, again capsizing en route. In 1977-78, he sailed to Cape Adare in the Ross Sea on the yacht *Solo* under the auspices of the Sydney-based Oceanic Research

Foundation. With five others in 1982, Lewis froze the steel yacht *Dick Smith Explorer* into an anchorage near Australia's Davis base and wintered aboard.

Gerry Clark

In 1983, Gerry Clark, a 56-year-old New Zealander, set off from NZ in the 10m wooden yacht *Totorore* to circumnavigate Antarctica. His three-year odyssey involved some remarkable single-handed yachting combined with adventures and ornithological work achieved with crews picked up in South America. Near Heard Island Clark's journey turned into a survival epic when *Totorore* lost its mast and rigging and he was lucky to make it to Fremantle, Western Australia.

Project Blizzard

Led by Bill Blunt, the Australian 'Project Blizzard' expedition twice visited Mawson's hut at Commonwealth Bay. The voyages, in 1984 (aboard *Dick Smith Explorer)* and 1985 (aboard *Southern Quest)* were undertaken to make an assessment of the historic hut's condition.

Ned Gillette

No survey of adventurous expeditions on the Southern Ocean would be complete without mentioning American Ned Gillette's four-member team, which *rowed* across the Drake Passage to Antarctica in March 1988. The men required 14 days to row *Sea Tomato* 1100km from Cape Horn to Nelson Island in the South Shetlands. Gillette traded *Sea Tomato* to the Chilean navy in exchange for a flight back to Punta Arenas. Sadly, in 1998, he was murdered in his tent during an expedition in Pakistan.

Solo Winters

The first-ever true solo winters in Antarctica both took place in 1990. Frenchman Hughes Delignières wintered on his 9m yacht *Oviri*, frozen into a bay near Pleneau Island along the Peninsula. He made adventurous winter sledging journeys south toward Marguerite Bay. Meanwhile, Brazilian Amyr Klink on *Paratii* wintered slightly farther north at Dorian Cove on Wienecke Island. (Some would say that Admiral Byrd's celebrated winter alone in 1934 at Advance Base on the Ross Ice Shelf was not really considered a solo, since Byrd was close to assistance from other expedition members, who indeed had to come to his rescue when he was afflicted by carbon monoxide poisoning.)

Wake of Shackleton

In 1993, during a tourist voyage on the Russian icebreaker *Kapitan Khlebnikov*, a replica of Shackleton's lifeboat *James Caird* was transported to Elephant Island. Led by Trevor Potts, three Englishmen and a woman then sailed the craft, which they called *Sir Ernest Shackleton*, 1480km to South Georgia. The 'Wake of Shackleton' team did not, however, attempt to cross the mountainous island. The group later became a burden on British authorities at Grytviken due to its poor planning and lack of finances.

Jean-Louis Etienne

No yacht had ever been south of Victoria Land's Cape Hallett until 1993, when Frenchman Jean-Louis Etienne returned, this time aboard the luxury steel yacht *Antarctica* instead of behind a dog team. The expedition made an ascent of Mt Erebus and shot footage on the Peninsula for children's educational TV.

Bernard Espinet

French yachtsman Bernard Espinet circumnavigated Antarctica in the yacht *Croustet* during a two-part voyage, sailing from Wellington in April 1996 and returning 15 months later in August 1997, having cruised 29,600km around the Southern Ocean. He was accompanied on the first leg to Cape Horn and the Falklands by 23-year-old New Zealander Matt Thorpe, but Espinet completed the voyage solo via South Georgia, Kerguelen and Hobart.

Don & Margie McIntyre

Australians Don and Margie McIntyre wintered in Antarctica in 1995, after being dropped off by their yacht at Commonwealth Bay (see their boxed text 'Expedition Ice-Bound' in the East Antarctica chapter).

'South Aris' Irish Antarctic Expedition

A second attempt to recreate Shackleton's open boat voyage from Elephant Island to South Georgia took place in January 1997, this time by a seven-member Irish crew led by Paddy Barry and Frank Nugent. Five of the team sailed on a replica of *James Caird* called *Tom Crean* after one of Shackleton's Irish crew members. Unlike the 'Wake of Shackleton' expedition in 1993 that set out without a support vessel, *Tom Crean* was shadowed by the charter yacht *Pelagic*. After capsizing repeatedly in huge waves, *Tom Cream* was abandoned and finally scuttled halfway to South Georgia and the crew taken aboard *Pelagic*. Landing in King Haakon Bay, four team members crossed South Georgia and descended to the now-derelict whaling stations on the north coast just as Shackleton's party had been forced to do 81 years before. A subsequent attempt to climb the virgin Mt Roots was abandoned.

Skydiving over the South Pole

What began as a spectacular stunt, intended to be a routine linkup of four skydivers 2500m above the South Pole, ended less than a minute after the jumpers bailed out of an ANI Twin Otter with the deaths of three of the total of six participating parachutists. In only the third parachute jump at 90° S – after the first in 1973 by US Navy personnel and the second in the mid-1990s – the three Americans, one Austrian and two Norwegians each paid ANI US$22,000 to make the jump. Hans Rezac and Ray Miller were experienced parachutists who had already jumped at the North Pole, while Steve Mulholland was a skilled BASE (Bridges, Antennas, Spans & Earth, or cliffs) jumper with past Antarctic work experience. All three died instantly, having failed to deploy their chutes after aborting the four-man linkup as they hurtled toward the glaring icescape at 320km/h. Of the four, only the survivor, Michael

Kearns, wore an automatic activation device (AAD), which was preset to release his chute at a safe altitude. AADs are normally used when low temperatures or hypoxia are expected to impair the judgement or physical function of the jumper, both significant factors at the South Pole, since the effective altitude at bailout was 6000m. The Norwegian pair, Trond Jacobsen and Morten Halvorsen, survived their tandem jump, the first at the South Pole.

The Future

Private expeditions to Antarctica are a spirited and valuable expression of our desire to travel in a great polar wilderness. Today, there is no excuse for poor planning. Expedition leaders must discuss objectives and support plans with their own government's Antarctic program administrators before departure. They have an obligation to leave Antarctica exactly as they find it: pristine. Above all, they must educate others upon their return of the dire need to treat Antarctica with the greatest respect.

Antarctic Gateways

Every trip to Antarctica, whether by ship or plane, leaves from a Southern Hemisphere city. Most cruise programs include one or more nights' stay in one of these Antarctic gateways.

The following information on Cape Town, Christchurch, Hobart, Punta Arenas, Stanley, and Ushuaia is adapted from material in other Lonely Planet guides. It is intended only as a very brief introduction to these cities, focusing on their Antarctic connections.

MONEY
Exchange Rates
At press time, exchange rates were:

country	unit		US dollars
Argentina	Arg$1	=	$1.00
Australia	A$1	=	$0.59
Canada	C$1	=	$0.68
Chile	Ch$100	=	$0.19
euro	€1	=	$0.92
France	FF1	=	$0.14
Germany	DM1	=	$0.47
Japan	¥100	=	$0.94
New Zealand	NZ$1	=	$0.49
South Africa	R1	=	$0.15
United Kingdom	UK£1	=	$1.56

Cape Town

• **population 860,000**

Cape Town, or Kaapstad, is one of the most beautiful cities in the world. No matter how long you stay, the image of the mountains and the sea will be seared into your memory. Dominated by 1000m flat-topped Table Mountain with its sheer cliffs, Cape Town is surrounded by superb mountain walks, vineyards and beaches. Located 40km from the Cape of Good Hope, near the southern tip of Africa, Cape Town is also one of the most geographically isolated of the world's great cities. Although it has a reputation for being South Africa's most open-minded and relaxed city – partly because blacks are in many ways culturally integrated – the scars of apartheid run deep.

History
The human history of the Cape began tens of thousands of years ago with Stone Age tribes, followed by the San, hunter-gatherers who left superb cave paintings. By the time the first Portuguese mariners arrived in search of a sea route to India and its spices, the Cape was occupied by seminomadic Khoikhoi, close relatives of the San. Bartholomeu Dias rounded the Cape in 1487, naming it Cabo da Boa Esperança (Cape of Good Hope). But by the end of the 16th century, the English and Dutch were beginning to challenge the Portuguese. In 1647, a Dutch East Indiaman was wrecked in Table Bay, and its crew built a fort and stayed for a year before being rescued.

The Dutch East India Company (Vereenigde Oost-Indische Compagnie or VOC) decided to build a permanent settlement, and Jan van Riebeeck, the man chosen to lead an expedition, reached Table Bay in 1652. He built a mud-walled fort not far from the site of the surviving stone castle and planted gardens that have now become the Botanical or Company's Gardens. While the population of whites did not reach 1000 until 1745, Cape Town thrived as the 'Tavern of the Seas,' a riotous port used by every ship traveling between Europe and the East (including Australia).

In response to the Napoleonic wars, the British decided to secure the Cape. In 1806, at Bloubergstrand north of Cape Town, they defeated the Dutch, and the colony was permanently ceded to the Crown in 1814.

The slave trade begun by van Riebeeck was abolished in 1808, and the remaining Khoisan, who had been treated as slaves, were given the explicit protection of the law (including the right to own land) in 1828. These events contributed to Afrikaners' dissatisfaction and helped motivate the Great Trek (1834-40), during which a steady steam of Boers migrated north and east, establishing independent Afrikaner states, including Natal.

The discovery and exploitation of diamonds and gold in central South Africa in the 1870s and '80s led to rapid changes. Cape Town was soon no longer the country's dominant metropolis, but as a major port it was a beneficiary of mineral wealth.

In 1860, construction of the Alfred Basin in the docks commenced, making the port storm-proof, but in 1869 the Suez Canal opened, diminishing Cape Town's maritime role.

After the 1899-1902 Anglo-Boer War – fought after Cecil Rhodes attempted to overthrow the South African Republic (Transvaal) and bring it into a federation under British control – the British made efforts to unify the separate South African provinces. The provinces, however, retained their existing systems for elections: blacks

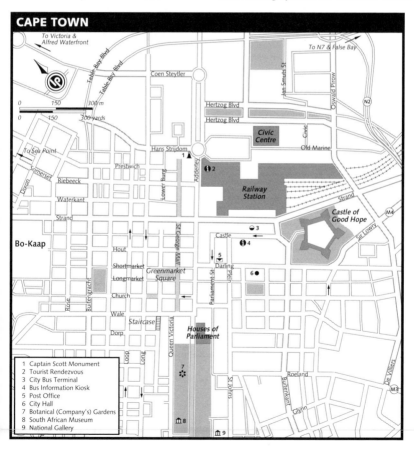

CAPE TOWN

To Victoria & Alfred Waterfront

To N7 & False Bay

Table Bay Blvd

Coen Steytler

Jan Smuts St

Oswald Pirow

N2

0   150   300 m
0   150   300 yards

Hertzog Blvd
Hertzog Blvd

Civic Centre

Old Marine

Civic

To Sea Point

Hans Strijdom

Prestwich

Somerset

Riebeeck

Waterkant

Strand

Dixon

Adderley

Lower Burg

1

2

Railway Station

Strand

Castle of Good Hope

M4

Sir Lowry

Bo-Kaap

Hout

St George's Mall

Castle

3

4

Shortmarket

Longmarket

Greenmarket Square

Church

Buitengracht

Rose

Wale

Dorp

Staircase

Parliament St

Plein

Darling

5

6

Houses of Parliament

Queen Victoria

Loop

Long

7

8

9

St Johns

Roeland

Buitenkant

Glynn

De Villiers

M3

1 Captain Scott Monument
2 Tourist Rendezvous
3 City Bus Terminal
4 Bus Information Kiosk
5 Post Office
6 City Hall
7 Botanical (Company's) Gardens
8 South African Museum
9 National Gallery

and colored people had a limited franchise in the Cape but could not vote elsewhere. Cape Town was made the seat of the legislature, Pretoria the administrative capital, Bloemfontein the seat of the Appellate Division of the Supreme Court, and the Union of South Africa was born in 1910.

In 1948, in the first election after WWII, the National Party campaigned on its policy of apartheid and narrowly won. After a series of bitter court and constitutional battles, coloreds lost their right to vote in the Cape, and the insane apparatus of apartheid was erected.

In 1960, the African National Congress and the Pan African Congress organized marches against the hated pass laws, which required blacks and coloreds to carry passbooks that authorized them to be in a particular area. In response, a warrant for the arrest of Nelson Mandela and other ANC leaders was issued. In 1964, Mandela was captured and sentenced to life imprisonment at the infamous Robben Island prison near Cape Town. In the early 1970s, rules were sufficiently relaxed to allow Mandela to write his now-famous prison notebooks and to teach politics.

Mandela was released from prison in 1990 after the ANC was declared a legal organization. In 1991 he was elected president of the ANC and began the long negotiations which would end minority rule. He shared the 1993 Nobel peace prize with FW De Klerk, and in the first free elections the following year he was elected president of South Africa.

Orientation

On first impression, Cape Town is surprisingly small. The city center lies to the north of Table Mountain and east of Signal Hill, and the old inner-city suburbs of Tamboerskloof, Gardens and Oranjezicht are all within walking distance of it. This whole area is sometimes referred to as the City Bowl.

Information

Tourist Offices At the Tourist Rendezvous, at the main railway station, you'll find the Captour Desk (☎ 418-5214/5), open week-

days 8:30 am to 6 pm, Saturday 8:30 am to 3 pm, and Sunday 9 am to 1 pm.

Money All prices quoted in the Cape Town section are in Rand (R). Money can be changed at any of the city's commercial banks, which are open weekdays 9 am to 3:30 pm, with many larger branches also open Saturday mornings.

Post The General Post Office, on the corner of Darling and Parliament Sts, is open weekdays 8:30 am to 4:30 pm, Saturday 8 am to noon.

Medical Services In an emergency you can go directly to the casualty department of Groote Schuur Hospital (☎ 404-9111), located at the intersection of De Waal (M3) and the Eastern Boulevard (N2) to the east of the city. Call the police (☎ 10111) to get directions to the nearest hospital.

Captain Scott Monument

Across from the Tourist Rendezvous, on the corner of Jan Strijdom Ave and Adderley St, opposite the fountain in the middle of the traffic circle, is a bronze model of a sailing ship on top of a stone plinth, a monument to Captain Scott. One side of the plinth is engraved 'In memory of Robert Falcon Scott RN who with four companions from *Terra Nova* perished March 1912 in returning from the South Pole.' On the opposite side are Scott's own closing lines: 'Had we lived, I should have had a tale to tell of the hardihood, endurance, and courage of my companions…These rough notes and our dead bodies must tell the tale.'

But there's a little mystery, too. An added plaque in English and Afrikaans reads: 'Replica of the memorial unveiled near this spot on 15th May 1916. The original monument of Elands River stone was irreparably damaged in June 1948.' No hint of what happened in 1948 – perhaps a Friday night driver?

South African Museum

The South African Museum (☎ 424-3330), at the mountain end of the Company's Gardens, is the oldest and arguably the most interesting museum in South Africa. Its holdings include Pacific Island artifacts left by Captain Cook, displays of indigenous culture, and a small section with sub-Antarctic birds in a Marion Island display, including a feral cat approaching a petrel burrow.

In the terrific **Whale Well** you can hear whale sounds while looking at extremely well-made (from casts) whale models suspended overhead. This room alone is worth a visit to the museum, which is open daily 10 am to 5 pm. Admission is R5 (free on Wednesdays).

National Gallery
This small but exquisite gallery (☎ 45-1628) in the Company's Gardens was always worth visiting for its architecture, but now it also has some very interesting exhibitions that begin to redress the imbalance from the apartheid days. There's a good shop and a pleasant café. Open 10 am to 5 pm daily – except Mondays, when it opens at 1 pm. Admission is free.

Houses of Parliament
On the south side of Government Ave (the Wale St end) are the Houses of Parliament, opened in 1885 and enlarged several times since. During the parliamentary session (usually January to June), gallery tickets are available; overseas tourists must present their passports, and reasonably decent dress is required. During the recess, there are free guided tours (☎ 403-2198) Monday to Friday at 11 am and 2 pm. Go to the Old Parliament Building entrance on Parliament St.

Castle of Good Hope
Built near the site of Jan van Riebeeck's 1652 mud-walled fort, the castle was constructed between 1666 and 1679 and is one of the oldest European structures in southern Africa. Within are a couple of museums with collections of furniture and paintings, mainly of Cape Town in the past. The castle opens at 10 am with the Ceremony of the Keys. Sentries change every half hour, and there is a full ceremonial **Changing of the Guard** at noon. Guided tours are offered

hourly between 10 am and 3 pm. The castle closes at 4 pm. Entry (from the Grand Parade side) is R5.

Table Mountain & Cableway
The cableway is such an obvious and popular attraction you might have difficulty convincing yourself that it is worth the trouble and expense. It is. The views from the top of Table Mountain are phenomenal, and there are some excellent walks on the summit. The mountain is home to over 1400 species of flowering plants, as well as rock dassies (hydraxes), curious rodentlike creatures whose closest living relative is the elephant. If you plan to walk, make sure you have warm and waterproof clothing as conditions can change quickly. There's a small restaurant and shop at the top.

A 1997 renovation to the cableway resulted in a much faster ride in smart, revolving cars – no matter where you stand, you get a panoramic view. The new cars also carry more passengers, so the four-hour queues have been cut drastically.

The cableway doesn't operate when it's too windy. Call in advance (☎ 24-5148 or 24-8409) to see if it is operating. Weather permitting, hours are 8 am to 9:30 pm in November; 7 am to 10:30 pm from December to mid-January; and 8 am to 9:30 pm from mid-January to the end of April. The best visibility and conditions are likely to be first thing in the morning, or in the evening. An adult round-trip ticket is R45.

Victoria & Alfred Waterfront
The Victoria & Alfred Waterfront is packed with restaurants, bars, music venues and interesting shops. The huge Victoria Wharf complex adds shops, cinemas, a produce market, and still more restaurants and bars, but also, unfortunately, a fair splash of the antiseptic atmosphere you'll find in rich white suburbs all over South Africa. Although the wharves are too small for modern container and passenger vessels, the Victoria Basin is still used by tugs, harbor vessels and fishing boats. The Waterfront is *the* place to go for night life. Although security is strict and it is safe to walk around,

people out alone should be cautious. There's an information center (☎ 418-2369) in the middle of the complex.

South African Maritime Museum

Part of the South African Cultural History Museum, this museum on the Victoria & Alfred Waterfront includes exhibits relating to the Southern Ocean. Among the highlights are shipwreck artifacts and an actual shipwreck. Postal stones – some on display date from as far back as 1632 – marked caches of letters left by ships' crews in the hope that they would be picked up before long by the next ship heading in the desired direction. They were engraved with the name of the ship and the names of those who sent the letters. The museum's John H Marsh Maritime Collection includes images of 9200 ships that called at Cape Town. The museum (☎ 419-2505/6; fax 419-7332; museum@maritimemuseum.ac.za) is open daily (except Good Friday and Christmas Day) 9 am to 4:45 pm. Admission is R5.

Shopping

There are craft shops all over town, but don't forget that few items come from the Cape Town area. There are, however, some township-produced items such as recycled tin boxes and toys which make great gifts. The **Siyakatala stall** in the craft market at the Waterfront sells items made by self-help groups in the townships, and the quality is very good.

Christchurch

• **population 310,000**

Christchurch is often described as the most English of New Zealand's cities. Punts glide down the picturesque River Avon, a grand Anglican cathedral dominates the city square and trams rattle past streets with oh-so English names (Oxford, Worcester, etc).

The city, particularly its port of Lyttelton, has strong connections to Antarctica going back to Scott's *Discovery* expedition of 1901-04 and continuing to this day

through the city's role as air-support center for the New Zealand, US and Italian Antarctic programs.

History

It is easy to forget that this epitome of Englishness is the capital of Te Wahipounamu, long-time ancestral home of the Ngai Tahu. The city's white settlement in 1850 was an ordered Church of England enterprise, and the fertile farming land was deliberately placed in the hands of the gentry. Christchurch was meant to be a working model of England in the South Pacific, complete with a class system, not just another scruffy colonial outpost of small landholders. Churches rather than pubs were built and wool made the elite of Christchurch wealthy. It was incorporated as a city in 1862, but its character slowly changed as other migrants and industry followed.

Orientation

Cathedral Square is the center of town. To find it, just look for the spire; once you're there, climb to the top to get your orientation. Christchurch is a compact city and walking around is easy.

Information

Tourist Offices The Christchurch/Canterbury Visitor Centre (☎ 379-9629; fax 377-2424) is by the Avon River on the corner of Worcester St and Oxford Terrace. Its hours are weekdays 8:30 am to 5 pm; weekends 8:30 am to 4 pm; later in the summer.

Across from the visitor center is the **Captain Scott Statue**, a white marble likeness of the explorer in polar clothes. Sculpted by his widow, Kathleen, it was unveiled May 21, 1917.

Money All prices quoted in the Christchurch section are in New Zealand dollars (NZ$). Hereford St has a collection of banks, open weekdays 9 am to 4:30 pm.

Post The post office, open 9 am to 5 pm weekdays, is in the southwest corner of Cathedral Square, as are pay phones.

Medical Services The Christchurch Hospital (☎ 364-0640) is on the corner of Oxford Terrace and Riccarton Ave.

Cathedral Square

Cathedral Square is the heart of Christchurch and the best place to start exploring the city. The square is dominated by **Christ Church Cathedral**, consecrated in 1881. Antarcticans have worshiped here before heading to The Ice since 1901, when Scott's *Discovery* sailed south. Memorial services have been held here for Scott's polar party

in 1913 and for the 257 people aboard the Air New Zealand DC-10 that crashed into Mt Erebus on Ross Island in 1979. Each spring (around October), a special service is held to mark the beginning of the Antarctic season.

For NZ$4, you can see the Cathedral's historical display and climb 133 steps to the viewing balconies 30m up the 63m-high spire of the cathedral. Take in the views – keeping in mind that the spire has been damaged by earthquakes several times, once sending the very top into Cathedral Square.

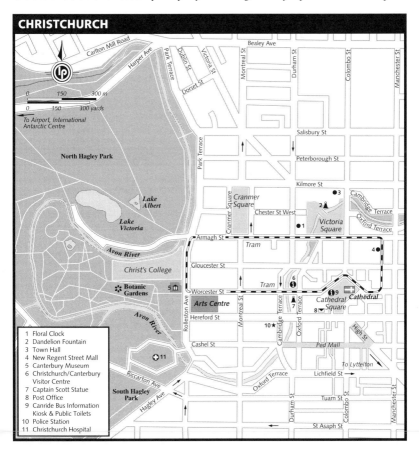

CHRISTCHURCH

1 Floral Clock
2 Dandelion Fountain
3 Town Hall
4 New Regent Street Mall
5 Canterbury Museum
6 Christchurch/Canterbury
  Visitor Centre
7 Captain Scott Statue
8 Post Office
9 Canride Bus Information
  Kiosk & Public Toilets
10 Police Station
11 Christchurch Hospital

Two **memorial plaques** have Antarctic connections. The first, on the outside wall directly below the spire, is dedicated to all those who have given their lives in Antarctica and was dedicated in 1973. Another, inside, was presented to the people of New Zealand by the US Operation Deep Freeze in 1955.

One of the city's most-visited attractions, the cathedral has embraced tourism with secular zeal. It has a souvenir shop, screens videos (NZ$2), charges for cameras (another NZ$2) and has a good café open weekdays. The cathedral is open weekdays 8:30 am to 8 pm, Saturday 9 am to 5 pm and Sunday 7:30 am to 8 pm.

Christchurch Tramway

Introduced to Christchurch in 1905, trams lasted as a means of transport for 60 years. Now, restored green and cream trams have been reintroduced as part of a 2.5km inner-city loop that takes in many of the city's best features and shopping areas. They operate daily from 8 am to 11 pm. Tickets are NZ$5 for one hour, NZ$6 for four hours, and NZ$7 for a full day (children NZ$2/3/4). It's probably quicker (and certainly cheaper) to walk. One plus is the fact that they pass through the historic precinct of **New Regent St**, which includes many examples of Spanish-style architecture.

Canterbury Museum

The Sir Robertson Stewart Hall of Antarctic Discovery at this fine museum, on Rolleston Ave at the entrance to the Botanic Gardens, houses perhaps the best collection of 'Heroic Era' material in the world. Among the many highlights are the Norwegian flag flown at the South Pole by Amundsen in 1911 and a box of cigars from Scott's last expedition, complete with a typed inscription: 'For final dash, compliments of the Sol factory, Havana.' (For further description of the Antarcticana collection, see boxed text below by the curator, Baden Norris.) There are also displays of

---

A Window on the 'Heroic Era'

New Zealand has been linked to Antarctica since the 1840s, when both the British explorer James Clark Ross and US Navy Lieutenant Charles Wilkes visited during their voyages to and from the continent.

In 1901 Robert F Scott used Lyttelton, the port of Christchurch, to prepare for his voyage south to Antarctica. Edward Wilson, the expedition's zoologist, worked at the Canterbury Museum while preparing albatross skins and other specimens collected during the voyage from England. Because of this association between Scott, Wilson and the museum, upon *Discovery*'s return from the Antarctic many of the items used on the expedition were deposited with the museum. At the Canterbury Museum's Sir Robertson Stewart Hall of Antarctic Discovery, these items are still the nucleus of the collection, which now ranks as the most comprehensive assembly of genuine relics from the Antarctic's past.

Nearly every subsequent expedition – including those led by Ernest Shackleton, Scott and Richard Byrd – left artifacts with the museum; later expeditions, such as the US's Operation Deep Freeze and the British Commonwealth Trans-Antarctic Expedition, continued that tradition. The result is that the gallery covers most of the important events in recent Antarctic history.

The Hall of Antarctic Discovery opened to the public in 1977. It is divided into three sections: geology, natural history and exploration. The extensive geology gallery is arranged in order of geological age and includes numerous fossils. The natural history section includes dioramas covering the life histories of penguins, whales and seals; there are also displays about huskies, the hard-working dogs that until recently provided welcome companionship for the continent's human population.

Antarctic natural history, including geology and wildlife. The museum (☎ 366-5000) is open daily 9 am to 5:30 pm (closed Christmas). Entry is by donation – NZ$5 is the suggested contribution.

Botanic Gardens
Beside the museum off Rolleston Ave, the gardens are open from 7 am to one hour before sunset, and offer 30 hectares of greenery alongside the Avon. The garden restaurant is open for lunch.

Arts Centre
Across from the Canterbury Museum is the Arts Centre, a great place to shop. The beautiful old Gothic buildings house an arts, craft and entertainment complex with a good selection of cafés and restaurants. The Galleria, one of the country's best craft centers, is open from 10:30 am to 4:30 pm and has dozens of craft stores selling pottery, jewelry, weaving, woolen goods, Maori carvings and handmade toys.

International Antarctic Centre
It doesn't come close to the real thing, but the International Antarctic Centre will either whet your appetite or bring back memories of the continent's magnificent sights, depending on whether or not you've been to The Ice. The center is only an eight-minute walk from the airport on Orchard Rd – follow the blue footprints. It's part of the huge complex built for administration and warehousing for the New Zealand, US and Italian Antarctic programs, which are supported by air from Christchurch. More than 135 flights depart from the airport to Antarctica every year.

Hands-on exhibits, video presentations and the 'sights and sounds' of Antarctica are all featured. The introductory Four Seasons Room, with the aid of freezing air blasts, special lighting, sound effects and holograms, allows visitors to 'experience' changes in weather and to see a penguin rookery.

You next see a model Scott Base before putting on heavy coats and shoes to enter the Snow and Ice Room, where temperatures

A Window on the 'Heroic Era'

The exploration gallery may be the Hall's most popular. It includes many fascinating relics, among them a dinner plate from James Clark Ross' ship *Erebus*, a medicine chest for sledge dogs and what is perhaps the collection's single most important item, the Polar Medal awarded to Scott in 1904, the first one ever presented.

Shackleton's expeditions are also well represented, with such artifacts as the red ensign flown from his ship *Nimrod*, tinned supplies recovered from the hut at Cape Royds, the Arroll-Johnston motor-sledge his Ross Sea party took with them on the ill-fated Imperial Trans-Antarctic Expedition of 1914-16 and a surprisingly modern-looking Primus stove taken on *James Caird* on its 1420km journey from Elephant Island to South Georgia after *Endurance* was crushed in the pack ice.

Roald Amundsen, victor in the race to the South Pole, is given prime billing in a display featuring the pocketknife used to sharpen a bamboo stake that Amundsen's party drove into the ice at the Pole to proudly support the Norwegian flag.

Items from Scott's *Terra Nova* expedition include pony snowshoes, a shaft from one of the motor-sledges and Wilson's microscope. Byrd's important role in Antarctic aviation is documented by a Primus lamp from his Advance Base and a champagne bottle covered with the signatures of many of the men who were involved in his first flight over the Pole.

Dominating the Hall are two large pieces: a Tucker Sno-Cat oversnow vehicle, one of four used by Vivian Fuchs in the first crossing of Antarctica; and a Ferguson farm tractor, one of three employed by Edmund Hillary to reach the South Pole.

– Baden Norris,
Antarctic curator at the Canterbury Museum

are maintained at -5°C and visitors are free to start their own snowball fight.

A fascinating polar aquarium – one of the very few in the world open to the public – displays Antarctic fish, starfish, sea anemones, sea spiders and sponges in a 2500-liter tank kept chilled at -0.2°C. There's also a stunning blue ice cave, fabricated from plaster, foam and acrylic and complete with delicate ice crystals.

The 13-minute 'Great White South' audiovisual show is very good, using 20 slide projectors to flash 900-odd images of Antarctica on a huge screen.

All the while you can listen to commentary about the displays over your own personal Snowphone, a telephone-like handset with 30 minutes' narration in your choice of English, German, Japanese, Korean, Mandarin or Thai.

Perhaps taking a page from Disneyland's book, the Centre recently added an odd new attraction: a 40-minute ride in a 16-seat Hägglunds BV206, a Swedish-made tracked vehicle used at many Antarctic stations. The ride offers a behind-the-scenes look at the logistics side of the International Antarctic Centre, taking visitors to see the cold-weather clothing warehouse for the US Antarctic Program, into the departure terminal where station members leave for The Ice, out to the tarmac to have a look at the Hercules, Galaxies and Starlifters which fly to Antarctica – and then onto an 'adventure course' with hills and mounds to demonstrate the vehicle's capabilities. The ride, priced separately from the visitor's center itself, departs hourly (NZ$20, and NZ$12 for children aged three to 15).

There is also a room for luggage storage, a souvenir shop and the 60° South Café & Bar. The center (☎ 358-9896, fax 353-7799, www.iceberg.co.nz) is open October to March 9:30 am to 8:30 pm; April to September 9:30 am to 5:30 pm. Admission is NZ$16. To get there catch a bus (every half hour) to the airport from the city; ask for the visitor center. Alternately, you can get a free shuttle from the domestic terminal at the airport by inquiring at the Antarctic Shop.

Operation Deep Freeze Totem Pole

The 9m **totem pole** at the airport on the corner of Memorial Ave and Orchard Rd was a gift to the city of Christchurch from the US state of Oregon in 1959. Carved by Chief Lelooska, it features a thunderbird, god of the storm, as well as a killer whale, eagle, grizzly bear and beaver. A bronze plaque recognizes the first airdrop at the South Pole and the 'warm hospitality extended to the officers and men of the US Air Force and US Navy' during Operation Deep Freeze, the annual US research expedition to Antarctica.

Air Force Museum

On display are a variety of aircraft used by the Royal NZ Air Force over the years, convincingly shown with figures and background scenery. A fine exhibit features the original Auster aircraft and a Beaver aircraft painted in the colors of the RNZAF Antarctic flight and other memorabilia. The Antarctic flight supported Sir Edmund Hillary's depot-laying for the British Commonwealth Trans-Antarctic Expedition during the IGY. The museum is at the former Wigram air base, a 15-minute drive south of the city on Main South Rd. A courtesy bus runs from the visitor center on Worcester St. It can also be reached by a Hornby bus Nos 8 or 25 from Cathedral Square. Open daily 10 am to 5 pm. Admission is NZ$9.

Ferrymead Historic Park

This working museum of transport and technology features several items with Antarctic connections. Chief among them is a cottage formerly sited on 'Warrimoo,' the Christchurch property of Sir Joseph Kinsey, a friend of Captain Scott's. The cottage contained a darkroom, which may have been used by self-described 'camera artist' Herbert Ponting. It now houses a photographic display. There's also an R4D-5 aircraft, which flew with the US Antarctic Program during the 1960s. Located southeast of the city center, at 269 Bridle Path Rd, Heathcote, Ferrymead is open daily 10 am to

4:30 pm. Admission is NZ$6. Take bus No 3 from Cathedral Square.

Lyttelton

Just 12km south of Christchurch, Lyttelton has important Antarctic connections. Bus No 28 from Cathedral Square goes to Lyttelton every half hour; hourly on weekends.

No 3 wharf was the last port of call for many British Antarctic expeditions in the early 1900s. Shackleton's *Nimrod* expedition in particular got a massive send-off here on New Year's Day 1908: an estimated 50,000 people – the largest crowd in Lyttelton's history – watched them depart.

The **Lyttelton Museum** (☎ 328-8972) on Gladstone Quay is a former seaman's mission which gave comfort to many mariners, including the crew of Scott's *Terra Nova*. It has colonial displays, a maritime gallery and an Antarctic gallery containing both 'Heroic Era' and modern Antarctic artifacts. Among the items of interest: artifacts from the Ross Island historic huts, clothing, sledges, geological specimens, personal items belonging to members of expeditions who lived in Lyttelton – and the mounted head of Deek, one of Captain Scott's sledging dogs. The museum is open 2 to 4 pm on Tuesday, Thursday, Saturday and Sunday; admission is free, though donations are appreciated.

On Reserve Terrace, the **Timeball Station** is one of only five still remaining in working order in the world. Built in 1876, it once fulfilled an important maritime duty. Daily for 58 years, the huge timeball was hoisted on a mast and then dropped at exactly 1 pm, Greenwich Mean Time, allowing ships in the harbor to set their clocks and thereby accurately calculate longitude. The Timeball Station (☎ 328-7311) is open daily 10 am to 5 pm. Admission is NZ$3.

On **Quail Island** in Lyttelton harbor, ponies, mules and dogs were quarantined and trained for Shackleton's *Nimrod*, Scott's *Terra Nova* and Byrd's Antarctic expeditions. Some dog kennels are still present. The island, accessible only by boat, is administered by the Department of Conservation (☎ 379-9758).

Hobart

• **population 128,600**

Hobart is the second-oldest, second-driest, smallest and most southerly of Australia's capitals. Straddling the mouth of the Derwent River and backed by mountains offering excellent views of the city, Hobart is one of the most enjoyable Australian cities, with its beautiful Georgian buildings, busy harbor and easy-going atmosphere.

History

The first inhabitants of the city area were members of the Aboriginal Mouheneer tribe, who lived a seminomadic lifestyle. The first European colony in Tasmania was founded in 1803 at Risdon Cove, but a year later Lt Col David Collins, governor of the new settlement in Van Diemen's Land, sailed down the Derwent River and decided that a cove about 10km below Risdon and on the opposite shore was a better place to settle. This, the site of Tasmania's future capital city, began as a village of tents and wattle-and-daub huts with a population of 262 Europeans. Hobart Town, as it was known until 1881, was proclaimed a city in 1842. Very important to its development was the Derwent River estuary, one of the world's finest deepwater harbors. Many merchants made their fortunes from the whaling trade, shipbuilding and the export of corn and merino wool.

Orientation

Hobart is sandwiched between the steep hills of Mt Wellington and the wide Derwent River. The city is about 20km long but very narrow. The center is small and simply laid out, and it is easy to find your way around. The streets in the city center are arranged in a grid pattern around the Elizabeth St Mall. Salamanca Place, the famous row of Georgian warehouses, is along the waterfront, while just south of it is Battery Point, the early colonial district.

Information

Tourist Offices The Tasmanian Travel & Information Centre (☎ 6230-8233) on the

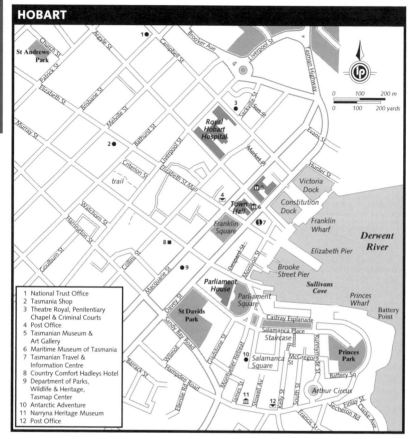

HOBART

1 National Trust Office
2 Tasmania Shop
3 Theatre Royal, Penitentiary
  Chapel & Criminal Courts
4 Post Office
5 Tasmanian Museum &
  Art Gallery
6 Maritime Museum of Tasmania
7 Tasmanian Travel &
  Information Centre
8 Country Comfort Hadleys Hotel
9 Department of Parks,
  Wildlife & Heritage,
  Tasmap Center
10 Antarctic Adventure
11 Narryna Heritage Museum
12 Post Office

corner of Davey and Elizabeth Sts is open weekdays 8:30 am to 5:15 pm, weekends and public holidays 9 am to 4 pm.

Money All prices quoted in the Hobart section are in Australian dollars (A$). Banks are open 9:30 am to 4 pm Monday to Thursday, until 5 pm on Friday. ATMs are available at all the major banks, near the mall on Elizabeth St.

Post The picturesque GPO, on the corner of Elizabeth and Macquarie Sts, is open weekdays 8 am to 5:45 pm. It has an interesting

link to Antarctic history: from here on March 8, 1912, Roald Amundsen – who had slipped ashore dressed as a simple Norwegian seaman from his ship *Fram*, anchored out in the Derwent – sent a telegram to announce his attainment of the South Pole.

Medical Services The Royal Hobart Hospital (☎ 6222-8308) on Argyle St has an emergency section.

Australian Antarctic Division

Located on Channel Hwy in the suburb of Kingston, the Australian Antarctic Division

(☎ 6232-3209), headquarters of Australia's Antarctic program, has a large one-room museum of Antarctic materials, open 9 am to 5 pm weekdays except public holidays. The centerpiece is a bright-orange Caterpillar D4 tractor used on a traverse to Russia's Vostok station near the Geomagnetic South Pole. There is also a mounted skin of an Adélie penguin you can touch, samples of Antarctic minerals, scale models of Australia's Antarctic stations, bits of wind-scoured timber taken from Mawson's Hut at Commonwealth Bay and a small souvenir shop.

Franklin Square

Although Sir John Franklin, the subject of the statue by the fountain in this square, did not himself go to Antarctica, he was governor of Van Diemen's Land (now called Tasmania) from 1837 to 1843, and played host to James Clark Ross' *Erebus* and *Terror* when they stopped here on their way south in 1839-40. Franklin, of course, later used these same ships in his ill-fated search for the Northwest Passage. Franklin Square has drawn Antarcticans for more than a century; signs here show photos of the visit by the 1898-1900 expedition led by Carsten Borchgrevink, first to winter at Cape Adare.

Tasmanian Museum & Art Gallery

The excellent Tasmanian Museum & Art Gallery (☎ 6235-0777), at 5 Argyle St (enter via 40 Macquarie St), incorporates Hobart's oldest building, the Commissariat Store, built in 1808. The museum features a collection of Antarctic and Southern Ocean artifacts, including whaling relics, as well as a Tasmanian Aboriginal display and artifacts from the state's colonial heritage, while the gallery has a good collection of Tasmanian colonial art. Open daily 10 am to 5 pm; free admission.

Narryna Heritage Museum

This is the oldest folk museum in Australia. Formerly called the Van Diemen's Land Folk Museum, it's based in Narryna, a fine Georgian home at 103 Hampden Rd, Battery Point. Dating from the 1830s, it stands on beautiful grounds and has a large collection of relics from Tasmania's pioneering days. The museum (☎ 6234-2791) is open Tuesday through Friday 10:30 am to 5 pm, weekends 2 to 5 pm. Admission is A$5.

Maritime Museum of Tasmania

This museum contains an extensive collection of photos, paintings, models and relics depicting Tasmania's – and particularly Hobart's – colorful shipping history, as well as information on early sealing and whaling voyages and Antarctic expedition ships. The museum is open daily (except Christmas Day and Good Friday) 10 am to 5 pm. Admission is A$6. It is located in the Carnegie Building at 16 Argyle St on the corner of Davey St in the Town Hall block (near Constitution Dock). The historic Carnegie Building, constructed in 1907, was the home of the Tasmanian Public Library until 1962.

Royal Tasmanian Botanical Gardens

Within the chilled Tasmania, Alpine and Sub-Antarctic House – the only such cold house of its kind in the world – is a plant display featuring the flora of Macquarie Island. The gardens are a short taxi drive north of the city center in the Queens Domain near the Tasman Bridge. Open daily 8 am to 4:45 pm; admission is free.

Historic Buildings

One of the things that makes Hobart so unusual among Australian cities is its wealth of old and remarkably well preserved buildings. More than 60 of them, featuring some of Hobart's best Georgian architecture, are on Macquarie and Davey Sts. The National Trust office is on the corner of Brisbane and Campbell Sts (☎ 6223-5200); it has a shop at 33 Salamanca Place, open Monday to Friday and on Saturday morning.

Close to the city center is **St Davids Park**, which has lovely old trees and some gravestones dating from the colony's earliest days. On Murray St is **Parliament House**, originally used as a customhouse. Hobart's prestigious **Theatre Royal**, at 29 Campbell St, was built in 1837 and is the oldest theater in Australia.

The historic **Penitentiary Chapel & Criminal Courts** are located at 28 Campbell St (☎ 6231-0911); tours are offered daily between 10 am and 2 pm. Admission is A$4.

Country Comfort Hadleys Hotel
You'll have your own accommodations as part of your Antarctic tour, but this hotel at 34 Murray St, once known as Hadley's Orient, is noteworthy as the place Amundsen stayed when he came ashore to wire his triumphant message. The 'Amundsen Suite' – tarted up from the simple room in which he lodged – combines rooms 201 and 202, at least one of which was Amundsen's. His photograph hangs above the bed in which he allegedly slept.

Waterfront
Hobart's busy waterfront area centers around **Franklin Wharf**, close to the city center. At **Constitution Dock** there are several floating takeaway seafood stalls, and it's a treat to sit in the sun munching fresh fish and chips while watching the harbor. The docks also have some fine sit-down restaurants. At the finish of the annual Sydney to Hobart and Westcoaster yacht races, around New Year's, and during the Royal Hobart Regatta in February, Constitution Dock really comes alive.

Salamanca Place
The row of beautiful sandstone warehouses on the harborfront at Salamanca Place is a prime example of Australian colonial architecture. Dating to the whaling days of the 1830s, the warehouses were the center of Hobart Town's trade and commerce. Today they house galleries, restaurants, nightspots and shops. Saturday mornings in summer a popular 300-stall **open-air craft market** is held from 8:30 am to 3 pm.

Australia's big red **Antarctic research vessel** *Aurora Australis* lies at anchor at Prince's Wharf when it is between voyages, just across the road from Salamanca Place.

Antarctic Adventure
This theme park and science center near the waterfront at Salamanca Square allows you to experience snow and temperatures as low as -15° C, view Antarctica's night sky in the planetarium and simulate performing a penguin census – but it's not Antarctica. Among the 50-odd exhibits are sample penguin and seal skins to touch, and climb-through displays of tents, huts and snow machines. Electronic headset guides with programs in English, German and Japanese can be rented. Antarctic Adventure (☎ toll-free 1-800-350-028, 24-hour information ☎ 6223-8383, www.antarctic.com.au) is open 10 am to 5 pm daily except Christmas Day. Admission is A$16.

Battery Point
Behind Princes Wharf and Salamanca Place is the historic core of Hobart, the old port area known as Battery Point. This area was a colorful colonial maritime village, home to master mariners, shipwrights, sailors, fishers, coopers and merchants. The houses reflect their varying lifestyles, ranging from tiny one- and two-room houses to large mansions. Battery Point is now made up of lots of great private homes with shops, museums and tourist attractions scattered through. Don't miss **Arthur Circus** – a small circle of quaint little cottages built around a village green – or **St George's Anglican Church**.

Shopping
The Antarctic Connection (☎ 6224-8233), at 29 Salamanca Pl in the Salamanca Maxilab photo store has a wide selection of Antarctic-related items, including books, bookmarks, postcards, magnets, stamps and stuffed toys. There's also a selection of historic photographs for sale. The store is open daily (☎ 6224-8244, www.southcom.com.au/~salmax/).

Many stores sell Tasmania-related items. Among the best is the Tasmania Shop (☎ 6231-5200, tasmaniashop@trump.net.au) at 108 Elizabeth St, which carries a wide variety of handsome handcrafted items.

DIRECCION PROVINCIAL DE PUERTOS
DELEGACION - PUERTO USHUAIA

BIENVENIDOS A LA CIUDAD MAS AUSTRAL DEL MUNDO. —
WELCOME TO THE SOUTHERN - MOST CITY IN THE WORLD.—
BENVENUTI NELLA CITTÁ PIU' A SUD DEL MONDO.—
BIENVENUS A LA VILLE PLUS AUSTRALE DU MONDE.—
WILLKOMMEN IN DER SÜDLICHSTEN STADT DER WELT. —
PASAJEROS DEL:— PASSENGERS OF:— PASSEGGERI DEL:—
PASSAGERS DU:— PASSAGIEREN DES:—   VAVILOV
                                PROF. MOLCHANOV

Ushuaia (Arc.-Antártida   1000 km
Punta Arenas (Chi-)Antártida   1300 km
Hobart (Aus)Antártida   2200 km
Crhistchurch (NZel)Antártida 2250 k

JEFF RUBIN

Sign in Ushuaia, Argentina, listing Antarctic tour ships in port

JEFF RUBIN

Russian-flagged tour ship rolling through the Southern Ocean

Cape Horn, the southernmost tip of South America

Ushuaia, Argentina, a main traveler gateway to Antarctica

Punta Arenas

• **population 113,000**

At the foot of the Chilean Andes on the western side of the Strait of Magellan, Punta Arenas (roughly 'Sandy Point') features many mansions and other impressive buildings dating from the wool boom of the late 19th and early 20th centuries. As one of the best and largest ports for thousands of kilometers, it attracts ships from the burgeoning South Atlantic fishery as well as Antarctic research and tourist vessels.

History

Ona, Yahgan, Alacaluf and Tehuelche Indians, sustaining themselves by fishing, hunting and gathering, were the area's original inhabitants. There remain very few individuals of identifiable Ona or Yahgan descent, while the Alacalufes and Tehuelches survive in much reduced numbers. In 1520, Magellan was the first European to visit the area, but early Spanish colonization attempts failed; tiny Puerto Hambre (Port Famine), on the strait south of Punta Arenas, is a reminder. Nearby, the restored

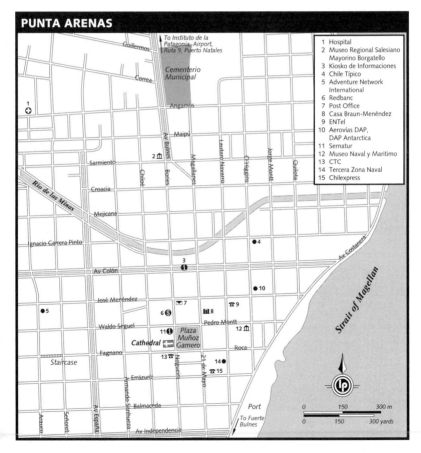

PUNTA ARENAS

To Instituto de la Patagonia, Airport, Ruta 9, Puerto Natales

Cementerio Municipal

Rio de las Minas

Strait of Magellan

Plaza Muñoz Gamero

Cathedral

Staircase

Port
To Fuerte Bulnes

1   Hospital
2   Museo Regional Salesiano Mayorino Borgatello
3   Kiosko de Informaciones
4   Chile Típico
5   Adventure Network International
6   Redbanc
7   Post Office
8   Casa Braun-Menéndez
9   ENTel
10 Aerovías DAP, DAP Antarctica
11 Sernatur
12 Museo Naval y Maritimo
13 CTC
14 Tercera Zona Naval
15 Chilexpress

0   150   300 m
0   150   300 yards

wooden bulwarks of Fuerte (Fort) Bulnes recall Chile's initial colonization in 1843, when President Manuel Bulnes ordered the army south to an area then only sparsely populated by indigenous peoples.

Founded in 1848, Punta Arenas was originally a military garrison and penal settlement, which proved conveniently situated for ships headed to California during the Gold Rush. Compared to the initial Chilean settlement at Fuerte Bulnes, 60km south, it had a more protected harbor and better access to wood and fresh water.

The area's economy did not take off until the late 19th century, after the territorial governor authorized the purchase of 300 purebred sheep from the Falkland Islands. This experiment's success encouraged others to invest in sheep, and by the beginning of the 20th century there were nearly 2 million sheep in the territory.

In 1875, the population of Magallanes province was barely 1000, but European immigration accelerated as the wool market boomed. Among the most notable immigrants was José Menéndez, an entrepreneur from Spanish Asturias who would become one of the wealthiest and most influential individuals in all of South America.

The opening of the Panama Canal in 1914 precipitated a decline in traffic around Cape Horn, which diminished Punta Arenas' importance.

Orientation

The city has spread north and south from its original center between the port and the Plaza de Armas, properly known as Plaza Muñoz Gamero. Street names change on either side of the plaza, but street addresses on the plaza itself bear the name Muñoz Gamero.

Most landmarks and accommodations are within a few blocks of the plaza. Mirador La Cruz, at Fagnano and Señoret, four blocks west of the plaza, provides a good view of town and the strait. Most city streets are one-way, though grassy medians divide Av Bulnes and a few other major thoroughfares.

Information

Tourist Offices Sernatur (☎ 22-5385), the Chilean state tourist agency, is at Waldo Seguel 689, just off Plaza Muñoz Gamero. It's open weekdays 8:30 am to 5:45 pm, and has a friendly, helpful and well-informed staff. The municipal Kiosko de Informaciones (Information Kiosk) (☎ 22-3798) in the 700 block of Av Colón, between Bories and Magallanes, is open weekdays 9 am to 7 pm, Saturday 9 am to 7 pm.

Money All prices quoted in the Punta Arenas section are in US dollars (US$). Money changing is easiest at cambios and travel agencies along Lautaro Navarro, which are open weekdays and Saturday mornings. Traveler's checks are easy to negotiate, but many hotels and restaurants also accept US dollars at a fair rate of exchange. Redbanc has an ATM at Bories 970, half a block north of the plaza, and there are several others in the area.

Post & Communications Correos de Chile, the central post office, is at Bories 911 near José Menéndez, a block north of the plaza. Chilean telephone companies provide offices from which you can call long-distance: CTC is at Nogueira 1116, at the southwest corner of the plaza; Chilexpress is at Errázuriz 856 and ENTel is at Lautaro Navarro 931.

Medical Services The Hospital Regional (☎ 24-4040) is at Arauco and Angamos.

Plaza Muñoz Gamero

This lovingly maintained plaza is landscaped with a variety of exotic conifers and a Victorian kiosk (1910). In the plaza's center, which was donated by wool baron José Menéndez in 1920, is a monument to the 400th anniversary of Magellan's voyage. Around the plaza are the **Club de la Unión** (once the Sara Braun mansion, built by a French architect and and since renovated as a hotel and restaurant), the **Cathedral** and other monuments to the city's early- 20th-century splendor.

Casa Braun-Menéndez

Also known as the Palacio Mauricio Braun, this opulent mansion testifies to the wealth and power of pioneer sheep farmers in the late 19th century. Much of it, including original furnishings, remains as it was when still occupied by the Braun-Menéndez family. The museum (☎ 24-4216) also has excellent historical photographs and artifacts of early European settlement. Open Tuesday to Sunday 11 am to 2 pm. Admission is US$2.

Museo Regional Salesiano Mayorino Borgatello

Especially influential in European settlement of the region, the Salesian order collected outstanding ethnographic artifacts, but this museum takes a self-serving view of the Christian intervention, portraying missionaries as peacemakers between Indians and settlers. The best materials are on the various indigenous groups, including Onas, Alacalufes and Yaganes. The museum (☎ 24-1096), Av Bulnes 374, is open daily except Monday 9 am to noon and 3 to 6 pm. Admission is US$2.

Museo Naval y Marítimo

Despite its overbearing military music and romantic view of Chile's presence in the southern oceans, Punta Arenas' naval and maritime museum has varied worthwhile exhibits on model ships, naval history (including the obligatory homage to patriotic icon Arturo Prat), the unprecedented visit of 27 US warships to Punta Arenas in 1908 and material on southern Patagonia's Canoe Indians. Particularly interesting is a very fine account of the Chilean mission that rescued Shackleton's *Endurance* expedition from Elephant Island. At Pedro Montt 981, the museum (☎ 20-5558) is open Tuesday through Saturday 9:30 am to 12:30 pm and 3 to 6 pm. Admission is US 75¢.

Cementerio Municipal

The walled municipal cemetery, at Av Bulnes 949, tells a great deal about the history and social structure of the region – and includes an intriguing Antarctic connection.

Close to the cemetery entrance gate, under a prominent cenotaph, rests Captain Adolfus Amandus Andresen (1863-1940), a Norwegian-born immigrant to Chile whose harpooning of a humpback whale in the Straits of Magellan in 1903 marked the beginning of modern whaling in the Southern Hemisphere. In 1906, Andresen established a base of operations at Deception Island in the South Shetland Islands northwest of the Antarctic Peninsula. His company, Sociedad Ballenera de Magallanes, was based in Punta Arenas. In a bit of Chilean chauvinism, his grave marker reads: 'Captain Adolfo Andresen…who, on Deception Island, let the Chilean flag wave as a sign of superiority, and thus established Chile's rights to Antarctica, an historic and geographical extension of the Republic.' (Thanks to Norwegian whaling historian Gustav Rossnes for this information.)

The first families of Punta Arenas flaunted their wealth in death as in life – wool baron José Menéndez's extravagant tomb is, according to Bruce Chatwin, a scale replica of Rome's Vittorio Emmanuel monument. But the headstones among the topiary cypresses also tell the stories of Anglo, German, Scandinavian and Yugoslav immigrants who supported the wealthy families with their labor. There is also a monument to the now nearly extinct Ona Indians. Open daily, the cemetery is about a 15-minute walk from the plaza, but you can also take any *taxi colectivo* from the entrance of the Casa Braun-Menéndez on Magallanes.

Magellanic Penguin Colonies

Also known as the 'jackass penguin' for its characteristic braying sound, the Magellanic penguin *(Spheniscus magellanicus)* comes ashore in spring to breed and lay its eggs in sandy burrows or under shrubs a short distance inland. There are two substantial colonies near Punta Arenas: the easiest to reach is the mainland pingüinera on **Seno Otway** (Otway Sound), about an hour northwest of the city, while the larger **Parque Nacional Los Pinguinos** is accessible only by boat. Since there is no scheduled public transport to either site, it is necessary to rent a car or take a tour to visit. Admission is US$4.

Shopping

Chile Típico (☎ 22-5827), Ignacio Carrera Pinto 1015, offers artisanal items in copper, bronze, lapis lazuli and other materials.

Stanley

• **population 1560**

Stanley, the Falkland Islands' capital, is little more than a village, which, by historical accident, acquired a political status totally out of proportion to its size. Because many of its houses were built from available materials – often locally quarried stone and timber from shipwrecks – it has a certain ramshackle charm, as the houses' metal cladding and brightly painted corrugated-iron roofs contrast dramatically with the surrounding moorland. Nearly all have large kitchen gardens where residents grow much of their own food and enough flowers to give the townscape color. The sweetish fragrance of peat fuel still permeates the town on calm evenings, though many households now use oil, gas and electricity for cooking and heating.

For information on the rest of the Falklands, see the Southern Ocean & Sub-Antarctic Islands chapter.

History

Stanley was founded in 1844, when the British Colonial Office ordered the removal of the seat of government from Port Louis on Berkeley Sound to the more sheltered harbor of Port Jackson, since renamed Stanley Harbour. Originally a tiny outpost of colonial officials, vagabond sailors and British military pensioners, the town grew slowly as a supply and repair port for ships rounding Cape Horn en route to the California Gold Rush. Some damaged vessels were forced to limp back into port, and their cargoes were legitimately condemned and sold, but the port acquired an unsavory reputation as ships were scuttled under questionable circumstances, which undoubtedly discouraged growth. Only as sheep replaced cattle in the late 19th century did Stanley begin to grow more rapidly, as it became the transshipment point for wool between the outlying sheep ranches and the UK.

As the wool trade grew, so did the influence of the Falkland Islands Company, already the Islands' largest landowner. FIC soon became the town's largest employer. From the late 19th century on, FIC's political and economic dominance was uncontested, as it ruled the town no less absolutely than the owners of the large sheep stations ruled the countryside (locally known as 'Camp'). At the same time, the company's relatively high wages and good housing provided a paternalistic security.

During the 1982 Falklands War, the capital escaped almost unscathed despite its occupation by thousands of Argentine troops. The two major exceptions were both sad and ironic: a British mortar round hit a house on the outskirts of town, killing three local women, while Argentine conscripts rioted against their officers after the surrender and burned the historic Globe Store, a business whose Anglo-Argentine owner had died only a few years earlier.

Stanley remains the service center for the wool industry, but since the declaration of a fisheries protection zone around the Islands, it has become an important port for the deepwater fishing industry, and many Asian and European fishing companies have offices here. The potential oil boom promises further changes.

Orientation

On a steep hillside on the south shore of Stanley Harbour, Port William's sheltered inner harbor on East Falkland, Stanley is surrounded by water and low hills. For protection from the prevailing southwest winds, the town has sprawled east and west along the harbor rather than onto the exposed ridge of Stanley Common to the south. Ross Rd, running the length of the harbor, is the main street, but most government offices, businesses and houses are within a few blocks of each other in the compact town center.

Information

Tourist Offices The Falkland Islands Tourist Board (☎ 22215, 22281, fax 22619, manager@tourism.org.fk) at the Public Jetty distributes an excellent guide to Stanley, as well as other useful brochures. Open weekdays 8 am to noon and 1:15 to 4:30 pm.

Money All prices quoted in the Stanley section are in British pounds (£). Standard Chartered Bank, on Ross Rd between Barrack and Villiers Sts, changes foreign currency and traveler's checks and is open weekdays 8:30 am to 3 pm. Most Stanley businesses readily accept traveler's checks, but credit cards are not generally accepted, except at the Falkland Islands Company, Ltd, which takes Visa and Mastercard, and the Philatelic Bureau, which takes only Visa. Remember that Falklands currency is valueless outside the Islands – change your local notes before leaving.

Post & Communications The post office (☎ 27180), in Town Hall on Ross Rd at Barrack St, is open weekdays 8 am to noon and 1:15 to 4:30 pm. Stamp collectors should visit the Philatelic Bureau (☎ 27159) in the same building, open weekdays 9 am to noon and 1:15 to 4 pm.

Easily identified by its satellite dish, Cable and Wireless PLC (☎ 20804) operates the Falklands' phone, telegram, telex and fax services from offices on Ross Rd near Government House. To make an overseas call from the booths in the office, purchase a magnetic card over the counter – this is cheaper than an operator-assisted call. Counter hours are 8:30 am to 5 pm weekdays, but public booths are open 24 hours.

Medical Services The King Edward VII Memorial Hospital (☎ 27328 for appointments, ☎ 27410 for emergencies), a joint military-civilian facility at the west end of St Mary's Walk, is one of the best in the world for a community of Stanley's size.

Government House

Probably Stanley's most photographed landmark, rambling Government House has been home to London-appointed governors since the mid-19th century. Once a very minor post within the UK's Foreign & Commonwealth Office, the governorship is much more significant now. It is traditional for all

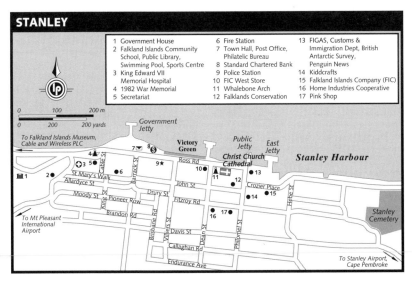

STANLEY

1 Government House
2 Falkland Islands Community School, Public Library, Swimming Pool, Sports Centre
3 King Edward VII Memorial Hospital
4 1982 War Memorial
5 Secretariat
6 Fire Station
7 Town Hall, Post Office, Philatelic Bureau
8 Standard Chartered Bank
9 Police Station
10 FIC West Store
11 Whalebone Arch
12 Falklands Conservation
13 FIGAS, Customs & Immigration Dept, British Antarctic Survey, Penguin News
14 Kiddcrafts
15 Falkland Islands Company (FIC)
16 Home Industries Cooperative
17 Pink Shop

0   100   200 m
0   200   200 yards

To Falkland Islands Museum, Cable and Wireless PLC

Government Jetty

Victory Green

Public Jetty

East Jetty

Christ Church Cathedral

Stanley Harbour

Ross Rd

Cable St

Barrack St

St Mary's Walk
Allardyce St
Moody St
King St
Pioneer Row
Drury St
John St
Fitzroy Rd
Brandon Rd
Brisbane Rd
Villiers St
Davis St
Dean St
Callaghan Rd
Endurance Ave
Crozier Place
Hebe St
Philomel St

To Mt Pleasant International Airport

Stanley Cemetery

To Stanley Airport, Cape Pembroke

visitors to the Falklands to sign the register of visitors, but this custom has declined with the increased passenger traffic of the postwar period. Government House is on Ross Rd West, set back 50m from the street.

Christ Church Cathedral

Completed in 1892 and undoubtedly the town's most distinguished landmark, the cathedral, on Ross Rd, is a massive brick-and-stone construction with a brightly painted corrugated-metal roof and attractive stained-glass windows. On the small square next to the cathedral, the recently restored **Whalebone Arch** commemorates the 1933 centenary of British rule in the Falklands.

Battle of the Falklands Memorial (1914)

On Ross Rd West just past Government House, this obelisk commemorates a naval engagement between British and German forces in WWI. Nine British ships, in Stanley for refueling, quickly responded to sink four of five German cruisers that had earlier surprised them in southern Chile.

1982 War Memorial

Just west of the Secretariat on Ross Rd is a wall honoring the victims of the 1982 Falklands conflict. Designed by a Falkland Islander living overseas, it was paid for by public subscription and built with volunteer labor. Somber ceremonies take place every June 14.

Falkland Islands Museum

Ironically, the facility that houses the Falklands museum was built for the Argentine Air Force officer who was the local representative of LADE, which until 1982 operated air services between Comodoro Rivadavia and Stanley. For several years after the war, it was the residence of the Commander of British Forces Falkland Islands (BFFI), but after the garrison moved to Mt Pleasant it became the new home of the local museum (☎ 27428). You'll find it on Holdfast Rd south of Ross Rd West, just beyond the 1914 Battle Memorial. Today the museum contains natural history specimens and artifacts from

everyday life in the Falklands. Curator John Smith's booklet *Condemned at Stanley* relates the stories of the numerous shipwrecks that dot Stanley Harbour. The museum is open Tuesday to Friday 10:30 am to noon and 2 to 4 pm, Sunday 10 am to noon. Admission is £1.50.

Stanley Harbour Maritime History Trail

See the tourist office on the Public Jetty for Graham Bound's brochure, which describes the various wrecks and condemned ships in Stanley Harbour. There are now informational panels near the remains of vessels such as *Jhelum*, a sinking East Indiaman deserted by her crew in 1871, *Charles Cooper*, an American packet from 1866 still used for storage by the FIC and *Lady Elizabeth*, a striking three-masted freighter that limped into Stanley after hitting a reef in 1913.

Shopping

You may find a few Falklands souvenirs, but most come from the UK. The exception is locally spun and knitted woolens. Try the Home Industries Cooperative on Fitzroy Rd, open weekdays 9:30 am to noon and 1:30 to 4:30 pm. Kiddcrafts (☎ 21301), 2A Philomel St, makes stuffed penguins and other soft toys appealing to children. The Pink Shop (☎/fax 21399), 33 Fitzroy Rd, sells gifts and souvenirs, Falklands and general-interest books (including a selection of Lonely Planet guides), excellent wildlife prints by owner-artist Tony Chater and work by other Falklands artists. Postage stamps, available from the post office and from the Philatelic Bureau, are popular with collectors. The Bureau also sells stamps from South Georgia and the British Antarctic Territory. The Treasury (☎ 27141), in the Secretariat on Thatcher Dr behind the 1982 War Memorial, sells commemorative Falklands coins.

Ushuaia

• **population 42,000**

Over the past two decades, fast-growing Ushuaia in Argentina has evolved from a village into a city, sprawling from its original site, but still located in one of the most dramatic settings in the world. It lies beneath the jagged glacial peaks of the Montes Martial, which rise from sea level to more than 1300m and are topped by Monte Olivia (1318m), an easily recognized sharp pinnacle.

Ushuaia's airport, officially called Aeropuerto Internacional Malvinas Argentinas, is located on the peninsula across from the waterfront. A 3800m runway permits planes larger than 737s to land, which have been made necessary by the city's growing popularity with tourists, Antarctic and otherwise.

More Antarctic tourists depart for The Ice from Ushuaia than from anywhere else by a wide margin, thanks mainly to the city's fortunate location almost directly across the 1000km-wide Drake Passage from the Antarctic Peninsula.

History

From the 16th-century voyages of Magellan through the 19th-century explorations of Fitzroy and Darwin in *Beagle*, and even to the present, this 'uttermost part of the Earth' has held a double-edged fascination for travelers. For more than three centuries, its climate and terrain discouraged European settlement, yet indigenous people considered it a land of plenty.

The Yahgan Indians, now few in number, built the fires that inspired Europeans to give this region its name, famous throughout the world: Tierra del Fuego, or Land of Fire. In 1520, when Magellan passed through the strait that now bears his name, neither he nor any other European explorer had any immediate interest in the land or its people. In search of a passage to the spice islands of Asia, early navigators feared and detested the stiff westerlies, hazardous currents and violent seas that impeded their progress. Consequently, the Ona, Haush, Yahgan and Alacaluf peoples who populated the area faced no immediate competition for their lands and resources.

All these groups were mobile hunters and gatherers. The Onas, also known as Selknam, and the Haush subsisted primarily on terrestrial resources, hunting the guanaco and dressing in its skins, while the Yahgans and Alacalufes, known collectively as 'Canoe Indians', lived on fish, shellfish, and marine mammals. The Yahgans, also known as the Yamana, consumed the 'Indian bread' fungus

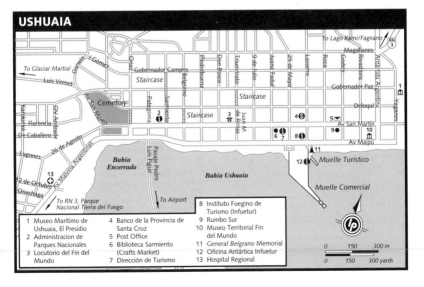

USHUAIA

To Lago Kami/Fagnano
Magallanes
RN 3

To Glaciar Martial
Luis Vernet
Gobernador Campos
Staircase
Staircase
Gobernador Paz   1
Cemetery
Staircase
Deloqui
Av San Martín
Florencia
2   3
De Caballero
6 7   8   9   10
Av Maipú
11
Bahía
Encerrada
12   Muelle Turístico
Bahía Ushuaia
Muelle Comercial
13
To RN 3, Parque
Nacional Tierra del Fuego
To Airport

0   150   300 m
0   150   300 yards

1 Museo Marítimo de Ushuaia, El Presidio	4 Banco de la Provincia de Santa Cruz
2 Administracion de Parques Nacionales	5 Post Office
3 Locutorio del Fin del Mundo	6 Biblioteca Sarmiento (Crafts Market)
	7 Dirección de Turismo
8 Instituto Fuegino de Turismo (Infuetur)	11 *General Belgrano* Memorial
9 Rumbo Sur	12 Oficina Antártica Infuetur
10 Museo Territorial Fin del Mundo	13 Hospital Regional

(Cytarria darwinii), which parasitizes the ñire, a species of southern beech. Despite frequently inclement weather, they wore little or no clothing, but constant fires (even in their bark canoes) kept them warm.

As Spain's control of its American empire dwindled, the area slowly opened to settlement by other Europeans, ensuring the rapid demise of the indigenous Fuegians, whom Europeans struggled to understand. Darwin, visiting the area in 1834, wrote that the difference between the Fuegians ('among the most abject and miserable creatures I ever saw') and Europeans was greater than that between wild and domestic animals. On an earlier voyage, though, Captain Robert Fitzroy of *Beagle* had abducted several Yahgans whom he returned after several years of missionary education in England.

Beginning in the 1850s, Europeans attempted to catechize the Fuegians. The earliest such instance ended with the death by starvation of British missionary Allen Gardiner. Gardiner's successors, working from a base at Keppel Island in the Falklands, were more successful, despite the massacre of one party by Fuegians at Isla Navarino. Thomas Bridges, a young man at Keppel, learned to speak the Yahgan language and became one of the first settlers at Ushuaia. His son, Lucas Bridges, born at Ushuaia in 1874, left a fascinating memoir of his experiences among the Yahgans and Onas titled *The Uttermost Part of the Earth* (1950).

Since no other European power had any interest in settling the region until Britain occupied the Falklands in the 1770s, Spain paid little attention to Tierra del Fuego, but the successor governments of Argentina and Chile felt differently. The Chilean presence on the Strait of Magellan (beginning in 1843), along with increasing British evangelism, spurred Argentina to formalize its authority at Ushuaia in 1884 and install a territorial governor the following year.

In 1870, the British-based South American Missionary Society made Ushuaia its first permanent outpost in the Fuegian region. Despite minor gold and lumber booms, Ushuaia was for many years primarily a penal settlement for both political prisoners and common criminals.

As early as 1884, Argentina's federal government established a military prison on Isla de los Estados (Staten Island), at the east end of Tierra del Fuego, partly to support its territorial claims in a region inhabited only by hunter-gatherers with no state allegiance. In 1902, it shifted the prison to Ushuaia and, in 1911, it merged with the Carcel de Reincidentes, which had incarcerated civilian recidivists since 1896. One of Ushuaia's most famous inmates was Russian anarchist Simón Radowitzky, who assassinated Buenos Aires police chief Ramón Falcón with a bomb after a police massacre on May Day in 1909. Too young for the death penalty, Radowitzky instead received a life sentence at Ushuaia. Héctor Cámpora, who served as Argentina's president before Juan Perón's last term (1973-74), also did time here.

Sheep farming brought great wealth to some individuals and families, and is still the island's economic backbone. Since 1950 the town has been an important naval base, supporting Argentine claims to Antarctica.

In 1978 Argentina and Chile nearly went to war over claims to three small disputed islands in the Beagle Channel. International border issues in the area were only finally resolved in 1984, when an Argentine plebiscite ratified a diplomatic settlement.

Orientation

Running along the north shore of the Beagle Channel, Av Maipú becomes Av Malvinas Argentinas west of the cemetery and, as RN 3, continues west to Parque Nacional Tierra del Fuego. Unlike most Argentine cities, Ushuaia has no central plaza. Most hotels and visitor services are on or within a few blocks of Av San Martín, the principal commercial street, one block north of Av Maipú. North of Av San Martín, streets rise very steeply, giving good views of the Beagle Channel.

Information

Tourist Offices The municipal Dirección de Turismo (☎ 24550) is at Av San Martín

660, between 25 de Mayo and Juana Fadul. Open weekdays 8 am to 9 pm, weekends and holidays 9 am to 8 pm. The Instituto Fueguino de Turismo (Infuetur, ☎ 23340) is on the ground floor of Hotel Albatros at Maipú and Lasserre.

The Oficina Antártica (☎ 54-29014-24431, fax 54-29014-30694, antartida@tierradelfuego .org.ar, tierradelfuego.org.ar/antartida/ indexeng.htm), on the waterfront Muelle Comercial at Av Maipú 505, has an extremely friendly staff (Andrea Barrio and María Gabriela Roldán) and sells postcards and an Antarctic Peninsula map (mostly in Spanish). There's also a modest display of artifacts from the Hope Bay party of Nordenskjöld's ill-fated Swedish South Polar Expedition of 1901. Across from the Oficina is a small post office and outdoor pay phones which can be used to call the US, Canada and Europe. The Oficina Antártica (Antarctic Unit), at Av Maipú 505 (☎ 54-29014-24431, fax 54-29014-30694, antartida@ tierradelfuego.org.ar, tierradelfuego.org.ar/ antartida/indexeng.htm) is nearly always open when Antarctic tour ships are in port.

Money All prices quoted in the Ushuaia section are in US dollars (US$). Several banks on Maipú and San Martín have ATMs; the best bet for traveler's checks (2% commission) is Banco de la Provincia de Santa Cruz, San Martín 396.

Post & Communications The post office is on Av San Martín, at the corner of Godoy. Locutorios are convenient places to make telephone calls. The Dirección de Turismo has a line for collect and credit card calls to Brazil, Chile, France, Italy, Japan, Spain, Uruguay and the US (AT&T, MCI, Sprint).

Medical Services Ushuaia's Hospital Regional (☎ 22950, emergencies ☎ 107) is at Maipú and 12 de Octubre.

The Harbor
Ushuaia's harbor is busy and not overly picturesque, though its margins are good for bird-watching. The wrecked tugboat is St Christopher, which arrived in 1953 to refloat the stranded cruise ship *Monte Cervantes*. Not only did it fail at this, it damaged itself so badly that it was unable to leave.

Museo Territorial Fin del Mundo
The Museo offers exhibits on Fuegian natural history, aboriginal life, the early penal colonies (complete with a photographic rogues' gallery), replicas of an early general store and bank – and a rare opportunity to see Andean condors, though unfortunately stuffed, not live. There is also a copy of Thomas Bridges' Yamana-English dictionary and a bookshop. On the waterfront at Av Maipú and Rivadavia, the museum (☎ 21863) is open Monday through Saturday 10 am to 1 pm and 3 to 8 pm. Admission is US$5.

Museo Marítimo de Ushuaia
The Museo Marítimo is within the military base, El Presidio. Closed as a penal institution since 1947, the present building at one time held as many as 800 inmates in 380 cells designed to hold one prisoner each. Some of the displays, which highlight local history and convict life and include a fascinating collection of handmade knives fashioned by the prisoners, are in the former cells. There is also a 1:1 scale model of the San Juan de Salvamento Lighthouse built in 1884 on Isla de los Estados, made famous by Jules Verne's novel, *The Lighthouse at the End of the World*.

Antarctic exhibits include stuffed penguins, a fur seal pelt you can touch and photos of Antarctic historical interest. Some artifacts from Nordenskjöld's expedition huts on Snow Hill Island and at Hope Bay are on display in several of the cells.

On the ground floor is a remarkable display of several dozen ship models, including Amundsen's *Fram*; Scott's *Discovery*; Charcot's *Le Français* and *Pourquoi-Pas*; Argentina's *Uruguay* (which rescued Nordenskjöld in 1903 and relieved Bruce's party in 1904); Argentina's *Bahia Paraiso* (wrecked in Antarctica in 1989) and the icebreaker *Almirante Irizar*. On the second floor there is an extensive exhibit of stamps and postcards from Antarctica, Tierra del

Fuego and Ushuaia, along with a 'relax zone' and gift shop.

Incorporated into the naval base at the east end of Av San Martín, the museum (☎ 37481) is open Monday to Sunday from 10 am to 1 pm and 3 to 8 pm during the summer. Admission is US$7. Use the entrance at Yaganes and Gobernador Paz rather than the base entrance at Yaganes and San Martín.

General Belgrano Memorial

At the foot of the Muelle Turistico is a small memorial to the Argentine cruiser *General Belgrano*, sunk in 1992 by Britain's Royal Navy during the Falklands War. A stylized gunsight and ship's bow memorialize the 368 crew members who died in the sinking.

Shopping

At Av San Martín 674, a crafts market operates outside the former **Biblioteca Sarmiento** (1926), Ushuaia's first public library.

Puerto Williams (Chile)
• population 2000

While sailing down the Beagle Channel on your way to Antarctica, you'll pass – on your right (south) side – Puerto Williams, Chile, on Ile Navarino.

British Captain Robert Fitzroy encountered Yahgan and Alakaluf Indians near here in 1828, four of whom – Jemmy Button, York Minster, Fuegia Basket and Boat Memory – he brought to England aboard *Beagle* for education. Missionaries in the 19th century and fortune-seekers during the local gold rush of the 1890s established a permanent European presence. Chile built a naval settlement here in 1953, and about

two-thirds of the population now is navy personnel and their families. A few people of Yahgan descent still reside 2km east of town at Ukika.

A dispute over the three small islands of Lennox, Nueva and Picton, east of Ile Navarino at the mouth of the Beagle Channel, nearly brought Argentina and Chile to war in 1978, but papal intervention defused the situation and the islands remain in Chile's possession.

Although it's unlikely that your ship will stop in Puerto Williams, there are two sites worth seeing: the prow of **Yelcho**, the tug commanded by Chilean hero Luis Alberto Pardo that rescued Shackleton's men from Elephant Island, now in an outdoor setting in front of the Chilean Navy supermarket; and the A-framed **Museo Martín Gusinde**, honoring the German priest and ethnographer who worked among the Yahgans in the early 1920s, with exhibits on natural history and ethnography.

Puerto Williams also has a small post office, three restaurants, several small groceries, a few guesthouses and two bars. Satellite TV helps to reduce the sense of isolation by bringing in about 100 channels in both English and Spanish.

Puerto Toro (Chile)
• population 10

This tiny fishing village, also on Ile Navarino, lies to the south of the Beagle Channel along the island's east coast, facing Ile Picton. During king crab season, June to November, the population triples. Your ship won't stop here, but Puerto Toro is notable as the southernmost town in the world – outside Antarctica.

Southern Ocean & Sub-Antarctic Islands

Antarctica is surrounded and isolated by the southern portions of the Atlantic, Indian and Pacific oceans. These are separated from the Southern Ocean by a surface oceanographic phenomenon called the Antarctic Convergence.

Southern Ocean

Although for many people crossing the Southern Ocean is the least interesting – and least comfortable – part of their trip to Antarctica, they should know the Southern Ocean is important to the biology and the climate of the continent in particular and of the Earth in general.

There is a psychological benefit to the Southern Ocean as well: sailing over it to Antarctica makes clear the continent's remoteness and immensity. The Southern Ocean allows time to prepare for Antarctica, to anticipate it. Antarctica is unveiled to the sea traveler slowly, just as it was to human knowledge – the first astonishing iceberg, then many icebergs, then an island, and finally, the continent ahead on the horizon.

First, there is the wide open sea. Most visitors to Antarctica must cross the Drake Passage, the narrow stretch of water separating South America from the Antarctic Peninsula. You may hear about the 'Roaring Forties,' but Tierra del Fuego is at about 55°S, so in fact you'll be passing through only half of the 'Furious Fifties' and part of the so-called 'Screaming Sixties.' Generally, the passage is quick, and if you are fortunate, you'll experience the quiet waters known as the 'Drake Lake.' Otherwise, prepare yourself for a 'Drake Shake,' also known as paying the 'Drake Tax.'

Sailing to Antarctica from Australia, New Zealand or South Africa requires a longer voyage. While there's a greater chance of encountering heavy weather on a longer voyage, there's also more time for birdwatching, stargazing and (perhaps) observing the aurora australis.

No matter where you embark, at some point on your voyage you'll pass over the Antarctic Convergence, also called the Polar Front. The ocean south of the Convergence differs greatly from northern waters in salinity, density and temperature. A great mixing occurs where northern and southern waters meet, with nutrients from the sea floor being brought to the surface, making the Convergence a highly productive area for algae, krill and the other small creatures at the base of the Antarctic food web.

The exact location of the Convergence varies slightly throughout the year, and from year to year. Despite what you may read, there is very little sign that you are crossing the Convergence. The sea does not get rougher, and there is usually no change in its appearance. The primary indicator is a dip of 1.7° to 2.8°C in the water temperature, a change that the ship's instruments will detect, though you almost certainly will not. The engine room crew generally detects it before the officers on the bridge – and changes the flow of cooling water appropriately.

An important feature of the Southern Ocean is the Antarctic Circumpolar Current. This is the world's biggest ocean current, flowing eastward at the rate of 153 million cubic meters per second, about a thousand times the Amazon River's flow.

CAPE HORN (CABO DE HORNOS)

Because most Antarctic tour ships depart from Ushuaia, passengers are often able to catch sight of the fabled Cape Horn – and occasionally to land there. Cape Horn is a synonym for adventure and the romance of the old days of sail – though for most of the poor sailors aboard ships attempting to double the Horn, there was no romance on a cold winter ocean with a gale blowing.

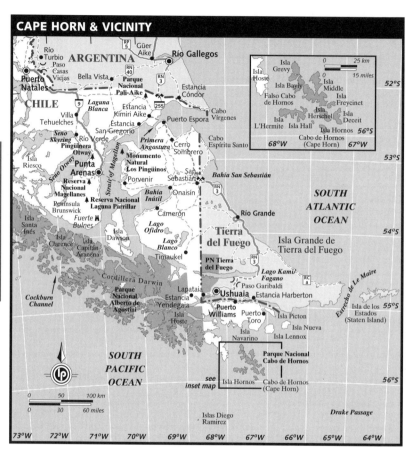

CAPE HORN & VICINITY

Cape Horn was discovered in January 1616 by Dutchmen Jakob Le Maire and Willem Schouten, sailing in *Unity*. They named the cape for their ship *Hoorn*, which had accidentally burned at Puerto Deseado on the Patagonian coast.

Horn Island, of which the famous cape forms the southernmost headland, is just 8km long. The cape itself rises to 424m, with striking black cliffs on its upper parts.

Though you may be one of the thousands each year who lands at Cape Horn and receives a certificate stating that you have done so, be aware of the distinction between 'rounding' the Horn and merely going ashore for a photo session. 'I like to draw a distinction for the visitors I take down there,' writes Skip Novak, skipper of *Pelagic*, a charter yacht often visiting the Antarctic Peninsula. 'I bring people to "see" the Horn, not to round it. My advice to them is that if they want to "round" the Horn, they had better start from somewhere like New Zealand.'

Landings at Cape Horn are infrequent. They are expensive to attempt, since ships are required to have a Chilean pilot for navigation in the shoal-filled offshore waters. Also, the weather seldom cooperates, since even on a calm day, the seas coming north from the Southern Ocean tend to make for choppy water.

When they are attempted, landings are usually made in the westward of the two bays located east of the Cape. A steep wooden stairway of about 110 steps leads to high ground above the beach.

Cabo de Hornos Light is a white fiberglass-reinforced plastic tower 4m high with a red band running around it. It's automated, but a nearby Chilean naval observation station, two huts with a conspicuous radio antenna about 1600m northeast of the light, is home to a few lonesome naval officers.

A **stone monument** on a plinth surrounded by heavy iron chains honors the ancient mariners who rounded Cape Horn.

Another monument, in the form of a large **abstract sculpture** depicts – in the negative space formed by four steel plates – an albatross in flight. It commemorates those lost in the treacherous seas off this headland. A poem by Sara Vial, translated from Spanish, is engraved on a metal plaque:

I am the albatross that waits for you

at the end of the earth.

I am the forgotten soul of the dead sailors

who crossed Cape Horn

from all the seas of the world.

But they did not die

in the furious waves.

Today they fly in my wings

to eternity

in the last trough of the Antarctic winds.

The great Andean condors can be seen here, as well as Magellanic penguins, which nest in burrows in the moss and tussock grass.

ISLAS DIEGO RAMIREZ

These Chilean islands, about 100km southwest of Cape Horn, became the most southerly known land in the world when they were discovered by two ships from a Portuguese expedition on February 12, 1619. They held that honor for more than 150 years, until Cook discovered the South Sandwich Islands in 1775.

The Chilean navy established a meteorological station on one of the islands in 1951. It is now resupplied by navy ships several times a year.

Sub-Antarctic Islands

These tiny specks of land include the most remote islands on Earth. Ecologically, they are extremely important – completely out of proportion to their size – for a large number of seabird, penguin and seal species, because they are often the only breeding places for many hundreds of kilometers in the vast ocean surrounding Antarctica.

Although many people consider a landing on the actual continent to be an essential part of their visit to Antarctica, the sub-Antarctic and ocean islands are in many ways more interesting than large sections of the continental coast. Most of them have more wildlife than Antarctica. While Antarctic tour operators make every effort to land passengers on the continent, most of these islands are properly thought of as part of the Antarctic as well.

No Antarctic voyage, even a circumnavigation of Antarctica, will be able to visit all of the sub-Antarctic and Southern Ocean islands – there are simply too many. But nearly every cruise will visit at least one of the following island groups, and there are even trips that visit *only* islands (see the Getting There & Away chapter).

Cruises from South America or the Falklands stop at the South Shetlands, while voyages sailing from Australia, New Zealand or South Africa will often stop at, respectively, Macquarie Island or Heard Island; New Zealand's sub-Antarctic islands; or the Prince Edward Islands. Resupply vessels visiting the three French sub-Antarctic islands take a limited number of tourists. Tristan da Cunha and Gough Island are usually visited on 'repositioning' cruises, when Antarctic ships sail to or from the Northern Hemisphere, where they ply Arctic waters during the austral winter. The most rarely visited islands are Bouvetøya, Peter I Øy and Scott Island.

OCEAN & ISLANDS

A Visit to Cape Horn

This is the headland sailors shun. We landed on a tiny beach covered with boulders in a cove filled with comb jellies and I wanted to put up a huge sign: IF YOU CAN READ THIS, YOU'RE TOO CLOSE.

Three oceans meet here at basalt cliffs where Magellanic penguins breed. Topsides, you wander the saddles among mounds of tussock grass higher than your head.

We humans are stunned, agape. You'd think we had never seen vegetation before. A hundred flowers bloom on the hillsides – white composites – and green leaves sprout and hang from every crevice in every cliff, and underfoot the wild geraniums and celery, the red berries, the white berries, the succulents that pack every rock, the heaths whose lives mingle with ours.

All over the rocks leaves with unique shapes pulse. What is this soft stuff made of sunlight and rainwater? You can even eat it. Songbirds live here, too, and insects – a dragonfly, on Cape Horn! And a white moth drowned in a pond.

Two Chileans man a base here, and a cat, a dog, and a puppy, who show and return the tenderness a succession of desolate men must have lavished on them. The only other pets I've seen as deeply loved as these lived in a monastery.

There is a tiny church here too, double-walled in bark-sided lumber. There is a stone slab altar, a wooden cross, six or eight short benches, a few garish saint pictures, and a few candles. By the door, in a vestibule smaller than a phone booth, hang four pegs for coats.

The sun is out, here where so many men have died, and there's no wind. An old Inuit poem repeats,

Let me see,
Is it real,
This life I am living?

– Annie Dillard,
member of the American Academy of
Arts and Letters (elected in 1998)

The sub-Antarctic and Southern Ocean islands are presented here in order, traveling eastward from the Prime Meridian.

BOUVETØYA

Bouvetøya is the most isolated island on Earth. Not counting its tiny off-lying neighbor to the southwest, Larsøya, the nearest land is more than 1600km away.

Bouvetøya is the tip of a volcano that rises out of the Southern Ocean, and although the volcano is dormant, there is still geothermal activity on the island. Another island, Thompson Island, was first sighted by 19th-century sealers northeast of Bouvetøya. It is believed to have been destroyed during a volcanic explosion in 1895 or 1896. Sometime between 1955 and 1958, a low-lying shelf of lava appeared on Bouvetøya's west coast, providing the only bird-nesting site of any size on the island. A scientific team landed on Bouvetøya in 1978 and measured a below-ground temperature of 25°C.

Bouvetøya covers about 54 sq km. The highest point is 780m Olavtoppen (Olav Peak). It and another high peak surround the ice-filled crater of an inactive volcano known as the Wilhelm II plateau. Glaciers cover 93% of the island and prevent landings on the south and east coasts, while steep cliffs as high as 490m block access to the north, west and southwest. These cliffs leave only a few places where landings can be made, and numerous offshore rocks serve to make navigation hazardous. Bouvetøya's weather is nearly always cloudy or foggy. The mean temperature is -1°C; in summer, the average high is 2.2°C.

The island is named after French navigator Jean-Baptiste-Charles Bouvet de Lozier, who, sailing in *Aigle*, first sighted it on January 1, 1739, but was unable to get a good fix to determine its position. It was not until 1808 that British whaling captains James Lindsay and Thomas Hopper, sailing in *Swan* and *Otter*, resighted it and proved that it was an island. Bouvetøya's precise position, however, was only pinned down 90 years later by the German Deep Sea Exploration Expedition in *Valdivia* of 1898, which did not succeed in landing.

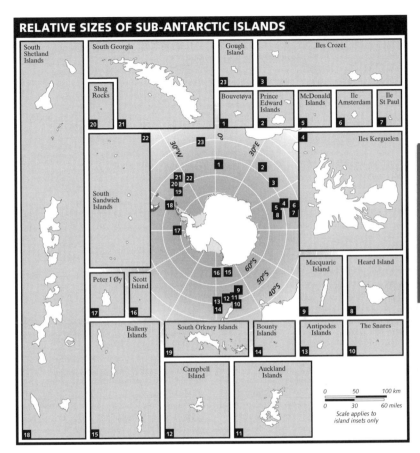

RELATIVE SIZES OF SUB-ANTARCTIC ISLANDS

OCEAN & ISLANDS

The first landing was made by an American sealing expedition led by Benjamin Morrell in *Wasp*, who came ashore on December 8, 1822, and took 172 fur seal skins, thus encouraging other sealers, who visited sporadically during the 19th century. Two British sealing ships, *Sprightly* and *Lively*, rediscovered Bouvetøya on December 10, 1825, and named it Liverpool Island, taking possession for the British crown.

Science, in the form of a Norwegian oceanographic expedition, first visited Bouvetøya in 1927. The island was claimed for Norway on December 1, and on January 23, 1928, it

was formally annexed by Norwegian royal proclamation. (The British Parliament wisely declined to get upset about such an unpromising dot of territory and renounced all claim to Bouvetøya later in 1928.) In 1971 the Norwegian government made the island a nature reserve.

The island has only rarely been visited, so its history is brief. Two events, however, are rather mysterious. First, a sunken lifeboat and assorted supplies were discovered on the island in 1964, but their origin could not be determined. Second, a thermonuclear bomb test seems to have occurred to the west of Bouvetøya in 1979. Though no country ever admitted setting off a bomb there, an orbiting satellite detected a brief, intense burst of light on September 22, 1979. Magnetic, seismographic and ionospheric evidence all pointed to a nuclear blast. Personnel at Australian Antarctic stations later detected radiation and radioactive debris.

Another island mystery surfaced in 1986 when a newspaper in the Norwegian capital of Oslo reported that US census records showed that, since 1959, 60 women and 26 men had emigrated from the uninhabited Bouvetøya to the US.

Three huts were set up by a Norwegian research expedition that spent four months on the island in 1978. They are no longer there, but in 1997 a shipping container brought to the island was converted to a small **Norwegian research station**.

PRINCE EDWARD ISLANDS

Bleak and barren in winter but lush and green in summer, the Prince Edward Islands consist of Prince Edward Island and the larger Marion Island, 22km to the southwest. The islands cover 316 sq km and are part of South Africa's Province of Cape of Good Hope. Dome-like Marion is dotted by more than 100 small hills and many small lakes. Prince Edward is more vertical, with dramatic cliffs towering to 490m high on the southwest coast. The islands' highest point, on Marion, is State President Swart Peak (1230m). The weather is depressingly constant: low temperatures throughout the year, extremely strong westerly winds, abundant snow and rain and skies usually at least three-quarters covered by clouds.

The Prince Edward Islands were declared Special Nature Reserves by the South African government in 1995. Even scientific research on Prince Edward Island is severely restricted. A group of not more than four people is permitted to land only once every three to five years, staying no more than two or three days.

The islands were first sighted by Dutchman Barent Barentszoon Lam (or possibly Ham) sailing in *Maerseveen* on March 4, 1663, who named the northerly island Dina,

and the more southerly Maerseveen. But a subsequent Dutch expedition could not find the islands in the latitude reported (41°S), and they were all but forgotten.

Frenchman Marc Macé Marion du Fresne, sailing in *Mascarin*, rediscovered them on January 13, 1772. Not realizing at first that they were islands, he called the larger one Terre de l'Espérance, but then changed it to Île de l'Espérance. He called the smaller one Île de la Caverne because of a large cave he saw while circumnavigating it. He also saw tiny white spots dotting Île de la Caverne, which he somehow mistook for sheep (they were nesting albatrosses). A collision with his accompanying ship *Marquis de Castries* prevented Marion du Fresne from making a landing to investigate. Sailing farther east, he discovered Îles Crozet (see the Îles Crozet section later in this chapter).

The ubiquitous Briton Captain James Cook searched for Île de l'Espérance and Île de la Caverne early in 1775, but couldn't find them. Meeting one of the few returning survivors of Marion du Fresne's expedition (which had been attacked by Maoris in New Zealand) in Cape Town, Cook obtained a chart showing the islands' location. On December 12, 1776, Cook spotted the islands – and noting that the chart gave them no name, took it upon himself to name them, calling them the Prince Edward Islands after the fourth son of the reigning British monarch. Unknowingly causing considerable confusion for latter-day scholars, Cook gave the name Marion and Crozet Islands to the islands that Marion du Fresne had found later on his voyage, the present-day Îles Crozet. Nineteenth-century sealers further confused the issue by transferring the appellation Marion Island back to the island now known by that name.

French sealers may have made the first landing, in about 1799, though this is not certain. Sealing continued throughout the 19th century and well into the 20th. During those times, like many other sub-Antarctic islands, the Prince Edwards saw their share of shipwrecks, and groups of hapless sailors were stranded for months at a time before being rescued, often by other sealers.

Despite the islands' discovery by the Dutch (and the French), in 1908 the British government felt it had enough proprietary rights over them to grant one William Newton a 21-year lease to exploit guano deposits believed to lie on the islands, but he never used the concession. In 1926, the islands, along with the Heard and McDonald Islands, were leased by the British government for 10 years to the Kerguelen Sealing and Whaling Co of Cape Town, which was granted exclusive rights to seals, whales, guano and minerals. The company worked in the islands until 1930.

If the French had any inclination to challenge these tacit British claims of sovereignty over the islands, their opportunity vanished in 1947, when a secret South African naval expedition code-named 'Operation Snoektown' raised the Union of South Africa's flag at Marion Island on December 29, 1947, and at Prince Edward Island on January 4, 1948. Also, a permanent meteorological station was established at Transvaal Cove on Marion's northeast coast. On January 12, 1948, the South African government issued a proclamation that the British Crown's rights over the islands would henceforth be controlled by His Majesty's Government in South Africa rather than His Majesty's Government in London.

The **met station**, operated continuously since 1947 despite a fire that destroyed the main living quarters and communications facilities in 1966, has gradually expanded its scientific program to include biology. Currently as many as 17 people winter there; during summer, the population swells to about 50. A volcanic eruption occurred in December 1980 but did not damage the scientific station. The possibility of constructing a landing strip was investigated in 1987, but, for environmental reasons, it was not built.

Introduced species have wreaked havoc on Marion's indigenous flora and fauna, just as on other sub-Antarctic islands. The diamond-backed moth (*Plutella xylostella*), for example, introduced itself to the island in 1986; it has badly damaged the Kerguelen cabbage. Mice, inadvertently brought by early-19th-century sealers, have also damaged plant and insect life. Far more damage, however, has been done by descendants of the five house cats brought to the meteorological station in 1949 to control rodents. By 1977, they had multiplied to an estimated 3400 animals and were ravaging the local bird population. The feline panleucopaenia virus, introduced in '77, brought a massive but temporary drop in the feral cat population. Other measures were taken (including shooting), and the cats have now been exterminated. As a result, the breeding success of burrowing petrels has increased rapidly.

Fur seals and elephant seals breed on the islands, as do hundreds of thousands of penguins (kings, gentoos, rockhoppers and macaronis), hundreds of thousands of petrels and thousands of albatrosses.

ÎLES CROZET

Îles Crozet are divided into two groups, L'Occidental (Île aux Cochons, Îlots des Apôtres, Île des Pingouins and the reefs Brisants de l'Héroïne) and L'Oriental (Île de l'Est and Île de la Possession, the largest of the Crozets), about 100km east. The islands cover 325 sq km. The highest point is 1090m Pic Marion-Dufresne on Île de l'Est. There are no glaciers. The islands are part of France's Terres Australes et Antarctiques Françaises and have been a national park since 1938. The Crozets' weather is generally cold, wet, windy and cloudy, but the winters are not severe.

Frenchman Marc Macé Marion du Fresne, sailing in *Mascarin*, discovered the islands on January 23, 1772. He went ashore the next day and took possession of them for France (on Île de la Possession), naming them for his second-in-command, Jules Marie Crozet.

The first sealers arrived in 1804, taking fur seal skins and sailing directly to Canton for sale and processing. Just two years later, a group of 14 wretched, stranded sealers was rescued from the Crozets by *Eliza*, sailing from Nantucket. Unscrupulous captains occasionally abandoned men to uncertain fates on the sub-Antarctic islands, increasing their voyage's profitability. Relentless slaughter soon took its toll on the once-teeming

OCEAN & ISLANDS

Nonexistent Antarctic Islands

Along with the 19 groups of isolated oceanic islands surrounding Antarctica – known as the peri-Antarctic islands – there are reports of a curious assortment of 18 nonexistent but putatively similar far southern islands: Aurora Islands, Burdwood's Island, The Chimneys, Dougherty's Island (also called Keats Island), Elizabethides, Emerald Island, Isla Grande, Macey's Island, Middle Island, New South Greenland, Nimrod Island, Pagoda Rock, Royal Company Island, Strathfillan Rock, Swain's Island, Thompson Island, Undine Rock and Trulsklippen. These have all been recorded in the Southern Ocean or the extreme southern limits of the adjoining oceans, and all have appeared on official charts. Several have been seen more than once, and three may once have existed but have become submerged following volcanic explosions.

Besides volcanoes, there are several reasons people may have supposed these islands existed. Many might be explained as sightings in dirty weather of icebergs that were carrying rocks and moraine. A captain, rightly erring on the side of safety, would report these (dirty ice, especially when extensive, can look convincingly like an island). Some sightings, however, were more likely the result of a bit too much rum. A few may have been deliberate hoaxes: sealers always tried to keep secret the locations of good sealing discoveries, especially new islands, in order to reduce the competition for a scarce resource. Some of the sealers may well have deliberately led others on wild goose chases. One island, New South Greenland, was probably invented to embellish a book by an author who was known as 'the greatest liar in the Pacific.'

The problem with all these nonexistent islands has been getting rid of them. If there was a possibility of a supposedly sighted island being a hazard to navigation, the British Admiralty and other maritime authorities were very reluctant to expunge it from the charts. It usually took a substantial hydrographic survey before this was done (although the satellite age has now simplified this). The persistence of nonexistent islands is phenomenal: Swain's Island, ordered to be deleted from the charts in 1920, could still be found in a 1995 comprehensive world atlas produced by a well-known publisher. Some nonexistent islands have even appeared in novels – there is a lot of writing that can be done with such a theme.

– Robert Headland

beaches, however, and by 1835 the American sealer *Tampico* reported that fur seals were rare in the Crozets.

The islands' first recorded shipwreck was the British sealer *Princess of Wales*, which came to grief in 1821; the crew was not rescued until 21 months later. After they wrecked on Île de l'Est in 1825, the company of the French sealer *Aventure* spent 17 months as castaways. The crew of the French ship *Tamaris*, which sank off Île aux Cochons on March 9, 1887, were the most inventive of the stranded seamen. During their seven-month unplanned sojourn on the island, they attached a message to a giant petrel, which was recovered seven months later near Fremantle, Western Australia, some 6500km away. According to the message they sent,

Tamaris' crew planned to set out for Île de la Possession, but they vanished without a trace.

Whaling soon replaced sealing as the islands' primary economic activity, and in 1841, 12 whaling expeditions from the US alone operated in the waters around Îles Crozet. During the 1843-44 season, the fleet of American whaling ships in the Crozets, as recorded by one sealer, grew to 18: *Aeronaut*, *Arab*, *Cicero*, *Dragon*, *Fenelon*, *France*, *Halcyon*, *Herald*, *John & Elizabeth*, *Majestic*, *Milwood*, *Neptune*, *Popmunnet*, *Romulus*, *Roscoe*, *Stonington*, *Superior* and *Tenedos*.

In the 20th century, after several visits to the Crozets to reassert its territorial sovereignty, France moved to consolidate its hold over its sub-Antarctic islands. In 1955, French law established the Terres Australes et Antarctiques Françaises, which includes Île St Paul, Île Amsterdam, Îles Kerguelen, Îles Crozet and Terre Adélie in Antarctica. In 1978, concerned about fishing by countries including Taiwan and the Soviet Union, France declared a 370km exclusive economic zone around each of the four archipelagos, patrolled by French naval vessels that arrest foreign ships for illegal fishing.

A temporary scientific camp was set up on Île de la Possession in 1961, and during the 1963-64 austral summer a station was established at Port-Alfred on the island's northeast coast, with an aerial cableway running from the beach to the station site. Now known as **Alfred-Faure station**, for its first leader, it houses 35 people over the winter.

As on the other sub-Antarctic islands where they were introduced by sealers and whalers, foreign species including cats, rats, rabbits and mice have damaged some of the islands' fragile ecosystems. Introduced pigs gave Île aux Cochons its name. They caused so much damage that they ate up all their food and became extinct, as did the goats landed on Île de la Possession.

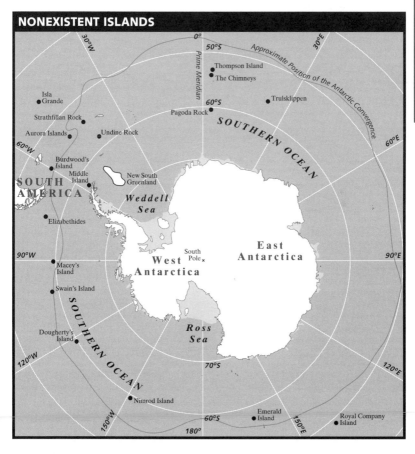

NONEXISTENT ISLANDS

OCEAN & ISLANDS

The Crozets are noted for their birdlife. Half of the world's king penguins breed here.

ÎLES KERGUELEN

Îles Kerguelen consists of one major island, Grande Terre (sometimes called Île Kerguelen), and about 300 tiny islets and rocks. The archipelago covers 7215 sq km, extending 195km from Îlot du Rendez-Vous in the north to Rochers du Salamanca in the south, and 145km from Îles de la Fortune in the west to the eastern tip of Péninsule Courbet on Grand Terre. A submarine shelf at a depth of 200m extends for many kilometers off Grand Terre's northern coast, evidence that Kerguelen was once a much larger landmass.

Grand Terre is heavily serrated by fjords along its northeast and southeast coasts, providing excellent anchorages. No point on the island is farther than 21km from the coast. Kerguelen is sculpted by glacier action, with deep valleys and lakes carved out of its high mountains and plateaus. The impressive Calotte Glaciaire Cook icecap, in the island's west, covers 10% of the island and is the remnant of the ice sheet that once covered the whole of Grande Terre. The island's highest point is Grand Ross (1850m), first climbed in 1975. Kerguelen has typically sub-Antarctic weather: rainy, cloudy, cold and windy, with the prevailing westerlies frequently rising to gale force.

Sailing in *Fortune* in 1772, French Captain Yves Joseph de Kerguélen-Trémarec sighted the archipelago for the first time on February 12, calling it La France Australe because he didn't realize he was looking at islands. Two days later, François Alesno, Comte de Saint-Allouarn, the commander of the accompanying *Gros-Ventre*, sent a boat ashore to claim the territory for King Louis XV. The two ships then separated, and Alesno died soon after his arrival at Mauritius.

With no one to challenge him upon his return to France, Kerguélen told wildly optimistic tales – indeed, outright lies – about his discovery. The lands, he boasted, 'appear to form the central mass of the Antarctic continent,' adding that they were perfectly suited to agriculture and promised abundant minerals and even precious gems. 'If men of a different species are not discovered,' he said, 'at least there will be people living in a state of nature.'

Understandably impressed, the French monarch dispatched Kerguélen on a second voyage in 1773, with three ships, *Rolland*, *Oiseau* and *Dauphine*, and 700 men to colonize 'La France Australe.' A second landing was made, in January 1774, and this time there was no hiding from the reality that Kerguélen's discovery was far from a southern motherland. Upon his second homecoming, a French court martial sentenced Kerguélen to 20 years in prison (later reduced to six) and dismissed him from the navy.

When British Captain James Cook landed on Christmas Eve 1776, one of his men found a bottle containing a parchment inscribed in Latin telling of Kerguélen's visits. Cook, however, was much more sanguine about the islands, calling them the Isles of Desolation.

The first sealers, from the US, arrived in 1791. They remained for 15 months, killing the thick-furred creatures on their breeding beaches. (The first Kerguelen shipwreck occurred just two years later, stranding *Eleanora*'s crew for seven months.) By 1804-05, eight British sealing ships were landing gangs in the Îles. Repeating the pattern of slaughter practiced on other islands, the sealers soon wiped out the giant colonies almost completely. By 1817, the British ship *Eagle* was able to find just four seals (which, naturally, they killed).

With the fur seals gone (to another island, the sealers always seemed to believe; the thought of extinction appeared never to cross their minds), the sealers turned to elephant seals, whose blubber they rendered into a valuable oil. In 1835-40, the British sealer *George Howe* visited Kerguelen, taking 3000 barrels of elephant seal oil, while the American *Columbia* took 3700 barrels in 1838-40.

From 1845-75, American sealers from the port of New London, CT, had a near-monopoly on the Kerguelen elephant seal trade, perhaps because of the island's notorious weather. 'Fogs and snow squalls alternate with great frequency,' wrote a medical doctor, Nathaniel William Taylor, who accompanied a whaling and elephant sealing voyage to Kerguelen in 1851-53. 'The gusts often occur so suddenly that one is obliged to prostrate himself on the ground or be driven along without the power to resist, when walking on shore.'

Unlike other sub-Antarctic islands, Kerguelen somehow appears to have induced labor in the occasional sealer's wife who visited there. On Christmas Day 1852, the wife of Henry S Williams, captain of *Franklin* (part of a fleet of seven American ships), gave birth to a daughter in the islands. In 1859 the wife of Tasmanian sealer James William Robinson, commander of *Offley*, gave birth to James Kerguelen Robinson.

Death was far more common than birth, however, and at Anse Betsy on the north coast of Péninsule Courbet a lonely cemetery is the final resting place for more than a dozen sealers and whalers.

In 1874 three separate expeditions, sent by the US, Britain and Germany, landed on Kerguelen to observe the December 9 transit of Venus across the face of the sun. This rare opportunity allowed astronomers to gather data used to calculate the distance between the Earth and the sun. Since the accuracy of the measurement depended on there being a variety of sightings, many countries participated in making observations from various parts of the world. (The next transits of Venus will occur in 2004 and 2012.)

A British company tried to develop a coal-mining operation on Kerguelen in 1877, but the coal was of poor quality and the attempt was abandoned.

In 1893 France formally annexed Îles Kerguelen. That same year, the French government granted an exclusive 50-year lease to the Frères Bossière, who in 1909 established **Port-Jeanne d'Arc**, a sealing and whaling station on Grand Terre's southeast coast. It operated from 1908 to 1925, with interruptions. Today some barracks are still in good condition, but the processing plant has collapsed. Another sealing and whaling station ran on the island from 1951 to 1956, and the French reestablished elephant sealing at Port-aux-Français from 1956 to 1960.

German Erich von Drygalski's *Gauss* expedition landed a scientific party on Grande Terre from 1902 to 1903. The group did extensive biological and survey work, although an outbreak of beriberi, a disease caused by lack of thiamine, killed several members.

During WWII, Kerguelen's myriad fjords provided valuable hiding places, and the Allies rightfully fretted about the possibility of the Germans or Japanese using them as a strategic submarine or cruiser base. In fact, in December 1940 and January 1941, the German *Atlantis* (also known as 'raider C') stopped at Kerguelen, where its crew buried a seaman ashore. Another German ship, *Pinguin* ('raider F'), was resupplied from an anchorage in the Îles. In 1941, HMAS *Australia* steamed to Kerguelen and laid mines at four places in the archipelago. This action helped force the Germans to abandon their plans to establish a meteorological station on Kerguelen. To this day, the mined waters remain dangerous places to anchor.

France set up **Port-aux-Français station** on Golfe Morbihan on the island's east coast in 1949-50. It has been permanently occupied since 1951, and can accommodate 80 expeditioners in winter and 120 in summer. Since 1994, the French National Center for Space Studies has operated a ground station for satellite tracking – identifiable by its two prominent white, spherical radomes – here.

Formerly administered as a dependency of Madagascar, Îles Kerguelen were incorporated into the Terres Australes and Antarctiques Françaises in 1955.

Rabbits, introduced in 1874 by the British Transit of Venus Expedition, have ravaged Grand Terre's native vegetation, but the namesake Kerguelen cabbage (once prized by sailors as an antiscorbutic) and tussock grasses are widespread. In 1955, myxomatosis, a viral disease, was introduced in an attempt to control the rabbits. After a large decrease in their population, they quickly recovered.

Other introduced animals have also caused severe damage to endemic species. Rats devour the eggs and chicks of petrels. Cats, which prey on petrel colonies, were introduced by sailors in the early 19th century

OCEAN & ISLANDS

and again in the 1950s. An eradication program was begun in 1972, but so far has not eliminated them. Dogs, mink, reindeer, mules, ponies, pigs and cattle have all also lived on Grand Terre at one time. Several hundred mouflon, a type of wild sheep from Corsica, survive from a failed wool-raising operation. Trout were introduced in 1958.

HEARD & MCDONALD ISLANDS

Heard and McDonald Islands, an external territory of Australia, consists of the main volcanic island of Heard, the tiny Shag Islands lying 11km north and the three small McDonald Islands (Flat and McDonald Islands and Meyer Rock) 43km west. Heard Island is a roughly circular active volcano, called Big Ben, with the 10km-long Laurens Peninsula extending northwest and the 7km Elephant Spit extending east. The island covers 390 sq km and is 80% glaciated. Big Ben erupted in 1910, 1950, 1985 and again in 1992. Its summit, the island's highest point, is Mawson Peak (2745m), first climbed in 1965 by a private Australian expedition. The volcano constantly emits steam, and its upper slopes are

nearly always shrouded in low cloud. In a discovery that surprised scientists, the McDonald Islands were also recently found to be volcanic, when a passing ship noted steam rising from rocks in 1997.

The climate, as on most of the other sub-Antarctic islands, is cold, wet and windy. In fact, winds blow almost continuously, with frequent gales. The mean annual temperature is - 1°C.

The date of the islands' first sighting is unknown. Cook noted 'signs of land' near their position in February 1773. Heard Island was possibly sighted in 1833 by Briton Peter Kemp, sailing in *Magnet*, and again, possibly, in 1848 by American Thomas Long, master of *Charles Carroll*.

John J Heard, captain of the American *Oriental*, definitely discovered the island that bears his name on November 25, 1853. Two months later, Briton William McDonald, sailing in *Samarang*, rediscovered Heard and discovered the McDonalds.

The islands were thrice rediscovered during the month of December 1854, by three British ships, *Earl of Eglinton*, *Herald of the Morning* and *Lincluden Castle*. Each ship's

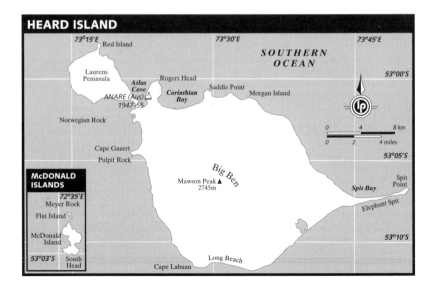

crew thought it was the first to see the islands, and each renamed them. In 1857, German Captain Johann Meyer, in *La Rochelle*, named them yet again, this time König Max-Inseln for the King of Bavaria.

American Erasmus Darwin Rogers, sailing in *Corinthian*, made the first recorded landing on Heard in January 1855, where he and the crews of six accompanying ships collected full loads of fur seal skins and 3000 barrels of elephant seal oil. There is questionable evidence that fur sealers had been working on the island before this. If the sealers were in fact there, they may have been reluctant to give competing companies any knowledge of their discovery, and may simply have left it out of their logbooks.

Later sealers also worked at the Heard Island beaches, shaking iron buckets filled with stones to frighten the elephant seals back up the beach and prevent their escape into the sea. Since there was no safe anchorage for ships, however, most of the sealers did not perform the laborious rendering of the blubber down to oil on Heard Island itself. Instead, they sailed down from Kerguelen and, after the seals were flensed, minced the blubber and put it in barrels to take back to Kerguelen for boiling. The cold air kept the blubber from going rancid en route.

Probably nothing kept the sealing gangs themselves from becoming rancid-smelling, however, given their smoky, sooty work of rendering the blubber and their low standard of personal hygiene. Captain James Robinson, master of the barque *Offley* from Hobart, left a sealing gang of 17 men to winter at Heard in 1858. 'No one,' he wrote in his log, 'is ever guilty of washing here.'

Elephant Spit's low sand-and-shingle beach, which rises less than 3m above sea level, is named for its abundance of elephant seals. Around 40,000 come ashore here each year for breeding – with more than 15,000 pups being born annually. Little wonder that the spit was Heard's prime hunting ground during the sealing era. At its peak in 1858, more than 15 vessels worked this area, putting hundreds of men ashore to kill and skin the seals and boil their blubber down in large iron try-pots.

In 1856 the first wintering party was landed by the American sealer *Zoe*, and in the same year, the American vessel *Alfred* became the first Heard shipwreck. Many others followed: *RB Coleman* (1859), *Mary Powell* (1859), *Exile* (1860), *Pacific* (1864), *ER Sawyer* (1866) and *Trinity* (1880).

Two exceptional artifacts from the sealing era have been found on Heard. A blubber press, one of the few surviving examples, was excavated and is now on loan to the Queen Victoria Museum and Art Gallery in Launceston, Tasmania. A carved basalt rock, the only one ever discovered in the sub-Antarctic or Antarctic, was found on Heard in 1985-86. It depicts the face of a bearded man, and it was carved by an unknown 19th-century sealer, possibly shipwrecked on the island. It is now displayed at the headquarters of the Australian Antarctic Division in Kingston, Tasmania.

In 1908, Heard and McDonald Islands were annexed by the British Government. On December 26, 1947 this sovereignty was transferred to the Australian Government. Also on this date, the first of the Australian National Antarctic Research Expeditions (ANARE), led by Stuart Campbell, established a base at Atlas Cove on Heard's northwest coast, using a WWII naval landing craft, which was driven onto the beach and unloaded through bow doors. Soon after, an aircraft used for aerial surveys of the island was destroyed by a storm after making a single flight. The first wintering party's experiences are chronicled in Arthur Scholes' *Fourteen Men: The Story of the Antarctic Expedition to Heard Island* (1952).

A group from the ANARE station completed the first journey on foot around the island in 1951. The station closed in 1955, transferring personnel and material to Mawson station on Antarctica. Today, collapsing early ANARE huts, dog pens, fuel drums, abandoned machinery and food supplies litter the black volcanic sand at Atlas Cove, along with the graves of two expedition members who died in 1952. Remnants of the Admiralty Hut, built by the British in 1929 as a refuge for shipwrecked mariners, also still stand at Atlas Cove.

Aurora Australis

Mysterious, beautiful, wonderful – colored profusion in visual chaos – ribbons of light snake across the night sky – batteries of celestial searchlights zero in on the magnetic zenith, waltzing to the music of the celestial spheres, forming an ever-changing crown in the heavens. Successive bands of increased light intensity move upwards, highlighting the display and flaming heavenwards – patches of light pulsate rhythmically; in another region of the night sky, other patches of light pulsate, out of phase – such is the aurora australis or southern lights at the height of a display.

– FR Bond, 'Background to Aurora Australis'

The aurora is the collective name (taken from the Roman goddess of the dawn) given to photons (light) emitted by atoms, molecules and ions that have been excited by energetic charged particles traveling along magnetic field lines into the Earth's upper atmosphere. The aurora results from the interaction of the solar wind with the Earth's magnetic field.

The colors in the aurora result from photons of specific energy level transitions in the excited atoms, molecules and ions of the upper atmosphere returning to their lowest energy state. There are hundreds of individual colors in an auroral display, but three are dominant in the visible spectrum. The brightest auroral line is generally a green line emitted by excited oxygen atoms. A red diffuse glow results from another oxygen atom transition. A purple color results from a transition in a nitrogen molecular ion. The mixture of the major green, red and purple emissions may combine to give an aurora a general whitish appearance.

Most commonly, auroral glows form a band aligned in a magnetic east-west direction. If sufficient numbers of energetic electrons are impacting the upper atmosphere, bands may have shimmering rays extending upward from them. These rays define magnetic field lines along which the auroral electrons travel into the atmosphere. The twisting of auroral rays and bands results from dynamic interaction of electric currents and magnetic fields in the upper atmosphere.

In active displays, multiple bands may be visible. These may break into small arcs. If rapid horizontal motion of the auroral form is apparent, the form may appear more purplish on its leading edge and greenish on its trailing edge. This results from a small delay (less than a second) between the peak intensity of the nitrogen molecular ion emission and the green oxygen atom emission. The active phase of an auroral display will last on the order of 15 to 40 minutes and may

Summer research programs have operated occasionally on the island since 1955, and two parties have wintered at Spit Bay since the Atlas Cove station closed: an American satellite-survey team in 1969 and an Australian expedition in 1992. An automatic weather station was established at Atlas Cove in 1990.

The first recorded landing on the McDonald Islands was on January 27, 1970, when two Australian researchers were placed on the main island by helicopter for a stay of less than an hour. An ANARE party of six men spent four days on the islands in 1980, after making the first landing by sea.

More than a million pairs of macaroni penguins breed on Heard Island, and another million pairs on the McDonald Islands. Long Beach on Heard's southern coast is the site of what may be the world's largest colony of macaronis. There are also approximately 1000 Heard Island sheathbills, a subspecies, in the islands. The rarest bird in the islands is the endemic Heard shag *Phalacrocorax nivalis*, of which fewer than 100 breeding pairs exist.

No known introduced species are present on Heard and McDonald Islands, which makes them highly unusual. For this reason, extreme care must be taken when visiting,

Aurora Australis

recur in two to three hours. Auroral band features may persist much longer. A red-dominated auroral glow will be very diffuse. It will fluctuate slowly in location and intensity (on timescales of half a minute or so). This results from a significant time delay in the emission of light by the atomic oxygen state, which smooths out any rapid variation in which the auroral electrons are impacting on the atmosphere.

If an auroral band has an easily discernible lower border, this will generally be at around 100km to 110km in altitude. Auroral rays may extend above the lower border for hundreds of kilometers. If the lower border has a pinkish edge (resulting from an emission of molecular nitrogen), the altitude may be around 90km to 100km. A diffuse red aurora occurs above 250km.

During an active auroral display, the intensity variations will be rapid and spectacular. A most dramatic variation is an increase in brightness moving up the auroral display. Faster electrons reach the atmosphere first and deposit their energy low in the atmosphere. These are followed by lower energy electrons, which are stopped at progressively higher altitudes giving an enhanced brightness moving upwards from the lower border. These variations may occur in rapid succession.

The global distribution of auroral activity is an oval around the magnetic poles in both hemispheres. As the level of disturbance of the Earth's magnetic field increases, the oval of auroral activity expands equatorward. The auroral oval in the Southern Hemisphere, the aurora australis, is linked by magnetic field lines to the auroral oval in the Northern Hemisphere, the aurora borealis.

Auroral electrons are often accelerated along magnetic field lines toward the opposite hemispheres from a region near the magnetic equator. The aurora australis and aurora borealis thus develop simultaneously, as near mirror images of each other. Aurora in the two hemispheres, if directly linked by the Earth's magnetic field, are said to be 'conjugate.'

Auroral displays are seen more often equatorward of their normal locations at times of high sunspot activity. Auroral occurrence in these regions has a broad two- to three-year maximum around the peak in the 11-year sunspot cycle, which is next expected in the middle of 2011.

– Dr Gary Burns,
Principal Research Scientist with the Australian Antarctic Division
– Dr Ray Morris,
Program Manager of the Atmospheric and Space Physics group at the Australian Antarctic Division

and anyone going ashore must wear thoroughly clean footwear and clothing.

Tourist visits to Heard Island are rare, thanks to its notoriously bad weather and the hazards of landing. Nevertheless, the Australian Antarctic Division, which administers Heard and McDonald Islands, carefully restricts tourism. Just 400 people are permitted to land at Heard annually, though currently far fewer visit each year. No more than 60 visitors are allowed ashore at one time, and once ashore they must remain in groups of 15 people. All landings require a permit from the Division (for contact details, see the Hobart section in the Gateways

chapter). The McDonald Islands, due to their almost completely untouched state, are off-limits to tourism.

ÎLE AMSTERDAM

An oval-shaped volcanic island, Île Amsterdam is part of France's Terres Australes et Antarctiques Françaises, like its neighbor Île St Paul, 89km to the south. All of Amsterdam's 85 sq km are unglaciated. The two highest points, Mont de la Dives (867m) and La Grande Marmite (730m), are part of the now-collapsed rim of the volcano that formed the island. The volcano's floor now forms a plateau about 600m high. Lava flows radiate from this plateau, spilling down to the sea where they end in cliffs above narrow shingle beaches. These headlands are generally less than 30m high, except on the west coast, where they tower to 700m.

Weather on Île Amsterdam is comparatively warm, windy, wet and humid. June, the coolest month, averages 10°C, while January and February, the warmest, average 15°C.

Juan Sebastián de Elcano, the Basque who completed the voyage of the great Portuguese navigator Fernão de Magalhães (Ferdinand Magellan) after Magellan was killed, discovered the Île on March 18, 1522, during the first-ever circumnavigation of the Earth. But Elcano did not give the island a name, a task left for Dutchman Anthonie van Diemen, sailing in *Nieuw Amsterdam* in 1633. The first landing was made by a three-ship Dutch survey expedition in 1696.

Oddly, sealers did not arrive on the island until almost two centuries after its discovery. *Nootka*, a British ship, started Île Amsterdam's fur rush, landing parties on Îles Amsterdam and St Paul for 17 months in 1791-92 and taking 15,000 fur seal skins. An American sealer, *Flora*, took 13,415 seals in 1792, while another American ship, *Mary*, took 44,517 in 1800.

Shipwrecks occurred on a fairly regular basis throughout the 19th century. Among those on record are *Lady Munro* (1833), *George* (1839), *Meridian* (1853), *Tuscany* (1855), *Vellore* (1865) and *Fernand* (1876).

In 1870-71, a Frenchman, along with his wife, children and four employees, inhabited the island for seven months in an abortive attempt to raise cattle. Three years later, Captain Coffin of the ship *Annie Battles* and two of his crew were rescued from Île Amsterdam after being abandoned there during a mutiny.

France has operated a permanent scientific station on the island's north coast since 1949, when 10 men led by Paul Martin de Viviès wintered there. Now called **Martin-de-Viviès station** for its first leader, it accommodates 30 people in winter, more in summer.

Île Amsterdam is one of the few sub-Antarctic islands with trees – *Phylica*

arborea. Records from an East India Company vessel visiting the island in 1770 describe a heavy tree cover, a French naval expedition in 1792 noted a forest fire. In 1825-26, two Tasmanian sealers started a fire that lasted several months, and in 1833 the survivors of the wreck of the American ship *Lady Munro* caused another conflagration that destroyed much of the island's forest. Today, semiwild descendants of introduced cattle are browsing on young saplings and the trees are disappearing.

The unusual long-crested rockhopper penguin lives on the island, and also on Île St Paul. Rock lobsters have been commercially harvested on Île Amsterdam since 1948.

ÎLE ST PAUL

Île St Paul is a volcanic cone, the eastern third of which has either been blown away by an eruption or eroded by wave action. What's left is an unglaciated island shaped like a right triangle with the coast running from northwest to southeast as its hypotenuse.

The volcanic crater has been breached by the sea, which enters to form the circular Bassin du Cratère. The crater's inner walls and the island's eastern coast are steep cliffs up to 200m high. The western and southern slopes of the volcano are much less steep and end in 30m sea cliffs. These are generally unclimbable, making landings on the island from these approaches very difficult. Île St Paul covers 7 sq km. Its highest point is Crête de la Novara (264m).

Dutchman Haevik Klaaszoon van Hillegom, sailing in *Zeewolf*, discovered Île St Paul on April 19, 1618, but it was later found marked as 'S Paulo' on an earlier Portuguese chart from 1559. The first landing was made by the Dutch in 1696.

In 1789 sealers first arrived from Britain, and the usual slaughter quickly wiped out most of the seal population. There have been at least three recorded shipwrecks: *Fox* (1810), *Napoléon III* (1853) and *Holt Hill* (1889).

A solitary Polish settler, Józef Kosciuszko, lived on St Paul between 1819 and 1830. For several years of that time, he was apparently all alone. Fishermen from Réunion lived on the island periodically during the mid-19th century, with their settlement reaching a peak population of 45 in 1845. In 1871, after the British troop transport ship HMS *Megaera* sprang a leak and beached at Île St Paul, 500 men were forced to live in a tent camp for three months. In 1874, on December 9, a French expedition observed the transit of Venus from the island.

Abundant rock lobsters thrive in Île St Paul's waters. From 1928 to 1931 a French fishing company, La Langouste Française, operated a lobster-fishing enterprise on the island. As many as 100 men spent the summers ashore, fishing and canning. But four of the seven winterers died in 1930, and the next year, 30 more men died of beriberi, so the settlement was abandoned. Today, a ship-based lobster fishery operates around Île Amsterdam and Île St Paul.

In 1955 the island was formally incorporated with Île Amsterdam, Îles Kerguelen, Îles Crozet and Terre Adélie in Antarctica as the Terres Australes et Antarctiques Françaises.

Among Île St Paul's bird species is the unusual long-crested rockhopper penguin, also found on Île Amsterdam. A recent rat eradication program, completed in 1997, appears to have been successful, and ground-nesting birds have begun returning.

MACQUARIE ISLAND

Australian Antarctic explorer Douglas Mawson, who first visited Macquarie Island in 1911, called it 'one of the wonder spots of the world.' Captain James Douglas, master of *Mariner*, which came from Sydney in company with three other sealers in 1822, disagreed, describing it as 'the most wretched place of involuntary and slavish exilium that can possibly be conceived – nothing could warrant any civilized creature living on such a spot.'

Located about halfway between Tasmania (which is 1467km to the northwest) and the Antarctic continent (1296km to the south), Macquarie is a good transition point between the two. The island's leading attractions are its residents: 100,000 seals, mainly

OCEAN & ISLANDS

OCEAN & ISLANDS

the blubbery elephant seals, and 4 million penguins, including about 850,000 breeding pairs of royal penguins, which breed nowhere else. To its human residents, the island is known as 'Macca.'

Rising in steep cliffs to a plateau 240m to 345m high, Macquarie is 34km long and between 2.5km and 5km wide, and covers 128 sq km. The highest point, 433m Mt Hamilton, is named for an early father-son team of naturalists. There are several small lakes on the plateau. The Judge and Clerk rocks lie 16km north and the Bishop and Clerk rocks lie 28km south – obviously some cartographer had a sense of humor.

The climate is one of the most equable (least-changing) on Earth, with mean annual temperatures ranging from 3.3°C to 7.2°C and strong westerly winds blowing nearly every day. There is no permanent snow or ice cover. The yearly precipitation (all 91cm) is spread out over more than 300 days and in a variety of forms: snow, rain, hail, sleet, mist and fog, sometimes all in the same day.

Vegetation is mainly tussock grass, and there are no trees or shrubs. Among Macquarie's unusual geological features are the 'featherbeds,' waterlogged areas on the highland plateau, which only just support the weight of a person. Also known as 'quaking bogs,' they are actually floating patches of vegetation covering pockets of water, which can be more than 6m deep. Crossing them is like stepping on a giant natural waterbed.

Geologically the island is very interesting, for it's the only place on Earth where rocks from the Earth's mantle, 6km below the ocean floor, are actively being exposed above sea level by the gradual but continuing upthrust of the plate. With all of this seismic activity, large earthquakes occur often.

The first recorded sighting of Macquarie was on July 11, 1810, when Captain Frederick Hasselborough of Sydney on the sealing brig *Perseverance* raised it. But Macquarie was most probably visited earlier by a sealer who kept his discovery secret so he alone could exploit its abundant fur seal population – for Hasselborough reported finding a shipwreck. He named the island after

Lachlan Macquarie, governor of the Australian colony of New South Wales (of which Tasmania was then a part) and collected 80,000 fur seal skins. He may also have tried to keep Macquarie Island a secret, but if so he failed badly.

By December 1810, just five months later, the island's location was printed in the *Sydney Gazette*. By 1812, a single ship recorded taking 14,000 fur seals. Naturally, such heavy harvesting quickly led to local extinction, and by 1830 it was no longer worthwhile for sealers to stop here, even for elephant seals, whose blubber could yield a valuable oil used for lubrication and lighting. During the boom years of Macquarie's seal trade, dozens of ships came annually, but between 1830 and 1874 there were fewer than half a dozen recorded visits. One of them, *Lord Nelson*, was wrecked at Hasselborough Bay in 1838, its survivors not rescued for two years.

Ships began calling at Macquarie again regularly in the mid- to late 1870s, when king and royal penguins were killed and boiled for their oil. Each bird yielded about half a liter. The royals were preferred, because their oil was not as highly saturated with blood, which tended to ferment and ruin the oil. At the penguin-oil industry's peak, in 1905, the factory at Nuggets Point could process up to 2000 birds at once. But the trade eventually became uneconomical – and conservation rules were applied to the island. Today, seals and penguins breed amidst the rusting remains of the cast-iron boilers used in the trade that nearly exterminated their ancestors.

At least nine ships have wrecked on the rocky coast, the oldest being the aptly named *Campbell Macquarie*, which wrecked at Caroline Cove on June 10, 1812, less than two years after Macquarie was discovered. The most recent wreck occurred on December 3, 1987, when the Danish ship MV *Nella Dan*, which had been chartered by ANARE for 26 years, ran aground at Buckles Bay. She was scuttled on Christmas Eve 1987, following unsuccessful salvage attempts.

Among the island's plants, perhaps most conspicuous is the yellow-flowered Macquarie Island cabbage *(Stilbocarpa polaris)*, once eaten by sealers to prevent scurvy.

Horses, donkeys, dogs, goats, pigs, cattle, ducks, chickens and sheep were brought to Macquarie by whalers and sealers, though none survive today. Rats, mice, cats, rabbits and wekas (a flightless bird from New Zealand) did thrive – and in recent years have heavily impacted the island's ecology. Although wekas were eradicated in 1988, the rats, mice, rabbits and cats remain. Introduction of the myxoma virus in 1978 has reduced the rabbit population by 93%.

Feral cats, which kill an estimated 60,000 prions and petrels annually, have been more difficult to get rid of. Licensed rangers now shoot, trap and gas the felines, and the Australian government is spending A$9000 per cat to rid the island of its last 100 very wily animals. Weighing up to 6kg and all muscle, the cats are mainly tabby, with a strain of ginger orange.

When Mawson landed a scientific party on the island during his Australasian Antarctic Expedition of 1911-14, he was met by the crew of *Clyde*, shipwrecked a month earlier and prepared to defend their sealing rights against what they initially thought were rival sealers. Once the mix-up was straightened out, Mawson used a wireless relay station set up on Wireless Hill in the first two-way communication with the Antarctic continent. One of the transmissions was a grim exchange of information: news of the death of Mawson's sledging companions, Belgrave Ninnis and Xavier Mertz, was sent from Commonwealth Bay to Macquarie, while word of Captain Scott's death was sent from Macquarie to the Australian explorers in Antarctica.

Other expedition leaders who stopped at Macquarie include Bellingshausen (who traded one of the sealers three bottles of rum for two albatrosses, one live parrot and two dead ones), Wilkes, Scott and Shackleton.

In 1948, a scientific station was established by ANARE at the isthmus on the site occupied by Mawson's men in 1911. About 15 to 20 people winter at the **ANARE station**; the number climbs to 40 during the summer. The very first woman ever to winter at an ANARE station, Zoe Gardner, was the station doctor in 1976.

The island's first tourists were four men carried by the New Zealand sealing ship *Gratitude* in 1891. Today, Macquarie is Australian territory, specifically a Tasmanian State Reserve, and permits to land must be obtained in advance from the Tasmanian Parks and Wildlife Service or TASPAWS (☎ 61-3-6233-6203, fax 61-3-6233-3477), 134 Macquarie St, Hobart. Ships or yachts that arrive unannounced are not allowed to put people ashore. There is a landing fee of US$100 per person, though most visitors are unaware of it, since it is included in the price of their cruise. Part of this fee pays for a color brochure distributed to visitors.

TASPAWS rangers oversee visits to the island. Boardwalks have been constructed in several places to prevent erosion, and regulations govern how many people can come ashore at once. At Sandy Bay, site of a royal penguin rookery, for instance, no more than 60 people may be landed simultaneously. At Lusitania Bay, home of a massive king penguin colony, no visitors are permitted on the beach, and Zodiacs must remain 200m offshore. All visitors to the island must leave by 7 pm, and no food or drink can be brought ashore. Just as in Antarctica, nothing – not even a pebble – may be removed.

BALLENY ISLANDS

These islands, 95% covered in ice and straddling the Antarctic Circle, are the tops of volcanoes, which rise from depths of 3km. Rarely visited by anyone, the Ballenys are the northernmost territory of New Zealand's Antarctic claim, the Ross Dependency. Young, Row, Borradaile, Buckle and Sabrina islands, and the Monolith and Sturge Island stretch some 195km from north to south. Brown Peak (1524m) on Sturge Island is the group's highest point.

The Ballenys are largely unlandable because of their steep basaltic cliffs, and so have been visited only a handful of times. Without large beaches to attract seals, they were ignored by sealers, who merely regarded them as hazards to navigation. English whaling captains John Balleny in the schooner *Eliza Scott* and Thomas Freeman in the cutter *Sabrina* were the first to visit. Freeman went ashore – or at least stepped into waist-deep water and collected some pebbles – probably on Sabrina Island, on February 9, 1839. This 'landing' was the first ever south of the Antarctic Circle. Unfortunately, *Sabrina* later became separated from *Eliza Scott* and was never heard from again, which helps to explain how the islands came to be called the Ballenys and not the Freemans.

Because of the islands' isolation, Sabrina Island was designated in 1969 as the fourth Specially Protected Area under the Antarctic Treaty. No landings can be made on it without special permission. About 500 Adélies nest each year, as well as the occasional chinstrap or macaroni penguin and numerous species of seabirds.

The first tourist landing was made in the Ballenys in 1968. An automatic weather station set up by the US on Brown Peak is checked annually by helicopter, but the mountain remains unclimbed.

An enormous earthquake – 8.1 on the Richter scale – occurred just offshore in March 1998, one of the biggest to occur anywhere that year. In comparison, the 1995 earthquake in Kobe, Japan that killed 6000 people measured 7.2 on the Richter scale.

Australian physicist Louis Bernacchi, who sailed past the Ballenys in 1899 on Borchgrevink's *Antarctic* expedition, was moved by their bleak aspect to write: 'I can imagine no greater punishment than to be "left alone to live forgotten and die forlorn" on that desolate shore.'

NEW ZEALAND'S SUB-ANTARCTIC ISLANDS

New Zealand maintains five sub-Antarctic island groups as National Nature Reserves: the Antipodes, Auckland, Bounty, Campbell and Snares groups. All are managed by the NZ Department of Conservation (☎ 64-3-214-4589), PO Box 743, Invercargill. Entry is by permit, issued only if the group is accompanied by a Department of Conservation representative. To prevent the accidental introduction of non-native species such as rats,

which could wipe out local bird and insect populations, no landings are allowed in the Antipodes or Snares groups, or on pristine islands of the Aucklands and Campbell Island groups. A NZ$200 per person fee is charged for landing, good for all of the islands on the same trip, which includes a handsome four-color, 74-page guidebook, *New Zealand's Sub-Antarctic Islands*, published by the Department of Conservation in 1991.

Antipodes Islands The Antipodes group consists of the eponymous main island, with the two Windward Islands lying appropriately to the west and Leeward Island to the east, and Bollons Island to the northeast. They were named 'the Penantipodes' on March 26, 1800, by their discoverer, Captain Henry Waterhouse of HMS *Reliance*, for being almost directly opposite the globe from London.

Sealing began in 1804, when a group landed by the American ship *Union* was stranded ashore for a year after the ship dropped them off and went on to Fiji, where it was wrecked and its crew massacred. The castaways on the Antipodes made profitable use of their time, killing 60,000 fur seals before being rescued by another American ship, *Favorite*, in 1806. The Antipodes fur seal trade peaked in 1814-15, when 400,000 animals were killed. One especially galling mistake was made during that season by the British sealer *Pegasus*, which took 100,000 skins to London. Upon arrival, it was found that the skins had rotted during the voyage due to insufficient salting, and the once-valuable cargo was sold for fertilizer.

The Antipodes, too, saw their share of shipwrecks. The survivors of the British ship *Spirit of the Dawn*'s wreck in 1893 spent nearly three months before being rescued. The 22-member crew of *President Félix Fauré*, wrecked while sailing from New Caledonia in 1908, survived two months before aid arrived.

No landings are allowed in the Antipodes, but there would be little room for people ashore anyway, as the islands are almost completely covered with the burrows and nests of seabirds. Along with the Bounty

Islands, the Antipodes are the only home of the world's estimated 200,000 pairs of erect-crested penguins. Also endemic to the islands is the Antipodes parakeet, which is found with, but does not breed with, the red-crowned parakeet (similar to the New Zealand species of this parakeet). In the short grass at the top of the islands, wandering albatross nest. The Antipodes' only introduced species are sheep and mice.

Auckland Islands The Aucklands, at 627 sq km the largest of New Zealand's sub-Antarctic island groups, consists of four main islands. Southernmost Adams Island, which has no introduced species, was declared a nature reserve in 1910 in recognition of its pristine state. Between Adams and the main island, Auckland Island, lies the superb three-armed natural anchorage of Carnley Harbor, once known as Sarah's Bosom after an early visitor, the British whaling ship *Sarah*, which stopped in 1807. The islands' highest point is Mount Dick (668m) on Adams Island.

Deep fjords serrate Auckland Island's east coast, while the windward west side features steep cliffs up to 300m high. At times the powerful westerlies striking the cliffs turn cascades there into 'reversible' waterfalls, actually blowing the water that has fallen part of the way down the cliffs back up onto the plateau, where the process is repeated as long as the wind keeps up. Disappointment Island lies to the west of Auckland Island, while Enderby Island, with its striking cliffs of columnar basalt, lies to its northeast.

The group was discovered on August 18, 1806, by Captain Abraham Bristow of the whaler *Ocean*, who named them for his friend Lord Auckland. As with other New Zealand sub-Antarctic islands, the early Maori may well have known about the Aucklands.

An odd near meeting occurred in 1840 in a natural harbor on Auckland Island's northeast tip: Charles Wilkes' US Exploring Expedition ship *Porpoise* landed on March 10 and set up a sign for anyone who might follow. Two posts were set in the ground at a promi-

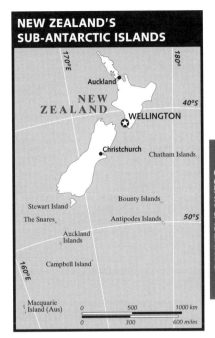

NEW ZEALAND'S SUB-ANTARCTIC ISLANDS

170°E · 180° · Auckland · NEW ZEALAND · 40°S · WELLINGTON · Christchurch · Chatham Islands · Stewart Island · Bounty Islands · The Snares · Antipodes Islands · 50°S · Auckland Islands · Campbell Island · 160°E · Macquarie Island (Aus) · 0 · 500 · 1000 km · 0 · 300 · 600 miles

OCEAN & ISLANDS

nent spot, and a message painted on boards was nailed to them. Incredibly, Frenchman Jules-Sébastien-César Dumont d'Urville came ashore just two days later and added to the sign a message of his own. Both communiqués were found eight months later by British explorer James Clark Ross. Still, the harbor came to bear Ross' – not Wilkes' or Dumont d'Urville's – name.

A group of Maori – with a group of Moriori slaves – moved to Port Ross in 1842, after finding it convenient to leave the Chatham Islands (located 770km east of Christchurch). The aboriginals were there to greet Charles Enderby, of the famous London whaling firm Samuel Enderby & Son, when he arrived in 1849 to set up a colony he called Hardwicke, hoping to duplicate the success of the Falkland Islands colony, which thrived on whaling and ship refitting. Perhaps he should have called it Hardworke instead. Though its peak population of nearly 300 people struggled mightily, the colony survived just three years. Crops failed, whale catches were minimal and few ships called in needing overhaul.

By 1852, the last colonists had departed, leaving behind a forlorn ghost town at Erebus Cove on Port Ross' northern shore. Two buildings stand there today, though neither is contemporary with the colony. One is a former depot for castaways, the other a boatshed now rather grandiosely called the **Erebus Cove Museum**, which contains island relics. Starting from just south of Erebus Stream, 10 minutes' walk up from the beach brings you to Hardwicke's cemetery, where half of the graves are of shipwrecked sailors. Farther east lie the settlement's overgrown cobblestone paths, and at Davis Bay (directly south of Davis Island) are glass-strewn ruins of the colony's house sites. Taking souvenirs is forbidden.

The Maori left soon after the Hardwickers did. Interestingly, there was no sign at their departure of the Moriori, who some

believe may have been eaten. By 1856 the islands were uninhabited again.

At least nine ships have wrecked on the Aucklands, including, most famously, *General Grant* in 1866. London-bound from Melbourne and the Australian goldfields, the American-flagged treasure ship was driven into a huge cavern on Auckland Island's west coast, ironically, not by a storm, but by very light winds which prevented her from steering away. When a rising tide and the cavern's roof forced the mainmast down through the hull, the 83 people aboard *General Grant* abandoned ship. Only 15 – including a woman – survived, but most of them lived the 18 months it took them to be rescued by a New Zealand whaling brig, *Amherst*. Also lost in the wreck: at least 70kg of gold, according to official records; rumor made the haul as large as eight tonnes. Despite at least 18 salvage attempts, no trace of anything of value from *General Grant* has ever been found, though the wreck has been located.

The Auckland Island Coracle

The New Zealand government periodically set up castaway huts with emergency supplies for shipwreck survivors on Auckland Island and nearby Enderby Island, but nobody imagined that a ship would manage to run ashore on tiny Disappointment Island, 7km west of Auckland Island.

Unfortunately for the 15 survivors from the barque *Dundonald*, that was where they ended up in March 1907. The ship's 12 other crew members, including the captain and his 16-year-old son, were drowned in the surf. By July the castaways were thoroughly fed up with life in grass huts. Using twisted branches, they constructed a flimsy coracle frame which they covered with fabric salvaged from their wrecked ship's sails. Three men sailed this ramshackle craft across the often-stormy strait.

Upon landing on Auckland Island, however, they were unable to penetrate the thick scrub and make their way to the castaway depot at Erebus Cove on Port Ross. Disheartened, they returned to Disappointment Island.

There they soon constructed a four-person coracle, but this second attempt failed when the little boat was wrecked upon launching. Making a third attempt, the crew managed again to cross the strait, but this time their craft was wrecked upon landing at Auckland Island, so finding a way to the depot became imperative. Finally, they managed to make it through the scrub to Erebus Cove.

With supplies from the castaway hut they were able to return to rescue the other survivors. Eventually the government steamer *Hinemoa* collected the castaways in November 1907 and returned them to New Zealand, along with their first crude coracle. Today the fragile little boat, which must have been one of the least seaworthy craft ever to sail Antarctic waters, can be seen in the Canterbury Museum in Christchurch, along with other relics from the crew of *Dundonald*.

– Tony Wheeler,
cofounder of Lonely Planet Publications

Wake of the Invercauld (Montreal: McGill-Queens University Press, 1997) is a fascinating memoir by Madelene Ferguson Allen, a descendent of one of the survivors of another Aucklands wreck *(Invercauld*, in 1864), who made her own trip to the island in the early 1990s.

Many other ships were lost during the years when the Great Circle Route – the name given to the shortest distance between any two points on the Earth's surface – was used to sail from Australia to New Zealand. So high was the danger of a ship coming to grief here that the New Zealand government set up castaway huts containing food, clothing, blankets and weapons (for procuring food) at various prominent places. 'Finger posts' – poles supporting wooden hands with pointing fingers – were placed on headlands to show the way. Pigs, rabbits, goats and other food animals were also released on the islands to provide emergency food sources for shipwrecked sailors. Since castaways sometimes spent up to two years waiting to be rescued, such measures saved many lives over the years. The oldest remaining such castaway depot, Stella Hut at Sandy Bay on Enderby Island, dates to 1880. New Zealand continued making annual cruises in search of castaways in all of the five sub-Antarctic island groups until 1927, when widespread radio technology rendered them unnecessary.

Pastoral leases were set up in the Aucklands in 1894, but the 2020 sheep that were imported did not thrive, and the last lease was forfeited in 1910. In the mid-1990s wild shorthorn cattle, descendants of an early rancher's herd, which survived by eating seaweed, were exterminated from Enderby by shooting. Fifty Agente de Champagne, or French blue, rabbits, the last of their type left in the world, were also removed and taken to New Zealand for breeding. Introduced goats, meanwhile, are being extirpated from Auckland Island by poisoning. Feral cats and mice, however, are on the island to stay.

During WWII, the secret Cape Expeditions set up coast-watching stations for the Allies on the islands to watch Ross and Carnley harbors to ensure that enemy ships weren't using the islands as a staging post for an invasion. Despite their bleak daily treks to observation areas (the stations were well inland to avoid detection), the coast watchers never saw a single enemy vessel. In 1955 one of them, Alan W Eden, wrote a book about his experiences with the revealing title *Islands of Despair*.

Among the twisted trunks of Enderby Island's red-flowering southern rata tree *(Metrosideros umbellata)* hides the elusive and solitary nesting yellow-eyed penguin. Rarest of the 17 species of penguin, the yellow-eyed numbers only about 5000 animals and prefers not to congregate in large colonies in the manner of most other penguins. More breed on Enderby than anywhere else.

Ninety-five percent of the global population of the Hooker's sea lion *(Phocarctos hookeri)* – the world's rarest sea lion with about 12,000 animals – breeds in the Auckland Islands. But Enderby's Sandy Bay – one of only three places in the world where it breeds – has illustrated the sea lions' fragility: rabbit burrows behind the beach once killed one of every 10 pups born each year after the baby sea lions crawled in and got stuck. Unfortunately, 70 to 100 adults are still killed each year in squid trawlers' nets, but New Zealand has instituted strict limits on the number of accidental net deaths that it will allow each year before closing the squid season.

The Aucklands are also home to the world's largest breeding population of wandering albatrosses, as well as 50,000 white-capped mollymawks (see the Wildlife Guide for more on the fauna and flora mentioned in this chapter).

Bounty Islands The Bountys are a sprinkling of some 22 islets, the largest of which is not more than 1 km across. Discovered on September 9, 1788 by the infamous Captain William Bligh of mutiny fame, they were named for his ship *Bounty*.

Here, as at many of the other islands, an onslaught of sealers arrived soon after the islands' discovery. By 1831, when British whaler-explorer John Biscoe visited, the

Bountys' fur seals had very nearly been exterminated.

British Captain George Palmer, in HMS *Rosario*, landed and took formal possession of the islands for Queen Victoria in 1870.

The erect-crested penguin breeds only here and on the Antipodes Islands. The Bountys are also home to 76,000 pairs of Salvin's albatrosses, a type of shy or white-capped albatross.

Campbell Island Most southerly of the five New Zealand sub-Antarctic island groups, Campbell Island covers 114 sq km. Of volcanic origin, it consists of a large main isle and two other tiny islets: Dent to the west and Jacquemart to the south. The highest point is 569m Mt Honey.

New Zealand is so proud of Campbell Island that it is featured on the back of the country's five-dollar notes, which have Everest conquerer and Antarctic crosser Sir Edmund Hillary on the front. The Campbell Island scene shows the yellow-eyed penguin (known to New Zealanders as the 'Hoiho'), the sub-Antarctic lily and the giant Campbell Island daisy.

Campbell was discovered by Captain Frederick Hasselborough in the ship *Perseverance* (for which Perseverence Harbour is named) on January 4, 1810, and named for the owner of his sealing company. Sadly, Hasselborough drowned in Perseverence Harbour exactly 10 months later – along with a woman and a young boy – when their small boat capsized. In a twist of fate, *Perseverance* was wrecked in the same place 18 years after that. Hasselborough was able to keep his discovery a secret for nearly a year, and to profit from the island's seal-rich beaches. But as on all the other sub-Antarctic islands, the sealing 'gold rush' eventually swept over Campbell, and by the 1820s the seal population had effectively been exterminated.

In 1839 a fur-sealing party of three men and a woman were rescued after being marooned for 27 months when their ship, *New Zealand*, wrecked after dropping them off here. The seals had been so depleted by that time that the castaways were able to find only 170 seals.

Two 19th-century scientific expeditions stopped at Campbell. Sir James Clark Ross' expedition of 1840-42 conducted the first plant and animal surveys of the island, while the French government's 1873-75 expedition to observe the transit of Venus visited Campbell twice on the frigate *Vire*. Clouds prevented any observation of the celestial phenomena, and the ship's engineer, Duris, died of typhoid and was buried opposite Venus Cove. In 1993 his grave was discovered under 30cm of peat, having last been seen in 1931. With a striking iron cross as its headstone, the grave is now fenced to keep out seals.

Pastoral enterprises fared better on Campbell than they did on Auckland. A lease was set up in 1895, and a rancher built a homestead at Tucker Cove on Perseverance Harbour. Wool-raising continued until 1931, when the island was abandoned to the 4000 remaining sheep. After the island became a nature reserve in 1954, a control program was begun to limit destruction of native vegetation. The Tucker Cove homesite is still visible, though the last sheep were shot in 1990.

The secret wartime Cape Expeditions set up a coast-watching station in 1941 to keep Perseverance Harbour under surveillance. Although no unauthorized vessel was ever spotted, the coast watchers performed valuable surveys on the island and maintained meteorological records. After the war, this work was continued. But because the coast-watching station was built 800m inland to avoid detection, the scientific station was moved in 1957 to Beeman Point on Perseverance Harbour. In 1992 the station's five members were on a snorkeling trip at Northwest Bay when a shark attacked, tearing off one man's arm. The station closed in October 1995, replaced, after 54 years of service, by automatic instrumentation.

From the landing dock at the station, a boardwalk leads about 5km up to the Col-Lyall Saddle, where a large colony of royal albatrosses nest. The meadows on both sides of the walk are filled with 'megaherbs' – flowering perennials with oversized blossoms and leaves: white alpine daisies *(Damnamenia vernicosa)*, violet and white Campbell Island daisies *(Pleurophyllum speciosum)*, yellow sub-Antarctic lilies *(Bulbinella rossii)*, pink broccoli-like Campbell Island carrots *(Anisotome latifolia)* and brown button daisies *(Pleurophyllum hookerii)*.

According to *The Guinness Book of World Records*, Campbell Island is the home of the 'world's loneliest tree.' A single 6m Sitka spruce, planted in 1902 by New Zealand's governor, is the only tree for hundreds of kilometers around.

The Snares This group consists of the Western Chain (Rima, Wha, Toru, Rua and Tahi) and Northeast Island and its adjuncts, Alert Stack, Broughton Island and Daption Rocks. The Snares were named for their unpleasant habit of 'snaring' ships eastbound on the Great Circle route from Australia to Cape Horn. A smaller group of rocks, the Traps, were equally deadly.

In a rare coincidence, the Snares were discovered independently – on the same day, November 23, 1791 – by two different shipmasters, Captain George Vancouver of *Discovery*, and Lieutenant Broughton of *Chatham*. Vancouver called the islands the Snares, while Broughton called them Knight's Islands.

Little more than a year later, in December 1792, Captain William Raven sailing in *Britannia* independently sighted the Snares and named them the 'Sunday Islands.'

Four men were marooned on the Snares between 1810 and 1817, having been forcibly put ashore from the ship *Adventure* by its master, Captain Keith. One man was murdered by the other three, who were rescued by the American ship *Enterprise* in 1817.

Literally millions of seabirds breed in the Snares group. Nearly 3 million pairs of sooty shearwaters alone shelter in burrows, where they hide from predators. Taking off at dawn on hunting flights and returning home before sundown, the great clouds of birds are an awesome sight. The Snares are the only home of the Snares crested penguin. Because of the abundance of wildlife, no landings are permitted on any of the islands.

SCOTT ISLANDS

Remote, barren and rarely visited, Scott Island is the remains of a volcanic crater. It includes an isolated offshore stack, the 63m Haggit's Pillar, about 800m west of the island. Covering a mere 40 hectares, Scott Island is just 370m long and 180m wide, with its long axis running north-south. The northern coast ends in cliffs 50m high, while the southern coast is barely above sea level. The island is entirely covered in snow and ice during the winter, but in summer large areas of bare rock are exposed.

Its location and extremely tiny size enabled Scott Island to evade detection until 1902, when it was found by British Captain William Colbeck, sailing in *Morning*, on Christmas Day. Colbeck, who was carrying stores to Robert F Scott in McMurdo Sound, sent a party ashore and claimed the island for Britain, calling it Markham Island after Sir Clements Markham, President of the Royal Geographical Society and the architect of Scott's *Discovery* expedition. (The name was later changed to memorialize Scott.)

Tourists were first landed on this inhospitable island in 1982.

PETER I ØY

Surrounded by thick pack ice nearly all year round, Peter the First Øy's 158 sq km are 95% glaciated. The highest point, 1640m Lars Christensentoppen (Lars Christensen Peak), is an extinct volcano. Glaciers extend tongues into the sea nearly all around the island, but in a few places narrow, rocky beaches are exposed. To the east of the island lie two flat-topped, ice-free columns, the Tvistein Pillars.

Peter I Øy was discovered on January 21, 1821, by the Russian Fabian von Bellingshausen, who named it for czar Peter the Great, founder of the Russian navy. It was the first land discovered south of the Antarctic Circle and thus the most southerly land known at the time.

Due to the island's extreme inaccessibility, the first landing on Peter I Øy took place more than a century after its discovery, when Norwegian Ola Olstad, leading the *Norvegia* expedition, went ashore February 2, 1929, and claimed it for Norway. It was formally annexed by Norwegian Royal Proclamation in 1933.

Beginning in 1980, several tourist ships have succeeded in landing passengers on the island.

SOUTH SHETLANDS ISLANDS

This major group of islands at the northern end of the Antarctic Peninsula is one of the continent's most visited areas, thanks to its spectacular scenery, abundant wildlife and proximity to Tierra del Fuego, which lies 1000km to the north across the Drake Passage. The 540km-long chain consists of four main island groups. From northeast to southwest, they are Clarence and Elephant islands; King George and Nelson islands; Robert, Greenwich, Livingston, Snow and Deception islands; and Smith and Low islands.

There are also 150-odd islets and rocks, many with picturesque names: Potmess Island, Hole Rock, Stump Rock, Sea Leopard Patch, Square End Island, The Watchkeeper, Desolation Island, Pig Rock, Salient Rock, Cone Rock, Conical Rock, The Pointers and Sewing-Machine Needles. The South Shetlands are about 80% glaciated and cover 3688 sq km. The archipelago's highest point is Mt Foster (2105m) on Smith Island, first climbed in 1996 by a group from the Canadian yacht *Northanger*.

William Smith, sailing in the British ship *Williams*, was blown off course while rounding Cape Horn for Valparaiso, Chile, and discovered the islands on February 19, 1819, but made no landing. Sailing eastward on his return from Chile he headed south again, but this time was too far west and missed the islands. But he returned later in the year and landed on King George Island on October 16, claiming the islands for King George III.

On Christmas Day that same year, the first British sealing ship arrived – with Joseph Herring, who had been the mate of *Williams* when the islands were first discovered. (He obviously saw his chance to make a fortune – and acted quickly.) This vessel was the advance party for a veritable navy, which proceeded to descend upon the seal-rich islands the next year.

During the summer of 1819-20, the senior British naval officer for the west coast of South America, William Henry Shirreff, chartered *Williams* from Captain Smith and placed Edward Bransfield aboard as the senior naval officer. Smith and Bransfield surveyed the island group and today the strait between the South Shetlands and the northwest coast of the Antarctic Peninsula (which he discovered) bears Bransfield's name. Bransfield landed on both King George Island (January 22, 1820) and Clarence Island (February 4) to claim them for the new sovereign, King George IV.

William Smith returned to the South Shetlands for a fifth time during the 1820-21 austral summer, this time on a sealing voyage designed to reap a rich harvest from his discovery – a goal he certainly achieved. His two vessels alone took 60,000 fur seal skins.

An incredible 91 sealing ships operated in the South Shetlands during that season, most of them British or American. The predictable result: the fur seals were almost completely gone by the end of 1821. It was half a century before sealers visited the islands again in great numbers. From 1871-74, a handful of American sealing ships returned to kill anew, taking another 33,000 fur seals from the slowly recovering populations. By 1888-89, the American sealer *Sarah W Hunt* reported taking just 39 skins in a season of South Shetland sealing; two years later, the same vessel could only find 41 fur seals in the islands.

As they sought unexploited new islands, the sealers must have ranged throughout the Bransfield Strait area, probably 'discovering' the Antarctic Peninsula several times over, but the finding of untouched sealing grounds was always a closely held secret, and no such discoveries were reported.

Death visited the sealers as well as the seals: with so many vessels operating in such treacherous waters, predictably there were many wrecks. Six ships – *San Telmo, Ann, Clothier, Lady Troubridge, Cora* and *Venus* – all foundered within just three years, 1819-21. Over the succeeding decades, there were more wrecks: *Richard Henry* (1845), *Catherine* (1847), *Lion* (1854), *Graham* (1924) and *Professor Gruvel* (1927).

In 1944, despite having its hands full with war in Europe, the British government took steps in the islands to detect enemy raiders and to underscore its sovereignty. Through the Falkland Islands Dependencies Government, it established permanent stations and issued postage stamps for four of the Dependencies (South Shetlands, South Orkneys, South Georgia and Graham Land, or the Antarctic Peninsula). Argentina and Chile naturally protested this show of ownership, since they had made rival claims to the territory.

Some of the first Antarctic tourism took place in the South Shetlands. The first Antarctic tourist flight, by LAN Chile in 1956, flew over the South Shetlands and the Antarctic Peninsula. Two of the earliest tourist cruises to Antarctica, by the Argentine ship *Les Eclaireurs*, reached the South Shetlands in January and February 1958. In 1959 the Argentine ship *Yapeyú* and the Chilean vessel *Navarino* both took passengers to the South Shetlands. In the earliest mass visit of tourists to the Antarctic, the Spanish cruise ship *Cabo San Roque* carried 900 passengers to the South Shetlands and the Peninsula in 1973. It visited again in 1974 and 1975, but made no landings.

Among the South Shetlands are several islands with noteworthy individual histories. They are described here from north to south.

Elephant Island Located at the archipelago's northeastern end, Elephant Island is notorious as the desolate place where 22 members of Shackleton's *Endurance* expedition, stranded in 1915 after their ship was crushed in Weddell Sea pack ice, spent 135 days. At Point Wild, where the men lived beneath two upturned boats, a **monolith and plaques** commemorate their rescue by the Chilean Navy cutter *Yelcho* on August 30, 1916. Elephant Island is also home to several chinstrap rookeries, and some very old moss colonies, dated at more than 2000 years old – with peat nearly 3m deep. Landings on the island, unfortunately, are extremely difficult.

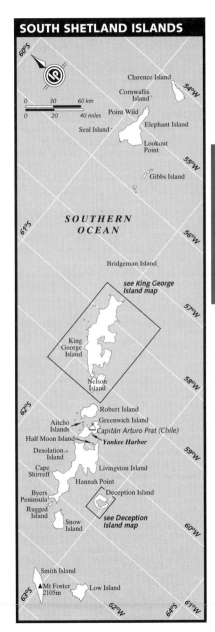

SOUTH SHETLAND ISLANDS

60°S

0   30   60 km
0   20   40 miles

Clarence Island

Cornwallis Island

54°W

Point Wild

Seal Island

Elephant Island

Lookout Point

55°W

Gibbs Island

SOUTHERN OCEAN

61°S

56°W

Bridgeman Island

see King George Island map

57°W

King George Island

Nelson Island

58°W

62°S

Robert Island

Aitcho Islands

Greenwich Island

Half Moon Island

Capitán Arturo Prat (Chile)

Yankee Harbor

Desolation Island

Cape Shirreff

Livingston Island

59°W

Hannah Point

Byers Peninsula

Deception Island

Rugged Island

Snow Island

see Deception Island map

60°W

Smith Island

▲Mt Foster 2105m

Low Island

63°S

62°W

64°W

67°W

OCEAN & ISLANDS

King George Island Sometimes called Antarctica's unofficial capital, thanks to the eight national winter stations crowded onto it, King George Island is the largest of the South Shetlands and the first stop in the Antarctic for many tourists. Less than 10% of the island's 1295 sq-km-area is ice-free, yet it supports year-round stations maintained by Argentina, Brazil, Chile, China, South Korea, Poland, Russia and Uruguay, all connected by more than 20km of roads and tracks. There are also Ecuadorian, German, Peruvian and US summer bases. The stations, some within walking distance of one another, are here because King George Island is so accessible to South America. This makes it an easy place for a country to build a station and perform scientific research, thus earning the status of a consultative party, or full member, of the Antarctic Treaty.

In 1906, however, before the island's station-building boom began, whalers set up operations at Admiralty Bay on the southern coast. Two years later the whaling supply vessel *Telefon* ran aground on Telefon Rocks at the entrance to Admiralty Bay and was abandoned. In 1909 it was salvaged and towed to Telefon Bay at Deception Island, where it was repaired.

The British were first to build a base on King George Island, in 1946-47, on Admiralty Bay, but it was closed in 1961. Base G, as it was known, was demolished and removed by members of the Brazilian Antarctic Expedition at Comandante Ferraz station during the 1995-96 austral summer.

Argentina built its **Teniente Jubany station** at Potter Cove in 1953, though it has been a year-round facility only since 1984. It is designed to hold a maximum of 80 people. Jubany is a good example of international scientific cooperation in Antarctica: the station often accommodates large numbers of visiting scientists from a number of nations, including Germany, the Netherlands and Italy. The summer-only **Dallman Laboratory**, opened in 1994 by Argentina, the Netherlands and Germany, is the first research facility in Antarctica designed as a multinational laboratory.

Russia set up its **Bellingshausen station** in 1968 on the nearly ice-free Fildes Peninsula at the island's southwestern tip. After a fuel tank farm was established, the station became a major fuel depot for the Soviet Antarctic fishing fleet. Bellingshausen has a normal population of only 25, despite its maximum capacity of 50. It has gained a reputation in recent years as a trading post, with station members often willing to swap or sell pins, flags and clothing. Unfortunately, due to Russia's ongoing economic troubles, the station is not well maintained. Waste and large amounts of scrap metal are in piles outdoors, awaiting return to Russia, so the station has a somewhat dumpy look. Efforts are being made to clean it up, but the process may take several years.

The construction boom continued with Chile's establishment of **Presidente Eduardo Frei Montalva station** in 1969, adjacent to Bellingshausen and separated from it by a small stream (though in places the two stations' buildings are intermixed). Ten years later, Chile built Teniente Rodolfo Marsh Martin station less than 1km across the Fildes Peninsula from Frei station, which Frei has incorporated. (Thus, the station's name appears either as Frei or Marsh on various charts; presently, Frei is in use.) Together with the Escudeoro base (described later in this section), Frei/Marsh is one of the Peninsula's largest and most complex stations.

As part of Chile's policy of trying to incorporate its claimed Territorio Chileno Antártico into the rest of the country as much as possible, the government has encouraged families to live at Frei station, and the first of several children was born there in 1984. Families are housed in an apartment comzplex around Villa Las Estrellas, built in 1984. Today the station accommodates about 80 summer personnel, nearly 25% of whom are children of primary-school age or younger. Parties of station kids sometimes greet tourists upon arrival.

When seen from afar, Frei looks like a small village with more than 40 buildings, including 15 chalets painted in bright colors on the slope of the hill. In the station center,

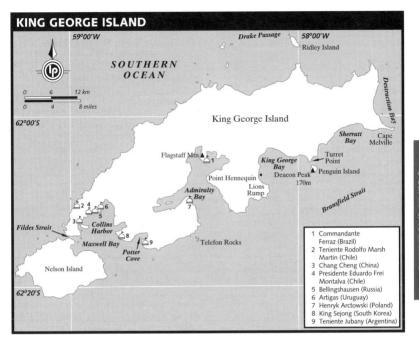

KING GEORGE ISLAND

59°00'W

Drake Passage

58°00'W

Ridley Island

SOUTHERN OCEAN

0   6   12 km
0   4   8 miles

62°00'S

King George Island

Sherratt Bay

Cape Melville

Flagstaff Mtn △ 1

King George Bay

Turret Point

Point Hennequin

Deacon Peak 170m

Penguin Island

Admiralty Bay

Lions Rump

7

Bransfield Strait

Fildes Strait

2 4   6
3   5

Collins Harbor

8

Maxwell Bay

9

Potter Cove

Telefon Rocks

Nelson Island

62°20'S

Destruction Bay

1 Commandante Ferraz (Brazil)
2 Teniente Rodolfo Marsh Martin (Chile)
3 Chang Cheng (China)
4 Presidente Eduardo Frei Montalva (Chile)
5 Bellingshausen (Russia)
6 Artigas (Uruguay)
7 Henryk Arctowski (Poland)
8 King Sejong (South Korea)
9 Teniente Jubany (Argentina)

OCEAN & ISLANDS

buildings are painted red-orange and include a hospital, school, bank, post office and a tourist shop. Also in the center is the original base complex, which houses a supermarket, canteen, kitchen and recreation area. Frei also has a chapel, a large gymnasium, accommodations for unmarried personnel and the station's administrative center, along with nearly 5km of gravel roads.

The Marsh section of the station includes a 1300m compacted gravel runway, a hangar, a garage, a hostel and a control tower. Wheeled Hercules aircraft have landed here since 1980, and several of the station's international neighbors on King George Island, including China, have flown personnel to their own stations using this airstrip. Charter flights to Frei/Marsh for tourists are available from Aerovías DAP, a Chilean regional airline (see the Getting There and Away chapter).

In 1982, Chile held the first international meeting in Antarctica, a conference at Marsh on Antarctic resources policy, with delegates from 12 countries attending. Chilean military ruler Augusto Pinochet visited the station in 1984 and officially opened its married quarters.

In what was certainly one of the first public concerts in Antarctica, Japanese pop singer Yasunori Sugawara held a concert at the station in March 1993 for about 100 people from Frei and the neighboring Uruguayan and Russian stations.

Rather revealingly, it was not until 1995 that a scientific annex was added to Frei's sprawl. The five attractive blue-roofed white buildings of the separate, summer-only **Professor Julio Escudeoro base** are located along the bottom of a steep hill southeast of Frei. The scientific annex can accommodate 16 people.

Poland's **Henryk Arctowski station**, opened in 1977, accommodates about 40 personnel. A handsome and well-illustrated 24-page color brochure (in English) sold at the station provides a brief history and proudly declares that 'visitors are honoured at Arctowski.' Women visitors were once presented with small bouquets of flowers grown in the station greenhouse, but this has been discontinued because growing of nonfood plants now requires special permission under the Antarctic Treaty.

Arctowski's legendary hospitality may have sown the seeds of its own destruction, however. During the summer of 1992-93, the station hosted 33 tourist ships, sometimes three a day, and station personnel were understandably less than enthusiastic about the invading hordes.

Thanks to all that traffic, sad evidence of humans' negative impact on Antarctica can be found at Arctowski station. Sun-bleached whalebones, relics of the whaling industry (which operated there long before the station opened), were once so numerous that the black pebble beach appeared white, and walking was difficult in places. The bones are noticeably absent today, however, taken by hundreds of selfish visitors – some of them scientists.

To help manage tourists, Arctowski has established several walking routes in the vicinity of the station. The large gentoo and Adélie rookeries are out of reach because they are encircled by protected moss beds. Only 50 tourists are allowed ashore at one time. Station personnel recently built a **tourist information center** out of recycled wood on the unnamed point situated beneath the small yellow-and-red striped lighthouse.

A protected area, Site of Special Scientific Interest No 8, lies 400m south of the station and is off-limits to visitors. A prominent 'No Entry' sign marks its boundaries.

The US has operated the small summeronly **Peter J Lenie field station** near Poland's Arctowski since 1985; it's also called 'Copacabana.'

Brazil's **Commandante Ferraz station**, on Admiralty Bay, opened in 1984 and is between an old whaling station and the site of the abandoned British **Base G**, which was removed in 1996. Ferraz' distinctive orangeroofed, pine-green buildings accommodate 33 people. There is also a small cemetery containing several graves and memorials.

Uruguay's **Artigas station**, established in 1983, accommodates 14 in winter and 32 in summer. The station is named for Uruguay's national hero, José Gervasio Artigas, a progressive early leader who redistributed land and abolished slavery.

China's **Chang Cheng station** (the Great Wall of China), was established in 1985 and can accommodate 50 people, though the recent winterover crews have been less than one-third of that number. One of Antarctica's oddest ceremonies was performed at the red-and-orange station during the 1987-88 season, when the Chinese introduced hundreds of domestic pigeons in a 'Dove of Peace' ritual. Nearly all died the same day.

South Korea set up **King Sejong station** at Marian Cove close to Maxwell Bay in 1987-88. It accommodates 80 people, though usually there are fewer than one-third of that number. Adélie and chinstrap rookeries lie 2km south.

Peru established its summer-only **Machu Picchu station**, which can accommodate 28 people, on Admiralty Bay in 1989. In 1977 Italy also set up a small hut on the island, which was later removed unilaterally by the Argentines, and Ecuador established its summer-only **Point Hennequin station** in 1987-88.

Tourism to King George Island, as to anywhere else in Antarctica, is not without its hazards. In 1972, *Lindblad Explorer*, the first passenger ship built specifically for polar cruising, ran aground in Admiralty Bay. The 90 passengers were rescued by a Chilean naval vessel, and a German tugboat towed the ship off the rocks 18 days later.

Among the most popular landing sites on King George Island today is **Turret Point**, at the eastern end of King George Bay on the island's south coast. The point takes its name from a group of prominent high rock stacks above the beach, a nesting area for Antarctic terns. You'll also find chinstraps, Adélies, blue-eyed shags and southern giant petrels. Beaches in the area have yielded evidence of 20th-century whaling, including harpoon heads.

Penguin Island Just offshore from Turret Point is Penguin Island. While there are many Penguin Islands scattered throughout the Antarctic, this one's pedigree is longer than most – it was named by Bransfield in 1820. Its highest point, 170m **Deacon Peak**, with its red cone, is easily identifiable; an extensive crater is at the summit. It's easy to climb, and so many people do that a path is worn into the ground early each season – even with the best of care, people *do* leave their mark on Antarctica. There's also a meltwater lake in a former volcanic crater. You'll see chinstrap penguins here, but Adélies also nest on an out-of-the-way beach.

Bridgeman Island A steep-sided, nearly circular volcanic island about 800m long, Bridgeman is located 37km east of King George Island. Its snow-covered summit (240m) is inclined toward the south, and its reddish-brown sides are nearly vertical on the north coast. Bridgeman was discovered by Bransfield on January 22, 1820 and named after Captain Charles O Bridgeman of the British Royal Navy. Volcanic activity was observed on the island by Captain George Powell in 1821, by Captain James Weddell in 1821 and then by Lieutenant Charles Wilkes in 1839. Charcot made the first landing, in 1909, and found proof of 'comparatively recent (volcanic) activity.'

Aitcho Islands Often visited in conjunction with other, larger islands in the South Shetland chain, the Aitcho Islands are named for the British Admiralty's Hydrographic Office ('HO'). Lying in the strait between Greenwich and Robert islands, the Aitchos are covered with extensive beds of moss and lichens and are home to gentoos and chinstraps.

Greenwich Island Sealers stalked the beaches of this island, as they did nearly all the South Shetlands, during the early 1800s. A British captain working here in 1821-22 reported finding a cave on Greenwich with the inscription 'J Macey 1820-21 & 22 but never more' along with several other names.

As early as 1820, circular **Yankee Harbor**, on the island's southwest side, was an important anchorage for sealers, who knew it as Hospital Cove. Somewhat confusingly, the harbor at Deception Island (described later in this section) was also known as Yankee Harbor. A stone and gravel spit extends nearly 1km in a wide curve, protecting Yankee Harbor and making it a favorite yacht anchorage. The spit is an ideal place for walking; look for an old sealer's try-pot on this strand. Farther up the beach, by the Argentine *refugio* built in the 1950s, several thousand pairs of gentoos nest.

Chile's **Capitán Arturo Prat station**, a collection of orange buildings on Discovery Bay on the north coast, was opened in 1947 as Soberanía station, and later renamed to honor the Chilean naval hero. The first head of state to visit Antarctica, Chile's Presidente Gabriel González Videla, stopped here in 1948 – with an entourage of 140. The station now accommodates 15 personnel and has a small **museum** displaying old photographs, early expedition equipment and a few whaling artifacts. It also features photos of Shackleton's *Endurance* expedition and

The Ice has many Penguin Islands.

OCEAN & ISLANDS

KERRY LORIMER

its Chilean rescuers. A bust of Prat stands outside the station, and nearby is a **cross and shelter** commemorating the 1960 station leader, who died while in he was in charge. A **cross and shrine to the Virgin of Carmen**, erected in 1947, is also in the vicinity.

Half Moon Island Crescent-shaped Half Moon, just 2km long, lies in the entrance of Moon Bay on the east side of Livingston Island. Here the Argentine Navy operates the summer-only **Teniente Cámara station**, built in 1953. Landings are usually made on the wide sweeping beach east of the station. A handsome wooden boat lies derelict on the shore below the large chinstrap colony. In 1961, 21 tourists were stranded here for three days when the landing craft from their chartered vessel *Lapataia* was damaged.

Livingston Island Livingston was a major early-19th-century sealing center, and the remains of primitive shelters and assorted artifacts have been found on many of its beaches. In fact, the entire Byers Peninsula on the island's western end is protected as Site of Special Scientific Interest No 6 under the Antarctic Treaty, because it contains the greatest concentration of 19th-century historical sites in Antarctica.

British Captain Robert Fildes, who survived the wrecks of two ships *(Cora* and *Robert)* while sealing in the South Shetlands in the early 1820s, wrote about the superabundance of fur seals on Livingston's north coast during that period:

... in many places it was impossible to haul a boat up without first killing your way, and it was useless to try to walk through them if you had not a club in your hand to clear your way and then twas better to go two or three together to avoid being run over by them ...

Fildes added that English sealers had taken more than 95,000 fur seal skins from that stretch of coast alone.

Hannah Point, on Livingston's south coast, is an extremely popular stop, with its large chinstrap and gentoo rookeries and the occasional macaroni pair nesting among them. The point is named after the British sealer

Hannah of Liverpool, which was wrecked in the South Shetlands on Christmas Day, 1820.

On a hill above the Hannah Point landing beach, you'll notice a prominent red vein of jasper running through the rock. From this lookout, you can survey a sheltered beach on the opposite side of the point where elephant seals bask and young male fur seals spar. But if there are elephant seals in the wallow on this lookout, do *not* walk up to them, as they might be intimidated and retreat – over the cliff, to their deaths onto the rocks below. Tourists have done this in the past, which accounts for the place's nickname, Suicide Wallow.

Walker Bay is occasionally used as a landing site instead of the overvisited Hannah Point to its east. On the broad beach is a fascinating collection of **fossils** left by researchers on a table-like rock among a group of boulders. There are also seal jaws and teeth and penguin skulls and skeletons. This open-air museum is right below the squarish outcrop on top of the ridge above.

Just east of Hannah Point lies Spain's **Juan Carlos Primero station**, a summer-only base established in 1987-88, which accommodates 15 personnel. It has one of the few alternative-energy systems at an Antarctic station, using both solar power and wind generators.

Bulgaria's **St Kliment Ohridskiy station** is less than 2km northeast of Juan Carlos Primero. A summer-only station, it was built in 1988 and accommodates 15 people.

Antarctica's worst loss of life occurred in September 1819 near Cape Shirreff on Livingston's north coast. The 74-gun *San Telmo*, a Spanish man-of-war sailing from Cadiz to Lima, encountered severe weather while crossing the Drake Passage and lost her rudder and topmasts. Although taken in tow by an accompanying ship, the hawsers parted and the ship was lost – along with 650 officers, soldiers and seamen. Circumstantial evidence points to *San Telmo*'s destruction on Livingston: an anchor stock and spars were found by sealers in 1820, and in the same year James Weddell (discoverer of the Weddell Sea) found evidence that survivors of a shipwreck had lived for a period on the island. A cairn on Livingston's north coast at **Half Moon Beach**, named by sealers in 1820, commemorates those lost in *San Telmo*, possibly the first people to die in Antarctica.

Deception Island Easily recognized on any map by its broken-ring shape, Deception's collapsed volcanic cone provides one of the safest natural harbors in the world – despite periodic eruptions.

To attain this secret haven, however, vessels must navigate a tricky 230m-wide break in the volcano's walls – known since the early-19th-century sealing days as **Neptunes Bellows** for the strong winds that blow through this strait. Even veteran captains sometimes smoke an entire pack of cigarettes during the brief passage through the Bellows, for hull-piercing Ravn Rock lies just 2.5m beneath the surface in the center of the channel – and foul ground lies between Ravn Rock and the southern headland, called En-

trance Point. Visible on the north coast of Entrance Point is evidence of how dangerous the narrow channel can be: the wreck of the British whale-catcher *Southern Hunter*, which ran aground on New Year's Eve 1957 while avoiding an Argentine naval vessel steaming in through the Bellows.

As you enter the harbor, notice the striking colors of the rock faces rising on either side. One of Deception's earliest visitors, the surgeon William HB Webster (who arrived in 1829 with the British *Chanticleer*), wrote that these cliffs 'present a curious and not unpleasing appearance.' It's true.

Upon reaching this interior sea, visitors land at Whalers Bay on a black sand beach cloaked in mysterious white clouds of sulfur-scented steam. Those with cold feet need only dig their boots down into the sand to warm them with the heat escaping from subterranean volcanic vents. The island's sloping, snow-covered walls, which reach 580m, tower above the beach.

OCEAN & ISLANDS

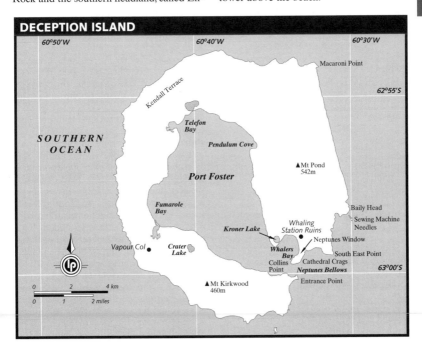

DECEPTION ISLAND

Early sealers used Deception's 12km-wide harbor as a base for operations. From the break in the caldera wall at **Neptunes Window**, American sealer Nathaniel Brown Palmer, who first explored the island and discovered its inner harbor, is thought to have seen the Antarctic Peninsula in 1820.

Chanticleer, commanded by Captain Henry Foster, entered the harbor now known as Port Foster in 1829, anchored at Pendulum Cove and performed magnetic experiments there for two months. Besides Webster, the first scientist to visit the Antarctic, *Chanticleer* also carried Lieutenant Edward Kendall, who made the first survey of the island and the first paintings of Antarctica.

In 1906, a Norwegian-Chilean whaling company established by Captain Adolfus Amandus Andresen, a Norwegian-born immigrant to Chile, began using an area on the north side of the caldera at **Whalers Bay** as a base for *Gobernador Bories*, his floating factory ship. (Floating factory ships were large vessels that processed whales brought to them by 'catcher' ships. The development of floating factories, which could operate at sea, heralded the decline of shore-based whaling stations.) Andresen was accompanied by his wife, family and pets: a parrot and an Angora cat. His company, Sociedad Ballenera de Magallanes, was based in Punta Arenas and used Whalers Bay for 10 years. (He is buried in Punta Arenas' municipal cemetery; see the Antarctic Gateways chapter.) In 1907, the company's factory ship was joined by two Norwegian whaling companies and another from Newfoundland, all of which operated factory ships at Deception.

Britain, which had formally claimed the island in 1908 as part of the Falkland Islands Dependencies, gave a 21-year lease to Hvalfangerselskabet Hektor A/S, a Norwegian whaling company based in Tønsberg, in 1911. One of the reasons for granting the license was to utilize the estimated 3000 whale carcasses that littered the shores of Port Foster. They had been abandoned by ships that had stripped them of their blubber but were unable to process the meat and bones, which

contain 60% of a whale's oil. British authorities hoped to end this terrible waste. Hektor established a shore station at Whalers Bay in 1912, though it was not fully operational until 1919, after World War I had ended.

By the peak season of 1914-15, thirteen floating factories and the shore station operated at Whalers Bay. The whalers themselves called it 'New Sandefjord' after the Norwegian whaling town. Unlike many other whaling stations, however, Whalers Bay only processed whale carcasses that had already been stripped of blubber, which was processed by the floating factories anchored offshore. Instead of rendering blubber into oil, the station boiled down meat and bones to get the oil.

Jean-Baptiste Charcot, the French Antarctic explorer who visited in 1908, described the bustling whaling station in operation:

We find two three-masters and two steam vessels, surrounded by several little steam-whalers, this fleet belonging to three different companies. Pieces of whale float about on all sides, and bodies in the process of being cut up or waiting their turn lie alongside the various boats. The smell is unbearable.

The shore station closed in 1931, partly because of a slump in whale oil prices and partly because technology had advanced. Floating factories could efficiently process an entire whale at sea, especially once the stern slipway was invented, allowing the entire carcass to be hauled aboard.

Today at Whalers Bay, where the beach is more than 300m wide in places, several crude wooden huts stand disintegrating. Wooden flensing boats and water barges lie buried to their gunwales in black volcanic sand. There is also a virtual outdoor museum of early-20th-century industry, where huge boilers and tanks that once processed and held the whale oil now stand rusting under the southern sky.

A **whalers' cemetery** once held the graves of 45 men (38 Norwegians, three Swedes, one Chilean, one Russian, one Briton and one of unknown origin) who died lonely deaths half a world away from their loved ones. The cemetery is now buried under several meters of sludge from a *lahar* or mudslide, released in 1969 when a volcanic eruption melted the glacier above. Sharp-eyed visitors who wander in the area behind the station may be surprised to find one of the cemetery's simple wooden coffins (empty), which was tossed about by the massive wave of mud and water.

A cross commemorating Tømmerman (carpenter) Hans A Gulliksen, who died in 1928, is far down the beach toward the 17m by 22m corrugated steel **aircraft hangar**. There was once a north-south runway alongside this hangar. Today the orange fuselage of a British survey aircraft, stripped of its wings, stands derelict outside.

Australian Hubert Wilkins made the first powered flight in Antarctica on November 16, 1928, taking off from this runway in his Lockheed Vega monoplane *Los Angeles* and flying for 20 minutes. A month later, on December 20, Wilkins and his pilot, Carl Ben Eielson, took off in his other Vega, *San Francisco*, and flew 2100km to about 71°20'S along the Peninsula.

Wilkins then prepared to return home, but decided to remain long enough to accept the hospitality of the Norwegian whalers who had been so helpful to his flights. New Years' Day at the whaling station, as recounted in Lowell Thomas' biography of Wilkins, was celebrated with enormously exuberant games, songs, eating, drinking – and much gunfire. Two drunk whalers climbed atop a pair of big sperm whales lying on the large flat expanse of the wooden flensing plan awaiting processing. The whales had been cooking themselves from the heat of the blood fermenting inside their bodies and were swollen with gas.

One of the whalers thrust his long knife into this veritable whale-balloon, which promptly exploded, hurling both men into the harbor, where they had to be rescued by some of the few sober observers. Meanwhile, two other whalers had decided to ignite an explosives barge that was moored to the beach. It contained 65 tonnes of black powder and other combustibles. Taking a 22kg keg of powder, they began laying a trail to the barge. One of the pair got impatient and lit the powder trail, which burned up to the half-empty keg, which had been dropped by the other man. The keg exploded, blowing both whalers some distance and burning off all their hair. Flames had ignited in the other direction, too, and were still burning steadily toward the barge. Fortunately, the powder trail stopped on the gangplank to the barge – not aboard it.

Just west of the old hangar toward the point and Kroner Lake is Site of Special Scientific Interest No 21, protected by the Antarctic Treaty. Entry is forbidden. No boundaries are marked, but to be safe, don't wander past the hangar toward the point. Go up the hill behind the hangar instead, to get a view into a small volcanic cone.

The **volcano** that formed Deception is only dormant, not extinct. Eruptions have occurred as recently as 1991-92. In 1923, water in the harbor boiled and removed the paint from ships' hulls, and in 1930 the floor of the harbor dropped 3m during an earthquake. In 1967, two eruptions forced the evacuation of the Argentine, British and Chilean research stations, and the Chilean station was destroyed. More eruptions occurred in 1969, forcing another round of evacuations and damaging the British station, and there were further eruptions in 1970.

There is a positive side to all this volcanic activity. **Pendulum Cove**, which takes its name from the experiments performed there by Captain Foster aboard *Chanticleer*, is a popular tourist site. The reason: you can doff your parka and go 'bathing' in the thermally heated waters. You can't really swim, though, and most people who take a dip do it mainly to be able to show photos of themselves later. But be forewarned: moving even a meter from the warm water can lead to a real shock – you may either scald yourself or else hit a patch of unheated (frigid) water.

Also at Pendulum Cove, which was once a much deeper inlet but has been much altered by volcanic activity, are the ruins of Chile's **Presidente Pedro Aguirre Cerda station**, which was destroyed by the 1967 eruption. Part of Site of Special Scientific Interest No 21, protected under the Antarctic Treaty,

OCEAN & ISLANDS

Deadly Debris

Despite Antarctica's remote location on the bottom of the globe, the seas surrounding it are becoming as polluted as waters in more populated regions. Sadly, even in the vastness of the Southern Ocean, people leave litter behind – with tragic consequences for wildlife. Every year, thousands of Antarctic seabirds and marine mammals are killed or injured by marine debris.

Dumping any garbage overboard south of 60°S is prohibited by the Antarctic Treaty agreements governing Antarctica. This includes all plastics, ropes, nets, paper, rags, glass, metal, bottles, crockery and even incineration ash – in short, anything. But many vessels ignore these regulations.

Fishing is the main source of Southern Ocean debris. Fishing boats either toss or lose overboard many types of litter: plastic packaging bands from bait boxes; fishing net panels, buoys, ropes and fishing lines – often with hooks still attached.

South Georgia alone has recently experienced a threefold increase in the amount of debris found on its beaches, according to the Commission for the Conservation of Antarctic Marine Living Resources (CCAMLR) – pollution directly related to increased fishing in the area.

Fur seals often become entangled in plastic debris, particularly in net fragments, packaging bands and six-pack rings. Because the plastic doesn't stretch, these items become deadly nooses for fur seals, slowly strangling them as they grow.

Albatrosses, penguins, gulls and shags can likewise be killed or injured when they eat plastic and other debris that can cause intestinal blockages or starvation. When used as a nesting material, the same debris can fatally entangle birds. Among South Georgia's wandering albatrosses, it is estimated that 20% of all chicks may have swallowed the large, heavy-duty steel hooks used in longline fishing.

Even debris left over from worthwhile scientific work, such as weather balloons used in atmospheric research, may be harmful. Antarctic stations launch 10,000 balloons every year. Within hours of their ascent, the balloons burst and fall, often into the sea. Others are blown into the water. Most weather balloons are made from highly durable polythene, and could last for decades in the chilly Southern Ocean. One researcher has calculated that every whale has a 7% chance of encountering a spent balloon during the course of a single year. Although no one is certain what effects might be suffered by a whale ingesting a balloon, whales have been found dead with plastic bags in their stomachs, and it's possible that they choked to death on them.

People are not immune from the threat posed by marine debris. In 1984, a fishing boat's propellers became fouled by the very nets it had earlier discarded overboard, putting both the vessel and her crew in peril.

lies 300m south of the station ruins. Although no boundaries are marked, to protect the abundant mosses the area is off-limits and entry is forbidden.

Telefon Bay is named for the whaling supply vessel *Telefon*, which ran aground in 1908 at the entrance to Admiralty Bay on King George Island. It was repaired here in 1909. Although there is no wildlife at Telefon Bay, it's a spectacular place to view the results of some recent volcanic activity.

Deception's strategic location and superb harbor have made it a contested piece of real estate. During WWII, a British naval operation mounted in 1941 to thwart German raiders destroyed coal and fuel oil depots at the whaling station. In 1942 Argentina sent its naval vessel *Primero de Mayo* to the island to take formal possession of all territory south of 60°S between 25°W and 68°34'W. The ship repeated the possession ceremony at two other island groups and left behind copper cylinders containing official documents claiming the islands for Argentina. In January 1943, Britain dispatched HMS *Carnarvon Castle* to Deception, where it removed evidence of the Argentine visit, hoisted the Union Jack and returned the copper cylinder and its contents to Argentina through the British ambassador in Buenos Aires. Two months later, *Primero de Mayo* was back, removing the British emblems and repainting the Argentine flag. At the end of 1943 the British once again removed Argentina's marks. They probably thought they were putting an end to all the territorial squabbling when they established a permanent meteorological station, **Base B**.

Today the ruins of the base's main timber building (30.6m by 10.4m), **Biscoe House**, can be seen just west of the whaling station at Whalers Bay. Biscoe was originally the main accommodation building for the whaling station. It was badly damaged by the 1969 mudslide, which carried away several sections of its walls.

Another structure, mostly intact, the 19.3m by 6.3m **FIDASE building**, housed the Falkland Islands and Dependencies Aerial Survey Expedition, which spent two years (1955-56 and 1956-57) taking aerial photographs of the South Shetlands and northern Peninsula for mapping purposes. Using Canso flying boat aircraft, FIDASE photographed nearly 90,000 sq km of territory.

Predictably, the bickering between Argentina and Britain continued after the establishment of Base B, and the Argentines built their own base **Decepción** in 1948. In 1952, the Argentines and Chileans both built refuge huts on Britain's airstrip (formerly Wilkins'). The British navy removed the huts the next year and deported two Argentines to South Georgia. In 1953-54, a detachment of Britain's Royal Marines arrived to 'keep the peace' and spent four months on Deception. In 1955, Chile formalized its presence on Deception, building its station at Pendulum Cove. In 1961, Argentina sent President Arturo Frondizi to show the country's official interest in the island. Today all three countries claim the island as their own, but official posturing aside, they get along pretty well.

Chinstraps are the most common penguins on Deception, with several rookeries exceeding 50,000 pairs in each rookery. Rookeries are found along the exterior coast at points on the east at **Baily Head** (also called Rancho Point) and **Macaroni Point** and on the southwest at **Vapour Col**. Aside from the occasional whale or seal, few marine animals venture into Port Foster, since numerous volcanic vents heat the water inside, making it several degrees warmer than the sea outside.

Today, Deception's only regularly open stations are both summer-only facilities. Spain's **Gabriel de Castilla station**, on the southern side of Fumarole Bay, accommodates 12, but is open only occasionally. About 1000m west is Argentina's **Decepción station**, occupation of which is becoming sporadic.

SOUTH ORKNEY ISLANDS

Four major islands (Coronation, the largest, and Signy, Powell and Laurie) make up the South Orkneys, along with several minor islands and rocks, as well as the Inaccessible Islands 29km to the west. The group covers 622 sq km, and 85% is glaciated. The highest point, 1265m Mount Nivea, was first scaled in 1955-56. The weather is cold, windy (westerlies) and overcast, and on average the sun shines less than two hours a day.

The South Orkneys were discovered jointly, by American sealer Nathaniel Brown Palmer sailing in *James Monroe* and British sealer George Powell in *Dove*, on December 6, 1821. Powell named the islands Powell's Group and took possession for the British crown the next day on Coronation Island. On December 12, British sealer Michael McLeod, sailing in *Beaufoy*, independently discovered the group. British sealer James Weddell, who visited in *Jane* in February 1822, gave the islands their present-day name in recognition of their position at the same latitude in the south that Britain's Orkney Islands occupy in the north.

Sealing took its usual course – until nearly every last animal had been killed. As late as 1936, a visitor to the islands found just one solitary fur seal.

In 1903 William Spiers Bruce, leader of the Scottish National Antarctic Expedition, wintered on mountainous Laurie Island, where he helped set up a meteorological

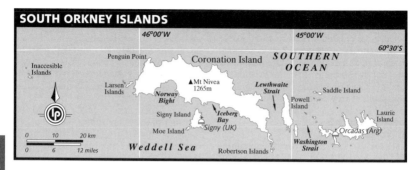

SOUTH ORKNEY ISLANDS

station, which opened April 1. The ruins of the stone hut where the expedition spent the winter, **Omond House**, are still visible at the end of the beach. When Bruce departed in February 1904, the met station was turned over to Argentina's Oficina Meteorologica, which has operated it ever since, making it the oldest continuously run research facility in Antarctica. It was renamed **Orcadas station** in 1951. The station includes a three-room **museum** in the Casa Moneta (1905), which features a replica of an early hut interior as well as an array of artifacts, some from Bruce's expedition. Chinstraps, Adélies and gentoos nest nearby.

Britain declared the islands part of its Falkland Islands Dependencies in 1908, a territorial claim later challenged by Argentina in 1925.

Whaling began in January 1912, when the Norwegian company Aktieselskabet Rethval of Oslo deployed the factory ship *Falkland* at Powell Island. The captain who took the first whale, Petter Sørlle, master of the whale-catcher *Paal*, surveyed the South Orkneys in 1912-13 and named low-lying Signy Island for his daughter. A Norwegian-Chilean enterprise, Sociedad Ballenera de Magallanes, sent a factory ship to Signy in 1911-12, and floating factory ships visited the archipelago until 1914-15. *Tioga*, the first ship to undertake open-ocean whaling in Antarctica, was wrecked at Signy in 1913. Whaling reopened in the South Orkneys in 1920-21, when a Norwegian company operated a station on Signy, and floating factories operated here from 1920 to 1930. About

3500 whales were caught in that decade. The shore station at Signy took the *skrotts*, or stripped carcasses, cast off by the floating factories and from them extracted the remaining oil – 60% of a whale's oil is in its meat and bones. The station also made 'guano,' or meat and bone meal, from the remains after oil extraction.

In 1933 the South Orkneys became one of the first Antarctic regions to receive tourists, when an Argentine naval voyage to relieve the Laurie Island meteorological station brought visitors.

Britain established a meteorological station in 1946-47, **Base H**, at Factory Cove, site of the old Norwegian whaling station on Signy Island. Over the years Signy expanded its program to include biological studies. The station is located on a site with particularly rich plant life, including steep moss-covered terraces rising behind it. In the station's wooden Tønsberg House is a marine biology aquarium. Until 1995, Signy was operated as a permanently staffed – though small – research base. Since 1996 it has operated on a summer-only program, accommodating about 24 personnel.

Signy's fur seals, which were nearly exterminated by hunting, have rebounded dramatically. In 1965 there were practically none. In 1995 researchers estimated that 22,000 lived on the island, which is just 6.5km by 5km. In fact, Signy's seal population was recently found to be 75% greater than its highest previous level, according to a report in *Nature* in 1997. A British researcher who counted seal hairs in sediment cores from

Signy going back at least 6000 years speculated that the precipitous decline in baleen whales has created a virtually limitless food supply for the seals, since krill is a primary prey of both species.

Tourist landings are often made at **Shingle Cove** on nearby Coronation Island, an excellent viewing area for wildlife.

SHAG ROCKS

Comprising six isolated, guano-covered rocks, along with Black Rock and another low-lying rock 20km to the southeast, the group known as Shag Rocks is the smallest of the sub-Antarctic islands. It's part of Britain's South Georgia and South Sandwich Islands territory. Covering only 20 hectares, Shag Rocks are 240km west of South Georgia. They rise straight out of the sea, reaching a peak elevation of 71m. Landings are nearly impossible.

Mislocated by their discoverer, the Spaniard Joseph de la Llana sailing in *Aurora* in 1762, the rocks were originally named the Aurora Islands. In 1819, American sealer James Sheffield in *Hersilia*, searching for the Auroras, found Shag Rocks. The first landing was not made until 1956, when an Argentine geologist was lowered by helicopter to spend a few hours collecting samples. The first tourists landed in 1991. Wildlife includes prions, wandering albatrosses and the eponymous shags.

SOUTH GEORGIA

Crescent-shaped South Georgia, 170km long and 40km wide at its broadest, was one of the first gateways to Antarctica and the center for the huge Southern Ocean whaling industry from 1904 to 1966. Several important expeditions to Antarctica called at the whaling stations en route to or from Antarctica, notably those of Ernest Shackleton.

With its sharp, heavily glaciated peaks, South Georgia presents a rugged appearance. The Allardyce Range forms the island's spine. The highest point is Mt Paget (2934m), first ascended in 1964. Glaciers cover 57% of the island, which covers 3755 sq km. The northeast coast, with many fjords, is protected by mountains from the prevailing

westerlies; this is where all of the whaling stations were built. Bird Island and the Willis Islands lie off South Georgia's northwest tip, Annenkov Island lies off the southwest coast, and Cooper Island off the east coast. The outlying Clerke Rocks are 72km southeast. South Georgia's weather is cold, cloudy and windy, with little variation between summer and winter.

London-born merchant Antoine de la Roche probably was the first to sight the island. In April 1675, while sailing from Lima to England, his ship was blown south as he rounded Cape Horn and he caught a glimpse of South Georgia's ice-covered mountains. The island was seen again in 1756 by Spaniard Gregorio Jerez, sailing in *Léon*, who called it 'Isla de San Pedro.'

Captain James Cook made the first landing on South Georgia on January 17, 1775, when he named it the Isle of Georgia after King George III and claimed it for His Majesty. Cook called it:

savage and horrible . . . the wild rocks raised their lofty summits until they were lost in the clouds, and the valleys lay covered with everlasting snow. Not a tree was to be seen nor a shrub even big enough to make a tooth-pick.

When Cook's account of South Georgia was published in 1777, his descriptions of fur seals there set off a stampede of British sealers, who began arriving in 1786. American sealers followed shortly after, and within five years there were more than 100 ships in the Southern Ocean taking fur seal skins and elephant seal oil. The British sealer *Ann*, for example, took 3000 barrels of elephant seal oil and 50,000 fur seal skins from South Georgia in 1792-93. In that same season, an American sealer hit upon the idea of taking fur seal skins from the Southern Ocean to the market in China, circumnavigating the Earth in the process. During the next season, eight British sealing ships worked in South Georgian waters. Just one, *Mary*, took 5000 fur seals, which we can reasonably assume was an average harvest.

South Georgia's rock-filled waters proved treacherous for ships, and many wrecked or sank near the island. These include *Sally*

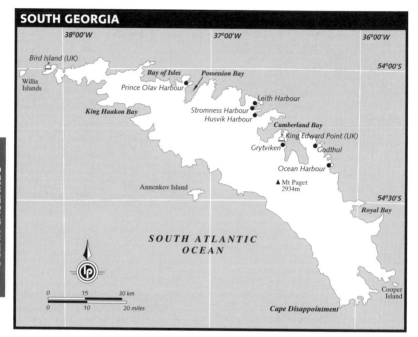

SOUTH GEORGIA

(1796), *Regulator* (1799), *Canada* (c1800), *Earl Spencer* (c1801), *Admiral Colpoys* (1817), *Hope* (1829), *Fridtjof Nansen* (1906) and *Ernesto Tornquist* (1950).

An amazing 57,000 fur seal skins were taken in 1800-02 by American sealer Edmund Fanning, in what was probably the most profitable sealing voyage ever made to South Georgia. Sixteen other British and US sealers worked at South Georgia that season. By 1831, the American ship *Pacific*, landing a sealing gang for eight months, found that fur seals were scarce. As late as 1909, when the American ship *Daisy* stayed for five months in what was probably the last fur-sealing visit to South Georgia, only 170 fur seals could be found.

Elephant seals likewise were slaughtered by the thousands for their oil, which was rendered from their thick blubber. A large elephant seal yielded one 170-liter barrel of oil (though a big bull could produce double that), so the 15,000 barrels taken in 1877-78 by the American sealer *Trinity* show the huge number of seals that could be exterminated in a single year by just one ship. By 1885-86, the American *Express* secured just two elephant seals and 123 'sea leopards' (probably Weddell seals), which all together produced only 60 barrels of oil.

Science intruded on this slaughter briefly in 1882-83, when the German International Polar Year Expedition, part of a 12-country effort to make scientific observations in the polar regions, set up a station at Royal Bay on the southeast coast. They worked for 13 months, and ruins of their hut remain today.

Whaling began in 1904, when the Compañía Argentina de Pesca, a Norwegian company based in Buenos Aires, established the first Antarctic whaling station at Grytviken (see the boxed text 'Grytviken Whaling Station' in this chapter). Using only one whale-catching ship, the Compañía took 183 whales its first year. This modest start quickly became an enormous industry that generated millions of kroner for its primarily Norwegian owners. This also marked the beginning of South Georgia's permanent occupation.

Eventually six shore stations were built on South Georgia – at Grytviken, Ocean Harbour, Leith Harbour, Husvik Harbour, Stromness Harbour, and Prince Olav Harbour – plus an anchorage for floating factory ships at Godthul. Grytviken was the first and longest-lived, operating until 1965. Godthul ran from 1908 to 1917 and from 1922 to 1929. Ocean Harbour, which opened in 1909, closed in 1920. Leith Harbour opened in 1909, closed for a year in 1933 and again during WWII, and closed for good in 1964. Husvik Harbour operated from 1910 to 1931 and again from 1945 to 1960, missing the 1957-58 season. Stromness Harbour operated from 1912 to 1931, and then became a repair yard until it closed in 1961. Prince Olav Harbour operated from 1917 to 1931.

Considering the whaling catch during just two of South Georgia's peak seasons, it's easy to understand why whales are so scarce today. In the 1925-26 season, there were five shore stations, one factory ship and 23 whale-catching ships. In that season, 1855 blue whales, 5709 fin whales, 236 humpbacks, 13 sei whales and 12 sperm whales were caught. The total catch made it a record year: 7825 whales, which produced 404,457 barrels of whale oil. During the 1926-27 season, the same number of catcher ships took 3689 blue whales (a record), 1144 fin whales, no humpbacks, 365 sei whales and 17 sperm whales. The total catch was 'only' 5215 whales, but they produced a then-record 417,292 barrels of oil. Of the total Antarctic whale catch, however, land stations took only 10%.

The Great Depression beginning in 1929, though it caused severe economic hardship in many parts of the world, proved fortuitous for the whales of Antarctica. Combined with a barely nascent realization that controls were needed, it put the brakes on the booming business of whale-hunting. By the 1931-32 season, the economic crisis, as well as severe overproduction the season before, forced Prince Olav and Stromness stations to close for good. Husvik Harbour

also closed, but it reopened in 1945. Leith closed only for the 1932-33 season, and Grytviken never closed.

By 1961-62, the Norwegian companies, which once dominated the trade – a 1909 census at Grytviken found that 93% of the 720 whalers were Scandinavian – could no longer make a satisfactory profit. The Japanese took over the South Georgia whaling operations the next season, but soon also found it unprofitable and closed the last shore station, Grytviken, in 1965.

South Georgia's total whale catch from 1904 to 1966 included 41,515 blue whales, 87,555 fin whales, 26,754 humpbacks, 15,128 sei whales and 3716 sperm whales: a total of 175,250 animals. One of them, a female blue whale landed at Grytviken in the 1911-1912 season, measured just over 33.5m – the largest animal ever recorded.

Elephant seals were also killed again during the whaling era. Their oil was mixed with inferior-quality whale oil to improve it. Grytviken was able to remain open longer than the other South Georgia whaling stations in part because it processed elephant seals. From 1905 to 1964, another 498,870 seals (most of them elephant seals) were killed at South Georgia for their oil.

Ernest H Shackleton achieved one of the greatest of his accomplishments on South Georgia, making the first major crossing of its 1800m range as the final lap in his rescue of the crew of his doomed *Endurance*. He returned to South Georgia again in January 1922, aboard *Quest*. At age 47, his health was failing him, and he died of a heart attack in his cabin aboard *Quest* at Grytviken on January 5. Even as his body was en route home to Britain, his widow, the Lady Emily Shackleton, decided that he should be buried at South Georgia, and he rests today in the **whaler's cemetery at Grytviken**, a must-see tourist site. Along with Shackleton's, there are 62 other graves, several of which may belong to 19th-century sealers. Most are of Norwegian whalers, including nine who died in a 1912 typhus epidemic. One grave holds the remains of an Argentine soldier killed during the Falklands War. The cemetery's abundant dandelions probably come from seeds in the soil, some of which was imported from Norway to allow the dead whalers to be buried in a bit of home.

Cruises that focus on Shackleton's *Endurance* voyage sometimes visit other South Georgia sites associated with the explorer, including **Cape Rosa**, where Shackleton and his men arrived after their voyage from Elephant Island; **Peggotty Camp**, at the head of King Haakon Bay, from which Shackleton

Grytviken Whaling Station

Grytviken means 'Pot Cove' and is named for the sealers' try-pots that were discovered there. As a 'bay within a bay,' it is the best harbor in South Georgia and was chosen by the Norwegian Captain Carl Anton Larsen as the site of the first whaling station in Antarctic waters. On November 16, 1904 Larsen arrived with a small fleet of ships to build a factory, and whaling started five weeks later. Although the company was Argentine-owned, the whalers were mostly Norwegians. Huge profits were made at first, but Grytviken was eventually forced to close because whales had become so rare.

During Grytviken's first years, only the blubber from the whale was utilized. Later meat, bones and viscera were cooked to extract the oil, leaving bone- and meat-meal as important by-products. Elephant seal oil was also produced from bull elephant seals, which were shot and flensed on the beaches around South Georgia. High quality seal oil was an important contribution to the economy of Grytviken.

Life for the station workers was arduous. The 'season' ran from October to March, and the workers put in 12-hour days. As many as 300 worked here during the heyday of the industry. A few stayed over winter to maintain the boats and factory. Transport ships brought down coal, fuel oil, stores and food for the workers and took away the oil and other products.

Attitudes toward whaling were very different a generation ago, and whaling was a highly respectable profession among Norwegians. Through the development of its whaling industry, Norway became a leading industrialized nation known for its shipbuilding and oil technology.

Warning Many parts of Grytviken are unsafe. Do not enter buildings that are boarded up and marked as off-limits. Fire is a serious hazard – so smoking is forbidden.

Visitors' Trail (To be read in conjunction with the map and walked only with the permission of the museum curators or marine officer) Start at the flensing plan, the large open space between the two main jetties. Whale carcasses were brought to the iron-plated whale slip at the base of the plan and hauled onto the plan by the whale winch. (The 40,815kg electric winch has been removed from the top of the plan.) The blubber was slit by flensers armed with hockey-stick-shaped flensing knives. Strips of blubber were ripped off the carcass, like the skin from a banana, by cables attached to steam winches, which you can still see.

The blubber went to the blubber cookery, the large building on the right of the plan. It was minced and fed into huge pressure cookers. Each cooker held about 24 tonnes of blubber, which was cooked for approximately five hours to drive out the oil. The oil was piped to the separator house for purification by centrifuging. The separator house, and the generator house behind it, have been destroyed by fire but you can still see the separators in the ruins. Finally, the oil was pumped into tanks behind the station. If there was a good supply of whales, about 25 fin whales, each 18m long, could be processed in 24 hours. They would yield 1000 barrels (160 tonnes) of oil.

When the whale had been flensed, the meat, tongue and guts were cut off by the lemmers, drawn up the steep ramp on the left of the plan to the meat cookery and dropped into rotating cookers. The head and backbone were dragged up another ramp at the back of the plan to the bone cookery, where they were cut up with large steam saws and also cooked. After oil extraction, the remains of the meat and bone were dried and turned into guano for animal feed and fertilizer.

and his two companions set out to cross the island; and **Stromness whaling station**, where they finally received aid.

In 1908, the British government consolidated earlier claims of sovereignty into a territory called Dependencies of the Falkland Islands, which includes South Georgia, the South Orkneys, the South Shetlands, the South Sandwich Islands and Graham Land on the Antarctic Peninsula. A magistrate

Grytviken Whaling Station

In later years meat extract was made by treatment with sulfuric acid in a plant next to the blubber cookery. Meat extract was used in dried soups and other prepared foods.

From the plan, turn to the right and walk along the shore past the boiler house and guano store to the slipway where *Petrel* lies. Built in 1928, she was used for whaling until 1956 and then converted for sealing. The catwalk connecting the bridge to the gun platform has been removed and the present gun is a recent addition. In this area of the station are the engineering shops, foundry and smithy, all of which enabled the whalers to repair their boats. Farther along the trail is the piggery, the meat freezer and, on the hillside, the hydroelectric power plant. On the shore is the burnt-out remains of the wooden barque *Louise*, a sailing ship built in 1869 at Freeport, Maine. She came to Grytviken in 1904 as a supply ship and remained as a coaling hulk, until she was burned as a training exercise by the UK's garrison at King Edward Point in 1987.

Whalers' Cemetery & Shackleton's Grave This is the resting place mainly of whalers, but there are a few graves of 19th-century sealers. At the back is the grave of Ernest Shackleton, who died on January 5, 1922 aboard his ship *Quest* moored in King Edward Cove. His granite stone bears the nine-pointed star that he used as a personal symbol. On the reverse of the stone is one of Shackleton's favorite quotations, from the poet Robert Browning: 'I hold that a man should strive to the uttermost for his life's set prize.' The cross on the hillside above commemorates Walter Slossarczyk of the *Deutschland* expedition. (This cross, a good location for taking photographs of Grytviken, can be reached by a path.)

Whalers' Church This is a typical Norwegian church and is the only building at Grytviken that retains its original function. It was consecrated on Christmas Day 1913. Inside are memorials to Carl Anton Larsen and to Ernest Shackleton, whose funeral was held here. There are also two bells, which visitors are invited to ring. The church's wooden structure has deteriorated over the years, and storm damage to the roof in 1994 prompted a major program of restoration, which is now complete. Note the remains of the ski jump on the hill behind the church and the football (soccer) pitch on the left.

The first pastor, Kristen Löken, had to admit that 'religious life among the whalers left much to be desired.' The church has been used for a few baptisms and marriages. The first baptism was on Christmas Day 1913, and 13 births have been registered on South Georgia. There have also been four marriages – the most recent in 1999 – but the church has been used more often for funerals. Twelve men died in 1912 of typhus brought by ship.

South Georgia Museum The Museum is housed in the former Manager's Villa. It was opened in 1992 and is supported by the South Georgia government. Material has been collected from Grytviken and other South Georgia whaling stations; exhibits illustrate the lives of the whalers, the history of the island, and its wildlife. The Museum has a shop where you can buy T-shirts, sweatshirts, patches, woolly hats, souvenirs, postcards, slide sets and books. US dollars, British pounds and German deutsche marks are accepted, as are Visa credit cards. Proceeds from sales assist further improvements to the Museum.

– Robert Burton,
past director of the South Georgia Museum

OCEAN & ISLANDS

has resided at Grytviken continuously from 1909, except briefly during the Falklands War in 1982.

In 1949-50, the Falkland Islands Dependencies Survey established a new base at King Edward Point on South Georgia's northeast coast. This station assumed responsibility for meteorological observations, which had been made since 1905 and continued throughout the whaling era. In the 1962-63 season, a large hospital and residential building, called 'Shackleton House,' was built at King Edward Point, but today no scientists work at the station; they're all out in field camps.

War intruded on South Georgia in 1982. On March 25, the Argentine naval vessel *Bahía Paraíso*, later to become infamous for spilling fuel at Anvers Island, arrived at Leith Harbour and set up a garrison in a clear challenge to Britain's claim of territorial sovereignty over South Georgia. On April 3, *Bahía Paraíso*, *Guerrico* and their accompanying helicopters landed 200 Argentine forces at King Edward Point, which was defended by just 22 Royal Marines. After a two-hour battle, the Argentines captured the station and took the Marines and scientists as prisoners to Argentina. Fifteen British researchers at four field stations were later relieved by the Royal Navy.

In response to the Argentine aggression, London dispatched six Royal Navy ships, including the nuclear submarine HMS *Conquerer* for reconnaissance. This force retook King Edward Point on April 25, and the Argentine garrison at Leith Harbor the next day. An Argentine submarine, *Santa Fé*, was sunk; 185 Argentines were taken prisoner and later released in Uruguay. During the Falklands War, the Royal Navy used South Georgia as a base. The 15 British troops remaining at King Edward Point were scheduled to be pulled out in 2000.

South Georgia's wildlife is varied and abundant, despite the incredible slaughter that took place just a century ago. During the 1960s and '70s, the Antarctic fur seal population increased about 15% annually. Today the South Georgia population is more than 3 million. Found mainly on the northwest coast, the seals are so numerous that they present a hazard to Zodiacs trying to land during breeding season.

More than 5 million pairs of macaroni penguins nest on the island. King penguins breed on the gravel beach at **St Andrews Bay** where a melt stream from the Ross Glacier runs through the rookery of 100,000 birds, South Georgia's largest king rookery. Kings also nest at **Salisbury Plain** in the Bay of Isles on the northwest coast.

Albatross Island and **Prion Island** in the Bay of Isles are home to the magnificent wandering albatrosses. Thousands of burrowing seabirds also thrive, since there are no rats on the islands. Three other rat-free islands, where tourist landings are prohibited, **Cooper Island** off the southeast coast, **Annenkov Island** off the south coast and **Bird Island** at the northwest end of the island, are also home to enormous seabird populations.

Two fascinating birds also reside on the island. The South Georgia pipit is the only songbird in Antarctica, while the South Georgia pintail is the world's only known carnivorous duck.

South Georgia's 2000 reindeer were introduced by whalers in 1911 and are confined by glaciers to two regions.

Visitors to South Georgia are charged a landing fee of £50, and without exception visits must be approved in advance. Tour companies take care of the paperwork for their passengers, but yachts will need to apply to the Commissioner for South Georgia and the South Sandwich Islands (☎ 500-27433, fax 500-27434, gov.house@horizon.co.fk), Government House, Stanley, Falkland Islands via UK.

Three excellent books offer more information: Tim and Pauline Carr's *Antarctic Oasis: Under the Spell of South Georgia* (New York: Norton, 1998) is a well-written photograph book by a couple who have lived on their yacht *Curlew* at Grytviken for many years. Robert Headland's *The Island of South Georgia* (Cambridge: Cambridge University Press; 1984) is a definitive study of the island, its history and geography. Sally Poncet's *Antarctic Encounter: Destination South Georgia* (New York: Simon & Schuster,

GRYTVIKEN WHALING STATION

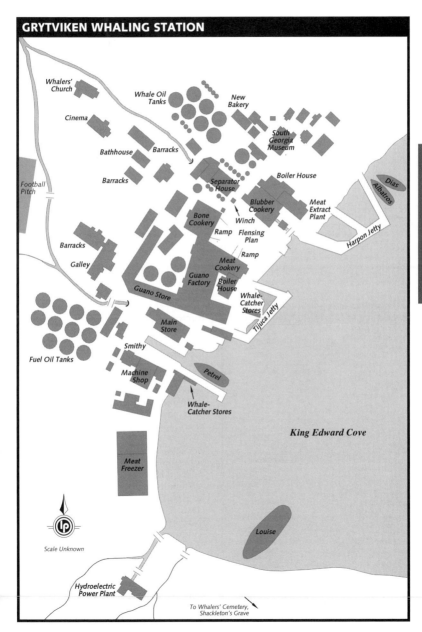

Whalers' Church

Cinema

Whale Oil Tanks

New Bakery

Bathhouse

Barracks

South Georgia Museum

Barracks

Separator House

Boiler House

Football Pitch

Bone Cookery

Blubber Cookery

Winch

Meat Extract Plant

Dias

Albatros

Ramp

Flensing Plan

Harpon Jetty

Barracks

Galley

Meat Cookery

Ramp

Guano Factory

Boiler House

Whale-Catcher Stores

Guano Store

Tijuca Jetty

Main Store

Smithy

Fuel Oil Tanks

Machine Shop

Petrel

Whale-Catcher Stores

King Edward Cove

Meat Freezer

Louise

Scale Unknown

To Whalers' Cemetery,
Shackleton's Grave

OCEAN & ISLANDS

1995) describes the island's wildlife and history through the eyes of three boys who explore it with their parents by yacht.

SOUTH SANDWICH ISLANDS

The 11 islands of the South Sandwich group are spread over a rough arc running north to south: Zavodovski, Leskov (the archipelago's smallest), Visokoi, Candlemas, Vindication, Saunders, Montagu (the largest), Bristol, Bellingshausen, Cook and Thule. Five of the islands (Thule, Cook, Bristol, Montagu and Visokoi) are mostly ice covered, while two (Saunders and Candlemas) are more than half covered with ice. The remaining four have almost no ice caps. Together the South Sandwiches cover 310 sq km. On the archipelago's convex eastern side is a deep-sea trench with a depth of 8265m. The highest point in the islands is 1375m Mt Belinda on Montagu Island.

Volcanoes formed all of the South Sandwiches a relatively short time ago. Volcanic

activity has been recorded in this century on all of the islands except Cook, Montagu and Vindication. In 1908, Norwegian whaler Captain Carl Anton Larsen was almost asphyxiated by volcanic fumes on Zavodovski Island.

In a dramatic demonstration of the islands' continuing volcanism, in January 1956 a group of Argentines at the Teniente Esquivel refuge hut on Thule Island witnessed an extraordinary sight: three jets of glowing material shot 300m into the air in a display that lasted 48 hours. The men understandably evacuated as soon as possible.

In 1962 the South African research ship *RSA*, beset by ice, was freed by shock waves believed caused by a volcanic eruption in the South Sandwiches, and in March of that year, rafts of pumice were sighted offshore of the islands. About 35km off the northwest end of the chain, there's a submarine volcanic cone just 25m underwater.

In recognition of its underworld-like landscape, the British Antarctic Survey has named the features of **Candlemas Island** Cauldron Pool, Demon Point, Chimaera Flats, Gorgon Pool, Lucifer Hill and Sarcophagus Point. Surveyors of **Zavodovski Island**, meanwhile, have named salient features in accordance with how they smell: Reek Point, Pungent Point, Fume Point, Stench Point, Acrid Point and Noxious Bluff.

Although they're more northerly than either the South Shetlands or the South Orkneys, the South Sandwich Islands have a much colder climate, thanks to a cold ocean current originating in the Weddell Sea. The sky is almost constantly cloud-covered.

The eight most southerly islands in the group were discovered on January 30, 1775, by British Captain James Cook, sailing in HMS *Resolution*. He named the islands 'Sandwich Land' after the 4th Earl of Sandwich, then the First Lord of the Admiralty. Ironically, Cook was killed in the Sandwich Islands, now called the Hawaiian Islands.

Sealers made the first landing in the South Sandwich group in 1818.

The three northernmost islands were first sighted by Russian Fabian von Bellingshausen in 1819. Bellingshausen landed on

SOUTH SANDWICH ISLANDS

28°W   26°W

○ Zavodovski Island

Traversay Islands

. Leskov Island   ○ Visokoi Island

57°S

Vindication Island ○ Candlemas Island

Candlemas Islands

SOUTH ATLANTIC OCEAN

○ Saunders Island

0   30   60 km
0   20   40 miles

59°S

○ Bristol Island

Southern Thule

Thule Island ○ ○ Bellingshausen Island
Cook Island

Zavodovski Island and named it for Lieutenant Ivan Zavodovski, captain of his flagship *Vostok*, on Christmas Eve 1819.

The islands are claimed by the British as part of the South Georgia and South Sandwich Islands territory, but they're also claimed by Argentina as part of its Islas del Atlántico Sur. These conflicting claims have occasionally threatened to erupt into violence. In 1976, Argentina established a 50-member naval station on Thule and occupied it for the summer without authorization from Britain. The next season the naval station, Corbeta Uruguay, opened for the winter. It remained active until June 20, 1982, when it was closed and its remaining personnel removed by the British navy because of its role as a staging point in the attack on South Georgia. The following January, the station (except for a refuge hut) was destroyed by British forces after they discovered an Argentine flag flying.

Tourists were first landed on the islands in 1982. Among the islands' attractions are 1.5 million breeding pairs of chinstraps. Some Antarctic tour brochures claim that more than 12 million chinstraps breed on Zavodovski Island alone, but this very rough estimate has been superceded by recent surveys of the South Sandwiches. Biologists say there are in fact about 1 million breeding pairs on Zavodovski – or about 2 million birds – which still makes it one of the world's largest penguin colonies.

TRISTAN DA CUNHA GROUP

You can call Tristan da Cunha 'the middle of nowhere,' for it is the world's most remote inhabited island.

Located midway between South Africa and Brazil, the volcanic islands of the Tristan da Cunha group stand astride the border between the sub-Antarctic and subtropical climatic zones. Tristan is often included on the 'repositioning voyages' at the end of the Antarctic tour season, in part because of the millions of seabirds that nest in the islands.

The northernmost of the group, Tristan Island, is also the largest, being roughly circular and covering 98 sq km. It has a steep volcanic cone that rises to 2060m, the group's

highest point. Tristan is the only inhabited island in the group. The settlement of Edinburgh is named for the island's first royal visit, by Prince Alfred, Duke of Edinburgh in 1867, and is home to about 300 Tristanians. Inaccessible Island is 40km to the westsouthwest and its neighbor, Nightingale Island, is 38km to the south-southwest; they lie 23km apart. Appropriately named Inaccessible Island covers 18 sq km and is almost completely ringed with vertical cliffs. Nightingale, covering less than 260 hectares, is the most densely populated with bird life. Nightingale also has two tiny off-lying islands, Middle and Stoltenhoff.

Portuguese Admiral Tristão d'Acunha, sailing in *Santiago*, discovered the islands in 1506 while traveling in company with 13 other ships. Dutchman Claes Gerritszoon Bierenbroodspot, sailing in *Heemstede*, made the first recorded landing on February 7, 1643.

Austrian Guilleme Bolts, sailing in *Joseph et Thérèse*, landed on Tristan da Cunha in 1775 and took possession for the Emperor of Austria, Joseph II.

The usual sad sequence of discovery, exploitation, extinction was repeated on Tristan da Cunha. The first sealers, Americans sailing in *Industry*, visited for eight months in 1790-91, industriously taking 5600 fur seal skins. By 1801-02, sealers sailing from the Cape Colony in *Phiamingi* were able to take fewer than 10 skins.

Three Americans landed by the sealing ship *Baltic* in 1810-12 established the first settlement on Tristan. One of them, Jonathan Lambert from Salem, Massachusetts, declared himself emperor and proclaimed that Tristan should henceforth be called 'the Islands of Refreshment,' a name he hoped would inspire passing ships to call in for reprovisioning. A copy of Lambert's personal flag can be seen in Tristan's museum. The three men began killing fur seals, hoping to sell the skins to passing vessels. After two of the men drowned in 1812, the lonely survivor, Thomas Curry, continued working. When a British naval vessel stopped in March 1813, two new settlers joined him. According to the official history notes at Tristan's website

OCEAN & ISLANDS

(website.lineone.net/~sthelena/tristan.htm), Curry 'aroused their interest with stories of buried treasure but never revealed its whereabouts. He died of drink, plied to him by the members of the garrison seeking the treasure!'

During the 1812-15 war between Britain and the US, the islands were used by American naval ships and privateers as a base for raids on British vessels. In one offshore gun-battle, USS *Hornet* sank HMS *Penguin*. Partly thanks to this unhappy state of affairs and partly to prevent a rescue of Napoleon – exiled on St Helena in 1815 – Britain set up a garrison and took possession of Tristan in 1816. After the garrison was withdrawn in 1817, three men, a woman and two children, all British, stayed on the island, along with horses and cattle. One of them, Corporal William Glass of Scotland, is recognized as Edinburgh's founder.

British artist Augustus Earle was stranded on Tristan in 1824 when en route to India his ship, *Duke of Gloucester*, was forced by a storm to shelter offshore. Anxious to see an island that, as he said, was 'hitherto un-visited by any artist,' Earle went ashore with his dog and a crew member for what they thought would be a day-long visit. Instead, the ship left without them when the weather worsened. Earle spent eight months on the island. The population was then six adults and several children, whom he tutored up until the time a passing ship took him on to Hobart. He was later briefly attached to Darwin's *Beagle* expedition as official artist before illness forced him to resign. Sixteen works from his exile on Tristan are now at the National Library of Australia in Canberra.

Shipwrecked sailors added to Tristan's tiny community, and by 1826 the island's population was 14: Glass, his wife, their seven children and five other men. The population began to rise fairly quickly after the bachelors negotiated with a ship captain to procure wives for them from the British colony of St Helena 2100km to the northeast. In addition, by the time Glass died in 1853, he had fathered a total of eight sons and eight daughters.

Edinburgh thrived as a convenient mid-ocean filling station – ships stopped for water, vegetables and meat from the islanders' sheep and cattle. Crews of passing ships often remarked upon the islanders' abstemiousness – they neither smoked nor drank, perhaps not surprising given their isolation. But Tristan's ship traffic dwindled as Atlantic and Pacific whaling came to an end and the Suez Canal opened in 1869, eliminating the need to sail around Africa to reach India and the Far East.

Nevertheless, residents of the settlement rescued dozens of mariners whose ships had foundered or burned offshore. In just 81 years, 19 ships wrecked at Tristan. These were HMS *Julia* (1817), *Sarah* (1820), *Blenden Hall* (1821), *Nassau* (1825), *Emily* (1836), *Joseph Somes* (1856), *Sir Ralph Abercrombie* (1868), *Bogata* (1869), *Beacon Light* (1871), *Czarina* (1872), *Olympia* (1872), *Mabel Clark* (1878), *Edward Vittery* (1881), *Henry B Paul* (1882), *Shakespeare* (1882), *Italia* (1892), *Allan Shaw* (1893), *Helen S Lea* (1897) and *Glenhuntley* (1898).

So many times did the islanders aid ship-wrecked sailors that as thanks the British government sent provisions in 1858 and a new lifeboat and other equipment in 1884. In 1879-80, a British naval voyage dropped off presents sent by US President Rutherford B Hayes in gratitude for the Tristanians' role in saving *Mabel Clark*'s crew two years before.

One of the island's most intriguing wrecks occurred in 1864 when the American ship *Lark* was caught in a hurricane. The crew managed to get ashore with £35,000 in gold and currency, at that time a considerable fortune. The loot was left on the island after the survivors were rescued, and although *Lark*'s captain died of smallpox on the voyage home, the first mate later returned for the stash.

To prevent overpopulation, in 1857 a British naval expedition removed 45 of Edinburgh's settlers, leaving 28 people. Ironically, fate took its own cruel measure 27 years later, when 15 men drowned while rowing out in a small boat to try to hail a passing ship for provisions after the potato crop failed. The tragedy left only three grown men on the island.

At least two of the ships that called in at Tristan had connections with Antarctic exploration. In 1893, Henrik Bull's *Antarctic* visited before heading south to the Ross Sea. In 1922, *Quest* landed at Tristan after Shackleton's death.

Annual voyages to bring mail and provisions to the island were begun by the British Colonial Office in 1927, and in 1938 British Letters Patent defined the Tristan da Cunha group and Gough Island as Dependencies of St Helena.

During WWII, the British navy established a meteorological and radio station on the island to prevent Nazi ships from using Tristan as a watering place. The detachment was withdrawn in 1946 and the South African Weather Bureau took over responsibility for the station.

A volcanic eruption in 1961, which followed more than two months of seismic activity, forced Edinburgh's evacuation on October 10. Two fishing boats took the entire population (289 people) to Nightingale Island. The next day they sailed for Cape Town, and later to England, where they remained until November 1963, when they returned home. Many Tristanians later said they found England too cold and too noisy.

Edinburgh's population today is just under 300, with 80 families sharing eight surnames. The Prince Philip Hall is the island's social center, with a weekly dance, a pub and indoor sports. There's an outdoor swimming pool and a café nearby, as well as two churches, a school with about four dozen students, a supermarket, a gym, a public library, a museum and a golf course. There is one public satellite telephone, and mail comes by ship approximately every three months. The Internet arrived in 1998, but no one does much net surfing, as the Inmarsat connection costs US$5 or more per minute.

Elections are held every three years for the eight positions on the Island Council, which also has three appointed members. The Administrator, appointed by the governor of St. Helena, is the head of government and must act in accordance with advice from the Island Council. At least one councillor must be female. The councillor who receives the most votes is named Chief Islander.

Employment consists of either a government job or working for the plant that processes the local catch of rock lobster (crayfish), which is exported to France, Japan and the US. Other exports include handicrafts and postage stamps prized by collectors all over the world. The island is almost completely self-supporting. There is no income tax.

Edinburgh, says Tristan's current Administrator, Brian Baldwin, 'is a very small community with the characteristics of small communities all over the world. But the isolation factor has required Tristanians to work at solving interpersonal relations in a realistic way.' Equality of opportunity, he adds, is important. 'No one islander will try to outdo another. This attitude derives from a very egalitarian declaration made by William Glass and the original settlers, the original of which is in the British Museum.' There is also no serious crime and people do not lock their doors.

In 1997 a study of the Tristanians' DNA found the cause of asthma suffered by about 30% of the population: a mutated gene, apparently passed down from an early settler.

The islanders' distinctive speech is characterized by slow enunciation. Their accent is thought to resemble that of English spoken in parts of Britain during the early 19th century. Words used on the island include cappie (hood) and gansey (pullover); the island's potato-growing section is called Patches.

A landing fee of £10 per person is charged. Although the island has no hotel and camping is not allowed, accommodations in island homes are available at £20 per night including three meals and laundry service. There are no reductions for long-term stays. For safety reasons, visits to parts of the island away from the settlement plain and to Nightingale Island can only be made with an island guide, for which a daily charge of £6 per person is made. Part of this fee goes to the island's conservation fund.

OCEAN & ISLANDS

GOUGH ISLAND

Oblong Gough Island rises steeply out of the sea 340km southeast of Tristan da Cunha. It covers 65 sq km, with several pillars and rocks lying offshore. Its coasts are nearly all steep cliffs, especially on the windward western side, where they stand nearly 460m high. At 910m, Edinburgh Peak is the highest point. There are no glaciers on the island. With the island's getting more than 3m of rainfall each year, and an average annual temperature of 11.7°C, a lush carpet of mosses, tussock grasses and ferns covers its slopes.

Gough was probably first sighted in 1505 by the Portuguese Gonçalo Alvarez when he was blown south while rounding the Cape of Good Hope. For this reason, the island is occasionally referred to as Gonzalo Alvarez. The Dutchman January Jakobszoon van Amsterdam examined Gough and the Tristan da Cunha group in 1655-56. The first landing on Gough was probably made when Antoine de la Roche, a London-born merchant, came ashore in May 1675, a month after he discovered South Georgia. Such mid-ocean discoveries were not always shared, however, especially among rival seafaring nations. British Captain Charles Gough, sailing in *Richmond*, rediscovered the island on March 3, 1732, naming it for himself, though he made no landing.

The first sealers arrived in 1804, and the island's resources were exploited throughout the 19th century. In 1881, for example, parties from Cape Town reported taking eight tonnes of guano, 4000 penguin eggs and 151 fur seal skins. In 1919 a group from Cape Town spent four months prospecting unsuccessfully for diamonds.

Shortly after British Letters Patent defined Gough Island as a dependency of St Helena in 1938, a formal territorial claim was made during a British naval visit by HMS *Milford*.

During WWII, Germany sent *Stier*, also known as 'Raider J,' to investigate Gough as a potential base of operations and prison camp. Britain quickly dispatched HMS *Hawkins* to ensure that the Germans would not be able establish a beachhead.

In 1955-56, a comprehensive exam of Gough was made by British scientists, who built a small station. In May 1956, the British scientific station was transferred to the **South African Weather Bureau**, which continues meteorological observations today.

The first tourist landing was made in 1970, and Gough was declared a Wildlife Reserve in 1976. In late 1995, after a comprehensive management plan was adopted, it was declared a World Heritage Site, the first Southern Ocean or sub-Antarctic island so designated. The unusual long-crested rockhopper penguin and two endemic birds, the Gough bunting and the Gough flightless moorhen, breed on the island. It is also one of the most northerly habitats for both the southern elephant seal and the wandering albatross.

FALKLAND ISLANDS (ISLAS MALVINAS)

Although they are not sub-Antarctic islands, the Falklands are a popular addition to the itinerary of many Antarctic voyages. Surrounded by the South Atlantic and by centuries of controversy, the Falklands lie 490km east of Patagonia. Consisting of two main islands, East and West Falkland, and about 700 smaller ones, they cover 12,173 sq km, about the same area as Northern Ireland or Connecticut. Except for the low-lying southern half of East Falkland, known as Lafonia, the terrain is generally hilly to mountainous. East Falkland's highest point is 701m Mt Usborne, West Falkland's is 697m Mt Adam. Among the most interesting geological features are the 'stone runs' of quartzite boulders that descend from many of the ridges and peaks on both East and West Falkland.

The climate is temperate, with frequent high winds. Maximum temperatures rarely reach 24°C, while even on the coldest winter days the temperature usually rises above freezing. Average annual rainfall at Stanley, one of the Islands' most humid areas, is only 600mm.

Grasslands and shrubs dominate the flora. There are no native trees. At the time of European discovery, extensive stands of the native tussock grass *Parodiochloa flabel-*

lata dominated the coastline, but very little remains today, although well-managed farms on offshore islands have preserved significant areas of it. Among the 13 endemic plants are several unusual species, including snake plant *(Nassauvia serpens)*, with its phallic-looking stalks and tiny leaves; Felton's flower *(Calandrinia feltonii)*, an annual until recently thought to be extinct in the wild; and vanilla daisy *(Leuceria suaveolens)*, which, while not endemic, is still very interesting: its flowers smell like chocolate.

Besides the five types of penguin (Magellanic, rockhopper, macaroni, gentoo and king) that breed here, there are many other birds, equally interesting and uncommon.

According to the 1996 census, the Falklands population is 2564, of whom about two-thirds live in Stanley (see the Antarctic Gateways chapter). The rest live in 'Camp,' the name for all of the Falklands outside Stanley. Only a few of the numerous smaller offshore islands are inhabited. About 60% of the population is native born, some tracing their ancestry back six or more generations. Most of the remainder are immigrants or temporary residents from the UK.

Since the advent of large sheep stations in the late 19th century, rural settlement in the Falklands has consisted of tiny hamlets (really company towns) built near sheltered harbors where coastal shipping could collect the wool clip. In fact, these settlements were the models for the sheep estancias of Patagonia, many of which were founded by Falklands emigrants. On nearly all of them, shepherds lived in 'outside houses,' which still dot the countryside.

Although there's evidence that Patagonian Indians may have reached the Falklands in canoes, the islands were officially discovered on August 14, 1592 by John Davis, master of HMS *Desire*, during an English naval expedition, though a 1522 Portuguese chart indicates knowledge of the islands. The Falklands' Spanish name, Islas Malvinas, derives from early French navigators from St Malo, who called the islands 'Les Malouines' after their home port.

No European power established a settlement until 1764, when the French built a garrison at Port Louis on East Falkland, disregarding Spanish claims under the papal Treaty of Tordesillas that divided the New World between Spain and Portugal. Unbeknown to either France or Spain, Britain soon set up a West Falkland outpost at Port Egmont, on Saunders Island. Spain, meanwhile, discovered and then supplanted the French colony after an amicable settlement. Spanish forces then detected and expelled the British in 1767. Under threat of war, Spain restored Port Egmont to the British, who only a few years later abandoned the area – without, however, renouncing their territorial claims.

For the rest of the 18th century, Spain maintained the islands as one of the world's most secure penal colonies. After it abandoned them in the early 1800s, only maverick whalers and sealers visited, until the United Provinces of the River Plate sent a military governor in the early 1820s to assert its claim as successor to Spain. Later, a naturalized Buenos Aires entrepreneur named Louis Vernet initiated a project to monitor uncontrolled sealers and exploit local fur seal populations in a sustainable manner.

Vernet's seizure of three American sealers triggered reprisals from a hotheaded US naval officer, who vandalized the Port Louis settlement beyond restoration in 1831. After Vernet's departure, Buenos Aires kept a token force there until early 1833, when it was expelled by British forces. Vernet pursued his claims for property damages in British courts for nearly 30 years, with little success.

Under the British, the Falklands languished until the mid-19th century, when sheep began to replace cattle, and wool became an important export commodity. Founded by Samuel Lafone, an Englishman from Montevideo, the Falkland Islands Company became the Islands' largest landholder, but other immigrant entrepreneurs occupied all other available pastoral lands in extensive holdings by the 1870s.

The steady arrival of English and Scottish immigrants augmented the early population, a mix of stranded mariners and gauchos from the Vernet era. Roughly half resided in

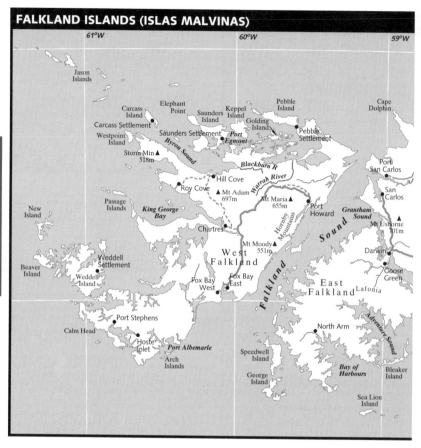

FALKLAND ISLANDS (ISLAS MALVINAS)

Stanley, with the remainder living as resident laborers on sheep stations. The population has never exceeded its 1931 peak of 2400.

Although Argentina had persistently affirmed its claim to the Falklands since 1833, successive British governments never publicly acknowledged that claim until the late 1960s. By then, the Foreign & Commonwealth Office and the military government of General Juan Carlos Onganía had reached an agreement, to begin in 1971, that gave Argentina a significant voice in matters affecting Falklands transportation, fuel supplies, shipping and even immigration.

Islanders (sometimes called 'Kelpers') and their supporters in Britain saw the Argentine presence as ominous. Only a few years earlier, right-wing guerrillas had hijacked an Aerolíneas Argentinas jet, which had crash-landed on the Stanley racecourse (the islands had no airport then). Afterward, the guerrillas briefly occupied parts of town. Concerned about Argentina's chronic political instability, Falklanders suspected the FCO of secretly arranging transfer of the islands to Argentina. They may have been correct.

This process dragged on for more than a decade, during which Argentina's brutal

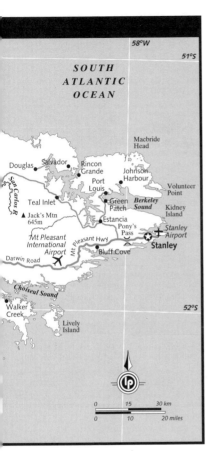

trained and poorly supplied Argentine conscripts. The most serious battle took place at Goose Green on East Falkland, but the Argentine army's surrender at Stanley averted the capital's destruction. Today, Britain spends about US$1 billion to maintain a 2000-troop garrison.

Since the war, most Falklanders want little or nothing to do with Argentina, which continues to send mixed messages to the islands. President Carlos Menem has repeatedly renounced the use of force to support his country's claim, yet he has also bragged that the Falklands will soon be Argentine once again. Foreign minister Guido di Tella, meanwhile, has carried out an ineffectual policy of sending the Falklanders Christmas cards and gifts, while at the same time proposing to pay US$100,000 or more per person if the islanders vote to accept Argentine sovereignty. Nearly all Falklanders dismiss his efforts as insulting, but many do not oppose a strictly economic relationship with Argentina.

The Falklands remain a colonial anachronism, administered by a governor appointed by the FCO in London. In local affairs, the eight-member elected Legislative Council (Legco) exercises power over most internal matters. Four of the eight members come from Stanley, the remainder represent Camp. The British government controls defense and international relations.

From the mid-19th century until 1986, the Falklands' economy depended almost exclusively on wool exports. However, fishing has eclipsed agriculture as a revenue producer under a licensing scheme established by the local government with the approval of the FCO. Asian and European fleets seeking squid and finfish have brought as much as £25 million per year into the Islands. Most of this money has paid for improvements in public services. Also, local government began permitting offshore seismic surveys for oil in 1993 and is considering issuing licenses for offshore petroleum exploration.

Most of Stanley's population works for the local government (FIG) or for the Falkland Islands Company (FIC), the major landowner and economic power in the islands for

Dirty War after 1976 gave Falklanders good reason to fear increasing Argentine presence. What was too fast for the Islanders was too slow for Argentina, especially the military government of Gen Leopoldo Galtieri, which invaded the nearly undefended Falklands on April 2, 1982. The seizure briefly united Argentina and made Galtieri a hero, but he never anticipated British prime minister Margaret Thatcher's decisive response.

The fight was one-sided, despite Britain's substantial naval losses. Experienced British troops landed at San Carlos Bay, routing ill-

more than a century. The FIC continues to provide shipping and other services, but it has sold all its pastoral property to the government for subdivision and sale to the local people. In Camp, nearly everyone lives on relatively small, widely dispersed family-owned units and is involved in wool-growing. (For more on Stanley, see the Antarctic Gateways chapter.)

Many books have been written since the 1982 war, but the most readily available general account is the third edition of Ian Strange's *The Falkland Islands* (David & Charles, 1983), which covers the islands' geography, history, and natural history. More recent are Paul Morrison's *The Falkland Islands* (Aston Publications, 1990) and Tony Chater's *The Falklands* (Penna Press, 1993), the latter with large format photographs. Based on unpublished materials from Cambridge University archives and other sources, Patrick Armstrong's *Darwin's Desolate Islands: A Naturalist in the Falklands, 1833 and 1834* (Picton, 1992) is of great historical interest. For a good contemporary account of the Falklands, see Robert Fox's *Antarctica and the South Atlantic: Discovery, Development and Dispute* (BBC Books, 1985). Of the numerous books on the war, one of the best is *Battle for the Falklands* by Max Hastings and Simon Jenkins (London, Pan, 1983). Visitors interested in wildlife should acquire Robin Woods' *Falkland Islands Birds* (Anthony Nelson, 1982), a field guide with excellent photographs, or his more detailed *Guide to Birds of the Falkland Islands* (Nelson, 1988). Ian Strange's *Field Guide to the Wildlife of the Falkland Islands and South Georgia* (Harper Collins, 1992) is also very good. Bluntisham Books (see the Books section in the Facts for the Visitor chapter) has published TH Davies and JH McAdam's *Wild Flowers of the Falkland Islands* (1989) and Julian Fisher's *Walks and Climbs in the Falkland Islands (1992)*.

What follows is a selection of sites and islands that commonly receive visits from ships on Antarctic trips.

East Falkland East Falkland has the Islands' most extensive road network, con-

sisting of a good highway to Mt Pleasant international airport and Goose Green. **Port Louis** is the Falklands' oldest settlement, dating from the French foundation of the colony by Louis de Bougainville in 1764. One of the oldest buildings is the ivy-covered 19th-century farmhouse, still occupied by farm employees. Scattered nearby are ruins of the French governor's house and fortress and Louis Vernet's settlement. Visit the grave of Matthew Brisbane, Vernet's lieutenant, murdered by gauchos and Indians after British naval officer JJ Onslow left him in charge of Port Louis in August, 1833. Brisbane, who twice survived being shipwrecked, was also the master of *Beaufoy*, which accompanied James Weddell's *Jane* on his furthest south of 74°15'S in February 1823, when Weddell discovered his namesake Sea. Sir James Clark Ross in 1842 dug up Brisbane's body from the rough grave in which the Indians had buried it and reinterred it, giving it a wooden marker. The grave marker, now in the museum at Stanley, was replaced in 1933 by a marble stone.

Sea Lion Island The most southerly inhabited island in the Falklands is little more than 1km across at its widest, but has more wildlife in a smaller area than almost anywhere in the islands. Here you will find all five species of Falklands penguins, enormous colonies of cormorants, giant petrels and the 'Johnny Rook' (more properly the striated caracara *Phalcoboenus australis)*, one of the world's rarest birds of prey. Elephant seals breed on the island's sandy beaches every spring, while sea lions line the narrow gravel beaches. For most of its history, Sea Lion's isolation has undoubtedly contributed to the continuing abundance of wildlife, but much of the credit has to go to Terry and Doreen Clifton, who farmed the island from the mid-1970s to the early 1990s, when they sold it. The Cliftons developed their 930-hectare farm with the idea that wildlife, habitat and livestock were compatible. Sea Lion Island is one of few working farms in the Falklands with any substantial cover of native tussock. Through improved fencing and conscientious management decisions, the Cliftons

Photographing elephant seals, King George Island

Cruising the Ross Sea

Zodiac drivers, Deception Island

Outdoor 'barbie,' Davis Station

MARK NORMAN

Megaherbs, Campbell Island

MARK NORMAN

Heard Island

MARK NORMAN

Scott Island, Ross Island

JEFF RUBIN

Taylor Valley, Dry Valleys, Victoria Land

JEFF RUBIN

Lone Adélie penguin

made the island both a successful sheep station and a popular tourist site.

Bleaker Island The northern part of Bleaker is a wildlife sanctuary; the rest is used for raising sheep. Rockhopper, gentoo and Magellanic penguins are resident, along with king cormorants, elephant seals and sea lions.

West Falkland Nearly as large as East Falkland, West Falkland's only proper road runs from Port Howard on Falkland Sound to Chartres on King George Bay, but there's also a system of rough tracks. **Port Howard** is West Falkland's oldest farm and one of very few large sheep stations to survive the major agrarian reform of the past decade. About 40 people live on the 81,000-hectare station, which has 42,000 sheep and 800 cattle. Unquestionably the most scenic part of the Falklands, **Port Stephens'** rugged headlands are open to the blustery South Atlantic and battered by storms out of the Antarctic. Thousands of rockhopper penguins, cormorants and other seabirds breed on the exposed coast, a short distance from the settlement's harbor.

Pebble Island Elongated Pebble, off the north coast of West Falkland, has varied topography, a good sampling of wildlife and extensive wetlands. There are also about 13,000 purebred Corriedale sheep.

Keppel Island In 1853 the South American Missionary Society established an outpost on Keppel Island to catechize Yahgan Indians from Tierra del Fuego and teach them to become potato farmers instead of hunter-gatherers. The mission was controversial because the government suspected that Indians had been brought against their will, but it lasted until 1898, despite the Indians' susceptibility to disease. One Falklands governor attributed numerous Yahgan deaths from tuberculosis to their

delicacy of constitution...developed owing to the warm clothing which they are for the sake of decency required to adopt after having been for 15 or 20 years roaming about in their canoes in a very cold climate without clothing of any kind.

It's likely that hard physical labor, change of diet, European-introduced diseases and harsh living conditions in their small, damp stone houses played a greater role in the Yahgans' demise than any inherent delicacy of constitution. The mission was undoubtedly prosperous, though, by 1877 bringing in an annual income of nearly £1,000 from its cattle, sheep and gardens. Although Keppel is now exclusively a sheep farm, several interesting ruins remain. The former chapel is now a wool shed, while the stone walls of the Yahgan dwellings remain in fairly good condition. The mission bailiff's house stands intact, though in poor repair. Keppel is also a good place to see penguins.

Saunders Island Only a few kilometers west of Keppel, Port Egmont on Saunders Island was the site of the first British garrison on the Falklands, built in 1765. In 1767, after France ceded its colony to Spain, Spanish forces dislodged the British from Saunders and nearly precipitated a war between the two countries. After the British left voluntarily in 1774, the Spaniards razed the settlement, including its impressive blockhouse. Remaining are jetties, extensive foundations and some of the buildings' walls, plus garden terraces built by the British marines. Saunders continued to be controversial in the late 1980s, when the property was passed by inheritance into the hands of Argentine descendants of the Scottish pioneer sheep farmer John Hamilton. For years Falklanders agitated for the farm's expropriation, but the owners sold the island to its local managers in 1987.

Carcass Island Despite its name, Carcass is a small, scenic island west of Saunders with a good variety of wildlife, including a large gentoo rookery. It's a popular weekend and holiday vacation spot for Stanleyites.

The island takes its name from HMS *Carcass*, which, along with HMS *Jason*, was dispatched by the British to the Falklands in 1765-67 to establish the settlement at Port Egmont on Saunders Island. HMS *Carcass*, a bomb vessel, was strongly built and designed for use in the bombardment of forts

and harbors. While establishing the Port Egmont settlement, the expedition made a hydrological survey of the Falklands, during which *Carcass* sounded the harbor on this island, to which it gave its name.

West Point Island A 2.5km walk past the main house of the settlement on this island brings you to rockhopper penguins and black-browed albatross in a natural amphitheater with the sea as its stage.

New Island The Falklands' most westerly inhabited island is also a unique wildlife area, with large colonies of penguins, albatrosses, petrels and seals.

The island comprises two properties but is effectively run as a wildlife reserve. New Island South is cared for by the New Island South Conservation Trust, which promotes the study of ecology and conservation and ensures that the reserve retains its status in perpetuity. Several long-term research projects are underway on New Island South. Privately owned New Island North is also run as a nature reserve.

In the late 18th century, New Island's excellent harbors and rich wildlife resources turned it into an important base for North American whaling and sealing vessels. The island's name originated from the voyagers'

New England home ports: New York, New Bedford and others.

It was on New Island that American sealer Captain Charles H Barnard, master of *Nanina*, was marooned. Captain Barnard had a disastrous encounter in the Falklands with the crew of a shipwrecked British vessel, *Isabella*, in April 1813, soon after the beginning of the 1812-15 war between Britain and the US. To thank him for rescuing them, all but two of the shipwreck survivors took over Barnard's ship, leaving him and four other men stranded on New Island for almost two years. But just as *Nanina* was being sailed away by the castaways-cumpirates, the British gun-brig *Nancy* arrived and took her as a prize of war. Barnard and his fellows, meanwhile, were left behind and not rescued until December 1814 by two British sealing ships, *Indispensible* and *Asp*.

Barnard published a book in 1829 about his ordeals, unimaginatively titled *A Narrative of the Sufferings and Adventures of Captain Charles H Barnard, In A Voyage Round The World, During The Years 1812, 1813, 1814, 1815 & 1816; Embracing An Account of the Seizure of His Vessel at the Falkland Islands, By An English Crew Whom He Had Rescued From The Horrors Of A Shipwreck; And Of Their Abandoning Him On An Uninhabited Island, Where He*

Resided Nearly Two Years. It was reprinted with an introduction by Bertha Dodge under the succinct title *Marooned* (Middletown, CT: Wesleyan University Press, 1979).

A Norwegian whaling company, based in Sandefjord, sent *Admiralen*, the first modern floating factory ship to reach the southern regions, and began whaling at New Island on Christmas Eve, 1905. The ship went to Admiralty Bay on King George Island in the South Shetlands in early 1906, returning to New Island in February.

A shore-based whaling station was operated on New Island by the whaling firm Salvesen's of Leith (in Scotland) from 1908 to 1916. The venture didn't last long because there weren't enough whales in the vicinity; the company subsequently set up operations on South Georgia. A few ruins of the station – building foundations and some machinery – remain about 3km south of the settlement on New Island's east coast.

Beached in Settlement Harbour lies *Protector*, built in Nova Scotia in the late 1930s/early 1940s as a minesweeper for the Canadian navy. She was brought down to the Falklands for a local sealing venture, which was eventually discontinued for lack of seals. The then-owner of New Island, a shareholder in the sealing venture, sailed *Protector* around the islands and eventually ran her onto the beach here.

A rough **stone hut** built up from the original structure built by Captain Barnard is just off the beach opposite *Protector*. It is being restored as a museum by the New Island South Conservation Trust.

On the island's precipitous west coast are large colonies of rockhopper penguins, king cormorants and black-browed albatrosses, as well as a large rookery of southern fur seals. Gentoo and Magellanic penguins also breed on New Island, which is also home to the Falklands' largest breeding ground for the thin-billed prion *(Pachyptila belcheri)*.

One or two people can be accommodated at the settlement in a self-contained cottage, but reservations must be made far in advance. Inquiries should be made to Ian and Maria Strange, (fax 500-21186, dolphins@ horizon.co.fk) PO Box 71, Stanley, Falkland Islands via UK.

Weddell Island Scottish pioneer John Hamilton, also a major landholder in Argentine Patagonia, acquired this western offshore island and others nearby to experiment with various agricultural improvement projects, including replanting of tussock grass, establishing forest plantations and importing Highland cattle and Shetland ponies. Hamilton, well-meaning but perhaps misguided, also introduced exotic wildlife such as guanacos (still present on Staats Island), Patagonian foxes (common on Weddell proper) and otters (apparently extinct). Saunders still hosts abundant local wildlife, including gentoo and Magellanic penguins, skuas, night herons, giant petrels and striated caracaras.

Antarctic Peninsula & Weddell Sea

ANTARCTIC PENINSULA

With its hundreds of tiny offshore islands, the Peninsula is one of Antarctica's richest breeding grounds for seabirds, seals and penguins. During the 19th century, it was extensively explored, not just by scientific expeditions but, in fact, primarily by sealers from Britain and the US.

Although there appears to be a wide variety of sites for Antarctic tour operators to choose from in deciding where to take their passengers, they all visit nearly the same places. The boxed text chart 'The Peninsula's Top Ten Most Visited Sites 1989-1999' gives an idea of how overused many of these places are. Of the 10,000 people now visiting Antarctica each year, almost half visit the same three tiny landing sites. That's because they offer what tour operators are looking for: easy access to wildlife, a station or a museum. The cumulative impact of all these tramping feet, unfortunately, is starting to become apparent.

Most tourist cruises to the Peninsula will visit a number of the following sites.

Astrolabe Island

Discovered by Dumont d'Urville's 1837-40 expedition and named for his chief ship, this island is home to several thousand pairs of chinstraps.

Cape Legoupil

One of the oldest stations on the Peninsula, Chile's **General Bernardo O'Higgins station**, stands on this ice-cliffed cape – or more precisely, 80m offshore on a small island. It was established in 1948, and inaugurated by Chilean president Gabriel González Videla, the first head of state to visit Antarctica. A wood-plank and wire suspension bridge for pedestrians links the island to the mainland. The station, which accommodates 50, is operated by the Chilean army. There are no scientific staff, and only meteorological and sea-temperature data are collected. There is a small museum in the stores building. Gentoos breed successfully right among the station buildings.

The separate **German Receiving Station** on the island was built by Germany in 1988-89. It accommodates nine people. The station, which is only operated periodically, acquires data from European Remote Sensing satellites via a large, white 9m parabolic dish.

Hope Bay

Hope Bay, on the northernmost tip of the Peninsula, is home to one of Antarctica's largest Adélie rookeries – 124,000 pairs, along with a few gentoos. The entrance to Hope Bay, reached via the Antarctic Sound, is often filled with tabular icebergs calved from the bay's glaciers.

Argentina built **Esperanza station** in 1951. The government expanded the station significantly in 1978 and began sending women and children to live there year-round as part of its efforts to establish 'sovereignty' over the territory. One of these women was Silvia Morello de Palma, wife of Army Captain Jorge de Palma, Esperanza's station leader. She was flown in from Argentina when she was seven months pregnant, and on January 7, 1978 she gave birth to Emilio Marcos de Palma, the first native-born Antarctican. In the five years following Emilio's birth, other women at the station gave birth to four boys and three girls.

Today usually about a dozen children live with their families year-round at the station, which can accommodate 79 people. Most station personnel are military, and about 35% of Esperanza's population is made up of spouses and children.

These families, along with the nature of the station itself, make Esperanza feel like a small village. Consisting of a small school building; a chapel; a post office; an infirmary; a graveyard with a stele in memory of Argentine expedition members who died in the area; 1.5km of bulldozed gravel roads;

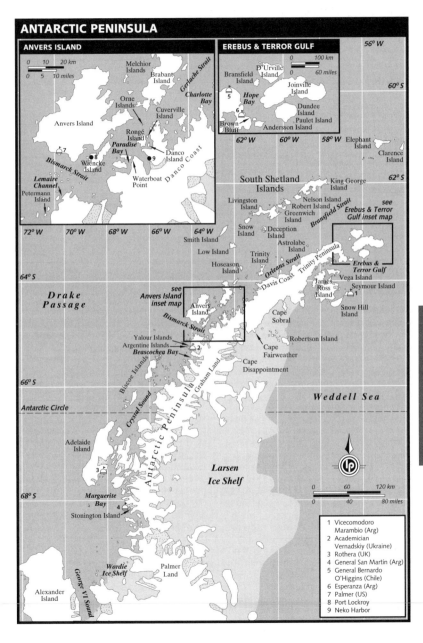

ANTARCTIC PENINSULA

ANVERS ISLAND

0   10   20 km
0   5   10 miles

Melchior Islands
Brabant Island
Gerlache Strait
Charlotte Bay
Orne Islands
Cuverville Island
Anvers Island
Rongé Island
Paradise Bay
Wiencke Island
Danco Island
Danco Coast
Bismarck Strait
Waterboat Point
Lemaire Channel
Petermann Island

7
8
9

EREBUS & TERROR GULF

0   100 km
0   60 miles

D'Urville Island
Bransfield Island
Joinville Island
Hope Bay
Dundee Island
Brown Bluff
Paulet Island
Andersson Island

5
6

62° W   60° W   58° W

56° W
60° S
62° S

Elephant Island
Clarence Island

South Shetland Islands

King George Island
Nelson Island
Robert Island
Greenwich Island
Livingston Island
Snow Island
Deception Island
Astrolabe Island
Smith Island
Low Island
Hoseason Island
Trinity Island
Orleans Strait
Davis Coast
Trinity Peninsula
Bransfield Strait

see Erebus & Terror Gulf inset map

Erebus & Terror Gulf

Vega Island
Seymour Island
James Ross Island
Snow Hill Island

1

72° W   70° W   68° W   66° W   64° W

Drake Passage

64° S

see Anvers Island inset map
Anvers Island
Bismarck Strait

Cape Sobral
Robertson Island
Cape Fairweather
Cape Disappointment

Yalour Islands
Argentine Islands
Beascochea Bay

2

Biscoe Islands

66° S

Crystal Sound

Antarctic Circle

Graham Land

Weddell Sea

Antarctic Peninsula

Adelaide Island

Larsen Ice Shelf

3

68° S

Marguerite Bay
Stonington Island

4

Wordie Ice Shelf

Palmer Land

George VI Sound

Alexander Island

0   60   120 km
0   40   80 miles

1   Vicecomodoro Marambio (Arg)
2   Academician Vernadskiy (Ukraine)
3   Rothera (UK)
4   General San Martín (Arg)
5   General Bernardo O'Higgins (Chile)
6   Esperanza (Arg)
7   Palmer (US)
8   Port Lockroy
9   Neko Harbor

ANTARCTIC PENINSULA

The Peninsula's Top Ten Most Visited Sites 1989-99

Location	1989-90	1990-91	1991-92	1992-93
	Number of Visitors per Season			
Whalers Bay, Deception Island	1682*	1496	2899	1711
Port Lockroy, Wiencke Island	796	1067	2615	2139*
Half Moon Island	1191	1011	2984*	1585
Cuverville Island	883	936	2565	1589
Pendulum Cove, Deception Island	587	1215	2011	1936
Hannah Point, Livingston Island	419	192	1632	1542
Petermann Island	761	1084	1376	1376
Argentina's Almirante Brown Station, Paradise Harbor	1191	1471	2899	1659
Chile's Gonzalez Videla Station, Paradise Harbor	1038	1965*	2398	1671
Paulet Island	772	240	2239	1498

* Antarctica's most visited tourist site in that season

and 13 chalets housing families, it *is* more a village than a scientific station, for there are only two modest-sized laboratories.

On two sides of the station there is a large Adélie rookery with more than 100,000 pairs, but much of it is protected and off-limits to visitors. Just 70 tourists are permitted to visit Esperanza at one time.

Two historic sites are nearby. Close to the jetty and behind ropes is the ruin of a **stone hut** where three members of Nordenskjöld's Swedish Antarctic expedition spent a desperate winter in 1903, surviving on seal. Nordenskjöld named the bay in honor of these three men. Some of the Esperanza staff rebuilt the hut in 1966-67. There is a small **museum** of historic relics in one of the buildings at the center of the station. Other historic equipment including sledges and an old Sno-Cat are kept outside near the stone hut.

On the hill about 500m from Esperanza station is **Trinity House**, a hut remaining from Base D, built by the UK's Operation Tabarin in 1944-45 and closed in 1963. The building was transferred to Uruguay in 1997 and is now being refurbished as **T/N Ruperto**

Elichiribehety Station, a summer-only facility accommodating 12 people. The station is named for the captain of the Uruguayan steam trawler *Instituto de Pesca No 1*, which Shackleton used in his second of three unsuccessful attempts to reach the castaways on Elephant Island before he was finally able to reach them in *Yelcho*.

Crosses in the cemetery close to the station mark the resting places of two men lost in a 1948 fire.

Brown Bluff

Brown Bluff is an ice-capped flat-topped 745m mountain on the Peninsula's northeast tip. It takes its descriptive name from a striking cliff of reddish-brown volcanic rock on its north face. Adélies and gentoos nest here.

Paulet Island

This circular volcanic island. just 2km in diameter, is one of Antarctica's most visited sites. Hundreds of thousands of Adélies nest here – along with blue-eyed shags and southern giant petrels.

The Peninsula's Top Ten Most Visited Sites 1989-99

1993-94	1994-95	1995-96	1996-97	1997-98	1998-99	Total
3480	5241*	5033	3012	5344	5427	35,325*
4274*	1769	3851	3110	6429*	6473*	32,523
2961	3017	5221*	2258	4382	3931	28,541
2174	3367	4343	3714*	4143	4087	27,801
3159	2803	3492	2725	3426	4676	26,030
2740	4010	3048	3480	3399	3982	24,444
2828	3406	3504	2576	3866	3305	24082
3513	1307	2244	2504	3991	1612	22,391
3248	1559	2384	1095	2998	3379	21,735
1664	2819	2315	2808	732	3722	18,809

Source: Office of Polar Programs, US National Science Foundation

Paulet was discovered by Briton James Clark Ross' expedition of 1839-43 and named for the Right Hon Lord George Paulet, a captain in the Royal Navy.

On February 12, 1903, Nordenskjöld's *Antarctic*, which had been crushed by the Weddell Sea pack ice for weeks, finally sank 40km east of Paulet. The men sledged for 14 days to reach the island. They built a 10m by 7m **hut** on the northeast coast, where all but one of them survived the winter. Today, the ruins are populated by Adélies.

Dundee Island

Lying 5km northwest of tiny Paulet Island is Dundee, where millionaire American aviator Lincoln Ellsworth took off on the first trans-Antarctic flight on November 22, 1935. With his quiet, pipe-smoking copilot, Herbert Hollick-Kenyon, Ellsworth flew – in five hops over two weeks – across the continent to the Bay of Whales on the Ross Ice Shelf.

Dundee was discovered in 1893 by British whaler Captain Thomas Robertson, who named it for his home port in Scotland.

Joinville Island

Immediately north of Dundee Island is Joinville, the largest of the three islands at the tip of the Peninsula.

Joinville was discovered in 1838 by the French explorer Jules-Sébastien-César Dumont d'Urville, who named it for a French nobleman, François Ferdinand Phillipe Louis Marie, Prince de Joinville, third son of the Duc d'Orléans.

Joinville Island's northerly neighbor, **D'Urville Island**, was charted by Nordenskjöld in 1902 and named for his predecessor, Dumont d'Urville.

Melchior Islands

Sixteen of the Melchior Islands are named for letters of the Greek alphabet: Alpha, Beta, Gamma, Delta, Epsilon, Eta, Theta, Kappa, Lambda, Omicron, Pi, Rho, Sigma, Tau, Psi and Omega (see the boxed text 'What's in a Name?' in this chapter). On Lambda Island is the first **lighthouse** built by Argentina in the Antarctic, Primero de Mayo, erected in 1942. It is now protected as a historic site by the Antarctic Treaty.

ANTARCTIC PENINSULA

Charlotte Bay

Some feel that Charlotte Bay, often filled with recently calved icebergs and one of the most beautiful spots along the Peninsula, rivals the photogenic Paradise Bay as an attraction. It is named for the fiancée of the second-in-command of de Gerlache's Belgian Antarctic Expedition of 1897-99. At the entrance to the bay, **Portal Point** is the former site of an old British Antarctic Survey hut, built in 1956 and now relocated to the Falkland Islands Museum in Stanley.

Orne Islands

This small archipelago just north of Rongé Island was probably named by early-20th-century whalers working in the area. It is home to a small colony of chinstraps.

Cuverville Island

Discovered by de Gerlache in 1897-99, and named for JMA Cavalier de Cuverville, a vice admiral in the French navy, this island is a popular stopover often made in conjunction with a visit to Rongé Island. Cuverville has several large gentoo rookeries, which comprise one of the largest gatherings of this species in Antarctica. University of Cambridge researchers conducted a three-year study at Cuverville in 1992-95 to try and determine the impact of their presence and the presence of tourists on the penguins. After monitoring the gentoos' heart rates and observing skuas and other species, the scientists concluded that the presence of well-conducted tour groups, with individuals observing the Guidelines for Visitors to the Antarctic (see the boxed text 'Guidance for Vistiors to the Antarctic' in the Facts for the Visitor chapter), had no detectable effects on breeding behavior or breeding success.

The slopes above the landing beach also shelter extensive and deep beds of moss, which shouldn't be stepped on.

Rongé Island

De Gerlache named this island for Madame de Rongé, a wealthy contributor to the expedition. It is home to several large colonies each of gentoos and chinstraps.

Danco Island

Danco Island, 1.5km long, has a wide, sloping cobblestone beach. It was charted by de Gerlache in 1897-99 and later named for the expedition's geophysicist, Émile Danco, who died in the Antarctic. A hut, built in 1955-56 as **Base O** by the Falkland Islands Dependencies Survey (forerunner of the British Antarctic Survey), is now maintained as a refuge and occasionally still used by researchers during short visits. There's a large anthracite dump in front.

Gentoos nest right up to the summit of the island's 180m peak.

Anvers Island

Mountainous Anvers Island, named for the Belgian province of the same name, was discovered in 1898 by de Gerlache's Belgian Antarctic Expedition. At 70km long, it's the largest and southernmost island in the Palmer Archipelago.

The US **Palmer station**, at Arthur Harbor on Anvers' southwest coast, was built in 1968. It replaced the prefabricated wood huts of 'Old Palmer' station, established in 1965, which were removed from Antarctica in 1991. The station is named for American sealer Nathaniel B Palmer, who in 1820 was one of the first to see Antarctica.

Due to local geography, the station is compact, with two main buildings, an aquarium with pumped seawater, a boathouse, a dive locker, workshops, a clean-air laboratory, a sauna and storage buildings all placed close together. The two-story BioLab also includes a dining area, offices, communications facilities, storage and sleeping facilities. The two-story GWR (garage, workshop and recreation) building also houses generators and sleeping facilities. Within the main station complex, raised wooden walkways set above the winter snow level connect the buildings. Gravel paths connect the outer buildings.

One amenity at Palmer may be unique for an Antarctic station: a hot tub made from a leaky circular fish tank which couldn't be repaired well enough to hold fish. It's outdoors on the deck behind the aquarium room in BioLab.

Palmer accommodates 43 people. During summer it's generally full, but only about 20 people winter over, because there's little research going on then other than remote sensing and instrument monitoring. Thanks to the station's relatively northerly location, it's accessible by sea year-round and is resupplied by ship every six weeks.

Research at Palmer focuses on long-term monitoring of the marine ecosystem, with an emphasis on seabirds and krill, atmospheric studies and the effects of increased ultraviolet radiation (caused by the 'ozone hole') on marine and terrestrial communities.

Until the US government began limiting tourist stopovers, Palmer was one of Antarctica's most heavily visited stations. In 1990-91, 12 tour ships visited. In 1969, about 70 American tourists from the chartered Chilean naval vessel *Aquiles* were marooned at Palmer for the night – a real strain on a station then designed to accommodate only 40 people!

The gentoo rookery at **Torgerson Island** is a popular site, often visited in conjunction with Palmer.

Antarctica's worst environmental disaster occurred near Palmer on January 28, 1989, when the 131m Argentine navy supply ship *Bahía Paraíso*, with 234 passengers and crew (including 81 tourists) aboard, ran into a submerged reef off DeLaca Island, 3km from the station. The reef ripped a 10m gash in the ship's hull, spilling 645,000 liters of diesel fuel and other petroleum products and creating a slick that covered 30 sq km. Although no one was injured, and two nearby cruise ships quickly rescued the passengers, the spill severely damaged seabirds and the marine environment. Blue-eyed shags and south polar skuas each experienced a nearly -100% loss of their chicks after the spill. Adélie numbers dropped 16% that season. Organisms in the rocky intertidal zone – mollusks, macroalgae – were also immediately damaged. Perhaps worst of all, the spill disrupted or destroyed research that in some cases went back two decades.

A joint Argentine-Dutch operation recovered the remaining 148,500 liters of fuel and some hazardous lubricants from the submerged tanks, but the spill had already caused great damage. If the spill had been crude oil rather than diesel and jet fuel, the effect would have been much worse.

In the course of the 1990s most local marine communities recovered, with the exception of the blue-eyed shags, which have not been able to regain their former numbers.

Today, *Bahía Paraíso*'s **nearly submerged hulk** is still visible. From the station as well as from approaching vessels, the ship's rusty hull can be seen between DeLaca and Janus Islands, in front of and slightly closer to DeLaca. Vessels enter Arthur Harbor between Bonaparte Point and Janus Island. Sharp-eyed observers can spot a 3m-long section of *Bahía*'s hull at high tide. At low tide, the section above the waterline is 10m long and half a meter high. The wreck is a reminder of the dangers of operating in Antarctica – and of our responsibility to try to prevent it from becoming sullied like the rest of the world.

Wiencke Island

Wiencke Island was named by de Gerlache in 1897-99 for Auguste-Karl Wiencke, a young seaman who fell overboard and drowned while trying to clear *Belgica*'s clogged scuppers.

Port Lockroy, an 800m-long harbor on Wiencke's west coast, is *the* most popular tourist stop in Antarctica, thanks to its former British station-turned-museum. During the 1998-99 season, 6,473 visitors came ashore here.

Visits are usually made in conjunction with landings at the gentoo rookery at **Jougla Point**, where other highlights include blue-eyed shags and a composite whale skeleton reconstructed on the shore.

Port Lockroy was discovered by Charcot's *Français* expedition of 1903-05 and named for Edouard Lockroy, vice president of France's Chamber of Deputies, who helped Charcot secure government funding for his expedition. Until about 1931, Port Lockroy was a major harbor for whalers. Evidence of that period, such as mooring chains embedded in rocks, can still be seen.

Don't Collect, Please!

One of the most difficult things in life is learning not to covet and collect things. Let's face it, the whole world is infected with capitalism, and few people are immune to the disease of acquiring things based on desire rather than need. At the same time, most of us recognize the innate goodness of those who manage to control feelings of temptation. As the Zen sages put it, 'desire is suffering.'

But the desire to collect little souvenirs of your trip to Antarctica can have a profound impact on the white continent.

The Antarctic Treaty encourages everyone who visits Antarctica to protect all its living creatures and to forgo any exploitation of mineral or other resources. The Treaty has been uniquely successful, more so than almost any other. Scientists, tourists, politicians, environmentalists, business-people, historians – all of their interests converge on maintaining the beauty and untrammeled nature of Antarctica.

And there we find a deep irony. No place on this planet is more awe-inspiring than Antarctica – how could you *not* want to bring a piece of it home with you? Exposure to Antarctica will profoundly affect you for the rest of your life. It's perfectly natural to want for that embrace to be represented by something tangible. The Treaty, however, is clear on this point: scientific study is the only reason samples of any kind may be removed from Antarctica. How can we reconcile the strong global mandate to protect Antarctica's pristine state with our powerful desire for a souvenir?

The key is to recognize that the physical things you bring home are nothing more than symbols or icons. The real value of your trip lies in simply having been to Antarctica. The most valuable things you can bring home are the changes that Antarctica has wrought upon you.

Don't try to fool yourself by rationalizing. It's easy to convince yourself that taking a pebble off a beach to give to a child may inspire the youngster, who may in fact want to be a scientist. That soggy little penguin feather, you may say, can educate someone about science. But this is false altruism. If you pick up that Antarctic stone 'just for the grandchildren,' you're setting a poor example for them. Show your respect for the special, unique nature of the Antarctic environment by resisting that temptation. Leave the rock, feather, bone, egg, fossil or artifact where you saw it.

Why should scientists get all the goodies? First of all, it's not as though scientists are allowed to take home anything they wish from Antarctica. In fact, without the deeply felt respect for the continent every Antarctic researcher has, Antarctic science would have ground to a halt long ago under the burden of permits, restricted procedures and off-limits areas imposed by the Treaty. But these restrictions ensure an undisturbed Antarctica where your grandchildren and mine can make new discoveries without wading around in the impact of past generations. Future tourists and scientists benefit when we restrain our 'collective' desires.

Instead of the rocks you trod upon, bring your grandchild the hat or gloves you wore in Antarctica. Rather than a feather, give your friends a photo of the penguin who came right up to you. Or, just to satisfy the capitalist system, go ahead and buy a T-shirt from a station or aboard ship. Do your part to preserve the irony.

– Dr Ralph P Harvey

After the Argentine navy ship *Primero de Mayo* left a cylinder at Port Lockroy in 1943 claiming the harbor and all territory between 25°W and 68°34'W south of 60°S, Britain moved to uphold its rival claim. In 1943-44, Britain's Operation Tabarin (named for a bawdy Parisian nightclub) removed the Argentine emblems and established a meteorological station, **Base A** on Goudier Island, in Port Lockroy. The base was staffed almost continuously until 1962; normal occupancy was four to nine people, with the usual tour of duty lasting two and a half years!

Port Lockroy's original station hut, **Bransfield House** – now surrounded by the nesting gentoos that have recolonized the island – was beautifully restored by the UK Antarctic Heritage Trust in 1996. Don't miss the full-length portrait of Marilyn Monroe painted on the back of the generator shed door, a memory aid to lonely winterers during Antarctica's all-male era. Displays on station history can be seen hanging inside Bransfield House, and two AHT staff members live at Port Lockroy in the summer to act as tour guides. These staff members also run a busy, well-stocked **post office and souvenir shop**, with the proceeds benefiting AHT.

Lemaire Channel

This steep-sided channel – just 1600m wide – runs for 11km between the mountains of Booth Island and the Peninsula. So photogenic that its nickname is 'Kodak Gap,' the passageway is only visible once you're nearly inside it.

The channel was discovered by a German expedition in 1873-74, but wasn't navigated until December 1898, when de Gerlache's *Belgica* sailed through. In a decidedly odd choice, de Gerlache named the channel for Belgian adventurer Charles Lemaire, who explored the Congo. Unfortunately, ice sometimes blocks the way, so ships may be forced to retreat and sail outside Booth Island. At the northern end of the Lemaire are two tall, rounded and often snowcapped peaks at **Cape Renard**.

Neko Harbor

Many passengers are especially glad to land at Neko Harbor, if only because it's on Antarctica itself, so they can officially 'bag' the continent. The glacier across from the landing site often calves with a thunderous roar, offering dramatic video footage for those lucky enough to be ready.

Neko Harbor was discovered by Adrien de Gerlache's Belgian Antarctic Expedition of 1897-99, but takes its name from a Norwegian floating factory whaling ship, *Neko*, which operated in the area for many seasons between 1911 and 1924.

The small orange hut with the Argentine flag painted on the side is a *refugio*, or refuge hut, built in 1949 and named Captain Fleiss. Wildlife here includes a small colony of gentoo penguins; sheathbills often nest in the rubbish outside the *refugio*. Look for the occasional starfish, krill or tiny urchin washed up on the beach.

Paradise Bay

Paradise Bay (officially called Paradise Harbor) is described in Antarctic tour brochures as 'the most aptly named place in the world.' That may be overstating the case – many more people would probably consider paradise to be a sun-drenched tropical island. Still, the harbor, with its majestic icebergs and reflections of the surrounding mountains, is undeniably beautiful. Even the early-20th-century whalers operating in this vicinity recognized its extreme beauty, for they gave the bay its name.

This is a favorite place for 'Zodiac cruising,' in which no landings are made and you simply motor around the sculpted pieces of ice calved from the glacier at the head of the bay. Your tour may pass beneath blue-eyed shags nesting on cliffs, which can be colored blue-green by copper deposits, emerald green by moss, and orange or yellow by lichens.

The original portions of Argentina's **Almirante Brown station** were destroyed on April 12, 1984 by a fire set by the station's physician/leader, who didn't want to stay another winter. The station personnel were rescued by the US ship *Hero*.

Thanks to its proximity to Paradise Bay, Almirante Brown is one of the most visited sites in Antarctica. The summer-only station is being rebuilt, and its personnel sell a particularly handsome T-shirt featuring a blue-eyed shag. Climb the hill behind the station for a great view of surrounding glaciers. Then save yourself the walk and slide back downhill.

Waterboat Point

Although it appears to be an island, Waterboat Point is separated from the mainland of the Peninsula only at high tide. At low water,

ANTARCTIC PENINSULA

it is possible to walk across a stretch of low rocks to reach the Peninsula.

Two British researchers, Thomas W Bagshawe and Maxime C Lester, spent a year here from January 1921 to January 1922 recording meteorological, tidal and zoological data. They supplemented their insufficient stores with penguin and seal meat, living in a rough shelter partially constructed from a whaler's upturned water boat left by a Norwegian factory ship a few years before. The pair were part of the smallest British expedition ever mounted to the Antarctic, a four-man effort led by John Cope; the other member was Hubert Wilkins. The expedition was intended to be much larger, but was unable to raise sufficient funds. A **ruin** of Bagshawe and Lester's hut remains. It is a historic site protected by the Antarctic Treaty.

The Chilean air force operates summer-only **Presidente Gabriel González Videla station** in the midst of a gentoo rookery. It's named for the Chilean president who in 1948 became the first head of state to visit Antarctica – with an entourage of 140.

Petermann Island

Home to the world's southernmost gentoo colony, Petermann is another of Antarctica's 10 most visited spots (see the boxed text). At 65°10'S, 64°10'W, it's one of the most southerly landings most expeditions make. Just under 2km long, the island was discovered by a German expedition in 1873-74 and named for German geographer August Petermann. Adélies, gentoos and blue-eyed shags nest here.

Charcot's French Antarctic Expedition of 1908-1910 wintered aboard *Pourquoi Pas?* at Port Circumcision, a cove on the southeast coast. It was discovered by Charcot on New Year's Day 1909 and named for the holy day of the Feast of the Circumcision, January 1st, when tradition says Christ was circumcised. While today none of the small huts constructed for scientific purposes by the expedition remain, a **cairn** it built can still be seen, as can an abandoned Argentine **refuge hut** built in 1955. Close by the hut is a **cross** commemorating three British Antarctic Survey men who died in 1982 while at-

tempting to cross the sea ice from Faraday station to Petermann.

Yalour Islands

This group, about 2.5km in extent, was named by Charcot for Lieutenant Jorge Yalour, an officer of the Argentine navy ship *Uruguay*, which came to the rescue of the Swedish Antarctic Expedition in 1903. About 8000 pairs of Adélies nest here. There are often beautiful examples of orange lichens and green mosses, as well as small clumps of Antarctic hair grass *(Deschampsia antarctica)*.

Argentine Islands

This island group was discovered by Charcot on his *Français* expedition and named for the Argentine Republic in thanks for its help.

Ukraine's **Academician Vernadskiy station**, which can accommodate 24 people, is located on Galindez Island in the archipelago. Transferred from the UK in 1996, the station was previously called Faraday. Currently it is the senior station open continuously in Antarctica. One popular remnant from its British era is the pub, with a dartboard, billiards table and magnificent carved wooden bar – built by station carpenters who were supposed to be working on something else. The islands offer several sheltered yacht anchorages.

Long-running weather records kept by the station show that mean annual temperatures along the Peninsula's west coast have risen by about 2.5°C since 1947. Local ice cover has also declined, and the number of plants – Antarctic hairgrass *(Deschampsia antarctica)* and Antarctic pearlwort *(Colobanthus quitensis)* – in the station vicinity has increased. These may be early warnings of global climate change.

Wordie House, built in 1947 as the first part of what would later become Faraday, is located about 1km from the station. It is a historic site protected by the Antarctic Treaty, and it was restored in the late 1990s by the British Antarctic Survey. The rooms have been returned to their early 1950s appearance, and contain artifacts and furniture from that period. Signs outlining the building's history line the walls.

Ernest Shackleton

Beascochea Bay

Discovered by the Belgian Antarctic Expedition of 1897-99, and more completely mapped by Charcot's *Français* expedition of 1903-05, this bay is named for Commodore Beascochea of the Argentine navy.

Crystal Sound

This island-dotted sound was named by the British because many of the geographical features in the sound, including several islands, are named after scientists who studied the structure of ice crystals.

Marguerite Bay

Few Antarctic tour ships make it as far south as this extensive bay on the west side of the Peninsula. Well below the Antarctic Circle, it was discovered by Charcot on his *Pourquoi Pas?* expedition in 1909 and named for his wife.

The UK's **Rothera station**, built in 1975 on Adelaide Island, occupies a small rocky peninsula. A 900m crushed-rock airstrip and hangar were added in 1990-91, making Rothera a Peninsula region logistics center for British Antarctic Survey operations using Twin Otter aircraft. The station is also resupplied by ships, which use a 60m wharf also built in 1990-91. Rothera can accommodate

ANTARCTIC PENINSULA

Deadly pack ice claimed many ships.

124 people and boasts one of the few aquariums in the Antarctic. The Bonner Laboratory complex, completed in 1997, includes a recompression chamber, a wet lab and a terrestrial biology lab. A large new sleeping quarters building, which can house 88 people, is being constructed at Rothera and should be completed by 2002. The 95m by 11m single-story building will be fitted out with triple-glazed windows and Swedish pine furniture.

At the northern tip of Rothera Point is **Site of Special Scientific Interest No 9**, its boundary marked with yellow drums. This area was put off-limits to allow monitoring of the station's local environmental impact.

Argentina's **General San Martín station**, the most southerly Peninsula station, was established in 1951 on Barry Island in the Debenham Islands, between Adelaide and Alexander islands. It closed between 1960 and 1975, but reopened and now accommodates 20 personnel.

Stonington Island

Stonington Island, named for the Connecticut home port of American sealer Nathaniel Brown Palmer, is something of an Antarctic ghost town. It's the site of two former stations, which are separated by about 200m. They are rarely seen by tourists, being too far south of the Antarctic cruise routes, but get occasional visitors from Rothera and San Martín stations.

The UK's **Base E**, established in 1945-46 and used until 1975, consists of two wooden huts and some steel mesh dog pens. The larger, two-story hut served as sleeping facilities, while the smaller was a generator shed. A **cross** on the point commemorates three young Britons who died in 1956 when the sea ice they were crossing during a dogsledding trip broke up beneath them.

The US's **East Base** was built during Richard Byrd's third Antarctic expedition, the US Antarctic Service Expedition of 1939-41. It was also used in 1947-48 by a private American venture, the Ronne Antarctic Research Expedition, which included the first women to winter in Antarctica, Edith Ronne and Jennie Darlington, who accompanied their husbands. Unfortunately, their men quarreled, so, out of loyalty, they also did not speak to one another. It must have been a long year. After the Ronne expedition departed, the UK used East Base until 1975.

The US government funded a historic preservation program at East Base in 1990-91. A small display of artifacts from the Ronne expedition has been set up in one of the three base buildings, marked as a museum.

WEDDELL SEA

The Weddell Sea is one of the least visited parts of Antarctica, since its extremely heavy pack ice rarely allows ships to penetrate to any great distance. This is where Shackleton's *Endurance* went down, and where at least four other ships have been crushed and sunk by pack ice. The Weddell's primary attractions are its emperor penguin rookeries and the Ronne and Filchner Ice Shelves, reachable by air.

British sealer James Weddell, sailing in the brig *Jane*, discovered the sea in February 1823 and named it 'King George IV Sea' for the British sovereign. German Antarctic historian Karl Fricker proposed the name Weddell Sea in 1900.

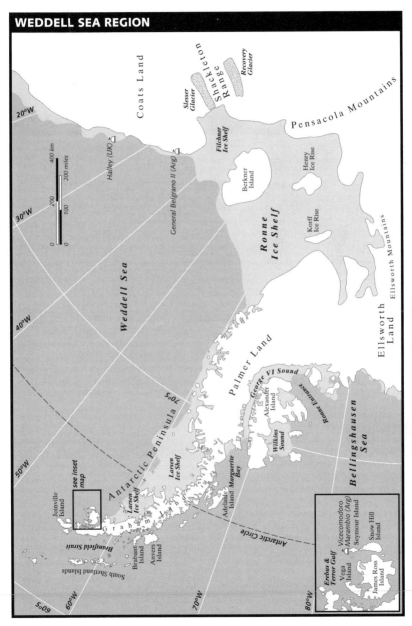

WEDDELL SEA REGION

Snow Hill Island

This descriptively named 395m-high island was discovered by James Clark Ross in 1843, who called it simply 'Snow Hill' because he was uncertain of its connection with the mainland. Nordenskjöld, who set up a winter base in February 1902, determined its insular nature.

Today the prefabricated black-walled **hut**, in which three Swedish and one Argentine scientist spent two years, is a historic site protected by the Antarctic Treaty. The group's second year was unplanned, forced upon them by the crushing and sinking about 100km away of Nordenskjöld's ship *Antarctic*. The 6m by 8m hut contains three

ANTARCTIC PENINSULA

Seymour Island: Antarctica's Rosetta Stone

Little did I know, when I landed on the mud runway at Marambio station on Seymour Island early in January 1975, that I would spend the rest of my life working on the scientific treasures of this unique island.

The landscape of this small, ice-free island off the northeast tip of the Antarctic Peninsula looks much like the Badlands of the southwestern US. In fact, when you're working here, the only signs that you're actually in Antarctica are the large tabular icebergs slowly drifting northward past the island and the occasional group of Adélie penguins walking along the beach.

Seymour Island is truly remarkable. The slopes of many of the hills, particularly on the western side, are literally paved with fossils. Not only are the rocks well exposed, but they also contain extremely rich and well preserved assemblages of marine invertebrates and terrestrial animals and plants. The problem of working on Seymour is not finding the fossils, but deciding which ones to collect.

Seymour is also the only place in Antarctica where rocks ranging in age from about 120 million to 40 million years are known. In terms of understanding the geologic history of Antarctica's last 100 million years and the role the continent has played in the evolutions of the modern faunas and floras of the Southern Hemisphere, Seymour is the Rosetta Stone of Antarctica.

Among the 800 fossils found here so far are 2m-tall giant penguins (now extinct, unfortunately), starfish, crabs, crinoids, corals and nearly 200 new mollusks, among them a 4m-long ammonite (related to the pearly nautilus). Another interesting find: a sea turtle that lived 40-45 million years ago and was the size and shape of a Volkswagen Beetle.

When we arrived in 1975, we planned to work on neighboring James Ross Island, but problems with the Argentine helicopters prevented our reaching it. That proved very fortunate, since we were forced to spend the entire field season on Seymour Island.

We were the first geologists to have the opportunity to look for fossils on Seymour since Swedish explorer Otto Nordenskjöld visited 75 years before. We found some remarkable fossils from the marine Eocene deposits (about 35 million years old) at the north end of the island. We also found bones of the giant penguins that Nordenskjöld first reported during his expedition. These penguins stood nearly 2m in height and may have weighed as much as 135kg. It must have been quite a sight to see thousands of these giants walking along the beach.

One of the major paleontological questions about Antarctica's history was whether land mammals lived there before the development of the ice sheets that cover the continent today. In 1981, we returned to continue our work at Seymour's north end and to carry out a survey of those rocks that seemed to have the greatest potential for containing fossil land mammals. Mike Woodburne, a noted vertebrate paleontologist, and his assistant, Bill Dailey, came along. While they meticulously searched the most likely localities, I worked on the Eocene marine faunas. Each day was an adventure and ended with backpacks full of fossils. In midseason I came across a unique fossil locality: an Eocene beach, exposed by erosion, which was covered with mollusks, shark teeth and bones of penguins and whales.

double-bunk rooms, a kitchen and a central living room. Two large metal signs in Spanish describe the site's historical importance, as do informative leaflets in English inside the hut. Two angled wooden planks, original to the design, support the northeast wall. The Argentine government, whose Vicecomodoro Marambio station is 21km northeast on Seymour Island, does a good job of maintaining the hut.

Seymour Island

Approximately 20km long and 3km to 9km wide, Seymour Island is remarkable for its lack of snow and ice cover. The island is ice-free because it lies in the lee of the high

Seymour Island: Antarctica's Rosetta Stone

Although Mike and Bill spent the entire season crawling on their hands and knees looking for mammal bones, they found only a few scattered fish bones. Two days before the end of the season, I suggested that they join me in collecting the abundant penguin bones at the Eocene beach deposit. After an hour and a half of walking into the wind, we reached the site and Mike sat down to rest. Looking at the surface, he immediately saw a tooth of the small primitive marsupial *Polydolops*.

This was the first discovery of a fossil land mammal in Antarctica. It also answered a question concerning the origin of Australian marsupials that had puzzled scientists since the 19th century: how did marsupials get to Australia? The oldest marsupials known were from rocks in Wyoming about 100 million years old, while Australia's oldest marsupials were only about 30 million years old. Mike's discovery helped prove that early marsupials migrated from North America through South America, then across Antarctica to Australia.

Seymour also contains one of the most important records of the circumstances surrounding the worldwide 'extinction event' 65 million years ago that wiped out 70% of the world's species, including the dinosaurs. Most scientists now generally accept that the mass extinction was related to a major meteorite impact in Central America. Today, the debate has shifted to whether it was the sole cause – or whether a conjunction of events, including the impact, led to the extinction. Conditions portrayed by supporters of the impact hypothesis were so extreme that I asked, How did any life survive? And why don't we see a layer of burnt and twisted dinosaur bones?

During the 1994-95 season, we found on Seymour the first documented victims of the mass extinction. We made a detailed map of the layer of iridium-rich sediments dating from the impact – known to geologists as the KT boundary. Nearly everywhere along the KT boundary, there were scattered bones of fish, killed by the impact 65 million years ago.

But the decline in the number of species of marine life on Seymour began approximately 8 million years *before* the impact, clearly showing that Earth's climate was cooling. Species of marine life that lived for millions of years before the impact disappeared first in the high southern latitudes, then in the temperate and middle latitudes. Approaching the KT boundary on Seymour, more and more species disappear. Just below the boundary, 55% of the remaining species vanish. And the fish bones above the KT boundary are in scattered concentrations over about 3m of section, suggesting that they represent not a single mass kill, but a number of mass kills due to unstable conditions that may have lasted for thousands of years after the impact.

So I believe that the Cretaceous-Tertiary extinction was not related to a single event, but was the result of a conjunction of events. The impact was only the final straw for an already stressed environment. You could almost use this as a model for the present: How long can we stress the biosphere before something small pushes things over the edge?

– Dr William J Zinsmeister,
a paleontologist at Purdue University in West Lafayette, IN,
who has spent eight field seasons on Seymour Island

ANTARCTIC PENINSULA

What's in a Name?

Because Antarctica has no native inhabitants and was discovered relatively recently, large swaths of territory were often mapped and named all at once. In some cases, groups of associated geographic features were given associated names.

British expeditions in particular used associated place names freely. The UK's Antarctic gazetteer lists 45 name groups comprising a total of 998 names, fully 23% of all official place names in Britain's Antarctic claim.

Names in the South Shetlands, appropriately enough, include 112 commemorating 19th-century sealers and their ships, while 16 of the Melchior Islands are named for **letters of the Greek alphabet** and nine names on Wilkins Coast and Bowman Coast commemorate **gods in Greek mythology**. Fifty-one names on southeastern Alexander Island commemorate **planets, their satellites and discoverers**, and 23 on Rymill Coast are named for **stars and constellations**. Another six on northeastern Alexander Island commemorate **Saxon Kings of England**.

Composers and their works lend their names to 67 features on Alexander Island. Literature is also well represented, with **Chaucer's** *Canterbury Tales* providing appellations for 10 features in the Wauwermans Islands, **Dickens'** *Pickwick Papers* giving 18 in the Pitt Islands, **Homer's** *Iliad* inspiring 15 on Anvers Island, **Kipling's** *The White Seal* supplying five on James Ross Island, **Melville's** *Moby Dick* furnishing 26 along Oscar II Coast, and **Verne's** *20,000 Leagues under the Sea* accounting for five on Pourquoi Pas Island.

Professions associated with Antarctic research get their due in the name game, including **glaciologists** (103 names), **geologists** (29), **Antarctic historians, bibliographers and cartographers** (23), **Antarctic oceanographers and marine biologists** (22), **Antarctic meteorologists and atmospheric physicists** (19) and **glacial geologists** (16), not to mention **biochemists and designers of sledging rations** (12) and **continental drift scientists** (eight).

Other name groups commemorate **pioneers of medicine** (Brabant Island), **pioneers of aviation** (Davis Coast and Danco Coast), **pioneers of photography** (Danco Coast), **pioneers of vitamin research** (Graham Coast), **pioneers of navigation** (Bowman Coast and Falliéres Coast) and **pioneers of ski-mountaineering** (Graham Coast). Even **pioneers of prevention of snow blindness** (Graham Coast and Loubet Coast) and **pioneer designers of oversnow vehicles** (Trinity Peninsula and Nordenskjöld Coast) are not left out.

mountains on the neighboring James Ross and Snow Hill islands. Seymour was discovered in 1843 by James Clark Ross, who gave it the name Cape Seymour after British Rear Admiral George Seymour. Norwegian whaler Captain Carl Anton Larsen determined in 1892-93 that Seymour was in fact an island.

In December 1902 Nordenskjöld, who was wintering at Snow Hill Island directly to the south, made some striking fossil discoveries at Seymour. He found the bones of a giant 1.5m-tall penguin, bolstering earlier fossil finds made by Larsen in 1893 (see the boxed text 'Seymour Island: Antarctica's Rosetta Stone').

At **Penguin Point** (one of three sites in Antarctica with that name) on the south coast, more than 20,000 pairs of Adélies breed.

Argentina's **Vicecomodoro Marambio station**, built in 1969-70, accommodates 22 people in winter and 150 in summer. Operated by the Argentine air force, the station boasts a 1200m airstrip, one of only three functioning hard-rock airstrips in Antarctica. Seymour was chosen as a station location for its large, flat surface. Marambio is primarily a logistics base, where Hercules C-130s can land during most of the year. In summer, Twin Otters and helicopters transport supplies and personnel to outlying stations and camps.

Ronne Ice Shelf

Together with its eastern neighbor, the Filchner Ice Shelf, this large ice shelf forms the Weddell Sea's southern coast. It was discovered by American naval commander Finn Ronne, leader of the private Ronne Antarctic Research Expedition in 1947-48. He named it for his wife, Edith, who accompanied the expedition at the last minute and spent a difficult year at Stonington Island (see Stonington Island, earlier in this chapter).

Germany's summer-only **Filchner station**, established on the Ronne Ice Shelf in 1982, accommodated 12 people. But the calving of an enormous iceberg that took the station with it was observed via satellite on October 13, 1998. Fortunately the station was unstaffed at the time. A 10-day recovery operation in February 1999 removed the sleeping facilities containers, laboratories and 170 tonnes of equipment, using the research vessel *Polarstern*.

Filchner Ice Shelf

German explorer Wilhelm Filchner, who discovered this ice shelf in January 1912, named it after his emperor, Kaiser Wilhelm, who promptly decided that the honor should go to Filchner. Berkner Island, which separates the Filchner from the Ronne Ice Shelf, is often the start of 'trans-Antarctic' ski expeditions.

General Belgrano II station

Argentina's Belgrano II station was built in 1979 and accommodates 18 people year-round. Its predecessor, General Belgrano station, was built as a meteorological center by the Argentine army in 1954-55. It became a scientific station in 1969-70. The original Belgrano station was abandoned in January 1980, having been nearly destroyed by snow buildup.

Halley Station

It was here in 1985 that British scientists first measured the ozone depletion of the Antarctic stratosphere. Their discovery that this critical protection from ultraviolet radiation had been decreasing from 1975 to 1985 made headlines around the world and spurred the international agreement on banning chlorofluorocarbons (CFCs).

Halley was established in 1956 on the Brunt Ice Shelf. It is built on a floating ice shelf and requires renewal every decade or so as it approaches the ice edge. To date, two stations (built in 1966 and 1972) have calved off, one (built in 1982) is about to, one (built in 1989) is buried and closed, and Halley V (built in 1994) remains. The station is built on stilts above the ice surface, which moves approximately 2m per day! The stilts can be jacked up so the station can be maintained 2m above the snow surface.

ANTARCTIC PENINSULA

Ross Sea

Sometimes called the 'Gateway to Antarctica,' the Ross Sea was the path by which explorers of the Heroic Era penetrated the continent. James Clark Ross, for whom the sea is named, pushed through the Ross Sea pack ice in February 1842, becoming the first to reach the Ross Ice Shelf. The Ross Sea has been little visited by tourists – despite its fascinating historic huts – until the last decade.

The first two tourist cruises to the Ross Sea, on the American-chartered Danish ship *Magga Dan* (also the first tour ship to cross the Antarctic Circle), were in 1968. Unfortunately, *Magga Dan* ran aground off Hut Point but was freed two days later with assistance from the US Coast Guard. *Lindblad Explorer* visited the Ross Sea in 1974, '79, '81 and '82, the only tourist vessel to do so during that period. By 1983, other ships had begun visiting infrequently, and in 1992 annual tourist cruises began, with two and sometimes three ships visiting in the same season. Even today, however, the Ross Sea gets nowhere near the traffic that the Peninsula does.

What makes the Ross Sea special are its historic huts, the Dry Valleys and the awe-inspiring Ross Ice Shelf. Nowhere else in Antarctica is there a richer Heroic Era heritage. If the Ross Ice Shelf didn't calve icebergs, there would be even more history to see: Amundsen's base at Framheim in the Bay of Whales, plus all five of Richard E Byrd's Little America stations, covered by drifting snow, have long since gone to sea inside giant tabular bergs.

Only by entering the historic explorers' huts can one truly sense what it must have been like on the early expeditions. In the black-and-white photos of the era, explorers crowd around a table or pack together in groups of bunks. When you step inside Scott's hut at Cape Evans, you suddenly realize: those men didn't crowd together just for the photographer – this was how they lived every day. Note also the rough construction of the huts' interiors. The buildings were only expected to be in use for two or three years, so they were built in a hurry, without having their corners squared off or rough edges sanded.

Today, the huts are all locked. A representative of New Zealand's Antarctic Heritage Trust (see Heritage Antarctica in the Useful Organizations section in the Facts for the Visitor chapter), which maintains and conserves the huts, will monitor your visit. The AHT representatives are not policemen, but caretakers. They're also very good guides, familiar with the huts through their restoration and conservation work, and they can point out things visitors would otherwise miss. One good suggestion, which the guides may share with you: keep backpacks, life jackets, fire extinguishers and other gear at least 10m from all huts so their modern look doesn't spoil your photos.

David Harrowfield's handsome book *Icy Heritage: Historic Sites of the Ross Sea Region*, available from AHT, is fascinating reading. It gives details on 34 sites and includes dozens of photographs, many in color and many published for the first time. The AHT representative on your ship will also distribute brochures about each hut.

CAPE ADARE

This northernmost headland at the entrance to the Ross Sea was named for Britain's Viscount Adare, Member of Parliament for Glamorganshire, by his friend James Clark Ross, who discovered the cape in 1841. Here is Antarctica's largest Adélie rookery – 250,000 nesting pairs – as well as two sets of historic huts. Unfortunately, Cape Adare is an extremely difficult landing, with heavy surf and strong offshore winds usual. Because of the penguin rookery, helicopters cannot be used except very late in the season. Between 200 and 500 people land at Cape Adare annually; the exact number varies with the weather.

One of the first landings on the Antarctic continent – approximately the fifth, in fact

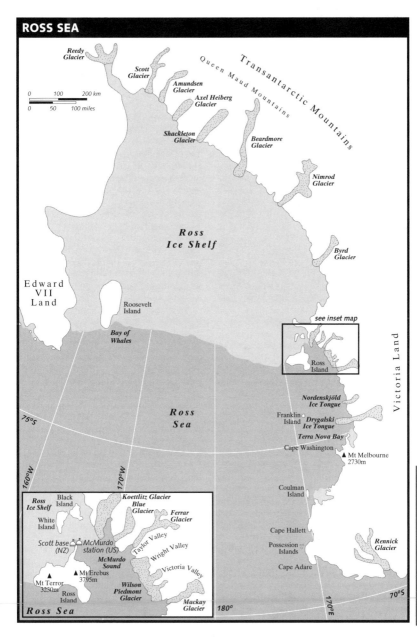

ROSS SEA

Reedy Glacier

Scott Glacier

Amundsen Glacier

Axel Heiberg Glacier

Queen Maud Mountains

Transantarctic Mountains

Shackleton Glacier

Beardmore Glacier

Nimrod Glacier

Ross Ice Shelf

Byrd Glacier

Edward VII Land

Roosevelt Island

see inset map

Bay of Whales

Ross Island

Victoria Land

Nordenskjöld Ice Tongue

Franklin Island

Drygalski Ice Tongue

Terra Nova Bay

Ross Sea

Cape Washington

▲ Mt Melbourne 2730m

75°S

160°W

170°W

Coulman Island

Cape Hallett

Possession Islands

Cape Adare

Rennick Glacier

70°S

170°E

Inset map:

Ross Ice Shelf

Black Island

White Island

Koettlitz Glacier

Blue Glacier

Ferrar Glacier

Scott base (NZ)

McMurdo station (US)

Taylor Valley

Wright Valley

Victoria Valley

McMurdo Sound

▲ Mt Terror 3230m

▲ Mt Erebus 3795m

Ross Island

Wilson Piedmont Glacier

Mackay Glacier

Ross Sea

180°

0   100   200 km

0   50   100 miles

KERRY LORIMER

Penguins at Cape Adare

On the ceiling were hanging guns, fishing tackle, knives, mittens, chains, and odds and ends. The bunks were closed after the plan followed by sailors on board whaling vessels, with a small opening, leaving yourself in an enclosure which can hold its own with our modern coffin; and, like this, it is private; for some minds it is absolutely necessary to be alone, out of sight and entirely undisturbed by others. It was by special recommendation from the doctor that I made this arrangement and found that it answered well.

Borchgrevink's huts have outlasted the 'Northern Party' Huts (see later in this chapter), even though they are 12 years older, because they were built from sturdier materials – interlocking boards of Norwegian spruce.

The accommodation hut, which housed all 10 men, was 5.5m by 6.5m. Upon entering, an office/storeroom is to your left and a darkroom to the right. Both were once lined with furs for insulation. Continuing inside, a stove stands to the left, a table and chairs are on the left past the stove, and five of the double-tiered coffinlike bunks line the remaining wall space. Borchgrevink's was in the back left corner, on top. The hut had papier-mâché insulation and a single double-paned window. Be sure to look for the fine pencil drawing of a young Scandinavian woman on the ceiling above one of the bunks. Despite Borchgrevink's careful planning, the huts were not, apparently, comfortable homes. Australian physicist Louis Bernacchi wrote of leaving Cape Adare: 'May I never pass such another 12 months in similar surroundings and conditions.'

The stores hut, to the west, is now roofless. It contains boxes of ammunition that Borchgrevink brought in case the expedition encountered large predators such as polar bears. (He was the first to winter on the continent.) Coal briquettes and stores barrels litter the ground outside this hut.

Today, the huts are completely surrounded by an Adélie colony, and care must be taken to avoid disturbing the penguins. The Antarctic Heritage Trust, which is working to conserve the huts, reroofed the accommodation hut and installed support braces during the 1989-90 season.

(see the boxed text 'Earliest Antarctic Landings' in the Facts about Antarctica chapter) – occurred here on January 24, 1895, when Captain Leonard Kristensen of the whaling ship *Antarctic* landed a party including expedition leader HJ Bull and Carsten Borchgrevink.

Borchgrevink's Huts

Four years after Kristensen's landing, Borchgrevink was back at Cape Adare as the leader of the *Southern Cross* expedition, which landed here in 1899. Two weeks later, two prefabricated wooden huts had been erected, the remains of which can be seen today on Ridley Beach, which Borchgrevink named for his mother. Here, a party of 10 spent one of the loneliest Antarctic winters ever, being the only humans on the continent, though they had the company of 90 dogs.

When they were occupied, the huts must have felt something like rustic fishing or hunting cabins. In *First on the Antarctic Continent*, Borchgrevink wrote:

To limit the possibility of damage, only four people (including the AHT representative, who will accompany your cruise or come over from Scott Base) are permitted inside the Cape Adare huts at one time. In any case, there's not much room inside. Only 40 people are allowed in the area of the huts at one time.

Hansen's Grave

The *Southern Cross* expedition's biologist, Norwegian Nicolai Hansen, died on October 14, 1899, probably of an intestinal disorder. His deathbed wish was to be buried on the ridge above Ridley Beach, so his expedition mates built a coffin and dynamited a grave up on the stone ridge for the first known human burial on the continent. Dragging Hansen's heavy coffin up the steep incline was a major effort.

When *Southern Cross* returned, a graveside memorial was held and an iron cross and brass plaque were attached to a boulder on the site. Later, when Campbell's men used the ridge as a lookout for *Terra Nova*, one of them spelled out Hansen's name with white quartz pebbles. Visitors to the site in 1982 restored the inscriptions.

The climb up the 350m ridge is very strenuous, and the 1.5km return trip to the grave can take well over two hours even in good weather and when there is little ice. Wind, loose rock, ice and drifting snow can make it impossible. Only very fit and agile people should attempt the climb. Many expedition leaders discourage it altogether in the interests of safety and time.

Access to the grave is by a rough trail at the north end of Ridley Beach. You'll see a large greenish boulder at the top. Keep going but head slightly to the right. The iron cross will come into view atop the boulder.

'Northern Party' Huts

Almost nothing remains of the hut built by Victor Campbell, a member of Scott's *Terra Nova* expedition of 1911-14. Cape Adare's raging winds have pretty well wrecked it. Its ruin lies east of Borchgrevink's huts. The prefabricated building, originally standing 6.4m by 6.1m, once housed six men.

POSSESSION ISLANDS

The group's two main islands, Foyn and Possession, were discovered by James Clark Ross. After pushing *Erebus* and *Terror* through the Ross Sea pack ice to open water, he was surprised to sight land on January 10, 1841. To Ross, this was quite unexpected, because he hoped to sail west from the Ross Sea to the area where the South Magnetic Pole was calculated to lie. In that era, the pole was in fact well inland.

Despite his disappointment, Ross landed a boat two days later on Possession Island and claimed it for Queen Victoria. It was, declared the expedition's 24-year-old naturalist Joseph Dalton Hooker, 'surely the whitest if not the brightest jewel in her crown.' A handsome engraving of the event shows penguins lined up even on the highest ridge of the island. Indeed the Adélies that nest on both islands today climb right to the top of the small hill on Possession.

In 1895, Carsten Borchgrevink found a lichen here, the first plant discovered in Antarctica.

A century later, in February 1995, a small modern wreck of unknown origin was discovered on the western side of Possession Island: a mystery.

CAPE HALLETT

Cape Hallett was discovered by James Clark Ross in 1841 and named for Thomas Hallett, *Erebus*' purser. When a scientific station jointly run by the US and New Zealand was built in January 1957 as part of the IGY, 8000 Adélie penguins were moved to another part of the cape to make way for the base. It accommodated 11 Americans and three New Zealanders for the winter. It operated year-round until 1964, when it became a summer-only facility after fire destroyed the main science building. The station was closed in 1973, and since the late 1970s the disused buildings have gradually been removed to allow the Adélies to return. Cape Hallett can usually only be visited by Zodiac, for helicopter landings are not permitted while the penguins occupy their rookery.

MOUNT MELBOURNE

This 2730m cone is one of the very few volcanoes on the Antarctic continent itself. All the others – including Mt Erebus, Mt Siple and Deception Island – are on off-lying islands. Like the Australian city of the same name, the volcano commemorates Lord Melbourne, British Prime Minister in the 1830s and '40s. Like so many other features in the Ross Sea region, it was discovered in 1841 by James Clark Ross.

TERRA NOVA BAY

This 65km-long bay was discovered by Scott's *Discovery* expedition and named for the relief ship *Terra Nova*. Italy operates the summer-only **Baia Terra Nova station**, which accommodates about 80 people. The station, a collection of blue buildings with orange trim, was established in 1986-87. A sea-ice runway, opened in 1990, is used by about 10 Hercules flights per season.

DRYGALSKI ICE TONGUE

Discovered by Robert Scott in 1902 and named for German explorer Erich von Drygalski, this ice tongue is the seaward extension of the David Glacier. It ranges from 14km to 24km wide and is nearly 50km long.

FRANKLIN ISLAND

The ubiquitous James Clark Ross landed on this 11km-long island on January 27, 1841, claiming the Victoria Land coast for Queen Victoria. He named the island itself for John Franklin, Governor of Van Diemen's Land (Tasmania), who had shown the expedition considerable hospitality when it called in at Hobart in 1840 on the way south. Affixed to only this tiny island in the Antarctic, Franklin's name is writ much larger in the history of the Arctic, where major discoveries were made by explorers searching for his missing ships, *Erebus* and *Terror*, the same vessels Ross used to explore this area. Franklin Island is home to a large Adélie rookery.

NORDENSKJÖLD ICE TONGUE

Discovered by Robert Scott's National Antarctic Expedition of 1901-04, this ice tongue is named for Swedish explorer Otto Nordenskjöld. It is the seaward extension of the Mawson Glacier.

DRY VALLEYS

The Dry Valleys are some of the most unusual places on Earth. No rain has fallen there for at least 2 million years – and possibly as long as 4 million years. They are magnificent spaces: huge, desolate, beautiful. As with other parts of Antarctica, it can be hard to comprehend the Dry Valleys' scale. What appears to be a nearby mountainside or glacier could in fact be several hours' walking distance.

From north to south, the three main Dry Valleys are Victoria, Wright and Taylor. The air is so dry in the Dry Valleys, which cover 3000 sq km, that they have no snow or ice. Such ice-free areas in Antarctica are called oases. The conditions required for an oasis are a retreating or thinning ice sheet, and a large area of exposed rock from which snow becomes ablated due to solar radiation absorbed by the rock. Although these valleys are the most prominent Antarctic oases, there are at least 20 others, including the Bunger, Larsemann and Vestfold Hills of East Antarctica. The Dry Valleys were formed when the terrain uplifted at a faster rate than glaciers could cut their way down through them. Eventually, the glaciers were stopped by high necks at the head of each valley.

Robert Scott accidentally discovered the first of the Dry Valleys in December 1903 and named it for geologist Griffith Taylor. Scott and two others had sledged up the Ferrar Glacier to the East Antarctic Ice Sheet. On their return, they became lost in thick cloud and descended the wrong valley. Because they were equipped for sledging, not hiking, they were forced to turn back after a brief exploration. In *The Voyage of the Discovery*, Scott wrote:

I cannot but think that this valley is a very wonderful place. We have seen today all the indications of colossal ice action and considerable water action, and yet neither of these agents is now at work. It is worthy of record, too, that we have seen no living thing, not even a moss or a lichen; all that we did find, far inland amongst the moraine heaps, was the skeleton of a Weddell seal, and how that came there is beyond guessing. It is certainly a valley of the dead; even the great glacier which once pushed through it has withered away.

Although the valleys appear lifeless, they harbor some of the most remarkable organisms on Earth. In 1976, American biologists discovered algae, bacteria and fungi growing *inside* Dry Valley rocks. This 'endolithic' vegetation grows in the air spaces in porous rocks. Light, carbon dioxide and moisture penetrate the rock, and the rock protects the organisms against excessive drying and harmful radiation. Some of these plants are believed to be 200,000 years old.

A collection of unusual ponds and lakes within the valleys also harbor life (at least some of them do). Although Taylor Valley's Lake Hoare is permanently covered by 5.5m-thick ice, dense mats of blue-green algae carpet its bottom. Lake Bonney, also in Taylor Valley, is freshwater at its surface, and at its bottom is 12 times more saline than the sea. Wright Valley's Lake Vanda, named for a sled dog, is 60m deep and 25°C at its bottom. Antarctica's longest river, the 30km

The Lions of the Dry Valleys

Although the Dry Valleys appear to be a completely lifeless void, there is abundant microfauna in the soils: primarily bacteria, yeasts, protozoa and nematodes. Picture an ecosystem teeming with as much life as Africa's Serengeti Plain – with its vast migrating herds – except invisible to the naked eye.

Nematodes are tiny, elongated, cylindrical worms measuring only about 0.1mm long. In most Dry Valley soils, just two or three nematode species occupy the top of a very simple food chain, leading some people to describe them as the 'lions of the Dry Valleys.' In stark contrast, most soils in temperate regions contain more than 100 species of nematodes and thousands of other organisms in a complex food web.

One nematode species, *Scottnema lindsayae*, has the highest population densities in the Dry Valleys in some of the most extreme soils – those containing virtually no water and high levels of salt. Nematodes need water to move, feed and reproduce, but *Scottnema* survives the winter in dry saline soils by coiling up into a state of reversible dormancy called anhydrobiosis (literally 'life without water'). Individuals can remain dormant for years – and then become active within minutes of getting wet. Although *Scottnema*'s longevity is not known, some species of nematodes have been in anhydrobiosis for as long as 60 years and have then become active again.

'Life without water' offers another advantage for this nematode: dispersal. Even in optimum conditions, nematodes travel only centimeters per year. By drying out like a tiny speck of dust, *Scottnema* can be carried many kilometers by the wind. It may be particularly well adapted to this form of dispersal, as it is smaller and lighter than the other species of nematodes in the Dry Valleys. Genetic analyses of the different populations throughout the region suggest that *Scottnema* can also adapt to 'local scale' variations in soils and environmental conditions.

These nematodes and their habitats are extremely vulnerable to human influence. Their numbers are reduced by one-third in soil on paths that are moderately trampled by people. Human activities – and disturbance to soils – in the Antarctic will undoubtedly increase. As more people enter the Dry Valleys, the fragile soil ecosystem will experience species loss, erosion and compaction. Additionally, the movement of soil and associated organisms will increase the rates of dispersal and introductions of new organisms into the remote regions, as has occurred in temperate ecosystems.

– Dr Diana Wall,
professor and director of the Natural Resource Ecology Laboratory (NREL) at Colorado State University, who has spent 11 field seasons in the Dry Valleys studying nematodes
– Dr Andy Parsons,
research associate at NREL, who has spent four seasons in the Dry Valleys

ROSS SEA

melt water stream called the Onyx River, flows into Lake Vanda from the glacier at the end of the valley. Don Juan Pond, also in Wright Valley, is only 10cm deep. It is the most saline lake in Antarctica, so salty that it never freezes – even at -51°C. White crusts of calcium salt crystals and of a rare mineral called antarcticite precipitate on Don Juan Pond's shores.

Another reason the Dry Valleys appear so otherworldly is the bizarre, sculptured form of the rocks. These 'ventifacts' are highly polished on their windward surfaces. Some have been carved by the wind into pocked boulders or thin, delicate wafers. Others fit into your hand so well that they resemble smoothly ground primitive tools. Although they feel good to pick up, the ventifacts should not be removed. As one scientist familiar with the Dry Valleys puts it: 'You either understand the ethics of such a place, or you don't.'

Mummified seals such as those seen by Scott are not uncommon in the Dry Valleys, though most appear to be crabeaters, not Weddells. They have been found as far as 40km inland, a remarkable journey for an animal as awkward on land as a seal. Given the number of seals, it's not difficult to believe that one or two per year might wander into the valleys and get lost. The occasional carcass of a disoriented Adélie has also been found in the Dry Valleys, as far as 50km from the sea. The remains of both seals and penguins become freeze-dried by the extreme aridity of the valleys, then eroded by the scouring wind, just like the ventifacts.

Scientists believe the Dry Valleys are the nearest equivalent on Earth to the terrain of Mars. NASA performed extensive research here from 1974 to 1976 before sending the Viking Lander spacecraft to Mars.

In addition to Victoria, Wright and Taylor valleys, several smaller valleys are also part of the region. Interestingly, the Americans call them the 'McMurdo Dry Valleys,' while the British prefer the 'Victoria Land Dry Valleys.' Most people just call them the 'Dry Valleys.' Tourists generally fly by helicopter into Taylor Valley, the most accessible from the Ross Sea. Large sections of the others

are protected areas under the Antarctic Treaty, and access is restricted or forbidden, even to scientists.

ROSS ISLAND

Both New Zealand and the US have their principal Antarctic stations on Ross Island. As part of NZ's Ross Dependency territorial claim, Ross Island is – as the joke goes – the only island in New Zealand without sheep. It's also the location of the three most famous historic huts.

Scott Base

New Zealand's Scott base is located at Pram Point, on the southeast side of Hut Point Peninsula. Pram Point was named by Scott's *Discovery* expedition because getting from there to the Ross Ice Shelf in summer requires a pram, or small boat.

An attractive collection of lime-green buildings, which accommodates 11 winterers and up to 70 people in summer, Scott base looks trim and tidy compared to McMurdo's 'urban sprawl.'

Tourists can easily overwhelm a smaller Antarctic station such as Scott base, where the staff must dedicate itself to accommodating a ship visit. Still, the New Zealanders are very friendly. Between 200 and 300 people visit annually.

Although there are no mail facilities at Scott base, phone calls can be made using the two **public telephones** in the foyer of the Command Centre. You can use phone cards purchased in the base shop, call collect or use a credit card. The shop accepts NZ and US currencies, Visa, Mastercard and American Express.

McMurdo Station

The US's McMurdo station is Antarctica's largest. It accommodates 1200 people in summer and 200 in winter. The station covers nearly 4 sq km between Hut Point and Observation Hill and has more than 100 buildings. McMurdo's structures are built on short stilts, and water, sewer, telephone and power lines all run aboveground.

The sprawling, industrial-looking station can be a shocking sight after Antarctica's clean white icebergs, bare mountains and scarce signs of human life. But in the past decade the US has actually made enormous strides in decreasing McMurdo's environmental impact. Before 1990, the station's accumulated trash – including junked vehicles, empty fuel barrels and scrap metal – was hauled out onto the sea ice each spring before the annual breakup. Today, this practice is a thing of the past.

Aluminum, clothing, construction debris, food waste, hazardous waste, heavy metals, light metals, magazines, newspapers, packaging, plastics, white paper and wood, which formerly would have been discarded, are now all recycled. Still, in the summer when the station's dusty ground mixes with melt water, the station resembles a mining town of the Old West. Some residents refer to it as 'McMuddo' or 'McMudhole.'

McMurdo was established in January 1956. The station takes its name from McMurdo Sound, which James Clark Ross named in 1841 after Lieutenant Archibald McMurdo of the ship *Terror*. The station was originally going to be at Cape Evans, but the death of a tractor driver whose Caterpillar D8 fell through the sea ice caused the

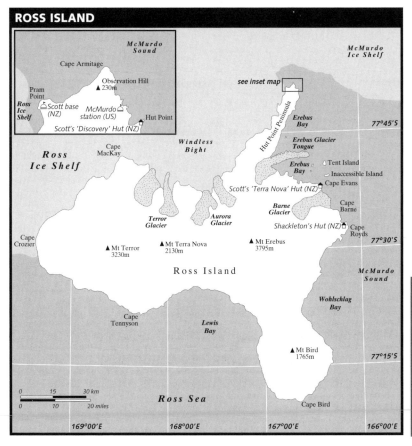

station's builders to reconsider their choice. The settlement was big right from the start: 93 men wintered over the first year.

Today, McMurdo is both a logistics center and Antarctica's premier scientific base. Researchers are flown to nearby field camps via helicopter and to remote field camps and the South Pole via ski-equipped LC-130 Hercules aircraft.

'You will find,' says a welcoming handbook issued to all new residents, 'that McMurdo Station resembles an urban center in its population diversity and hectic pace.' Called MacTown (or just 'Town') by its residents, the station has the feel of a bustling village – with all of the problems and benefits of a small town. The station's oldest section is called 'Downtown McMurdo' or 'the historic district.' Nearly 80 vehicles (excluding heavy equipment) roll through its streets, though not very quickly: The station speed limit is 30 km/h.

Compared to the modest facilities at many other Antarctic stations, McMurdo is almost overwhelming. It has its own hospital, church, post office (for residents only), library, barbershop, video store and automatic teller machines (ATMs). There is a coffee shop, as well as two clubs: the Erebus Club (the former enlisted-men's club from McMurdo's US Navy days) and Gallagher's Pub (formerly called the Southern Exposure but renamed to commemorate a McMurdo resident who died in 1997). The base has a 24-hour shuttle bus to various parts of McMurdo as well as Scott base. It is also home to a seawater reverse-osmosis desalination plant, video teleconferencing facilities, a diving recompression chamber, a 220m-long Ice Pier, a fuel tank farm with a total capacity of 30 million litres and a hydroponics greenhouse.

McMurdo once also boasted the continent's only large nuclear power plant, a 1.8 megawatt experimental reactor known colloquially as 'Nukey Poo.' It was deployed on Observation Hill in December 1961 and went on-line in March 1962. Unfortunately, the reactor experienced numerous problems, and in 1972, faced with a large repair bill, the US decided to shut it down. Eventually, some 10,000 tonnes of radioactively contaminated soil and rock were removed from the site, though some scientists say that the rock in that area was naturally radioactive.

McMurdo housing is allocated through a points system, in which position and previous months on The Ice determine your berth. Scientists and others 'moving frequently between the field and town' will probably bunk in one of the large dorms overlooking the helicopter pad. Two of these dorms are picturesquely named the 'Hotel California' and the 'Mammoth Mountain Inn.' There are newer dorms that overlook the Ice Pier.

The station's newspaper, the *Antarctic Sun*, is published weekly during the summer. There's also 'The Scroll,' a televised list of the day's activities, announcements, weather information, movie schedules and other station news, which can be viewed on one of the station's several dozen TVs. Other media include Radio McMurdo (104.5 on your FM dial), and two TV broadcast channels, 8 and 13.

Recreation opportunities for station personnel abound: McMurdo offers aerobics, basketball, bingo, bowling, chili cook-offs, country dancing, darts, soccer, softball, table tennis, tae kwon do, volleyball and (in good weather) bicycle rental (US$5 a day). For golfers, there's the McMurdo Open tournament. For runners, there are several races: the 5km Run Across Ross Island, the McMurdo Midsummer Midnight Mile and the 7.25km Scott's Hut race.

There are Sunday Science Lectures, computer classes, cardiopulmonary resuscitation (CPR) training, Alcoholics Anonymous meetings, Town Choir rehearsals, the Ross Island Drama Festival, the Ross Island Art Show, the 'Icestock' rock and comedy festival, meetings of the McMurdo Historical Society and even occasional tours of Scott's *Discovery* Hut. Also available are outings to breathtakingly beautiful ice caves formed during the summer by wave action eroding part of the Erebus Glacier Tongue, made accessible by winter sea ice. Station residents may also win a lottery to go on a very special vacation from McMurdo by taking a space-available flight to South Pole station, a

McMURDO STATION

1 Scott's 'Discovery' Hut
2 Frozen Food Storage
3 Galley, Accommodation,
   Store, Laundry, Library
4 Power Plant
5 Water Plant
6 Chapel of the Snows
7 Coffee House
8 Playhouse
9 Gallagher's Pub
10 Erebus Club
11 Medical Building
12 Firehouse &
    Telephone Exchange
13 Crary Laboratory
14 National Science
    Foundation Chalet
15 Gymnasium

········ Walking Tour

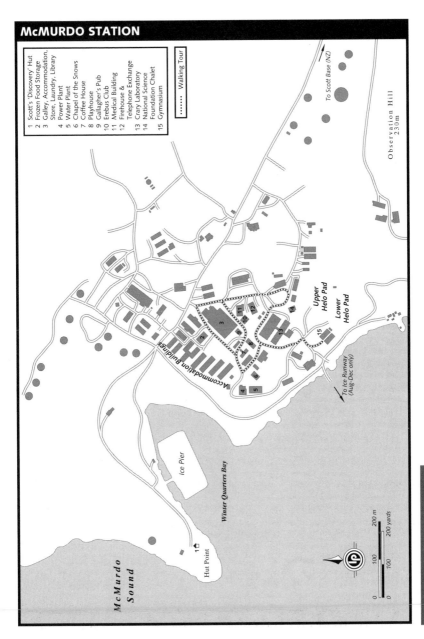

To Scott Base (NZ)

Observation Hill
230m

Upper
Helo Pad

Lower
Helo Pad

Accommodation Buildings

To Ice Runway
(Aug-Dec only)

Ice Pier

Winter Quarters Bay

McMurdo
Sound

Hut Point

0   100   200 m
0   100   200 yards

unique reward that is known locally as a 'sleigh ride.'

McMurdo is served by three different airport facilities, each operating at different times of the year. In the spring, a landing field is laid out on the annual sea ice of McMurdo Sound for use by wheeled aircraft flights in October, November and early December. There is one local hazard found at almost no other airfield in the world: penguins and seals that occasionally wander across the ice runway, causing all flights to be canceled. Later in December, as summer temperatures weaken the sea ice, flight operations shift to **Williams Field**, a 3000m skiway on the Ross Ice Shelf. Also known as Willy Field or just plain 'Willy,' it was named for Richard T Williams, who died during Operation Deep Freeze I (1955-56) when his 30-tonne tractor broke through sea ice off Cape Royds. Williams Field is located 16km from the station. This being McMurdo, there's an

Diving in McMurdo Sound

I'm finning slowly over the bottom, nearly 40m down. It's early spring and far overhead the sea surface is a solid, 2m-thick sheet of ice. In the distance, I can clearly see our safety line with its flashing strobe lights. It marks the manmade hole that is our only access to the surface.

Ahead of me, my dive partner is a shadow in the darkness. The sea ice permits only 1% of the sunlight that falls upon it to penetrate to the water below. Yet that water is so clear that even in the dim light the visibility is astounding – perhaps 245m. Strange, irregular shapes project upward from the dull, blue-brown seafloor. When I snap on my underwater light, the colors leap out – bright reds, vibrant greens, luminescent yellows, glaring whites.

The bottom is literally covered with a garden of life. Most of the conspicuous animals are sponges, in a multitude of shapes and colors. A yellow rope sponge thrusts its slim fingers toward the sky. A white volcano sponge the size of an armchair sits at a curious angle, its single giant osculum gaping like an open mouth. A large colony of pink staghorn sponge resembles a pile of discarded elk antlers.

I'm diving in the frigid waters of McMurdo Sound as part of a team of scientists trying to unravel the mysteries of this little-understood environment. The richness and diversity of the seafloor community we've found is mind-boggling: the bottom is as thick with living creatures as some tropical reefs.

Getting into the water wasn't easy, though. We used a diesel-powered auger to drill a 1.25m diameter hole through the ice, then positioned a mobile hut over it to protect us from blizzards and bitter cold while we prepared to dive.

Scuba diving in Antarctica presents other dangers, too. Unprotected exposure to the water will cause severe hypothermia in minutes, so even a minor equipment malfunction can become life-threatening. If a regulator freezes up or a dry suit zipper fails, a diver may have only a few moments to get to the dive hole. For this reason, our dives are limited to 40m or less. Deeper dives frequently require decompression stops. In case of an equipment failure, that could force us to choose between hypothermia and the bends.

One reason for the density and diversity of the creatures here is the remarkable stability of the marine environment, thanks to two main factors. First, the massive Ross Ice Shelf keeps the temperature in McMurdo Sound from fluctuating more than 0.2° C. Second, every year with unerring predictability, the seafloor here is bathed with a rich rain of food. By mid-December, the height of the Antarctic summer, the midnight sun has fueled a stupendous growth of plankton in the nutrient-rich ocean. A southerly current carries this plankton under the ice, where it drifts down to nourish the hundreds of species of sponges and other suspension feeders that live on the sea bottom.

airport bus to transport the large number of new arrivals to the station. Huge TerraBus vehicles carry passengers to the station over a snow road called Antarctic 1. A third airfield, the Pegasus blue ice runway (named for Pegasus, a US Navy C-121 Super Constellation that crashed nearby during the 1970-71 season; everyone aboard survived the crash, and the wrecked plane is still there today) is about 45 minutes' drive from McMurdo. It was completed in 1992 and can be used nearly year-round, except during the height of the summer, when warm temperatures cause pitting and melting of the surface.

About 250 flights from Christchurch land at McMurdo each year, using C-130 Hercules, C-5 Galaxies, C-141 Starlifters and LC-130 ski-equipped Hercules. While most flights occur between early October and late February, some land in late August during the latter part of the austral winter, in an operation called 'Winfly,' or Winter Fly-In.

Diving in McMurdo Sound

We often see Weddell seals – they swim slowly by, studying us from a safe distance and perhaps wondering what we odd, bubbling creatures are. Leopard seals, fortunately for me, cannot survive under the fast ice. They're very aggressive, fear only orcas, and have been known to harass divers.

I peer down the steeply sloping bottom into the depths. Between my position here at the 40m diving limit and about 80m, where the dim light disappears and everything fades to black, I see an endless forest of sponges. Some look big even from this distance, and so must be huge. Remotely operated vehicles (ROVs) sent into these depths of more than 200m have brought back videos of an incredible kingdom. Giant, knobby vase sponges litter the stygian depths like the trunks of an ancient forest. Strange creatures abound, some of which have not yet even been named: 2m-long white stalks, strange purple mollusks, orange blobs on sticks.

The seafloor around Ross Island is separated into three distinct zones. Sponges and accompanying organisms rule the depths below 30m. At 30m, the sponge community abruptly gives way to bare rock and beds of frilly soft corals and orange sea anemones. Above 15m, I find only motile animals such as common red sea stars, science-fiction-ugly crustaceans called giant isopods, and slimy, meter-long nemertean worms.

Most benthic ecologists believe that the cause of this zonation is the annual formation of anchor ice each spring. If anything gives this environment an otherworldly aspect, it is the anchor ice. The water in McMurdo Sound is the coldest liquid water on Earth. At -1.8° C, it cannot get much colder and remain liquid. In the spring, however, the pattern of currents occasionally shifts to allow supercooled water to flow north from deep under the Ross Ice Shelf. This water is at -1.9° C and, amazingly, that mere 0.1° C has a profound effect on the surrounding water. Tiny ice crystals begin to form, shimmering like a million diamonds in the faint light. On the sea bottom, ice begins to crystallize on rocks, and even on some unfortunate animals. This ice quickly grows into a maze of interlocking plates 20cm to 25cm across. Soon it covers the seafloor in the shallows, forming a glittering, brittle blanket.

On occasion, the mass of ice will grow so large that the item to which it is attached is no longer heavy enough to keep it down. Like a hot-air balloon, the ice and its cargo float up and stick to the underside of the sea ice, ultimately freezing in. When this happens to either an urchin or sea star, the animal often does not survive. It's easy to see why sponges and soft corals cannot grow in the shallow water: any settling larvae are scoured off by the anchor ice.

I fin over this surreal coating of ice on my way back to the dive hole. For a moment it feels as though I'm in an underwater crystal cave, sandwiched top and bottom by glittering ice. It's a sight every bit as wonderful and mysterious as the sponge garden I left behind in the depths.

– Jim Mastro,
who has made 250 dives in Antarctic waters

ROSS SEA

Code of Conduct for Visiting Historic Antarctic Huts

These guidelines have been established to minimize the deterioration and damage that can result from the intrusion of visitors. Please observe this code at all times.

• Reduce floor abrasion. Thoroughly clean grit and scoria, ice and snow, from boots before entering.
• Salt particles accelerate corrosion of metal objects. Remove any clothing wetted by seawater, and any sea ice crystals from boots.
• Create an airlock when entering. Close exterior doors before opening interior doors and moving into huts.
• Do not handle or remove any items or furniture in the huts.
• When moving around the sites, take great care not to tread on any items. Many may be partially covered by snow. Do not disturb or remove anything from around the huts.
• Smoking in or around the huts is strictly forbidden.
• All visitors should record their names in the book.
• Flash photography *is* permitted inside the huts.

– from the Antarctic Heritage Trust

Until recently, midwinter airdrops of mail and supplies were made in June, but funding for the flight was cut for the 1996 season. (LC-130s, the workhorses of the US Antarctic Program, cost US$3500 per hour to operate.)

Tourists, of course, will only glimpse a tiny slice of the station's busy life, including the **Chapel of the Snows**, a 64-seat house of worship with a unique penguin motif stained-glass window and the station's only organ. It's the third chapel raised at McMurdo; the first two were destroyed by fire.

Crary Laboratory This science laboratory, completed in 1991, is named for Albert P Crary, a geophysicist and glaciologist who was the first to visit both the North and South Poles. The 4300 sq meter building houses work space for biological studies, Earth science and atmospheric science. The lab's equipment is state-of-the-art, with facilities as good as or better than those found at major research universities. It's a bit disconcerting to go straight from a penguin rookery to a place where scientists have digital card keys to their offices, but then again, this is the Big City! The Crary Lab also has a darkroom, freezers for processing

ice cores, an electronics workshop, a library, a seismic observatory that monitors Mt Erebus (it's a volcano after all) and three large aquariums, often shown to tourists, filled with McMurdo Sound marine life. The street in front of the Crary Lab is called Beeker St. Although 'beaker' is a nickname for scientists, the spelling on the street sign leads one to believe it's a clever pun on Bleecker St in New York City's Greenwich Village – or else a simple misspelling.

Ships Store No, this isn't on a ship, but since the Navy used to run it, this is the ship's store nevertheless. They sell postcards, calendars, batteries, ceramic sculptures, T-shirts, sweatshirts and other souvenirs. Liquor and cigarette prices are quite reasonable, at least compared to those aboard ship, but the clerks might not sell these items to you, as that depletes the station stock. Note that the US Antarctic Program does not carry tourist mail on its ships or aircraft, so you can't send letters or postcards from McMurdo.

Scott's *Discovery* Hut
Robert Scott's National Antarctic Expedition built this hut in February 1902. The prefabricated building, purchased in Australia,

Dusk, Antarctic Peninsula: long summer sunsets last for hours

Purposeful penguins waddling on in single file

US Geological Survey research team's polar pyramid tent during a blizzard

Kapitan Khlebnikov pushing through heavy pack ice in the northern Ross Sea

is of a type still found in rural Australia, with a wide overhanging veranda on three sides. Despite the building's expense and the effort required to erect it, Scott's men never used it for accommodation, since it was difficult to heat efficiently. Instead it was used for storage, repair work and as an entertainment center, when it was called 'The Royal Terror Theatre.'

In fact, the *Discovery* Hut was used more heavily by several expeditions that followed *Discovery*. Shackleton's *Nimrod* expedition, based at Cape Royds, found it a convenient en route shelter during sledge trips to and from the Ross Ice Shelf in 1908. Scott's *Terra Nova* expedition also used it in 1911 for the same purpose.

The Ross Sea party of Shackleton's ill-fated Imperial Trans-Antarctic Expedition benefited most from the hut. Their arduous task was to lay depots for the party crossing the continent from the Weddell Sea side to use on the second half of their journey. Unfortunately, *Endurance* was crushed and sunk by the Weddell Sea ice, so the depots were never used (see the story of *Endurance* in the Facts about Antarctica chapter). The Ross Sea party, meanwhile, holed up in the hut in 1915 and again in 1916. Unfortunately, the men were unaware of vast quantities of stores buried in the ice that had accumulated in the hut, and nearly starved – despite the hidden bounty lying literally underfoot. But they did find some food, cigars, Crème de Menthe, sleeping bags and a pair of long underwear. The interior of the hut is soot-blackened from the smoky blubber stove they used to try to stay warm.

Because it is the hut closest to McMurdo station and has received the most visitors (and souveniring) over the years, the *Discovery* Hut is the least interesting of the three Ross Island historic sites. The Antarctic Heritage Trust estimates that 1000 people visit the hut each year.

There are few artifacts in the dingy hut, which smells strongly of burnt seal blubber. Stores line the right-hand wall as you enter. The central area is occupied by a stove, piles of provisions and a sleeping platform. Much of the hut feels empty. A square hole in the floor was used for pendulum experiments. A mummified seal lies on the open southern veranda, its back covered in liquefying blubber. The hut sharply conveys the hardships endured by the early explorers.

For conservation purposes, only eight people are permitted inside the hut at the same time. Only 40 people are allowed in the area of the hut at one time. Make sure you sign the visitor's book, which helps Antarctic Heritage Trust maintain its records.

Vince's Cross

About 100m from the *Discovery* Hut, an oak cross stands as an enduring memorial to Able Seaman George T Vince, who fell to his death over an ice cliff into McMurdo Sound on March 11, 1902.

Observation Hill

The 3.5m cross surmounting this 230m volcanic cone was raised in memory of the five men who perished on the return from the South Pole: Henry Bowers, Edgar Evans, Laurence Oates, Robert Scott and Edward Wilson. Its fading inscription is the closing line from Tennyson's poem *Ulysses* – 'To strive, to seek, to find, and not to yield.' Erected on January 20, 1913, the cross has been blown over by storms at least twice. At the last re-erection, in January 1994, it was placed in a concrete base.

Cape Evans

In stark contrast to the *Discovery* Hut, Scott's Hut from the *Terra Nova* expedition is filled with an incredible feeling of history. Erected in January 1911 at the place Scott named Cape Evans after his second-in-command, Edward Evans, the prefabricated hut is 14.6m long and 7.3m wide. It accommodated 25 men in fairly crowded conditions, though it is the largest of the three historic huts on Ross Island. It must have been chilly inside, despite the insulation of seaweed sewn into jute bags.

This is the real thing, what you came for, the reason you paid thousands of dollars and suffered through long days of seasickness. Here, dog skeletons bleach on the sand in the Antarctic sun, chiding memento mori of

ROSS SEA

Antarctica during the 'Age of Reptiles'

The first Antarctic terrestrial vertebrate fossil was discovered in 1967. Since the finding of that single jaw fragment in Early Triassic age sediments (245 million years old) near the Beardmore Glacier, four different Mesozoic terrestrial vertebrate assemblages – including several species each – have been collected from Antarctica.

The Early Triassic assemblage is dominated by synapsids, an extinct group of animals that links primitive reptiles to mammals. Perhaps the best known member of this assemblage is *Lystrosaurus*, a small herbivore also found on most of the other southern continents and in China and Russia. Its discovery in Antarctica in the early 1970s added strong support to the theory of plate tectonics.

In 1985 a vertebrate community of Middle Triassic age (235-240 million years old) was found near the first Early Triassic *Lystrosaurus* site in the central Transantarctic Mountains. This assemblage is dominated by larger synapsids than those from the Early Triassic and includes the wolf-sized carnivore *Cynognathus*. At least two large capitosaurids with skulls nearly a meter long also occurred in the Middle Triassic. Capitosaurs were semiaquatic and, although they resemble very large crocodiles, are actually amphibians, distant relatives of frogs and salamanders.

The first discoveries of Antarctic dinosaurs were made during the late 1980s in Late Cretaceous (65-70 million years old) deposits on James Ross and Vega islands. These remains included partial skeletons of a nodosaurid ankylosaur (armored dinosaur) and a hypsilophodontid (a small herbivorous ornithopod dinosaur). A few small limb pieces have also been referred to the Theropoda (carnivorous dinosaurs). In 1998, a single tooth from a hadrosaur ('duck-billed' dinosaur) was collected from the same area on James Ross Island. It is the first hadrosaur found in Antarctica; others are known from South America, North America and Eurasia.

A fourth terrestrial vertebrate community was found in 1990, again near the Beardmore Glacier. This Early Jurassic (190-200 million years old) assemblage includes the nearly 7m-long bipedal carnivorous dinosaur, *Cryolophosaurus* ('frozen-crested reptile'). Represented by the most complete dinosaur skeleton known from Antarctica, Cryolophosaurus is also the only dinosaur

Scott's death march from the Pole. Inside the hut, unquiet ghosts glide soundlessly through memories of sledging pennants, the rustle of pony harnesses and a sighing wind. It's an absolutely amazing and eerie feeling to stand at the head of the wardroom table and recall the famous photo of Scott's final birthday party, with the men gathered around the huge meal spread out before them, and their banners hanging behind. You definitely feel their ghostly presence! Between 700 and 800 people land at Cape Evans each year, making it the most frequently visited Ross Sea tourist site.

Located on the beach at what Scott called Home Beach, the hut stands close to the shore of McMurdo Sound. A long, narrow building (the latrines, with separate facilities for officers and men) stands in front of the hut.

After Scott's last expedition, 10 members of the Ross Sea Party of Shackleton's Imperial Trans Antarctic Expedition were stranded here in May 1915, when their ship *Aurora* was blown from its moorings. The men passed a very difficult 20 months before *Aurora* was able to return.

Entering the hut, you pass through an outer porch area. To the left are the stables on the hut's beachfront side. Still in the porch today are a box of penguin eggs, big piles of suppurating seal blubber, lots of shovels and implements hanging on the walls, and geologist Griffith Taylor's bicycle.

Inside the hut proper, your eyes will take a while to adjust to the half-light. Stand quietly for a moment and take it all in. You're standing in what the expedition called the mess deck. In keeping with Royal Navy practice, Scott segregated expedition

Antarctica during the 'Age of Reptiles'

known to be unique to the continent (the Cretaceous dinosaurs are too incomplete to determine whether or not they represent new genera). The Latin term 'loph' was included in the generic name *Cryolophosaurus* because of a unique bony display crest on the top of the head above the eyes. The Latin 'cryo' was included because although Antarctica wasn't frozen when the dinosaur lived there, we nearly froze to death while collecting it.

Parts of a prosauropod dinosaur were found with the skeleton of *Cryolophosaurus*. In fact, ribs of the prosauropod were in the mouth of the cryolophosaur when it died, leading to the assumption that the carnivore may have choked to death on its last meal. Prosauropods were smaller (7.5m-long) predecessors to the well-known large sauropods *(Apatosaurus, Brachiosaurus)* of the later Jurassic.

After the cryolophosaur died along an Antarctic riverbank 200 million years ago, smaller carnivorous theropods scavenged the skeleton. Gnaw marks were found on some of the bones and small broken theropod teeth were collected nearby. Other members of the Jurassic fauna are represented by single elements, including a tooth from a rodentlike synapsid and the upper arm of a small pterosaur (flying reptile).

These vertebrate assemblages suggest that Antarctic climates were relatively mild during the Mesozoic and also that connections once existed between Antarctica and the other southern continents. Since Antarctica was part of the supercontinent Gondwana for much of the Mesozoic, it was also farther north, which partially explains the milder climate. During the Triassic and Jurassic, however, the paleolatitude of the continent was still fairly high, probably between 65° and 70° south. Although some of the larger animals may have migrated north during the winter months, the ectothermic ('cold-blooded') semiaquatic amphibians would have been restricted to limited watersheds, suggesting that ice-free rivers and lakes existed all year.

– Dr William R Hammer,
Fritiof Fryxell professor and chair of the department of Geology at Augustana College
in Rock Island, IL, who discovered *Cryolophosaurus* with William Hickerson

members into officers and men. In the mess deck lived Edgar Evans, Crean, Keohane, Ford, Omelchenko, Gerov, Clissold, Lashly and Hooper. To the right as you enter the hut is the galley with a large stove.

Continuing farther into the hut, past what was once a dividing wall made out of packing cases, you're in the wardroom. Straight in back is the darkroom and Ponting's bunk. To the right is the laboratory, along with Wright's and Simpson's bunks. To the left of the wardroom table from front to back of their alcove were: Bowers (top bunk) and Cherry-Garrard; Oates (no bunk beneath); and Mears (top) and Atkinson. To the right of the wardroom table were (front to back): Gran (top bunk) and Taylor; a small geology lab; Debenham; and Nelson (top bunk) and Day. A special note about Day's bunk: it was used by Dick Richards during the Ross Sea

Party's occupation of the hut. Look for the depressing notation he made on his bunk wall after three of the party's members had died:

RW Richards August 14th, 1916

> Losses to date--
> Hayward
> Mack
> Smith

The back left corner of the hut is the sanctum sanctorum. Scott's bunk, to the left, is separated from the bunks of Wilson and Edward Evans by a work table covered with an open book and a fading stuffed emperor penguin.

Throughout the hut are provisions and photographic supplies. There's a strong, not unpleasant musty smell, like that of dusty old books and pony straw. Boxes hold candles

ROSS SEA

Polar Posts: A Brief History of Antarctic Philately

Antarctic philately began at the start of the Heroic Age of Antarctic exploration. Many early expeditions issued picture postcards, both for promotion and for their members' use. Expedition organizers found that the public greatly enjoyed these cards, and it was not long before series of them were being issued to raise funds. The earliest cards showing Antarctic scenes come from the Belgian Antarctic Expedition of 1897-1899.

The first item of mail posted from the Antarctic with a distinctive Antarctic postmark came from the 1902-04 Scottish National Antarctic Expedition. A postcard with an Argentine postmark from February 20, 1904 reading 'Orcades Del Sud/Districto 24 (Gallenos)' bears the signatures of 13 expedition members. It was sold at auction in New Zealand in 1998 for a record US$4940.

The first Antarctic postage stamp was issued on January 15, 1908, during Shackleton's Nimrod expedition. The New Zealand one penny stamp, specially overprinted with the words 'King Edward VII Land,' was first used aboard *Nimrod* just south of the Antarctic Circle when the mail was transferred to the accompanying *Koonya*, which was returning to New Zealand. This mail contained only 131 envelopes, mostly first-day covers addressed to expedition sponsors and friends in the UK.

Scott's *Terra Nova* expedition used a penny stamp and a half-penny stamp, each overprinted 'Victoria Land.' Today the half-penny is one of the rarest Antarctic stamps, selling for US$800 in perfect condition. Filchner's 1911 German South Polar Expedition produced Antarctica's first local post, or 'cinderella,' stamp: a red stamp showing the expedition vessel *Deutschland*.

Today Antarctic expeditions get requests from philatelists around the world for mail bearing expedition cachets, postmarks or signatures of expedition members. Some expeditions have quite ornate rubber-stamped cachets that are highly sought after by collectors, especially if the expedition is a small one.

When collecting modern Antarctic covers, the most important thing to consider is, has the item actually been to the Antarctic? A first-day cover of Antarctic stamps can be postmarked in Moscow or Santiago and can give the appearance of being an Antarctic cover. Careful reading of the date-stamp, however, is required to determine the cover's origins. The best covers have proof of Antarctic origins, such as a postmark applied at an Antarctic station.

In recent years, a number of interesting events have been recorded with Antarctic expedition covers. Covers exist from the Russian research vessel *Mikhail Somov*, which was trapped in the ice for five months in 1985. The private expedition vessel *Southern Quest* was crushed by ice and sunk in the Ross Sea in 1986. Fortunately, the crew members were safely rescued – along with their mail, which is now prized by the receivers. The Air New Zealand flight that crashed into Mt. Erebus in 1979, killing all 257 people aboard, also carried a small number of commemorative covers. Although many auction houses and dealers decline to handle these covers, those that have reached the market have sold for around US$1000.

In 1998, the US Postal Service provided collectors with another desirable item, a new postmark at McMurdo with Antarctica misspelled as 'Antartica.' It wasn't long before the authorities realized they had left the 'c' out, and the datestamp was replaced at the start of the 1998-99 summer season.

– Steven McLachlan,
professional philatelist and owner of Shades Stamp Shop in Christchurch

that could be used today without problem. The name brands on many of the supplies are still familiar, with label designs that are hardly changed even now. Be sure to look for the telephone, which connected this hut with the *Discovery* Hut using bare wire laid across the sea ice.

Only 12 people are permitted inside the Cape Evans hut at one time, and only 40 people are allowed ashore at once.

Other Sites at Cape Evans

During the site's occupation by the Ross Sea Party of Shackleton's Imperial Trans Antarctic Expedition, three of the party's members perished while returning from a trip laying depots for the Weddell Sea party, which they were expecting to arrive from across the continent. The Rev Arnold Spencer-Smith died of scurvy on March 9, 1916, and two others, Aeneas Mackintosh and Victor Hayward, vanished in a blizzard while walking on thin sea ice on May 8, 1916. They are commemorated by the **Cross on Wind Vane Hill**. Two of *Aurora*'s **anchors** remain embedded in the sand on Home Beach, one directly in front of the hut, the other 25m north of it.

The environmental organization Greenpeace had a year-round base at Cape Evans between 1987 and 1982. It was dismantled and removed in 1991-92. A rather difficult to find **Greenpeace Base Plaque** is now all that marks the site. You need to walk north up the beach to find it.

Cape Royds

Besides being the home of Shackleton's *Nimrod* expedition, Cape Royds also harbors a rookery of 3500 pairs of Adélies. The cape was named by Robert Scott for *Discovery*'s meteorologist, Charles Royds. The small pond in front of the hut is called Pony Lake, because the expedition kept its ponies tethered nearby.

Shackleton erected his hut here in February 1908. Unlike the class-minded Scott, he imposed no division between officers and men at Cape Royds, though as 'The Boss' he did invoke executive privilege to give himself a private room near the hut's front door. Fifteen men lived in the hut, which is much smaller than Scott's at Cape Evans.

The feeling inside is still very ghostly, though perhaps not as eerie as Cape Evans with its lingering sense of tragedy. All of Shackleton's men, after all, left here alive. Apparently they did so in a hurry – when members of the *Terra Nova* expedition visited in 1911, they found socks hanging to

Shackleton's *Nimrod* expedition hut on Cape Royds

Antarctica's Hot Spots

Beneath the icy exterior of Antarctica is a dynamic continental geologic plate. Tectonic forces are at work within the Antarctic plate, and in places the continent is slowly being torn apart by rifting, much like East Africa. As the Earth's crust is extended and thinned, deep hot mantle rises and partially melts to form basaltic magma, which rises and is often stored within the crust in magma chambers. Where the magma reaches the surface, it is erupted as lava or volcanic ash and volcanoes are formed.

Active volcanoes are found today in three areas of Antarctica: the western Ross Sea, West Antarctica and along the Antarctic Peninsula. There remains a high probability that significant volcanic eruptions could occur at any time in Antarctica.

In the western Ross Sea region, most volcanism occurs on or along the front of the Transantarctic Mountains. Many small volcanic vents have been detected beneath the Ross Sea as magnetic anomalies, but none of these vents are currently active. Among a group of volcanic cones and domes called **The Pleiades** high in the Transantarctic Mountains of northern Victoria Land is a very young-looking dome, which probably erupted less than 1000 years ago. **Mt Melbourne** near Terra Nova Bay has steaming ground at its summit and an ash layer showing it erupted less than 200 years ago.

In Marie Byrd Land of West Antarctica, only **Mt Berlin** is considered active. There is also a possibility that an eruption is currently ongoing beneath the ice of the West Antarctic ice sheet. Airborne studies have shown a circular depression consistent with melting of the ice by a volcanic vent. The presence of a volcano beneath the depression is confirmed by studies, which show magnetic rocks typical of volcanoes.

In the Antarctic Peninsula region, volcanic **Deception Island** can be found at the southern end of Bransfield Strait.

Antarctica's best known volcano is **Mt Erebus** on Ross Island, discovered by British explorer Sir James Clark Ross in 1841. Ross noted in his journal that Erebus was erupting,'…emitting flame and smoke in great profusion…some of the officers believed they could see streams of lava pouring down its sides until lost beneath the snow.' Erebus is one of the largest volcanoes in the world, ranking among the top 20 in size.

Erebus has many unique features, the most notable being a permanent convecting lake, 10m to 20m in diameter, of molten magma with a temperature of 1000°C. The magma, which is very rich in sodium and potassium, is called phonolite. This name comes from the German and refers to rocks that ring like a bell when hit. Also unique to Erebus is the occurrence of large crystals in the magma. They can exceed 10cm in length and take many different forms. Easily eroded out from the soft

dry and a meal still on the table. Members of Shackleton's Ross Sea party also stopped by, collecting tobacco and soap, among other items.

Although the hut has been cleaned up since these long-ago stopovers (snow filled it during one long interval between visits), there's still a strong historical presence about the place. If you're tall, you'll need to duck slightly as you step inside so you don't hit your head on the acetylene generator over the entryway. It once powered the hut's lamps.

Cape Royds is the least visited of the Ross Island historic huts. About 700 people land each year.

A freeze-dried buckwheat pancake still lies in a cast-iron skillet on top of the large stove at the back of the hut, beside a tea kettle and a cooking pot. Colored glass medicine bottles still line several shelves. One of the few surviving bunks, to the left toward the back, has its fur sleeping bag laid out on top. Many tins of food with unappetizing names like Irish brawn (head cheese), boiled mutton, Army Rations, Aberdeen marrow

Antarctica's Hot Spots

glassy matrix of volcanic bombs erupted from the volcano, the crystals litter the upper crater rim like a carpet. They are of a mineral type called feldspar and belong to the anorthoclase variety. The anorthoclase is spectacular, and among the most perfect and largest crystals found in volcanic rocks anywhere on Earth.

Small eruptions are common from Erebus' magma lake, occurring six to 10 times daily since the mid-1980s. The eruptions are referred to as Strombolian eruptions, after the volcano Stromboli near Sicily. Only rarely since 1984 have bombs been ejected outside the 600m-diameter crater.

But beginning in September 1984, a four-month episode of more violent eruptions showered bombs more than 3km from the vent inside the crater. Scientists had to abandon a small research facility near the crater rim while volcanic bombs – some as big as cars – rained down around the summit crater, forcing the scientists to keep their distance. The bombs whistled as they fell, but the most memorable part of the eruption was the sound of the sharp explosions that threw the bombs from the volcanic vent. Upon landing, the bombs crackle as they cool. The interior of the bombs can be very hot, and if you break one open, you can pull the plastic hot lava out like taffy candy.

Today a network of nine seismic stations monitors Erebus, recording its small explosions and the occasional earthquake within its bowels. The seismometers should allow scientists to predict the next episode of eruptions. While there's no evidence in the geologic record of huge eruptions of the magnitude of the 1980 eruption at Mt St Helens in the US state of Washington, the presence of volcanic ash from Erebus in blue ice near the Transantarctic Mountains several hundred kilometers from the volcano attests to its potential for larger eruptions.

Erebus' summit features beautiful fumarolic ice towers. These can be observed with binoculars from sea level on the upper summit plateau of the volcano. The ice towers represent places where heated gases, rich in water, vent to the surface along fractures. When the gas reaches the cold air, the water freezes and forms bizarre shapes of varying size. Beneath the ice towers it is common to find tunnels and caves melted into the underlying snow and ice. These ice caves are warm and steamy and in some cases feel like a sauna. Access to the cave system can be difficult and may require an abseil (a rappel) of more than 20m. During the summer, when the sun dips toward the horizon around midnight, the ice towers look spectacular, as steam slowly ascends through the hollow towers and vents out the top.

– Dr Philip Kyle,
a professor of geochemistry at the New Mexico Institute of Mining and Technology,
who has spent 28 field seasons in Antarctica

fat, lunch tongue and pea powder lie on the floor next to the walls, along with still-bright red tins of Price's Motor Lubricant. The dining table, which was lifted from the floor every night to create extra space, is gone. It may have been burned by one of successive parties who ran out of fuel. A bench still piled with mitts and shoes stands on the right.

Ask your AHT guide to point out Shackleton's signature in his tiny bunk room. It's upside down on a packing crate marked 'Not for Voyage' that he made into a headboard for his bunk.

Outside the hut, remnants of the pony stables and the garage built for the Arrol-Johnson motorcar (Antarctica's first) are tumbling into ruin. Pony oats spill from feed bags onto the ground. One of the car's wheels leans up against a line of provision boxes, its wooden spokes scoured by the wind. Two wooden doghouses are likewise being eroded.

On the hut's south side, the wood has weathered to a handsome bleached grey color. Nail heads that were once pounded flush now stick out a centimeter or more.

Boxes of rusting food tins stand against the side and back. Although rust has completely destroyed the labels, one wooden carton is literally spilling its beans.

Cables running over the hut lash it to the ground, and the AHT attached rubber sheathing to the roof in 1990 for further protection. For conservation reasons, only eight people are permitted inside at one time, and only 40 people are allowed ashore at once.

Mts Erebus & Terror
Mt Erebus, the world's most southerly active volcano, is 3795m high. Its lazily drifting plume of steam is a familiar sight in the Ross Sea region. It gives a good indication of wind speeds at altitude. Mt Erebus was first climbed in 1908 by a party from Shackleton's *Nimrod* expedition.

Modern-day visitors will understand the awe of Erebus as it was expressed by Joseph Hooker, the young botanist on James Clark Ross' expedition, in a letter written to his father in 1841:

To see the dark cloud of smoke, tinged with flame, rising from the volcano in a perfectly unbroken column, one side jet black, the other giving back the colours of the sun, sometimes turning off at a right angle by some current of wind, and stretching many miles to leeward…was a sight so surpassing everything that can be imagined, and so heightened by the consciousness that we had penetrated into regions far beyond what was ever deemed practicable, that it really caused a feeling of awe to steal over us at the consideration of our own comparative insignificance and helplessness, and at the same time, an indescribable feeling of the greatness of the Creator in the works of His hand.

A geological curiosity, Erebus emits about 80g of metallic gold crystals each day.

The volcano is more famous as the site of Antarctica's worst air tragedy. All 257 people aboard Air New Zealand Flight 901 were killed when their DC-10 slammed into Mt Erebus on November 28, 1979. The crash site has been declared a tomb by the Antarctic Treaty members. One edge of the crash site is marked by a stainless steel cross, where memorial services are held.

Mt Terror, an extinct volcano separated from Mt Erebus by Mt Terra Nova, rises to 3230m.

ROSS ICE SHELF
Covering 520,000 sq km – an area roughly the size of France – the Ross Ice Shelf was discovered on January 28, 1841 by James Clark Ross, who called it the Victoria Barrier in honor of Queen Victoria. Since then it has been called many things, namely the Barrier, the Great Barrier, the Great Ice Barrier, the Great Southern Barrier, the Ice Barrier, the Icy Barrier, the Ross Barrier, the Ross Ice Barrier and, these days, the Ross Ice Shelf.

Its mean ice thickness is 335m to 700m, but where glaciers and ice streams meet it, the shelf is up to 1000m thick. At the ice front facing the Ross Sea, it's less than 100m thick. It is rather hard to believe, but the whole ice shelf is actually *floating*.

It moves as fast as 1100m per year, and calves an estimated 150 cubic km of icebergs annually, out of its total of 23,000 cubic km of ice. In 1987, a berg measuring 155km by 35km calved from the eastern side.

Another giant iceberg, code-named B-15, calved from the Ross Ice Shelf in March 2000. Measuring 298km by 37km and covering an area of some 11,000 sq km, it was the largest iceberg ever recorded. Although an iceberg sighted by USS *Glacier* in 1956 was reported to be 335km by 97km and cover nearly 32,500 sq km, researchers now believe these measurements were incorrect and that the berg was far smaller. The error persists in many sources, however, including the *Guinness Book of World Records*.

Scientists regard the calving of gigantic bergs as part of a normal process in which the ice sheet maintains a balance between constant growth outward from the continent and periodic loss by icebergs breaking off.

The Ross Ice Shelf has inspired many awestruck responses. The blacksmith aboard *Erebus* in 1841 was uncharacteristically moved to write a couplet: 'Awful and sublime, magnificent and rare/No other Earthly object with the Barrier can compare.' Ross himself called it 'a mighty and wonderful object far beyond anything we could have thought or conceived.'

Roald Amundsen was moved to write on January 11, 1911:

At 2:30 pm we came in sight of the Great Ice Barrier. Slowly it rose up out of the sea until we were face to face with it in all its imposing majesty. It is difficult with the help of the pen to give any idea of the impression this mighty wall of ice makes on the observer who is confronted with it for the first time. It is altogether a thing which can hardly be described...

Louis Bernacchi, the Australian physicist on Borchgrevink's *Southern Cross* expedition, climbed to the top of the shelf in 1900 with William Colbeck, the British surveyor. 'Nothing was visible,' Bernacchi later wrote, 'but the great ice cap stretching away for hundreds of miles to the south and west. Unless one has actually seen it, it is impossible to conceive the stupendous extent of this ice cap, its consistency, utter barrenness, and stillness, which sends an indefinable sense of dread to the heart.'

Borchgrevink himself found the Barrier to be much smaller than it appeared when Ross discovered it. In fact, at a place located at about 164°W (Scott later called it 'Discovery Inlet,' after his ship), the ice shelf was only 4.5m above the water. In 1900, Borchgrevink landed stores, sledges and dogs here. With two members of his expedition, William Colbeck and Per Savio, he trekked to 78°50'S, at the time the farthest south ever reached.

Roosevelt Island, 130km long and 65km wide, is completely covered by ice and is identifiable mainly by a central ridge of ice 550m above sea level. The island, of which the northernmost point is just 5km south of the Bay of Whales, was discovered by Byrd in 1934 and named for Franklin D Roosevelt, then president of the US.

East Antarctica

East Antarctica derives its name from the fact that nearly all of it lies in the Eastern Hemisphere. Although it's sometimes called Greater Antarctica, since it is the larger half of the continent, the name East Antarctica, coined by Antarctic historian Edwin S Balch in 1904, is preferred. East Antarctica is a high plateau covered by a vast, thick ice sheet, and is divided from West Antarctica by the Transantarctic Mountains.

In tourist brochures East Antarctica is often called Antarctica's 'Far Side' (these same brochures urge you to 'get away' from the 'crowded' Antarctic Peninsula!). Thanks to its isolation and the long voyages required to reach it, the region has been all but unvisited by tourists until very recently, with the first tour ships calling at the three Australian stations only during the 1992-93 season.

For tourists, the presence of numerous emperor penguin rookeries is a primary attraction. The largest penguin, the emperor is the only animal to breed during the long Antarctic night. The sight of one of their rookeries, with the tall, dignified-looking adult birds and their downy silver-and-black chicks, is one of Antarctica's most stunning.

East Antarctica includes regions claimed by Norway, Australia and France. Much of the Norwegian claim (called Dronning Maud Land and extending from 20°W to 45°E) was explored by Norwegian whalers. During the 1930-31 whaling season alone, about 265 whaling ships, most of them Norwegian, worked the Southern Ocean in the area between 20°W and 50°E. Although exploration was only their second line of work, these whalers discovered much of the Dronning (Queen) Maud Land coast, naming sections of it for members of the Norwegian royal family, including Kronprinsesse Martha Kyst (Crown Princess Martha Coast), Prinsesse Astrid Kyst (Princess Astrid Coast) and Prinsesse Ragnhild Kyst (Princess Ragnhild Coast).

Australia's claim, called the Australian Antarctic Territory (or AAT), extends from 45°E to 160°E, except for the thin slice of France's Terre Adélie. It was explored by Australians including Douglas Mawson, George Hubert Wilkins and Phillip G Law. Reflecting its numerous other discoverers, the region includes Enderby Land, Kemp Coast, Mac.Robertson Land, Princess Elizabeth Land, Wilhelm II Coast, Queen Mary Coast, Wilkes Land and George V Coast.

Terre Adélie, France's Antarctic claim, extends from 136°E to 142°E and is wholly within Australia's claim. This section of the coast is distinguished by its French names: Cap Bienvenue, Glacier du Commandant Charcot, Glacier du Français.

The principal sites of interest that have a describable human history are spread out rather sparsely along the thousands of kilometers of East Antarctica's coast. But the coast itself, with its enormous white grounded bergs and massive iceberg tongues, is magnificent. Below are some of the coast's main features, beginning at the western end.

NEUMAYER STATION

The first Georg von Neumayer station was built in 1981 and named for one of the promoters of the First International Polar Year, 1882-83. After it was buried by drifting snow, a replacement was completed about 10km away in 1992. The new facility, called simply Neumayer station, is on the Ekström Ice Shelf and operates year-round. Nine people generally winter over.

In December 1990 Georg von Neumayer station was staffed by the first all-female group to winter on Antarctica. It consisted of two meteorologists, two geophysicists, two engineers, a radio operator, a cook and a medical doctor who also served as the station leader. The women spent 14 months on The Ice, including nine in complete isolation.

Neumayer has little to show on the surface, apart from its wind-powered generators. Buried 3m beneath the snow surface of the 200m-thick ice shelf, it consists of two parallel galvanized steel tubes, each 90m

EAST ANTARCTICA

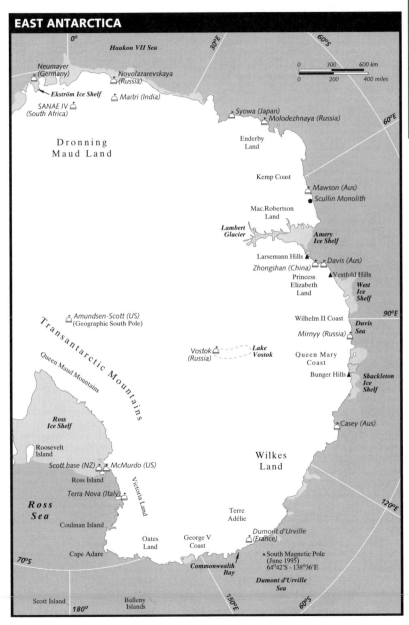

0°

Haakon VII Sea

30°E

60°S

0   300   600 km

0   200   400 miles

Neumayer
(Germany)

Novolazarevskaya
(Russia)

Ekström Ice Shelf

Maitri (India)

SANAE IV
(South Africa)

Syowa (Japan)

Molodezhnaya (Russia)

60°E

D r o n n i n g
M a u d   L a n d

Enderby
Land

Kemp Coast

Mawson (Aus)

Scullin Monolith

Mac.Robertson
Land

*Lambert
Glacier*

*Amery
Ice Shelf*

Larsemann Hills

Davis (Aus)

Zhongshan (China)

Vestfold Hills

Princess
Elizabeth
Land

*West
Ice
Shelf*

Tr a n s a n t a r c t i c   M o u n t a i n s

Amundsen-Scott (US)
(Geographic South Pole)

Wilhelm II Coast

*Davis
Sea*

90°E

Queen Maud Mountains

Vostok
(Russia)

*Lake
Vostok*

Mirnyy (Russia)

Queen Mary
Coast

*Ross
Ice Shelf*

Bunger Hills

*Shackleton
Ice
Shelf*

Roosevelt
Island

Casey (Aus)

Scott base (NZ)

McMurdo (US)

W i l k e s
L a n d

Ross Island

Terra Nova (Italy)

Victoria Land

*R o s s
S e a*

Terre
Adélie

Coulman Island

Oates
Land

George V
Coast

Dumont d'Urville
(France)

×South Magnetic Pole
(June 1995)
64°42'S - 138°36'E

Cape Adare

*Commonwealth
Bay*

*Dumont d'Urville
Sea*

70°S

120°E

Scott Island

Balleny
Islands

180°

150°E

60°S

long and 8.4m in diameter, and connected by two transverse tubes. Inside are shipping containers that are outfitted as living quarters, a kitchen, a hospital, laboratories and workshops. About 22 people can be accommodated in the sub-ice station and another 36 during the summer in above-ice huts.

SANAE IV

SANAE stands for South African National Antarctic Expedition. The first SANAE base was occupied in December 1959, when Norway handed it over to South Africa after deciding its work was finished there. Since then, there have also been SANAE II and SANAE III bases. The latter, which was closed for wintering in December 1994, had over the years been buried by 14m of drifting snow on the surface of the Fimbul Ice Shelf on which it was built. It became unsafe, as it was slowly being crushed by the compacted snow's weight.

The newest station, SANAE IV, is located on a nunatak, or rocky outcrop, at Vesleskarvet (Norwegian for 'little barren mountain') on the Ahlmann Ridge, about 170km from the coast. Hence the station's nickname of 'Vesles.'

SANAE IV is probably the most modern station in Antarctica. Its main 176m-long building is painted blue on the bottom to absorb solar energy and help keep the area beneath it snow-free. The roof is painted orange for visibility from the air. Built on 3m stilts above the rock surface, it's expected to last much longer than SANAE III did. It was occupied by its first wintering team in 1997 and accommodates about 20 winterers and 80 summer personnel. The station is re-supplied by tractor trains unloading from ships at the ice shelf.

NOVOLAZAREVSKAYA STATION

Russia's Novolazarevskaya station, opened in 1961, is named for Mikhail Petrovich Lazarev, the second-in-command of Bellingshausen's expedition and captain of *Mirnyy*. Soviet/Russian activity in the area dates to the establishment of the Lazarev base in 1958. The current station replaced the old Novolazarevskaya in 1979. It can accommo-

date about 57 winterers and 60 summer personnel, but far fewer people live on station now. Novolazarevskaya is only 1km from the former East German Georg Forster station and 4.5km east of Maitri station.

MAITRI STATION

India's first Antarctic station, Dakshin Gangotri, was initially established as a refuge hut in January 1982. In January 1984, another Gangotri was constructed farther inland, and the first group wintered over. Today's Indian Antarctic expedition members live at Maitri (Hindi for 'Friendship'), established well inland in 1989 to replace Gangotri, which was becoming crushed and buried in ice. The winter complement is 26; summer, 65. A bust of Mahatma Gandhi was installed in 1997. Maitri is located on Priyadarshini Lake in the Schirmacher Hills, a line of low coastal hills about 18km long and dotted with numerous melt-water ponds. Dakshin Gangotri is now used as a supply base and transit camp, and – since it is buried beneath the ice – as a storage area for ice cores.

SYOWA STATION

Japan's Syowa station was established in 1956-57, and has been used continuously since then except for a four-year period from 1962-66. It's built on the northern half of East Ongul Island, 4km off the mainland coast. Syowa is a collection of about 50 brightly colored structures. The main building, built in 1992, is a four-story structure topped by a domed skylight over a central stairway. Syowa is the logistics base for two inland summer stations (Dome Fuji and Mizuho) and many field parties. Its winter complement is 31 people. Syowa has adopted the admirable practice of employing grey water from dishwashing and showers for the station toilets, making for low water consumption on the base.

The season after Syowa was built, its first wintering crew was flown by helicopter to the relief ship *Soya*, which could not approach the station closer than 100km because of heavy pack ice. Helicopters ferried personnel and equipment to the ship, but when the last helicopter flew off the station on February 11, 1958, severe weather prevented it from returning to Syowa with the new wintering crew from the ship.

Tragically, the station's 15 sledge dogs had been chained up and given a small amount of food while they awaited the arrival of the new station personnel. Although the ship waited for weeks to try to fly the men ashore, it was impossible to get to the station. Even the US icebreaker *Burton Island*, called to assist, was unable to help. With winter approaching, the possibility that *Soya* could become beset was a real danger, so the station relief effort was reluctantly abandoned. The dogs were left to fend for themselves.

When the next station team returned in January 1959, two dogs – Taro and Jiro – were found alive. Since neither penguins nor seals remain ashore in the Syowa region over the winter, it is unknown how the dogs managed to survive for a full year. Even the possibility that they ate some of their dead fellows does not explain the feat, since seven dogs were found still chained up, untouched.

For their amazing survival, Taro and Jiro became famous in Japan. Although Jiro died at Syowa the following year, Taro was returned in 1961 to Japan, where he lived another nine years at the University of Hokkaido and received thousands of visitors each week. A film made about the canine pair, Koreyoshi Kurahara's *Antarctica*, was Japan's biggest movie in 1984 – and probably the most moving of all Antarctic films. (Thanks to Baden Norris, curator of Antarctic history at the Canterbury Museum in Christchurch, for this information.)

In 1979, from January 28 to February 3, the first live TV transmission from Antarctica was broadcast from Syowa to Tokyo.

One part of the research done at Syowa in recent years is a study of the microclimates in Antarctic moss beds. In 1996, Japanese scientists were startled to find a 20cm-high flowering plant growing in a rock fissure about 25km south of Syowa, creating concern that global warming might be behind the plant's ability to thrive. Also nearby is **Yukidori Valley**, named for the large numbers of snow petrels which nest in the area, protected as **Site of Special Scientific Interest No 22** by the Antarctic Treaty.

MOLODEZHNAYA STATION

Molodezhnaya, established in 1962, in 1970 replaced Mirnyy as the premier Russian Antarctic station. At its peak, a winter population of 120 was usual, with as many as 400 in summer. It also had an intercontinental airport with a 2645m compacted snow runway where aircraft used to arrive from Lorenco Marques in Mozambique and, later, from Cape Town. Some of these planes crashed, and can still be seen beside the runway. Presently, Molodezhnaya is all but closed, due to Russia's difficult financial situation. A staff of 10 continues meteorological observations. The station takes its name from the *molodezh*, or young people, who helped to construct it. Molodezhnaya has major **rocketry facilities** for upper atmospheric studies that were coordinated with similar observatories along the meridian all the way to the Arctic.

MAWSON STATION

Australia's Mawson station was established in February 1954. Named for Douglas Mawson, it is the oldest continuously occupied station south of the Antarctic Circle. Mawson is approached through Iceberg Alley, a channel lined with huge tabular bergs that have run aground on underwater banks. Horseshoe Harbour is the best natural harbor for thousands of kilometers, protected by two projecting arms of land.

Mawson's high-latitude location makes it a good place for studying cosmic rays. This research is done in an underground vault in solid rock, 20m below the surface. The station was also the principal home of Australia's much-loved Antarctic huskies, before the Antarctic Treaty's Protocol on Environmental Protection forced their removal. Many of the dogs now live in northern Minnesota in the US.

As at the other two Australian stations in Antarctica, a massive construction program has modernized the station buildings during the past decade. Each structure is color-coded and vividly visible against the white Antarctic snows. The large living quarters building at Mawson, in the same way as its counterparts at Davis and Casey stations, is known as the 'Red Shed.'

One of the few surviving buildings from 'old' Mawson station is the small wooden **Weddell hut**, the second building erected at the station and originally erected at Heard Island but later moved. Attached to its ceiling are 92 nude pinups cut out of American magazines between 1972 and 1988 by station personnel. The small gallery is irreverently known as 'the Sistine Ceiling.'

The longest golf drive on Earth (the lunar golf drive record is longer) was made at Mawson in 1956, when Norwegian dogsled driver Nils Lied whacked a black-painted golf ball 4km across new and extremely smooth sea ice. 'For once, I made a good hit,' Lied later told Tim Bowden, author of *Antarctica and Back in Sixty Days*. 'It was a beauty!...So we saddled up Oscar, my lead dog, with a sledge behind him. We knew if any dog could sniff the ball out, Oscar would. And he did.'

SCULLIN MONOLITH
Scullin Monolith, 180km east of Mawson, is known for its remarkable bird life, with the highest concentration of breeding Antarctic petrels (157,000 pairs) and an extensive Adélie rookery.

The crescent-shaped monolith was named for Australian Prime Minister James H Scullin by Mawson, who discovered it on

his BANZARE expedition in 1931. At about the same time, a group of Norwegian whalers named the feature for Norwegian whaling captain Klarius Mikkelsen. As the result of a later compromise, the highest point (420m) on Scullin Monolith is known as Mikkelsen Peak.

AMERY ICE SHELF
The Amery Ice Shelf is the seaward extension of the **Lambert Glacier**. At up to 65km wide and 400km long, the Lambert is the world's largest glacier, draining about 8% of the Antarctic ice sheet out into Prydz Bay. Named in 1957 for Bruce Lambert, Australia's director of National Mapping, it was originally called Baker Three Glacier for the photo reconnaissance air crew who discovered it during 'Operation Highjump' in 1946-47. West of the Lambert Glacier is **Fram Bank**, where huge tabular bergs frequently become grounded on the shallow bottom.

LARSEMANN HILLS
The Larsemann Hills, 11 rocky peninsulas discovered by Norwegian Captain Klarius Mikkelsen in 1935, are an ice-free oasis extending 15km from the Daålk Glacier. Mikkelsen named the hills after young Lars Jr, son of expedition organizer Lars Christensen. The Larsemanns, which reach a maximum elevation of 160m, contain about 200 lakes, including some with water that is among the freshest in the world.

China's year-round **Zhongshan station** was founded in 1989 and accommodates about 22 people in winter. Very close by are two other facilities: Australia's summer-only **Law base**, named for Phillip Law and established in 1986-87, and Russia's **Progress II base**, opened in 1989 and recently designated as Russia's main Antarctic station. Progress II accommodates a maximum of 77 people in summer and 20 in winter. An earlier Progress I base nearby is now abandoned.

DAVIS STATION
Australia's Davis station opened in January 1957. Located on the edge of the Vestfold Hills, Davis is named for Captain John King

Davis (1884-1967), master of ships used on expeditions led by Shackleton and Mawson. During its first years, Davis accommodated very small wintering parties: in some cases, just four or five men stayed through the long polar night. In January 1965, Davis was closed temporarily to allow Australia to concentrate its efforts on the building of Casey station. It reopened in February 1969 and has been operated continuously since then. It currently accommodates 80 people. Compared to those at its two Australian sister stations, Davis' climate is relatively mild, a fact that has earned it the nickname 'Riviera of the South.' Among the unusual (for Antarctic stations) recreation activities available to Davis residents are ice-skating on the station tarn and rock climbing on the climbing wall in the Green Store building. The most southerly known nesting site of the giant petrel is a few kilometers south of Davis on **Hawker Island**.

VESTFOLD HILLS
The Vestfold Hills, which cover 400 sq km, are an oasis, or area of ice-free rock. These hills, 25km across with a maximum elevation of 159m, are especially beautiful when viewed from the air, revealing long, black volcanic dikes striping the bare rock. The first woman to set foot in Antarctica, Caroline Mikkelsen, came ashore here on February 20, 1935 with her husband, Klarius Mikkelsen, captain of the Norwegian whaling support ship *Thorshavn*. The Mikkelsens named the Vestfolds for their home county in Norway, the center of the country's whaling industry.

The Vestfolds are biologically unique, dotted with a series of remarkable lakes, both freshwater and saline. Some of the hypersaline lakes are more than 13 times as salty as seawater, and have freezing points as low as -17.5°C. In winter, when the ice on these lakes acts as a lid trapping solar energy absorbed by the saline water, the temperature of the bottom water can reach 35°C. Life in these lakes is highly specialized – and rare. In Deep Lake, for instance, only two species have been found, an alga and a bacterium. Because no burrowing animals disturb the lake-bottom sediment, cores taken here provide an unparalleled record going as far back as 5000 years.

At nearby **Marine Plain**, fossils of whales and dolphins have been found. The area is protected by the Antarctic Treaty as **Site of Special Scientific Interest No 25**.

MIRNYY STATION
Russia's Mirnyy ('Peaceful') station, opened in 1956, was Russia's first on the Antarctic continent. It's named for Bellingshausen's

Totality in 2003

A total solar eclipse will occur over East Antarctica in late 2003. Eclipse specialists are excited by the prospect of observing the phenomenon in the region's clear air. Total solar eclipses are extremely rare: between 2000 and 2035 there will only be 26 worldwide, including annular total eclipses, in which a thin, outer ring of the sun's disk is not completely covered by the moon.

Totality will begin southeast of Heard Island at 22:19 UTC (Coordinated Universal Time) on November 23, 2003 (at Heard Island, the time will be around sunrise the next day). The rapidly moving shadow of the moon will fall first on the Antarctic coast at Russia's Mirnyy station, where totality will last just under two minutes. The zone of totality will then curve inland over the polar plateau, crossing near Japan's Dome Fuji station (77°S, 40°E) before exiting the continent in the vicinity of India's Maitri and Russia's Novolazarevskaya stations.

No detailed plans for viewing the eclipse had been developed at the time of this writing, although one group is seeking sponsors for an expedition which, in addition to making general observations, proposes to provide a live broadcast on the Internet.

Antarctica's most recent total solar eclipse was on November 12, 1985, although little of the continent experienced it. After 2003, the next total solar eclipse in Antarctica will occur December 4, 2021.
– Martin Betts

Colored & Striped Icebergs

Every once in a great while, visitors to Antarctica – particularly East Antarctica, south of Australia and Africa – are shown a rare and exceptional wonder: a green iceberg. As many as 10% of all icebergs from this region may be green, but they are only rarely seen.

Pure ice is blue in color because it absorbs red light most efficiently, green light less efficiently and blue light minimally. When sunlight, which is white, shines upon pure ice, only the blue light is reflected back to your eye as the other wavelengths are absorbed. Glacial ice ranges in color from white to milky blue because air bubbles trapped in the ice scatter white light very efficiently. Thus all colors of light are reflected to your eye before they have a chance to be absorbed by the ice. The more bubbles the ice contains, the whiter it appears; the fewer bubbles, the bluer it appears.

Until recently, however, scientists couldn't satisfactorily explain what causes the beautiful jade or bottle-green icebergs. We have now learned that icebergs can be blue or green for the same reason seawater can be blue or green: both contain organic material from the degradation of marine plants and animals. This organic material absorbs blue light very efficiently, green light less so and red light only minimally. When this organic material is frozen into ice, blue light is absorbed by the organic material, red light is absorbed by the ice, and only green wavelengths of light are left over to be reflected to our eyes. The more organic material, the greener the ice or the seawater.

How does this organic material become trapped in the ice? Under very special conditions – found primarily in East Antarctica – the organic material in seawater can become frozen into icebergs. The story begins high on the Antarctic continent where thousands of years worth of snowfall is compressed into ice. This ice flows toward the sea as glaciers. Upon reaching the sea, the glaciers float and are called ice shelves. Because the density of glacial ice, with all of its air bubbles, is less than that of water, approximately 90% of the ice shelf is underwater and only 10% is visible to us.

That nine-to-one ratio of ice underwater to ice above water means that some of the underwater ice is at great depth. In the case of the Amery Ice Shelf in East Antarctica – a source of green icebergs – the ice shelf's cliffs are approximately 50m in height above the water, suggesting that the base of the ice

ship. Its 200m main street was once officially called Lenin Ulitsc (Lenin Street), though what it might have been called by the locals is an interesting thought. The original station was replaced in 1970-71 and now lies under 2m of ice. An imposing cemetery with graves of Russian, Czech, German and Swiss members of Soviet and Russian Antarctic expeditions is located on **Buromskiy Island** just offshore from Mirnyy. Amidst an Adélie rookery, 30 coffins and four memorials are bolted to the exposed rock, because there is no soil in which to bury them.

BUNGER HILLS

The 780-sq-km Bungers caused a sensation when their discovery was announced. Because they are an oasis, or area of ice-free rock, newspaper headlines blared 'Antarctic Shangri-La,' which may explain why some science fiction movies about Antarctica depict a tropical region inhabited by dinosaurs. The hills are named for US Navy pilot David Bunger, who landed a seaplane on an unfrozen lake here in February 1947 while on a photographic mission for Operation 'Highjump.' Dotted with numerous melt-water ponds, they are bisected by Algae Lake. The hills reach a maximum elevation of 180m and are surrounded on all sides by 120m walls of ice.

CASEY STATION

Australia's Casey station was established in February 1959, when Australia took overall responsibility for the US's Wilkes station, built in 1957 for the IGY and named for Lieutenant Charles Wilkes, leader of the US Exploring Expedition. Ten years later, when its main building was covered over by snow,

Colored & Striped Icebergs

shelf is 450m deep. At that depth and pressure, seawater slowly freezes to the underside of the ice shelf, forming 'marine ice.' At its greatest, the accumulation of marine ice can be tens of meters thick.

Icebergs that calve from the edge of the ice shelf are composed of two kinds of ice literally stuck together: glacial ice made of compressed snow that originated from the continent and flowed down to become the ice shelf, and marine ice from the freezing of seawater on the underside of the ice shelf. If an iceberg becomes unstable due to uneven melting, it list and then turn over, exposing its marine ice underside.

Green icebergs are rarely seen because not all ice shelves have the right conditions for marine ice to form, and also because the icebergs have to turn over and show their verdant bellies before the marine ice underside is melted by the relatively warm waters that circulate around Antarctica.

Marine ice's most striking characteristic – even more than its color – is its unbelievable clarity, caused by the absence of air bubbles. Observers often comment that they can see 'meters and meters' into the marine ice. At the depth and pressure that marine ice forms, air is highly soluble in seawater. This is in sharp contrast to sea ice, which is formed by the freezing of seawater at the ocean surface. At the surface, air is not so soluble in seawater and air bubbles are trapped in the forming ice. Thus sea ice contains lots of bubbles and has a milky appearance.

While green icebergs are spectacular in appearance, observers should also look for variations in the color of marine icebergs ranging from deep indigo to jade to yellow-brown, depending upon the amount of organic material that is trapped in the ice. The different colors are due to the changing concentrations of organic material in the seawater that was frozen into the marine ice.

An even rarer phenomenon is the striped iceberg. These form when seawater fills up and freezes in crevasses occurring on the bottom side of ice shelves. The result is a bubbly, milky-blue iceberg with dark blue or green stripes.

– Dr Collin Roesler,
oceanographer at Bigelow Laboratory for Ocean Sciences in West Boothbay Harbor, ME

Australia replaced Wilkes with Casey station, 3km to the south across the bay. Casey was a radical innovation in Antarctic design. It was built on stilts to allow snow to blow through beneath, and had a long corrugated iron tunnel on the windward side connecting all the buildings, which were built separately as a safety measure in case of fire. Casey was first known as 'Repstat,' or replacement station, but its name was changed to honor Australia's Governor-General Richard (later Lord) Casey, a staunch supporter of Australia's fledgling Antarctic program.

Casey itself had to be replaced in the late 1980s when corrosion threatened its metal supports. The new station, also called Casey, was built 1km away and completed in December 1988. The old Casey was dismantled in 1991-92 and 1992-93 and returned to

Australia. Casey accommodates 17 people in winter and 70 in summer.

One of the first direct flights from Australia to Australia's claimed territory in Antarctica was made in November 1988 by electronics mogul and *Australian Geographic* magazine publisher Dick Smith along with copilot Giles Kershaw (cofounder of Adventure Network International), when the pair flew from Hobart to Casey. They went on to the South Pole and proceeded to circumnavigate the globe via the North Pole.

A large emperor penguin colony was sighted in late 1994 among the grounded icebergs of **Petersen Bank**, offshore of Casey. Despite more than 40 years of operations, including helicopter flights over the bank during station resupply visits, the bank is so large that the penguins had remained undiscovered until then.

DUMONT D'URVILLE STATION

France's Dumont d'Urville station, named for French explorer Jules-Sébastien-César Dumont d'Urville, is located on Pétrel Island in the Géologie Archipelago. It was built in 1956 to replace Port Martín station, which burned down on the night of January 24, 1952, without injury to anyone.

Colloquially known as 'Du-d'U' ('doo-doo'), the station sensibly allows only 30 to

Expedition Icebound: A Year at Commonwealth Bay

In the period from 1911 to 1914, Douglas Mawson spent two winters at Cape Denison in Commonwealth Bay, one of the most inhospitable spots on Earth. He was well equipped and had a number of companions. Though tragedy struck during his foray onto the Antarctic ice cap, Mawson and the rest of his men fared well in the relative comfort of their hut. Could a privately funded and much smaller expedition winter as successfully?

That was the question in Don's mind after he returned from a voyage to Cape Denison early in 1993. We decided to find out, launching what we called Expedition Ice-Bound in February 1994.

Living for a year at the windiest place on the planet would be more than just a simple camping trip. Among other preparations, it required nearly 10 months of negotiations with the Australian Antarctic Division. We submitted a full report on our proposed activities to the Division's policy section, and we sought in every way to meet the same criteria that official government activities must. We assessed all impacts on flora, fauna, ecological processes, ice, air, water and the heritage qualities of Cape Denison, along with the waste-handling methods we would use while living there.

On January 15, 1995, we reached Commonwealth Bay in our 18m expedition support vessel, *Spirit of Sydney*. On board were 4.5 tonnes of equipment, including a two-year supply of food and fuel and a prefab 2.4m by 3.6m box that was to be our home. Before the month was out, the yacht's five-member crew sailed home and we were left alone in the world's last great wilderness.

Only days later, the wind worked itself up into a screaming fury and the first blizzard struck. The roar of the wind would rise to a howling climax in a gust, and there was no way we could hide from the sound. It filled our world, needling us second by second, worrying, tormenting, wearing us down. All we could do was sit and wonder how long the hut, which we called Gadget Hut (after one of Mawson's huskies), could stand the punishment. Battered by winds that exceeded 240 kph and gripped by temperatures as low as -38°C, our tiny hut shook and creaked and grew a lining of frost as thick as that found in any home freezer. At times, the interior temperature dropped to -18°C and our breath froze to our sleeping bags.

We had come in search of adventure. We were alone together without any possibility of rescue, yet we were able to share our experience daily with thousands of schoolchildren around the world, thanks to our sponsor, COMSAT, who provided a satellite telephone system. (Despite this connection to the outside world, we sometimes found ourselves feeling depressed on Sunday nights when we left the telephone on and no one called!) We also spent time writing, observing wildlife, recording weather data and, in Margie's case, hand-sewing 86 teddy bears to be auctioned for charity.

There were dangers, difficulties and disappointments. On two occasions we

Gadget Hut

40 people to come ashore at one time. Ice and strong katabatic winds often prevent landings, either by Zodiac or helicopter. The station accommodates 30 winterers and 120 during the summer.

Dumont d'Urville became the focus of international attention in 1983 when the French government began construction of a 1100m crushed-rock airstrip. Unfortunately, Lion Island and two adjacent islets were

Expedition Icebound: A Year at Commonwealth Bay

were made sick by carbon monoxide poisoning when our roof ventilators iced up. Whenever we cooked or turned on the heater, the ice on the walls and ceiling melted, creating rain inside the hut. We had to cover the bed every day to catch the melt water, and pools of water puddled the floor. When we opened what we thought was our last can of potatoes, which we had been hoarding, we were crestfallen to discover (the label had fallen off) that they were in fact asparagus.

As autumn gave way to lifeless winter, the psychological pressure increased. For three months we lived in almost complete darkness, and for 21 days we didn't see the sun at all. Margie suffered bouts of profound despondency, particularly when we

Holiday celebrations broke the monotony of the Antarctic winter.

were confined indoors for long periods; she cried for six months, from March until October, and felt sorry for Don when she couldn't stop the crying. Once, we were stuck inside for 20 days in a row. We'll never forget the roar of the wind – it will stay with us forever. We had to shout just to talk to each other in bed.

With the arrival of spring came life – killer whales, seals and penguins – and days of never-ending sunshine. Occasionally, we had such brilliant days that the stunning panoramas outside inspired moods close to euphoria. We would sit for hours watching the penguins and seals, who became our friends. At night, we were impressed by the aurora, with its green and yellow 'waterfall' effects. On Christmas, we were visited by a US helicopter – the first people we had seen in 12 months!

Our adventure cost us around A$600,000, including the purchase of *Spirit of Sydney*. You could say that our hut was the most expensive – and smallest – hotel room in the world. But we felt we were privileged to be staying at the most remote and beautiful place in the world.

We found that we are two sides of the same coin; we have our differences, but we make a formidable unit. Today Don is 45 and Margie is 39; we have been married for 16 years. We didn't have a single fight all year – except for what we'd term two 'debates.' That's pretty incredible, considering that we were never more than 100m apart for a whole year. We really had to support each other to survive, which meant that we had to become closer. Yet our differences came to an extraordinary climax at the end of our stay, when Don pleaded with Margie to let him stay on for another year, completely alone. It was another testing time for our relationship, which survived stronger than ever. (Don came home with Margie.)

We are now seeking couples worldwide to spend a year in our hut. By means of satellite technology, we hope to create a dynamic and adventurous education program with live videoconferencing from what is presently the only private year-round base in Antarctica.

– **Don & Margie McIntyre,**
authors of *Two Below Zero: A Year in Antarctica*

dynamited to level them and provide material to fill in the sea separating them. Greenpeace made headlines around the world when it visited the runway construction site during the 1983-84 season and obtained photos of dead penguins killed by flying rock shrapnel. The airstrip was completed – at a cost of 110 million francs – in early 1993 and was due to be used for test flights the next season. In January 1994, however, the nearby Astrolabe Glacier calved, causing an enormous wave that destroyed an equipment support building. The French government subsequently decided not to utilize the airstrip.

There are major emperor and Adélie rookeries in the area of the station, but they're off-limits to visitors.

COMMONWEALTH BAY

Mawson's Australasian Antarctic Expedition was based here from 1912 to 1914. Mawson named Commonwealth Bay after the Commonwealth of Australia, while Cape Denison commemorates one of the expedition's main supporters, Hugh Denison. Mawson called the Cape's two points of attachment to the mainland Land's End and John O'Groats, letting his Anglophilia show.

The same furious katabatics that caused Mawson to call this region the 'Home of the Blizzard' can make a landing impossible here. Because of these violent winds, conservation of Mawson's huts is much more difficult than it is for historic buildings elsewhere in Antarctica, for instance on Ross Island.

No more than 20 people are allowed to come ashore at one time here. Visitors to the Main Hut are asked not to climb on structures and must not take any materials of any kind from the site.

Areas where artifacts (building materials, domestic and scientific equipment, food, packaging, clothing and other historic rubbish) are scattered on the ground between the Main Hut and the Boat Harbor are off-limits and should be avoided.

Two ANARE buildings are located at Cape Denison: Sørenson Hut (1986), east of Mawson's Hut, and Granholm Hut (1978) to the northwest.

From January 1995 to January 1996, an Australian couple named Don and Margie McIntyre wintered at Cape Denison, the first to do so since Mawson. They lived in a 2.4m by 3.7m cabin they built near Mawson's Hut (see the boxed text 'Expedition Ice-Bound: A Year at Commonwealth Bay').

Warning: Explosives left over from the expedition lie approximately 50m southwest (or inland) of the Main Hut. Keep away from the area.

Main Hut Mawson originally intended to have two separate huts, one housing 12 men, the other 6. But it was decided instead to join the two, creating an accommodation area and a workshop. The larger building, about 53 sq meters, was surrounded on three sides by a veranda, which held stores, food and biological supplies. A central dining table was surrounded by Mawson's room, a photographic darkroom and the cook's table and stove. Bunks were placed along the perimeter, and four unfortunate men had to sleep next to the bacteriological research area.

The smaller workshop, covering roughly 30 sq meters, was connected by a door on the north side of the larger building. The workshop contained generators, biology and geology labs, a mechanics' bench, a lathe, a sewing machine and a wireless operating bench, along with another stove. Dogs were housed in kennels on the east veranda, while the west veranda contained a meat cellar, a roof door for winter entrance and a latrine. The entrance to the whole hut complex was through a 'cold porch' on the west veranda, with the door facing north to avoid the furious winds coming from the south.

Lighting consisted of acetylene lamps and skylights. Winter snowdrifts kept the quarters at a frosty 4-10°C.

Magnetograph House & Magnetic Absolute Hut Cape Denison's location close to the South Magnetic Pole makes it an ideal place to observe the Earth's magnetic field. These huts northeast of the Main Hut are where this work was conducted. The magnetograph house, the best-preserved building at Cape Denison, was protected by a stone wall built on its windward side, which helps explain its good condition.

Transit Hut East of the Main Hut, this building was used as shelter while taking sights from stars to determine the exact position of Cape Denison.

Memorial Cross Erected by the expedition in the spring of 1913, this memorial honors Mertz and Ninnis, who perished on the Far Eastern Journey with Mawson, an ordeal from which Mawson himself barely escaped with his life.

VOSTOK STATION
Russia's Vostok Station – an outpost if ever there was one – is located near the South Geomagnetic Pole, where the flux in the Earth's electromagnetic field is manifested. It was built in 1957 and named for one of Bellingshausen's two ships, *Vostok* (East). The station was resupplied by semiannual tractor-train expeditions that took a month to travel the 1400km from the coast. Like Russia's other Antarctic stations, Vostok has seen its operations and personnel substantially reduced in recent years.

The station sits atop the southern end of the under-ice **Lake Vostok**, to which it gave its name. Lying under ice that is nearly 4km thick, the lake is 280km long and 60km wide. The deepest ice core ever drilled comes from Vostok station. It is 3611m deep – with an estimated age of 420,000 years at the bottom. Drilling stopped 150m above the

The Under-Ice Lakes

Beneath the ice sheet, which is more than 4km thick in places, lies the rock of Antarctica. Geothermal heat from the Earth's core raises the temperature of the base of the ice sheet. This melts enough ice to form freshwater lakes in some basins. Glaciologists have identified 79 under-ice lakes all over East Antarctica. The largest, Lake Vostok, is comparable in area to Lake Ontario and may be up to 500m deep, with sediment on its bottom.

Because they are cut off from the sea, and because they are melted from ice possibly hundreds of thousands of years old, the under-ice lakes may contain important information about previous climates. They might even contain ancient microbes with special features no longer present in today's world. Currently, however, nobody knows what is in these under-ice lakes, since the technical problem of how to sample the water without contaminating the lake remains unsolved.

– Dr David Walton,
Editor in Chief of the international journal
Antarctic Science

surface of Lake Vostok to avoid contaminating the lake with the kerosene used as an antifreeze in the drilling fluid.

No tourists have ever visited Vostok, but it's of interest as the site of the lowest temperature that has ever been recorded on Earth: -89.6°C on July 21, 1983. Vostok's record *high* temperature is -22°C.

South Pole

'Great God! This is an awful place!' British explorer Robert Falcon Scott famously wrote in his diary on the day in 1912 that he reached the South Pole – only to discover that his Norwegian rival, Roald Amundsen, had arrived 35 days before. Scott's exclamation reflected not only his anguish over losing the great polar race he had labored for a decade to win, but also his awe of the near-mythical spot itself. He had good reason to marvel.

Almost nothing lives here. The two exceptions are a species of algae and a species of bacteria, which were probably blown in from somewhere else, as there are no indigenous species at the Pole. Only four other animal species have ever visited: humans, sledge dogs, hamsters (experiment subjects) and a few presumably very lost skuas, which may have followed the vapor trails of aircraft resupplying the station here. (Plus a few other invertebrates that hitchhiked in with shipments of vegetables: a bee, a ladybug, flies, spiders, gnats and worms.)

Just a few years ago, the South Pole (known to its denizens simply as 'Pole') was still accessible only to the US government and the small number of other national expeditions that made long traverses from the coast. A handful of adventurers launched private expeditions at a cost of hundreds of thousands of dollars – and their safe return was doubtful. Now, anyone with a reasonably thick wallet can visit this remote redoubt in the high Antarctic desert. Still, in recent years, fewer than 40 tourists annually have reached the Farthest South.

HISTORY

Robert F Scott's *Discovery* expedition of 1901-04 was the first to set off with the explicit goal of reaching the Pole – and to have a reasonable chance of doing so. After an initial push to the south with a large supporting party, Scott and two fellow Britons, Edward Wilson and Ernest Shackleton, set off on what they hoped would be the final push to the Pole. But the untrained men's attempts at driving their sled dogs were inefficient, and they failed miserably, reaching only 82°16.5'S. Though this was a record for farthest south, it was more than 725km from the mark.

Shackleton tried again in 1908. His *Nimrod* expedition was a close scrape with death, part of an emerging pattern for South Polar exploration that by this time was becoming all too familiar (and in hindsight, with better planning completely unnecessary). Shackleton and three companions – Eric Marshall, Jameson Adams and Frank Wild – trekked on foot to within 180km of the elusive destination before they calculated that their dwindling provisions would make suicide the price of reaching the Pole. Making a decision that would haunt him for the rest of his life, Shackleton ordered a retreat. Later he told his wife, Emily: 'I thought you'd rather have a live donkey than a dead lion.' They returned to base in extremely poor condition and with all their supplies exhausted.

It was generally believed that the next expedition to tackle the Pole, strengthened by knowledge gained from the previous attempts, would most likely reach it. Scott, therefore, felt justifiably confident when he set sail for the south again in 1910, on his *Terra Nova* expedition. Unfortunately, as had Shackleton, Scott drew the wrong conclusion from his earlier ill-fated attempts at dog sledging. He tried several methods of travel – including motor-sledges, ponies and dogs – but eventually selected manhauling. This brutal exercise – walking or skiing while pulling sledges heavily laden with supplies – is among the most strenuous human activities possible.

Once again, it was a race with death. Scott and four companions arrived at the Pole to find, in his words, that they had done so 'without the reward of priority.' Amundsen's dark green tent, topped with the Norwegian flag, made that painfully clear. The grim photo Scott's party snapped of themselves

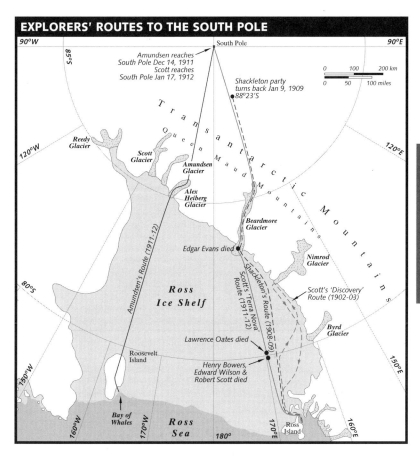

EXPLORERS' ROUTES TO THE SOUTH POLE

90°W

85°S

South Pole

90°E

Amundsen reaches
South Pole Dec 14, 1911
Scott reaches
South Pole Jan 17, 1912

Shackleton party
turns back Jan 9, 1909
88°23'S

0   100   200 km
0   50   100 miles

120°W

Reedy
Glacier

T r a n s

Q u e e n

M a u d

120°E

Scott
Glacier

Amundsen
Glacier

Alex
Heiberg
Glacier

a n t a r c t i c

M o u n t a i n s

M o u n t a i n s

Beardmore
Glacier

Edgar Evans died

Nimrod
Glacier

Amundsen's Route (1911-12)

80°S

*Ross
Ice Shelf*

Scott's 'Terra Nova'
Route (1911-12)

Shackleton's Route (1908-09)

Scott's 'Discovery'
Route (1902-03)

Byrd
Glacier

Lawrence Oates died

150°W

Roosevelt
Island

Henry Bowers,
Edward Wilson &
Robert Scott died

150°E

160°W

170°W

Bay of
Whales

*Ross
Sea*

180°

170°E

Ross
Island

160°E

SOUTH POLE

tells it all. Complete, hollow-eyed despair darkens their faces. Some now wonder if the explorers didn't deliberately martyr themselves on their desperate return journey, preferring the converse of Shackleton's simple equation.

Certainly one of the men did just that, sacrificing himself in the hope that his three remaining companions might live. On the morning of his 32nd birthday, his feet badly frostbitten, Captain Lawrence 'Titus' Oates hoped not to wake. When he found that he had lived through the night, he walked out into a raging blizzard, excusing himself to his

companions with the courtly exit line: 'I am just going outside and may be some time.' They never saw him again.

Meanwhile, their own fate was sealed. Just two days later, another severe blizzard pinned them down in their tent – just 18km from a major cache of provisions they called One Ton Depot. They remained trapped for 10 days, their supplies gradually dwindling to a single sputtering lamp. By its light, Scott, who may or may not have been the last to die, scrawled his immortal words: 'It seems a pity, but I do not think I can write more…For God's sake, look after our people.'

A search party found their bodies the following November. Buried in the tent beneath a snow cairn by the search party, the bodies will reach the Ross Sea in a few hundred years. Because of the accumulated snowfall on the icecap as it advances toward the sea, Scott, Wilson, Bowers and their tent will reach the sea through the *bottom* of the Ross Ice Shelf, making it extremely unlikely that they will be spotted by human eyes. All in all, a fitting grave.

Roald Amundsen, Scott's rival, was a polar technician. His approach was slow, methodical, proven (though he made one false start, trying to leave his coastal base too early in the season, and was forced to retreat with severe frostbite). He carried spare food, extra fuel and backups for all essential equipment. Most importantly, he brought dogs to do the heavy pulling, saving the men's strength. He also coldly calculated the worn-out dogs as food for the others.

Amundsen had a different problem than Scott: He actually wanted to reach the North Pole. His expedition left Norway with that stated intention. But after American Robert Peary announced that he had attained the North Pole on April 6, 1909, Amundsen secretly turned his ambition 180°. In his diary, he remarked upon this irony after reaching the South Pole on December 14, 1911:

The goal was reached, the journey ended. I cannot say – though I know it would sound much more effective – that the object of my life was attained. That would be romancing rather too bare-facedly. I had better be honest and admit straight out that I have never known any man to be placed in such a diametrically opposite position to the goal of his desires as I was at that moment. The regions around the North Pole – well, yes, the North Pole itself – had attracted me from childhood, and here I was at the South Pole. Can anything more topsy-turvy be imagined?

In contrast to the Britons' desperate race against starvation, the Norwegians' return trip from 90°S was little more than a bracing ski outing. After three days spent at the Pole making weather observations and precisely calculating their position, they headed north, reaching their base on the coast 'all hale and hearty.'

Amundsen's polar camp also remains buried under the annual accumulations of snow, and by now should be about 12m down. In 1993, a Norwegian group came to the Pole with hopes of recovering the tent, Norwegian flag and sledge for display at the 1994 Winter Olympics in Lillehammer. The group had to give up when one of its members fell 40m down a crevasse and was killed. The huts Amundsen left at his camp on the Ross Ice Shelf at the Bay of Whales long ago disappeared as pieces of the ice shelf calved and floated out to sea.

American Richard E Byrd, next to claim to have seen the Pole, reported flying over with three other men on November 29, 1929. Byrd pretty well summed up the quixotic quality of all quests, polar and otherwise: 'One gets there, and that is about all there is for the telling. It is the effort to get there that counts.' He dropped a rock wrapped in the American flag out the window of his Ford Trimotor plane and flew back to his camp at Little America. Although the navigation of Byrd's flight has been questioned by some authorities, the point is actually moot, for Byrd himself was among the six men in two aircraft who definitely flew over 90°S on February 15, 1947.

On neither of his flights did Byrd land, however, meaning that after Amundsen and Scott, the Pole lay untouched for another 44 years. During that interval, two world wars raged, and a third at times appeared imminent. On October 31, 1956 an American ski-equipped plane set down on the ice, making the first aircraft landing at the Pole. Pilot Conrad 'Gus' Shinn landed his Navy R4D (the military version of a DC-3) named *Que Sera Sera*, along with Admiral George Dufek and five other US Navy men who surveyed the area for a permanent scientific base. Construction began the next month, and the first South Pole station was completed by February 1957. It has operated ever since.

Three modified Ferguson farm tractors, outfitted with rubber tracks, were the first motor vehicles to reach the Pole overland, on January 4, 1958, led by New Zealander Edmund Hillary of Mt Everest fame.

Farthest South

Claims of having reached the North Pole were made in 1908 by Frederick Cook and in 1909 by Robert Peary. Though both claims are doubted by most polar historians today, their presumed authenticity at the time served to divert attention to attaining the South Pole.

The following notes describe successive penetrations leading up to Roald Amundsen's attainment of the Pole in December 1911, as well as subsequent landmark voyages.

1603 Gabriel de Castilla (Spain), with a ship's company, probably penetrated the Southern Ocean south of Drake Passage. Subsequently several Spanish and other merchant vessels reported being blown south of 60°S rounding Cape Horn in severe weather.

1773 James Cook (UK), with companies aboard HMS *Resolution* and HMS *Adventure*, crossed the Antarctic Circle (66.55°S) off Enderby Land on January 17 and later reached a farthest south of 71°10'S off Marie Byrd Land on December 30, 1774.

1842 James Clark Ross (UK), with companies aboard HMS *Erebus* and HMS *Terror*, reached 78.17°S in the Ross Sea on February 23.

1900 Hugh Evans (UK) and three others from *Southern Cross* sledged to 78.83°S on the Ross Ice Shelf on February 23. This was the first southern penetration by land.

1902 Robert Scott (UK) and two others sledged to 82.28°S, near the foot of the Beardmore Glacier, on December 30.

1909 Ernest Shackleton (UK) and three others sledged up the Beardmore Glacier to 88.38°S on January 9. This was approximately 160km from the South Pole – but insufficient supplies necessitated their return.

1911 Roald Amundsen (Norway) and four others dog-sledged to 90°S on December 14.

1912 Robert Scott and four others sledged to 90°S on January 17. They arrived 33 days after the Norwegians had departed and all perished during the return journey. Their bodies and notes were found in November that same year.

1929 Richard Byrd (US), with an aircraft crew, claimed to have flown over the South Pole from the Ross Ice Shelf on November 29, but the navigation has been questioned. On February 15, 1947, he definitely flew over it, with crew aboard two aircraft from Little America IV station, which was located on the Ross Ice Shelf.

1956 John Torbert (US) and six others flew across Antarctica via the South Pole (Ross Island to Weddell Sea and back, without landing) on January 13. On October 31, Conrad Shinn (US), with an aircraft crew, landed at the South Pole. A permanent station was established and sustained by aircraft.

1958 Vivian Fuchs (British Commonwealth), with an expeditionary party, reached the South Pole by motor vehicles and dog sledges on January 20, and continued across Antarctica (Weddell Sea to Ross Sea).

Subsequently, several expeditions have crossed the Antarctic through the South Pole by surface, and many have made one-way surface journeys to the Pole, departing by aircraft. Most adventurers' South Pole journeys during the past decade have used aircraft, and many started well inland, far from any place that a ship could reach.

– **Robert Headland**

Amundsen – first to the Pole

Hillary's team was laying depots for the first successful crossing of the continent, by British explorer Vivian Fuchs' Commonwealth Trans-Antarctic expedition.

Women were notably absent from these expeditions. Most governments operating in Antarctica had an all-but-official ban on women in Antarctica for decades. This is perhaps better understood today when we recall that expeditions were often staffed by members of the military – a group that was then all-male. Still, Antarctic sexism was often justified by lame rationalizations about physical strength, sexual frustrations and even the difficulty of providing separate toilet facilities. The influence of the male expedition members' wives back home may have had something to do with the policy.

The first women joined the US Antarctic Program in 1969. The first women to reach the Pole arrived by US Navy aircraft on November 11 that year. The six of them – not wishing for one to later claim she had been first out of the aircraft – linked arms and walked out the back of the plane together. They spent a few hours visiting the station before flying back to McMurdo. Another two years passed before the first woman actually spent a 'night' at the Pole, in December 1971. She was Louise Hutchinson, a reporter for the *Chicago Tribune*, and she only got to stay because weather delayed her flight out. But two years later, two American women, Nan Scott and Donna Muchmore, became the first women to work at the Pole. By 1979, the Pole station had a female physician, Dr Michele Eileen Raney, the first woman to winter at 90°S. On January 6, 1995, Norwegian Liv Arnesen arrived at the Pole after skiing unaccompanied from the edge of the continent in 50 days, the first woman to accomplish the feat.

The 300 Club

One day, it was announced that the temperature was steadying at around -101°F (-73.9°C). So a group of us – 15 men and four women – gained our exclusive membership in the 300 Club. We crowded into the sauna – cranked up to 200°F (93°C) – and began to work up a sweat. About 15 minutes later, we burst through the door, down the hallway and out of the Dome – a sheer drop of 300°F. I wore nothing but socks, tennis shoes and a neck gaiter over my nose and mouth so my lungs wouldn't get frostbitten while I ran. Someone was taking pictures – I could see the flash going off but not much else, thanks to all the steam coming from our bodies. Once outside, I ran up the slight snow incline to the surface. Some people stopped there, took a few photos and returned to the sauna. A few of us continued. I stopped halfway across the taxiway because I couldn't run any farther, but six people made it to the Ceremonial Pole, and one made it all the way to the Geographic Pole. Then it was a mad dash back inside. I'm glad I did it, though I did get a touch of frostbite on my thumbs (of all places) – nothing serious. Better my thumbs than somewhere more important!

– **Ricardo Ramos,**
1995-96 station science leader at Amundsen-Scott South Pole station

Tourists first arrived at the South Pole in 1968, when a chartered Convair flew over both poles from November 22 to December 3 as part of a fund-raising effort for a Boston museum. The South polar leg left Christchurch, landed at McMurdo Sound for a few hours' look at both Scott's Hut and McMurdo station, then flew over the Pole at a low altitude and on to Argentina. The first tourist flight to land at the Pole was on January 11, 1988, when a pair of DHC-6 Twin Otters operated by Adventure Network International, also known as 'Antarctic Airways' (see the Getting There & Away section), brought the first 15 paying passengers to 90°S – for a cool US$25,000 or US$35,000 each. The higher price was paid by the seven tourists who wished to be in the first plane, which landed 15 minutes before the other.

GEOGRAPHY

Unlike its northern conjugate, which sits in the middle of the Arctic Ocean, the South Pole lies amid a mind-bending wasteland of monotonously flat snow-covered ice called the polar plateau. The Pole itself is among the most isolated spots on Earth, surrounded by thousands of square kilometers unrelieved by a single feature to interest the eye. In every direction you look, there is only unbroken horizon.

CLIMATE

Temperatures on the Polar Plateau range from -82°C to -14°C. The mean temperature is -49°C. Winter wind chills can plummet down to -110°C. The elevation is 2835m, but the cold and polar location make the air pressure the equivalent of 3230m. New arrivals are often exhausted after even gentle exercise until they become acclimated. The average wind speed is just 20 km/h, a summer breeze compared to the 320 km/h katabatic winds found on the coast. The extreme cold and very low absolute humidity (0.03%) combine to make this the world's driest desert.

Very little snow actually falls in Antarctica's interior, thanks to this extreme cold and low humidity. The most common form of precipitation is ice crystals, also called

South Pole Weather Data

The following data are derived from records dating from 1957 to 1999

Avg Snow Accumulation (fallen & drifted): 23 cm/year
Avg Liquid Equivalent: 8.6 cm/year
High Temperature: -13.6°C (Dec 1978)
Low Temperature: -82.8°C (June 1982)
Avg Annual Temperature: -49.4°C
Highest Pressure: 719.0 millibars (Aug 1996)
Lowest Pressure: 641.7 millibars (July 1985)
Avg Pressure: 681.4 millibars
Avg Wind Speed: 20.0 kph
Peak Wind Speed: 88.5 kph (Aug 1989)
Source: Amundsen-Scott South Pole Station Meteorology Department

'diamond dust.' These often fall out of a clear sky, sometimes creating beautiful sundogs, sun pillars and other refractions around the sun and the moon.

The sun ends a spectacular weeks-long sunset and dips below the horizon on about March 22, though the extreme atmospheric refraction sometimes allows it to be seen for a day or two more, and twilight lingers for another six or seven weeks. Then the potentially depression-inducing unbroken darkness sets in, lightened only by the surreal sky show of the aurora australis and the stars. On about September 22, pale, sunshine-deprived winterers rejoice at sunrise, though up to seven weeks of dawn precede the actual arrival of *El Sol*. All year round, South Polarites can fall victim to a peculiar form of polar pathology called 'Big Eye,' a period of disorientation and sleeplessness caused by the lack of a regular light-dark cycle.

The disintegration of the ozone layer – the notorious 'ozone hole' – allows powerful ultraviolet rays to penetrate the atmosphere, causing severe sunburn to unprotected skin.

VISITING THE SOUTH POLE

Because of the Pole's extreme altitude, many visitors experience altitude sickness upon arrival (at least, those who do not arrive on

SOUTH POLE

foot or skis). Shortness of breath, lack of energy and very painful headaches are among the symptoms. The first 24 hours are the worst, it is said, but since most tourists remain at the Pole for only a few hours, that fact doesn't help much. Some visitors recommend taking three or four aspirin on the flight to the Pole to ease the headache.

At 90° S, you'll probably first visit the Ceremonial Pole and the Geographic Pole to take your 'hero pictures.' You can also expect to be invited inside the Dome for a visit to the dining room and possibly a quick look around the station. While there's no shop at which to buy anything, you can have letters or postcards stamped with the station postmark.

No tourists stay overnight at the Pole, because there's no room under the Dome for extra people. All visitors are expected to be completely self-sufficient, so Adventure Network International – currently the sole tour operator offering Polar visits – carries a full complement of emergency equipment and food to enable their clients to camp for several days if necessary.

Ceremonial Pole

This red-and-white-striped 'barber' pole, capped by a chromium globe, is surrounded by the flags of the original 12 Antarctic Treaty signatories, so it offers the perfect photo-op. But it's not the real thing – it's just for show.

Geographic Pole

Because the ice at the Pole moves about 10m per year in the direction of 43°W, the Geographic Pole marker has to be moved each austral summer. At this rate of movement, the ground now at the Pole will drop into the Southern Ocean in 120,000 years. The 'new' South Pole is recalculated annually using a combination of old-fashioned science (the shadow tip method) and the latest technology (global positioning satellites). The marker is about 4m long, but two-thirds of it gets pounded into the ice with a

SCOTT POLAR RESEARCH INSTITUTE ARCHIVES

Amundsen's tent tells Scott he's not first at the Pole.

special Day-Glo orange mallet during the brief annual Pole-moving ceremony. Afterward, South Polar denizens rush back indoors for medicinal hot chocolate. The long line of markers stretching off into the distance marks the former South Poles. Due to snow buildup, they appear to be sinking into the ground.

The American flag is conspicuously planted about a meter from the Pole marker, which reads

Geographic South Pole/Roald Amundsen, December 14, 1911
'So we arrived and were able to plant our flag at the geographical South Pole'

Robert F Scott, January 17, 1912
'The Pole, Yes, but under very different circumstances from those expected'

Elevation: 9301ft (2835m)

You may hear about three other Poles while in Antarctica:

- The South Magnetic Pole (located at 64° 42'S, 138° 36'E in 1995), off the coast near Commonwealth Bay, is where a magnetic compass needle will try to point straight down. Its position moves about 10km to 15km a year presently in a north to north-westerly direction. Tourist ships to the region typically sail right over it. The south magnetic pole, then on land, was first reached in 1909 by Douglas Mawson, Edgeworth David and Alistair Mackay.
- The South Geomagnetic Pole (located at 79° 18'S, 108° 30'E in 1995) is where the flux in the Earth's electromagnetic field is manifested. Russia's Vostok station is nearby.
- The Pole of Maximum Inaccessibility (84°S, 65°E) is the point farthest from any Antarctic coast.

AMUNDSEN-SCOTT SOUTH POLE STATION
The Dome

The Dome, as it's universally known, was built from 1971 to 1970. Measuring 50m in diameter at its base and 15m high, the silver-grey aluminum geodesic dome covers three structures, each two stories high, which provide accommodations, dining, laboratory

and recreation facilities. The Dome protects these buildings and their occupants from the wind, but not the cold; it's unheated and has a packed snow floor. A line of steel arches runs off to the left and to the right of the Dome's entryway. They house the garage complex, gymnasium, carpenter shop, power plant, biomedical facility and main fuel storage, which consists of double-contained steel tanks holding 1.7 million litres. Sub-ice utility corridors, called utilidors, carry glycol heat-circulation pipes between facilities, as well as water, sewage, phone, computer and electric lines.

In the summer, South Pole station can accommodate as many as 220 people, with up to 190 crowded into the above-ground Summer Camp, located 140m from the Dome. During winter, 28 people inhabit the Dome. From mid-February to late October, no flights can make it in, so they are physically cut off from the rest of the world. These South Polar 'winterovers,' as they are called, are members of one of the most elite groups in the world, numbering fewer than 700 people.

The hierarchy at the station can be confusing. The person in charge of station operations in the summer goes by the unfortunate acronym of SPAM: South Pole Area Manager. The Winter Site Manager usually takes the role of station leader during the cold and dark. Also during the winter, the Station Science Leader is in charge of the scientists, while in the summer, science teams are run by individual Field Team Leaders. During the summer, highest overall rank is held by the National Science Foundation Representative, or NSF Rep – someone you could call top dog at the bottom of the world.

Walking down the long ramp into the Dome through the huge garagelike doors about 6.5m below the snow surface, you can't help notice the sign overhead: 'The United States of America Welcomes You to Amundsen-Scott South Pole Station.' This causes many people to ask, 'No one owns the South Pole, do they?' The answer, of course, is no. But Amundsen-Scott South Pole Station is, among other things, an ice-and-aluminum

SOUTH POLE

SOUTH POLE

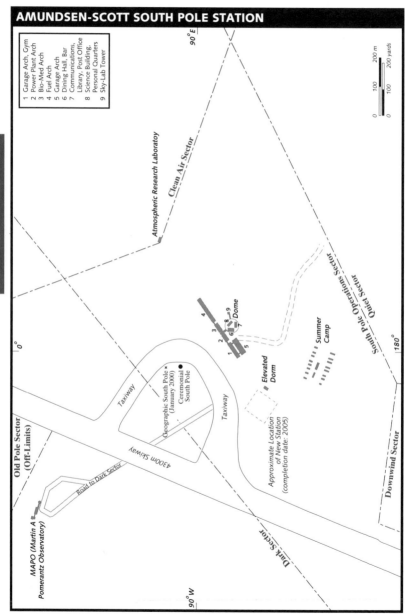

AMUNDSEN-SCOTT SOUTH POLE STATION

1 Garage Arch, Gym
2 Power Plant Arch
3 Bio-Med Arch
4 Fuel Arch
5 Garage Arch
6 Dining Hall, Bar
7 Communications,
   Library, Post Office
8 Science Building,
   Personal Quarters
9 Sky-Lab Tower

lesson in Antarctic realpolitik. While no certain ownership of Antarctica exists, and the Antarctic Treaty agrees to set aside the territorial claims made by seven countries, the stark reality is that some countries are more equal than others in Antarctic politics. Before its collapse, the Soviet Union, for example, maintained a ring of research bases that encircled the continent, while the US's Pole station sits astride all the lines of longitude, neatly occupying all time zones – and six of the seven Antarctic claims – at once. (Amundsen-Scott station, by the way, uses New Zealand time since resupply flights to the Pole and McMurdo station originate in Christchurch, and this simplifies logistics.)

In the recent past, private expeditions arriving at the Pole were greeted by the Americans with a decidedly chilly welcome, one that had nothing to do with the subzero temperatures. Not that the scientists, technicians and support staff at Amundsen-Scott disliked visitors. In fact, just the reverse was true. But thanks to the official US government prohibition of support to nongovernmental activities in Antarctica (the reasoning is that scientists are disrupted by tourists and that the inevitable accidents require costly search-and-rescue), the station staff were told to have no contact with visitors. Now, thankfully, a more enlightened policy operates – a warm welcome is offered by the South Polarites, though the official no-support policy continues.

Three sky divers free-fell 2500m to their deaths over the South Pole in 1997 when they failed to open their parachutes. Because station members had the grisly task of excavating the bodies from the 1.2m-deep craters they made in the snow, such 'adventure tourism' remains a point of controversy.

Life Under the Dome

South Polar living is difficult. It takes some people two or three weeks simply to adjust to the Pole's altitude, as the body strives to produce more red blood cells to handle the oxygen-thin air. Extreme cold limits the time one can spend outdoors, and the darkness and even more extreme cold of the polar winter can be very hazardous to human life.

(Station members, however, routinely go outside the Dome even on the coldest and darkest days. Flag lines – bamboo poles with small flags attached to the top and spaced every 2m – guide the way from the Dome to outlying buildings.) During the summer, showers are limited to two minutes' running water and can be taken only twice a week. Fire is an omnipresent danger in the thin, dry atmosphere, which can turn wood-construction buildings into tinderboxes. That same dry air cracks skin, lips and the inside of nostrils, so petroleum jelly must be used to keep them moist.

The isolation can be overwhelming. Wintering at the Pole is in some ways similar to being an astronaut, albeit one who has a bit more room to walk around and can use email. The accommodation probably doesn't help much, since the rooms – which at least are private for winterovers – are smaller than the average prison cell.

During the summer ham radio phone patches allow station members to talk with family at home, but the calls can only be originated at the station – no one can call the Pole this way. But during the winter, atmospheric conditions sometimes don't allow for good signal propagation, so the ham radio is unreliable. In any case, as newer technologies have taken over, the ham patch appears to be losing popularity. Now station members can also use high-frequency radio to patch calls via McMurdo station. Internet telephone technology produces high-quality calls, and the station also has two Iridium satellite telephones.

A psychologist who has studied Antarctic winterovers and helped in their selection sums up their isolation like this: 'The normal ways we deal with things when we're fed up – either withdrawing and shutting the door or going out to seek other people – are not available.'

Indeed, on cloudy, moonless winter nights, station residents may feel they're on another planet. One recent winterover described walking outside on such a night. 'I couldn't see anything…It was so dark I couldn't see my own hand in front of my face,' he said. 'I might as well have been walking with my

Coping with Isolation

Although it's rarely a problem for tourists, Antarctica's remoteness can be difficult to handle for many winterers. Several mental health coping mechanisms are common. To relieve the boredom of the polar winter, expeditioners sometimes shave their heads or pierce their ears or nose, knowing they can revert back to their 'old selves' before returning home. Sometimes whole research bases indulge in a kind of collective cultism, in which a certain song or movie is replayed over and over, with station members memorizing the entire dialogue and playing particular roles. A film version of Jane Austen's *Pride and Prejudice* assumed bizarre importance for a wintering party at one sub-Antarctic island. A group of winterers at a continental station became fairly infatuated with a ZZ Top music video. For obvious reasons, drag enjoys a long history in Antarctica, from Scott's *Discovery* expedition's Royal Terror Theatre to Australian stations' four-decade tradition of performing bawdy versions of *Cinderella*. Perhaps flirting with a little paranoia, winterover crews at the South Pole usually screen *The Thing* immediately after the departure of the year's last plane out. *The Shining* is also popular.

eyes closed. It took my eyes at least three minutes to adjust enough so that I could see even very faint outlines of nearby buildings.'

That kind of sensory deprivation is also evident in the fact that one of the biggest treats enjoyed by Pole station members is opening magazines to find the perfume sample strips that are included in some advertisements.

On the plus side, of course, there are no bills, traffic jams, biting insects or waiting in line. On clear nights, the stars and aurora australis provide a spectacular show, and the winterover crew gets treated to the Green Flash (caused by the prism-like effect of the Earth's atmosphere on the rays of the setting sun) in March and early April.

South Polarites eat very well – steak and lobster are often on the menu – even though

frozen, dried and canned food obviously form the majority of meals. One chef with a finely honed sense of humor started a custom he called 'Dog Day' by serving hot dogs for lunch on the day that Amundsen had to shoot his remaining dogs on his journey to the Pole. The custom, however, appears not to have taken hold. Through the long dark winter, chocolate is a favorite. One popular dessert is 'buzz bars,' which are not what some people might guess but rather brownies with chocolate-covered expresso beans baked into them. Ice cream is also a local favorite, but since it's stored outdoors, it has to be warmed in a microwave before it can be eaten. Despite the effort put into procuring and preparing top-quality food, the South Pole is apparently a *very* good place to lose weight. Even with three full meals a day plus numerous snacks, many people still manage to lose several kilograms during their stay, with losses of 20kg not uncommon in a 16-week summer!

Interestingly, the station now gets its water from a well, a welcome improvement over the former inefficient system of melting clean snow, which required large amounts of fuel and time. The well, more than 120m deep, is created by using waste heat from the power plant to make a hot-water 'drill.' Below the firn layer, the snow is no longer porous, so adding heat melts the ice, but the water can't seep out into the surrounding ice. As a result, a large pool of water is created that can be pumped out and used. Of course, the water is also very old, since the well is so deep. There's an unusual side benefit to the well: the filtered water has yielded hundreds of thousands of micrometeorites for scientific study.

Recreation opportunities on the polar plateau are naturally limited, but inventive South Polarites have come up with improvisations such as volleybag, a version of volleyball that uses a beanbag instead. Radio darts, played against other winter stations around the continent (scores are communicated by radio), is also popular despite its heavy dependency on trust – though one early participating station was later found not to even have a dartboard! 'Dome sledding' is done on the back side of the Dome. The station library houses more than 1000 videos and 3000 books. On Christmas Eve, the 4.4km Race Around the World circles the Pole in -23°C temperatures, challenging runners, joggers, walkers, skiers and even snowmobilers. The 1995 winner (on foot) had an impressive time of 13:55. Christmas itself is marked by a 'Yankee gift exchange,' at which station members can either take a wrapped gift from the table, or take an opened gift from someone else.

The South Pole station bar is a small lounge on the second floor of the galley building, boasting a beautiful oak-and-brass bar. It's the only place under the Dome where smoking is allowed. There's no bartender, so residents bring their own refreshments and operate on an honor system. If they leave something there, it's open to everyone, and if they have a drink from something left there, they replenish it. The system seems to work well, even with as many as 200 people on station in summer. Liquor and beer are sold in the station store. Most of the beer is from New Zealand, since that's the most cost-effective place from which to transport it. Another popular hangout is the small, volunteer-run hydroponic greenhouse. As one veteran says, 'The lights, warmth, plants and humidity make it a nice place to get away from the normal reality of daily life at the South Pole.' While the garden's actual yield is modest – 500g of fresh vegetables a week, enough for small salads in the winter – tending the plants is a nice diversion for some station members.

Then there's the unique membership known as the 300 Club (see the boxed text 'The 300 Club' in this chapter). To join, you simply wait until the temperature drops below -100°F (-73°C) – which happens only during the deepest cold of winter. After you steam in a 200°F (93°C) sauna until you begin to sweat, you streak naked (shoes, however, are highly recommended) out of the Dome and up to the snow surface. Some members push on even farther, going about 100m out of the Dome and around the Ceremonial Pole. While some people claim that the rime of flash-frozen sweat actually acts

as insulation, if you fall, the feeling of the ice against your reddened skin is similar to that of a severe burn and as rough as falling on granite. Induction into the 300 Club requires photographic documentation – but with so much steam rising from the hot bodies, most pictures turn out to be rather foggy.

Building the New Station

The Dome has had a hard life under harsh conditions. Parts of the under-ice complex are now unsafe. Occasional power brownouts and fuel leaks also threaten station security, as does drifting snow, which will eventually crush the Dome. Because of all these problems, the US government is building a new 6129-sq-m above-ground facility to replace it.

The project, which began in 1997, requires 80 construction workers working round-the-clock shifts during the 24-hours-of-sunlight summer days. The winterover population, meanwhile, has nearly doubled, the extra staff devoted to construction. To bring in all the necessary building materials, the number of annual flights to the Pole has jumped from 230 to 330. The new station should be completed in 2005 at a cost of US$153 million.

Two separate horseshoe-shaped modules will be connected by flexible walkways and raised on stilts to prevent the destructive snow buildup. The stilts will be able to be jacked up as snow accumulates underneath and eventually rises to the level of the buildings. Being on the surface, the new station will also prevent the claustrophobic 'cabin fever' induced by living underground. It will accommodate 110 people, with the option (if additional funding is available) to house 150.

One module will house living quarters, dining room, bar, hospital, laundry, store, post office and greenhouse. In the other will be offices, labs, computers, telecommunications, emergency power plant, conference rooms, music practice rooms and a gym. Reading rooms and libraries will be scattered throughout both units.

The old Dome is to be dismantled in 2004 or 2005 and taken back to the US for disposal or re-erection, perhaps as the centerpiece of a national Antarctic museum.

SOUTH POLE

Science Facilities

Most, if not all, of the scientific facilities at the Pole are off-limits to visitors, in order to prevent disruption to the research. Time is at a premium for most scientists working here. If they're unable to complete their work in the time allotted, they may not be able to win a grant to return to Antarctica. Other laboratories are off-limits because their delicate instrumentation could be contaminated or decalibrated by unauthorized visitors. Still, it's interesting to know what science is being done at Pole.

Among the most important research is work on the notorious 'ozone hole,' the thinning of the atmosphere's ozone layer, caused by halocarbons and other synthetic chemicals (see the Antarctic Science chapter). Scientists at the Atmospheric Research Observatory, located several hundred meters

Life at the South Pole

Pic and I were walking back from preparing some bad batteries from the emergency power plant for return to the States. It was a clear night, the moon was full and there was hardly any wind, though it was -70° C. Through the smoke of the power plant, we noticed a slight green glow. We crossed over to the other side of the exhaust plume and saw the sky beginning to come alive with aurora.

The two of us stood there watching the aurora grow until it almost covered half the sky, lighting up with all the colors of the spectrum, colors that can never be reproduced or described. It danced around like a curtain blowing in the wind, continuing to shift and flicker, darting upward and all across the sky from horizon to zenith. After 15 minutes, our boots froze solid. It felt as if we were wearing wooden shoes, but we didn't pay any attention to the cold. The display was so impressive that our gaze remained skyward for 45 minutes. When the aurora died down, we strolled inside the Dome, thinking how unfortunate some people were, since they would never get to experience such a magnificent show.

This is the reason we come down here and endure the winter temperatures and not being able to see the sun for six months. Seeing the aurora or the dust glow from the arms of the Milky Way galaxy or the stars in the night sky makes the temperatures – which can drop to -80° C – bearable. It's magical standing out on this barren plateau of ice. The 41 of us here – nine women and 32 men – live from mid-February to early November with no physical contact with the outside world. All that breaks our 8½ months of isolation is the Internet and ham radio.

Winter at the South Pole can be described as one of the world's best-kept secrets. During the long dark night, people must use their imaginations to keep themselves entertained. Brewing beer, watching movies, building models and studying a foreign language are just some of the activities people enjoy here. There is always an abundant amount to do as long as you keep the right attitude. The best way of dealing with the isolation and darkness is to stay busy. One favorite activity is sitting around the galley looking at an atlas and discussing travels and home – if a place to call home even exists.

Just arriving on station can take its toll. Every year, some people are sent back to McMurdo with altitude sickness. The actual altitude at Pole is 2835m, but due to atmospheric effects, the air is thinner, so the physiological altitude can vary from 2800m to 3690m. As the physiological altitude increases in the middle of winter, many people find themselves lying in bed at night unable to sleep.

Our food is set outside around the inside of the geodesic dome that we live in. With no animals to consume it and temperatures that never get above freezing, we have the perfect environment for food storage. Many nights while sitting around the galley, eating either hamburgers or steaks, you realize that the conditions down here are not bad. We have a warm place to live and always plenty of good food. We even manage to have a barbecue occasionally, although it can be difficult even getting the barbecue lit in this intense cold.

upwind of the Dome, study some of the purest air on Earth in hopes of learning about pollution and how it spreads around the globe. Another group in this observatory is using LIDAR, or light radar, to study the formation of polar stratospheric clouds, which act as the seeds for the depletion of ozone each austral spring.

The South Pole is a world center for astronomy, thanks to its high altitude and thin, dry atmosphere. The centrifugal force of the earth's rotation flattens out the atmosphere at both poles, and the extreme cold freezes water vapor out of the air. The astronomical instruments are located about 1km from the Dome in the so-called Dark Sector, where extraneous light, heat and electromagnetic radiation are prohibited, so as not to disturb the experiments. Noise and other Earth-shaking activity, meanwhile, are banned in

Life at the South Pole

Winterovers are given their own rooms. It's a very small space, but a very big necessity in coping with life here. The rooms are as small as 1.8m x 3.0m, but that space becomes treasured as the year progresses. Because everything must be shared during the winter, your room is the only place to go that is your own private space.

Holidays are celebrated with great enthusiasm. At Christmas there is a gift exchange and a 'race around the world.' New Year's is kind of a free-for-all party. The main celebrations during the times of isolation are sunrise, sunset and solstice. Since there is only one sunset and one sunrise during the year, both are celebrated. The solstice is the middle of the period of darkness, the point when the sun starts its slow return back up above the horizon. The solstice is very symbolic for the winterover crew, since it means that it will be only another three months until we get to see the sun again. This year we celebrated the solstice with a formal dinner. Every year these events are celebrated differently, as determined by the ever-changing crew.

The people here are from all walks of life. They maintain the generators, repair broken equipment, cook, construct new buildings and operate the science experiments. The crew is selected from across the US, with some scientists coming from other countries. Watching the last plane leave for the winter, you realize that these 41 people are your new family, upon which your life depends.

Everyone must work closely together, especially in emergencies. When the fire alarm goes off or when a generator stops working, the entire crew stops its normal day-to-day operations and responds. Fire is one of our biggest dangers – even the smallest fire in the wrong area could produce a life-threatening situation. When the fire alarm goes off or the power goes out, one of the things running through your mind is that we're on our own – there is no way out!

The South Pole is an unknown element to most of the world, something that very few understand. When companies try to design items to be used down here, they have a difficult time. Most have nothing to which to compare these conditions and cannot imagine what it is like here. Everything from bulldozers to computers has to be modified or specially treated in order to operate here. The simplest things become extremely difficult with the altitude, dryness, six months of daylight, then six months of darkness, and the lowest temperatures on Earth.

Wintering over at the South Pole teaches you a great deal and helps you appreciate things back home that most people overlook: a rainy day, the smell of fresh-cut grass and watching the sun rise and set every day. Most important, it teaches you that getting along with your neighbors can make life so much more enjoyable.

– Mike Masterman,
winter site manager at South Pole Station for 1998-99,
who has wintered over at the Pole twice and sent this article via email

SOUTH POLE

the Quiet Sector, where seismological studies are done.

Perhaps because their highly technical work may appear dull to the uninitiated, scientists sometimes like to jazz up the names of their experiments for the general public – and their funding governments. Astronomers at the South Pole's CARA, the Center for Astrophysical Research in Antarctica, use telescopes with cool-sounding names. SPIREX, the South Polar Infrared Explorer, seeks infrared radiation from deep space that signals young galaxies. One experiment, called VIPER (which doesn't stand for anything), looks for small variations in the temperature of microwave radiation dating back to just 1 million years after the Big Bang. This may reveal mysteries about the structure of the universe. AMANDA, the Antarctic Muon and Neutrino Detector Array, is a collection of 200m-long strings of instruments called photomultipliers lowered into holes drilled up to 2180m down into the ice with hot water. AMANDA looks for ultra-

high-energy subatomic particles called neutrinos that pass through the Earth and interact with atoms in the ice – perfectly transparent at that depth – creating blue flashes of light detected by the photomultipliers. Neutrinos may shed light on the power sources of galaxies and the workings of supernovae, the massive explosions of stars. AST/RO, the Antarctic Submillimeter Telescope and Remote Observatory, surveys emissions of carbon atoms from the large clouds of gas and dust that lie between stars. Researchers hope to learn more about how the collapse of these dust clouds gives birth to stars. Finally, SPASE-2 (South Pole Air Shower Experiment, part 2) searches for sources of gamma radiation out in the universe.

All of these instruments detect radiation not visible to the human eye. There are, of course, several telescopes at the Pole in the visible range of light. Taking advantage of the thin atmosphere, they peer far into the Pole's star-filled night sky.

Appendix: The Antarctic Treaty

The Antarctic Treaty was made on December 1, 1959, and came into force June 23, 1961.

TEXT OF THE ANTARCTIC TREATY

The Governments of Argentina, Australia, Belgium, Chile, the French Republic, Japan, New Zealand, Norway, the Union of South Africa, the Union of Soviet Socialist Republics, the United Kingdom of Great Britain and Northern Ireland, and the United States of America,

Recognizing that it is in the interest of all mankind that Antarctica shall continue forever to be used exclusively for peaceful purposes and shall not become the scene or object of international discord;

Acknowledging the substantial contributions to scientific knowledge resulting from international cooperation in scientific investigation in Antarctica;

Convinced that the establishment of a firm foundation for the continuation and development of such cooperation on the basis of freedom of scientific investigation in Antarctica as applied during the International Geophysical Year accords with the interests of science and the progress of all mankind;

Convinced also that a treaty ensuring the use of Antarctica for peaceful purposes only and the continuance of international harmony in Antarctica will further the purposes and principles embodied in the Charter of the United Nations;

Have agreed as follows:

Article I

1. Antarctica shall be used for peaceful purposes only. There shall be prohibited, inter alia, any measure of a military nature, such as the establishment of military bases and fortifications, the carrying out of military maneuvers, as well as the testing of any type of weapon.

2. The present Treaty shall not prevent the use of military personnel or equipment for scientific research or for any other peaceful purpose.

Article II

Freedom of scientific investigation in Antarctica and cooperation toward that end, as applied during the International Geophysical Year, shall continue, subject to the provisions of the present Treaty.

Article III

1. In order to promote international cooperation in scientific investigation in Antarctica, as provided for in Article II of the present Treaty, the Contracting Parties agree that, to the greatest extent feasible and practicable:

(a) information regarding plans for scientific programs in Antarctica shall be exchanged to permit maximum economy of and efficiency of operations;

(b) scientific personnel shall be exchanged in Antarctica between expeditions and stations;

(c) scientific observations and results from Antarctica shall be exchanged and made freely available.

Article IV

1. Nothing contained in the present Treaty shall be interpreted as:

(a) a renunciation by any Contracting Party of previously asserted rights of or claims to territorial sovereignty in Antarctica;

(b) a renunciation or diminution by any Contracting Party of any basis of claim to territorial sovereignty in Antarctica which it may have whether as a result of its activities or those of its nationals in Antarctica, or otherwise;

(c) prejudicing the position of any Contracting Party as regards its recognition or non-recognition of any other State's rights of or claim or basis of claim to territorial sovereignty in Antarctica.

2. No acts or activities taking place while the present Treaty is in force shall constitute a basis for asserting, supporting or denying a claim to territorial sovereignty in Antarctica or create any rights of sovereignty in Antarctica. No new claim, or enlargement of an existing claim, to territorial sovereignty in Antarctica shall be asserted while the present Treaty is in force.

Article V

1. Any nuclear explosions in Antarctica and the disposal there of radioactive waste material shall be prohibited.

2. In the event of the conclusion of international agreements concerning the use of nuclear energy, including nuclear explosions and the disposal of radioactive waste material, to which all of the Contracting Parties whose representatives are entitled to participate in the meetings provided for under Article IX are parties, the rules established under such agreements shall apply in Antarctica.

Article VI

The provisions of the present Treaty shall apply to the area south of 60°S Latitude, including all ice shelves, but nothing in the present Treaty shall prejudice or in any way affect the rights, or the exercise of the rights, of any State under international law with regard to the high seas within that area.

Article VII

1. In order to promote the objectives and ensure the observance of the provisions of the present Treaty, each Contracting Party whose representatives are entitled to participate in the meetings referred to in Article IX of the Treaty shall have the right to designate observers to carry out any inspection provided for by the present Article. Observers shall be nationals of the Contracting Parties which designate them. The names of observers shall be communicated to every other Contracting Party having the right to designate observers, and like notice shall be given of the termination of their appointment.

2. Each observer designated in accordance with the provisions of paragraph 1 of this Article shall have complete freedom of access at any time to any or all areas of Antarctica.

3. All areas of Antarctica, including all stations, installations and equipment within those areas, and all ships and aircraft at points of discharging or embarking cargoes or personnel in Antarctica, shall be open at all times to inspection by any observers designated in accordance with paragraph 1 of this Article.

4. Aerial observation may be carried out at any time over any or all areas of Antarctica by any of the Contracting Parties having the right to designate observers.

5. Each Contracting Party shall, at the time when the present Treaty enters into force for it, inform the other Contracting Parties, and thereafter shall give them notice in advance, of

(a) all expeditions to and within Antarctica, on the part of its ships or nationals, and all expeditions to Antarctica organized in or proceeding from its territory;

(b) all stations in Antarctica occupied by its nationals; and

(c) any military personnel or equipment intended to be introduced by it into Antarctica subject to the conditions prescribed in paragraph 2 of Article I of the present Treaty.

Article VIII

1. In order to facilitate the exercise of their functions under the present Treaty, and without prejudice to the respective positions of the Contracting Parties relating to jurisdiction over all other persons in Antarctica, observers designated under paragraph 1 of Article VII and scientific personnel exchanged under sub-paragraph 1(b) of Article III of the Treaty, and members of the staffs accompanying any such persons, shall

be subject only to the jurisdiction of the Contracting Party of which they are nationals in respect of all acts or omissions occurring while they are in Antarctica for the purpose of exercising their functions.

2. Without prejudice to the provisions of paragraph 1 of this Article, and pending the adoption of measures in pursuance of sub-paragraph 1(e) of Article IX, the Contracting Parties concerned in any case of dispute with regard to the exercise of jurisdiction in Antarctica shall immediately consult together with a view to reaching a mutually acceptable solution.

Article IX

1. Representatives of the Contracting Parties named in the preamble to the present Treaty shall meet at the City of Canberra within two months after the date of entry into force of the Treaty, and thereafter at suitable intervals and places, for the purpose of exchanging information, consulting together on matters of common interest pertaining to Antarctica, and formulating and considering, and recommending to their Governments, measures in furtherance of the principles and objectives of the Treaty, including measures regarding:

(a) use of Antarctica for peaceful purposes only;

(b) facilitation of scientific research in Antarctica;

(c) facilitation of international scientific cooperation in Antarctica;

(d) facilitation of the exercise of the rights of inspection provided for in Article VII of the Treaty;

(e) questions relating to the exercise of jurisdiction in Antarctica;

(f) preservation and conservation of living resources in Antarctica.

2. Each Contracting Party which has become a party to the present Treaty by accession under Article XIII shall be entitled to appoint representatives to participate in the meetings referred to in paragraph 1 of the present Article, during such times as that Contracting Party demonstrates its interest in Antarctica by conducting substantial research activity there, such as the establishment of a scientific station or the despatch of a scientific expedition.

3. Reports from the observers referred to in Article VII of the present Treaty shall be transmitted to the representatives of the Contracting Parties participating in the meetings referred to in paragraph 1 of the present Article.

4. The measures referred to in paragraph 1 of this Article shall become effective when approved by all the Contracting Parties whose representatives were entitled to participate in the meetings held to consider those measures.

5. Any or all of the rights established in the present Treaty may be exercised as from the date of entry into force of the Treaty whether or not any measures facilitating the exercise of such rights have been proposed, considered or approved as provided in this Article.

Article X

Each of the Contracting Parties undertakes to exert appropriate efforts, consistent with the Charter of the United Nations, to the end that no one engages in any activity in Antarctica contrary to the principles or purposes of the present Treaty.

Article XI

1. If any dispute arises between two or more of the Contracting Parties concerning the interpretation or application of the present Treaty, those Contracting Parties shall consult among themselves with a view to having the dispute resolved by negotiation, inquiry, mediation, conciliation, arbitration, judicial settlement or other peaceful means of their own choice.

2. Any dispute of this character not so resolved shall, with the consent, in each case, of all parties to the dispute, be referred to the International Court of Justice for settlement; but failure to reach agreement on reference

to the International Court shall not absolve parties to the dispute from the responsibility of continuing to seek to resolve it by any of the various peaceful means referred to in paragraph 1 of this Article.

Article XII

1.–(a) The present Treaty may be modified or amended at any time by unanimous agreement of the Contracting Parties whose representatives are entitled to participate in the meetings provided for under Article IX. Any such modification or amendment shall enter into force when the depository Government has received notice from all such Contracting Parties that they have ratified it.

(b) Such modification or amendment shall thereafter enter into force as to any other Contracting Party when notice of ratification by it has been received by the depository Government. Any such Contracting Party from which no notice of ratification is received within a period of two years from the date of entry into force of the modification or amendment in accordance with the provision of subparagraph 1(a) of this Article shall be deemed to have withdrawn from the present Treaty on the date of the expiration of such period.

2.–(a) If after the expiration of thirty years from the date of entry into force of the present Treaty, any of the Contracting Parties whose representatives are entitled to participate in the meetings provided for under Article IX so requests by a communication addressed to the depository Government, a Conference of all the Contracting Parties shall be held as soon as practicable to review the operation of the Treaty.

(b) Any modification or amendment to the present Treaty which is approved at such a Conference by a majority of the Contracting Parties there represented, including a majority of those whose representatives are entitled to participate in the meetings provided for under Article IX, shall be communicated by the depository Government to all Contracting Parties immediately after the termination of the Conference and shall

enter into force in accordance with the provisions of paragraph 1 of the present Article.

(c) If any such modification or amendment has not entered into force in accordance with the provisions of subparagraph 1(a) of this Article within a period of two years after the date of its communication to all the Contracting Parties, any Contracting Party may at any time after the expiration of that period give notice to the depository Government of its withdrawal from the present Treaty; and such withdrawal shall take effect two years after the receipt of the notice by the depository Government.

Article XIII

1. The present Treaty shall be subject to ratification by the signatory States. It shall be open for accession by any State which is a Member of the United Nations, or by any other State which may be invited to accede to the Treaty with the consent of all the Contracting Parties whose representatives are entitled to participate in the meetings provided for under Article IX of the Treaty.

2. Ratification of or accession to the present Treaty shall be effected by each State in accordance with its constitutional processes.

3. Instruments of ratification and instruments of accession shall be deposited with the Government of the United States of America, hereby designated as the depository Government.

4. The depository Government shall inform all signatory and acceding States of the date of each deposit of an instrument of ratification or accession, and the date of entry into force of the Treaty and of any modification or amendment thereto.

5. Upon the deposit of instruments of ratification by all the signatory States, the present Treaty shall enter into force for those States and for States which have deposited instruments of accession. Thereafter the Treaty shall enter into force for any acceding State upon the deposit of its instruments of accession.

6. The present Treaty shall be registered by the depository Government pursuant to Article 102 of the Charter of the United Nations.

Article XIV
The present Treaty, done in the English, French, Russian and Spanish languages, each version being equally authentic, shall be deposited in the archives of the Government of the United States of America, which shall transmit duly certified copies thereof to the Governments of the signatory and acceding States.

In witness thereof, the undersigned Plenipotentiaries, duly authorized, have signed the present Treaty.

Done at Washington this first day of December, one thousand nine hundred and fifty-nine.

Antarctic Treaty Parties
Country, Date Ratified or Acceded to Treaty

Argentina, June 23, 1961
Australia, June 23, 1961
Austria, August 25, 1987
Belgium, July 26, 1960
Brazil, May 16, 1975
Bulgaria, September 11, 1978
Canada, May 4, 1988
Chile, June 23, 1961
China, June 8, 1983
Colombia, January 31, 1989
Cuba, August 16, 1984
Czech Republic, June 14, 1962[1]
Dem People's Rep of Korea, January 21, 1987
Denmark, May 20, 1965
Ecuador, September 15, 1987
Finland, May 15, 1984
France, September 16, 1960
Germany, February 5, 1979[2]
Greece, January 8, 1987
Guatemala, July 31, 1991
Hungary, January 27, 1984
India, August 19, 1983
Italy, March 18, 1981
Japan, August 4, 1960
Netherlands, March 30, 1967
New Zealand, November 1, 1960
Norway, August 24, 1960
Papua New Guinea, March 16, 1981
Peru, April 10, 1981
Poland, June 8, 1961
Rep of Korea, November 28, 1986
Romania, September 15, 1971
Russian Federation, November 2, 1960[3]
Slovak Republic, June 14, 1962[1]
South Africa, June 21, 1960
Spain, March 31, 1982
Sweden, April 24, 1984
Switzerland, November 15, 1990
Turkey, January 24, 1995
Ukraine, October 28, 1992[4]
United Kingdom, May 31, 1960
United States, August 18, 1960
Uruguay, January 11, 1980

Notes:

1. The Czech and Slovak Republics inherited Czechoslovakia's obligations; Czechoslovakia ratified the Treaty on June 14, 1962.

2. The German Democratic Republic united with the Federal Republic of Germany on October 2, 1990; the GDR had acceded to the Treaty on November 19, 1974.

3. Following the dissolution of the USSR, Russia assumed the rights and obligations of being a party to the Treaty.

4. Ukraine has asserted that it has succeeded to the Treaty following the dissolution of the USSR.

Glossary

A Factor – The Antarctic Factor; Murphy's Law in Antarctica.

ablation – The loss of snow or ice by melting or evaporation.

ANARE – Australian National Antarctic Research Expeditions.

anchor ice – Submerged ice that is attached to the sea bottom.

Antarctic 10 – A man – or more often, a woman – who is described as being quite beautiful in Antarctica, but 'just a plane ride away from being ordinary.'

Antarctic Convergence – The region where the colder Antarctic seas meet the warmer waters of the northern oceans; also called the Polar Front.

apple – A small, round, red prefabricated hut used in Australian and other government field camps in Antarctica; by adding additional panels to make an apple hut larger, you get 'melons,' 'zucchinis' and 'cucumbers.'

Bag Drag – (American) A designated time before leaving McMurdo station when station members' luggage is put on a pallet and weighed for loading onto departing aircraft.

banana belt – A warmer part of Antarctica, especially the Antarctic Peninsula.

BAS – British Antarctic Survey.

beachmaster – A large, dominant male seal who guards – and breeds with – a harem (qv) on a breeding beach.

beaker – An American nickname for a scientist.

berg – An iceberg.

bergy bit – A piece of floating ice rising 1m to 5m out of the water.

Big Eye – A period of sleeplessness caused most often by the 24-hour daylight of Antarctic summertime, but also by the 24-hour darkness of winter.

blat – (British) *v* To shoot, with either a camera or a gun.

blegs – (British) Bits of dirt on transparencies or photos.

blinder – (British) An astonishing act of foresight, a smart move.

blizz static – Electric charge that builds up because of the dry atmosphere, high winds and blowing snow in a blizzard.

blow – A blizzard.

boffin – An Australian nickname for a scientist.

BOLOW – (Australian) Burnt-Out Left-Over Winterer.

bondu – (British & Australian) An anonymous or featureless countryside.

bondu-bashing – Traveling over bondu (qv); cross-country traveling.

boomerang – (American) To start on a flight to or from Antarctica, only to be forced by inclement weather to return.

brash ice – The wreckage of larger pieces of ice.

bummock – A submariner term for a ridgelike ice formation hanging down from beneath pack ice; a hummock that is under water (qv).

bunk-ride – *v* What many passengers prefer to do in rough seas; to sleep.

bunny boots – (American) Huge inflatable boots that make their wearer resemble a cartoon character.

cairn – A pyramid of stones or pieces of ice or cut snow raised as a marker.

calve – The breaking off of an iceberg from a glacier or ice shelf.

Camp – Falkland Islands term for the countryside; all areas outside of Stanley.

CCAMLR – The Convention for the Conservation of Antarctic Marine Living Resources.

Chch – Pronounced 'Cheech'; Christchurch, gateway to Antarctica for the US, New Zealand and Italian national Antarctic programs.

chompers – (Australian) Snacks.

collapso – (British) Cheap wine from South America.

crack – A crevasse.

crèche – A group of penguin chicks attended by a small group of adults while most of the parents are out at sea hunting for food.

crud – A flu-like illness that strikes the wintering-over crew of an Antarctic station when a new group arrives, caused by the weakening of the winterers' immune systems, which have not been stimulated by any germs for many months.

dhobi – (British) *n* Laundry.

dieso – (Australian) A (diesel) mechanic.

Dome or **The Dome** – The main building at Amundsen-Scott South Pole Station, a geodesic dome. Used in phrases such as 'Dome Sweet Dome' and 'It's time to go Dome.'

Dome slugs – South Pole station members whose jobs do not require them to leave the Dome.

donga – (Australian) An individual bedroom at an Antarctic station.

'doo – (British) A skidoo or snowmobile.

driftiness – Slowed thinking and speech and an inability to concentrate experienced by some Antarctic station members.

DV – Distinguished Visitor; bureaucratic parlance for politician or bureaucrat visiting The Ice through the auspices of a national research program.

ECW gear – (American) Extreme Cold Weather gear.

fast ice – Sea ice attached to the shore or between grounded bergs (qv).

FID – A British Antarctic worker (this term is still in use today, even though the Falkland Islands Dependencies Survey from which the name derives was replaced by the name British Antarctic Survey in 1962).

firn – *See névé.*

flense – To strip (as a whale or seal) of blubber or skin.

FNG – (American) Pronounced 'fingie'; stands for (expletive deleted) New Guy; a new member of an Antarctic station.

frazil ice – Needle-shaped ice crystals forming a slush in the water.

freezer suit – A windproof insulated jumpsuit.

freshies – Fresh fruits and vegetables, much-appreciated commodities in Antarctica and rare between resupplies.

frost smoke – Condensed water vapor that forms a mist over open water in cold weather.

gash – (British) Rubbish or trash.

googy – (Australian) A fiberglass field hut resembling a spheroid UFO.

GPS – Global Positioning System; a satellite-based system that employs triangulation to determine geographic location to within 10m.

grease ice – Ice in a later stage of freezing than frazil ice; takes its name from the matte appearance it gives to the sea.

greenout – The shock experienced by Antarctic station members upon returning home and seeing trees and grass.

Grid – The coordinate system designed to allow navigation at the South Pole, where all 'directions' are north. Grid North is the Prime Meridian, Grid South 180° longitude, and so forth.

growler – Small – and therefore difficult to see or pick up on radar – piece of ice awash with waves and thus a hazard to shipping.

guano – (1) Bird excrement. (2) The remains of whalemeat and bones that were dried and turned into meal after the oil extraction process.

Hägglunds – A Swedish-made, tracked vehicle used at many Antarctic stations.

ham patch – Ham radio telephone patches from Antarctic stations to home.

harem – A group of female seals jealously guarded on a breeding beach by a beachmaster (qv).

helo – American station lingo for helicopter (never 'chopper').

herbie – A blizzard, especially at McMurdo station.

Herc – A Hercules C-130 cargo plane, which can be equipped with skis as well as wheels, commonly used for resupplying Antarctic stations.

hero picture – (American) Photograph taken of oneself standing by the sign marking the Geographic South Pole.

Hollywood shower – (American) Term of derision for a shower lasting longer than the allotted two minutes at many Antarctic stations; originally a US Navy term.

homer – Home-brewed beer popular on Australian stations.

hoosh – A thick hot stew made usually of pemmican (qv), crumbled dry sledging biscuits (qv) and boiled water, eaten on early expeditions.

house mouse – The duty, rotated among station members at the US's South Pole and Palmer stations, of cleaning up common areas.

hummock – An area where ice floes have rafted, or piled atop one another, often reaching heights of several meters.

IAATO – International Association of Antarctica Tour Operators, the industry trade association.

ice blink – A lighter, brighter section on the underside of clouds, caused by light reflected up from ice below; used by early explorers to detect and thus avoid the pack ice.

Ice time – The amount of Antarctic experience one has; how long one has lived on The Ice.

ice window – The short summer season when the fast ice has broken out, allowing ships to near the Antarctic coast.

IGY – The International Geophysical Year, which ran from July 1, 1957 to December 31, 1958.

INMARSAT – International Maritime Satellite; used to make telephone calls and send faxes and email aboard ship.

jobbie – (Australian and British) Feces.

jolly – (Australian and British) A pleasure or sightseeing trip, often made by helicopter.

katabatic – A gravity-driven wind caused by colder, heavier air rushing down from the polar plateau.

knot – One nautical mile (1.15 statute miles or 1.85km) per hour.

Kodachrome poisoning – A phenomenon experienced by heavily photographed Antarctic wildlife such as Adélie penguins.

LARC – (Lighter Amphibious Resupply Cargo) A five-tonne combination boat/truck used by Australia to service ships and bases; the driver is a LARCie.

lead – A section of open water within pack ice between large floes.

manhaul – (archaic) *v* To pull a sledge carrying supplies and food on a South Polar journey, while either skiing or walking.

mank – (British) *v* To turn bad or deteriorate (said of weather).

manky – (British) *adj* Bad or foul (said of weather).

me-pickie – (Australian) A photo of oneself.

mid-rats – (American) Midnight rations, served at McMurdo station for late-shift workers.

moon dog – A 'false moon,' or paraselena: an optical phenomenon caused by the refraction of moonlight by ice crystals suspended in the air; see *sun dog*.

moraine – Rock debris moved and deposited by a glacier; lateral (at the sides); medial (at the center) or terminal (at the foot).

nelly – A member of either of the two species of giant petrel.

névé – Literally, 'last year's snow.' Hard granular snow on the upper part of a glacier that hasn't yet turned to ice; firn.

NGO – Nongovernmental organization.

NSF – National Science Foundation, the part of the US government in charge of the US Antarctic program.

nilas – A thin crust of floating ice that bends with waves but does not break; the darker its appearance, the thinner the nilas is.

nunatak – A mountain or large piece of rock sticking up through an ice sheet.

OAE – Old Antarctic Explorer; used to describe someone who has worked at an Antarctic station.

oasis – An area of bare rock without ice or snow caused by a retreating or thinning ice sheet and ablation of any snow that does fall; examples include the Bunger Hills, Dry Valleys, Larsemann Hills and Vestfold Hills.

old ice – Sea ice that is more than two years old; up to 3m thick.

pancake ice – Discs of young ice, formed when waves jostle them against one another, rounding their edges.

pax – Passengers.

pemmican – Ground dried meat mixed with equal parts lard. This concentrated food was a primary ration on early expeditions.

PI – Principal Investigator; the lead scientist on a project.

polynya – An area of open water within the pack ice that remains free of ice throughout the winter.

pyramid – A double-skinned pyramid-shaped tent used in field work in Antarctica.

quad, quike – A four-wheeled motorized vehicle.

Red Shed – The living quarters on an Australian Antarctic station, named for its color.

rotten ice – Older ice that has severely weakened prior to melting.

RTA – (Australian) *v* To Return to Australia supplies, materials or specimens.

sastrugi – Furrows or irregularities formed on a snow surface by the wind. They can be more than a meter in height.

SCAR – Scientific Committee on Antarctic Research; originally the Special Committee on Antarctic Research.

scradge – (British) Food.

shuga – Spongy white ice lumps, formed from grease ice or slush.

skijouring – Being pulled on skis by one or more dogs in harness; no longer possible in Antarctica since dogs were banned.

skua – (American) (1) *n* A nickname for frozen chicken, a staple on Antarctic station menus; (2) *v* To swipe or scavenge; after the skua's propensity to scavenge food from Antarctic stations.

sledging biscuits – Dry, crackerlike food usually made from wheat.

slot – A crevasse.

slushy – (Australian) Station kitchen hand, a rotating duty.

smoko – (Australian and British) Tea break.

snow blindness – A debilitatingly painful inflammation of the eyes, with a resulting (usually temporary) loss of sight; caused by the glare of sunlight reflected off ice or snow.

snow bridge – The crustlike lid that often covers a crevasse; formed when windblown snow builds up on the leeward wall of the crevasse.

souvenir – *v* To remove (steal) artifacts or natural history specimens; the term is usually used to refer to the theft of historic items from an early explorer's hut for a personal collection, an act performed mainly by visitors from nearby scientific stations, as they were the only people who had access to these huts.

SPA – Specially Protected Area; may not be entered without a permit.

SSSI – Site of Special Scientific Interest; a place that may not be entered without a permit.

starchy – A thrush common to the Tristan da Cunha group.

sublimate – To pass from the solid state directly to vapor. Ice and snow commonly sublimate in dry areas of Antarctica.

sun dog – A 'false sun,' or more correctly, a parhelion: an optical phenomenon caused by the refraction of sunlight by tiny ice crystals, themselves known as 'diamond dust,' suspended in the air.

sun pillar – Another solar phenomenon, this one a vertical shaft of light from the rising or setting sun, also caused by ice crystals in the atmosphere.

tabular berg – An iceberg with vertical sides and a flat top, indicating that it has calved relatively recently.

Terres Australes et Antarctiques – France's sub-Antarctic islands and territorial claim in Antarctica, Terre Adélie.

The Ice – Antarctica.

tide crack – A crack separating sea ice from the shore, caused by the rise and fall of the tide; often too wide to cross safely.

toasted, toasty – Burned out; what many winterovers (qv) feel before leaving The Ice.

try-pot or **tryworks** – A cauldron for rendering the blubber of whales, seals or penguins into oil.

ventile – Windproof outer clothing.

wallow – *n* A muddy, noxious-smelling hollow made by seals, especially elephant seals.

water sky – Dark section on the underside of clouds, indicating open water below; used by early explorers to help penetrate the pack ice.

Wellies – Calf- or knee-high rubber boots worn by most Antarctic tourists to go ashore.

whiteout – A condition in which overcast sky descends to the horizon, causing a blurring between ground and sky and eliminating all points of perspective; described by pilots as 'like flying in a bowl of milk.'

Winfly – Winter Fly-In; flights made by the US Antarctic program in mid-August to bring supplies and new personnel to McMurdo station to help prepare it for the summer season.

winterovers – Station members who remain in Antarctica through the long dark winter.

wobbly – (British) A panic attack, as in 'to chuck a wobbly.'

WYSSA – Australian slang for a message sent to or received from home, from code letters used in telex messages meaning All My Love Darling.

Zodiac – An inflatable rubber dinghy powered by an outboard engine and used for making shore landings.

NOTE: Several of these entries are taken from *A Dictionary of Antarctic English (DANTE),* compiled by Australian Bernadette Hince.

Acknowledgments

THANKS

Many thanks to the following travelers (apologies if we misspelled your name) who read the First edition of this book and took the time to write to us about their experiences in Antarctica:

Alain Caradec, Allan White, Anne L Erdmann, Anthea Wallhead, Bill Essig, Caroline Hall, Caron Patterson, Catherine Rutter, Charles Bobbish, Clare Kines, Dave Burkitt, Donald & Sandy Komito, Dr Kou Kusunoki, Elizabeth Chipman, Gillian M Lindsay, Gregg Kaczmarczyk, HC Lee, J Max Creswell, Jacques Belge, Jean Maurice Silagy, John R Taylor, John Jacobsen, Jono Feldman, Katherine Winter, Les Bonwell, M Gommans & C Cruysberg, Mary Stripling, Massimo Bisiacchi, Max Corry, Mike Hergert, Roland Thanner, Stephen Pendleton, Suzanne Southon, Terry Last, Tim Hendley

Index

Text

A

AAT 330
Abercrombie & Kent 108-9
Academician Vernadskiy station 301
accommodations 103
life aboard a polar ship 110-11
activities 102
Adelaide Island 23
Adventure Associates 109
Adventure Network International (ANI) 109, 125-8, 202-3
air travel 114, 124-8
Aitcho Islands 265
Albatross Island 278
albatrosses 59, 141-6, 164, 257, 278
Alfred-Faure station 243
algae 181-2
Almirante Brown station 294, 299
American Polar Society 99
American Women's Expedition 205
Amery Ice Shelf 334
Amundsen, Roald 24, 25, 29, 40, 41, 42, 45, 48, 83, 196, 219, 308, 329, 342, 344, 345, 346, 348, 349
Amundsen-Scott South Pole station 55, 349-56, **350**
ANARE 42-3, 49, 247-8
ANARE Club 99
ANARE station 253
Andresen, Adolfus Amandus 227
ANI. See Adventure Network International
Annenkov Island 278

Antarctic Adventure 224
Antarctic Convergence 54, 176, 235
Antarctic Peninsula 24-5, 292-302, **293**
Antarctic Site Inventory project 56-7
Antarctic Society of Australia 99
Antarctic Treaty 60-1, 72, 172
parties to 361
Protocol on Environmental Protection 55, 56-7, 59, 61, 104-5, 165, 169
text of 357-61
Antarctica Project 99-100
Antarctican Society 100
Antarcticana 86-7
Antipodes Islands 254-5
Anvers Island 23, 296-7
Arctowski station 263-4
Argentine Islands 301
Artigas station 264
Astrolabe Island 292
astronomy 192-3
Auckland Islands 255-7
aurora australis 64, 89, 248-9
Aurora Expeditions 109-11
Australian Antarctic Division 222-3
Australian Antarctic Territory (AAT) 330

B

Baia Terra Nova station 312
Balchen, Bernt 47, 48
Balleny Islands 253-4
Barnard, Charles H 290-1
Beardmore Glacier 39
Beascochea Bay 301
Belgrano II station 307
Bellingshausen, Fabian von 18, 19, 22, 23, 25, 259, 280-1
Bellingshausen station 262
binoculars 70
biographies 83

Bird Island 278
birds 57, 137-58, 178
albatrosses 59, 141-6, 164, 257, 278
books 83-4
cormorants 156
kelp gulls 157
penguins 84, 107, 137-41, 227-8, 248, 252, 257, 278, 281, 296, 309, 310, 330
petrels 146-53, 154-6, 164, 334
prions 152
shearwaters 153-4
sheathbills 156-7
skuas 158
terns 157-8
Biscoe, John 23-6, 257
Bjaaland, Olav 40
Bleaker Island 289
blizzards 55
books 76-88
Borchgrevink, Carsten E 18, 29, 32-3, 36, 310, 329
Bounty Islands 257-8
Bouvetøya 238-40
Bowers, Henry 'Birdie' 24, 41, 321, 344
Bransfield, Edward 18, 22-3, 24, 260, 265
Bridgeman Island 265
Brown Bluff 294
Bruce, William Spiers 37, 88
Bull, Henrik Johan 18, 29, 34, 283, 310
Bunger Hills 336
Buromskiy Island 336
Byrd, Richard Evelyn 24, 25, 47-8, 88, 89, 206, 308, 344, 345

C

Campbell Island 258-9
camping 111, 116, 127-8
Candlemas Island 280

Canterbury Museum 218-9
Cape Adare 308, 310-1
Cape Denison 340
Cape Evans 321-5
Cape Hallett 311
Cape Horn 235-7, 238, **236**
Cape Legoupil 292
Cape Renard 299
Cape Royds 170-1, 325-8
Cape Town, South Africa
    212-6, **213**
Carcass Island 289-90
Casey station 168, 336-7
CD-ROMs 90-1
CDs 80-1
Chang Cheng station 264
Charcot, Jean-Baptiste 24, 32,
    37-8, 265, 268, 297, 300,
    301
Charlotte Bay 296
children
    books for 84-5
    traveling with 98-9
Christchurch, New Zealand
    216-21, **217**
Clark, Gerry 209
claustrophobia 102
climate 54-5, 188
Clipper Cruise Line 111-2
clothing 69
Coats Land 37
Colbeck, William 33, 36, 259,
    329
collecting 86-7
Commonwealth Bay 338-9,
    340-1
Commonwealth Trans-
    Antarctic Expedition 197
conduct 62-3, 320
continental drift 12
Convention for the Conserva-
    tion of Antarctic Marine
    Living Resources
    (CCAMLR) 163-4
Cook, Frederick A 29, 32, 345
Cook, James 16-7, 18, 174,
    196, 237, 240, 244, 273,
    280, 345
Cooper Island 278
cormorants 156

Coronation Island 23
costs 73
credit cards 73-4
cruises 65-6, 108-18
Crystal Sound 301
'currency' 73
customs 72-3
Cuverville Island 294, 296

D

da Gama, Vasco 13
Dakshin Gangotri station 332
Dallman Laboratory 262
Danco Coast 29, 32
Danco Island 296
David, TW Edgeworth 39
Davis, John King 43, 49,
    334-5
Davis station 43, 334-5
de Gerlache, Adrien 29, 32,
    37, 296, 299
Deacon Peak 264
Decepción station 271
Deception Island 23, 64, 227,
    267-71, 294, 326, **267**
dehydration 95
Delignières, Hughes 209
Días de Novaes, Bartholomeu
    13
disabled travelers 98
Disappointment Island 256
diving 102, 109-10, 113, 115,
    116, 318-9
documents 71-2
The Dome 349-53
Drake, Francis 15
Drake Passage 15, 235
drinks 103-5
Dronning Maud Land 207-8,
    330
Dry Valleys 41, 64, 207, 312-4
Drygalski, Erich von 33-4
Drygalski Ice Tongue 312
Dumont d'Urville, Jules-
    Sébastien-César 22, 24, 26,
    27, 255, 292, 295
Dumont d'Urville station 168,
    338-40
Dundee Island 295
D'Urville Island 295

E

East Antarctica 330-41, **331**
East Falkland 288
ecology. See environmental
    issues
Eielson, Carl Ben 46
electricity 94
Elephant Island 261
Elichiribehety station 294
Ellsworth, Lincoln 25, 43, 47,
    48-9, 197, 295
employment 102-3
environmental issues 55-6,
    161-73
    exploitation of wildlife 58-
        9, 161-4
    global warming 166, 191-2
    impact of science 166-70
    impact of tourism 55-6,
        170-2
    mining 59, 164-5
    ozone depletion 165-6,
        190-1
    pollution 56, 165-6, 189,
        270
    species conservation 57-8
    your presence 173
Escudeoro base 263
Esperanza station 292, 294
Espinet, Bernard 210
Etienne, Jean-Louis 204, 210
Evans, Edgar 41, 321
exchange rates 212
expeditions, private 196-211
Expeditions Inc 112
exploration. See history;
    individual explorers
eye hazards 95

F

Falkland Islands 228-30, 284-
    91, **229**, **286-7**
Fallières Coast 38
fauna. See wildlife
fax 74
Ferraz station 264
fiction 78-9
Fiennes, Ran 77, 205
Filchner, Wilhelm 44-5, 307
Filchner Ice Shelf 307

Filchner station 307
films 88-90
fish 158-9, 179-80
fishing industry 59, 162, 163-4
flightseeing 124-5, 126-7
flora. See plants
food 103
Footsteps of Scott expedition 77, 201
fossils 12, 185-6, 266, 304-5, 322-3
Fram Bank 334
Franklin, John 27, 28, 223
Franklin Island 312
Frei station 125, 262-3
Fuchs, Arved 77, 203-4
Fuchs, Vivian 88, 197, 219, 345

G

Gabriel de Castilla station 271
gateway cities
    Cape Town 212-6, **213**
    Christchurch 216-21, **217**
    Hobart 221-4, **222**
    Puntas Arenas 225-8, **225**
    Stanley 228-30, **229**
    Ushuaia 230-4, **231**
geography 53-4
geology 54, 185-7
geomagnetism 192
geomorphology 186-7
German Receiving Station 292
Gillette, Ned 209
glaciology 14-5
global warming 166, 191-2
Gondwana 12
González Videla station 294, 300
Gough Island 284
government 59-62
Graham Land 24-5
Grande Terre 244
Greenpeace 168-9, 325
Greenwich Island 265
Grytviken whaling station 275, 276-7, **279**

guidebooks 76-7

H

Half Moon Beach 267
Half Moon Island 266, 294
Hallett station 167, 169
Halley station 307
Hannah Point 266, 294
Hansen, Nicolai 33, 311
Hanssen, Helmer 40
Hapag-Lloyd Kreuzfahrten 112-3
Harvey, Peter 23
Hassel, Sverre 40
Hawker Island 335
health 94-8, 193-4
Heard Island 246-8, **246**
helicopters 66, 112
Heritage Antarctica 100
Heritage Expeditions 113, 115
highlights 64
Hillary, Edmund 197, 199, 219, 258, 344
history. See also individual explorers
    ancient 13
    explorers 13-9, 21-9, 32-49
    contemporary 49, 52-3
    books 79-82
Hobart, Australia 221-4, **222**
Hope Bay 292, 294
huts 64, 295, 304, 308, 310-1, 320-8, 334
hypothermia 95

I

IAATO 100, 108
ice sheet 14-5, 54
    drilling into 14-5, 188
    thickness **15**
icebergs 28
    colored & striped 336-7
    largest 328-9
    research on 189
IGY 49, 60, 197
Île Amsterdam 249-50
Île St Paul 250-1
Îles Crozet 241-4
Îles Kerguelen 244-6
immunizations 95

Infante, João 13
INMARSAT 74
insomnia 95
insurance 72, 94-5
International Antarctic Centre 219-20
International Association of Antarctica Tour Operators (IAATO) 100, 108
International Geophysical Year (IGY) 49, 60, 197
International Trans-Antarctic Expedition 204
Internet resources 75
Islas Diego Ramírez 237
Islas Malvinas. See Falkland Islands
isolation, coping with 352

J

James Caird Society 101
Joinville Island 22, 295
Jougla Point 297
journals 91
Juan Carlos Primero station 266
Jubany station 262

K

Kagge, Erling 205
katabatics 55
kayaking 110, 116
kelp gulls 157
Keppel Island 289
Kershaw, Giles 201, 203, 208
King Edward VII Land 36
King George Island 23, 262-4, **263**
King George V Land 43
King Sejong station 264
Klink, Amyr 209
krill 57, 58-9, 159, 162, 163-4, 180-1
Kristensen, Leonard 18, 310
Kristensen, Monica 202

L

Lake Vanda 184, 313
Lake Vostok 341
lakes

Bold indicates maps.

surface 184, 313-4
under-ice 341
Lambert Glacier 54, 334
landings, earliest 18
Larsemann Hills 334
Larsen, Carl Anton 28-9, 34,
35, 276, 306
laundry 94
Law base 334
Lazarev, Mikhail 18, 332
legal matters 102
Lemaire Channel 64, 299
Lenie field station 264
Lewis, David 77, 208-9
Lindblad, Lars-Eric 11, 83
Lindblad Special Expeditions
115
Livingston Island 266-7, 294
Louis Philippe Land 22
'low-latitude' sites 24-5, 100
Luitpold Coast 45
Lyttelton 221

M

Machu Picchu station 264
Macquarie Island 55, 251-3,
251
Mac.Robertson Land 44
magazines 91
Magellan, Ferdinand 13, 231
mail 74
Maitri station 332
maps 66-9
Marambio station 168, 169,
206
Marguerite Bay 38, 301-2
Marine Expeditions 115
Marine Plain 335
Marion Island 240-1
marriages 102
Martin-de-Viviès station 250
Mawson, Douglas 42, 43-4,
49, 83, 209, 251, 253,
334, 338, 340-1
Mawson station 42-3, 49, 55,
333-4
McDonald Islands 246-8,
246
McIntyre, Don & Margie 210,
338-9, 340

McMurdo station 168, 169,
314-20, **317**
medical research 97, 193-5
Melchior Islands 295
Mertz, Xavier 44, 341
Messner, Reinhold 77, 203-4
meteorites 30-1, 44, 187
microbes 183-4
Mikkelsen, Caroline 52, 335
Mikkelsen, Klarius 52, 334,
335
minerals 59, 164-5, 185
Mirnyy station 335-6
Modre, Sjur & Simen 204-5
Molodezhnaya station 333
money 73-4, 212
Montreal Antarctic Society
101
Mountain Travel-Sobek 115
mountaineering 77, 102, 128,
196, 197-9, 202, 206-8
Mt Berlin 326
Mt Erebus 27, 39, 326-7, 328
Mt Herschel 199
Mt Melbourne 312, 326
Mt Terror 27, 328
Mt Vaughan 206-7
museums 24, 67

N

names 306
Neko Harbor 299
nematodes 313
Neptunes Bellows 267
Neumayer station 330, 332
New Island 290
New Zealand Antarctic Society
101
Ninnis, Belgrave 44, 341
Nordenskjöld, Otto 25, 29,
34-5, 38, 294, 304, 306
Nordenskjöld Ice Tongue 312
Novolazarevskaya station 332

O

Oates, Lawrence 24, 41, 321,
343
Oates Land 41
Oceanwide Expeditions 116
O'Higgins station 292

Operation Deep Freeze 220
Operation Highjump 49, 334,
336
Operation Windmill 49
Orcadas station 272
organizations 99-101
Orient Lines 116
Orne Islands 296
Ousland, Børge 77
ozone depletion 165-6, 190-1

P

packing 69, 71
paleontology 185-6, 304-5.
See also fossils
Palmer, Nathaniel Brown 19,
23, 24, 268, 271
Palmer Land 23, 24-5
Palmer station 296-7
Paradise Harbor 64, 294, 299
passports 71
Patriot Hills 128
Paulet Island 294-5
Peary, Robert 344, 345
Pebble Island 289
Pendulum Cove 269, 294
Penguin Island 264
Penguin Point 306
penguins 84, 107, 137-41,
227-8, 248, 252, 257, 278,
281, 296, 309, 310, 330
Peregrine Expeditions 116
permits 72
Peter I Øy 19, 259-60
Petermann Island 294, 300-1
Petersen Bank 337
petrels 146-53, 154-6, 164,
334
philately 62, 75, 101, 106, 324
photography 92-4
planning 64-71
plants 56, 160, 181-2, 183-4
The Pleiades 326
Point Hennequin station 264
Pole of Maximum Inaccessibility 349
politics 59-62, 82-3
pollution 56, 165-6, 189, 270
population 62
Port Howard 289

Port Lockroy 38, 294, 297-9
Port Louis 288
Port Stephens 289
Portal Point 296
Port-aux-Français station 245
Port-Jeanne d'Art 245
Possession Islands 27, 311
postal services 74
Powell, George 19, 23, 271
Prat station 265-6
Prince Edward Islands 240-1
Prion Island 278
prions 152
Progress II base 334
Project Blizzard 209
protected areas 58, 104
Protocol on Environmental
    Protection 55, 56-7, 59,
    61, 104-5, 165, 169
Puerto Toro 234
Puerto Williams 234
Puntas Arenas, Chile 225-8,
    225

Q

Quark Expeditions 116-7

R

resupply vessels 122-4
Rongé Island 296
Ronne Ice Shelf 307
Roosevelt Island 329
Ross, James Clark 24, 27-8,
    218, 219, 223, 255, 258,
    295, 308, 311, 312, 315,
    345
Ross Ice Shelf 27, 64, 328-9
Ross Island 27, 314-28, **315**
Ross Sea 308-29, **309**
Rothera station 301-2

S

Saddle Island 21
safety 101-2, 104-5
San Martín station 302
SANAE IV 332
Saunders Island 289

Bold indicates maps.

Sayre, Woodrow Wilson 197-8
science 174-95. *See also*
    stations
    astronomy 192-3
    atmospheric 190-2
    books 84
    environmental impact of
        166-70
    future of 195
    geology, geomorphology &
        paleontology 185-7
    geomagnetism 192
    land & sea ice 188-90
    medical research 97, 193-5
    oceans & marine life 176-82
    reasons for 174
    terrestrial life 183-4
    weather forecasting 190
Scott, Robert Falcon 24, 25,
    35-7, 39, 40, 41, 83, 89,
    201, 214, 218, 219, 221,
    311, 312, 320-4, 342-4,
    345, 348, 349
Scott base 314
Scott Island 259
scuba diving. See diving
Scullin Monolith 334
sea ice 189-90, **21**
Sea Lion Island 288-9
sea lions 257
seafloor communities 182,
    318-20
sealing industry 17, 18, 19,
    58, 161, 162, 240, 241,
    244-5, 247, 250, 252, 254,
    258, 260, 266, 273-4, 281
seals 134-7, 178-9, 251-2,
    272-3, 278
seasickness 95-8
senior travelers 98
Seymour Island 304-6
Shackleton, Ernest Henry 24,
    25, 32, 36, 38-9, 40, 45-6,
    82, 83, 200, 209, 219, 221,
    261, 275-7, 301, 302, 321,
    325, 342, 345
Shackleton Ice Shelf 26
Shag Rocks 273
shags 156
shearwaters 153-4

sheathbills 156-7
Shinn, Conrad 344, 345
Shirase, Nobu 42
shopping 105-7
Sites of Special Scientific
    Interest (SSSIs) 58
size 53-4, **20**
skuas 158
skydiving 210-1
Smith, Dick 208
Smith, William 22-3, 260
The Snares 259
snow accumulation **21**
Snow Hill Island 304-5
social rules 62-3, 320
Society Expeditions 117
soils 187
solar eclipses 335
South Aris expedition 210
South Geomagnetic Pole 349
South Georgia 16, 207, 273-
    80, **274**
South Magnetic Pole 27, 39,
    349
South Orkney Islands 23,
    271-3, **272**
South Pole 40, 41, 196, 342-
    56, **343**
    climate 347
    geography 347
    history 342-7
    life at 354-5
    station 55, 344, 349-56
    visiting 347-9
South Sandwich Islands 16,
    237, 280-1, **280**
South Shetland Islands 18,
    260-71, 261
Southern Ocean 57, 120-1,
    176-7, 235-7
souvenirs 72-3, 105-7, 298
special events 102
Specially Protected Areas
    (SPAs) 58
species conservation 57-8
squid 163-4, 180
St Kliment Ohridskiy station
    266
Stanley, Falkland Islands
    228-30, **229**

stations *See also individual stations*
environmental impact of 55-6
life in 175-6
locations of **50-1**
population of 62
visiting 62-3
Steger, Will 204
Stonington Island 302
Stroud, Mike 77, 205
sub-Antarctic islands 237-91
Aitcho Islands 265
Antipodes Islands 254-5
Auckland Islands 255-7
Balleny Islands 253-4
Bounty Islands 257-8
Bouvetøya 238-40
Bridgeman Island 265
Campbell Island 258-9
Candlemas Island 280
Deception Island 23, 64, 227, 267-71, 294, 326, **267**
Elephant Island 261
Gough Island 284
Greenwich Island 265
Half Moon Island 266
Heard & McDonald Islands 246-8, **246**
Île Amsterdam 249-50
Île St Paul 250-1
Îles Crozet 241-4
Îles Kerguelen 244-6
King George Island 23, 262-4, **263**
Livingston Island 266-7, 294
Macquarie Island 55, 251-3, **251**
New Zealand's 254-9, **255**
nonexistent 242, **243**
Penguin Island 264
Peter I Øy 19, 259-60
Prince Edward Islands 240-1
relative sizes **239**
Scott Island 259
Shag Rocks 273
The Snares 259
South Georgia 273-80, **274**

South Orkney Islands 23, 271-3, **272**
South Sandwich Islands 16, 237, 280-1, **280**
South Shetland Islands 18, 260-71, **261**
Zavodovski Island 64, 280-1
sunburn 95
sunglasses 95
Syowa station 332-3

T

Tasman, Abel Janszoon 16
Telefon Bay 270
telephones 74
terns 157-8
Terra Nova Bay 312
Terre Adélie 22, 330
Tierra del Fuego 13, 231-2, 235
time 94
tipping 74
Tollefsen, Ivar 77, 207
Torbert, John 345
tourism
environmental impact of 55-6, 170-2
increase in 11
tourist office 71
Transglobe Expedition 200-1
travel insurance 72, 94-5
traveler's checks 73-4
Trinity Island 23
Trinity Peninsula 18
Tristan da Cunha group 281-3
Tunzleman, Alexander 18
Turret Point 264

U

Ui-te-Rangiora 13
Ushuaia, Argentina 230-4, **231**

V

Vaughan, Norman 98, 206-7
Vestfold Hills 335
videography 92-4

videos 88-90
Vinson Massif 197-9, 202
visas 71, 72
volcanoes 326-7
Vostok station 341

W

Wake of Shackleton expedition 209
Walker Bay 266
Waterboat Point 299-300
weather forecasting 190
websites 75
Weddell, James 19, 21-2, 266, 271, 302, 334
Weddell Island 291
Weddell Sea 302-7, **303**
Wegener, Alfred 12
West Falkland 289
West Point Island 290
Whalers Bay 268, 294
whales 84, 130-4, 179, **163**
whaling industry 29, 58, 82, 161-2, 163, 179, 227, 242, 268-9, 272, 274-7, 291, 330
whiteouts 55
Wiencke Island 294, 297-9
wildlife 56-7, 130-60. *See also* birds
books 83-4
exploitation of 58-9, 161-4
fish 158-9, 179-80
krill 57, 58-9, 159, 162, 163-4, 180-1
photographing 93-4
protected areas 58
sea lions 257
seals 134-7, 178-9, 251-2, 272-3, 278
species conservation 57-8
squid 163-4, 180
terrestrial invertebrates 159-60, 184
watching 57, 93-4, 105, 171-2
whales 84, 130-4, 179, **163**
WildWings 117

Wilkes, Charles 22, 26-7, 83, 218, 255
Wilkes station 43, 336
Wilkins, Hubert 46-7, 48, 49, 83
Wilson, Edward A 24, 36, 41, 218, 321, 342, 344
winds 55
Wisting, Oscar 40

women 52-3, 88, 176, 202, 205, 330, 346
Wordie House 301
work 102-3

yacht voyages 118-22
Yalour Islands 301

Yankee Harbour 265
Yukidori Valley 333

Zavodovski Island 64, 280-1
Zegrahm Expeditions 117-8
Zhongshan station 334
Zodiacs 122-3

Boxed Text

Air Travel Glossary 114
Antarctic Medicine 96-7
Antarctic Museums 67
Antarctic Site Inventory 56-7
The Antarctic Treaty: A Unique Pact for a Unique Place 60-1
Antarctic 'Visas' 72
Antarctica: A Discography 80-1
Antarctica – The Bar 100
Antarctica during the 'Age of Reptiles' 322-3
Antarctica in Fiction 78-9
Antarctican Dollars: The Coolest Cash 73
Antarctica's Hot Spots 326-7
The Auckland Island Coracle 256
Aurora Australis 248-9
Choosing and Using Binoculars 70
Code of Conduct for Visiting Historic Antarctic Huts 320
Collecting Antarcticana 86-7
Colored & Striped Icebergs 336-7
The Continent in a Day 126-7
Coping with Isolation 352
Deadly Debris 270
Diving in McMurdo Sound 318-9
Don't Collect, Please! 298
Earliest Antarctic Landings 18
Expedition Icebound: A Year at Commonwealth Bay 338-9
Farthest South 345
Glaciology 14-5

Grytviken Whaling Station 276-7
Guidance for Visitors to the Antarctic 104-5
Helicopter Safety 112
Icebergs 28
Life Aboard a Polar Ship 110-1
Life at the South Pole 354-5
The Lions of the Dry Valleys 313
A Low-Latitude Antarctic Gazetteer 24-5
Nonexistent Antarctic Islands 242
'Oh My God, It's Female!' 52
On Top of the Bottom of the World 198
The Origins of ANARE 42-3
Patriot Hills, Antarctica 128
The Peninsula's Top Ten Most Visited Sites 1989-99 294-5
Polar Posts: A Brief History of Antarctic Philately 324
Seymour Island: Antarctica's Rosetta Stone 304-5
South Pole Weather Data 347
Southern Ocean Yachting 120-1
Taking Photos in the Antarctic 92-3
They Come from Outta Space 30-1
The 300 Club 346
Totality in 2003 335
The Under-Ice Lakes 341
A Visit to Cape Horn 238
Warning 108
What's in a Name? 306
A Window on the 'Heroic Era' 218-9
Zodiacs 122-3

Bold indicates maps.

MAP LEGEND

BOUNDARIES

```
·· ■ ·■ ·■ ·■    International
··· ■ ·■ ·■ ··    State, Province
· · ─ · ─ · ─ ─    County
```

HYDROGRAPHY

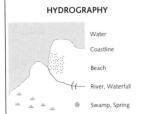

Water

Coastline

Beach

River, Waterfall

Swamp, Spring

ROUTES & TRANSPORT

Freeway

Toll Freeway

Primary Road

Secondary Road

Tertiary Road

Unpaved Road

Pedestrian Mall

Trail

Chair Lift

Ferry Route

Railway, Train Station

Mass Transit Line & Station

ROUTE SHIELDS

| RN 3 | Argentina Ruta Nacional | N2 | South Africa Highway |
| RP 21 | Argentina Ruta Provincial | 5 | Chile Ruta Nacional |

AREA FEATURES

Cemetery

Ecological Reserve

Glacier

Golf Course

Park

Plaza

✪ **NATIONAL CAPITAL**

◉ **State, Provincial Capital**

● **LARGE CITY**

● **Medium City**

● Small City

● Town, Village

■ Place to Stay

▲ Campground

⌂ Chalet or Hut

▼ Place to Eat

☗ Bar (Place to Drink)

MAP SYMBOLS

✈ Airfield

✕ Airport

∴ Archaeological Site, Ruins

⑤ Bank

⌂ Base Station

Ბ Beach

✦✦ Border Crossing

◒ Bus Depot, Bus Stop

⊞ Cathedral

⛵ Canoe

⌒ Cave

✝ Church

◎ Embassy

⟩─⟨ Footbridge

ᘐ Fish Hatchery

⚘ Garden

⛽ Gas Station

✛ Hospital, Clinic

❶ Information

⛨ Lighthouse

☼ Lookout

☗ Mine

♠ Monument

▲ Mountain

⛫ Museum

⊖ Observatory

◄ One-Way Street

♣ Park

P Parking

⟩(Pass

⊓ Picnic Area

★ Police Station

▭ Pool

☒ Post Office

❖ Shopping Mall

⛷ Skiing (Alpine)

⛷ Skiing (Nordic)

▥ Stately Home

☎ Telephone

⚐ Trailhead

⚘ Winery

☗ Zoo

Note: Not all symbols displayed above appear in this book.

LONELY PLANET OFFICES

Australia

Locked Bag 1, Footscray, Victoria 3011
☎ 03 8379 8000 fax 03 8379 8111
email talk2us@lonelyplanet.com.au

USA

150 Linden Street, Oakland, California 94607
☎ 510 893 8555, TOLL FREE 800 275 8555
fax 510 893 8572
email info@lonelyplanet.com

UK

10a Spring Place, London NW5 3BH
☎ 020 7428 4800 fax 020 7428 4828
email go@lonelyplanet.co.uk

France

1 rue du Dahomey, 75011 Paris
☎ 01 55 25 33 00 fax 01 55 25 33 01
email bip@lonelyplanet.fr
www.lonelyplanet.fr

World Wide Web: www.lonelyplanet.com *or* AOL keyword: lp
Lonely Planet Images: lpi@lonelyplanet.com.au